Collective Labour Law

Collective Labour Law

Gillian S Morris LL.B. (Bristol), Ph.D (Cantab)
Professor of Law, Brunel University;
Barrister, 11 King's Bench Walk Chambers

and

Timothy J Archer M.A. (Oxon)
Solicitor, Head of Employment Law Department at Richards Butler

·H A R T·
PUBLISHING

OXFORD – PORTLAND OREGON
2000

Hart Publishing
Oxford and Portland, Oregon

Published in North America (US and Canada) by
Hart Publishing c/o
International Specialized Book Services
5804 NE Hassalo Street
Portland, Oregon
97213-3644
USA

Distributed in the Netherlands, Belgium and Luxembourg by
Intersentia, Churchillaan 108
B2900 Schoten
Antwerpen
Belgium

Hart Publishing Ltd is a specialist legal publisher based in Oxford, England.
To order further copies of this book or to request a list of other
publications please write to:

Hart Publishing Ltd, Salter's Boatyard, Oxford OX1 4LB
Telephone: +44 (0)1865 245533 or Fax: +44 (0)1865 794882
e-mail: mail@hartpub.co.uk
www.hartpub.co.uk

British Library Cataloguing in Publication Data
Data Available
ISBN 1 84113–096–6 (cloth)
1 84113–177–6 (paperback)

Typeset in Times 10pt by Hope Services (Abingdon) Ltd.
Printed and bound in Great Britain on acid-free paper by
Biddles Ltd, www.biddles.co.uk

Preface

The past two years have witnessed fundamental changes in the field of collective labour law. The Employment Relations Act 1999 has introduced a procedure for the compulsory recognition of trade unions, additional protection for employees dismissed while taking part in industrial action, and changes to industrial action ballots and notices. Significant changes have been made to the requirements for consultation prior to collective redundancies and transfers of undertakings, and the European Works Councils Directive has been implemented in domestic law. The Human Rights Act 1998 has important implications for collective labour law, and focuses attention not only on the jurisprudence of the European Convention on Human Rights but also on other international treaties relating to this field.

This book aims to provide a detailed and integrated analysis both of these developments, and of pre-existing common law and statute. It is thus designed to be a comprehensive study of the field. Each chapter begins with an overview of the area with which it is concerned; detailed discussion of topics within each chapter is also, where appropriate, prefaced by a summary of the sources and general principles governing that topic. We have sought, throughout the text, to draw attention to relevant international provisions, and to indicate those respects in which we consider the development of domestic law may be affected by the Human Rights Act 1998. The importance which we attribute to that Act is evidenced by the material in the first chapter in the book, where we highlight some controversial and, in our view, neglected issues.

In analysing ambiguous provisions of the legislation, or explaining legislative policy, we have incorporated references to parliamentary debates. It will be noted that references to Standing Committee debates on internet material refer to the time at which a speech was made (in blocks of fifteen minutes) rather than columns, the practice in the printed version. We have assumed that the majority of our readers will obtain their parliamentary material from internet sources, and have therefore adopted its mode of citation in this work.

For the sake of clarity, we have used the nomenclature of the new Civil Procedure Rules throughout, regardless of whether the case with which we are concerned was subject to these rules. Thus, 'plaintiffs' become 'claimants', 'interlocutory' injunctions are 'interim'.

In April 2000 one of us, Gillian Morris, was appointed a deputy chairman of the CAC. This work is written entirely in a personal capacity and its contents should not be taken to represent the views of the CAC unless indicated otherwise in the text.

The law of England and Wales is as stated at 1 July 2000, with two exceptions. At the time of writing, the right to be accompanied in disciplinary and grievance proceedings is due to take effect on 4 September 2000; the revised provisions on industrial action ballots and notice to employers on 18 September 2000. The relevant Codes of Practice have, at the time of writing, been laid before Parliament, and as they are highly unlikely to be changed we have included discussion of their provisions in the text.

GSM
TJA
July 9 2000.

Contents

Table of Cases

Table of Legislation

Table of Statutory Instruments

Table of Codes of Practice

Table of EU Secondary Legislation

Table of Treaties

List of Abbreviations

ACAS	Advisory, Conciliation and Arbitration Service
CA	Court of Appeal
CAC	Central Arbitration Committee
ChD	Chancery Division
CIE	Committee of Independent Experts (of the European Social Charter)
CO	Certification Officer
CS	Court of Session
CPR	Civil Procedure Rules
DC	Divisional Court
DETR	Department of Environment, Transport and the Regions
DTI	Department of Trade and Industry
EAT	Employment Appeal Tribunal
EC	European Community
E Com HR	European Commission of Human Rights
ECHR	European Convention on Human Rights and Fundamental Freedoms
ECJ	European Court of Justice
ECSR	European Committee of Social Rights
ECtHR	European Court of Human Rights
ESC	European Social Charter
EWC	European Works Council
HL	House of Lords
HSC	Health and Safety Commission
HSE	Health and Safety Executive
ICP	Information and Consultation Procedure
ICCPR	International Covenant on Civil and Political Rights
ICESCR	International Covenant on Economic, Social and Cultural Rights
ILO	International Labour Organisation
KBD	King's Bench Division
NHS	National Health Service
NI CA	Court of Appeal, Northern Ireland
NIRC	National Industrial Relations Court

PC	Privy Council
QBD	Queen's Bench Division
RSC	Rules of the Supreme Court
SNB	Special Negotiating Body
TUC	Trades Union Congress
UDHR	The Universal Declaration of Human Rights
CJPOA	Criminal Justice and Public Order Act 1994
DPA	Data Protection Act 1998
DDA	Disability Discrimination Act 1995
ECA	European Communities Act 1972
ERA 1996	Employment Rights Act 1996
ERA 1999	Employment Relations Act 1999
ETA	Employment Tribunals Act 1996
HSWA	Health and Safety at Work etc Act 1974
HRA	Human Rights Act 1998
ICTA	Income and Corporation Taxes Act 1988
LGA	Local Government Act 1988
NMWA	National Minimum Wages Act 1998
RRA	Race Relations Act 1976
SDA	Sex Discrimination Act 1975
TICER	Transnational Information and Consultation of Employees Regulations 1999
TULRCA	Trade Union and Labour Relations (Consolidation) Act 1992
TURERA	Trade Union Reform and Employment Rights Act 1993
TUPE	Transfer of Undertakings (Protection of Employment) Regulations 1981.

1

Collective Labour Law and Human Rights

INTRODUCTION

1.1 At an international level human rights have long been central to collective labour law. The major human rights conventions all guarantee the right to freedom of association, and an important element of that right is the freedom of workers to associate in order to further and defend their interests. The Universal Declaration of Human Rights (UDHR), adopted by the United Nations General Assembly in 1948, proclaims that '[e]veryone has the right to form and to join trade unions for the protection of his interests', a right which was given effect in international law by the International Covenant on Economic, Social and Cultural Rights (ICESCR) and the International Covenant on Civil and Political Rights (ICCPR) of 1966. Freedom of association has been a core principle of the International Labour Organisation (ILO) since its inception in 1919, and it is also included in treaties agreed at regional level, including the European Convention on Human Rights and Fundamental Freedoms (ECHR) 1950 and the European Social Charter (ESC) 1961,[1] each negotiated under the auspices of the Council of Europe. Unlike most other rights, therefore, workers' freedom to associate is regarded as significant both in treaties which deal with civil and political rights and those which guarantee rights of an economic, social and cultural nature. There is greater variation between treaties in the extent to which they explicitly guarantee other rights relevant to collective labour law. Thus, ILO Conventions and the ESC alone include an obligation upon contracting states to promote collective bargaining machinery, and only the ICESCR and ESC guarantee the right to strike. However this has not prevented more extensive rights than those specified in the treaty text being developed in the relevant jurisprudence. Thus, although ILO Conventions do not explicitly protect the right to strike, the ILO supervisory bodies have derived this right from the right to organise, of which it is seen as an essential ingredient; similarly the UN Committee on Economic, Social and Cultural Rights has derived an obligation on states to promote collective bargaining from the right of unions to function freely.

The UK has ratified all these instruments and is therefore bound in international law to give effect to the rights which they contain.[2] As examples given throughout this book reveal, however, its record of compliance with its obligations in this area is patchy, even when supervisory bodies have confirmed the failure of domestic law to reflect international standards (the exception to this pattern being judgments of the European Court of Human Rights (ECtHR)). Prior to the Human Rights Act 1998, these rights could not be enforced directly in domestic law unless they had been transposed into statute or subordinate legislation or fell within the scope of EC law. The Treaty on European Union now explicitly binds the EU to respect fundamental rights as guaranteed by the ECHR (and as they result from the constitutional traditions common to the Member States) as general principles of Community law.[3] However, even before that time the ECHR was significant in determining the scope of fundamental rights, which were regarded by the ECJ from an early stage as integral to the general principles of EC law.[4] Outside these situations, international obligations are relevant in domestic law if courts are required to construe legislation which is ambiguous, in the sense of being 'open to two or more different constructions',[5] when the (rebuttable) presumption that Parliament intended to comply with the UK's international obligations will apply.[6] UK courts have also on occasion taken cognisance of such obligations when interpreting the common law.[7]

The Human Rights Act 1998 enables rights contained in the ECHR which previously could be invoked in domestic courts only in these limited circumstances to be relied upon directly in a much wider range of situations. Under the Act, legislation must be 'read and given effect' in a way which is compatible with 'the Convention rights' 'so far as it is possible to do so', and it is unlawful for public authorities (including courts and tribunals) to act in a way which is incompatible with a Convention right unless, as a result of the provisions of primary legislation, they could not have acted differently.[8] However although the Human Rights Act relates to rights contained in the ECHR, those guaranteed by other international treaties may henceforth also have greater relevance in domestic law. The Act instructs domestic courts, in interpreting the scope and application of the Convention rights, to 'take into account' relevant decisions and opinions of the ECtHR, and of other bodies which previously made decisions relating to the ECHR,[9] which to date have generally adopted a restrictive approach to the interpretation of the Convention in the sphere of collective labour law, particularly when compared with the supervisory organs of the ILO. However the Human Rights Act does not require the courts to follow these decisions and opinions, and whilst a more restrictive interpretation of a particular article than that reflected in ECHR jurisprudence, if upheld on appeal, will probably provoke an application to the ECtHR, there is nothing to prevent domestic courts adopting a more expansive view.[10] In addition, national courts will inevitably be faced with questions which have not previously arisen in ECHR jurisprudence, or which have done so only in a modified form. It is highly likely, therefore, that in being called upon to interpret the scope of Convention rights in the area of collective labour law the courts will be presented with arguments derived from other international instruments, particularly where these accord workers more extensive rights than those which have been derived from the ECHR. Moreover, the ECHR jurisprudence itself has on occasion taken account of other international standards, such as those of the ILO, in interpreting the scope of the right to join trade unions, although with variable consequences.[11]

We have attempted throughout this work to integrate discussion of relevant international standards, and of the implications of the Human Rights Act, into our analysis of domestic law. We do not, therefore, provide an exhaustive analysis of these provisions in this chapter. Rather, our aim here is to provide a framework within which the points of detail raised in later chapters can be located. The chapter starts by outlining the procedure for bringing a complaint under the ECHR and the remedies which can be granted, with particular reference to complaints relating to collective labour law. It then explains the scope of collective rights guaranteed by the Convention, and the general criteria which are used to assess whether an interference with the exercise of any of these rights is justified. This is followed by an analysis of the application of the ECHR in the sphere of employment, focussing in particular upon the circumstances in which state liability may be engaged. This involves examining both the basis of state responsibility and the nature of the acts for which liability potentially may lie. As the analysis indicates, the ECHR jurisprudence has to date drawn a distinction between denial of access to employment, which has been regarded as outwith the Convention, and dismissal and other disciplinary acts during employment, a distinction which in our view is indefensible. Finally in this section we examine the important question of the extent to which the right to exercise a right which the ECHR guarantees can be excluded or modified by contract, an area which, again, we regard as inadequately reasoned in ECHR jurisprudence. The second section discusses the implications of the Human Rights Act 1998 for collective labour law, and explains the legal contexts in which the Convention rights may influence the interpretation given to domestic law and the exercise of judicial discretion. The final section gives an overview of the standards relevant to collective labour law which are guaranteed in the remaining international instruments—ILO Conventions, and the ESC, ICCPR and ICESCR—and the mechanisms for monitoring compliance with such standards.

---

1. The ESC was revised in 1996. At the time of writing the UK has signed, but not ratified, the revised Charter.

2. Although States are not required to be bound by every article of the ESC, the UK has accepted those contained in the 1961 version relevant to collective labour law: see further para **1.21**.

3. Article 6(2) EU.

4. Case 11/70 *Internationale Handelsgesellschaft v Einfuhr- und Vorratsstelle für Getreide* [1970] ECR 1125, at 1134; Case 4/73 *Nold v Commission* [1974] ECR 491, para 13. For examples relevant to employment law see Case 222/84 *Johnston v Chief Constable of the Royal Ulster Constabulary* [1986] ECR 1651; Case C–13/94 *P v S and Cornwall County Council* [1996] IRLR 347; Case C–249/96 *Grant v South-West Trains Ltd* [1998] IRLR 206. Note that the absence of a preliminary reference procedure from the ECJ to the ECtHR means that the two bodies may differ as to the interpretation of particular articles: cf. Case 46/87 *Hoechst v Commission* [1989] ECR 2859, in which the ECJ held that Article 8 did not extend to business premises, and *Niemietz v Germany*, judgment of 16 December 1992, (1993) 16 EHRR 97. In case of conflict a UK court would be required by the ECA 1972, s 3(1) to follow the decision of the ECJ.

5. *R v Home Secretary ex parte Brind* [1991] 1 All ER 720, Lord Ackner at 734.

6. Cf the more positive formulation of this principle by the Privy Council in *Matadeen and Pointu v Minister of Education and Science* [1998] 3 WLR 18.

7. See, for example, *A-G v Guardian Newspapers Ltd (No 2)* [1988] 3 All ER 545, Lord Goff at 660; *Middlebrook Mushrooms Ltd v TGWU* [1993] IRLR 232, CA, Neill LJ at 235; *DPP v Jones* [1999] 2 All ER 257, Lord Irvine LC at 266, and for a wider discussion Browne-Wilkinson, 1992; Laws, 1993; Hunt, 1997. It has been stated that between 1964 and July 1999 the Convention, although unincorporated, was referred to in over 650 English cases: Grosz *et al*, 2000, para 1–03. Note also that some rights are regarded as fundamental by the common law and can be overridden only if a statute makes clear Parliament's intention to do this by express words or necessary implication: for an overview see de Smith, Woolf and Jowell, 1995, paras 6-053-6-058 (and 1998 supplement).

8. HRA 1998, ss 3, 6. The Act uses the term 'the Convention rights' to mean the rights and freedoms guaranteed in the articles which have effect for the purposes of the Act: s 1(1),(2).

9. HRA 1998, s 2(1).These other bodies are the EComHR and the Committee of Ministers. The former has been abolished, the latter no longer has the right to make decisions: see further para **1.3**.

10. ECHR, Article 53. See para **1.13** for the different sources of jurisprudence referred to in the HRA 1998.

11. See, for example, *Cheall v UK* App No 10550/83, (1986) 8 EHRR 74; *Sigurour A. Sigurjonsson v Iceland* judgment of 30 June 1993, (1993) 16 EHRR 462, discussed at para **1.6**. See also *National Union of Belgian Police v Belgium* judgment of 27 October 1975, (1979–80) 1 EHRR 578 at para 38, discussed at para **1.6**.

THE EUROPEAN CONVENTION ON HUMAN RIGHTS AND FUNDAMENTAL FREEDOMS

Overview and Procedure

1.2 The ECHR was adopted in 1950 and came into force in 1953.[1] At the time of writing 41 states have ratified it. The rights guaranteed by the Convention are predominantly civil or political in nature. They include the right to life, liberty and security; freedom from torture or inhuman or degrading treatment, slavery and forced labour; the right to respect for private life; freedom of expression; freedom of assembly and association; and freedom of thought, conscience and religion. However the Convention also strays into the field of economic, social and cultural rights in guaranteeing the rights to property and education (and freedom of association can also be regarded as straddling these categories). A complaint that a contracting state has violated a right guaranteed by the Convention may be referred to the ECtHR by another state party or (much more commonly in practice) by individuals; the right of individuals to complain, initially optional (it was accepted by the UK in 1966), is now mandatory for all states.[2] Individual applications may be presented by 'any person, non-governmental organisation or group of individuals claiming to be the victim of a violation by one of the High Contracting Parties of the rights set forth in the Convention or the protocols thereto'.[3] The term 'victim' has been taken in the Strasbourg jurisprudence to require the applicant to be 'directly affected' by the matter complained of, so preventing individuals challenging a law or practice purely on public interest grounds.[4] The location of the boundary between those directly and remotely affected by a measure has proved 'shifting and uncertain'.[5] However two principles of particular relevance to collective labour law emerge. First, the ECtHR has held in a variety of contexts that individuals may be directly affected by a provision in the absence of any specific measure of implementation, or where they run the risk of being directly affected by it.[6] Thus if the state in its role as employer were to threaten active trade unionists with disciplinary action, for example, workers subject to this threat could probably claim to be 'victims' even if no disciplinary measures had yet been imposed upon them on the basis either that they ran the risk of being directly affected by this measure, or faced the choice of abstaining from the exercise of the right or risking disciplinary reprisals. Secondly, pressure groups, trade unions and other representative bodies may present an application only if they as organisations are in some way affected by the measure complained of; that their members are affected will not suffice. Thus, in a complaint that restrictions on the political activities of local government staff constituted a violation of their rights under the ECHR, the EComHR held that the officers affected were victims but their union was not.[7] Applications are admissible only if all domestic remedies available to provide redress for the alleged wrong have been exhausted,[8] reflecting the principle that states should be afforded the opportunity to put right the wrongs they are alleged to have committed. This requires recourse to remedies which are likely to be adequate and effective to provide redress, and in principle victims should take their case to the highest domestic court prior to an application being made although this may not be necessary if it is clear that no legal remedy exists.[9] Applications must be presented within six months from the date on which the final decision was taken.[10] The 'final decision' for this purpose will normally be the final domestic decision rejecting the applicant's claim, but where no adequate and effective remedy is available it will be the act or decision complained of.[11] In the case of continuing situations, such as a legislative provision or administrative practice which constantly interferes with the exercise of a right, the six-month rule does not apply unless and until the interference ends.

---

1. The most comprehensive texts in English on the ECHR are Harris *et al*, 1995 (at the time of writing a new edition is expected later in 2000); and van Dijk and van Hoof, 1998; also useful is Lawson and Schermers, 1999.

2. Articles 33, 34. The Secretary General of the Council of Europe may also require a Contracting Party to explain the manner in which its law ensures the effective implementation of any provision of the Convention: Article 52. For details of the procedure for bringing an application to the Court, see Clements *et al* 1999.

3. Article 34.

4. There is extensive case law on the concept of a victim: see Harris *et al*, 1995, 632–638; Van Dijk and van Hoof, 1998, 44–58.

5. Harris *et al*, 1995, 633.

6. *Klass and others v Germany*, judgment of 6 September 1978, (1979–80) 2 EHRR 214, para 33; *Marckx v Belgium*, judgment of 13 June 1979, (1979–80) 2 EHRR 330, para 27; see also *Dudgeon v UK* judgment of 22 October 1981, (1982) 4 EHRR 149, para 41; although cf. the Commission decision in *Leigh, Guardian Newspapers Ltd and Observer Ltd v UK* App. No. 10039/82, 38 DR 74 (1984).

7. *Ahmed et al v UK*, App No 22954/93, noted [1997] 6 *EHRLR* 670; cf *National Union of Belgian Police v Belgium* judgment of 27 October 1975 (1979–80) 1 EHRR 578; *Council of Civil Service Unions v UK* App No 11603/85, 50 DR 228 (1987).

8. Article 35.

9. Harris *et al*, 1995, 608–621; Reid 1998, 21–24; Clements *et al* 1999, 25–33. Note that Article 13 obliges states to afford everyone whose rights and freedoms guaranteed by the Convention are violated 'an effective remedy before a national authority notwithstanding that the violation has been committed by persons acting in an official capacity'. This obscurely-worded provision requires provision of a remedy for 'arguable' claims: see further Harris *et al*, 1995, Chapter 6.

10. Article 35.

11. Harris *et al*, 1995, 623. Note that there is ECHR case law on when the date of the 'final decision' is determined.

1.3 Until 1 November 1998 all applications were initially examined by the European Commission of Human Rights (EComHR), whose members (as many as there were contracting parties) were required from 1990 onwards to possess the qualifications required for high judicial office or to be persons of recognised competence in national or international law.[1] The primary role of the Commission was to decide whether cases were admissible, under the terms of the ECHR, including whether they were 'manifestly ill-founded'; there was no avenue of appeal against its decision to reject a complaint as inadmissible. In respect of cases which were deemed admissible, the Commission was charged with establishing and verifying the facts of the case; conciliating between the parties with a view to securing a 'friendly settlement' of the matter; and, where no settlement was reached, preparing a (non-binding) legal opinion as to whether the Convention had been violated. The Commission then drew up a report for the Committee of Ministers, the executive organ of the Council of Europe consisting of the Foreign Ministers of Member States or their deputies. The case could then be referred to the ECtHR within three months of the report being presented to the Committee of Ministers by, variously, the Commission; the Contracting Party whose national was alleged to be a victim; the Contracting Party which referred the case to the Commission; the Contracting Party against which the complaint had been lodged; and, latterly, the victim of the violation (provided that the Contracting State had agreed to this[2]). In the event that the question was not referred to the Court, the Committee itself was required to decide whether there was a violation. It is notable that the Human Rights Act 1998 directs domestic courts to take into account admissibility decisions of the Commission, and its opinions, as well as decisions of the Committee of Ministers,[3] in addition to those of the ECtHR (although as no reasons were produced for the decisions of the Committee of Ministers, nor were they the subject of a hearing, it is difficult to see what weight can usefully be attached to them). Since 1 November 1998, all applications proceed immediately to the ECtHR, which is now composed of full-time judges;[4] the Commission has been abolished and the Committee of Ministers confined to supervising the execution of judgments of the Court.[5] Each application is assigned to a designated Judge Rapporteur who may take the case initially before a three-judge committee which is empowered, by a unanimous vote, to rule the application inadmissible, a decision against which there is no appeal.[6] Alternatively (or if the committee is not unanimous) the case goes before a seven-judge Chamber which may examine both the admissibility and the merits of the application.[7] The judgment of the Chamber is final unless any party to the case, within three months from the date of judgment, requests that the case be referred to a seventeen-judge Grand Chamber.[8] This request must be accepted if a panel of five Grand Chamber judges finds that the case 'raises a serious question affecting the interpretation or application of the Convention . . . or a serious issue of general importance'.[9] A case may also go before the Grand Chamber if the seven-judge Chamber decides to relinquish jurisdiction in its favour. This may be done if the case 'raises a serious question affecting the interpretation of the Convention . . . , or where the resolution of a question before the Chamber might have a result inconsistent with a judgment previously delivered by the Court'.[10] However any party to the case has the right to veto such relinquishment, a provision apparently inserted to ensure that a party cannot be deprived involuntarily of the opportunity to seek a second-stage hearing.[11] The judgment of the Grand Chamber is final.[12] Contracting states undertake to abide by the final judgment of the Court in any case to which they are parties; such judgments are transmitted to the Committee of Ministers which supervise their execution.[13]

---

1. Eighth Protocol to the Convention.
2. Ninth Protocol to the Convention, into force 1 October 1994.
3. S 2(1); see further para **1.13**.
4. See generally ECHR Articles 19–51; ECtHR Rules of Court, 4 November 1998.
5. Article 46(2).
6. Article 28.
7. Article 29. The decision on admissibility is to be taken separately unless the Court, in exceptional cases, decides otherwise. If an application is deemed admissible the Court must also place itself at the disposal of the parties with a view to 'securing a friendly settlement of the matter on the basis of respect for human rights . . .': Article 38(1)(b).
8. Article 44.
9. Article 43.
10. Article 30.
11. Rowe and Schlette, 1998.
12. Article 44.
13. Article 46.

1.4 If the ECtHR finds that a decision or measure taken by a respondent state conflicts with its obligations under the Convention, and the internal law of that state allows only partial reparation to be made for the consequences of such a decision or measure, 'the decision of the Court shall, if necessary, afford just satisfaction to the injured party'.[1] This provision has been interpreted by the Court to enable the award of financial compensation to successful complainants to cover legal costs and damages for pecuniary and non-pecuniary loss. Thus, when the dismissal of employees who refused to join a closed shop union was found by the Court to violate Article 11, the applicants were awarded in 1982 loss of earnings, pension rights and travel expenses as items of pecuniary loss, together with sums ranging between £2,000 and £6,000 for non-pecuniary loss, such as the harassment and humiliation to which they had been subjected, stress and anxiety compounded by the difficulties in obtaining alternative employment, and deterioration in their way of life and that of their families.[2] In general, however, it is difficult to discern any coherent principles relating to the availability and amount of compensation in the ECHR jurisprudence.[3] In some cases the finding of a violation has itself been regarded as just satisfaction; the conduct of the applicant has also on occasion been regarded as material (the Court has been reluctant to award compensation to prisoners), although little justification has been given for this approach.[4] Research published in 1997 showed that applicants had a relatively low success rate in obtaining compensation, and that even when awards are made they tend to be lower than those claimed. However, claims for costs and expenses fared better, provided that applicants could establish that costs had actually been incurred and were for a reasonable amount.[5] The Court has no power to provide any form of redress other than financial compensation. Thus it cannot, for example, require states to take any specified form of action; rather, it is for the state to choose the means to be used in its domestic legal system to redress the situation. Neither does the Court have formal power to award binding interim relief, although the Chamber or, where appropriate, its President may indicate to the party any interim measure which it considers should be adopted in the interests of the parties or the proper conduct of the proceedings,[6] and in practice states normally comply with such requests.

---

1. ECHR, Article 41. Claims for just satisfaction must be set out in the written observations on the merits or, if none are filed, in a special document filed no later than two months after the decision declaring the application admissible, unless the President of the Chamber otherwise directs: ECtHR Rules of Court, rule 60.

2. *Young, James and Webster v UK* (Article 50), judgment of 18 October 1982.

3. See generally Mowbray, 1997.

4. In *McCann v UK* judgment of 27 September 1995, (1996) 21 EHRR 97, however, the Court explicitly affirmed that it did not consider it appropriate to make an award in respect of the death of terrorist suspects who were intending to plant a bomb in Gibraltar.

5. Mowbray, 1997. Note that lawyers who agree to work *pro bono* cannot make a retrospective claim under Article 41, so it is preferable to bill clients but suspend collection of fees until after Article 41 has been applied.

6. ECtHR Rules of Court, rule 39; see *Cruz Varas v Sweden* judgment of 20 March 1991, (1992) 14 EHRR 1. Van Dijk and van Hoof, 1998, argue (at 104) that the obligation not to hinder the effective exercise of the right to apply to the Court may in some circumstances imply an obligation to comply.

The ECHR and Collective Labour Law

1.5 There are two articles of the ECHR which are of particular relevance to collective labour law. Article 11(1) provides that:

> [e]veryone has the right to freedom of peaceful assembly and to freedom of association with others, including the right to form and to join trade unions for the protection of his interests.

In addition, Article 10, which guarantees the right to freedom of expression, may apply to some forms of collective activity such as discussing trade union matters, standing for union office and picketing.[1] Other articles of the ECHR may also be relevant in specific contexts: for example, differences in access to recognition or consultation rights for trade unions may raise issues under Article 14, which provides that the rights and freedoms set forth in the Convention should be secured without discrimination,[2] and industrial action may interfere with a wide range of Convention rights, including the right to liberty, to a fair and public hearing within a reasonable time, and freedom of expression, thereby possibly attracting state responsibility to take measures to ensure that these rights are otherwise safeguarded.[3] In this chapter, we focus upon the general principles of the jurisprudence relating to the scope of the right to join trade unions and the criteria which are used to assess whether an interference with the exercise of the rights to freedom of association and freedom of expression is justified, leaving discussion of specific aspects of these and other rights to relevant points in later chapters.

---

1. In *Vogt v Germany* judgment of 26 September 1995, (1996) 21 EHRR 205, para 67 and *Ahmed v UK* judgment of 2 September 1998, [1999] IRLR 188 standing for political office was regarded as involving the exercise of freedom of expression.

2. Although Article 11 does not afford trade unions or their members a right to recognition or consultation, where this means of making the Article 11 right 'possible and effective' has been chosen it must be implemented without discrimination: see *National Union of Belgian Police v Belgium* judgment of 27 October 1975, (1979–80) 1 EHRR 578, discussed further at para **1.6**.

3. See *Ashingdane v UK* App No 8225/78 (complaint that the applicant's continued detention in Broadmoor instead of a local psychiatric hospital because of a union ban on admitting particular categories of patient admissible); cf *Pafitis v Greece* judgment of 26 February 1998 (delay caused by strike called by members of the Athens Bar could not be attributed to the state). See further para **1.18**.

1.6 The right to form and join trade unions appears in the ECHR as a sub-division of freedom of association, not as an independent right. The jurisprudence relating to its scope is relatively sparse and undeveloped by comparison with that relating to ILO Conventions, the ICESCR and the ESC. It is clear Article 11 requires the state not to prevent the establishment of unions, or individuals from joining them. It does not, however, confer a right to join the union of one's choice, irrespective of that union's rules; the EComHR has affirmed that unions should be free to draw up their own rules and administer their own affairs, and to decide, in accordance with their rules, questions of admission and expulsion, subject to those rules not being 'wholly unreasonable or arbitrary' or their application not resulting in exceptional hardship such as job loss.[1] There is support in the jurisprudence for the view that Article 11 extends to the participation in the activities of a union, including holding union office,[2] although such activities may alternatively (or additionally) be regarded as involving the exercise of freedom of expression.[3] It is notable that Article 11 states that an individual has the right to join a union 'for the protection of his interests'. The ECtHR has accepted that this safeguards the 'freedom to protect the occupational interests of trade union members by trade union action, the conduct and development of which the Contracting States must both permit and make possible', from which it follows that union members have a right, in order to protect their interests, 'that the trade union should be heard'.[4] However it has not implied from this right a specific right for unions to be recognised or even consulted by employers, nor, *a fortiori*, is there a right to conclude collective agreements. Rather each state has 'a free choice of the means to be used towards that end'. Thus, while consultation, or the conclusion of a collective agreement is one means by which a union can be heard,

> there are others. What the Convention requires is that under national law trade unions should be enabled, in conditions not at variance with Article 11, to strive for the protection of their members' interests.[5]

The Court has also indicated that:

> In view of the sensitive character of the social and political issues involved in achieving a proper balance between the competing interests and, in particular, in assessing the appropriateness of State intervention to restrict union action aimed at extending a system of collective bargaining, and the wide degree of divergence between the domestic systems in the particular area under consideration, the Contracting States should enjoy a wide margin of appreciation in the choice of the means to be employed.[6]

On the basis of the reasoning in these cases it would be possible to argue that if there is no mechanism whatsoever by which a particular union could be 'heard' by a state employer this would violate its members' rights under Article 11, even if there is a channel for receiving the views of other unions.[7] It is also strongly arguable that, on the basis of the case law, there is an obligation on the state to provide a mechanism by which the right of a union to be 'heard' by employers in the private sector is secured.[8] However, a requirement to ensure that all relevant unions can be 'heard' does not entail according them *equal* status as negotiating or consultative partners. Article 14 provides that the enjoyment of the rights and freedoms set forth in the Convention

> shall be secured without discrimination on any ground such as sex, race, colour, language, religion, political or other opinion, national or social origin, association with a national minority, property, birth or other status.

However, differences in treatment between unions are unlikely to violate Articles 11 and 14 together provided that the employer can demonstrate a legitimate aim, such as the desire to avoid a large number of consultation or bargaining partners, and the action is proportionate to that aim.[9] By contrast if the employer's aim is to attempt to reduce support for a 'militant' union which has a substantial membership among the workforce this may be more difficult to justify. There is no reference to the right to strike in Article 11, and the ECtHR has refused to imply such a right. In *Schmidt and Dahlström v Sweden* the Swedish Government concluded a collective agreement which denied retrospective benefits to members of two unions which had taken strike action. The Court rejected their claim that this violated Article 11, affirming that while the 'grant of a right to strike' represents 'one of the most important' of the means by which the occupational interests of trade union members may be protected by trade union action, 'there are others'.[10] Hendy has argued that if a union had no other means of conveying its members' interests a right to strike could be implied.[11] We consider it somewhat unlikely that the ECtHR would accept this reasoning, particularly given the attendant problems of establishing the appropriate limits of such a right, unless it was prepared to draw heavily upon the jurisprudence of more specialist supervisory bodies. However the matter cannot be regarded as free from doubt. Finally, Article 11 does not specify a right not to join a union and the *travaux préparatoires* indicate that it was not intended to be covered. Despite this, the ECtHR, invoking the principle that the Convention is a 'living instrument which must be interpreted in the light of present-day conditions', has concluded that Article 11 does encompass a negative right, although without determining whether this should be considered on an equal footing with the positive.[12] In doing so, it invoked the jurisprudence of the ILO, which states that union security arrangements imposed by law violate freedom of association principles. Although the case before the ECtHR was itself concerned with an obligation imposed by law, the judgment appears to extend more widely to embrace all instances of compulsory union membership, regardless of their source.

---

1. *Cheall v UK* App No 10550/83, (1986) 8 EHRR 74. In this case the Commission drew upon the terms of ILO Convention 87.

2. *X v Ireland* App No 4125/69: threats of dismissal to make an employee relinquish the office of shop steward could, in certain circumstances, seriously restrict or impede the lawful exercise of freedom of association.

3. See para **1.5**, note 1, above.

4. *National Union of Belgian Police v Belgium* judgment of 27 October 1975, (1979–80) 1 EHRR 578 at para 39.

5. *Ibid.*, *Swedish Engine Drivers' Union v Sweden* judgment of 6 February 1976, (1979–80) 1 EHRR 617, para 40.

6. *Gustafsson v Sweden* judgment of 28 March 1996, (1996) 22 EHRR 409, para 45. In this case the Court affirmed that the Convention did not guarantee a right not to enter a collective agreement.

7. In *Swedish Engine Drivers' Union v Sweden*, above, note 5, although it was not incompatible with Article 11 for the Swedish National Collective Bargaining Office to restrict the number of organisations with which collective agreements were concluded, it was material that the applicant union was still able to make representations to the government for the protection of its members' interests.

8. See the text above notes 4 and 5; see also *Gustafsson v Sweden*, above, note 6, para 52; *Young, James and Webster v UK* judgment of 13 August 1981, (1982) 4 EHRR 38, para 49, discussed para **1.9** below.

9. *Swedish Engine Drivers' Union v Sweden*, above, note 5 paras 44–48; see also *National Union of Belgian Police v Belgium*, above, note 4 at paras 43–49.

10. Judgment of 6 February 1976, (1979–80) 1 EHRR 632, para 36. See also *X v Germany* App No 10365/83, (1985) 7 EHRR 461 (disciplinary proceedings against a civil servant who participated in a strike not a violation of Article 11). Cf Ben-Israel, 1988, 28–29, who argues that the Court provided 'powerful support' for the argument that freedom to strike is essential for freedom of association.

11. Hendy, 1998. In *NATFHE v UK* App No 28910/95 the EComHR concluded that the requirement to divulge the names of members likely to vote in an industrial action ballot contained in TULRCA 1992, s 226A prior to its amendment by ERA 1999 did not constitute a 'significant limitation on the right to take collective action'. Hendy argues that this suggests that a more inhibiting provision would have been regarded as such a violation. It is unquestionably the case that the decisions of both the Commission and the Court in this area are delphic in their phraseology.

12. *Sigurour A. Sigurjonsson v Iceland* judgment of 30 June 1993, (1993) 16 EHRR 462, para 35; cf. *Sibson v UK* judgment of 20 April 1993, (1994) 17 EHRR 193, where the applicant was not subjected to a form of treatment 'striking at the very substance' of freedom of association (see para **3.17**). See further Deakin and Morris, 1998, 740–744.

1.7 The right to freedom of association (and freedom of assembly) guaranteed by Article 11 applies to 'everyone'. However the article does not 'prevent the imposition of lawful restrictions on the exercise of these rights by members of the armed forces, of the police or of the administration of the State'. The exclusion of 'members . . . of the administration of the State' is anomalous given that the ESC, which was intended to complement the Convention in trade union matters, contains no such exception; indeed, besides the ECHR, it appears only in the ICESCR.[1] The scope of this category is uncertain. In *Council of Civil Service Unions v UK*[2] the applicants claimed that the ban on membership of national civil service unions at Government Communications Headquarters (GCHQ) violated Article 11. The EComHR held that workers at GCHQ were 'members . . . of the administration of the state' because the purpose of GCHQ 'resemble[d] to a large extent that of the armed forces and the police insofar as GCHQ staff directly or indirectly, by ensuring the security of the . . . Government's military and official communications, fulfil vital functions in protecting national security'. By contrast, in the later case of *Vogt v Germany* the ECtHR warned that the concept should be interpreted 'narrowly, in the light of the post held by the official concerned'.[3] It should be noted that in the case of all excepted groups the article merely authorises the imposition of lawful restrictions on the exercise of the rights it guarantees. However in the *CCSU* case the Commission rejected the applicants' argument that 'restrictions' did not extend to a complete ban. It also found that the restrictions in question met the test of being 'lawful'. The applicants argued that this test did not merely require the measure to have a basis in national law; it also needed to be proportionate. The Commission held that even if the term went beyond the first of these requirements, containing, in particular, a prohibition upon arbitrariness, such a condition had been met in this case. It emphasised in this connection the wide discretion afforded to states when ensuring the protection of their national security.[4]

---

1. See Morris, 1994a, for a comparison of the scope of the exceptions in the respective treaties. All these treaties exclude the armed forces, and all but the ESC the police (which has been interpreted by the Committee of Independent Experts (now called the European Committee of Social Rights) to mean that their freedom to associate must be left intact in its essentials: Article 5).

2. App No 11603/85, 50 DR 228 (1987).

3. Judgment of 26 September 1995, (1996) 21 EHRR 205, para 67. The Commision found that the applicant secondary school teacher was outside this exception; the Court did not find it necessary to determine this.

4. For more detailed discussion of this case, and a comparison with the treatment of the issue by the ILO and ESC Committee of Independent Experts, see Morris, 1994a.

1.8 Interference with the exercise of the rights guaranteed by both Articles 11 and 10 may be justified by reference to specific aims. Thus, Article 11(2) provides that

No restrictions shall be placed on the exercise of these rights other than such as are prescribed by law and are necessary in a democratic society in the interests of national security or public safety, for the prevention of disorder or crime, for the protection of health or morals or for the protection of the rights and freedoms of others.

Article 10(2) states that:

The exercise of these freedoms, since it carries with it duties and responsibilities, may be subject to such formalities, conditions, restrictions or penalties as are prescribed by law and are necessary in a democratic society in the interests of national security, territorial integrity or public safety, for the prevention of disorder or crime, for the protection of health or morals, for the protection of the reputation or rights of others, for preventing the disclosure of information received in confidence, or for maintaining the authority and impartiality of the judiciary.

These provisions set up three main requirements. The first is that the restriction is 'prescribed by law'. This means at a minimum that it must have some basis in domestic law.[1] In addition, the ECtHR has said that it must be adequately accessible to the citizen: he or she must be able to have an indication that is adequate in the circumstances of the legal rules applicable to a given case. Furthermore,

a norm cannot be regarded as a 'law' unless it is formulated with sufficient precision to enable the citizen to regulate his conduct: he must be able—if need be with appropriate advice—to foresee, to a degree that is reasonable in the circumstances, the consequences which a given action may entail.[2]

However, provided that these tests are met, there is no requirement that the restriction be contained in statute; unwritten law is covered,[3] and where a wide discretionary power is given, non-statutory guidance may set out the manner in which the discretion is to be exercised provided, again, that this is accessible to those concerned.[4] Moreover, the degree to which the law is required to be predictable in its application may vary with the circumstances; the ECtHR has acknowledged that 'the level of precision required of domestic legislation—which cannot in any case provide for every eventuality—depends to a considerable degree on the content of the instrument in question, the field it is designed to cover and the number and status of those to whom it is addressed'.[5] However, where a wide discretion is granted, the Court will investigate the extent to which there are adequate safeguards against abuse.[6] The second requirement is to show a legitimate aim as prescribed in Article 11(2) or 10(2), as the case may be. In practice, the Court has generally been reluctant to gainsay states in this regard. Instead, most cases turn upon the interpretation of the third requirement, that the interference is 'necessary in a democratic society'. 'Necessary' has been said to imply a 'pressing social need', the interference must be 'proportionate to the legitimate aim pursued' and reasons adduced by the national authorities must be 'relevant and sufficient'.[7] In relation to all these elements, the state is accorded a 'margin of appreciation', justified on the basis that, by reason of their direct and continuous contact with the vital forces of their countries, State authorities are in principle in a better position than the international judge to give an opinion on the exact content of these requirements as well as on the 'necessity' of a 'restriction' or 'penalty' intended to meet them.[8]

However, this does not mean that state discretion is unlimited; rather the Court is empowered to give a final ruling on whether a restriction is justified: the 'domestic margin of appreciation thus goes hand in hand with a European supervision'.[9] The scope of the 'margin of appreciation' varies depending on the context; relevant factors include the importance of the right at stake, the particular purpose pursued by the state, and the extent to which there can be said to be a 'European consensus' relating to the matter.[10] In the context of the right to join a union, because, as we explain in para **1.6**, the jurisprudence has adopted a restrictive approach to the scope of the substantive right, the case law on justification is largely confined to interference with the exercise of the right *not* to join, which is likely to prove difficult to justify. Thus in *Sigurour A. Sigurjonsson v Iceland*[11] for example, the government's reasons for the requirement of compulsory membership of the 'Frami Automobile Association' by the applicant taxidriver were regarded as relevant but not sufficient to show that it was 'necessary' to compel him to be a member on pain of losing his licence and contrary to his own opinions; notwithstanding Iceland's margin of appreciation, the measures complained of were disproportionate to the aim pursued. By contrast to the jurisprudence on Article 11, virtually all the case law concerned with Article 10 turns on whether the restriction in question can be justified, given that 'expression' has been accorded a wide interpretation. Here, the context of the expression has been important; in particular, the ECtHR has accorded a much narrower margin of appreciation to the state in relation to expression which is regarded as contributing to the democratic process or 'public' or 'general' interest[12] than artistic expression whose constraint is justified by reference to morals,[13] or information of a purely commercial nature.[14] As we discuss in para **6.80**, this may be material when considering the implications of the Human Rights Act 1998 for picketing.

---

1. See, for example, *Halford v UK* judgment of 25 June 1997, (1997) 24 EHRR 523, where the UK was unable to justify the interception of the applicant's telephone calls from her office which in the circumstances was contrary to Article 8 ECHR, because domestic law at that time did not provide any regulation in relation to calls outside the public network.

2. *Sunday Times v UK* judgment of 26 April 1979, (1979–80) 2 EHRR 245, para 49. In *Hashman and Harrup v UK* judgment of 25 November 1999 the ECtHR held that it could not be said that an order by which the applicants were bound over to keep the peace and not to behave *contra bonos mores* conveyed with sufficient precision what the applicants were being bound over not to do.

3. *Sunday Times v UK,* above, para 47.

4. *Silver v UK* judgment of 25 March 1983, (1983) 5 EHRR 347.

5. *Vogt v Germany* judgment of 26 September 1995, (1996) 21 EHRR 205, para 48.

6. See, for example, *Olsson v Sweden (No 1)* judgment of 24 March 1988, (1989) 11 EHRR 259.

7. *Handyside v UK* judgment of 12 December 1976, (1979–80) 1 EHRR 737, paras 48–50.

8. *Ibid.*, para 48.

9. *Ibid.*, para 49.

10. See, for example, *Sunday Times v UK*, above, note 2, para 59; *Dudgeon v UK* judgment of 22 October 1981, (1982) 4 EHRR 149, paras 59–62. For a critique of this doctrine see Jones, 1995; Lavender, 1997; Lester, 1998a; cf. Mahoney, 1997.

11. Judgment of 30 June 1993, (1993) 16 EHRR 462, para 41.

12. See, for example, *Lingens v Austria* judgment of 8 July 1986, (1986) 8 EHRR 103; *Castells v Spain* judgment of 23 April 1992, (1992) 14 EHRR 445; *Thorgeir Thorgeirson v Iceland* judgment of 25 June 1992, (1992) 14 EHRR 843. See further Tierney, 1998.

13. *Müller v Switzerland* judgment of 24 May 1988, (1991) 13 EHRR 212.

14. *Markt Intern Verlag v FRG* judgment of 20 November 1989, (1990) 12 EHRR 161, although cf. *Hertel v Switzerland* judgment of 25 August 1998, (1999) 28 EHRR 534.

The Application of the ECHR in the Sphere of Employment

1.9 There are two fundamental questions which require investigation when considering the application of the ECHR to the sphere of employment. The first is to identify the circumstances in which the responsibility of the state, which alone can constitute the respondent to complaints brought under the Convention, can be engaged in relation to a violation of the rights of an individual victim. The second, which we discuss in para **1.10** *et seq.*, is to identify the nature of the acts for which liability can lie. Article 1 of the ECHR imposes upon signatory states the obligation to 'secure to everyone within their jurisdiction the rights and freedoms defined in . . . [the] Convention', and Article 13 provides that everyone whose rights and freedoms are violated 'shall have an effective remedy before a national authority notwithstanding that the violation has been committed by persons acting in an official capacity'. These articles have been interpreted to mean that state liability may be engaged under the Convention in one of two ways. First, it may result from the perpetration of an interference with the exercise of a Convention right by an individual or body for which the state has direct responsibility. It is clear that these bodies include the legislature, executive (including the civil service), armed forces, courts, police, prisons, and local government. Beyond these, however, the position is much less clear. In EC law, the ECJ has developed principles for determining when a body constitutes an 'organ of the state' against which individuals can invoke directly effective provisions of directives in national courts.[1] By contrast, the ECHR jurisprudence is surprisingly undeveloped as to the criteria which should be used to judge whether organisations such as nationalised industries have a sufficiently close relationship with the state for its responsibility to be engaged.[2] In cases involving the provision of education[3] and legal aid[4] the ECtHR emphasised that the state could not evade its own responsibilities by contracting out its functions to private sector bodies, and held the respondent states potentially liable for the respective violations which were alleged. This approach would almost undoubtedly be applied in any cases where core state functions, such as those of law enforcement and prison management, are shared with or handed over to private sector operators. Clearly, however, it does not assist in determining the prior question of the services for which the state should be regarded as properly responsible. In some cases the Convention organs have been able to avoid the need to address this issue by relying upon the second basis of state liability, that of a failure to take positive measures to protect individuals against interference by other private parties with the right in question. An early example of this process came out of a case relating to collective labour law. In *Young, James and Webster v UK*, employees of the former (nationalised) British Rail were dismissed for refusing to join a union when their employer concluded a closed shop agreement with the rail unions. They alleged that their dismissal constituted a violation of Article 11, which they argued protects the right not to join a union in addition to the right to join.[5] The ECtHR held that

> Although the proximate cause of the events giving rise to this case was the 1975 agreement between British Rail and the railway unions, it was the domestic law in force at the relevant time that made lawful the treatment of which the applicants complained. The responsibility of the respondent State for any resultant breach of the Convention is thus engaged on this basis.[6]

The same principle was invoked in *Plattform 'Ärzte für das Leben' v Austria*, in which the ECtHR held that the right to freedom of peaceful assembly was not confined to a mere duty for the state not to interfere with its exercise, but also required 'reasonable and appropriate' positive measures, such as protection against counter-demonstrators, to enable lawful demonstrations to proceed peacefully.[7] The doctrine that the state owes a positive obligation to protect individuals against interference with the exercise of the right by other private individuals has also been adopted in relation to a number of other articles of the Convention.[8] In relation to collective labour law one clear example of the UK failing to fulfil its positive obligations would appear to be the confinement of protection against dismissal and other forms of detriment for reasons relating to union membership to 'employees', rather than extending it to 'everyone' as Article 11 requires.[9]

1. Case C–189/89 *Foster v British Gas* [1990] ECR 3313, para 20. The Court of Appeal has warned against treating this test as definitive, however: *NUT v Governing Body of St Mary's Church of England (Aided) Junior School* [1997] IRLR 242, Schiemann LJ at 248.
2. Initially the Commission determined whether a body was a state organ by reference to national law: see, for example, App No 1706/62 *X v Austria*, (1971) 9 Yearbook 112 at 162–164. The issue of state responsibility for the BBC has never been decided: App No 4515/70 *X and the Assoc. of Z v UK* (1971) 14 Yearbook 538; App No 12015/86 *Hilton v UK* (1988) 57 DR 108; see also App No 4125/69 *X v Ireland* (1971) 37 DR 38 (not necessary to decide whether the Irish state was responsible for acts of the Electricity Supply Board). In *Malone v UK* judgment of 2 August 1984, (1985) 7 EHRR 14 the issue of state responsibility for the acts of the Post Office, a public corporation, was not put before either the Commission or the Court.
3. *Costello-Roberts v UK* judgment of 25 March 1993, (1995) 19 EHRR 112 (UK responsible for matters of discipline in independent schools).
4. *Van der Mussele v Belgium* judgment of 23 November 1983, (1984) 6 EHRR 163, para 29 (Belgium could not relieve itself of the obligation under Article 6 to provide free legal aid in some circumstances by imposing this obligation on the Order of Advocates).
5. See now *Sigurour A. Sigurjonsson v Iceland* judgment of 30 June 1993, (1993) 16 EHRR 462, discussed at para **1.6** above.
6. Judgment of 13 August 1981, (1982) 4 EHRR 38, para 49.
7. Judgment of 21 June 1988, (1991) 13 EHRR 204, paras 32–34. The Court emphasised that States could not guarantee absolutely that demonstrations would be permitted to proceed, and had a wide discretion in the choice of means to be used.
8. See, for example, *X and Y v The Netherlands* judgment of 26 March 1985, (1986) 8 EHRR 235 (Article 8); *A v UK* judgment of 23 September 1998, (1999) 27 EHRR 611 (Article 3).
9. See further para **3.2** *et seq.*

1.10 In cases where state responsibility is engaged for the acts of a specific body, it is well established that the Convention applies to the actions of that body as employer, regardless of whether the employment relationship is governed by public or private law.[1] Somewhat surprisingly, however, the Court has not regarded all employment-related actions by the State as capable of attracting liability;[2] in particular it has differentiated between the treatment of those already in employment and candidates for public service posts, regarding only acts relating to the former as covered by the Convention. Thus dismissing or subjecting to the threat of dismissal a public servant for activities which fall within the scope of a right which the ECHR guarantees, such as union membership or expressing support for union activities, will constitute an interference with the exercise of that right;[3] lesser penalties, such as suspension or a reprimand,[4] or the threat of disciplinary action,[5] have also been found sufficient. However the argument that denial of employment, or confirmation of employment, for exercising a Convention right is capable of constituting an interference with the exercise of that right has so far been rejected on the ground (in our view, spurious) that the drafters of the Convention deliberately decided against including a right of equal access to the public service, in contrast to the UDHR and ICCPR, where such a right is expressly guaranteed.[6] Thus, in *Glasenapp v Germany* and *Kosiek v Germany*, where probationary civil servants had been dismissed because of their political views, the Court held by a 16 to one majority that 'access to the Civil Service . . . [lay] at the heart of the issues submitted to the Court'.[7] In refusing access to the applicants the authorities took account of their opinions and activities merely in order to determine whether they 'possessed one of the necessary personal qualifications for the post in question'.[8] That being so, there had been no interference with the exercise of the right to freedom of expression. The omission of the right of equal access to the public service from the Convention was explained by some members of the Court as due to the 'great difficulty of bringing before an international court the problem of recruitment and the arrangements for selection and access, which by their very nature differ considerably in Council of Europe member states according to national tradition and the system governing the civil service'.[9] However, to deduce from this that regarding refusal of employment as an interference would contradict the intention of those drafting the Convention is erroneous.[10] To recognise a meaningful right of equal access to the public service would indeed allow Convention organs to scrutinise the criteria and procedures used by signatory states to select their public servants, and require the development of jurisprudence stipulating what such a right entailed. However, this is very different from deciding that access to the public service should not be impeded by the state on grounds protected by the ECHR, a point emphasised by the one dissenting member of the Court, Judge Spielmann. It is also notable that actions of the state in other areas outside the main body of the Convention, such as immigration and extradition, can be capable in some circumstances of interfering with the exercise or enjoyment of Convention rights.[11] *Glasenapp* and *Kosiek* were distinguished by the ECtHR in *Vogt v Germany*,[12] where a permanent civil servant was dismissed from her secondary school teaching post because of her political activities. The Court held that, although the refusal to appoint a civil servant could not provide the basis for a complaint, this did not mean that a person who had been appointed and dismissed could not complain if dismissal violated a right under the Convention, given that the rights and freedoms it guaranteed applied to 'everyone'.[13] In holding that her dismissal was disproportionate to the aim pursued, it noted that it would be well nigh impossible for teachers in this situation to find another job, since in Germany teaching posts outside the civil service were scarce.[14] The Court did not explain the basis of distinguishing *Glasenapp* and *Kosiek*, beyond the blank assertion that the latter were essentially concerned with access to the public service, and in reality there seems no basis. The Convention does not specify a right not to be dismissed from the public service any more than it specifies a right of access, yet both are equally capable of interfering with the exercise of a Convention right, particularly in occupations or geographical locations where the state is a monopoly or quasi-monopoly employer or the individual has a strong ideological commitment to the concept of public service. Moreover, retention of the distinction may require some fine judgments to be made: on which side of the line would fall denial of promotion, for example, or non-renewal of a fixed term contract for exercising a right which the Convention guarantees? The artificiality of the dividing-line is well illustrated by the more recent case of *Wille v Liechtenstein*,[15] where the declared intention by the Prince of Liechtenstein not to appoint the President of the Administrative Court to any future public office because of his views on constitutional matters was held by the Court to be a reprimand for opinions previously expressed and therefore, again, distinguishable from *Glasenapp* and *Kosiek*.

---

1. *Swedish Engine Drivers' Union v Sweden* judgment of 6 February 1976, (1979–80) 1 EHRR 617, para 37; see also *Schmidt and Dahlström v Sweden* judgment of 6 February 1976, (1979–80) 1 EHRR 632.

2. For a fuller analysis of this issue see Morris, 1999, upon which the following paragraphs draw heavily.

3. *Vogt v Germany* judgment of 26 September 1995, (1996) 21 EHRR 205, para 44. Whether or not the restriction is justified in the circumstances is, of course, another matter.

4. *B v UK* App No 10293/83, (1985) 45 DR 41; *Morissens v Belgium* App No 11389/85, (1988) 56 DR 127. Cf. *Sibson v UK* judgment of 20 April 1993, (1994) 17 EHRR 193 (relocation of the applicant at another depot in accordance with his contract).

5. *Young, James and Webster v UK* judgment of 13 August 1981, (1982) 4 EHRR 38.

6. Article 21(2) of the UDHR provides that '[e]veryone has the right of equal access to public service in his country'; Article 25 of the ICCPR states that every citizen shall have the right and the opportunity to 'have access, on general terms of equality, to public service in his country'.

7. Judgment of 28 August 1986, (1987) 9 EHRR 25, para 53 and judgment of 28 August 1986, (1987) 9 EHRR 328, para 39 respectively. See also *Leander v Sweden* judgment of 26 March 1987, (1987) 9 EHRR 433, paras 59 and 72.

8. *Ibid.*

9. Joint Concurring Opinion of Judges Bindschedler-Robert, Pinheiro Farinha, Pettiti, Walsh, Russo and Bernhardt.

10. It is also notable that the drafting history of the Convention has not prevented the Court from reaching the opposite view to that originally intended in other contexts, such as the 'negative right of association' under Article 11, where the 'living instrument' approach has been applied: see *Sigurour A. Sigurjonsson v Iceland*, judgment of 30 June 1993, (1993) 16 EHRR 462, paras 33–35, discussed para **1.6** above.

11. See, for example, *Berrehab v The Netherlands* judgment of 21 June 1988, (1989) 11 EHRR 322; *Soering v UK* judgment of 7 July 1989, (1989) 11 EHRR 439.
12. Judgment of 26 September 1995, (1996) 21 EHRR 205.
13. *Ibid.*, paras 43, 44.
14. *Ibid.*, para 60.
15. Judgment of 28 October 1999.

1.11 The analysis in *Glasenapp* and *Kosiek* stands in marked contrast to the approach of the US courts to this issue. Initially the US jurisprudence followed the approach summarised in Holmes J's famous dictum that a policeman 'may have a constitutional right to talk politics, but he has no constitutional right to be a policeman'.[1] Thus in *Adler v Board of Education* the US Supreme Court concluded that a teacher denied employment because of membership of a listed organisation was:

> not thereby denied the right of free speech and assembly. His freedom of choice between membership in the organisation and employment in the school system might be limited, but not his freedom of speech or assembly, except in the remote sense that limitation is inherent in every choice.[2]

However in a number of subsequent decisions the Supreme Court rejected the argument that public employment could be made conditional on the surrender of constitutional rights which could not be abridged by direct governmental action.[3] Importantly it emphasised that the application of this principle did not depend upon the applicant being able to demonstrate a 'right' to the benefit which is being denied. Thus, in *Perry v Sindermann* the Court affirmed that:

> For at least a quarter-century, this Court has made clear that, even though a person has no 'right' to a valuable governmental benefit and even though the government may deny him the benefit for any number of reasons, there are some reasons upon which the government may not rely. It may not deny a benefit to a person on a basis that infringes his constitutionally protected interest, especially his interest in freedom of speech. For if the government could deny a benefit to a person because of his constitutionally protected speech or associations, his exercise of those freedoms would in effect be penalised or inhibited. This would allow the government to 'produce a result which [it] could not command directly' (*Speiser* v *Randall* 357 US 513 at 526) . . . Such interference with constitutional rights is impermissible.[4]

On this basis it was immaterial to his free speech claim that the petitioner, a college professor employed on a series of one year contracts, had no contractual right to re-employment. In *Rutan et al v Republican Party of Illinois* the Court emphasised that the burdens on free speech and association caused by hiring based on patronage were no less than those imposed by dismissal:

A state job is valuable. Like most employment, it provides regular paychecks, health insurance, and other benefits. In addition, there may be openings with the State when business with the private sector is slow. There are also occupations for which the government is a major (or the only) source of employment, such as social workers, elementary school teachers, and prison guards. Thus, denial of a state job is a serious privation.[5]

There is no barrier in the text of the Convention to the ECtHR adopting similar reasoning to recognise that being barred from State employment can constitute a weighty penalty for exercising a Convention right. *A fortiori* this course of action is open to domestic courts under the Human Rights Act 1998. This may be highly material in relation to discrimination on grounds of participation in union activities by 'public authorities' at the hiring stage, unless (as we argue in para **3.14**) domestic legislation, which covers only union membership, is interpreted to cover this.

---

1. *McAuliffe v Mayor of New Bedford* 155 Mass 216 at 220; 29 NE 517 (1892).
2. 342 US 485 at 492 (1952).
3. *Shelton v Tucker* 364 US 479 (1960); *Keyishian v Board of Regents* 385 US 589 (1967), 605. For an influential critique of the previous position, see Van Alstyne, 1967–1968.
4. (1972) 408 US 593, at 597.
5. (1990) 497 US 62, 77.

Rights Guaranteed by the ECHR and Contract

1.12 A further important question, which has yet to be satisfactorily resolved in ECHR jurisprudence, is whether acceptance of employment with an employer on terms which restrict the exercise of a right which the Convention guarantees precludes the worker later claiming that this restriction constitutes a violation of the right in question. This issue is probably of lesser relevance to domestic collective labour law than to the individual employment relationship (where it has enormous significance in areas such as the right to respect for private life and freedom of expression) because domestic legislation renders 'contracting-out' of statutory rights invalid, but it is possible to imagine circumstances not currently covered by legislation where it may arise.[1] There is authority from the ECtHR to suggest that Convention rights can be waived provided that such waiver is unequivocal[2] and has been obtained freely and without constraint.[3] This would appear to lend support to the argument that waiver clauses would preclude a subsequent challenge if workers have unambiguously and specifically assented to them. However it is submitted that the application of these principles should not save waivers in the context of employment save, perhaps, in highly unusual circumstances. First, the requirement that the waiver should be entered into without constraint may be difficult to prove: many groups of workers may claim with justification that the inequality of bargaining power inherent in the employment relationship prevents this condition being satisfied even if no overt threat of disciplinary action or damage to promotion prospects accompanies the 'invitation' to waive.[4] Moreover, there are ECtHR authorities to support the view that an act done against a background of compulsion may not estop an individual from claiming that the obligation to perform the act in question constitutes a violation of a Convention right.[5] Secondly, not all Convention rights are susceptible to waiver; the ECtHR has held that the right to liberty cannot be waived,[6] and it is notable that the decisions of the Court in this area generally relate to rights guaranteed by Article 6 (the right to a fair and public hearing). It may be possible to argue that other rights are so fundamental to a democratic society that they cannot be waived by agreement, or only to a limited extent. Finally, there is a decision of the EComHR which suggests that restrictions on freedom of expression which strike at the substance of the freedom require justification, an analysis which is equally applicable to other articles.[7] In this case a doctor employed in the hospital of a Catholic foundation was dismissed for having expressed in the press an opinion on abortion which was diametrically opposed to that of the Catholic Church. His contract imposed a duty of loyalty to the Church. As the Church was a private employer, the state could not be held directly responsible for its actions, but the applicant argued that, because the German courts had failed to provide him with a remedy against dismissal, the state had thereby failed to take the requisite positive measures to safeguard his freedom of expression. The Commission rejected the government's argument that the courts were not required to protect the applicant because he had waived this freedom in his employment contract; acceptance of the post of doctor in a Catholic hospital could not deprive him of the protection afforded by Article 10. It affirmed that 'in principle' the Convention permits contractual obligations which limit freedom of expression to a certain extent 'if they are freely entered into by the person concerned' and enforcement of the sanctions for breaching such obligations with the assistance of the state authorities did not, as such, constitute an 'interference by public authority' with the exercise of the right. However, this did not mean that the state had no responsibility in this area; rather, it owed an obligation to protect 'an employee against compulsion in matters of freedom of expression which would strike at the very substance of this freedom', in an analogous way to that found by the ECtHR to have been owed in *Young, James and Webster*,[8] described in para **1.9** above. This case raises the interesting question whether state parties to the Convention should provide a remedy for all employees to challenge the propriety of contractual clauses which they consider 'strike at the very substance' of the freedom to exercise a right which the Convention guarantees, without having to await the imposition of a disciplinary sanction, on the ground that the existence of the restriction in itself inhibits the exercise of the right. For the purpose of considering the relationship between Convention rights and contract, however, a positive obligation to safeguard employees against contractual terms which undermine the essence of a right would appear to indicate that the presence of such a term in a contract with a state employer should not, *per se*, prevent an individual from alleging that it constitutes an interference with the right in question, any more than would be the case if the restriction were imposed by legislation. For the purposes of domestic law, it is submitted that, equally, the presence of such a term should not prevent a court or tribunal inquiring into whether the interference with the right is justified.

---

1. For example, a restriction on participation in picketing, or articulating support for industrial action or union activities outside the scope of the statutory protection.

2. *Neumeister v Austria* judgment of 7 May 1974, (1979–80) 1 EHRR 136, para 36.

3. *Deweer v Belgium* judgment of 27 February 1980, (1980) 2 EHRR 439.

4. It is also submitted that waiver by collective agreement should not suffice: see *Young, James and Webster v UK* judgment of 13 August 1981, (1982) 4 EHRR 38.

5. *Sigurour A. Sigurjonnson v Iceland* judgment of 30 June 1993, (1993) 16 EHRR 462, para 36; *Van der Musselle v Belgium* judgment of 23 November 1983, (1984) 6 EHRR 163.

6. *De Wilde, Ooms and Versyp v Belgium (No. 1)* judgment of 18 June 1971, (1979–80) 1 EHRR 373; see also *H v Belgium* judgment of 30 November 1987, (1988) 10 EHRR 339, para 54.

7. *Rommelfanger v Federal Republic of Germany* App No 12242/86, (1989) 62 DR 151. Cf. *Vereniging Rechtswinkels Utrecht v The Netherlands* App No 11308/84, (1986) 46 DR 200; see also *Ahmad v UK* App No 8160/78, (1982) 4 EHRR 126; *Konttinen v Finland* App No 24949/94, (1996) 87 DR 68 (no interference with Article 9(1) right to manifest religion when workers were refused time off during working hours for religious observance); *Stedman v UK* App 29107/95, 23 EHRR CD 168 (no interference with Article 9(1) right when worker dismissed for refusing on religious grounds to sign a new contract of employment with employer which included Sunday as a working day). All these cases are analysed (and criticised) in detail in Morris, 1999.

8. Above, note 4.

COLLECTIVE LABOUR LAW AND THE HUMAN RIGHTS ACT 1998

General Principles

1.13 The Human Rights Act 1998 enables rights contained in the ECHR ('the Convention rights') to be relied upon in English courts and tribunals much more extensively than heretofore.[1] First, it requires all legislation to be 'read and given effect in a way which is compatible' with 'the Convention rights' '[s]o far as it is possible to do so'. Secondly, it will be unlawful for a public authority (including a court or tribunal) to act in a way which is incompatible with a Convention right unless, as the result of the provisions of primary legislation, it could not have acted differently. This has three major consequences for collective labour law. First, it will mean that the acts of at least some public authorities as employers will be susceptible to direct challenge even if they occur in contexts which are traditionally regarded as private for the purposes of judicial review. Secondly, the application of the duty to courts and tribunals is widely understood to mean that they will have an obligation to take cognisance of Convention rights when developing the common law. Thirdly, the obligation will be relevant to the exercise of judicial discretion; thus, in deciding whether an injunction should be granted, for example, a court will be required to consider whether the act which it is sought to restrain constitutes the exercise of a Convention right or, conversely, in some cases at least, whether that act itself interferes with the Convention right of another individual or body. We discuss each of these provisions in greater detail below. A court or tribunal determining a question which has arisen in connection with a Convention right must 'take into account' any judgment, decision, declaration or advisory opinion of the ECtHR; opinion or decision of the EComHR; or decision of the Committee of Ministers whenever made or given, so far as it appears relevant to the proceedings in which that question has arisen.[2] On the face of it, the Act accords equal weight to each of these sources. In practice, however, greater weight will be accorded to decisions of the Court, at least where it has found that a particular measure constitutes a violation of a right; if a domestic court failed to follow such a finding and this was upheld on appeal, the applicant could seek a remedy before the ECtHR. The converse, however, does not necessarily apply; it was not uncommon for the EComHR to find a violation when the Court did not,[3] and it will be open to domestic courts and tribunals to follow the Commission's view or, indeed, to take a more expansive view than either body, in the sense of according greater scope to the substantive right or lesser scope to that of the permissible exceptions to it. As we indicated in para **1.8**, the concept of the 'margin of appreciation' has often been important in the determination of whether a state is regarded as having acted in breach of the Convention. It is generally recognised that the concept in the form in which it is used in the ECHR jurisprudence, where it is concerned with the discretion accorded to a national authority by an international court, is inappropriate for use in a domestic court.[4] However, domestic courts will need to decide the scope of the discretion which they afford to the state or other body which seeks to justify an interference with a Convention right; this will almost certainly vary, depending upon the context.[5] It will almost certainly be argued (in our view, correctly) that ECHR decisions which have turned on the state having been accorded a wide margin of appreciation should not be regarded as unduly persuasive in domestic law, and that domestic courts should accord closer scrutiny to the matter.

---

1. See para **1.1** for a summary of the pre-existing position. Note that Articles 1 and 13 of the Convention (see para **1.9**) are not included in the Convention rights. The omission of Article 1 was uncontroversial—it was clearly inappropriate; that of Article 13 was not. The fourth and seventh Protocols to the ECHR are also omitted. There is already a voluminous literature relating to the Act. In this section we confine our discussion to the contexts in which Convention rights relevant to collective labour law may be raised before courts and tribunals. Note HRA 1998, s 22(4) for the relevance of acts of public authorities prior to 2 October 2000, the date the Act comes fully into force.

2. HRA 1998, s 2(1); see para **1.3** for the role played by each of these bodies. Cf the stronger obligation under the ECA 1972, s 3(1).

3. EComHR decisions on admissibility can also be a useful source of jurisprudence on case law relating to the concept of a 'victim' and on the scope of Convention rights, particularly where the application was regarded as 'manifestly ill-founded'. For the reasons we explain in para **1.3**, decisions of the Committee of Ministers are unlikely to be useful. No advisory opinions have been, or are likely to be, given by the Court (and see Article 47(2) ECHR for the restrictive scope of this power). All the ECHR jurisprudence is available on the ECtHR web-site: see App 5 .

4. See Pannick, 1998; Singh *et al*, 1999; Leigh and Lustgarten, 1999, 514–517.

5. See para **1.8** for the criteria which are used to assess justification. Note the provisions in HRA 1998 ss 12(4)–(5) and 13 relating to freedom of expression and freedom of thought, conscience and religion, although *quaere* how much difference in practice these provisions will make.

Interpretation of Legislation

1.14 As we indicated in para **1.1**, traditionally the scope for interpreting legislation in the light of international obligations has been confined to situations where that legislation is regarded as ambiguous. The Human Rights Act 1998 imposes a much more far-reaching interpretative principle in stating that '[s]o far as it is possible to do so, primary legislation and subordinate legislation must be read and given effect in a way which is compatible with the Convention rights'.[1] This requires the courts and tribunals (among others) to strive to find an interpretation of legislation which is consistent with the Convention rights; the government intended the conclusion that the legislation was incompatible with such rights to be a 'last resort', whilst not 'contort[ing] the meaning of words to produce implausible or incredible meanings'.[2] The obligation applies regardless of when the legislation was enacted; thus even legislation enacted after the Human Rights Act 1998 comes into force is subject to this interpretative principle (although note also that pre-existing primary legislation which is inconsistent with a Convention right is not impliedly repealed).[3] It means that previous authorities concerning the interpretation of legislation can no longer be regarded as binding where that interpretation is inconsistent with the Convention. Thus, to take an example we discuss in Chapter 3, the statutory protection against dismissal or subjection to other forms of detriment, or discriminatory hiring, on grounds of union membership and taking part in union activities will now be subject to interpretation in the light of ECHR jurisprudence, and tribunals will be free to depart from the narrow interpretation of 'membership' enunciated by the House of Lords on that basis if they are persuaded by the arguments which we propound.[4] The interpretative principle will be important in determining the scope of statutory discretions; thus, in the case of employers whose power to employ is derived from statute, such as local authorities or NHS Trusts, the statutory discretion accorded to determine the terms upon which they do so[5] will need to be exercised in the light of the Convention rights. The interpretation of the statutory concept of constructive dismissal[6] is another context in which it will be significant; it is strongly arguable that this provision should be given effect to in such a way that conduct of an employer which breaches a Convention right should be deemed to constitute a breach of the implied contractual duty of trust and confidence. In this connection, those authorities which support the view that employees can claim to have been constructively dismissed (or, indeed, directly dismissed for statutory purposes) and so mount an unfair dismissal claim (provided that other qualifications to claim are met) without resigning from the employment altogether on the basis that their existing employment *contract* has been breached may be particularly helpful.[7] Convention rights may also be important in determining whether a dismissal is unfair; to give effect to the Convention rights, the interpretation of 'some other substantial reason' for dismissal, and whether the employer has acted reasonably in the circumstances in dismissing, should render a dismissal which constitutes a violation of a Convention right unfair.[8] However, where it is impossible for a court or tribunal to read legislation compatibly with the Convention, the applicant will have no remedy. The legislation restricting the circumstances in which unions can admit to, or expel, from membership would seem to fall into this category.[9]

1 HRA 1998, s 3(1). See Hunt, 1997; Lester, 1998b. 'Primary' and 'subordinate' legislation are defined in s 21. Note that the s 3(1) obligation is not confined to courts and tribunals.

2 Mr. Jack Straw, Home Secretary, HC Debs Vol 313 , cols 421–422, 3 June 1998.

3 *Ibid.*, s 3(2)(a). A Minister in charge of a Bill in either House of Parliament must, prior to Second Reading, make a statement to the effect that in his or her view the provisions of the Bill are compatible with the Convention rights, or that although such a statement cannot be made, the government nevertheless wishes the House to proceed with such a Bill: s 19. For an example of the latter, see the Local Government Bill (H.L.) 1999.

4 See paras **3.5** and **3.7**.

5 Local Government Act 1972, s 112; National Health Service and Community Care Act 1990, Sched 2, para 16(1)(d).

6 ERA 1996, s 95(1)(c).

7 *Hogg v Dover College* [1990] ICR 39, EAT; *Alcan Extrusions v Yates* [1996] IRLR 327, EAT.

8 ERA 1996, s 98.

9 See para **2.24** *et seq.*

1.15 Specified courts—the House of Lords, the Judicial Committee of the Privy Council, the Courts-Martial Appeal Court, the High Court or the Court of Appeal—are empowered to make a 'declaration of incompatibility' if they conclude that primary legislation, or subordinate legislation where the primary legislation prevents removal of the incompatibility, is incompatible with the Convention.[1] The restriction to these courts means that for cases which are brought initially before employment tribunals, appeal would need to be taken to the Court of Appeal before a declaration of incompatibility could be made. However this does not mean that an employment tribunal, or the EAT, may not express its opinion on the compatibility of specific legislation; indeed, if a Convention right is raised in argument the tribunal will need to consider whether there is an incompatibility before considering whether it can interpret it away. The making of a declaration permits a government Minister to invoke a 'fast-track' procedure to amend the legislation to remove the incompatibility, subject to specified procedures being followed.[2] However it does not affect the validity, continuing operation or enforcement of the provision in question, and is not binding on the parties to the proceedings in which it is made.[3] Thus, the litigant whose proceedings lead to a declaration of incompatibility obtains no relief. It has been suggested that in these circumstances a court should use its discretion to award costs to such a litigant which, otherwise, he or she would need to go to the ECtHR to recover, at least where the opposing party was a public authority.[4]

1. HRA 1998, s 4. There are also provisions relating to courts in Scotland and Northern Ireland. The EAT is not part of the High Court, but it is a superior court of record: ETA 1996, s 20(3).
2. *Ibid.*, s 10; Sched 2.
3. *Ibid.*, s 4(6).
4. Grosz *et al*, 2000, para 3-51. Where a court is considering whether to make a declaration of incompatibility a Minister is entitled to be joined as a party to the proceedings, (HRA 1998, s 5) and it is suggested at para 3–51 that in these circumstances the justice of the case may require that he or she pay the costs of both the winning and the losing party.

Direct or Collateral Challenge against Public Authorities

1.16 It is unlawful for a 'public authority' to act in a way which is incompatible with a Convention right.[1] However, an authority's act will not be unlawful if, as a result of the provisions of primary legislation, it could not have acted differently or in the case of provisions of or made under primary legislation which cannot be read or given effect in a way which is compatible with the Convention rights, the authority was acting so as to give effect to or enforce those provisions.[2] An 'act' includes a failure to act, but does not include a failure to introduce in, or lay before, Parliament a proposal for legislation, or make any primary legislation or 'remedial order'.[3] A person who claims that a public authority has acted, or proposes to act, unlawfully may bring proceedings against the authority in the 'appropriate court or tribunal' or rely on the Convention right or rights concerned in any legal proceedings.[4] Controversially, the right to bring proceedings, or rely on the right in proceedings brought by a public authority, is confined to a 'victim' of the unlawful act, and a person is a victim for this purpose only if he or she would be so for the purposes of the proceedings before the ECtHR in respect of that act.[5] This appears to require domestic courts to follow, not merely to 'take into account', the ECHR jurisprudence on this matter. As we discussed in para **1.2**, that jurisprudence requires the individual to be 'directly affected' by the matter complained of, but the application of this term has not always proved easy to predict. However it is clear that it permits trade unions and other representative organisations to bring proceedings only if they as organisations are affected by a measure, and that it excludes challenges on public interest grounds. In general, it is a narrower test than the 'sufficient interest' required to bring an application for judicial review,[6] and it was maintained in the course of Parliamentary debates it would serve to 'hamper the proper administration of justice, unnecessarily increase the legal costs of judicial review proceedings and create legal uncertainty'.[7] However, the right to bring forms of proceedings other than those designated by the Act (such as judicial review) is expressly left unaffected,[8] and it has been argued that the restrictions which the victim test imposes may have been exaggerated. As Grosz *et al* explain, the limitation:

> does not therefore affect applications based on common law and probably not those in English courts based on an infringement of EC law. It will also not affect the rights of public interest groups or others with a sufficient interest—such as a public authority directed to enforce or give effect to legislation which it considers incompatible with Convention rights—to seek relief based on other provisions of the Act, including interpretative declarations, the quashing of unnecessarily incompatible subordinate legislation or the making of a declaration of incompatibility. Applications of this nature are grounded not on the duty contained in section 6 but on the interpretative obligation contained in section 3, which applies in all cases, and to which the restrictions on standing do not apply.[9]

The designation of bodies which constitute an 'appropriate court or tribunal' in which proceedings may be brought await determination in rules to be made by the Lord Chancellor or Secretary of State, as appropriate.[10] Thus, at the time of writing it is unclear whether employment tribunals will have this jurisdiction although a Consultation Paper issued by the Lord Chancellor's Department in March 2000 on Rules and Practice Directions relating to the Human Rights Act 1998 suggests that free-standing claims may be brought only in courts. Proceedings against public authorities must be brought within a year beginning with the date on which the act in question took place, or such longer period as the court or tribunal considers just and equitable in the circumstances, subject to any rule imposing a stricter time limit in relation to the procedure in question.[11] Thus, if a challenge is brought by way of an application for judicial review, the shorter time limit applicable in that context will apply.[12] Where a public authority is found to have acted unlawfully (or to have proposed to do so), a court or tribunal may grant such relief or remedy within its powers as it considers just and appropriate; a Minister may add to the relief or remedy a tribunal may afford in order to ensure that it can provide an 'appropriate remedy'.[13] However an award of damages may be made only by a court which has the power to award damages, or order the payment of compensation, in civil proceedings, and only where, in all the circumstances (including any other relief or remedy granted and the consequences of any decision) the court is satisfied that the award is necessary to afford 'just satisfaction' to the person in whose favour it is made.[14] In determining whether to make an award, and the amount, the court or tribunal is to 'take into account' the principles applied by the ECtHR.[15] As we indicated in para **1.4**, coherent principles in this context are difficult to discern; it is difficult to imagine that domestic courts will not adopt a more rigorous approach in this context. The capacity to raise the argument that a public authority has acted incompatibly with a Convention right, as well as according an important right of action, will also be significant as a defence in the area of collective labour law; thus, a picket who was prosecuted for obstructing a constable in the execution of his duty, for example, could plead as a defence that the constable was acting unlawfully in interfering with his or her freedom of expression, and thereby not acting in the execution of his duty.[16] We discuss in para **1.18** the implications of courts and tribunals being designated 'public authorities' for the implications of proceedings between private parties and the exercise of judicial discretion.

---

1. HRA 1998, s 6(1). See para **1.17** for the definition of a 'public authority'. Note s 9 in relation to proceedings relating to 'judicial acts'.
2. *Ibid.*, s 6(2). 'Primary' and 'subordinate' legislation are defined in s 21.
3. *Ibid.*, s 6(6).
4. *Ibid.*, s 7(1).
5. *Ibid.*, s 7(1),(7).
6. See Marriot and Nicol, 1998; Grosz *et al*, 2000, paras 4.30–4.44 (who point out (at 4.32) that in one respect the 'victim' test may be wider, in that one can be a victim even though others are more affected by the measure in question, whereas for judicial review purposes the position of an applicant in this position would be very weak).
7. Lord Lester HL Debs Vol 583, col 828, 24 November 1997.
8. HRA 1998, s 11.
9. Grosz *et al*, 2000, para 4.42.
10. HRA 1992, s 7(2),(9),(10).
11. *Ibid.*, s 7(5).
12. For judicial review, applications must be made 'promptly and in any event within three months from the date when the grounds for the application first arose': CPR Sched 1: RSC, Order 53, r 4(1).
13. HRA 1998, ss 8(1), 7(11).
14. *Ibid.*, s 8 (2),(3),(6).
15. *Ibid.*, s 8(4).
16. See para **6.78**.

1.17 The Government chose not to define 'public authority' for the purposes of the Act,[1] leaving this for determination by the courts, and existing principles of judicial review are likely to constitute a starting point for inquiring which bodies fall within the term, although the categories will not be wholly co-extensive (some bodies which have been regarded as excluded from the purview of judicial review because they are constituted by contract are likely to be regarded as having public functions, for example).[2] In the White Paper, *Rights Brought Home*, which preceded the legislation, central government, local government, the police, immigration officers and prisons were regarded as clearly being included,[3] and there seems little reason to think that the courts will gainsay this view. The Act affirms that a 'public authority' includes 'any person certain of whose functions are functions of a public nature'.[4] However, it then provides that a person is not a public authority *by virtue only* of this provision 'if the nature of the act is private'.[5] This means that there are effectively two categories of public authority for the purposes of the Act. First, there are 'pure' public authorities, all of whose acts will be susceptible to challenge even if they occur in the context of relationships which are traditionally regarded as private in nature for the purposes of judicial review.[6] Secondly, there are bodies with 'mixed' functions, where it will be necessary to decide whether the act in question lies in the public or the private realm. The first step, therefore, which employment lawyers may need to determine is the category into which a body falls. An issue may arise about the position of NHS Trusts in this regard. On one view, a court should regard as purely 'public' any organisation whose actions would attract state liability before the ECtHR (although, as we indicated in para **1.9**, the principles for determining this are not wholly clear). However it is arguable that a body may seek to be purely public if it is empowered to conduct activities of a commercial nature. Trusts are empowered to undertake such activities in making accommodation and services available to the public for payment, and in that respect they compete with the private sector.[7] The Lord Chancellor took the view that general practitioners would be 'public authorities' in relation to their NHS functions but not their private patients,[8] a view which would classify them as falling within the 'mixed' public/private category. However, it appears to be assumed within government that NHS Trusts are 'pure' public authorities, in which case the argument may not be put. Standard examples of bodies with 'mixed' functions are privatised prisons, contractors performing services for other areas of central government, and the public utilities. In their case it is widely assumed that all employment-related actions would be classified as private in nature, on the basis of authorities relating to judicial review, and therefore not susceptible to direct challenge. We do not accept this argument for three major reasons. First, the policy arguments which underlie the judicial review authorities on the dividing line between public and private acts, such as the provision of alternative remedies in the 'private' sphere, are not applicable in this context (and the dividing-line has, in any case, been removed for 'pure' public authorities). Secondly, even on the basis of the criteria which that case law has produced many of the cases involving alleged violations of Convention rights would fall within the 'public' realm because, for example, of the generalised impact of the act in question, its 'public element', or its statutory underpinning.[9] Thirdly, the ECHR jurisprudence does not distinguish between the 'public' and the 'private' acts of the state, and as we indicated in para **1.9** the ECtHR has affirmed that the state cannot evade its own responsibilities by contracting out its functions to private sector bodies (an approach reflected also in EC law).[10] Whilst this doctrine does not address the prior question of the boundaries of state functions, it would undoubtedly embrace areas of the civil service, such as prisons, so preventing the state arguing that it had no responsibility for the acts occurring within prisons run by private sector operators. It seems wholly undesirable to interpret 'private' acts in a way which is anything other than co-extensive with the scope of state responsibility before the ECtHR.

---

1. Cf, for example, the Race Relations (Amendment) Bill (H.L)1999, Sched 1.
2. See generally de Smith, Woolf and Jowell, 1995, and supplement 1998; Supperstone, 1997.
3. *Rights Brought Home: The Human Rights Bill* Cm 3792, 1997, para 2.2.
4. HRA 1998, s 6(3)(b).
5. *Ibid.*, s 6(5).
6. See Fredman and Morris, 1991; Poole, 2000.
7. National Health Service and Community Care Act 1990, Sched 2, para 14. Although they are empowered to do this only if it will not interfere with their duties to comply with directions given by the Secretary of State or the performance of their NHS obligations (paras 6,5), an argument based on the fact that these activities are subsidiary to their statutory duties could also be applied to privatised utilities which have a duty to supply on demand and whose capacity to diversify their activities may be limited by the need to fulfil this duty.
8. HL Debs, Vol 583, col 811, 24 November 1997.
9. See *McLaren v The Home Office* [1990] IRLR 338, Woolf LJ at 342; *R v London Borough of Hammersmith and Fulham, ex parte NALGO* [1991] IRLR 249, Nolan LJ at 256; *R v British Coal Corporation and the Secretary of State for Trade and Industry, ex parte Vardy* [1993] IRLR 104; R *v CPS ex parte Hogg* (1994) 6 Admin LR 778. see further Morris, 1998, 299–303.
10. Case C–189/89 *Foster v British Gas* [1990] ECR 3313, para 20.

Implications for Actions between Private Parties

1.18 The Human Rights Act 1998 does not provide an independent cause of action against private individuals for breach of the Convention rights. However, the obligation on courts and tribunals to act compatibly with Convention rights is widely understood to mean that the common law should be interpreted in a way which does not violate the Convention, even in actions between private individuals.[1] Thus, if a court is faced with proceedings involving an invasion of individual privacy, based on breach of confidence or trespass, for example, it should have regard to the terms of the right to respect for private life enshrined in Article 8 of the ECHR in interpreting the common law. This obligation may have important implications for the interpretation of the employer's managerial prerogative and the corresponding duty on employees to obey lawful and reasonable orders; it is submitted that this should be interpreted subject to the Convention rights, so that if an employer issued an instruction to employees of a nature which constituted a *prima facie* breach of such a right, such as a requirement to submit to intimate body searches, this would require justification on the basis of the principles set out in para **1.8**. As we argue in para **1.12**, we consider that express contractual powers which interfere with the exercise of a Convention right should also require justification by employers, but the ECHR jurisprudence on this matter is currently not wholly clear on this point. The duty to act compatibly with the Convention also has important implications for the exercise of judicial discretion. One context where this will be important in relation to collective labour law is that of the circumstances in which injunctions may be granted and the terms of those injunctions. As we argue in Chapter 6, we consider that the previous tendency of the courts to grant injunctions to restrain picketing by more than six persons at an entrance, in accordance with the Code of Practice on Picketing issued by the Secretary of State, could be challenged as incompatible with the right to freedom of expression under Article 10 and freedom of assembly under Article 11.[2] A more difficult issue is the implications of the Act for restraining the organisation of industrial action itself. As we explained in para **1.6**, the ECtHR has not regarded the right to strike as an essential element of freedom of association, but rather as only one of the variety of means by which a union may be 'heard' by an employer. It is possible that a domestic court may be persuaded to take a broader view, particularly on the basis of ILO jurisprudence, but this cannot be predicted with confidence.[3] Conversely, where industrial action itself threatens interference with the exercise of another Convention right, such as freedom of expression or, possibly, the right to life, this may well be a factor which, when assessing the balance of convenience, persuades a court in favour of granting the injunction and, indeed, in relation to some, at least, of the Convention rights there may be a positive obligation for it to do so.[4]

---

1. See generally Hunt, 1998 (who makes the point that existing causes of action will thereby metamorphose over time in order to comply with the Convention); Leigh, 1999; Markesinis, 1999; Bamforth, 1999; Wade, 1998.

2. See para **6.67**.

3. Note also *Collymore v AG of Trinidad and Tobago* [1970] AC 538, where the Privy Council held that constitutional protection of freedom of association does not extend to collective bargaining and the right to strike, and case law on the application of the Canadian Charter of Rights and Freedoms, 1982.

4. See para **1.9**. The Articles in relation to which the ECtHR has so far found a positive obligation should not be regarded as an exhaustive list: the same arguments of principle apply to others. It is instructive to compare the vulnerability of industrial action in this context to the position in EC law. In EC Council Regulation 2679/98, OJ [1998] L337/8, concerned with the safeguarding of free trade in the single market, Article 2 provides that '[t]his Regulation may not be interpreted as affecting in any way the exercise of fundamental rights, as recognised in the Member States, including the right or freedom to strike' (quoted Barnard and Hare, 2000).

OTHER INTERNATIONAL STANDARDS RELEVANT TO COLLECTIVE LABOUR LAW

International Labour Organisation Conventions

1.19 The most numerous and specific international labour standards emanate from the ILO, which was established in 1919 and is based upon a tripartite structure of governments, and representatives of employers and workers.[1] A state which ratifies an ILO Convention (of which there are more than 180) is obliged to 'take such action as may be necessary to make effective' its provisions,[2] although, at certain intervals, it may be open to states to denounce previously ratified Conventions. The 185 Recommendations aim at providing guidance to policy, legislation and practice, and are currently 'used mainly to supplement Conventions, in order to indicate in greater detail the manner of giving effect to their provisions or to advocate the establishment of higher standards'.[3] Freedom of association and effective recognition of the right to collective bargaining are regarded as fundamental principles of the ILO, and are laid down, primarily, in Convention 87 on Freedom of Association and Protection of the Right to Organise (1948) and Convention 98 on the Right to Organise and Collective Bargaining (1949).[4] Each state is required by the ILO Constitution to supply reports at regular intervals (in the case of freedom of association, every two years) on the measures taken to implement the Conventions it has ratified. These are examined by an independent Committee of Experts whose reports are submitted to a tripartite Committee on the Application of Conventions and Recommendations, established at each session of the International Labour Conference (which normally meets once a year), before which government representatives may appear. In addition to these regular monitoring procedures, there is provision for complaints, either by one Member State against another co-signatory to a Convention or by the ILO Governing Body (which has 56 members, 28 representing governments, the remainder equal numbers of employer and worker representatives), either of its own motion or at the instigation of a delegate to the Conference. It is also open to workers' and employers' representatives to make representations that a state is not securing the application of a ratified Convention; such representations are considered initially by a three-member committee of the Governing Body and then by the Governing Body itself. The importance of respect for the principles of freedom of association for the effective functioning of the ILO is reflected in the special machinery which has been developed to deal with alleged failures of compliance in this area. Two bodies are concerned with this. First, there is a tripartite Committee on Freedom of Association, composed of nine members appointed by the Governing Body, which has dealt with a large number of individual cases, mainly based on written submissions but sometimes involving oral hearings or visits to the countries concerned. Secondly, there is a Fact-Finding and Conciliation Commission, composed of independent persons, which may undertake more extensive investigations, similar to a commission of inquiry, provided that the Member State consents. These procedures can be invoked against governments which have not ratified all or any of the freedom of association Conventions because it is assumed that the very fact of ILO membership carries with it an obligation to respect those principles.[5]

1. For the history of the ILO, see Alcock, 1971; for an overview see Ewing, 1994. On its constitution and structure, see Valticos and Samson, 1998; Valticos and von Potobsky, 1995; Swepston, 1997. For an overview of the areas covered by ILO Conventions and Recommendations, see Valticos and Samson, 1998, paras 30–64. The ILO has a very useful web-site: see App 5.
2. ILO Constitution, Article 19(5)(d).
3. Valticos and Samson, 1998, para 16.
4. See also the Convention (No 135) and Recommendation (No143) on the Protection and Facilities to be afforded to Workers' Representatives in the Undertaking (1971); The Rural Workers' Organisations Convention (No 141) and Recommendation (No 149) of 1975; The Labour Relations (Public Service) Convention (No. 151) and Recommendation (No 159) of 1978, and Convention (No 154) and Recommendation (No 163) on The Promotion of Collective Bargaining (1981). Convention No 154 has not been ratified by the UK.
5. See now the *ILO Declaration on Fundamental Principles and Rights at Work and its Follow-UP*, ILO, 1998. States that have ratified a freedom of association Convention are also subject to the normal supervisory procedures relating to ratified Conventions.

1.20 Convention No 87 on Freedom of Association and Protection of the Right to Organise provides that all workers 'without distinction whatsoever, shall have the right to establish and, subject only to the rules of the organisation concerned, to join organisations of their own choosing without previous authorisation'.[1] Workers' organisations have the right to draw up their constitutions and rules, to elect their representatives in full freedom, to organise their administration and activities and to formulate their programmes; they may also establish and join federations and confederations and affiliate with international organisations of workers.[2] Member States undertake to take 'all necessary and appropriate measures' to ensure that workers may exercise freely the right to organise, and domestic law shall not impair the guarantees in the Convention.[3] Convention 98 provides that workers should enjoy adequate protection against acts of anti-union discrimination in respect of their employment, and their organisations should enjoy adequate protection against interference by employers or employers' organisations in their establishment, functioning or administration.[4] Again, there is an obligation to establish 'machinery appropriate to national conditions', where necessary, to ensure respect for the right to organise.[5] The Convention also states that measures appropriate to national conditions should be taken, where necessary, to encourage and promote collective bargaining machinery.[6] There is no express reference in either Convention to the right to strike. However, ILO supervisory bodies have consistently affirmed that this is one of the essential and legitimate means by which workers and their organisations may promote and defend their economic and social interests and, as such, it is an integral part of the free exercise of the rights which the Conventions guarantee (except in the case of public officials, where recognition of the freedom to associate does not necessarily imply the right to strike).[7] These bodies have developed an extensive jurisprudence on the scope and limits of the right to strike, covering issues such as the conditions for the exercise of the right (ballots and prior notice, for example, are acceptable); legitimate objectives of a strike (purely political strikes are excluded); sympathy strikes (which should be permitted where the initial strike is lawful), strikes in essential services and compensatory guarantees for workers who are denied the right to strike; and protection against dismissal and other forms of detriment for individual strikers. As we indicate in later chapters, there are a number of respects in which the UK has been found to be in breach of this and other aspects of the right to freedom of association and the right to organise.[8] As our discussion shows, breaches have not, in the main, been cured by the Employment Relations Act 1999.[9] The willingness of the ILO to recognise the right to strike as an essential means by which workers may promote their interests stands in marked contrast to the restrictive approach of the ECtHR to this issue; this is not an area, unlike some others, where that Court has been prepared to draw upon ILO standards in order to interpret the scope of the right guaranteed by the Convention.[10] The tripartite structure of the ILO, which ensures that the social partners as well as governments participate in the formulation of standards, and its long and specialist experience, accord it considerably greater legitimacy in this area than the ECtHR, which deals only with the case before it and has shown itself to be heavily orientated towards an individualistic perspective. There will be little to be lost in raising arguments derived from the ILO jurisprudence before UK courts in proceedings relating to industrial action once the Human Rights Act 1998 comes fully into force, but we cannot predict with confidence that they will be regarded as heavily persuasive in the face of the narrow view of the scope of the right to join trade unions accorded by the ECtHR.

1. Article 2.
2. Articles 3, 5.
3. Articles 11, 8.
4. Articles 1, 2.
5. Article 3.
6. Article 4. Both Conventions No 87 and 98 each provide that the extent to which the guarantees provided for in the Convention apply to the armed forces and the police is for determination by national laws or regulations: Article 9(1) and 5(1) respectively. Convention No 98 also 'does not deal with the position of public servants engaged in the administration of the State', although it should not 'be construed as prejudicing their rights or status in any way': Article 6. On the position of public servants, see further Convention No 151 (see para **1.19** note 4), and for a comparative discussion of the exceptions from freedom of association principles from the respective international treaties, see Morris, 1994a.
7. For the jurisprudence on the right to strike, see *Freedom of Association and Collective* Bargaining, ILO, 1994; *Decisions and Principles of the Freedom of Association Committee of the Governing Body of the ILO*, 4th ed., ILO, Geneva, 1996; and for a very useful broad analysis, see Gernigon, Odero and Guido, 1998.
8. See generally Ewing, 1994; Creighton, 1993; D Brown and A McColgan, 1992; Mills, 1997; Novitz, 2000.
9. See also Novitz, 1998; 2000.
10. See paras **1.1**, note 11; **1.6**.

The European Social Charter

1.21 The ESC of 1961, which constitutes the economic and social counterpart to the ECHR, protects collective rights much more extensively.[1] Signatory states need not undertake to be bound by every article of the Charter, but the UK has accepted those relevant to collective labour law. Unlike the ECHR there is no avenue for individuals to enforce rights guaranteed by the Charter; in 1995 a Protocol providing for a system of collective complaints by management, labour and non-governmental organisations was added,[2] but this has not been signed by the UK. This leaves as the only mechanism of enforcement scrutiny by a committee of seven independent experts (the 'ECSR', formerly known as the 'CIE'), assisted by an ILO representative in a consultative capacity, of reports on law and practice which each government supplies, although trade unions and employers' organisations have an opportunity to comment on them.[3] The ECSR has developed an extensive jurisprudence relating to the Charter.[4] There are two articles of the ESC relevant to collective labour law. First, Article 5 provides that:

> With a view to ensuring or promoting the freedom of workers . . . to form local, national or international organisations for the protection of their economic and social

interests and to join those organisations, the Parties undertake that national law shall not be such as to impair, nor shall it be so applied as to impair, this freedom.

The ECSR has stated that this implies both a positive and a negative obligation: the absence of any domestic law or practice that impairs freedom of association, together with 'adequate legislative or other measures' on the part of the state 'to guarantee the exercise of the right to organise, and in particular to protect workers' organisations from any interference on the part of employers'.[5] Secondly, under Article 6, contracting states undertake to promote joint consultation between workers and employers; to promote, where necessary and appropriate, collective bargaining machinery; to promote the establishment and use of appropriate machinery for conciliation and voluntary arbitration for the settlement of labour disputes; and to recognise 'the right of workers and employers to collective action in cases of conflicts of interest, including the right to strike, subject to obligations that might arise out of collective agreements previously entered into'. Both Articles 5 and 6 are subject to Article 31, which provides that the exercise of these rights 'shall not be subject to any restrictions or limitations . . . except such as are prescribed by law and are necessary in a democratic society for the protection of the rights and freedoms of others or for the protection of public interest, national security, public health or morals'.[6] We indicate in later chapters important respects in which the UK has been found not to be in compliance with the Charter by the ECSR. Ironically, the ESC, because it allows contracting states some discretion as to the articles they accept, has been invoked by the ECtHR to reinforce its narrow interpretation of Article 11 ECHR. Thus, in *National Union of Belgian Police v Belgium*, the ECtHR reasoned that because a state may not have chosen to accept Article 6 of the Charter, to conclude that a right to joint consultation derived directly from Article 11 would 'amount to admitting that the . . . Charter took a retrograde step in this domain'.[7] The fallacy of this argument is shown by the fact that Article 5 ESC includes the right to form and join trade unions guaranteed by Article 11 ECHR, yet it cannot be maintained that a state which has chosen not to accept Article 5 of the Charter is thereby not bound by any element of Article 11.

---

1. A revised ESC, which accords additional rights in the field of employment, was open for signature in May 1996. The UK signed the revised Charter in November 1997, but at the time of writing has not ratified it. Articles 5 and 6, and the terms of Article 31, remain the same in both versions of the Charter; Article 31 is Article G in the new Charter.

2. ETS No 158; see Brillat, 1996.

3. For critiques of this system see Harris, 1984; O'Higgins, 1991. We refer throughout this work to the ECSR although this committee was until recently known as the CIE.

4. For a useful overview, see Samuel, 1997. Recent ECSR Conclusions are on the ESC web-site: see App 5.

5. Conclusions I (1969–70), 31.

6. Article 5 leaves the application of the right to organise to members of the armed forces to national laws or regulations, but the CIE has concluded from the wording of the provision relating to the police and the *travaux préparatoires* that while a state may be permitted to limit the freedom of the police to organise, it cannot deprive them of all the guarantees provided in the article: Conclusions I (1969–70), p 31.

7. Judgment of 27 October 1975, (1979–80) 1 EHRR 578 at para 38.

The International Covenant on Economic, Social and Cultural Rights and the International Covenant on Civil and Political Rights

1.22 The protection of human rights is one of the purposes of the United Nations. The UDHR was adopted by the General Assembly in 1948, and the ICESCR and ICCPR, adopted in 1966, expand and define the Declaration's terms and establish legal obligations to which states may bind themselves. The ICESCR contains the more comprehensive provisions relating to collective labour law. Signatory states undertake to ensure the right of everyone to form and join the trade union of their choice, subject to that union's rules; the right of unions to join federations, confederations and international union organisations; and the right of unions to function freely (from which an obligation to promote collective bargaining has been implied).[1] The Covenant also explicitly guarantees the right to strike, although this is subject to the proviso that 'it is exercised in conformity with the laws of the particular country'.[2] By contrast, the ICCPR, like the ECHR, is confined to an affirmation of the right of 'everyone' to join trade unions for the protection of his or her interests, which, again, is treated as a sub-division of a broader freedom to associate.[3] In the case of the UK, compliance with both covenants is monitored by means of reports from signatory states.[4] Each contains a clause providing that nothing in the articles in question shall authorise states parties to ILO Convention No 87 to take legislative measures which would prejudice, or apply the law in such a manner as would prejudice, the guarantees provided for in that Convention. On one view, this is of 'negligible [legal] value' in that the obligations in the ILO Convention could not in any case be derogated from on the basis of the Covenant,[5] but in emphasising the importance of the ILO as a source of standards it may serve a useful purpose.[6] For advocates before domestic courts, reference to these instruments, particularly the ICESCR, is useful in reinforcing the universal nature of the rights which they uphold, but the jurisprudence of the ILO supervisory bodies is likely to prove a more fruitful and subtle source of argument.

1. Article 8(1)(c); on the history and jurisprudence of Article 8, and exceptions to the rights therein contained, see generally Craven, 1998, Chapter 7.

2. Article 8(d).

3. Article 22. In *J.B. et al v Canada* the majority of the Human Rights Committee expressed the view that a communication claiming that the general prohibition on strikes by public employees imposed by the Alberta Public Employee Relations Act 1977 violated Article 22 was inadmissible *ratione materiae* because the right to strike was not within the scope of freedom of association: see McGoldrick, 1994, para 4.60.

4. In the case of the ICCPR, there is an optional inter-state procedure and an individual communications procedure to the Human Rights Committee, but this has not been accepted by the UK.

5. Craven, 1998, 260.

6. Cf the case study of the discrepant treatment by the ILO, EComHR and ECSR (then the CIE) of the ban on membership of national civil service unions at Government Communications Headquarters in Morris, 1994a, 45–49.

2

The Legal Regulation of Trade Unions

INTRODUCTION

2.1 Historically, the nature and extent of the legal regulation of trade unions in Britain has varied greatly.[1] Like other Western European states, the UK sought initially to suppress the growth of collective organisation by workers by invoking the criminal law.[2] During the eighteenth century, several statutes forbade combinations in specific trades and places,[3] and at the turn of the century the Combination Acts of 1799 and 1800 made all combinations of workmen unlawful. All such legislation was repealed in 1824–1825, but the removal of the threat of criminal prosecution did not accord workers' organisations the right to exist, and in the famous case of *Hornby v Close*[4] trade union purposes were found to be illegal because they were in restraint of trade. A Royal Commission established in 1867 to investigate the issue of trade unionism showed the starkly differing policy directions which could be taken. The majority report considered that unions should be subject to a highly restrictive regime; the minority, consisting of union sympathisers, recommended that unions should have the legal protection which they required to function as such, but otherwise should be free from legal supervision. The Liberal Government of the day preferred the minority view, and the resulting Trade Union Act 1871 affirmed that the purposes of unions should not be deemed unlawful by reason only of being in restraint of trade so as to render any member liable to criminal prosecution, and stipulated that the restraint of trade doctrine should not render union agreements or trusts void or voidable. A further provision, which precluded any union agreements from being directly enforceable or subject to damages for breach, was designed to exclude union rules from the purview of the courts. However, due to tortuous drafting it achieved only partial success in this endeavour.[5]

The Trade Union Act 1871 reflected the principle that unions were autonomous bodies which should be free to determine and enforce their own constitutions. This is regarded as a fundamental principle in ILO Convention

No. 87 on Freedom of Association and Protection of the Right to Organise (1948), Article 3 of which proclaims the right of workers' (and employers') organisations to 'draw up their constitutions and rules, to elect their representatives in full freedom, to organise their administration and activities and to formulate their programmes' free from any interference by the public authorities which would restrict this right or impede its lawful exercise. The policy of abstinence from statutory regulation of union conduct remained intact in Britain for about a century, with the exception of union political activities and mergers. However, the form of protection the 1871 Act accorded—that of immunity against specified common law liabilities—was limited in its impact; in particular, it did not grant a positive right for unions to exist or for individual workers to form and join them. This immunities approach left unions vulnerable to the resurgence of common law doctrines, as shown by *Edwards v SOGAT*, for example, in which it was suggested that a rule which enabled unions to act in a 'capricious and despotic' manner was not proper to the purposes of a union and was therefore unprotected by the statutory immunity.[6] It also meant that workers had no protection in the event that their freedom to join unions was curtailed; thus, when the right to join national civil service unions was removed from workers at Government Communications Headquarters in 1984, there was no substantive right which they or their unions could invoke.[7] Finally, the legislation was insufficient to prevent judicial incursions into the autonomy of unions. In purporting to enforce their constitutions, the courts adopted a highly interventionist approach which favoured individual over collective interests, based on the dual perspectives that unions had functions whose significance far outweighed that of the social clubs whose legal structure they reflected, and that the ordinary union member had no influence on the composition of the union's rules. The power to imply terms into the union rule book, and to strike out those regarded as contrary to public policy, also proved highly significant in this context; in particular the courts imposed on unions through these mechanisms the duty to comply with public law standards of procedural fairness in exercising their decision-making powers.

Although its importance should not be underestimated, the degree of external regulation emanating from the common law was modest compared with the extensive statutory constraints on union conduct which now exist. The first break with the non-interventionist tradition came with the Industrial Relations Act 1971 enacted by the Heath Conservative Government, although notably its provisions were primarily concerned with requiring unions to include rules on specific matters rather than requiring these rules to take a specified form.[8] With the return of a Labour Government in 1974 the principle of union autonomy was to a large extent restored, the major exception being the application of the sex and race discrimination legislation to unions in their dealings with applicants and members. From 1980 onwards, however, the activities of unions were subjected by successive Conservative governments to an increasing degree of external regulation. This process began slowly, with the institution by the Employment Act 1980 of protection against 'unreasonable' exclusion or expulsion from a union where a closed shop was in operation. The Trade Union Act 1984 brought much more extensive regulation, with the introduction of statutory requirements to hold periodic elections for specified union offices; ballots before industrial action; and periodic ballots to retain existing political funds for expenditure on 'political objects', in addition to the requirement for a ballot to establish such a fund in the first place which had existed since the Trade Union Act 1913. The Employment Act 1988 imposed additional obligations in relation to the balloting procedures, and introduced further rights for individual union members, most notably restrictions on the types of conduct for which they could be disciplined by their unions, including refusing, and encouraging others to refuse, to participate in industrial action even if that action had been approved by a majority in a ballot. This Act also brought the creation of a Commissioner for the Rights of Trade Union Members to assist individuals who wished to bring legal proceedings against their union. In the Employment Act 1990 and Trade Union Reform and Employment Rights Act 1993 further provisions relating to the conduct of ballots were introduced; the 1993 legislation also constrained unions from excluding or expelling individuals from membership except in circumstances permitted by statute. In all cases the statutory provisions were deemed to prevail over anything in the union rule book, so diminishing very significantly the scope of union autonomy. The justifications for introducing these provisions varied, but a central theme was the need for legislative imposition of democracy within unions, predicated on the assumption (for which no evidence was supplied) that union leaders did not adequately reflect the views of their members and that, in the light of the special 'privileges' and immunities which unions enjoyed, it was particularly important to ensure that the rights of individual members were adequately protected and that there was proper accountability for the use of union power.[9]

A number of the statutory constraints introduced by the Thatcher and Major Conservative Governments (although not those pertaining to union elections) are regarded as incompatible with freedom of association by the ILO Committee of Experts on the Application of Conventions and Recommendations, and have also attracted condemnation from the ECSR (formerly the CIE) of the ESC. In addition, the EComHR has affirmed that the right to join a union guaranteed by Article 11 of the ECHR does not accord a general right to join the union of one's choice, regardless of the union rules.[10] Despite this, the incoming Labour Government has done nothing to alter the substantive framework regulating union conduct inherited from its predecessors. The very detailed statutory regulation affords little scope for modifying the application of these provisions by reference to arguments based upon the Human Rights Act 1998 in this context, although, as we indicate later in the chapter, the Act may have some part to play in relation to common law regulation.

We start the chapter by considering the powers of the Certification Officer, a statutory officer with responsibility for union affairs whose jurisdiction was extended and allied more closely with that of the courts by the Employment Relations Act 1999, as a concomitant of the abolition of the Commissioner for the Rights of Trade Union Members. We next examine the definition and legal classification of trade unions, and the nature of their legal status. This is followed by an analysis of the common law regulation of unions which, despite the scope of statutory regulation, still remains significant. The remainder of the chapter examines the statutory regulation of unions, including the restrictions on their powers to admit, discipline and expel members; restrictions against unlawful discrimination; and controls over elections and expenditure on 'political objects'.

---

1. For a brief overview, see Elias and Ewing, 1987, Chapter 1. Sidney and Beatrice Webb found no instance of the use of the term 'trade union' in the first third of the nineteenth century: Webb and Webb, 1920, 113.

2. See Jacobs, 1986.

3. See Orth, 1991, Chapter 2.

4. (1867) LR 2 QB 153.

5. See Elias and Ewing, 1987, 6–12.

6. [1971] Ch 354, per Sachs LJ at 382. Protection against the restraint of trade doctrine was extended to trade union rules in the Trade Union and Labour Relations Act 1974 and this has continued ever since: see now TULRCA 1992, s 11.

7. *CCSU v Minister for the Civil Service* [1985] AC 374, HL. The House of Lords accepted that the unions had a right to be consulted before their members' terms and conditions of employment were varied, but this was not specifically related to the nature of the freedom being curtailed (and in the circumstances was outweighed by the interests of the state in national security).

8. See Weekes *et al*, 1975, Chapter 3.

9. See, variously, the Green Papers *Democracy in Trade Unions*, Cmnd 8778, 1983; *Trade Unions and their Members*, Cm 95, 1987; *Industrial Relations in the 1990s*, Cm 1602, 1991. For a more detailed analysis, and powerful critique, of the assumptions upon which these statements rest, see Fredman, 1992. On the background to, and impact of, the balloting provisions see P Smith *et al*, 1993; Undy *et al*, 1996.

10. *Cheall v UK* App No 10550/83, (1986) EHRR 74.

THE ROLE OF THE CERTIFICATION OFFICER

2.2 The Certification Officer is an independent officer with statutory responsibility for an extensive range of functions relating to trade unions and employers' associations.[1] He or she is appointed by the Secretary of State after consultation with ACAS. The first Certification Officer was appointed in 1975 and took over the role previously performed by the Registrar of Friendly Societies under earlier union legislation. The functions of the Certification Officer now include maintaining lists of unions and employers' associations and ensuring that they comply with their accounting and auditing obligations; determining whether unions meet the statutory test of 'independence'; ensuring observance of the procedures governing the establishing and operation of political funds and approving the ballot rules of unions intending to conduct political fund review ballots; supervising union mergers; and, where appropriate, initiating investigations into unions' financial affairs. The Certification Officer is also charged with adjudicating upon complaints by union members[2] that a union has failed to comply with its statutory obligations in a wide range of areas, including those relating to the accuracy and confidentiality of its register of members; elections of its senior officers and members of its executive (and ensuring that they have not been convicted of specified offences); provisions governing political fund ballots and the administration of political funds; and merger ballots. Prior to the Employment Relations Act 1999 the Certification Officer's jurisdiction was confined to breaches of specified statutory obligations. However it has now been extended to cover breaches or threatened breaches of union rules concerning the appointment or election of a person to, or removal of a person from, office; disciplinary proceedings; ballots on any issue other than industrial action; and the constitution or proceedings of any executive committee or any decision-making meeting.[3] This extension of jurisdiction was considered by the government to be appropriate in the light of the abolition of the Commissioner for the Rights of Trade Union Members, an office established by the Conservative Government in 1988 to provide assistance to union members considering or bringing court proceedings against their union in relation to specified matters, including breaches of union rules.[4] Members who wish to complain that they have been denied access to union accounting records, or that a union which does not have a 'political fund' has spent money on political objects contrary to statute, have also been given the option of going to the Certification Officer instead of only to the High Court. Members retain the capacity to seek redress from the High Court instead of the Certification Officer in all areas where this was previously permitted, but in contrast to the position before the Employment Relations Act 1999, when an individual could pursue both avenues, they are now mutually exclusive; the Certification Officer may not consider an application if the applicant has applied to the court in respect of the same matter; conversely, once an application has been made to the Certification Officer the same matter may not be put to the court by that applicant even if the application to the Certification Officer is withdrawn.[5] This does not prevent another member raising the same claim in the alternative forum, but if this is done, the Certification Officer or the court, as the case may be, is generally required to have regard to any declaration, order, observations or reasons made or given in relation to the failure in question which is brought to its attention.[6] Applying to the Certification Officer is likely to be a cheaper, quicker and less formal mechanism than applying to the High Court unless interim relief, which only the High Court can grant, is sought. The procedure for doing so is relatively simple. Applicants are required to set out the basis of their claim in writing, if possible identifying which part of the legislation or which rules have allegedly been breached and why, and including supporting documents and other evidence.[7] There is a registration form available which helps to ensure that the requisite information is provided. The Certification Officer then forwards details of the application to the union for comment, and any comments are then copied to the applicant for observation.[8] The Certification Officer makes such enquiries as he or she thinks fit in relation to an application, and can ask for information to be furnished by a specified date, although the application can still be determined if that information is not provided unless the Certification Officer considers that would be inappropriate.[9] He or she is required to give the parties to the application an opportunity to present their case at a hearing;[10] in practice, hearings are held in public, and the parties are able to question each other. The Certification Office pays expenses incurred by applicants and their witnesses in attending hearings, but does not pay legal costs. There is no power to order witnesses to attend. The Certification Officer is required to ensure, so far as reasonably practicable, that an application is determined within six months of being made.[11] Full written reasons are given for his or her decision.[12] If the Certification Officer upholds the application, he or she must grant a declaration and, unless this is considered inappropriate, an 'enforcement order' which requires the union to take specified steps within a specified time to remedy the declared failure and/or to abstain from specified acts in future.[13] Such enforcement orders may be enforced as if they were orders of the court, so rendering the union liable for contempt of court in the event of non-compliance.[14] Either party may appeal against a decision of the Certification Officer to the EAT, within 42 days of the Certification Officer's decision being issued.[15] Decisions of the Certification Officer have no precedent value, but may serve as useful guidance as to how matters may be viewed.

1. TULRCA 1992, s 254. We discuss each of the areas of the Certification Officer's jurisdiction relating to unions in detail at appropriate points in the text, and do not, therefore, provide statutory references here. The law relating to employers' associations is beyond the scope of this work.

2. It is not always easy to determine whether an individual is a union 'member', particularly where unions have different categories of membership, such as 'full', 'honorary', 'limited' and 'retired'. In *NUM (Yorkshire Area) v Millward* [1995] IRLR 411, the EAT affirmed that the provisions of the rule book may not always be determinative for statutory purposes; in each case the relevant provision must be examined 'textually and contextually' (415). Returns submitted by unions for 1998 indicated that the total number of contributing members was around 6 per cent less than the figure for total membership as a result of the latter including retired and unemployed members, members on long-term sick and maternity/child care leave and those on career breaks: *Annual Report of the Certification Officer for 1999–2000*, para 4.8.

3. TULRCA 1992, s 108A. Other matters may be included by order of the Secretary of State. Industrial action ballots were excluded because they would draw the Certification Officer into deciding matters involving relations between unions and employers: Mr. Michael Wills, Minister for Small Firms, Trade and Industry, Official Report of Standing Committee E, 4 March 1999, 4.15pm. Misuse of union funds, on which the Certification Officer is empowered to investigate and report, and cases regarding the dismissal or disciplinary proceedings against union employees are also excluded (the former by implication).

4. *Ibid.*, ss 109–114 (now repealed).

5. However if the Certification Officer refuses to determine a complaint brought by a 'vexatious litigant' pursuant to the powers in TULRCA 1992, s 256A, such persons can still seek special leave from the courts to have their cases heard by the courts s 256B.

6. See, for example, TULRCA 1992, ss 25(11), 26(8). Cf., however, ss 108A and 108B, relating to breach of rules, where no such requirement is stipulated.

7. See App 5 for details of how to contact the Certification Office.

8. The identity of an applicant will be disclosed to the union unless the Certification Officer thinks that the circumstances are such that it should not be, and to such other persons as the Certification Officer thinks fit: TULRCA 1992, s 256(2A).

9. See, for example, *ibid.*,s 25(2),(7).

10. For example, *ibid.*, s 25(2).

11. For example, *ibid.*, s 25(6).

12. For example, s 25(5). Reasons may be accompanied by written observations on any matter arising from or connected with the proceedings.

13. For example, *ibid.*, s 25(5A).

14. For example, *ibid.*, s 25(10). See para **6.61** *et seq.* for the penalties for contempt of court. In some cases the order can be enforced by any member who was a member at the time the order was made (for example, s 25(5B)); in others (for example, s 31) no such provision is made.

15. See, for example, *ibid.,* s 45D. Appeals are on a question of law only (cf. the position on listing and independence, discussed in paras **2.5** and **2.6**).

THE DEFINITION AND LEGAL CLASSIFICATION OF TRADE UNIONS

Sources and General Principles

2.3 It is crucial to know whether an organisation falls within the definition of a 'trade union', since a number of important legal consequences, most of which are laid down in the Trade Union and Labour Relations (Consolidation) Act 1992, follow if it does. Some are beneficial, others onerous. On the one hand, unions are protected against certain common law liabilities: their rules and purposes are protected against the doctrine of restraint of trade; their liability in tort (with some exceptions) is subject to statutory limits in any set of proceedings; and certain categories of union property are protected against awards of damages, costs or expenses.[1] On the other, only unions are subject to the intricate statutory requirements governing the selection of their executive committees; restrictions upon whom they admit to, and expel from, membership; and the grounds upon which they discipline their members.[2] 'Employers' associations' share some of the legal attributes of unions, but only a few of the burdens.[3] Unions themselves sub-divide into different categories. First, they may be listed or unlisted. 'Listed' unions are those which appear on the Certification Officer's list of unions;[4] while not compulsory, being listed brings significant advantages. Secondly, they may be 'independent'[5] or 'non-independent'. 'Independent' unions have important rights not shared with the non-independent, including being able to present a request for recognition under the statutory recognition procedure (see further Chapter 4). Independence is significant also for their 'employee' members, who are accorded protection against dismissal or subjection to any other detriment by their employer on the grounds of their union membership or activities.[6] A third distinction is whether a union is recognised or unrecognised. Unlike whether the organisation constitutes a 'trade union', or whether it satisfies the test of 'independence', recognition is relevant only to the status of the union in relation to a particular employer; a union may be recognised by one employer but not by another. We discuss the definition of a 'recognised' trade union, and the rights which recognition brings, in Chapter 4.

---

1. TULRCA 1992, ss 11, 22, 23.
2. *Ibid.*, ss 46–61; 174–7; 64–67. We discuss the compatibility of these provisions with international standards at appropriate points in the text.
3. See App 1 for the definition of an 'employers' association'.
4. TULRCA 1992, ss 2–4.

5. *Ibid.*, s 5.
6. See para **3.2** *et seq*. Only members of independent unions have a statutory right to time off for union duties and activities.

The Definition of a Trade Union

2.4 A 'trade union' means an organisation (whether temporary or permanent) which consists wholly or mainly of workers of one or more descriptions and whose principal purposes include the regulation of relations between workers of that description or those descriptions and employers or employers' associations.[1] The stipulation that the organisation must consist wholly or mainly of 'workers' excludes organisations of persons working for professional clients, such as solicitors;[2] the police and armed forces are also specifically excluded.[3] The inclusion in the definition of 'worker' of those who seek to work means that, in theory, an organisation composed solely of the unemployed could constitute a union, although it may have difficulty in satisfying the other elements of the definition. The need to engage in the 'regulation of relations' probably requires the organisation directly to regulate relations between employers and workers rather than simply engaging in political activities which may influence industrial relations, or eschewing collective bargaining in favour of statutory regulation of terms and conditions. Although the organisation need only be temporary, and thus may include a committee formed to deal with a single issue, it has been suggested that it must at least have sought recognition from employers.[4] In *Midland Cold Storage Ltd v Turner*[5] the issue arose as to the status of a shop stewards' committee whose apparent activity was to recommend the taking or abandonment of industrial action in the London docks and organising any industrial action which might be recommended. There was no evidence that it sought recognition from the employers; rather, it left the conduct of negotiations to the established union machinery. The court held that no body whose principal purposes included the regulation of relations between workers and employers could fail at least to seek recognition from employers.[6] To constitute a 'trade union', the organisation need not be of a minimum size or demonstrate any particular effectiveness or frequency of intervention in regulating relations, however; the crucial point is that its principal purpose includes such regulation.[7] Moreover, that purpose need not be stated expressly in its constitution provided that it can be inferred from all the circumstances. Thus, the British Association of Advisers and Lecturers in Physical Education was found to be a 'trade union', despite the fact that its constitution merely stated that it should be 'concerned with the professional interests of its members', since in practice it concerned itself with the pay and working conditions of its employed members through national negotiating machinery.[8] Although the definition of a trade union focuses heavily upon the traditional role of unions as engaging and seeking to engage in collective bargaining, there is nothing to prevent a union having other lawful objects, including political objects. However where a union wishes to spend money on 'political objects' as legislatively defined it must establish a separate 'political fund' in accordance with a statutory procedure.[9] Organisations which themselves consist wholly or mainly of trade unions or representatives of trade unions, and whose principal purposes include the regulation of relations between workers and employers or employers' associations, or the regulation of relations between their constituent or affiliated organisations, are also defined as 'trade unions'.[10] Thus the TUC and the Iron and Steel Trades Confederation, for example, are trade unions. From the opposite end of the scale, the courts have held that a branch or division of a union can itself constitute a 'trade union' where it satisfies the statutory criteria, despite the fact that members of the branch are also members of the main trade union.[11] This may be significant in relation to the statutory limit on damages payable by a union in tort, for example.[12]

---

1. TULRCA 1992, s 1(a). See ss 295 and 122, and App 1 of this work, for the definition of 'employer' and 'employers' association'.

2. 'Worker' is defined in *ibid.*, s 296; see further App 1. On the exclusion of solicitors, see *Carter v Law Society* [1973] ICR 113, but *quaere* whether an organisation of employed solicitors could constitute a trade union. Specified health service practitioners are included within the definition: TULRCA 1992, s 279.

3. TULRCA 1992, ss 280, 274.

4. *Midland Cold Storage Ltd v Turner* [1972] ICR 230, NIRC.

5. *Ibid.*

6. For the legal definition of 'recognition', see para **4.3**. For an example of a recognition agreement, see App 6.

7. *BAALPE v NUT* [1986] IRLR 497, CA.

8. *Ibid.*

9. See further para **2.45** *et seq.*

10. TULRCA 1992, s 1(b). Note that some provisions which apply to trade unions as defined in s 1(a) do not apply to these organisations or apply with modifications: see s 118.

11. *BAALPE v NUT*, above, note 7; *News Group Newspapers Ltd v SOGAT '82 (No 2)* [1986] IRLR 337, QBD.

12. See para **6.65**.

Listed Trade Unions

2.5 The Certification Officer maintains a list of trade unions.[1] Listing is voluntary, but any organisation which satisfies the definition of a 'trade union' and which complies with specified formalities is entitled to have its name entered on the list.[2] Being listed has a number of advantages for a union. It is evidence (although not conclusive evidence) that the organisation is, indeed, a trade union;[3] it entitles the union to tax relief on income tax, corporation tax and chargeable gains applied for the purpose of 'provident benefits',[4] and there is a simplified procedure for vesting union property in newly appointed trustees.[5] Moreover, inclusion on the list is an essential preliminary to an application for a certificate of independence.[6] Thus, although listing is theoretically voluntary, in practice a union would be well advised to seek entry to the list. It is irrelevant to a union's application that there may be other organisations which already recruit members in the same area of work, although if the organisation's name is the same as that of a listed union or so closely resembles it as to be likely to deceive the public, listing will be refused.[7] The Certification Officer may remove an organisation from the list if he or she considers that it is not a union (after allowing the organisation to make representations), or if the organisation requests removal, or he or she is satisfied that it has ceased to exist (for example, as a result of merger with another union).[8] There is a right of appeal to the EAT against the Certification Officer's decision not to list an organisation, or to remove it from the list.[9] Unusually, such appeals may be taken on questions of either fact or law. If it upholds the appeal, the EAT must grant a declaration and direct the Certification Officer to list the organisation.[10] At the end of March 2000 there were 221 listed unions and a further 22 which had not sought to be listed.[11] Being unlisted does not limit an organisation's statutory responsibilities (although 'federated' trade unions, whether listed or unlisted, are exempted from several statutory obligations).[12] The Certification Officer takes steps to investigate whether organisations which come to his or her attention which are unlisted and do not submit returns are, in fact, trade unions and so subject to the relevant statutory obligations.[13]

---

1. TULRCA 1992, s 2.
2. *Ibid.*, s 3. Unions listed under the Trade Union and Labour Relations Act 1974, s 8 (now repealed) were automatically entered on the list: s 2(1)(a).
3. *Ibid.*, s 2(4).
4. ICTA 1988, s 467, as amended by the Finance Act 1991, s 74 and TULRCA 1992, Sch 2, para 37. For the definition of 'provident benefits' see s 467(2).
5. TULRCA 1992, ss 13, 14.
6. *Ibid.*, s 6(1); see para **2.6** below.

7. *Ibid.*, s 3(4).

8. *Ibid.*, s 4.

9. *Ibid.*, s 9. By analogy with appeals against refusal of a certificate of independence, the EAT may consider information which was not available at the time of the decision by the Certification Officer: see para **2.6**, note 7.

10. *Ibid.*, s 9(3).

11. *Annual Report of the Certification Officer for 1999–2000*, paras 1.8 and 1.12; App 1 and App 1a.

12. TULCRA 1992, s 118. At the end of March 2000 there were three unions in this category: *Annual Report of the Certification Officer for 1999–2000*, para 3.3, App 1 and 1a.

13. *Ibid.*, para 1.13.

Independent Trade Unions

2.6 Once a union has been entered on the Certification Officer's list, it is eligible to apply to him or her for a certificate of independence. Applications must be made in such form and manner as the Certification Officer may require, and accompanied by a prescribed fee.[1] Satisfying the test of 'independence' (which refers to independence from employers rather than the state) is essential for access to a number of statutory rights: only ('employee') members of independent unions are protected against dismissal or subjection to a detriment by their employers on grounds of their union activities; only independent unions may invoke the statutory recognition procedure; and only independent recognised unions have specified rights to information and consultation, and their members the right to time off work to participate in union duties and activities. In broad terms the concept is intended to preclude access to such rights by employer-dominated 'house unions' or 'staff associations', and its importance is emphasised by ILO Convention No. 98 on the Right to Organise and Collective Bargaining.[2] A certificate of independence is not a prerequisite of independent status, but it constitutes conclusive proof of such and if the question of the independence of a non-certificated union arises in any proceedings before a court, the EAT, the CAC, ACAS or an employment tribunal these proceedings must be stayed pending a decision by the Certification Officer on the matter.[3] On receiving an application for a certificate, which is entered on a record open to free public inspection at all reasonable hours, the Certification Officer must make such inquiries as he or she thinks fit and take into account any relevant information submitted by any person.[4] No decision may be reached for at least a month after the application has been entered on the record.[5] If a certificate is refused, the Certification Officer must give reasons for this decision; he or she may also withdraw a certificate at any time after notifying the union of this intention and following a similar procedure to that laid down for applications.[6] An appeal lies to the EAT against the Certification Officer's decision to refuse, or withdraw, a certificate of independence; as in the case of listing, the appeal may be on a question of fact or law.[7] If the EAT upholds the appeal it must grant a declaration and direct the Certification Officer to issue, or not withdraw, a certificate.[8] A union which has been refused a certificate may reapply at a later stage, although it would be well advised to scrutinise carefully its constitution, finances and conduct before it does so. There is no right of appeal for a third party which wishes to contest the granting of a certificate (in the past to prevent the union concluding enforceable closed shop agreements, now perhaps to prevent it invoking the statutory recognition procedure).[9] The only way in which such a third party could proceed would be to attempt to obtain an order for judicial review to overturn the Certification Officer's decision, but as this would require showing that the decision was vitiated by a procedural irregularity, illegality, or 'irrationality' it would probably be a difficult task.[10]

---

1. TULRCA 1992, ss 6(1). see *Guidance for Trade Unions Wishing to Apply for a Certificate of Independence* (Certification Office, 2000) for further details about the procedure which is followed.

2. Article 2 affirms the need for workers' and employers' organisations to enjoy adequate protection against any acts of interference by each other or each others' agents or members in their establishing, functioning or administration. In particular, acts which are designed to promote the establishment of workers' organisations under the domination of employers or employers' organisations, or to support workers' organisations by financial or other means, with the object of placing such organisations under the control of employers or employers' organisations, are deemed to constitute acts of interference.

3. TULRCA 1992, s 8(4). The body before whom the proceedings are stayed may itself refer the question of independence to the Certification Officer: s 8(5).

4. *Ibid.*, s 6(2),(4).

5. *Ibid.*, s 6(4).

6. *Ibid.*, ss 6(5),(6), 7.

7. *Ibid.*, s 9. The EAT considers the issue afresh and may take into account information unknown or non-existent at the time of the decision by the Certification Officer: *Association of HSD (Hatfield) Employees v Certification Officer* [1978] ICR 21, EAT; *A Monk and Co Staff Association v Certification Officer* [1980] IRLR 431, EAT.

8. *Ibid.*, s 9(3).

9. *GMWU v Certification Officer* [1977] ICR 183, EAT.

10. See generally de Smith, Woolf and Jowell, 1995, and supplement, 1998.

2.7 A trade union is 'independent' if it is not under the domination or control of an employer or group of employers or one or more employers' associations and is not liable to interference by an employer or any such group or association (arising out of the provision of financial or material support or by any other means whatsoever) tending towards such control.[1] This test directs attention therefore both to whether the employer in fact exercises domination or control over the union, and whether it is exposed to the risk of interference tending towards such control. 'Liable to interference' has been interpreted by the courts as 'vulnerable to interference'; thus there is no need to show that such interference is likely in the circumstances.[2] Beyond this general test the statute does not specify the criteria relevant to independence, although further guidance is available from the decisions of the Certification Officer and the courts. Among the factors which the Certification Officer considers relevant are the strength and sources of the union's finances; the extent of any assistance given by the employer in establishing and maintaining the organisation; whether the constitution allows for interference by the employer in the union's affairs; the scope of the union's membership base; and the union's negotiating record.[3] These criteria were referred to with approval in the judgment of the EAT in *Blue Circle Staff Association v Certification Officer*,[4] a case where the decision of the Certification Officer to refuse a certificate of independence was confirmed. In that case the EAT warned that a staff association which had historically been heavily dominated by the employer could not change its position overnight; rather, the association should recognise that 'the process of asserting genuine and effective independence after some years of such domination by management . . . is likely to be protracted'.[5] It is important to emphasise that the criteria listed by the Certification Officer are only guidelines whose relevance and weight may vary depending on the circumstances; thus, whilst single company unions, for example, are scrutinised more carefully because their membership base makes them more vulnerable to employer interference, they are not precluded altogether: the National Union of Railwaymen[6] and the National Union of Mineworkers were not refused certificates. Similarly, the provision of facilities by an employer is not of itself a bar to independence, and, indeed, the ACAS Code of Practice on Time Off for Trade Union Duties and Activities recommends that employers should make available facilities such as notice boards, a telephone, accommodation for meetings and office space.[7] The crucial question would seem to be whether the union could survive if its facilities were suddenly withdrawn. As the Certification Officer's *Guidance for Trade Unions Wishing to Apply for a Certificate of Independence* explains,

> A distinction can properly be drawn between a broadly-based union which could continue to function even if an employer withdraws facilities from one or more of its branches and a single company union which might well find it difficult or even impossible to carry on at all if such action were taken by the firm which employs its entire membership.[8]

A 'robust attitude in negotiation' and a good negotiating record are regarded as indicative of independence, although, again, this varies with the circumstances;

in the case of a 'good, tactful and sensitive employer' these could be difficult to demonstrate.[9] Willingness to take industrial action is not a criterion of independence, and organisations whose rules forbid this have been granted certificates.[10] In the light of the importance placed upon independence in order for a union to gain access to important statutory rights (see para **2.6** above), it is ironical that where no independent union is recognised by the employer its obligations to inform and consult in a number of areas can be fulfilled by informing and consulting worker representatives whose position may not comply in a number of respects with the criteria of independence outlined above, not least because it is a condition that they are employed by the employer at the time of their selection as such representatives (see further Chapter 5).

---

1. TULRCA 1992, s 5. See ss 295 and 122, and App 1 for the definition of 'employer' and 'employers' association'.

2. *Squibb UK Staff Association v Certification Officer* [1979] IRLR 75, CA. In *Government Communications Staff Federation v Certification Officer and CCSU* [1993] IRLR 260, the EAT confirmed the decision that the association formed at Government Communications Headquarters in the wake of the ban on membership of national civil service unions (see Fredman and Morris, 1989, 99–102) was 'vulnerable to interference' because of its dependence upon the continued approval of the director of GCHQ. A further application in January 1996 was also refused, on a variety of grounds see *Annual Report of the Certification Officer for 1996*, para 2.9.

3. *Guidance for Trade Unions Wishing to Apply for a Certificate of Independence*, Certification Office, 2000.

4. [1977] IRLR 20, EAT.

5. *Ibid.*, at 24.

6. Now the National Union of Rail, Maritime and Transport Workers.

7. Para 28; see further para **3.29**

8. Above, note 3. See also *Annual Report of the Certification Officer for 1996*, para 2.9.

9. *Blue Circle Staff Association v Certification Officer* above, note 4, at 23. A union which is seeking a certificate of independence may find it worthwhile to retain agreed minutes of meetings concerned with negotiations, and other meetings, with the employer.

10. In view of this it is notable that legislation clarifying the position of prison officers, which also removed their freedom to take industrial action, states that the Certification Officer should disregard their inability lawfully to take industrial action in determining whether their unions are independent: CJPOA 1994, s 127(7). See further Morris, 1994b.

The Legal Status of Trade Unions

2.8 At common law a trade union is an association of individuals bound together by a contract of membership which regulates the relationship between those members. However, although this remains the legal basis, in reality unions are subject to a wide range of statutory provisions which modify the common law position in most important areas.[1] The significant features of the legal status of unions (both listed and unlisted) can be divided into four broad categories. First, all property belonging to the union must be vested in trust for the union (not, notably, for its members).[2] Secondly, although statute prohibits unions from being incorporated (apart from 'special register bodies', described later in this paragraph), they have been accorded many of the attributes of incorporated bodies by legislation.[3] Thus they are capable of making contracts; they can sue[4] and be sued, and are amenable to criminal prosecution, in their own name; and judgments, awards and orders may be enforced against any property held in trust for the union (although certain property is protected against the enforcement of any award of damages, costs or expenses).[5] Thirdly, they have statutory protection against the doctrine of restraint of trade, without which it would be impossible for most unions to function lawfully;[6] the purposes of a union are not, by reason only that they are in restraint of trade, unlawful so as to make any member liable to criminal proceedings, or so as to make any agreement or trust void or voidable, nor is any union rule unlawful or unenforceable on that ground.[7] Finally, although unions have been potentially liable in tort since the Employment Act 1982, there are statutory limits on the amount of damages which may be awarded against a union in any proceedings in tort (with specified exceptions).[8] There is an exception to the general rule that unions cannot be incorporated in the case of the 13 'special register bodies', which are companies registered under the Companies Act 1985 or incorporated by charter or letters patent whose names appeared on a special register maintained under s 84 of the Industrial Relations Act 1971 (now repealed).[9] These organisations are bodies whose principal purposes are to maintain professional standards or training, but which also became involved in negotiating terms and conditions of employment for their members. Most are in the public services; they include the Royal College of Nursing and the British Medical Association. In so far as they relate to the regulation of such relations, their rules and purposes, like those of all unions, have immunity from the doctrine of restraint of trade.[10] Special register bodies whose principal purposes do not include employer–worker relations cannot be listed or seek a certificate of independence. There are various exceptions and modification to the legislation governing unions in the case of special register bodies.[11]

1. The bulk of this chapter is concerned with these provisions. Note that we refer only to the modern law; for further detail on the history of the law in this area see Elias and Ewing 1987 and references therein.

2. TULRCA 1992, s 12: see *Hughes v TGWU* [1985] IRLR 382, ChD (individual members have no interest severable or in common in union 'property', which means any form of property including documents and records). Cf. the puzzling wording of s 23(2)(b), which refers to 'property belonging to any member of the union otherwise than jointly or in common with the other members'. On provisions governing the transfer of property, see ss 13 and 14. The law relating to trustees is outside the scope of this work; but see McGhee, 2000, Chapters 10–12.

3. TULRCA 1992, s 10(1),(2). Any registration of a union (other than a special register body) under the Companies Act 1985 or under the Friendly Societies Act 1974 or the Industrial and Provident Societies Act 1965 (whenever effected) is void: s 10(3).

4. There has been some doubt whether unions can sue in defamation: in *EETPU v Times Newspapers Ltd* [1980] 1 All ER 1097, QBD it was held they could not, but cf *NUGMW v Gillian* [1946] KB 81, CA, cited without adverse comment in *Derbyshire County Council v Times Newspapers Ltd* [1993] 1 All ER 1011, HL.

5. TULRCA 1992, s 12(2). 'Protected property' is defined in s 23; see further para **6.65**.

6. In *Hornby v Close* (1867) LR 2 QB 153 it was held that the purposes of a union whose rules enabled a majority to control the terms on which all members disposed of their labour were unlawful.

7. TULRCA 1992, s 11. Statutory protection against the restraint of trade doctrine was introduced in 1871. The Trade Union Act 1871 granted protection as far as trade union purposes were concerned. In *Edwards v SOGAT* [1971] Ch 354, CA, it was suggested that this did not protect rules in restraint of trade, and protection was extended to rules in the Trade Union and Labour Relations Act 1974 (now repealed). Any reference to union 'rules' in the legislation, except where the context otherwise requires, includes the rules of any branch or section of the union: TULRCA 1992, s 119.

8. *Ibid.*, ss 22. The Employment Act 1982 (now repealed) repealed the Trade Union and Labour Relations Act 1974, s 14, which itself continued an immunity (with specified exceptions) which dated back to the Trade Disputes Act 1906. Because these limits are most likely to be relevant to the organisation of industrial action we discuss them in Chapter 6; see further para **6.65**. See para **6.12** *et seq.* for the circumstances in which a union is deemed liable in tort.

9. *Ibid.*, s 117. The register was closed in 1974; no new 'special register bodies' can be created. The figure of 13 is correct as of May 2000.

10. *Ibid.*, s 117(3)(b).

11. Ibid., s 117(3), (4), (5).

Returns and Accounts

2.9 All trade unions, even those which are not listed,[1] are subject to detailed obligations in respect of their accounting practices. They must keep proper accounting records in respect of their transactions, assets and liabilities and must establish and maintain a satisfactory system of control of their accounting records, cash holdings and all their receipts and remittances.[2] The records must be adequate to give a true and fair view of the state of affairs of the union and to explain its transactions.[3] Where a union is divided into branches or sections, its obligation to keep such records is discharged to the extent to which a branch or section does this instead.[4] Unions[5] must also submit an annual return to the Certification Officer in a prescribed form; in general this should be sent before 1 June in the calendar year following that to which it relates but the Certification Officer may, if he or she considers appropriate, direct that the return should relate to a different annual period, and this is usually done if the normal timetable would cause serious inconvenience to the union concerned.[6] The return must include revenue accounts and such other accounts as the Certification Officer requires, together with a balance sheet, each of which must give a true and fair view of the matters to which it relates.[7] Funds held at branch, as well as head office, level must also be included.[8] Union accounts must be audited by a professionally qualified auditor,[9] and the auditor's report should accompany them in the return.[10] Since 1993, details of the salary paid to, and other benefits provided to or in respect of, the president, general secretary and each member of the executive by the union during the period to which the return relates must also be included in the return.[11] The Conservative Government which introduced this requirement indicated that it was intended to require 'details of all salary payments expressed in cash amounts and all other benefits that could either be expressed in terms of cash equivalent figures or in terms of an adequate description of the benefits concerned, if that is more appropriate or practical'.[12] 'Benefit' is not defined; the Government indicated that any benefit to a person 'over what is required for his [*sic*] official duties' should be shown.[13] The Certification Officer requires that payments or benefits on termination of the employment of union officers should be included, including a payment or benefit to be provided in future financial years.[14] The position regarding facilities for both official and personal use (eg a car or mobile telephone) remains unclear,[15] but unions would be best advised to include these and similar items in the return. Lastly, the return should contain a copy of the union rules, and unions required to maintain a register of members' names and addresses must state the number of names on the register at the end of the period and the number of names which were not accompanied by the requisite address.[16] The rights of union members to apply to the Certification Officer or the court where they claim that their union has failed to comply with its duty to maintain an adequate register are discussed at para **2.29**.

---

1. See para **2.5**.

2. TULRCA 1992, s 28(1).Federated unions consisting wholly or mainly of representatives of constituent or affiliated organisations are excluded from this duty: s 118(4). For provisions relating to superannuation schemes by unions, see ss 38–42. At the end of March 2000 there were 20 members' superannuation schemes maintained by 12 unions, only five of which had assets exceeding £250,000: *Annual Report of the Certification Officer for 1999–2000*, para 5.3; App 6.

3. TULRCA 1992, s 28(2).

4. *Ibid.*, s 44(1), (2). Any duty failing upon a branch or section by virtue of its being a 'trade union' is treated as discharged to the extent to which the union of which it is a branch or section discharges it instead: s 44(4).

5. Other than those in existence for less than 12 months: TULRCA 1992, s 43(1)(b). The same provision is made for branches and sections as described in note 4 above: see s 44(2) and (4).

6. *Ibid.*, s 32(4)(a). He or she may also substitute another deadline for the return: s 32(4)(b).

7. *Ibid.*, s 32(3). The return should also show changes in the union's officers or in the address of the head or main office: *ibid.*

8. *Annual Report of the Certification Officer for 1997*, para 3.11.

9. TULRCA 1992, ss 33, 34. Persons not so qualified may act as auditors if the union's membership, assets, receipts and payments are below a specified level or certain special circumstances apply: s 34(2). There are detailed statutory provisions as to the appointment and removal of auditors and their rights and obligations in relation to the union: ss 34–37. Note that ss 33–35 do not apply to special register bodies (see para **2.8**) which are incorporated under the Companies Act 1985: s 117(4); this avoids duplication of obligations but an auditor's report which complies with TULRCA 1992 must still be supplied.

10. *Ibid.*, ss 32(3)(b), 36. The Certification Officer does not require a statement of where union funds are kept unless the auditor thinks that this is important to give a fair and balanced view. Thus, there is no requirement for a union to indicate whether its funds are invested in the UK or overseas.

11. TULRCA 1992, s 32(3)(aa).'President', 'general secretary' and 'executive' are defined in s 119; 'member of the executive' in s 32(7); see further para **2.32**. The salary and benefits of union general secretaries or equivalents appear in the Annual Reports of the Certification Officer.

12. Mr Michael Forsyth, Minister of State, Department of Employment, HC Debs, Vol 219, col 244, 16 February 1993.

13. *Ibid.*

14. *Annual Report of the Certification Officer for 1996*, para 3.14.

15. See HL Debs, Vol 543, cols 1425–1429, 16 March 1993.

16. TULRCA 1992, s 32(3)(d); see further para **2.29** on the duty to maintain a register.

2.10 Trade unions must supply any person with a copy of their most recent annual return on request, either free or on payment of a reasonable charge, and the Certification Officer must keep copies of all annual returns available for public inspection.[1] In addition, unions must take all reasonable steps to secure that members are supplied with a statement containing specified information not later than eight weeks after their annual return is sent to the Certification Officer.[2] This may be done either by sending individual copies of the statement to members or by any other means (whether by including the statement in a union publication or otherwise) which it is the practice of the union to use when information of general interest to all its members needs to be provided to them.[3] The statement must specify the total income and expenditure of the union for the period to which the return relates; how much of the income for that period consisted of payments in respect of membership; the total income and expenditure for that period of any political fund of the union; and the information on salary and benefits which must appear in the annual return.[4] The statement must not say anything inconsistent with the contents of the return.[5] In addition, the statement must set out in full the auditor's report on the accounts in the return, together with the auditor's name and address.[6] It may also include any other matter which the union considers may significantly assist a member to make an informed judgment about its financial activities during the period to which the return relates.[7] Finally the statement must include the following:

> A member who is concerned that some irregularity may be occurring, or have occurred, in the conduct of the financial affairs of the union may take steps with a view to investigating further, obtaining clarification and, if necessary, securing regularisation of that conduct.
>
> The member may raise any such concern with such one or more of the following as it seems appropriate to raise it with: the officials of the union, the trustees of the property of the union, the auditor or auditors of the union, the Certification Officer (who is an independent officer appointed by the Secretary of State) and the police.
>
> Where a member believes that the financial affairs of the union have been or are being conducted in breach of the law or in breach of rules of the union and contemplates bringing civil proceedings against the union or responsible officials or trustees, he should consider obtaining independent legal advice.[8]

Although the use of this form of words is mandatory, there is nothing to prevent a union from commenting upon them or indicating any respect in which the wording was not wholly applicable (eg the reference to trustees in the case of special register bodies).[9] The statement may also include such other details of the steps which a member may take for the purpose mentioned in the mandatory form of words as the union considers appropriate.[10] The union must send the Certification Officer a copy of the statement provided to its members as soon as reasonably practicable after it has been provided.[11]

---

1. TULRCA 1992, s 32(5), (6).

2. *Ibid.*, s32A(1). The same exceptions apply as in relation to returns and accounts: ss 43(1)(b) and 118(4)(c). Where either situation described in para **2.9**, note 4 applies, the duties imposed by s 32A in relation to the return are treated as those of the branch or section, or the union of which it is a branch or section, by which that duty is in fact discharged: s 44(5).

3. *Ibid.,* s 32A(2). In addition, the union must supply as soon as practicable a copy of the statement, free of charge, to any member who so requests within two years of the return being sent to the Certification Officer: s 32A(9). In *In the matter of complaints against MSF* (8 April 1998, unreported), CO, the Certification Officer found that the despatch of material to branch secretaries for them to disseminate to members satisfied the statutory requirement because it was the union's normal practice, although he pointed to the likelihood that some information would fall through the net because the practice depended upon branch secretaries having the time and resources to fulfil this task.

4. *Ibid.,* s 32A(3). See para **2.46** *et seq.* for the regulation of unions' 'political funds'.

5. *Ibid.,* s 32A(4). The Conservative Government which introduced this provision claimed that a misspelling or printing error would not constitute an offence: Baroness Denton, HL Debs, Vol 543, col 1430, 16 March 1993; see para **2.11**.

6. *Ibid.,* s 32A(5).

7. *Ibid.*

8. *Ibid.,* s 32A(6)(a). The text of the statement was amended by ERA 1999, s 28(3), to reflect the abolition of the Commissioner for the Rights of Trade Union Members.

9. Baroness Denton, HL Debs, Vol 543, cols 1432–1433, 16 March 1993.

10. *Ibid.,* s 32A(6)(b).

11. *Ibid,.* s 32A (7). Where the same form of statement is not provided to all members, a copy of each form of statement provided to any of them must be sent to the Certification Officer: s 32A(8).

2.11 If a trade union refuses or wilfully neglects to perform any duty specified in paras **2.9** and **2.10** relating to accounting records, the annual return and audit, and the information to be provided to members, it commits an offence, punishable by a fine not exceeding level 5 on the standard scale.[1] Where the union is guilty of such an offence, the offence is deemed also to have been committed by any union officer who is bound by the rules to discharge the relevant duty or, if there is no such person, every member of the general committee of management of the union.[2] However, it is a defence for an officer or member to prove that he or she had reasonable cause to believe, and did believe, that some other person who was competent to discharge that duty was authorised to discharge it instead, and had done or would do so.[3] Any person who wilfully alters or causes to be altered a document which is required for the statutory purposes with intent to falsify it or to enable a union to evade any of the statutory requirements is also guilty of an offence for which the punishment may include up to six months' imprisonment and a fine.[4] The Certification Officer is responsible for enforcing the statutory requirements, but does not generally undertake prosecutions for offences such as theft or fraud which would normally be dealt with by other prosecuting authorities.[5] The Certification Officer has very extensive powers of investigation in relation to unions' financial affairs, including the power, in specified circumstances, to appoint an inspector (either from within or outside the Certification Office) to conduct an investigation.[6] A member may complain to the Certification Officer that there are circumstances which suggest that an inspector should be appointed; if the Certification Officer decides against this course, he or she must notify the member of this and, if he or she thinks fit, give the reasons for that decision.[7] Inspectors must report to the Certification Officer as he or she directs and their final report must be published.[8] Any person convicted on a prosecution as a result of an investigation may in the same proceedings be ordered to pay some or all of the expenses of conducting the investigation.[9] Up to April 2000, the Certification Officer has used his powers to appoint inspectors on two occasions.[10] A variety of offences related to the obstruction of the conduct of any investigation have been created; these, again, are punishable by up to six months' imprisonment and a fine.[11] A union must ensure that any person convicted of any of the offences referred to in this paragraph does not hold any of the positions which are covered by the statutory election requirements;[12] in the case of those offences punishable only by a fine, the ban lasts for five years from the conviction; in the case of the remainder, ten.[13] A member who claims that the union has failed to comply with this requirement may apply to either the Certification Officer or the court (but not both) for a declaration to that effect.[14] The procedure to be followed by the Certification Officer is set out in para **2.2**. Where either the Certification Officer or the court makes a declaration, an order must also be made imposing on the union a requirement to take steps within a specified period to remedy the failure, unless this is considered inappropriate.[15] Provision for the enforcement of such an order, and for appeal, are described in para **2.2**. Any union member may enforce compliance with the order provided that he or she was in membership at the time the order was made and still remains in membership.[16]

---

1. TULRCA 1992, ss 45, 45A. At the time of writing £5,000 is currently level 5 on the standard scale established by the Criminal Justice Act 1982, s 37(2), as substituted by the Criminal Justice Act 1991, s 17(1). Note that this offence and penalty also applies to a refusal or wilful failure to supply a copy of the union's rules on request (s 27) and offences relating to members' superannuation schemes (ss 38–42).

2. *Ibid.*, s 45(2).

3. *Ibid.*, s 45(3). In this connection, it is desirable for there to be written job specifications for each union officer, and for there to be minutes of meetings recording decisions relating to the discharge of these duties.

4. *Ibid.*, ss 45(4), s 45A(1)(b).

5. *Annual Report of the Certification Officer for 1999–2000*, para 3.11. As of May 12 2000, prosecutions have been brought against five unions, and individual officials of those unions for failing to comply with statutory requirements (in 1991, 1998, 1999 and 2000): information supplied by the Certification Office.

6. TULRCA 1992, ss 37A–37E. Note that the Certification Officer is a 'prescribed person' for the purposes of ERA 1996, s 43F (protection for 'whistleblowers') in relation to fraud and other irregularities relating to the financial affairs of unions: The Public Interest Disclosure (Prescribed Persons) Order 1999, SI 1999/1549.

7. *Ibid.*, s 37E.

8. *Ibid.*, s 37C.

9. *Ibid.*, s 37D.

10. *Annual Report of the Certification Officer for 1997*, para 3.19, *Annual Report of the Certification Officer for 1998*, para 3.23.

11. TULRCA 1992, ss 45(5)–(9), 45A.

12. *Ibid.*, s45B; see further paras **2.34** and **2.35** . This applies to special register bodies on the same restricted basis as the election requirements: s 117(5).

13. *Ibid.*, s 45B(1).

14. *Ibid.*, s 45C. Where a different applicant pursues a claim on the same matter in the alternative forum, the Certification Officer or the court, as the case may be, must have regard to any declaration, order, observation or reasons made or given by the other body which is brought to its notice: ss 45C(5A),(5B).

15. *Ibid.*, s 45C(5),(5A).

16. *Ibid.*, s 45C(6).

COMMON LAW REGULATION

Sources and General Principles

2.12 When individuals join a trade union they enter a contract of membership which serves as the 'constitution' of the union. This contract, like other contracts, is subject to enforcement in the courts.[1] The contract of membership generally covers a wide variety of matters: the rights and obligations of individual union members; the powers and composition of various bodies within the union; the purposes for which union funds can be expended; and the powers of union officers. The primary source of the contract is the union rule book, which unions have a statutory obligation to supply to any person on request either free or on payment of a reasonable charge.[2] Rule books may vary considerably in the degree of detail they contain. Nevertheless even if ostensibly comprehensive, they may be supplemented by implied terms and by custom and practice within the union. The capacity to imply terms into union rule books, as into other contracts, can be an important mechanism of judicial control over union conduct. Another such mechanism is the capacity of courts to strike out rules on grounds of public policy. In some instances the justification for striking out has been common to all contracts; in others it has been grounded in the view that unions have important functions which exceed those of other private bodies, such as social clubs. One area in particular where the courts have exercised their discretion to strike out rules is where they conflict with natural justice. Where a member alleges that a union has acted, or threatens to act, in breach of the union rules, he or she may seek a remedy either in the High Court or, with some exceptions, from the Certification Officer.[3] Proceedings before the Certification Officer are likely to be the cheaper and the quicker route, but the time limit for applying to the Certification Officer is shorter than the courts, and, unlike the courts, the Certification Officer cannot grant damages or interim relief. In many important areas of union government, such as admission to and expulsion from the union, the power to discipline members for specified types of conduct, elections to certain offices, and industrial action ballots, unions are now subject to statutory restrictions which apply notwithstanding anything to the contrary in their rules. For this reason, we have given greater prominence in this work to the statutory provisions in those areas,[4] although we examine the general principles which inform the common law, and suggest some possible new and significant directions which the common law may take in the future in the area of implied terms and in the light of the Human Rights Act 1998. We also indicate, where appropriate, the situations in which a common law action may have advantages over a statutory complaint. We conclude this section by considering briefly the potential liability of unions in the tort of negligence to their members, an issue which may become of greater significance in the area of industrial action, in particular.

---

1. It is unclear whether the other party to the contract is the union or all the other members. Before the Industrial Relations Act 1971, unregistered unions were incapable of contracting in their own right, while the judges were divided about whether registered unions had sufficient corporate status to contract or not. In *Bonsor v MU* [1956] AC 104, the majority of the House of Lords considered that the contract of membership was a contract between the members *inter se* rather than between the member and the union. Under the Industrial Relations Act 1971, registered unions were incorporated bodies and so could contract; since that Act was repealed, all unions, listed and unlisted, can contract: see para **2.8**. However, it does not necessarily follow from this that the contract is *with the union* (and TULRCA 1992, s 20(7), in defining union rules, speaks of the 'contract between a member and the other members'). It would seem preferable to adopt the view that the contract is with the union, but 'even if the courts do not take this approach, *Bonsor* shows that the member will have no difficulty in enforcing the contract—even if it is with the members *inter se*': Elias and Ewing, 1987, 46.

2. TULRCA 1992, s 27. Failure to supply a copy of the rules is a criminal offence, punishable by a fine not exceeding level 5 on the standard scale established by the Criminal Justice Act 1982, as substituted by the Criminal Justice Act 1991, s 17(1) (at the time of

writing, £5,000): s 45A. Unions which have been in existence for less than 12 months, and those failing within s 1(b), are excluded from this obligation s 43(1)(a).

3. TULRCA 1992, ss 108A, 108B; see further para **2.2**.

4. The contractual rights of union members in relation to industrial action are discussed in para **6.110** *et seq.* For more extended discussion of the common law, see Elias and Ewing, 1987; Kidner, 1983; Harvey, 1972, as updated.

The Judicial Approach Towards the Contract of Membership

2.13 The primary source of the contract of membership is the union rule book, which is likely to be subject to amendment from time to time, with either the approval of the membership directly or that of their elected representatives. Union rule books are unlikely to have been drafted by lawyers, a feature which has been recognised by the courts when required to interpret them, although with differing conclusions drawn from this. In *Heatons Transport (St Helens) Ltd v TGWU*, Lord Wilberforce pointed out that:

> [t]rade union rule books are not drafted by parliamentary draftsmen. Courts of law must resist the temptation to construe them as if they were; for that is not how they would be understood by the members who are the parties to the agreement of which the terms, or some of them, are set out in the rule book . . .[1]

However, in *British Actors' Equity Association v Goring* Viscount Dilhorne affirmed that the same canons of construction should be applied to rule books as to any 'written documents. Our task is to construe them so as to give them a reasonable interpretation which accords with what in our opinion must have been intended'.[2] In *Jacques v AUEW (Engineering Section)* Warner J attempted to reconcile these approaches by stating that:

> the rules of a trade union are not to be construed literally or like a statute, but so as to give them a reasonable interpretation which accords with what in the court's view they must have been intended to mean, bearing in mind their authorship, their purpose, and the readership to which they are addressed.[3]

This dictum has been cited frequently in subsequent cases. However, in the context of the exercise of union disciplinary powers, where much of the case law has arisen, the courts have, in practice, tended towards an interpretation which protects the interests of the individual union member. In doing so, they have frequently prayed in aid a dictum of Lord Denning MR that union rule books are

> not so much a contract . . . but . . . much more a legislative code laid down by some members of the union to be imposed on all members of the union. They are more like by-laws than a contract. In those circumstances the rules are to be construed not only against the makers of them, but further, if it should be found that if any of these rules is contrary to natural justice . . . the courts would hold them to be invalid.[4]

This dictum can be criticised as overlooking the role which members play in formulating and changing rules. It has nevertheless played an important part in shaping judicial attitudes towards unions as bodies against whom members are in need of protection. In an earlier judgment in *Lee v Showman's Guild of Great Britain* Denning LJ pointed out the difference between social clubs and bodies like unions of ostensibly identical legal status:

> In the case of social clubs the rules usually empower the committee to expel a member who, in their opinion, has been guilty of conduct detrimental to the club, and this is a matter of opinion and nothing else. The courts have no wish to sit on appeal from their decisions on such a matter any more than from the decisions of a family conference. They have nothing to do with social rights or social duties. . . . It is very different with domestic tribunals which sit in judgment on members of a trade or profession. They wield powers as great, if not greater, than any exercised by courts of law. They can deprive a man [*sic*] of his livelihood. . . . They are usually empowered to do this for any breach of their rules which . . . are rules which they impose and which he has no real opportunity of accepting or rejecting. In theory their powers are based on contract. The man is supposed to have contracted to give them these great powers; but in practice he has no choice in the matter.[5]

This case also highlighted the degree to which the courts could intervene in union decision-making through the mechanism of interpreting the contract of membership. Although a domestic union body may be regarded as the final arbiter of facts, Denning LJ pointed out that the application of the rules to the facts and the construction of the rules were often inextricably linked. Thus:

> the question whether the committee has acted within its jurisdiction depends . . . on whether the facts adduced before them were reasonably capable of being held to be a breach of the rules. If they were, then the proper inference is that the committee correctly construed the rules and have acted within their jurisdiction. If, however, the facts were not capable of being held to be a breach and yet the committee have held them to be a breach, then the only inference is that the committee have misconstrued the rules and exceeded their jurisdiction.[6]

This approach has afforded the courts the opportunity to give their own interpretation of disciplinary offences such as conduct 'rendering an individual unfit for membership' or 'detrimental to the interests of the union', so, effectively, pronouncing on what union interests require.[7] Under the Human Rights Act 1998 it may be possible to argue that this approach is inconsistent with the terms of Article 11 of the ECHR, which guarantees the right to form and join trade unions.[8] In *Cheall v UK*[9] the EComHR took into account the terms of ILO Convention 87, which affirms the right of unions to draw up their own rules and to organise their administration and activities, in concluding that unions should remain free to decide, in accordance with union rules, questions concerning admission to and expulsion from the union, subject to the obligation on the State to protect individuals against abuse of a dominant position where rules were wholly unreasonable or arbitrary or where exclusion or expulsion resulted in exceptional hardship such as job loss.

---

1. [1972] ICR 308 at 393, HL.
2. [1978] ICR 791 at 794–795, HL.
3. [1986] ICR 683 at 692.
4. *Bonsor v Musicians' Union* [1954] Ch 479 at 485–486.
5. [1952] 2 QB 329 at 343.
6. *Ibid.*, at 345.
7. *Esterman v NALGO* [1974] ICR 625, ChD, is a particularly notable example of this and see also *Porter v NUJ* [1980] IRLR 404, HL, but cf *Longley v NUJ* [1987] IRLR 109, CA. All these cases, which relate to participation in industrial action, are discussed at para **6.112** and **6.113**.
8. See further Chapter 1.
9. App No 10550/83, (1986) EHRR 74. See also the judgment of Lord Diplock in this case, discussed at para **2.26**.

2.14 The courts have adopted the approach that union rule books, like other documents, do not necessarily contain a comprehensive list of contractual terms, and have drawn on custom and practice within the union, and on implied terms, to supplement the rules. In *Heatons Transport (St Helens) Ltd v TGWU* Lord Wilberforce stated that:

> it is not to be assumed, as in the case of a commercial contract which has been reduced into writing, that all the terms of the agreement are to be found in the rule book alone: particularly as regards the discretion conferred by the members upon committees or officials of the union as to the way in which they may act on the union's behalf. What the members understand as to the characteristics of the agreement into which they enter by joining a union is well stated in the section of the TUC handbook on the Industrial Relations Act which gives advice about the content and operation of unions' rules. Paragraph 99 reads as follows: 'Trade union government does not . . . rely solely on what is written down in the rule book. It also depends upon custom and practice, by (sic) procedures which have developed over the years and which, although well understood by those who operate them, are not formally set out in the rules. Custom and practice may operate either by modifying a union's rules as they operate in practice, or by compensating for the absence of formal rules. Furthermore, the procedures which custom and practice lays down very often vary from workplace to workplace within the same industry, and even within different branches of the same union.'[1]

It is notable, however, that this statement was made in the context of industrial action proceedings where the court held the union liable for the acts of its shop stewards despite the lack of any authority for their actions in the rules. It has been observed that in other contexts the courts have shown much greater reluctance to take account of union practices, to the extent that 'the gap between the practical operation of the constitution and the way it works in theory, as reflected in the formal constitution, is effectively disregarded . . .'[2] Moreover, in accordance with general contractual principles, while custom and practice may moderate the operation of a rule, it cannot entitle a union to act in conflict with it.[3]

---

1. [1972] ICR 308 at 393, HL. See further para **6.16**.
2. Elias and Ewing, 1987, 33.
3. *Porter v NUJ* [1980] IRLR 404, HL, Viscount Dilhorne at 410; *Taylor v NUM (Derbyshire Area)* [1985] IRLR 99, ChD.

2.15   In addition to custom and practice, terms may also be implied into the contract of membership on other general contractual principles.[1] However the courts have shown that they are most unlikely to imply terms which extend the duties of members as against those of the union. Thus, in *Radford v NATSOPA*,[2] for example, Plowman J refused to accept the argument that the applicant was in breach of an implied obligation he was alleged to owe to the union given the very specific circumstances indicated in the rules as to when expulsion could be justified. Again, in *Leigh v NUR*[3] Goff J rejected the contention that qualifications for nomination to the office of president specified in the union rules were subject to additional qualifications as a matter of implication. One area which has been relatively unexplored to date is the extent to which terms may be implied into the contract regarding access by members to union services, in particular representation. This may become an increasingly contentious area in the light of the new right for workers to be accompanied at disciplinary and grievance hearings by the companion of their choice where they reasonably request this,[4] and the increasing number of other legal rights which workers may expect their union to assist them to enforce. Given the number of requests to which they may be subject, unions are unlikely to be able to afford assistance in every case, and will therefore need to be selective. The question then arises whether there may be any legal constraints upon the ways in which they exercise their discretion. As we describe in para **2.17**, the courts have required unions to adhere to the public law principles of natural justice, and there is some authority to suggest that they may also be subject to public law standards of decision-making in relation to the substantive exercise of their discretions.[5] Moreover, in contexts analogous to those of unions, such as mutual insurance, 'contractual discretions have been held not to be unfettered, but to be subject to common law principles of procedural propriety (ie fairness or natural justice), "*Wednesbury*" reasonableness (or rationality), bona fides, propriety of purpose and relevancy'.[6] Thus, in *The Vainquer Jose*,[7] for example, which concerned the exercise of discretion by a mutual insurance association of shipowners, Mocatta J emphasised the need for the committee to exercise its discretion in dealing with a claim in accordance with the principles of fairness, reasonableness, bona fides, and absence of misdirection in law. Again, in *Shearson Lehman Hutton Inc v Maclaine Watson and Co Ltd*[8] the powers given to the London Metal Exchange, an administrative and regulatory body, by contract were held to be subject to challenge on these grounds, the court affirming that the differences between public and private law rights relate to the procedures by which they are protected rather than their substance. It is possible to envisage a similar approach being taken to the exercise of discretion by unions. Further ammunition for such an approach may come from case law relating to the exercise of contractual discretion by employers in relation to their employees, where the implied obligation of good faith has proved important.[9] To date, there appears to have been only one case where a common law challenge to the use of union resources has been raised.[10] In *Iwanuszezak v GMBATU*[11] the claimant, who was disabled, argued, *inter alia*, that the union had breached the contract of membership in failing to bring its collective strength to bear in negotiations with his employer to safeguard his existing conditions of employment. The Court of Appeal held that the claim should be struck out as disclosing no reasonable cause of action. In doing so, Lloyd LJ observed that it was the primary obligation of a union to look after the collective interests of its members and where these conflict with those of the individual, it makes sense that the collective interests should prevail.[12] Similarly in *The Vainquer Jose*, the court acknowledged that the committee could legitimately consider the interests of the members as a whole in reaching its decision on an individual claim.[13] However, it is submitted that neither of these dicta is inconsistent with the argument that where resources are made available to some members but not others, the basis of selection should withstand scrutiny by reference to standards of substantive and procedural fairness.

---

1. Broadly speaking, this may be done to give effect to the presumed intention of the parties (the 'officious bystander' or 'business efficacy' tests enunciated in *Shirlaw v Southern Foundries (1926) Ltd* [1939] 2 KB 206, CA, MacKinnon LJ at 227, and *The Moorcock* (1889) 14 PD 64, CA at 68 respectively) or as a legal incident of the relationship in question. See generally Chitty, 1999, Chapter 13.

2. [1972] ICR 484, ChD.; see also *Spring v NASDS* [1956] 1 WLR 585, ChD. Cf., however, *McVitae v UNISON* [1996] IRLR 33, ChD, where Harrison J implied a power for the defendant union, created upon amalgamation of three existing unions, to discipline

members for conduct prior to the amalgamation when such conduct was contrary to the rules both of the amalgamating union of which they were a member and of UNISON.

3. [1970] Ch 326, ChD.

4. ERA 1999, ss 10–15.

5. *Edwards v SOGAT* [1971] Ch 354, CA; *Breen v AEU* [1971] 2 QB 175, CA; *Cheall v APEX* [1982] IRLR 362, CA, at 367.

6. Beatson, 1995, at 269. See also Oliver, 1999, 180–185.

7. *CVG Siderurgicia del Orinoco SA v London Steamship Owners' Mutual Insurance Association Ltd (The Vainquer Jose)* [1979] 1 Lloyd's Rep 557, QBD. See also *Equitable Life Assurance Society v Hyman*, judgment of 20 July 2000, HL.

8. [1989] Lloyd's Rep 570.

9. See, for example, *Imperial Group Pension Trust Ltd v Imperial Tobacco Ltd* [1991] IRLR 66,ChD; *Clark v BET plc* [1997] IRLR 348, QBD.

10. See para **2.30** for arguments raised under discrimination legislation.

11. [1988] IRLR 219, CA.

12. At 220. In view of the claimant's argument that this consideration was irrelevant it was put to one side by the court.

13. See note 7, above.

2.16 A further means by which the courts may control the conduct of union affairs is by striking out rules which conflict with public policy. One area where this power has proved significant is in relation to terms which attempt to exclude the jurisdiction of the courts; a rule which provides that the decision of an internal body shall be final will be void as contrary to public policy.[1] In theory, a rule that members should attempt to exhaust internal remedies before resorting to the courts could also be construed as an attempt to oust their jurisdiction, albeit temporarily. In practice at common law the courts took the view that where such a rule did exist, it was for the claimant to show cause why the contractual position should not be adhered to,[2] the protection afforded to the member pending the exhaustion of internal procedures being material here.[3] The position in this context is now subject to statutory provisions which we discuss in para **2.20**. Another important area where the courts have exercised their discretion to strike out rules, although the basis of doing so is more controversial,[4] is where they provide for union bodies to act in conflict with the principles of natural justice. In the context of disciplinary hearings these principles, broadly speaking, require members to be given notice of the charge against them, an opportunity to be heard, and a fair hearing by an unbiased judge. In the past, the courts also sought to circumvent union rules governing admission to the union where these conflicted with the 'right to work' although the basis for this was questioned both by judges and by commentators. This concept is discussed in further detail in para **2.18** below.

---

1. *Lee v Showman's Guild of Great Britain* [1952] 2 QB 329, CA, Denning LJ at 342; *Lawlor v UPW* [1965] Ch 712, ChD.
2. *Leigh v NUR* [1970] Ch 326 at 334, ChD (cf *White v Kuzych* [1951] AC 585, PC).
3. *Leigh v NUR*, above; see also *Hiles v ASW* [1968] Ch 440 at 453, ChD.
4. See Elias and Ewing, 1987, 35–37.

Trade Union Membership and Discipline

2.17 The power of a trade union to discipline its members is restricted by the Trade Union and Labour Relations (Consolidation) Act 1992, ss 64–67 and 174–177, and the lawfulness of any disciplinary action should always be considered in the light of those restrictions, which are enforced by way of complaint to an employment tribunal.[1] However, the statutory restrictions are in addition to, not a substitute for, other rights,[2] and there may be situations where union action, although not contrary to the statute, constitutes a violation of its rules. Moreover, under statute the union cannot be required to halt disciplinary proceedings or to revoke a disciplinary penalty; the ultimate remedy is financial. By contrast, the courts and the Certification Officer may issue orders restraining a union from taking disciplinary action or from treating a disciplinary penalty as effective.[3] The common law still remains important, therefore, in some contexts, and where a remedy other than damages is sought, recourse to the Certification Officer where union action is alleged to violate both legislation and the rules is likely to prove the quickest option. If members wish to challenge a union's decision to expel them from union membership or subject them to some other disciplinary penalty, at common law the first question to consider is what the union rule book states. The power to discipline the member for the conduct in question must (usually) be present in the rules, and the penalty which may be imposed for that offence must be clearly expressed.[4] As we discussed in para **2.13**, although the rules may make the domestic tribunal the final arbiter of the facts, the court can inquire into the application of the rules to the facts,[5] and this has, in practice, afforded them considerable discretion to interpret union rules, even those which appear to give the union considerable discretion (for example, offences of conduct rendering an individual 'unfit for membership' or which is 'detrimental to the interests of the union').[6] The grounds upon which a member may challenge disciplinary penalties imposed in the context of industrial action are discussed in para **6.110** *et seq.* In all cases, any stipulation in the rules as to the procedure for disciplinary action must be followed to the letter.[7] In addition, regardless of the union rules, the courts will require the union to apply the rules of natural justice.[8] These require a member to be given notice of the charge,[9] an opportunity to be heard, and a fair hearing by an unbiased judge.[10] If the initial hearing failed to comply with natural justice, it seems that this cannot be cured by a fair appeal within the union.[11]

---

1. See further paras **2.24** *et seq.* and **2.27** *et seq.*
2. TULRCA 1992, s 64(5).
3. See para **2.20** and **2.21** . The Certification Officer is not empowered to grant interim relief, however.
4. See, for example, *Spring v NASDS* [1956] 1 WLR 585. Cf, however, *McVitae v UNISON* [1996] IRLR 33, ChD, para **2.15**, note 2, although the circumstances in that case—the amalgamation of three unions—were unusual, and the court implied a power to discipline for pre-amalgamation conduct only where the conduct contravened the rules both of the individual's pre-existing union and of the amalgamated union.
5. *Lee v Showman's Guild of Great Britain* [1952] 2 QB 329, Denning LJ at 342.
6. See, for example, *Esterman v NALGO* [1974] ICR 625, ChD.
7. See, for example, *Bonsor v MU* [1956] AC 104, HL; *Santer v NGA* [1973] ICR 60, QBD.
8. *Lee v Showman's Guild of Great Britain*, above note 5; *Hiles v ASW* [1968] Ch 440, ChD; *Lawlor v UPW* [1965] Ch 712, ChD; *Roebuck v NUM* [1977] ICR 573, ChD. Cf *Maclean v WU* [1929] 1 Ch 602 at 623–624.
9. *Annamunthodo v OWTU* [1961] AC 945.
10. *Maclean v WU*, above, note 8; *Taylor v NUS* [1967] 1 WLR 532, ChD; *Roebuck v NUM,* above, and *ibid (No 2)* [1978] ICR 676, ChD.
11. *Leary v NUVB* [1971] Ch 34 at 49, ChD. A more liberal approach has been supported by the Privy Council in *Calvin v Carr* [1979] 2 All ER 440 but the court indicated that the approach in *Leary* was probably appropriate for trade union cases. In *McKenzie v NUPE* [1991] ICR 155, ChD, it was held that in the context of disciplinary proceedings against one of its members it was an implied term of the contract that a tribunal which had once heard a disciplinary matter should be entitled to reopen or rehear it whenever, in all the circumstances, justice required it.

2.18 The position of those who are refused entry to trade union membership at common law is more complex given that they have no contractual relationship with the union, nor will the union have committed any tort against them provided that it is acting in what it perceives to be its own legitimate interests and no unlawful means are used.[1] In situations where membership of an organisation was necessary for access to, or retention of, employment the courts developed the concept of a 'right to work'[2] which meant that an application for membership should not be rejected arbitrarily or capriciously. In a departure from existing principle,[3] in the landmark case of *Nagle v Feilden*[4] the Court of Appeal held that the claimant female trainer had an arguable case for a declaration that the unwritten rule of the Jockey Club, which controls horseracing on the flat, of refusing to grant licences to women was void as being in restraint of trade. This concept was later applied to a union when in *Edwards v SOGAT*[5] Lord Denning declared that all union rules which impose an unwarranted encroachment on the right to work were *ultra vires* and void. This decision ran counter to an earlier House of Lords decision.[6] It also raised difficulties in relation to the relationship between the 'right to work' and the doctrine of restraint of trade, against which unions are protected by statute,[7] although if the right to work is 'more than simply a positive reformulation of the negative doctrine of restraint of trade'[8] this would not be problematic. In the light of the statutory restrictions upon the enforcement of closed shops, which we discuss at para **3.17** *et seq.*, the concept of the 'right to work' is probably otiose in the context of union membership. However, it is possible that, even in the absence of a closed shop, unions may continue to be subject to the public law concept of the 'duty to act fairly', which requires a decision to be made honestly and without caprice in considering applications for membership.[9] However, as this concept does not require an applicant to be given reasons if an application is refused, its use is likely to be limited unless the decision is patently arbitrary. In practice the introduction of the statutory right not to be excluded from a union contained in the Trade Union and Labour Relations (Consolidation) Act 1992, ss 174–177 is more likely to be invoked, although the common law principles remain relevant where the exclusion falls within a category permitted by the statute.

---

1. *Allen v Flood* [1898] AC 1, HL.
2. The basis of the 'right to work' was questioned both by judges and by commentators: see *McInnes v Onslow Fane* [1978] 3 All ER 211, ChD, Megarry J at 217; *Forbes v New South Wales Trotting Club Ltd* (1979) 25 ALR 1 (Aust HC), Barwick CJ at 17; Hepple, 1981a, 78–81.
3. Cf. *Weinberger v Inglis (No 2)* [1919] AC 606, HL.
4. [1966] 2 QB 633, CA.
5. [1971] Ch 354, CA.
6. *Faramus v Film Artistes Association* [1964] AC 925, HL.
7. TULRCA 1992, s 11; see para **2.8**. In *Faramus*, above, the court held that even if an arbitrary rule of exclusion was in restraint of trade at common law, it would be protected by the statutory provision. The earlier statutory protection in the Trade Union Act 1871 only covered the 'purposes' of a union and in *Edwards* Sachs LJ at 382 suggested that a rule which enabled 'capricious and despotic action' could not be proper

to the 'purposes' of a union. This circumvention of the statutory protection was blocked by the inclusion of union 'rules' as well as purposes in the Trade Union and Labour Relations Act 1974 and subsequent legislation.

8. Hepple, 1981b, 111. This broader interpretation was suggested by Slade J in *Greig v Insole* [1978] 3 All ER 449, at 510.

9. In *McInnes v Onslow Fane*, above, note 2, the application of the duty was based upon the fact that the body in question exercised monopoly control over boxing managers, but it was suggested (at 216) that the duty may also apply to bodies which exercise control over activities which are important to many people both as a means of livelihood and for other reasons. *Quaere* whether the duty to act fairly could be extended to invalidate union rules themselves. For discussion of the case, see Elias, 1979.

The Right to Control Trade Union Government

2.19 The trade union rule book serves as the constitution of the union and members have a contractual right to have the union governed in accordance with its terms, subject to the statutory restrictions on trade union government.[1] Most rule books lay down rules about the functions of various bodies within the union, the powers of officials, and the proper procedure for taking action, and it is open to any member to challenge the validity of union conduct or expenditure on the ground that it is not authorised by the union rules and thereby constitutes a breach of contract.[2] The application of these principles in the context of industrial action is discussed at para **6.109** *et seq*. The role of the courts in relation to union elections has been largely confined to ensuring that the union rules are observed. In *Leigh v NUR*[3] the claimant was successful in obtaining an injunction to prevent an election taking place without his name being included on the list of candidates after he successfully argued that he met the qualifications for nomination specified in the rules. In two cases involving election to the office of shop steward, however, the duty to act fairly was successfully invoked by individuals who had been elected by their fellow workers but whose election was not given the requisite approval by higher bodies within the union.[4] As we describe at paras **2.33** *et seq.*, elections to the posts of union president, general secretary and member of the executive are now governed by detailed statutory procedures. However if the rules impose restrictions which exceed, or do not conflict with, the statutory provisions, the common law will still be important. Thus, in *Wise v USDAW*,[5] for example, a decision by the executive council that a candidate for election to the office of general secretary must be nominated by not fewer than 25 of the branches of the union was a breach of a rule that 'all branches shall have the right to make nominations' for the office of general secretary. Again, in *Ecclestone v NUJ*[6] the union was found to have breached its rules in excluding the claimant from the shortlist for election to the post of deputy general secretary on the ground that he lacked the 'required qualifications' because he lacked the confidence of the union's national executive council. Moreover, the statutory provisions apply only to a limited range of officers; in particular they do not apply to the office of shop steward. To date, however, there have been relatively few cases in the area of union elections pursued at common law.

---

1. See para **2.23** *et seq.*
2. Occasionally the rule in *Foss v Harbottle* (1843) 2 Hare 461 will deny the member a remedy in cases where the action is not totally outside the powers of the union, but has not been taken by the properly-constituted body as the rules require. See Elias and Ewing, 1987, Chapter 4. On expenditure of union funds without the authority of the rules, see *YMA v Howden* [1903] 1 KB 308, CA, [1905] AC 256, HL; *Taylor v NUM (Derbyshire Area) (No 3)* [1985] IRLR 99, ChD; see further para **6.111**.
3. [1970] Ch 326, ChD.
4. *Breen v AEU* [1971] 2 QB 175; *Shotton v Hammond* (1976) 120 Sol Jo 780. However in *Meacham v AEU* [1994] IRLR 218, a union member who was not allowed for economic reasons to take up a full-time union post to which he had been elected was held to have no remedy other than his right to damages for breach of contract in the same way as any other prospective employee; the union was not obliged to act in accordance with natural justice in considering contracts of employment 'unless questions of vires arise, or the conduct or character of the member of the union was called into question' (at 226).
5. [1996] IRLR 609, ChD. See also *Douglas v GMPU* [1995] IRLR 426, QBD (no power in the union rules for the executive council to cancel an election after the candidate with the highest number of votes had been declared elected).
6. [1999] IRLR 166, ChD. The claimant was also held to have been unreasonably excluded contrary to TULRCA 1992, s 47; see further para **2.37**.

Remedies for a Breach or Threatened Breach of the Contract of Membership

2.20 A union member who alleges that the union has acted or threatens to act in breach of the contract of membership may seek a remedy in the High Court or, with some exceptions, apply to the Certification Officer (see para **2.21**).[1] The remedies which may potentially be sought from the High Court, depending upon the context, are a declaration, an injunction and damages.[2] Where time is of the essence—an impending election allegedly involving unlawful expenditure, or expulsion from the union, for example—a claimant may seek an interim injunction to restrain the union from carrying out or continuing an allegedly unlawful act. The procedure for applying for interim injunctions, the principles which govern the discretion to grant them, and the penalties for breaching them, are discussed at para **6.52** *et seq*. As in the context of proceedings brought by employers to halt industrial action, the courts have tended to conclude that the balance of convenience lies with the claimants in actions against unions.[3] It is notable that the statutory limits on damages awards which apply to proceedings in tort do not apply in this context.[4] Damages are most likely to be sought when a member is unlawfully expelled from a union. In practice there are very few reported cases dealing with this remedy.[5] The statutory restrictions upon enforcement of the closed shop, which mean that members cannot lawfully be deprived of their employment through loss of union membership, will probably make a claim in damages even more rare; there would be considerable difficulty in quantifying such a claim. As we discussed in para **2.16**, where a union rule requires a member to exhaust internal remedies before resorting to the courts, the courts have considered that the claimant should show cause why the contractual position should not be followed, the protection afforded to the member pending the exhaustion of internal procedures being material in this context. This rule is now subject to a statutory right not to be denied access to the courts.[6] Notwithstanding anything in the rules of the union[7] or in the practice of any court, if a member or former member of a union brings proceedings in a court with respect to a matter to which this statutory right applies, then, provided specified conditions are met, rules requiring or allowing the matter to be submitted for determination or conciliation, and the fact that any 'relevant steps'[8] remain to be taken under the rules, must be regarded as irrelevant to the question whether the legal proceedings should be dismissed, stayed or adjourned. The right applies where:

> a matter is under the rules of a trade union required or allowed to be submitted for determination or conciliation in accordance with the rules of the union, but a provision of the rules purporting to provide for that to be a person's only remedy has no effect (or would have no effect if there were one).[9]

The terms in which this right is framed are puzzling. The right clearly covers the situation where the rules attempt to oust the jurisdiction of the courts completely, and would also apply where the rules are silent; whether it applies where the rule merely provides for prior exhaustion of internal remedies is unclear, although it was the express intention of the Conservative Government which introduced the legislation that it should.[10] Two further conditions must be satisfied for the right to apply: the member or former member must have made a 'valid application' to the union for the matter to be submitted for determination or conciliation in accordance with the union's rules,[11] and the court proceedings must not have been commenced sooner than six months after the union received the application.[12] Once this period has expired, the court has no discretion to dismiss or adjourn the proceedings on the ground that internal remedies have not been exhausted (unless there has been delay in furthering the proceedings caused by the unreasonable conduct of the member[13]) although its discretion to do so on other grounds remains unaffected. The discretion of the court on general common law principles to grant a remedy before the statutory time limit has expired also remains unaffected,[14] although it is possible that the courts may be guided by the statutory period and refuse to intervene before that period has expired.

---

1. Note that a complainant must choose between these avenues of redress: TULRCA 1992, s 108A.

2. For more detailed discussion of the issues raised by these remedies in relation to unions, and the basis on which unions may be liable for the acts of their officials, see Elias and Ewing, 1987, 44–57.

3. See, for example, *Porter v NUJ* [1980] IRLR 404, HL.

4. TULRCA 1992, s 22; see further para **6.65**.

5. Elias and Ewing, 1987, 55. The leading case is *Edwards v SOGAT* [1971] Ch 354, CA, a case of expulsion in the context of a closed shop.

6. TULRCA 1992, s 63.

7. In this context, references to union rules include references to any arbitration or other agreement entered into in pursuance of any requirement imposed by or under the rules: *ibid.,* s 63(5)(a).

8. 'Relevant steps' include any steps falling to be taken in accordance with the rules for the purposes of, or in connection with, the determination or conciliation of the matter, or any appeal, review, or reconsideration of any determination or award: *ibid.,* s 63(5)(b).

9. *Ibid.,* s 63(1).

10. See, for example, Mr Patrick Nicholls, House of Commons, Official Report of Standing Committee F, col 62, 17 November 1987.

11. TULRCA 1992, s 63(2)(a). An application is deemed to be valid unless the union informs the applicant, within 28 days of receipt, of the respects in which the application contravened the requirements of the rules: s 63(3).

12. *Ibid.,* s 63(2)(b).

13. *Ibid.,* s 63(4). If a court is satisfied that any delay in the taking of relevant steps under the rules is attributable to unreasonable conduct of the person who commenced the proceedings, it may extend the six month period before which proceedings may not be brought by such further period as it considers appropriate: *ibid.*

14. *Ibid.* s 63(6).

2.21 The right of a member to apply to the Certification Officer where he or she alleges a breach or threatened breach of union rules was introduced by the

Employment Relations Act 1999.[1] It applies where the breach or threatened breach relates to the appointment or election of a person to, or the removal of a person from, any office; disciplinary proceedings (including expulsion); the balloting of members on any issue other than industrial action;[2] and the constitution or proceedings of any executive committee[3] or of any decision-making meeting.[4] The Secretary of State may add to this list by order.[5] As well as industrial action ballots, dismissal and disciplinary proceedings against an employee of the union are excluded, as are, by implication, allegations relating to the misuse of funds.[6] In contrast to High Court proceedings, which may normally be brought up to six years after the breach, a tight time limit applies to applications to the Certification Officer: the application must be made within a six month period starting with the day on which the breach or threatened breach is alleged to have taken place, or, if within that period any internal union complaints procedure is invoked to resolve the claim, within a six month period starting with the day on which the procedure is concluded, or the last day of the period of one year beginning with the day on which the procedure is invoked, whichever is the earlier.[7] Interestingly, the legislation reflects a preference for the use of internal complaints procedures where these exist; the Certification Officer may refuse to accept an application unless he or she is satisfied that the applicant has taken all reasonable steps to resolve the claim by these means.[8] The procedure which the Certification Officer is required to follow in dealing with such claims is described in para **2.2**. If the complaint is upheld, the Certification Officer must make, unless it is considered inappropriate, an enforcement order requiring the union to take specified steps to remedy the breach or withdraw the threat of a breach within a specified period, and/or to abstain from specified acts with a view to securing that a breach of the same or a similar kind does not occur in future.[9] Provision for enforcing such an order, and appeals, are also described in para **2.2**. Recourse to the Certification Officer is likely to prove a much speedier and cheaper option, unless the applicant seeks interim relief or damages, in which case he or she will have no alternative but to commence High Court proceedings.

---

1. TULRCA 1992, s108A,108B; see further para **2.2**. The applicant must be a member of the union or have been one at the time of the alleged breach or threatened breach: s108A(3). On the meaning of 'member', see further para **2.2** note 2. 'Rules' include the rules of any branch or section of the union: s108A(8).

2. This is defined as 'a strike or other industrial action by persons employed under contracts of employment': *ibid.*, s 108A(9). This does not advance matters very far: see further paras **6.91** and **6.115**.

3. Note that this goes beyond the 'principal committee' (defined *ibid.*, s 119), and extends to any union committee which has power to make executive decisions on behalf of the union or a constituent body; a committee of a major constituent body which has power to make executive decisions on behalf of that body; or a sub-committee of a

committee falling within either of these categories: s 108A(10). A 'constituent' body means 'any body which forms part of the union, including a branch, group, section or region'; a 'major constituent body' is such a body which has more than 1,000 members: s108A(12).

4. TULCRA 1992, s 108A(2). A decision-making meeting means a meeting of members of the union concerned (or the representatives of such members) which has power to make a decision on any matter which, under the union rules, is final as regards the union or which, under the union rules or those of a constituent body is final as regards that body, or a meeting of members of a major constituent body (or the representatives of such members) which has power to make a decision on any matter which, under the rules of the union or that body, is final as regards that body: *ibid.,* s 108A(11). See note 3 for the definition of 'constituent body' and 'major constituent body'.

5. *Ibid.,* s108A(2)(e),(13).

6. *Ibid.,* s 108A(5). See para **2.2** for the rationale of these restrictions. Complaints relating to a failure to comply with political fund rules must be brought under *ibid.,* s 80: s 108A(4).

7. TULRCA 1992, s 108A(6),(7).

8. *Ibid.,* s108B(1).

9. *Ibid.,* s 108B(3),(4).

Trade Union Liability in Negligence

2.22 To date, it does not appear to have been common for trade union members to bring proceedings against their unions in negligence. However in *Friend v IPMS*[1] the court approved the argument that a union advising and/or acting for a member in an employment dispute would owe a duty of care in tort to act with ordinary care and skill, although once the union engages solicitors on the member's behalf the duty on the union falls away. Unions which give advice to members in relation to compromise agreements, settling claims, must ensure that there is a contract of insurance in place to cover potential claims by employees in relation to the provision of advice.[2] The right of workers to be accompanied at disciplinary and grievance hearings by the companion of their choice, who may be a union official, when they reasonably request this[3] may lead, in practice, to an extension of their advisory services; members are unlikely not to wish to discuss with the official both before and after the hearing the implications of matters raised there. Another context in which the liability of unions to their members may become an issue in the future is the organisation of industrial action. As we discuss in Chapter 6, the statutory protection of those taking industrial action against unfair dismissal for so doing depends upon that action being protected against liability in tort.[4] Unions can lose that protection on a variety of grounds, including their conduct of the pre-industrial action ballot and by failing to ensure that the relevant employers receive the requisite pre- and post-ballot notices. A member who takes industrial action on the understanding that it is 'protected industrial action' who is then dismissed without a remedy because the action turns out not to be 'protected' because the union has not complied with the statutory procedures may well be tempted to seek a remedy against the union in tort.[5] Whether such a remedy could be sought would depend, in the first instance, on whether a duty of care was found to be owed by the union to its members in these circumstances, which involves enquiry into whether the harm was foreseeable, the claimant and defendant were in a relationship of 'proximity', and the imposition of the duty is 'fair, just and reasonable'. Space does not permit full consideration of the factors which may be influential in this context.[6] However, in our view it is certainly arguable that the union could be taken to have assumed responsibility for providing a service to its members who relied on that service, and that this relationship of itself could give rise to a duty of care.[7] Even if this were to be the case, it does not, of course, mean that liability would automatically lie; in particular, it may be difficult to show that the union had acted negligently. Nevertheless, this is another area in which unions may wish to consider insuring themselves against such claims.

---

1. [1999] IRLR 173, QBD.

2. ERA 1996, s 203(3),(3A). The relevant officer, official, employee, or member of the union must be certified in writing by the union as competent to give advice and authorised to do so on behalf of the union: s 203(3A)(b).

3. ERA 1999, ss 10–15. Note that the official must be either employed by the union or an official whom the union has reasonably certified in writing as having experience of, or as having received training in, acting as a worker's companion at disciplinary or grievance hearings: s 10(3)(a),(b). The ACAS Code of Practice on Disciplinary and Grievance Procedures para 60 advises that even where a union official has experience of acting in the role there may still be a need for periodic refresher training.

4. TULRCA 1992, s 238A; see further para **6.98** *et seq*.

5. *Quaere* whether there would also be a claim in contract based on breach of an implied term for the union to act with reasonable care.

6. See further Clerk and Lindsell, 1995, Chapters 1 and 7, and supplements.

7. See, in particular, *Henderson v Merrett Syndicates Ltd* [1994] 3 All ER 506, HL.

STATUTORY RIGHTS OF TRADE UNION MEMBERS

Sources and General Principles

2.23 There are a wide range of statutory rights which trade union members may exercise in relation to their union, regardless of the terms of the union rules.[1] The majority of these rights are contained in the Trade Union and Labour Relations (Consolidation) Act 1992. They can be divided into four broad categories:

(1) Rights relating to *union membership and discipline*, which we discuss in para **2.24** *et seq*. Individuals who are excluded or expelled from a union other than in circumstances expressly permitted by the legislation, or who are 'unjustifiably disciplined', may seek a remedy from an employment tribunal and may be awarded substantial financial compensation.[2] In addition, there is a statutory right to terminate union membership on giving reasonable notice and complying with any reasonable conditions.[3]

(2) Rights *not to be discriminated against* in relation to union membership and the benefits of membership: (a) where a union has a 'political fund', contribution to the fund cannot be made a condition of admission to the union, nor may non-contributors be placed at any disadvantage as compared with other members except in relation to the control or management of the fund;[4] (b) EC law requires that workers who are nationals of a Member State who are employed in another Member State must be given equal treatment as regards membership of unions and the exercise of rights attaching to membership;[5] (c) the Sex Discrimination Act 1975, Race Relations Act 1976, and Disability Discrimination Act 1995 make it unlawful for any 'organisation of workers' to discriminate, respectively, against women (or men) or married persons, on 'racial grounds', or against a disabled person in specified ways.[6] We discuss the first of these rights in greater detail in para **2.50**; the remainder in para **2.30**.

(3) Rights which may be exercised in the event that a union fails to comply with its statutory obligation to hold *appropriately conducted ballots* in relation to elections to specified offices; approval of the union adopting 'political objects' and periodic reapproval of an existing political fund; industrial action; and union amalgamations and 'transfers of engagements'.[7] We discuss the first and second of these rights in paras **2.33** *et seq*. and **2.46** *et seq*. respectively; the third in para **6.30** *et seq*. We do not consider the highly specialist area of amalgamations and transfers of engagements, which lie beyond the scope of this work.

(4) *Miscellaneous rights*. Members have the right to ascertain whether there is an entry on the register which unions are required to maintain relating to themselves, and to request the independent scrutineer required to supervise elections to inspect the register.[8] In addition, they have the right to inspect the accounting records of the union or any of its branches or sections.[9] These rights are discussed in paras **2.31**, **2.40** and **2.32** respectively. The rights of members to complain if disqualified persons hold specified positions in the union, and the right not to be denied access to the courts[10] are discussed in paras **2.11** and **2.20** respectively. Finally, members may bring High Court proceedings on the union's behalf where the union unreasonably fails to

recover payments unlawfully made to individuals in relation to the commission of an offence or contempt of court, and may also apply to the court to restrain the union's trustees from allowing unlawful application of the union's property or from complying with an unlawful direction to them under the union's rules.[11] These rights are most likely to be exercised in the context of industrial action, and we therefore discuss them in Chapter 6.

---

1. See para **2.2** for the concept of a union member, and para **2.4** for the definition of a 'trade union'.
2. TULRCA 1992, ss 174–177; 64–67.
3. *Ibid.*, s 69.
4. *Ibid.*, s 82(1)(c).
5. EC Regulation 1612/68, as amended.
6. Ss 12, 11 and 13 respectively. Note that the definition of 'organisation of workers' is wider than that of a trade union: see further para **2.30**.
7. TULRCA 1992, ss 46–61; 73–81; 62; and 97–106, respectively. Under a transfer of engagements, the transferor union loses its legal identity while the organisation to which it transfers continues in being with its legal identity unchanged. An amalgamation produces a new organisation replacing the amalgamating bodies, which then cease to exist.
8. *Ibid.*, ss 24–26.
9. *Ibid.*, ss 30–31.
10. *Ibid.*, ss 45C, 63.
11. *Ibid.*, ss 15, 16.

Rights Relating to Trade Union Membership and Discipline

The right not to be excluded or expelled from a trade union

2.24 An individual has the right not to be excluded or expelled from a trade union other than in circumstances specifically permitted by s 174 of the Trade Union and Labour Relations (Consolidation) Act 1992.[1] If a union fails either to grant or refuse an application for membership before the end of the period within which it might reasonably be expected to be granted, the applicant is treated as having been excluded from the union on the last day of that period.[2] There are now only four situations in which exclusion or expulsion is permitted:

(1) If the individual does not satisfy, or no longer satisfies, an 'enforceable membership requirement' contained in the union rules.[3] A requirement is 'enforceable' if it restricts membership solely by reference to one or more of

three sets of criteria: employment in a specified trade, industry or profession; occupational description (including grade, level or category of appointment); or the possession of specified trade, industrial or professional qualifications or work experience.[4]

(2) If the individual does not qualify, or no longer qualifies, for membership of the union because it operates only in a particular part or parts of Great Britain.

(3) In the case of a union whose purpose is the regulation of relations between its members and one particular employer or a number of associated employers,[5] if the individual is not, or is no longer, employed by a relevant employer. This enables 'house' unions to confine their membership to a single employer.

(4) If the exclusion or expulsion is entirely attributable to the individual's conduct. 'Conduct' is not defined, but it excludes being or ceasing to be: a member of another union; employed by a particular employer or at a particular place; or a member of a political party.[6] It also excludes any conduct for which an individual has the statutory right not to be 'unjustifiably disciplined'.[7] A union could not, therefore, exclude an individual who expressed an intention never to take part in industrial action, for example. An individual who under the union rules ceases automatically to be a member on the occurrence of a specified event is treated as having been expelled.[8] Thus, loss of membership pursuant to a rule providing for automatic loss of membership on non-payment of subscriptions will be treated as expulsion. Non-payment of subscriptions would be a permitted reason for expulsion, but a union could face difficulties in showing that it was 'entirely attributable' to the member's conduct if, for example, he or she had not taken part in recent industrial action.

---

1. See para **2.4** for the definition of a 'trade union'. In this context organisations falling within TULRCA 1992, s 1(b) are not included: TULRCA 1992, s 177. For an evaluation of this right, see Simpson, 1993. The ECSR of the ESC has condemned these provisions as incompatible with the right to organise.; see also para **6.115**.

2. TULRCA 1992, s 177(2)(a). In *NACODS v Gluckowski* [1996] IRLR 252, Maurice Kay J held that 'exclusion' refers to a refusal to admit and not to expulsion. He thought it unlikely that constructive expulsion would be covered by the statute (and see *McGhee v TGWU* [1985] IRLR 198, EAT).

3. This includes the rules of any branch or section of the union: TULRCA 1992, s 119.

4. *Ibid.*, s 174(3). *Quaere* whether, when the lines of demarcation between unions organising within the same general area is unclear, they can reach an understanding about the meaning of trade, industry, occupation, etc in relation to a particular activity and exclude individuals accordingly (see HL Debs, Vol 545, cols 34–38, 26 April 1993). On the face of it, there seems no reason why this should not be possible.

'Employment' in this context includes any relationship whereby an individual person-ally does work or performs services for another person: TULRCA 1992, s 177(1).
5. See App 1.
6. TULRCA 1992, s 174(4)(a). 'Conduct' includes statements, acts and omissions: *ibid.*, s 177(1)(b). For discussion of the meaning of 'political party', which is not defined in this context, see para **2.48**. *Quaere* whether membership of an anti-union think tank could, of itself, constitute 'conduct' justifying exclusion or expulsion.
7. *Ibid.*, s 174(4)(b); see para **2.27** *et seq.* A member or former member may also have a right of action under those provisions, but a claim which is declared well-founded under one section may not then be proceeded with under the other: ss 66(4), 177(4). Note that organisations falling within TULRCA 1992, s 1(b) are not excluded from the provisions relating to unjustifiable discipline.
8. *Ibid.*, s 177(2)(b).

2.25 An individual who claims to have been excluded or expelled from a trade union in contravention of the legislation may complain to an employment tri-bunal.[1] The complaint must be presented within six months of the date of the exclusion or expulsion or within such further period as the tribunal considers 'reasonable' where it is satisfied that it was not 'reasonably practicable' for the complaint to be presented within six months.[2] Where the tribunal upholds the complaint it must make a declaration to this effect.[3] An individual who has obtained a declaration may then apply for an award of compensation from the union.[4] The application should be made to a tribunal if the applicant has been admitted or re-admitted to the union by this time; otherwise it is made directly to the EAT.[5] The award is to be such as the tribunal or EAT 'considers just and equitable in all the circumstances', subject to a maximum award of £56,900 and, in the case of an application to the EAT, a minimum of £5,300.[6] Where the tri-bunal or EAT finds that the applicant has caused or contributed to the refusal or expulsion, it shall reduce the amount by such proportion as it considers 'just and equitable'.[7] In relation to applications for compensation, as in other con-texts, there is a right of appeal from tribunals to the EAT on questions of law.[8] The statutory right not to be excluded or expelled forms an addition to, not a substitute for, other rights which may be available to the individual,[9] so if expul-sion, for example were to infringe the union rules as well as the legislation it would still be open to the member to sue the union for breach of contract.[10]

---

1. *Ibid.*, s 174(5).
2. *Ibid.*, s 175; see App 2 for the meaning of 'reasonably practicable'.
3. *Ibid.*, s 176(1).

4. *Ibid.*, s 176(2).

5. *Ibid.* Applications must be made no earlier than four weeks, and no later than six months, from the date of the declaration: s 176(3).

6. *Ibid.*, s 176(4), (6). Figures as of 1 February 2000 and at the time of writing.

7. *Ibid.*, s 176(5).

8. ETA 1996, s 21. Thenceforth, with permission, to the Court of Appeal.

9. TULCRA 1992, s 177(5) (although where a complaint relating to an expulsion is upheld, no complaint of unjustifiable discipline should be pursued: s 177(4)).

10. See further paras **2.20** and **2.21** (and note the difference in remedies). The only remedy for infringement of the statutory right itself is that conferred by the statute: s 177(3).

2.26 The introduction of the right not to be excluded or expelled from a union necessitated revision of the TUC's Bridlington Principles, first promulgated in 1939 to minimise disputes between affiliated unions over membership issues. Although not intended to constitute a legally enforceable contract, they are 'accepted by all affiliated organisations as a binding commitment for their continued affiliation to the TUC'.[1] Before the 1993 revision these rules provided, *inter alia*, that the membership forms of all unions should inquire about the applicant's membership of other unions; that no union should accept as members applicants who were or had recently been members of any other affiliated union without inquiry of that union; that if that union objected, the applicant should not be accepted into membership; and that in the case of dispute the matter should be notified to the TUC and could be referred for adjudication by an internal Disputes Committee, composed of senior officials of affiliated unions. The Committee could issue an award that individuals accepted into membership in breach of the Principles should be expelled, and advised to join or rejoin the appropriate union. Expulsions to give effect to decisions of the Disputes Committee were upheld at common law provided that the decision was properly one which fell under the terms of the Committee's remit and the expulsion was authorised by the union rules.[2] In *Cheall v APEX* the House of Lords rejected the argument that these arrangements contravened public policy in restricting the right of an individual to join and remain a member of the union of his choice; in giving the judgment of the court, Lord Diplock affirmed that 'freedom of association can only be mutual; there can be no right of an individual to associate with other individuals who are not willing to associate with him'.[3] The argument that the expulsion breached Article 11 of the ECHR also failed, the EComHR affirming that the right to join a union did not confer a general right to join the union of one's choice, regardless of the union rules.[4] Revised Principles were drafted to accommodate the statutory restriction on exclusion and expulsion; initially promulgated in 1993, these now appear in the 2000 edition of the Principles.[5] They affirm that all TUC affiliates accept 'as a binding commitment to their continued affiliation to the TUC that they will not knowingly and actively seek to take into membership existing or "recent" members of another union by making recruitment approaches, either directly or indirectly, without the agreement of that organisation'. Unions must continue to include in their membership application form questions regarding past or present membership of another union, and if that other union has cause to object to the recruitment of its present or former members it should request a meeting with the prospective recruiting union. The effort at resolution will include a moral obligation on the part of the respondent union to 'offer compensation to the complainant union for any loss of income that it has suffered as a consequence of any knowing and active recruitment of its members'. In case of continuing disagreement the issue will be referred to the TUC which, if other attempts at settlement fail, may refer it to the Disputes Committee. If it finds in its favour, the Committee may adjudicate on the financial compensation to be paid to the complainant union, up to a maximum of two years' loss of contributions, and/or may censure the respondent union and require it to print the censure in a prominent place in its journal. However the Committee no longer has power to require the expulsion of those admitted to unions in breach of the Principles.

---

1. *TUC Disputes Principles and Procedures*, TUC, 2000.
2. Cf *Spring v NASDS* [1956] 1 WLR 585, which led to the TUC recommending unions to adopt a model rule permitting expulsions to comply with decisions of the Disputes Committee. See generally Simpson 1993, 189–193 and Elgar and Simpson, 1994, for an evaluation of the operation of the Principles before revision.
3. [1983] IRLR 215 at 218. The claimant's argument that the termination of his membership was void as being in breach of natural justice because he was not able to make representations to the Disputes Committee also failed.
4. *Cheall v UK* App No. 10550/83, (1986) 8 EHRR 74. Although the state was required to protected an individual against a dominant position by unions, which could occur if there was a closed shop or the union rules were wholly unreasonable or arbitrary, this was not the case here.
5. For an analysis of these changes, see Simpson, 1994.

The right not to be unjustifiably disciplined

2.27 An individual who is, or at any time has been, a member of a trade union has the right not to be 'unjustifiably disciplined' by that union, regardless of anything in the union rules.[1] Discipline is 'unjustified' if the actual or supposed conduct which constitutes the reason, or one of the reasons, for it is a form of conduct listed in the legislation or something which is believed by the union to amount to such conduct.[2] The statutory right is additional to any other rights which may be available to the individual,[3] so if disciplinary action were to infringe the union rules as well as statute it would still be open to the member to sue for breach of contract.[4] Recourse to the Certification Officer for breach of the union rules may be a speedier option than going to an employment tribunal (see para **2.21**), but he or she has no power to award financial compensation. Where disciplinary action infringes only the union rules, or the challenge is based exclusively upon the procedure followed by the union, the common law will be the only avenue available. A member may also wish to rely upon the common law if the challenge is based upon the procedure followed by the union rather than the substantive reason for the disciplinary action. Disciplinary action is 'unjustified' for conduct (which includes 'statements, acts and omissions)[5] which consists in:[6]

(1) failing to participate in or support a strike or other industrial action[7] (whether by members of the union or by others) or indicating opposition to or a lack of support for such action;

(2) failing to contravene, for a purpose connected with such a strike or other industrial action, a requirement imposed on the individual by or under a contract of employment;[8]

(3) asserting that the union, any official or representative of it or a trustee of its property has contravened, or is proposing to contravene, a requirement which is, or is thought to be, imposed by or under the rules of the union or any other agreement or by or under any enactment or any rule of law.[9] Encouraging or assisting a person to make or attempt to vindicate any such assertion is also protected. However the protection does not apply if the assertion was false and the individual believed that or was otherwise acting in bad faith.[10] There is no requirement that the member should have had reasonable grounds to believe that the assertion was true. Where the assertion was not false, the presence of bad faith is irrelevant;

(4) encouraging or assisting a person to perform an obligation imposed on him or her by a contract of employment.[11] This is most likely to be relevant to industrial disputes;

(5) contravening a requirement imposed by or in consequence of a determination which infringes the individual's or another individual's right not to be unjustifiably disciplined;

(6) failing to agree, or withdrawing agreement, to the check-off;[12]

(7) resigning or proposing to resign from the union or from another union, becoming or proposing to become a member of another union, refusing to become a member of another union, or being a member of another union;[13]

(8) working with, or proposing to work with, individuals who are not members of the union or who are or are not members of another union;

(9) working for, or proposing to work for, an employer who employs or who has employed individuals who are not members of the union or who are or are not members of another union;

(10) requiring the union to do an act which it is, under the Trade Union and Labour Relations (Consolidation) Act 1992, required to do on the requisition of a member;[14]

(11) consulting or asking advice or assistance from the Certification Officer on any matter, or which involves consulting or asking advice or assistance from any other person with respect to a matter which forms, or might form, the subject matter of any assertion mentioned in (3), above;

(12) proposing to engage in, or doing anything preparatory or incidental to, conduct falling within (1)–(11) above.

A member is treated as 'disciplined' if a 'determination' is made, or purportedly made, under the union rules, or by a union official or persons including an official, that he or she should be expelled from the union or a branch or section of it; should make any payment, or that subscriptions paid should be treated as unpaid or paid for a different purpose; should be deprived to any extent of any benefits, services or facilities which would otherwise be available; that another union, or branch or section, should be encouraged not to accept him or her as a member; or that he or she should be subjected to 'some other detriment'.[15] The EAT has held that 'determination' means a decision which disposes of the issue; thus, a recommendation by a union's Regional Council to the General Executive Council that a member should be expelled from the union, which required affirmation by the latter, was not a 'determination'.[16] Naming a member as a strikebreaker in a branch circular to cause her embarrassment has been held to constitute a 'detriment';[17] banning a member from standing for, or holding union office, would almost certainly be included, as would preventing an individual from attending a branch meeting.

---

1. TULRCA 1992, s 64(1). See para **2.4** for the definition of a 'trade union'. This right applies even to full-time union officials who have a contract of employment with the union, provided they have been members. The ILO Committee of Experts on the Application on Conventions and Recommendations has condemned this provision as being in conflict with Article 3 of ILO Convention 87 because it prevents unions disciplining members who refuse to participate in lawful industrial action, and it is regarded by the ECSR, which supervises compliance with the ESC, as incompatible with the right to organise. Although it seems strongly arguable that it conflicts with Article 11 of the ECHR (see *Cheall v UK* App No. 10550/83, (1986) 8 EHRR 74; Leader 1991), there seems little scope for modifying the application of these provisions by reference to arguments based upon the Human Rights Act 1998 in this context because the legislation is so specific in its terms.

2. *Ibid.*, s 65(1).

3. *Ibid.*, s 64(5). The only remedies for infringement of this right are those conferred by the statute (s 64(4)), subject to s 64(3) (where a determination which infringes an individual's right requires a payment of a sum or performance of an obligation, no person

in any proceedings may rely on that determination to recover the sum or enforce the obligation). Where a complaint relating to an expulsion presented under this provision is found to be well-founded, no complaint in respect of the expulsion can be proceeded with under s 174 (see para **2.24** above): s 66(4).

4. See para **2.12** *et seq.* (and note the difference in remedies). Note also that the statutory right arises only when a disciplinary 'determination' has been made; it does not allow the individual to forestall the disciplinary process, although if *Longley v NUJ* [1987] IRLR 109, CA, is followed (see para **6.113**), this may not make any practical difference.

5. TULRCA 1992, s 65(7).

6. *Ibid.*, s 65(2)–(4). Note that the statutory protection against such discipline does not apply if it shown that individuals would be disciplined by the union for such conduct irrespective of its connection with conduct for which discipline is unjustified: s 65(5). This provision is designed to protect unions, such as the Royal College of Nursing, which may discipline members in order to protect professional standards.

7. See further para **6.115**, where other forms of conduct relating to non-participation in, or opposition to, industrial action are discussed in further detail.

8. This includes any agreement between the individual and a person for whom he or she works or normally works: TULRCA 1992, s 65(7). Persons holding office or employment under the Crown are deemed to have contracts of employment for this purpose: s 65(8).

9. 'Official' is defined in *ibid.*, s 119, and is wide enough to include shop stewards. 'Representative' means any person acting or purporting to act in his or her capacity as a member of the union or on the instructions or advice of a person acting or purporting to act in that capacity or in the capacity of an official of the union: s 65(7).

10. *Ibid.*, s 65(6).

11. See note 8 above.

12. See paras **3.24** and **3.25** for rights against employers.

13. The Conservative Government which introduced this provision maintained that this would not prevent an individual who sought to persuade other members to resign and join a different union being disciplined: Mr Patrick McLoughlin, Standing Committee F, cols 189, 191, 10 December 1992.

14. 'Require' in this context includes 'request or apply for': TULRCA 1992, s 65(7).

15. *Ibid.*, s 64(2). See note 9 above for the meaning of 'official'. The provision for union officials to bind the union means that the union may be held responsible even if the determination is made by persons who have no express or implied authority to act on its behalf in this regard.

16. *TGWU v Webber* [1990] IRLR 462, EAT. Note that there may be more than one 'determination' within the expulsion process, eg suspension leading to deprivation of benefits prior to the decision to expel: *ibid.* However, where this occurs there will be a need to keep a careful eye on time limits: see further para **2.28**.

17. *NALGO v Killorn* [1990] IRLR 464, EAT. In that case the EAT expressed the view (at 469) that whether a member suffered detriment was the sort of question that employment tribunals were 'peculiarly suited to answer'. See para **3.10** for the meaning of 'detriment' in other contexts.

2.28 An individual who claims to have been 'unjustifiably disciplined' by a trade union may complain to an employment tribunal.[1] A complaint must be presented within three months of the date of the making of the determination which the individual claims infringes his or her right, although this may be extended to a period the tribunal considers 'reasonable' where it is satisfied either that it was not 'reasonably practicable' for the complaint to be presented within three months or that any delay in making the complaint is wholly or partly attributable to a reasonable attempt to appeal against the determination or to have it reconsidered or reviewed.[2] Where such an appeal is made, there is no requirement for it to be stated in any particular form, and the EAT has indicated that tribunals should look at the reality and intention of a member's communication with the union rather than the use of specific wording.[3] Where the tribunal upholds the complaint, it must make a declaration to this effect,[4] whereupon the applicant may apply for an award of compensation from the union. Such an application should be made to a tribunal, or, where at the time of the application, the 'determination' has not been revoked or the union has not taken all necessary steps to reverse anything done to give effect to it, directly to the EAT.[5] Whether the 'necessary' steps have been taken may itself be a matter of dispute.[6] There is a power to transfer the application from the EAT to a tribunal or vice versa, and a transferred application is to be treated as if made to the appropriate tribunal at the time it was originally made.[7] The compensation is such amount as the tribunal or EAT considers 'just and equitable in all the circumstances', subject in either case to a maximum award of £56,900 and, in the case of an application to the EAT, a minimum of £5,300.[8] An award may be reduced where the applicant has failed to mitigate his or her loss (according to the principles applicable to common law damages)[9] and where the tribunal finds that the applicant has caused or contributed to the infringement, it shall reduce the amount of compensation by such proportion as it considers 'just and equitable'.[10] In relation to applications for compensation, as in other contexts, there is a right of appeal from tribunals to the EAT on questions of law.[11]

---

1. TULRCA 1992, s 66(1).
2. *Ibid.*, s 66(2). As Kidner, 1991, points out time limits may be problematic in this area, particularly as a 'determination', for example to exclude an individual from a meeting, may not be applied immediately. See App 2 for the meaning of 'not reasonably practicable'.
3. *NALGO v Killorn* [1990] IRLR 464, EAT (member's letter to the branch chairman expressing dissatisfaction with the decision to suspend her an 'appeal' even though it did not use that term).
4. TULRCA 1992, s 66 (3). If the complaint relates to an expulsion, no complaint may then be proceeded with under s 174: s 66(4).

5. *Ibid.*, s 67(1)(a), (2). Where an individual has paid the union a sum in accordance with an unlawful 'determination', he or she may apply for this to be repaid: s 67(1)(b). Applications must be made no earlier than four weeks, and no later than six months, from the date of the declaration: s 67(3).

6. In *NALGO v Courteney-Dunn* [1992] IRLR 114, the EAT rejected the argument that necessary' meant 'requisite' or 'indispensable'; the union was required to put the member back into the same position he was in before the wrongful expulsion and the fact that the member himself could have done this (here, restored resumption of the check-off) was irrelevant.

7. TULRCA 1992, s 67(4).

8. *Ibid.*, s 67(5)–(8); figures as of 1 February 2000. See *Bradley v NALGO* [1991] IRLR 159, EAT, discussed Kidner 1991, where the EAT expressed the view that the measure of compensation for injured feelings, if recoverable, would fall within a modest bracket provided that the cause arose solely from the expulsion itself and not from other activities.

9. TULRCA 1992, s 67(6); see McGregor, 1997. Note that there is no duty to mitigate under s 176: see para **2.25**.

10. *Ibid.*, s 67(7).

11. ETA 1996, s 21. Thenceforth, with permission, to the Court of Appeal.

The right to resign

2.29 There is a term implied by statute into the contract of membership of all trade unions that a member should have the right to terminate his or her union membership on giving reasonable notice and complying with any reasonable conditions.[1] It has been suggested that where subscriptions are collected monthly, at least one month's notice should be given.[2] It has been accepted that resignation may be postponed until the completion of any disciplinary action which is pending and that a member can be required to make up any arrears of subscription.[3] The union may inquire as to the member's reason for resigning, but giving reasons cannot be made a condition of resignation.[4]

---

1. TULRCA 1992, s 69. See para **2.4** for the definition of a 'trade union'.

2. *Ashford v ASTMS* [1973] ICR 296, NIRC (decided under the comparable provision of the Industrial Relations Act 1971). Resigning without notice cannot be 'reasonable notice' nor, on the facts, was seven days' notice reasonable: *ibid.* Kidner, 1983, 26, n 96 suggests that where a union collects an annual subscription, a member may resign on reasonable notice of less than a year but cannot recover any part of the subscription.

3. *Ashford v ASTMS,* above. A member may attempt to seek an injunction to forestall disciplinary proceedings, although see para **6.112** and **6.113** for the approach of the courts towards such attempts.

4. *Ashford v ASTMS*, above.

Rights Not to be Discriminated Against in Relation to Trade Union Membership and the Benefits of Membership

2.30 There are three sets of provisions which prohibit discrimination in relation to union membership and the benefits of membership. First, where a union has a 'political fund', contribution to the fund cannot be made a condition of admission to the union, nor may non-contributors be placed at any disadvantage as compared with other members except in relation to the control or management of the fund.[1] We analyse this provision in para **2.50**. Secondly, EU law requires that a worker who is a national of a Member State who is employed in the territory of another Member State shall enjoy equality of treatment as regards membership of unions and the exercise of rights attaching to membership, including the right to vote and to be eligible for the workers' representative bodies in the undertaking.[2] Thirdly, it is unlawful for any 'organisation of workers' to discriminate against women (or men) or married persons, on 'racial grounds', or against a disabled person in admitting to membership; the terms on which membership is offered; access to benefits; or by subjecting the member to 'any other detriment'.[3] The organisation is liable for unlawful discriminatory acts committed by persons in the course of their employment with the union or its authorised agents.[4] There are exceptions to this general principle which enable the union to encourage persons of a particular sex or racial group to join, or to encourage or assist them to hold union office, where, respectively, they are significantly underrepresented within the organisation or as holders of such posts.[5] In addition, positions on elected bodies may be reserved for members of one sex where this is considered necessary to secure a reasonable lower limit to the number of members of that sex serving on them.[6] However, it is unlawful to discriminate in arrangements for determining entitlement to vote in an election to such a body or in membership of the organisation itself.

---

1. TULRCA 1992, s 82(1)(c).
2. Council Regulation 1612/68, Article 8. 'Worker' has a 'Community meaning' and includes part-time workers: Case 75/63 *Hoekstra (nee Unger)* [1964] ECR 177; Case 53/81 *Levin v Staatssecretaris van Justitie* [1982] ECR 1035.
3. SDA 1975, s 12; RRA 1976, s 11 and DDA 1995, ss 13–15. Note that the concept of an 'organisation of workers' is broader than that of a trade union: in particular no specific purposes are stipulated (cf para **2.4**). The fact that the organisation need not be permanent means that 'any branch or other division of a . . . union might constitute an organisation of workers, including unofficial workplace co-ordinating committees' (Doyle, 1996, paras 4.2.4–4.2.5). In *FTATU v Modgill* [1980] IRLR 142, the EAT held that the fact that the union was alleged not to provide sufficient support to its Asian members, or dealt with them inefficiently, did not constitute evidence that they had

been treated less favourably than any other group of workers; see also *FBU v Fraser* [1998] IRLR 697, CS (no evidence that the union's refusal to provide legal assistance to the male member who was the subject of a sexual harassment complaint was on the grounds of his sex rather than because he was the accused and not the complainant). There is an exception under the SDA 1975, s 12(4) for provision made in relation to the death or retirement from work of a member. In *Diakou v Islington Union 'A' Branch* [1997] ICR 121, the EAT emphasised that the RRA 1976, s 11 does not expressly cover constructively depriving an individual of membership.

4. SDA 1975, s 41; RRA 1976, s 32; DDA 1995, s 58. In relation to employees (see App 1) it is a defence to prove that the union took all such steps as were reasonably practicable to prevent the employee committing that act or such acts.

5. SDA 1976, s 48(2),(3); RRA 1976, s 38(3)–(5).

6. SDA 1976, s 49.

Miscellaneous Rights[1]

Rights relating to the trade union's register of names and addresses

2.31 Trade unions have a statutory duty to maintain a register of the names and addresses of their members and to secure, so far as is reasonably practicable, that the entries in the register are accurate and kept up-to-date.[2] The register may be kept by means of a computer.[3] No precise figure can be said to satisfy the criterion of 'reasonable practicability'; the exact percentage error is probably less relevant than whether the union can demonstrate that it has established a proper system for keeping the register and updating it regularly.[4] The Certification Officer has affirmed that the duty to keep the register up-to-date includes an obligation to operate a system for removing the names of those who no longer wish to be union members.[5] The Certification Officer has also held that there is no requirement to maintain a centrally held single register; the register may be compiled on a disaggregated basis, although the union cannot devolve its statutory duty to compile and maintain the register on local branches or associations and it should be kept in a schematic way under the direction of the union.[6] Union members have a right to ascertain, free of charge and at any reasonable time, whether there is an entry on the register relating to them after giving the union reasonable notice of their intention to do this.[7] The union must also supply a member with a copy of that entry on request as soon as reasonably practicable after the request is made, either free of charge or on payment of a reasonable fee.[8] A union member who claims that the union has failed to comply with its statutory duties relating to the register may apply either to the Certification Officer or the High Court (but not both) for a declaration to that effect.[9] The procedure which the Certification Officer is required to follow in dealing with such claims is described in para **2.2.** Where the Certification Officer or the court grants a declaration, an enforcement order must also be made requiring the union to take specified steps to remedy the declared failure within a specified period, and/or to abstain from specified acts with a view to securing that a failure of the same or a similar kind does not occur in future, unless this is considered inappropriate.[10] Provision for enforcing such an order, and appeals, are also described in para **2.2.**[11] The powers of the Certification Officer are identical to those of the court, except that the court is also able to grant interim relief.[12] Unless interim relief is being sought, recourse to the Certification Officer is likely to prove a much speedier and cheaper option. The powers and duties of the independent scrutineer appointed to supervise elections in relation to the membership register, and the rights of members to request examination or inspection of the register by the scrutineer, are discussed at para **2.40**.

---

1. In this section we deal with rights which are not dealt with elsewhere in this work. For a full list of such rights, see para **2.23**.

2. TULRCA 1992, s 24(1). See para **2.4** for the definition of a trade union. A member's address means either his or her home address or another address which he or she has requested the union in writing to treat as his or her postal address: s 24(5). Unions consisting wholly or mainly of constituent or affiliated organisations, or representatives of such organisations, are excluded from the duty to maintain a register if they have no individual members (other than representatives of such organisations) or if any individual members are all merchant seamen the majority of whom are ordinarily resident outside the United Kingdom; s 118(6).

3. *Ibid.*, s 24(2).

4. In *Cooper v AEU* (31 March 1987, unreported), CO, the union, composed of some 900,000 members with up to 50,000 joining and a similar number leaving each year, relied on members themselves and on branch secretaries to keep the register up to date. The Certification Officer emphasised that, in a union of that size and turnover, there could not be a precise borderline between what was, and what was not, reasonably practicable. Taking the situation overall, there was no breach of duty in that case.

5. *In the matter of complaints against MSF* (8 April 1998, unreported), CO.

6. *In the matter of a complaint against the AUT* (7 July 1993, unreported), CO.

7. TULRCA 1992, s 24(3)(a).

8. *Ibid.*, s 24(3)(b).

9. *Ibid.*, s 24A(6).

10. *Ibid.*, ss 25(5A), 26(4).

11. The order may be enforced by any member who was a member at the time when it was made: *ibid.*, ss 25(5B), 26(5).

12. *Ibid.*, s 26(6).

The right to inspect the trade union's accounting records

2.32 The duty of trade unions to keep proper accounting records, and to supply members with a statement about their financial affairs, is discussed at paras **2.9** and **2.10**. In addition to these obligations, unions must keep their accounting records available for inspection from their creation until the end of a six-year period beginning with 1 January following the end of the period to which the records relate.[1] A union member has the right to request access to those records provided that they relate to a period for at least part of which he or she was a member of the union.[2] This includes the right to inspect the records of any particular branch or section even though he or she is not a member of it.[3] The union must make arrangements with the member to allow inspection of the relevant records before the end of the period of 28 days from the request being made and allow inspection in accordance with those arrangements.[4] The inspection must be at a reasonable hour and at the place where the records are normally kept unless the parties agree otherwise.[5] The member must be allowed to take, or be supplied with, such copies of, or extracts from, the records as he or she requires.[6] The union may charge the member for inspecting, copying or supplying copies of the records provided that the charge does not exceed the reasonable administrative expenses incurred by the union, and the member was told of the charge and the principles for determining it before the arrangements were made.[7] The member may be accompanied for the purpose of the inspection by an accountant, unless the accountant fails to enter into such agreement as the union may reasonably require to protect the confidentiality of the records.[8] It is notable that there is no statutory provision allowing the union to impose a requirement of confidentiality on the union member; if the union sought to impose this as a condition of inspection against the will of the member, this would seem to constitute a breach of the statutory right. A member who claims that the union has failed in any respect to comply with a request to inspect its records may complain to the Certification Officer or the High Court (but not both); where the complaint is upheld, an order must be made to ensure that complainant is allowed to inspect the records in the company of an accountant and is allowed to take, or is supplied with, such copies of or extracts from the records as he or she may require.[9] The court, unlike the Certification Officer, is empowered to grant interim relief;[10] unless this is sought, recourse to the Certification Officer is likely to prove the cheaper and the speedier option. In addition to the remedies which individual members may seek, unions should note that it is a criminal offence for a union to refuse or wilfully neglect to perform its statutory duties to keep accounting records available for inspection.[11]

---

1. TULRCA 1992, s 29. The duty covers those records of the union, or of any branch or section, which are required to be kept under s 28: see para **2.9**. See para **2.4** for the

definition of a 'trade union'. Unions which consist wholly or mainly of constituent or affiliated organisations, or representatives of such organisations, and which have no members other than constituent or affiliated organisations or representatives of such organisations, are excluded from this provision: TULRCA 1992, s 118(5).

2. *Ibid.*, s 30; see further para **2.2**. 'Member', in relation to a union consisting wholly or partly of, or of representatives of, constituent or affiliated organisations, includes a member of any of the constituent or affiliated organisations.

3. *Ibid.*

4. *Ibid.*, s 30(2).

5. *Ibid.*, s 30(3).

6. *Ibid.*, s 30(2)(c).

7. *Ibid.*, s 30(6).

8. *Ibid.*, s 30(2)(b), (4), (5).

9. *Ibid.*, s 31. For the procedure to be followed by the Certification Officer, and provision for enforcement and appeals, see para **2.2**.

10. *Ibid.*, s 31(3).

11. *Ibid.*, ss 45, 45A, 45B; see further para **2.11**.

TRADE UNION ELECTIONS: THE STATUTORY REQUIREMENTS

Sources and General Principles

2.33 The Trade Union and Labour Relations (Consolidation) Act 1992, ss 46–61 require trade unions to ensure that their president, general secretary and every 'member of the executive' hold office by virtue of an election conducted in accordance with complex statutory requirements. Certain other persons who may attend meetings of the executive, whilst not being in formal membership, are included within the statutory definition of 'member'. The statutory requirements apply notwithstanding anything to the contrary in the union's rules or practices (although there is nothing to prevent a union adopting more stringent requirements in its rules).[1] No officer subject to election may continue to hold office for more than five years without being re-elected.[2] Unless the election is uncontested, the union must hold a fully postal ballot. In all cases the election must be supervised by an independent 'scrutineer' who satisfies specified conditions,[3] and the union may not publish the election result until it has received the scrutineer's report. A union member or a candidate in the election who alleges that the union has failed to comply with the statutory requirements may apply either to the Certification Officer or the High Court for a declaration to that effect; if the application is successful, an enforcement order requiring the union, *inter alia*, to remedy the defect will also normally be made. The High Court is additionally empowered to grant interim relief, so a member or candidate could

apply to prevent an election which is alleged to breach the statutory require-
ments being held. However, non-compliance with the legislation does not affect
the validity of anything done by a person improperly elected or appointed, so
any resolutions passed by the executive committee, for example, remain in force.
The statutory regime of elections imposes considerable costs upon unions.
Perhaps surprisingly, it has been found by the ILO Committee of Experts on the
Application of Conventions and Recommendations not to breach Article 3 of
ILO Convention No 87 on Freedom of Association and Protection of the Right
to Organise, which affirms the right of workers' organisations to 'draw up their
constitutions and rules, to elect their representatives in full freedom, to organise
their administration and activities, and to formulate their programmes'. The
Committee regarded it as within the range of measures which is acceptable as
'intended to promote democratic principles within trade union organisations or
to ensure that the electoral procedure is conducted in a normal manner and with
due respect for the rights of members in order to avoid any dispute arising as to
the result of the election'.[4] That being so, it would probably be difficult to challenge successfully under Article 11 of the ECHR.[5]

---

1. TULRCA 1992, s 46(6). See further para **2.20** and **2.21** for the remedies where a
union acts in breach of its rules.
2. Subject to specified exceptions: see para **2.36**.
3. The Certification Officer has held that this duty applies even where the election is
uncontested: *In the matter of a complaint against the Offshore Industry Liaison
Committee* (25 November 1994, unreported), CO; see further para **2.39**.
4. Report of the Committee of Experts on the Application of Conventions and
Recommendations, Report III (Part 4A), ILO, Geneva, 1985, 197.
5. See Chapter 1 for discussion of the relationship between Article 11 and other international standards.

The Application and Consequences of the Duty to Conduct Elections

2.34 All 'trade unions'[1] are covered by the statutory requirements to hold elections, with three exceptions: new unions of less than one year's standing, including those formed by amalgamation,[2] and those consisting wholly or mainly of
constituent or affiliated organisations, or representatives of such organisations
('federated trade unions'), and which either have no individual members, such as
the TUC, or whose individual members are all merchant seamen and the majority are ordinarily resident outside the United Kingdom.[3] 'Special register

bodies'[4] need only elect 'voting members' of their executive: those persons are entitled in their own right to attend meetings of the executive, and to vote on matters on which votes are taken (even if they are not entitled to attend all meetings or to vote on all matters or in all circumstances).[5] The election requirements apply to the union's president, general secretary, and 'members of the executive', including *ex officio* members.[6] Persons holding the position of president or general secretary on an honorary basis, with no voting rights, are not subject to election, but this applies only where the holder changes on an annual basis and certain other conditions are satisfied;[7] any individual appointed for a second term on an annual basis would not be able to rely on this provision. The term 'executive' means 'the principal committee of the union exercising executive functions, by whatever name it is called'; this requires there to be one, but only one, such body;[8] other bodies which may exercise executive functions within the union which are subordinate to the 'executive' are not subject to the legislation. Holders of senior posts within a union are sometimes permitted by the union rules to remain on the executive for a period after leaving office, possibly with voting rights. Provided that they can be regarded as having been elected to both offices at the time of the initial election, the Certification Officer has taken the view that there is no need to hold a fresh election to the second office.[9] There is no obligation to hold a ballot for an uncontested election.[10]

---

1. See para **2.4** for the definition of a 'trade union'.

2. TULRCA, s 57(1). In the case of unions formed other than by amalgamation, the date of formation is the date on which the first members of the executive are first appointed or elected. In the case of mergers there are also special provisions regarding individuals: see s 57(2),(3); see para **2.36**.

3. *Ibid.*, s 118(6). 'Merchant seaman' means 'a person whose employment, or the greater part of it, is carried out on board seagoing ships: *ibid.* This exception was inserted at the request of the International Transport Workers' Federation.

4. *Ibid.*, s 117(1); see further para **2.8**.

5. *Ibid.*, ss 117(5), 46(5).

6. *Ibid.*, s 46(2). Where the union does not have a president or general secretary, the obligation applies to the holder of the equivalent or nearest equivalent: s 119.

7. *Ibid.,* s 46(4), where the detailed conditions are laid down.

8. *Ibid.*, s 119. For a decision on which of two union bodies should be designated the executive, see *Stone v NATFHE* (30 June 1987, unreported), CO. Note that before TULRCA 1992, the 'executive' was termed the 'principal executive committee' in the legislation.

9. *Paul v NALGO* [1987] IRLR 43, CO.

10. TULRCA 1992, s 53.

2.35 It is not wholly clear when individuals will be deemed to be 'members of the executive'. The term clearly includes those designated as such by the union's rules, either on an ordinary or *ex officio* basis.[1] It also includes:

> any person who, under the rules or practice of the union, may attend and speak at some or all of the meetings of the executive, otherwise than for the purpose of providing the committee with factual information or with technical or professional advice with respect to matters taken into account by the executive in carrying out its functions.[2]

This was intended by the Conservative Government which introduced this provision to cover all those who 'act as though they are members of the . . . [executive]' and who participate in the decision-making process.[3] This may not be an easy group to classify; it may vary according to the role of an individual office holder within a union, and possibly the behaviour of an individual incumbent; thus one cannot state that all national or regional officers, for example, need, or need not, be elected. Unions wishing to minimise uncertainty and unnecessary elections should define in writing the roles of individual office holders with care, although it is hard to exclude the possibility of legal challenge altogether. There are four major ambiguities: the meaning of 'may . . . attend and speak', which may mean by entitlement,[4] but could mean 'not prohibited from attending' or 'it is theoretically possible may attend'; the meaning of 'practice', the longevity or consistency of which is unspecified; the number of meetings an individual may attend without attracting the requirements for election;[5] and whether attendance only at specific parts of meetings is sufficient.[6] The exception of those providing information or advice was intended to exclude individuals who offer merely 'supporting advice' to the committee, rather than participating in 'decision-taking', but the line between the two activities may be easily crossed.[7] Union legal officers who advise on the legal consequences of a proposed course of action and research and regional officers who merely give factual information, for example, would appear not to require election, but their position may be jeopardised if they stray into a discussion of union policy and its implications based on their advice or report. Thus, it will be important for the chair of meetings, and the individuals concerned, to guard against transgressions of this boundary.

---

1. See TULRCA 1992, s 46(2)(b), which brings within the duty to elect 'any position by virtue of which a person is a member of the executive'.
2. *Ibid.*, s 46(3).
3. Lord Trefgarne, Joint Under-Secretary of State for Employment, HL Debs, vol 486, cols 484–485, 28 March 1988.
4. Mr. John Cope, Minister of Employment, saw the provisions as covering those who could attend and speak without challenge (House of Commons, Official Report of Standing Committee F, cols 373, 391, 17 December 1987), but there is no such provision in the legislation (cf the definition of 'voting member' in s 46(5): see para **2.34**).

5. Mr. Cope considered that the salient point was whether the individual was 'one of those who are controlling the union and guiding its affairs' and that someone attending only occasionally was unlikely to require election (*ibid.*, col 366, 15 December 1987), but this is not reflected clearly in the statute.

6. Mr. Cope implied that attendance at specific parts would not attract the duty (*ibid.*, col 374, 17 December 1987). If this is correct, unions should ensure that matters with which unelected officers are concerned are included within a wider agenda rather than calling meetings which deal exclusively with such issues.

7. In *In the matter of a complaint against the GPMU* (11 March 1993, unreported), CO, the Certification Officer accepted the General Secretary's assurance that particular individuals fell within the exception in the absence of any evidence from the applicant to the contrary. This case shows the importance of ensuring that the union rules do not describe such individuals as members of the executive. Cf. *In the matter of a complaint against SOGAT 82* (31 July 1991, unreported), CO, where under the union rule book officers who spoke only for the purpose of technical or professional advice were members of the executive.

2.36 Individuals who fail to be re-elected can no longer hold their positions. However, they need not leave the post immediately; the trade union may allow their membership of the committee to continue for a period of up to six months after the election in order to give effect to the result.[1] Any term or conditions governing the official's employment with the union which conflicts with the obligation to leave office—for example, if he or she can be dismissed only on specific grounds, or is employed on a fixed-term contract for a longer period—cannot affect the statutory position.[2] This means that unions must ensure that the contracts of persons subject to election expire when the post falls due for election. It also means that unions are unable to offer any job security to individuals who may have been chosen for a particular office, in particular that of general secretary, for administrative rather than political skills. There are two situations where an individual who would otherwise be covered by the election requirements need not face election. They are both highly specific and we mention them in outline only. First, where unions amalgamate, a person who had been elected to a position to which the statutory requirements apply in one union who, under the instrument of transfer, holds such an office in the amalgamated union need not be re-elected until such time as he or she would have needed to stand for re-election in the former union.[3] Secondly, there are complex provisions governing those who are within five years of retirement. Such persons need not be re-elected provided that they have been elected to their position in accordance with the statutory requirements within the previous five years; are full-time employees of the union by virtue of their position, and have been so for at least ten years (which need not be continuous); and the union rules entitle them to continue in the position until retirement age without standing for re-election.[4]

1. TULRCA 1992, s 59.
2. *Ibid.*, s 46(6).
3. TULRCA, s 57(2). Note also s 57(1) (see para **2.34**). The Certification Officer has held that there is nothing to limit this provision to one merger during an individual's period of office: *In the matter of a complaint against PCS* (16 March 2000, unreported), CO. Similar provisions apply in the case of a transfer of engagements: s 57(3).
4. *Ibid.*, s 58. See App 1 for the definition of 'employee'. 'Full-time' is not defined in this context. 'Retirement age' means the age fixed by, or in accordance with, the union rules, or the age which is for the time being pensionable age for the purposes of paragraph 4 of Schedule 4 to the Pensions Act 1995, whichever is the earlier.

The Selection of Candidates and Election Addresses

2.37 No trade union member may be 'unreasonably excluded' from standing as a candidate at an election.[1] Exclusion is not 'unreasonable' if it is because the member belongs to a class all of whose members are excluded by the union rules.[2] This means that unions may require a minimum number of years' membership of the union, or apply a maximum age limit, for example; the exclusion of those who would be disqualified by statute from holding the position in question were they to be successful in the election would also be valid on this basis.[3] However, excluded classes must be stipulated in the union rules, and any rule which provides for such a class to be determined by reference to whom the union chooses to be excluded must be disregarded.[4] On this basis, the High Court held that the exclusion of persons in whom the national executive council did not have confidence was unreasonable, as it was essentially a class determined by reference to those whom the union chose to exclude.[5] A further statutory restriction is that no candidate may be required, directly or indirectly, to be a member of a political party.[6] Thus a union cannot require candidates to be members of the Labour Party or to attend the Labour Party conference, which is open only to members. Notably, however, it does not prevent the exclusion of members of a particular party from standing; thus unions may lawfully exclude members of the Communist or the Conservative Party, for example. The Certification Officer has held that it is not unreasonable for a union to demand a certain level of support from fellow members as a precondition of standing for election.[7] Thus a union may require a candidate to be nominated by a branch or a minimum number of branches, although where branches vary in size, reasonableness may demand that candidates be permitted to seek nomination from branches other than their own.[8] He has also held that a branch need not notify members in advance that nominations will be taken at a particular branch meeting provided that members are notified of the meeting in question in the usual manner,[9] although where branches are asked to invite nominations, allowing an unreasonably tight timetable for doing this may constitute unreasonable exclusion.[10] Finally, he has held that procedures which have the effect of precluding the possibility that ordinary members will put themselves forward for election could be unreasonable, even in the absence of evidence that a would-be candidate has actually been excluded.[11]

---

1. TULRCA 1992, s 47(1). Overseas members are outside this requirement: see s 60(3) (and see para **2.41** for the meaning of 'overseas member'.)

2. *Ibid.*, s 47(3). See, for example, *Flavin v UCATT* (17 February 1987, unreported), CO (exclusion of regional officers, who were full-time paid officers, under the union rules not unreasonable). In *In the matter of a complaint against the RMT* (10 June 1993, unreported), CO, the Certification Officer held that in appropriate circumstances it may be proper to consider that a long standing custom or practice had established a rule. (For the approach of the courts towards union rules see para **2.13** *et seq.*).

3. *Ibid.*, s 45B; see para **2.11**.

4. *Ibid.*, s 47(3).

5. *Ecclestone v NUJ* [1999] IRLR 166, ChD. The court also held that, even if this were wrong, the procedure followed by the union was so unfair that the claimant would have been unreasonably excluded on the ground of procedural unfairness under s 47(1). However, s 47(3) is absolute in its terms; if the candidate is a member of a class of which all the members are excluded, there seems no room to argue that the exclusion was unfair on general principles.

6. TULRCA 1992, s 47(2). See para **2.48** for discussion of the meaning of 'political party'.

7. *Paul v NALGO* [1987] IRLR 43, CO.

8. *Ibid.*; see also *In the matter of complaints against BETA* (21 December 1990, unreported) CO.

9. *Corti v TGWU*, 28 October 1986, CO.

10. *In the matter of a complaint against NATFHE* (12 August 1988, unreported) CO; *In the matter of complaints against ISTC* (21 December 1990, unreported) CO.

11. *Paul v NALGO*, above, note 7 (nominations to the post of Junior Vice-President technically open, but in practice the procedure made it very hard for ordinary union members to stand).

2.38 Trade unions must give every candidate in an election the opportunity to prepare an election address in his or her own words and to submit it to the union, which must ensure, so far as reasonably practicable, that a copy of each address is sent by post with the voting paper to each member who is entitled to vote.[1] It is unclear whether the statute requires unions to bring the right to prepare an address to candidates' attention or whether they should merely afford candidates who wish to submit an address the opportunity to do so; the former is the more likely, and the safer, view. The union must ensure that no modification is made to an address except at the request, or with the consent, of a candidate or 'where the modification is necessarily incidental to the method adopted for producing that copy',[2] an exception probably restricted to minor editorial amendments such as the translation of figures to word form. Any facilities and restrictions regarding the preparation or modification of an address must be applied equally to each candidate, and the same method of producing copies (which must be done free of charge) must be applied to each.[3] Unions may set a maximum limit for the length of addresses, subject to a minimum of 100 words, and may also provide that the address may incorporate only such photographs and 'other matters not in words' (eg diagrams and drawings) as they may determine.[4] Unions have no power to reject an address, regardless of its contents, unless, possibly, the material has so little connection with the election that it did not constitute an 'election address' at all, an argument it may be difficult to substantiate. Thus, unions may be required to distribute information which officials may regard as incorrect, and conceivably even libellous, particularly if it attacks the credibility or credentials of other candidates. The legislation protects unions against liability for defamation by providing that no person other than the candidate shall be subject to any civil or criminal liability in respect of any publication of a candidate's election address which is required by the statute.[5] Notwithstanding this provision, the union may find itself in difficulties if it continues with an election where one candidate argues that he or she has been prejudiced by the circulation of defamatory material. The statutory provisions regarding election addresses are clearly designed to ensure equal treatment between candidates. Nevertheless, there seems nothing to prevent a union from distributing additional material indicating, for example, those candidates whom the executive supports, a view echoed by the Certification Officer on a number of occasions.[6]

---

1. TULRCA 1992, s 48(1)(a). Unions may set a time limit for submission of election addresses but this must be no earlier than the latest time by which a person may become a candidate: s 48(2). In *In the matter of a complaint against USDAW* (13 January 1994, unreported), CO, the Certification Officer held that 'in his own words' did not prevent the candidate choosing someone else's words written on his behalf or to have published a letter written (on its face) by other persons endorsing his candidature.
2. TULRCA 1992, s 48(4).
3. *Ibid.*, s 48(6),(7).
4. *Ibid.*, s 48(3). In *In the matter of a complaint against the TGWU* (19 June 1996, unreported), CO, the Certification Officer held that a long-established practice of not including photographs in addresses was sufficient, in the absence of any contrary indication, to establish that provision had been made.

5. *Ibid.*, s 48(8).

6. See, for example, *In the matter of a complaint against the CPSA* (17 May 1995, unreported). In *In the matter of complaints against PCS* (6 March 1999, unreported), CO the Certification Officer suggested that the freedom to include extraneous material with the ballot paper was not an absolute one. Thus, if the paper and election address were swamped with a huge mass of advertising so as effectively to invite destruction of the package, this could be considered an interference with members' voting contrary to s 51(3)(a); see further para **2.42**.

Independent Scrutiny of Elections

2.39 Elections covered by the statutory procedure must be supervised by an independent 'scrutineer'.[1] Only persons specified in regulations issued by the Secretary of State are potentially qualified to act as scrutineers.[2] Three bodies are specified by name: Electoral Reform (Ballot Services) Ltd; The Industrial Society; and Unity Security Balloting Services Ltd. In addition, solicitors who have a current practising certificate and chartered and certified accountants who are qualified as auditors are potentially qualified to act, although specified connections with the trade union, or previous activities, may disqualify them.[3] Unions make their own choice of scrutineer from among those qualified.[4] The terms of the scrutineer's appointment must include specified functions, which we describe in para **2.40**. The union may also stipulate additional functions provided it ensures that nothing in the terms of appointment will make it reasonable for any person to call into question the scrutineer's independence in relation to the union.[5] The name of the independent scrutineer must be stated on the voting paper.[6] In addition, before the scrutineer begins to carry out his or her functions the union must either send a notice naming him or her to every union member (not just voters) to whom it is reasonably practicable to send one, or take all such other steps for notifying members of the name as it is the practice of the union to take when matters of general interest to all its members need to be brought to their attention.[7] Thus a circular or union journal should suffice provided that notice can be given in time. There is no provision for replacement of a scrutineer or appointment of a deputy if the named scrutineer becomes indisposed, so unions would be best advised to choose a qualified partnership or one of the three named organisations rather than a single individual.

---

1. TULRCA 1992, s 49(1). The Certification Officer has held that this duty applies even where the election is uncontested: *In the matter of a complaint against the Offshore Industry Liaison Committee* (25 November 1994, unreported), CO, emphasising that

the provision relating to unreasonable exclusion of candidates (see para **2.37**) applied equally to both a contested and an uncontested election.

2. *Ibid.*, s 49(2)(a); the Trade Union Ballots and Elections (Independent Scrutineer Qualifications) Order 1993, SI 1993/1909.

3. See 1993/1909, articles 3–6. Such persons are disqualified if, *inter alia*, they, or any present partner of theirs, has during the preceding 12 months been a member, officer (other than an auditor) or employee of the union concerned.

4. The union must have no grounds for believing that the scrutineer will not carry out his or her functions competently or that his or her independence, in relation to the union or election, might reasonably be called into question: TULRCA 1992, s 49(2)(b).

5. *Ibid.*, s 49(4).

6. *Ibid.,* s 51(2)(a).

7. *Ibid.*, s 49(5). See para **2.10**, note 3. Where a notice is sent the duty is discharged when it is sent rather than received (see *In the matter of complaints against CPSA* (10 September 1998, unreported), CO), and there is no obligation to use the post.

2.40 Trade unions have a duty to ensure that the independent scrutineer duly carries out his or her functions, but without interfering in a way which would make it reasonable for any person to question the scrutineer's independence in relation to the union.[1] It is possible to envisage situations where these two duties may conflict, although this is less likely to happen if a union selects an experienced scrutineer who requires little supervision. There is no provision which expressly allows a union to replace an unsatisfactory scrutineer, and the position if the union sought to do this mid-way through the election process is unclear; on the one hand replacement could be seen as failing to comply with the duty to appoint a scrutineer before an election is held; on the other it could be argued that, by appointing a scrutineer, albeit an unsatisfactory one, before that time the union had discharged its obligation. The union must comply with all reasonable requests by the scrutineer connected with the performance of his or her functions;[2] this probably entails, for example, allowing the scrutineer to look at records, obtain relevant information and visit any premises as appropriate. The mandatory functions of the scrutineer include supervising the production and distribution[3] of the voting papers and being the person to whom voting papers are returned, making a report to the union about the conduct of the election which covers specified matters, and retaining custody of the voting papers for at least a year after the announcement of the result of the election.[4] Apart from the ability to issue a critical report, the scrutineer has no power to direct the union to change its procedures or to call a halt to the election because of any defect. The scrutineer has extensive powers relating to the union's register of names and addresses. The union must give the scrutineer a copy of the register at the 'relevant date',[5] and comply with any request by the scrutineer to inspect the actual register.[6] The scrutineer should inspect the register or examine the copy whenever it appears to him or her appropriate, in particular when requested to do so by a union member or candidate who suspects that the register is not 'accurate and up-to-date', provided that the scrutineer does not consider the suspicion 'ill-founded'.[7] It is difficult to imagine how the scrutineer could dismiss such a request without examining the register unless a previous examination had already been conducted.[8] The member may make this request up to the day before the scrutineer makes his or her report to the union;[9] as the union may not declare the result of the election until it has received the report, this could, in theory, considerably delay the declaration of the election result. The scrutineer must state in the report whether the register was inspected or a copy examined; if so, whether on his or her own initiative or at the request of a member or candidate; whether any requests were declined; and whether the inspection or examination revealed anything that the union should know about to assist it in securing that the register is accurate and up-to-date.[10] A critical report on this matter may provide ammunition for challenging the election on the basis that not all those entitled to vote received voting papers, although this is subject to a test of 'reasonable practicability'.[11] It may also inspire a member's application to the Certification Officer or the court in relation to the register although the general duty to maintain the register is also qualified by the concept of 'reasonable practicability'.[12] The union must impose a duty of confidentiality on the scrutineer in relation to the register, and a member who claims that the union has failed to comply with this obligation may complain to the Certification Officer or the court.[13] The duty of confidentiality is stated by the statute to be owed by the scrutineer as a duty to the union.[14] However, if it duty were broken in relation to an individual member, and the union failed to act, it is possible that that member may have a right of action on the contract under the Contracts (Rights of Third Parties) Act 1999,[15] or for breach of confidence.[16]

---

1. TULRCA 1992, s 49(6)

2. *Ibid.*, s 49(7).

3. Unless he or she is appointed under TULRCA 1992, s 51A to undertake distribution: see para **2.43**.

4. *Ibid.*, s 49(3). See para **2.44** for the scrutineer's report.

5. 'Relevant date' means, where the union has rules determining who is entitled to vote in the election by reference to membership on a particular date, that date; otherwise, the date, or the last date, on which voting papers are distributed for the purposes of the election: *ibid.*, s 49(8).

6. *Ibid.*, s 49(5A). Where the register is kept by computer the union should supply either a legible printed copy or, if the scrutineer prefers, a copy of the computer data and the use of the computer to read it: s 49(5B).

7. *Ibid.*, s 49(3)(aa), (3A). There is no definition of 'accurate and up-to-date'.

8. There is no statutory remedy if the scrutineer refuses to comply with this request. *Quaere* whether the member could enforce the term under the Contracts (Rights of Third Parties) Act 1999, s 1.

9. TULRCA 1992, s 49(3B). A request may be made from the first day on which a person may become a candidate in the election or, if later, the day on which the scrutineer is appointed: *ibid.*

10. *Ibid.*, s 52(2A). Where this was done at the request of a member or candidate, the name of that person should not be given.

11. See para **2.42**.

12. See para **2.31**.

13. TULRCA 1992, ss 24A(6), 25, 26; see further para **2.31**. See s 24A(3),(4) for the scope of this duty.

14. *Ibid.*, s24A(5).

15. S 1(1).

16. Note also the implications of the DPA 1998, s 2(d); Sched 2, para 5(b); and Sched 3, para 7(1)(b); see further Jay and Hamilton, 1999.

The Balloting Constituency for Elections

2.41 As a general rule, entitlement to vote must be accorded equally to all members of the union.[1] This rules out any system of branch, block or delegate voting, or election to a body which then selects representatives to sit on the executive.[2] However, a union may lawfully restrict the balloting constituency in certain specified respects if it so chooses. First, provided that the union rules so provide, it may exclude all those who belong to one of three classes, or to a class falling within one of such classes, these being the unemployed; those in arrears with their subscriptions or contributions; and apprentices, trainees, students or new members.[3] It may also decide, it seems on an *ad hoc* basis, whether 'overseas members' are included, those being members (other than merchant seamen or offshore workers) who are outside Great Britain throughout the period during which votes may be cast.[4] The union may thus exclude members who are resident in Northern Ireland or the Republic of Ireland and also those who are absent on holiday.[5] There is nothing to prevent the union discriminating between categories of overseas member, provided that this is not contrary to the discrimination legislation. Secondly, a union may restrict voting entitlement to members falling within a class determined by reference to a trade or occupation; a geographical area; or one which is, under the union rules, treated as a separate section within the union.[6] It may also construct the constituency by reference to any combination of these factors.[7] However, these restrictions must, again, be specified in the union rules, and should not have the effect of excluding any individual member from voting in all elections.[8] It is notable that there is no provision for balloting constituencies based upon the employers of members.

---

1. TULRCA 1992, s 50(1). See para **2.2** for the interpretation of 'member'.
2. For a discussion of the variety of voting methods before the Act, see Undy and Martin, 1984.
3. TULRCA 1992, s 50(2). Note that nothing in the legislation fixes or allows the union to fix the qualifying date for entitlement to vote. What, then, is the position, for example, of the unemployed member who obtains employment, or the member in arrears who pays his or her back subscription, the day before the election? Kidner, 1984, 200, suggests that unions should be allowed to set qualifying dates a reasonable period before the election to allow time for the union's administrative machinery to operate.
4. TULRCA 1992, s 60(1), (2). 'Merchant seaman' means a person whose employment, or the greater part of it, is carried out on board sea-going ships; 'offshore worker' means a person in offshore employment, other than one who is in such employment in an area where the law of Northern Ireland applies: *ibid*.
5. Cf the provisions relating to industrial action ballots, discussed in para **6.34**.
6. TULRCA 1992, s 50(3). A 'section' may be a part of the union which is in itself a trade union: *ibid*. 'Occupation' is not defined (cf. s 174(3)(b)).
7. *Ibid*.
8. *Ibid*., s 50(4).

The Conduct of the Election

2.42 Election ballots must be conducted by the marking of a voting paper, and must be conducted entirely by 'post', which is defined in terms which exclude delivery by hand, internal mail or private courier.[1] The legislation recognises that it is unrealistic to expect a union to guarantee delivery to every member: *so far as reasonably practicable* every person entitled to vote must have sent to him or her by post a voting paper, which either lists the candidates or is accompanied by a separate list of those candidates; specifies the address to which, and the date by which, it is to be returned; and names the independent scrutineer.[2] In assessing 'reasonable practicability' in this context, the Certification Officer has regarded as highly material the efforts made by the union to maintain an accurate register of members' addresses, and other efforts to publicise the election, to inform members what to do if they fail to receive a ballot paper, and to enable members to vote.[3] In the context of industrial action ballots, since the Employment Relations Act 1999 accidental failures which are on a scale which is unlikely to have affected the result of the ballot are be disregarded.[4] However, in the past the Certification Officer has indicated that it could be correct to afford a remedy in relation to election ballots in circumstances which would be *de minimis* for industrial action purposes, given that an order could relate solely to the procedure for future elections.[5] The ballot must be conducted so as to ensure, so far as reasonably practicable, that those voting do so in secret,[6] and there are statutory requirements as to the numbering of voting papers.[7] So far as reasonably practicable, voters must be enabled to vote without incurring any direct cost to themselves;[8] this has been regarded as requiring that the cost of return postage must be borne by the union.[9] Voters must be allowed to vote without interference from, or constraint imposed by, the union or any of its members, officials or employees.[10] The Certification Officer has generally interpreted this provision as excluding conduct that would 'intimidate or put a member in fear of voting, or amount to physical interference'.[11] Thus, when a union member alleged that a member of her union's executive committee had telephoned her at home and asked whether she knew who to vote for as 'they' wished to keep the same people on the Committee, the Certification Officer decided that these words fell short of such conduct.[12] Moreover there is nothing to prevent the union indicating which candidates the executive supports, or those supported by particular branches.[13] However, in 1996 an election was found to be inherently compromised because ballot papers before and after completion fell into the hands of union officials, even though there was no evidence of intimidation.[14] It is notable that the legislation does not prohibit employers or third parties interfering with the conduct of the election or attempting to put pressure on individuals to vote a particular way.

---

1. TULRCA 1992, s 51(1), (4). 'Post' means a postal service which is provided by the Post Office or under a licence granted under the British Telecommunications Act 1981 or which does not by virtue of an order made under s 69 of that Act infringe the exclusive privilege of the Post Office: s 298. The voting paper must be sent to the individual's home address or another address which he or she has requested the union in writing to treat as his or her postal address: s 51(4).

2. *Ibid.*, s 51(2),(4).

3. See *In the matter of complaints against COHSE* (17 August 1990, unreported), CO, where the Certification Officer indicated that the test of reasonable practicability involved 'deciding whether a particular step would involve disproportionate time, trouble or expense in view of the benefit likely to be gained' (para 29); *In the matter of a complaint against ACTT* (21 December 1990, unreported), CO; *In the matter of a complaint against the AUT* (7 July 1993, unreported) CO.

4. TULRCA 1992, s 232B; see para **6.41**.

5. *In the matter of complaints against COHSE*, note 3, above, para 24. However, in *In the matter of complaints against ATL* (30 March, 2000) the Certification Officer held

that the exclusion of 1.8% of the membership entitled to vote did not constitute an unreasonable figure in an organisation that depended on individual members to report changes of address.

6. TULRCA 1992, s 51 (5)(a). Members should not, therefore, be required to sign for a voting paper against a particular serial number nor should there be any identifying mark on the voting paper.

7. *Ibid.*, s 51(2).

8. *Ibid.*, s 51(3)(b).

9. *Paul v NALGO* [1987] IRLR 43, CO. The Certification Officer regards it as a 'cost' to a member to pay and reclaim the cost of a stamp. Thus, for overseas members, unions must use an international reply coupon or some other method to avoid this situation.

10. TULRCA, 1992, s 51(3)(a).

11. *Rey v Film Artistes' Association* (11 April 1986, unreported), CO.

12. *Ibid.*

13. *Paul v NALGO*, above, note 9; see also cases in para **2.38**.

14. *In the matter of complaints against the Prison Officers Association* (9 August 1996, unreported), CO.

2.43 Votes must be fairly and accurately counted, although any inaccuracy which is accidental and on a scale which could not affect the result of the election may be disregarded.[1] The union must ensure that the storage and distribution of voting papers and the counting of votes cast are undertaken by one or more independent persons appointed by the union.[2] This function may be fulfilled either by the scrutineer or by some other person who the union has no grounds to believe will not carry out his or her functions competently or whose independence in relation to the union, or the election, might reasonably be called into question.[3] The legislation imposes similar requirements, *mutatis mutandis*, on the terms of appointment as those which apply to the scrutineer, including a duty of confidentiality in relation to the union register.[4] In practice it will probably be simplest for unions to require the scrutineer to conduct these functions. The result of the election must be determined solely by counting the number of votes cast directly for each candidate by those voting (although the use of the single transferable vote is expressly permitted).[5] In *R v The Certification Officer for Trade Unions and Employers' Associations, ex p EPEA*[6] the House of Lords held that the legislation did not necessarily mean that the 'first past the post' system must be uniformly applied. The union's rules allowed a maximum of four members of any one of its nine geographical divisions to serve on the national executive committee. Nine members of the committee were elected in divisional ballots, the remaining 15 in a national ballot. The rule meant that if there were more than three candidates from any one division in the national ballot, only the three who polled the greatest number of votes as between themselves could be elected, even if the fourth candidate in that division polled more than a successful candidate in another division. The court held that the statutory provision was designed to secure that the only votes which would determine the outcome of an election were those directly cast by individuals; it did not mean that a bare count of votes determined the result of the election without recourse to the union rules. Any other construction would have been an 'unreasonable result which the legislature could not sensibly have intended'.[7]

---

1. TULRCA 1992, s 51(5)(b).
2. *Ibid.*, s 51A(1). It is important that any such persons are appointed *by the union*: see *In the matter of complaints against the PCS* (3 June 1999, unreported), CO.
3. *Ibid.*, s 51A(2).
4. *Ibid.*, s 51A(3–6). Where the person is not the scrutineer, the appointment must require him or her to send the voting papers back to the scrutineer as soon as reasonably practicable after counting has been completed: s 51A(5). A member may complain if the union fails to impose the duty of confidentiality on the independent person: see para **2.40**.
5. *Ibid.*, s 51(6), (7).
6. [1990] IRLR 398, HL.
7. *Ibid.*, Lord Bridge at 400.

2.44 The independent scrutineer must make a report to the union about the conduct of the election, which must include specified information: the number of voting papers distributed; the number returned; the number of valid votes cast for each candidate; the number of spoiled or otherwise invalid voting papers returned; the name of the independent person (or persons) appointed to conduct the functions indicated in para **2.43** above; and information relating to inspection of the union's register (see para **2.40**).[1] The report must also indicate whether the scrutineer is satisfied that there are no reasonable grounds for believing that there was any contravention of a statutory requirement in relation to the election; that the arrangements made for producing, distributing and handling voting papers, and for counting votes, included all such security arrangements as were reasonably practicable to minimise the risk of any unfairness or malpractice; that he or she has been able to carry out the requisite functions without such interference which would make it reasonable for any person to call into question his or her independence in relation to the union; and, where applicable, whether he or she is satisfied with the performance of any person appointed by the union to carry out the function indicated in para **2.43**.[2] Reasons must be given if the scrutineer is not satisfied of any of these matters. The union must not publish the result of the election until it has received the scrutineer's report, and within three months of receipt it must notify the contents of the report to its members by either sending a copy to every member of the union to whom it is reasonable practicable to send one, or by taking all such other steps for notifying its contents to members as it is the practice of the union to take when matters of general interest to all its members need to be brought to their attention.[3] The union must ensure that any notification is accompanied by a statement that the union will, on request, supply any member with a copy of the report either free of charge or on payment of a reasonable specified fee.[4] A critical report does not of itself make the election invalid but it will draw the attention of members to the existence of possible grounds on which they may seek to have the election set aside.

––––––––––––––––

1. TULRCA 1992, ss 49(3), 52(1); see paras **2.38** and **2.39** for other functions of the scrutineer.
2. *Ibid.*, s 52(2); s 52(2)(b).
3. *Ibid.*, s 52(3),(4); see para **2.10**. See *England v PSTCU* and *Boxshall v PSTCU*, EAT 24/98 and 25/98, 2 March 1998, unreported.
4. *Ibid.*, s 52(5). The union must supply a copy to any member who makes such a request and pays the fee (if any): s 52(6).

Remedies for Breach of the Statutory Requirements

2.45 A trade union member, or a candidate in the election, who alleges that the union has failed to comply with the statutory requirements may apply either to the Certification Officer or to the High Court (but not both) for a declaration to that effect.[1] Applications which relate to an election which has already been held must be made within one year of the union announcing the result.[2] The procedure which the Certification Officer is required to follow in dealing with such claims is described in para **2.2**. Where either the Certification Officer or the court grants a declaration, an enforcement order should also be granted, unless this is considered inappropriate.[3] This order should require the union to secure the holding of an election in accordance with the order; and/or to take any other specified steps to remedy the declared failure; and/or to abstain from specified acts with a view to securing that the same or a similar failure does not recur. Provision for enforcing such an order and appeals are also described in para **2.2**. The powers of the court are identical to those of the Certification Officer, except that the court is also empowered to grant interim relief,[4] which may be appropriate if the applicant wishes to halt an election before it is completed. Unless interim relief is being sought, recourse to the Certification Officer is likely to prove the cheaper and the speedier option. In relation to an election which has taken place, non-compliance with the legislation does not affect the validity of anything done by a person improperly elected,[5] so any resolutions passed by the executive committee, for example, remain in force.

---

1. TULRCA 1992, s 54(1),(2). Where the application is made by a union member and relates to an election which has been held the applicant must have been a member at the time of the election and of the application; in any other case he or she must be a member at the time of the application. See para **2.2** on the meaning of member. (Earlier decisions of the Certification Officer in this context include *In the matter of a complaint against SOGAT* (5 October 1990, unreported; *ibid.*, 31 July 1991: retired member with free membership, who was not entitled to vote could apply); and *In the matter of complaints against COHSE* (17 August 1990, unreported: overseas member with entitlement to vote in the election could apply—although consistency with *SOGAT* would suggest that voting entitlement may not be required).

2. *Ibid.*, s 54(3). The Trade Union Act 1984, which TULRCA 1992 repealed and incorporates, stated that the remedy for breach of the statutory requirements 'shall be by way of application under this section and not otherwise' (s 5(10)). TULRCA 1992, s 54(1), which states that the remedy 'is by way of application' to the Certification Officer or the court, is intended to reflect this provision. *Quaere* whether it precludes an application for breach of contract where the statutory requirements have been incorporated into the union rules; if so, this would afford a longer period to complain to the High Court (see paras **2.20** and **2.21).** In *Veness and Chalkley v NUPE* [1991] IRLR 76, QBD (decided under the Trade Union Act 1984) a claim brought in contract on the basis of an alleged breach of the union's rules was struck out as disclosing no cause of action. It was stated by the court that had there been any impropriety in the holding of the election the appropriate course would have been for an application to have been made under the statute within the statutory time limit. The Certification Officer has held that it is irrelevant that a representative whose election is the subject of complaint resigns before a decision on the case is reached: *Whiteman v TASS* (3 February 1987, unreported), CO.

3. TULRCA 1992, ss 55(5A), 56(4).

4. *Ibid.*, 56(7).

5. *Ibid.*, s 61(2).

POLITICAL ACTIVITIES

Sources and General Principles

2.46 The definition of a 'trade union' requires the organisation's principal purposes to include the regulation of relations between workers and employers, but does not prevent the union pursuing other lawful objects.[1] However, unions which wish to spend money on 'political objects' have been subject to statutory regulation since the Trade Union Act 1913.[2] The relevant provisions are now contained in the Trade Union and Labour Relations (Consolidation) Act 1992. Unions[3] that wish to spend money on 'political objects' must first ballot their members on whether the union should adopt such objects. If a majority voting in a ballot are in favour, the union may adopt rules to establish a separate political fund which alone may be used for financing such objects. Unions must also hold a fresh ballot at least once every ten years in order to retain an existing political fund. The rules governing each ballot must be approved by the Certification Officer, and must reflect the complex requirements of the legislation. A union member who claims that a ballot (or proposed ballot) does not comply with those rules may apply to the Certification Officer or the High Court for a declaration; if successful, an 'enforcement order' requiring the union to remedy the defect will normally also be made. The High Court may also grant interim relief. Once the establishment of a political fund has been approved, there are tight controls over its operation. In addition, the fund rules must allow any union member a right not to contribute to the fund without suffering any disadvantage (except in relation to the control and management of the fund), and contribution to the fund must not be a condition of admission to the union. A member may complain to the Certification Officer or the High Court that a union has breached the political fund rules. Curiously, however, if the Certification Officer makes an order it cannot automatically be enforced as an order of the High Court, which is now the usual position; rather, it may be enforced in the same way as an order of the county court on being recorded in that court.[4] Where the complaint relates to a breach of statutory requirements, such as an allegation that a union which does not have a political fund has spent money on political objects, again complaint may be made either to the Certification Officer or the High Court.[5] However, if the political fund rules include provisions which are permissible but not required by statute, it seems that the member would be able to complain only to the High Court.[6]

---

1. TULRCA 1992, s 1; see para **2.4**.
2. The Trade Union Act 1913 enabled unions to have political funds by permitting

them to have objects additional to their statutory objects, so overruling *ASRS v Osborne* [1901] AC 87, HL, but subject to a regime of statutory regulation.

3. The provisions apply also to unions falling within TULRCA 1992, s 1(b), but in those cases the individual members of all the component unions must be balloted: s 118(7).

4. TULRCA 1992, s 82. See para **2.2** for the provisions which generally govern the Certification Officer's jurisdiction.

5. Jurisdiction was extended to the Certification Officer by the Employment Relations Act 1999: see now TULRCA 1992, s 72A. In this context, unlike others, there is no specific authority for recourse to the High Court, but this seems implicit from s 72A(11).

6. TULRCA 1992, s 82(2) applies only to rules made *in pursuance of this section,* and breach of rules relating to political funds is not covered by s 108A.

Establishing and Retaining a Political Fund

2.47 The funds of a trade union may not be applied, either directly or indirectly,[1] in furtherance of 'political objects' as defined by statute unless the furtherance of those objects has been approved as an object of the union by a resolution supported by a majority of those voting in a ballot.[2] If the object of the expenditure does not fall within the statutory definition, it may be supported from the union's general fund if the union rules so permit. The rules governing a 'political objects' ballot must be approved by the Certification Officer each time a ballot is to be held; thus the union cannot automatically rely on rules approved for a previous ballot.[3] These rules must reflect specified statutory requirements which are in most respects identical to those governing union elections described in para **2.33** *et seq.*[4] Thus, the ballot must be fully postal and supervised by an independent scrutineer, so imposing substantial costs upon the union. The major difference is in relation to the balloting constituency; all members of the union are entitled to vote, with none of the exclusions permitted in relation to election ballots, the only exception being overseas members where the ballot is to continue an existing political fund.[5] If the resolution to establish political objects is approved, the union may then adopt rules, which are subject to approval by the Certification Officer, to establish a political fund.[6] The Certification Office will supply an information pack including model rules free of charge. The rules must provide that payments furthering political objects must be made exclusively from the political fund, and they must safeguard the position of non-contributors.[7] The rules have effect as rules of the union, even if the rules of the union as to the alteration of rules or the making of new rules have not been complied with provided that the Certification Officer is satisfied, and certifies, that they have been approved by a majority of the members or by a majority of delegates at a meeting called for the purpose.[8] In practice, when a union seeks to establish a political fund it is usual to pass a combined resolution at the outset which adopts the ballot rules; agrees to hold a ballot; and agrees that political fund rules will be adopted if the procedure is successful. A resolution approving political objects automatically ceases to have effect (if not previously rescinded) ten years from the date of the ballot by which it was passed;[9] thus, unions must hold a ballot to re-approve an existing political fund at least once every ten years. The passage of a new resolution automatically rescinds the old,[10] so the ten-year period commences at this point. Where the new resolution is not passed, the old resolution expires two weeks after the date of the ballot.[11] The Certification Officer gives advice on request on the procedures for establishing political funds and for holding review ballots, and has issued free guidance on these matters.[12] At the end of March 2000 there were 36 political fund resolutions in force.[13]

---

1. For example in conjunction with any other trade union, association, or body: TULRCA 1992, s 71(2).

2. *Ibid.*, s 71. The Certification Officer has taken the view that the test of 'furtherance' is objective (*Richards v NUM* [1981] IRLR 247, CO; *Coleman v POEU* [1981] IRLR 427, CO) but the EAT has left the matter open: *ASTMS v Parkin* [1983] IRLR 448, EAT.

3. *Ibid.*, s 74

4. *Ibid.*, ss 75–78. See para **2.45** for provision for complaint in the event that the ballot rules are breached.

5. *Ibid.*, ss 76, 94. See para **2.2** for the interpretation of 'member'. 'Overseas member' is defined in s 94(3); see para **2.41** (the definition in s 60(3) is identical). Note that the dispensation in relation to overseas members is restricted to situations where a political fund resolution is currently in force; thus overseas members may not be excluded where the previous resolution has expired.

6. *Ibid.*, ss 71, 73(2).

7. *Ibid.*, s 82(1).

8. *Ibid.*, s 92.

9. *Ibid.*, s 73(3). Where votes may be cast on more than one day, the 'date of the ballot' means the last of those days: s 96. For the position regarding amalgamated unions, see s 93.

10. *Ibid.*, s 73(4)(a).

11. *Ibid.*, s 73(4)(b).

12. *Guidance for Trade Unions and Employers' Associations Wishing to Establish a Political Fund*; *A Guide to Political Fund Review Ballots*, available free of charge.

13. *Annual Report of the Certification Officer for 1999–2000*, para 7.12; App 8. At the end of 1998, returns showed that over 4.6 million trade unionists contributed to such funds, which contained a combined total of £15.8 million: *ibid.*, paras 7.15–7.16; App 8. See generally Leopold, 1997.

The Definition of 'Political Objects'

2.48 The 'political objects' which may be furthered exclusively by the expenditure of money from a trade union's political fund fall into six broad categories:[1]

(1) Any contribution to the funds of a political party, or on the payment of expenses incurred directly or indirectly by it. 'Contribution' includes affiliation or membership fees and loans,[2] and also extends to investments made on a commercial basis.[3] 'Expenses' would cover such matters as salaries, rents and administration. There is no statutory definition of a political party, and the issue has not, as yet, arisen for decision in this context;[4]

(2) The provision of any service or property for use by or on behalf of any political party. 'Property' could include equipment, such as computers; 'service' the provision of staff.[5]

(3) Expenditure in connection with the registration of electors, the candidature of any person (including prospective candidature), the selection of any candidate or the holding of any ballot by the union in connection with any election to a political office. 'Political office' covers members of the UK and European Parliaments and of a local authority, and also includes any position within a political party.[6] It therefore covers internal party elections, such as the nomination of parliamentary candidates or prospective candidates.

(4) Expenditure on the maintenance of any holder of a political office. 'Maintenance' means the maintenance of a person as a politician and is not confined to expenses incurred to stay alive; it also covers expenses to facilitate the conduct of political functions, such as a grant for research, travel or secretarial expenses.[7]

(5) Expenditure on the holding of any conference or meeting by or on behalf of a political party or of any other meeting the main purpose of which is the transaction of business in connection with a political party. Expenditure incurred by delegates or participants in connection with their attendance at such conferences or meetings is expressly included.[8]

(6) Expenditure on the production, publication or distribution[9] of any literature, document, film, sound recording or advertisement, the main purpose of which is to persuade people to vote, or not to vote, for a political party or candidate.

This sixth category, first introduced by the Trade Union Act 1984, represented a particularly significant extension of the previous definition; under the Trade Union Act 1913, expenditure on political literature was required to be financed from a political fund only if it was directly and expressly in support of a political party.[10] In expanding the definition, the Conservative Government's primary target was 'the electoral expenditure of public sector unions concerned to protect their members' interests in the face of privatisation and cuts'.[11] It claimed that the 'main purpose' test would ensure that campaigns on matters such as jobs and other matters affecting members' interests could still be financed from unions' general funds; they would only need to be paid for out of political funds if their main purpose was to influence voting behaviour. The only case on this provision to date, *Paul v NALGO*,[12] lends some support to this view. NALGO, a public service union, organised a campaign during the run-up to local authority elections and in anticipation of a general election. Pursuant to this, it issued leaflets which drew attention to the impact of government cutbacks and privatisation policies on public services and pointed out that readers had a vote. The leaflets specifically disclaimed any intention of seeking or opposing the election of particular candidates but their distribution was concentrated in marginal Conservative constituencies. In finding that expenditure on the leaflets from the general fund was unlawful, the court dismissed the union's claim that this was a non-partisan campaign designed merely to persuade people that public services were a good thing; the only rational conclusion to be drawn from the literature was 'If you accept the message of the leaflet, vote against the Conservatives' and this being so the disclaimer was not effective to avoid liability. However, the court emphasised that it was the linkage of disapproval of Government policies in a biased way with the invitation to vote at the time of an election which had made the campaign a 'political object', and stressed that:

> nothing in th[e] judgment should be taken as suggesting that a publicity campaign . . . at times other than an election and therefore at a time when neither directly nor indirectly can the union be inviting anybody to exercise a vote at the time, is unlawful, merely because it expresses disapproval of the Government's policy.[13]

Notwithstanding this limitation, many public service unions have established political funds in order to fend off the possibility of their campaigns being susceptible to legal challenge.[14]

---

1. TULRCA 1992, s 72(1), (2). In determining whether a union has incurred expenditure of this kind, no account is to be taken of the ordinary administrative expenses of the union: s 72(3). For a complaint where the union's attempt to rely upon this exclusion failed, see *In the matter of a complaint against the ISTC* (13 October 1994, unreported), CO.

2. *Ibid.*, s 72(4).

3. *ASTMS v Parkin* [1983] IRLR 448, EAT (investment on commercial terms in developing a site for the new Labour Party headquarters).

4. The Registration of Political Parties Act 1998 does not directly define a 'political party', but only those parties which declare an intention to have one or more candidates at a 'relevant election' (parliamentary elections; elections to the European Parliament or to Scottish Parliament, Welsh or Northern Ireland assembly; and local

government elections) can appear on the register; see also the Political Parties Elections and Referendum Bill (H.C.) 2000 and the SDA 1975, s 33(1). On the meaning of 'political purpose' in the context of charity law, see *McGovern v AG* [1981] 3 All ER 493, Slade J at 509; see also *R v Radio Authority ex parte Bull* [1997] 2 All ER 561, CA.

5. Elias and Ewing, 1987, 170.

6. TULRCA 1992, s 72(4). 'Local authority' means a county council, district council, a London borough council or a parish or community council. Local Government Act 1972, s 270, as amended.

7. *ASTMS v Parkin*, above, note 3.

8. TULRCA 1992, s 72(2).

9. The Certification Officer has held that 'distribution' includes not only distribution to the public but also to members and officials of the union, although limited circulation within a union office may not be covered: *McCarthy v APEX* [1980] IRLR 335, CO. Where a 'political' article features in a publication covering other issues, such as a union journal, this decision would suggest that the main purpose of the journal as a whole should be examined.

10. *Coleman v POEU* [1981] IRLR 427, CO.

11. Elias and Ewing, 1987, 172.

12. [1987] IRLR 413, ChD.

13. *Ibid*, at 421.

14. *Annual Report of the Certification Officer 1999–2000*, App 8; Fredman and Morris, 1989, 126–128.

Assets and Liabilities of the Political Fund

2.49 As we stated in para **2.47**, a trade union's political fund rules must stipulate that any payments in furtherance of 'political objects' are made only from the political fund.[1] It seems that the political fund may be used for general purposes if the fund rules so permit, but if the rules are silent the position is less clear.[2] There are three major statutory restrictions governing the assets and liabilities of the fund. First, when there is a political fund resolution in force, property may be added to the fund only from two sources: contributions by members or persons other than the union, and property which accrues to the fund in the course of administering its assets (for example, interest).[3] This means that unions cannot add to their political fund income generated by the investment of other funds; it may also prevent them borrowing money for political activities.[4] Secondly, once a political fund resolution has ceased to have effect, members cannot be required to contribute to the fund,[5] and no property may be added to it other than that contributed to the fund before the date of cessation but not yet deposited in it, and that accruing in the course of administering the assets of the fund.[6] The former exception allows contributions deducted by employers through the check-off but not yet forwarded to the fund to be added to it,[7] but does not permit contributions paid by members after the date of cessation, even if they were due for payment before that time. Lastly, regardless of whether there is a resolution in force, no liability of the fund may be discharged out of any other union fund, irrespective of whether any asset of that fund has been charged in connection with that particular liability.[8] Thus, a creditor will be unable to secure payment of a political fund debt out of the general fund of the union or out of the assets of that fund, notwithstanding any term or condition on which liability was incurred.

---

1. TULRCA 1992, s 82(1)(a).
2. Kidner, 1983, 215–216. If the political fund is not prohibited by the rules from financing industrial action it ceases to be 'protected property' for the purposes of TULRCA 1992, s 23(2)(d); see para **6.65**.
3. TULRCA 1992, s 83(1).
4. *ASTMS v Parkin* [1983] IRLR 448, EAT.
5. TULRCA 1992, s 83(2).
6. *Ibid.*, s 89(3).
7. See paras **3.24** and **3.25** for the provisions governing the check-off.
8. TULRCA 1992, s 83(3).

The Right of Exemption from Contribution

2.50 A trade union's political fund rules must allow any member to be exempted from an obligation to contribute to the political fund,[1] and unions must notify their members of their right of exemption in a form specified by statute.[2] Where a member gives an exemption notice within one month of members being notified of their right to do so, and at the time of the political resolution ballot no political resolution is in force, the exemption takes immediate effect; in all other cases it takes effect from 1 January after the notice is given.[3] In 1984, in return for the government agreeing not to re-introduce 'contracting-in',[4] the TUC issued a 'statement of guidance on political fund arrangements' designed to ensure that union members are informed about and able to exercise their right to contract out from contributing. The right of an exempted member not to have the political fund contributions deducted by an employer through the check-off system is discussed at para **3.25**. The political fund rules must provide that a member who is exempt from the obligation to contribute shall not be excluded from any benefits of the union or placed directly or indirectly under any disability or disadvantage as compared with other members of the union except in relation to the control or management of the political fund.[5] A union may not exclude a non-contributor from holding office in the union by failing to separate control of the fund from other union activities.[6] Thus a union has three choices: it may institute separate management in the case of the political fund; allow exempt members to hold office and participate in decisions about the fund; or adopt rules which allow exempt members to hold office involving control of the political fund, but which require them to refrain from participating in decisions relating to it.[7] The rules must also provide that contribution to the political fund should not be a condition of admission to the union.[8] The protection of non-contributors against discrimination continues after a political fund expires.[9]

---

1. TULRCA 1992, s 82(1)(b). Exempt members must be relieved of the political fund element of the normal periodical contributions, unless contributions to the political fund are collected by a separate levy: s 85(1). The rules should also make provision for enabling every union member to know what portion, if any, of his or her periodical contribution is a contribution to the political fund: s 85(2)(b).

2. *Ibid.*, s 84(1),(2). The union rules may provide that notice need not be given to overseas members: s 94(1)(b); for the definition of 'overseas member', see s 94(3). Notice of the right must be given whenever a political resolution is renewed (s 73), but a member's exemption notice continues to have effect until it is withdrawn: s 84(5). It has been held that members may write out their own forms and hand them to the appropriate officials (*Valentine and the ETU*, Registrar's Annual Report, 1957); see also Elias and Ewing, 1987, 179.

3. *Ibid.*, s 84(4).

4. Between 1927 and 1946 a system of contracting-in was in force. The contributions to political funds rose from 38% of members of TUC unions in 1945 to 60% in 1948: Wedderburn, 1986, 762.

5. *Ibid.*, s 82(1)(c). The disadvantage must be more than merely technical: *Reeves v TGWU* [1980] IRLR 307, EAT (although note that TULRCA 1992, s 86 now makes the practice in that case unlawful); *Richards v NUM* [1981] IRLR 247, CO (although note now TULRCA 1992, s 30).

6. *Birch v NUR* [1950] Ch 602, ChD.

7. Kidner, 1983, 227.

8. TULRCA 1992, s 82(1)(d).

9. *Ibid.*, s 91(4).

Remedies for Breach of the Political Fund Provisions

2.51 There are four major categories of complaint which may arise in relation to expenditure for political objects. All but the third can be pursued before either the Certification Officer or the High Court. The procedure to be followed by the

Certification Officer, the usual effect of orders made by him or her and provision for appeal are discussed in para **2.2**. The first is a complaint relating to a breach of the union's political fund rules. In this context, unusually, any order made by the Certification Officer cannot be automatically enforced as an order of the High Court; rather it may be enforced in the same way as an order of the county court on being recorded in that court.[1] The second relates to a breach of the statutory provisions governing political funds, such as a complaint that money has been spent on 'political objects' without a political resolution being in force.[2] However, if the political fund rules include provisions which are permissible but not required by statute, it seems that complaints of breaches of those rules may be taken only to the High Court.[3] Complaints about political resolution ballots may, like those relating to elections, be made to the Certification Officer or the High Court.[4] Applications which relate to a ballot which has already been held must be made within one year of the union announcing the result.[5] In the case of a successful application, an 'enforcement order' requiring the union to remedy the defect will normally also be made. In all areas of its jurisdiction, the High Court is empowered to grant interim relief,[6] which may be particularly helpful if the complainant seeks to halt a ballot or restrain unlawful expenditure. Where interim relief is not being sought, recourse to the Certification Officer is likely, in this as in other contexts, to prove the cheaper and the speedier option.

---

1. TULRCA 1992, s 82(4). This right survives expiry of the political fund: see para **2.52**.
2. The Certification Officer's jurisdiction in this area was introduced by ERA 1999; see now TULRCA 1992, s 72A. It is notable that in this context no specific provision is made for the High Court to have jurisdiction, but s 72A(11) implies that it is intended to exist.
3. TULRCA 1992, s 82(2) applies only to rules made *in pursuance of this section*, and breach of rules relating to political funds is not covered by s 108A.
4. *Ibid.*, s 79.
5. *Ibid.*, s 79(3).
6. TULRCA 1992, s 81(7). Even if this is not in the statute, this is part of the High Court's inherent jurisdiction.

Expiry of a Political Fund

2.52 Where a political fund resolution expires without a new resolution replacing it, a number of provisions come into effect. First, as we indicated in para **2.49**, there are restrictions on adding to the fund; members cannot be required to continue their contributions to it, and no property may be added other than that contributed to the fund before the date of cessation and that accruing in the course of administering its assets.[1] The trade union must take the necessary steps to ensure that the collection of contributions to the fund is discontinued as soon as reasonably practicable;[2] this is likely to require telling employers to modify their check-off arrangements.[3] Where contributions continue to be received after the date of cessation then, notwithstanding anything in its rules, the union may pay any of these into its general fund, but any member who applies is entitled to a refund of such contributions.[4] Any member, not only a contributor to the fund, may apply to the High Court for a declaration that the union has failed to comply with its duty to ensure that the collection of contributions is discontinued; if successful, the court may make an order requiring the union to take, within a specified time, specified steps to ensure compliance if it considers it appropriate to do so.[5] Any such order may be enforced by any member who was a member at the time that it was granted.[6] The second issue on expiry of a resolution is the destination of the remaining assets of the fund. The union may decide to freeze the fund in the hope that members will approve a new resolution at some time in the future. If this happens, the frozen fund may be added to the new fund but no other money or property may be added.[7] Alternatively, it may transfer all or part of the money to other funds.[8] However, neither of these options allow the union to repay any existing debts, given that only the political fund may be used for political objects. There is a limited exception to this: where a ballot was held before the expiry of a political resolution and a new resolution was not passed, the union may continue to use the fund for political objects for up to six months from the date of the ballot, but this does not authorise payments which would put the fund in deficit or increase any existing deficit.[9] Finally, on expiry of the resolution the political fund rules cease to have effect on cessation of the resolution, unless the ballot was held while an existing resolution was in force, in which case they cease to have effect six months from the date of the ballot.[10] The right of members to complain to the Certification Officer about an alleged breach of the rules while they remained in force remains unaffected.[11]

---

1. TULRCA 1992, ss 83(2), 89(3).
2. *Ibid.*, s 90(1).
3. See paras **3.24** and **3.25**.
4. TULRCA 1992, s 90(2),(3).
5. *Ibid.*, s 90(4),(5).
6. *Ibid.*, s 90(5).
7. *Ibid.*, s 89(5).
8. *Ibid.*, s 89(4). This applies notwithstanding any rules or any trusts on which the political fund is held.

9. *Ibid.*, s 89(2).

10. TULRCA 1992, s 91(2).However, those rules which are required to enable the political fund to be administered at a time when there is no political resolution in force continue to have effect: s 91(1).

11. *Ibid.*, s 91(3).

3

Trade Unions and Employers

INTRODUCTION

3.1 In Chapter 2 we examined the legal status of trade unions and the provisions governing their relationship with their members. In this chapter we analyse the rights which individual union members and those who participate in union activities are accorded in relation to employers. We also discuss the protections for those who do not wish to join a union, which are crucial to understanding the development of the law in this area. The rights accorded to unions, rather than their individual members, in relation to collective bargaining and consultation are analysed in Chapters 4 and 5 respectively. As we discussed in Chapter 2, unions became lawful in this country in that they no longer attracted automatic liability under the criminal and, later, the civil law, during the nineteenth century. However this absence of constraint by the state means little in practical terms if employers are free to refuse to employ, or dismiss or otherwise discriminate against, union members. This point is emphasised by International Labour Organisation Convention No 98 which states that '[w]orkers shall enjoy adequate protection against acts of anti-union discrimination in respect of their employment', more particularly in relation to acts 'calculated to (a) make the employment of a worker subject to the condition that he shall not join a union or shall relinquish trade union membership; (b) cause the dismissal of or otherwise prejudice a worker by reason of union membership or because of participation in union activities outside working hours or, with the consent of the employer, within working hours'.[1] However, despite the fact that the UK ratified this Convention in 1950, the first statutory support for freedom of association in the employment relationship came only in 1971. The government in its capacity as employer gave active encouragement to union membership from the end of the First World War, and hoped in doing so to set an example to the private sector,[2] but many employers, particularly in the white-collar sectors, resisted this.[3] Employer strategies to discourage union organisation ranged from making it a term of the contract of employment that employees should not join unions, denying promotion and pay increases to union members, and continuously transferring active unionists between departments, for example, to establishing 'company unions' to ward off external organisations and offering rewards to 'loyal' employees on the other.[4] Greater direct encouragement to employers to allow trade unionism was given by the 1946 House of Commons Fair Wages Resolution which, unlike its predecessors of 1891 and 1909, affirmed that government contracts with private employers should require contractors to recognise the freedom of their workers to be union members, but, although symbolically significant, this seems to have been of little practical effect in influencing employment practices due to inadequate monitoring and enforcement.[5]

The first statutory protection for workers against discrimination by employers on grounds of union membership and activities was granted by the Industrial Relations Act 1971 (which also bestowed correlative rights not to join). However as these rights were restricted to membership of unions which had 'registered' under the Act, and it was TUC policy not to register, they had little practical effect. They were maintained in an amended form in the 1974–1979 Labour Government's 'Social Contract' legislation, and have continued in force, with significant modifications, ever since. They were joined in 1975 by the introduction of a statutory obligation on employers to grant officials of recognised independent unions a reasonable amount of paid time off work for industrial relations duties and training, and members of such unions time off (which need not be paid) to participate in union activities or to represent the union. Perhaps surprisingly, these provisions remained in force during the period in office of the 1979–1997 Conservative Government, although the duties for which officials could claim time off were narrowed. The survival and, indeed, extension of the provisions preventing discrimination on union grounds in a political climate hostile to collective organisation is explicable on the basis that the government's real target was the protection of the right not to join, of which the right to join was perceived as a corollary. Thus, when protection was accorded against discrimination against non-union members at the hiring stage, as well as during employment, this was extended by analogy to union members. Those dismissed on grounds of union membership and activities also benefited from high compensation levels designed essentially to deter compulsory union membership. The principle of reciprocity was also reflected in provisions relating to contract compliance; when it became unlawful to specify in contracts for the supply of goods and services that work should be done exclusively by union labour, the same protection was extended to non-union labour. However, this 'even-handedness' was not universally applied. The prohibition on requiring recognition of, or consultation with, unions in contracts for the supply of goods and services was not paralleled by a prohibition on requirements not to recognise or consult. Moreover, when a judicial decision threatened the ability of employers lawfully to induce employees to transfer from contracts incorporating the terms of collective agreements to 'personal contracts',[6] the government responded by inserting a late amendment to the Trade Union Reform and Employment Rights Act

1993 to make clear that such action (if taken in relation to employees as a 'class') was not to be regarded as deterring union membership.

The Employment Relations Act 1999 has left the framework of protection essentially in place, although some amendments have been made. First, the impact of a House of Lords' decision that 'action short of dismissal' on grounds of union membership or activities did not include 'omissions', such as a failure to promote, has been overturned.[7] Secondly, the Secretary of State is empowered to issue regulations to prohibit the compilation, supply or use of 'blacklists' of union members and those who have taken part in union activities. Thirdly, the Secretary of State is empowered to issue regulations about cases where a worker is dismissed or subjected to detriment by his or her employer on the ground that he or she refuses to enter into a contract which includes terms which differ from the terms of a collective agreement which applies to him or her. However, this is subject to the proviso that it should not be regarded as a detriment to those who so refuse that higher wages or other monetary benefits are paid to other workers, provided that these benefits are not linked to the prohibition of union membership and reasonably relate to services provided by those workers under a contract of employment. Moreover, the provision for employers to 'further a change in . . . [their] relationship' with any class of their employees without this constituting an unlawful detriment to union members still remains intact, the Labour Government having concluded that employers should be free to change their bargaining arrangements without impediment. Thus, the government has maintained the distinction between union membership and collective bargaining reflected in the legislation which it inherited. The final significant change in this area is the abolition of the enhanced levels of compensation payable to those who seek reinstatement or re-engagement after having been unfairly dismissed on grounds of union membership or activity, or non-membership of a union. Compensation is now assessed on the same basis as dismissal for other reasons (unlike in the case of 'whistleblowers' and those dismissed for reasons relating to health and safety, where there is no limit on the compensatory award).[8]

The first section of this chapter analyses the scope of the protections afforded to union members and those who participate in their activities against discrimination by employers. We then examine the provisions which secure the right not to join a union. This is followed by a survey of the relevant legislation relating to contract compliance. The final section analyses the remaining rights of union members in relation to employers: provisions governing the deduction of union subscriptions at source, and rights to time off work for union duties and activities.

---

1. ILO Convention No 98 on the Right to Organise and Collective Bargaining (1949), Article 1. Interestingly, the *Report of the Royal Commission on Trade Unions and*

Employers' Associations 1965–1968, Cmnd 3623, 1968 pointed out (at para 243) that ILO Conventions in this area were not drafted in terms which required legislation; 'successive British Governments' had taken the view that the union movement was sufficiently strong to make legislation unnecessary, and the TUC had not pressed for it.

2. See generally Fredman and Morris, 1989, Chapter 4. In some areas of the public service, such as the Post Office, unionism was encouraged at an earlier stage: see Hans ((4th ser) vol CLIX, col 396, 21 June 1906.

3. See the *Report of the Royal Commission on Trade Unions and Employers' Associations 1965–1968*, above, note 1, paras 213–224.

4. See Bain, 1970, 131–135, who divides such strategies into those of 'forceful opposition' and 'peaceful competition'.

5. See Bercusson, 1978, Chapter 17.

6. *Wilson v Associated Newspaper Ltd*; *Palmer v Associated British Ports* [1993] IRLR 336, CA. This decision was reversed by the House of Lords: see note 7 below.

7. *Associated Newspapers Ltd v Wilson*; *Associated British Ports v Palmer* [1995] IRLR 258, HL.

8. ERA 1996, s 124(1A).

THE RIGHT TO ORGANISE

Sources and General Principles

3.2 At common law all workers are free to form and join trade unions apart from the police, who are forbidden to do so by statute.[1] This mere absence of constraint does not provide any enforceable rights, however, in the event that employers deny employment to union members. Legislation now affords trade unionists limited protection against discrimination before and during employment, although some categories of worker are excluded from these provisions.[2] First, the Trade Union and Labour Relations (Consolidation) Act 1992, ss 152 and 153 give employees the right not to be dismissed (or, in specified circumstances, selected for redundancy) on account of their membership of an independent trade union or participation in the activities of such a union at an appropriate time. Secondly, s 146 of that Act gives employees the right not to be subjected to any detriment by any act, or deliberate failure to act, to penalise or deter such membership or activities.[3] Lastly, s 137 makes it unlawful to refuse a person employment because he or she is a member of a union (but does not proscribe refusal based on union activities). To date, these provisions have been accorded a restrictive interpretation by the courts, although the application of s 146 has recently been extended by the Employment Relations Act 1999. The protections contained in the Trade Union and Labour Relations (Consolidation) Act 1992 have also been reinforced by a power accorded to the Secretary of State by s 3 of the Employment Relations Act 1999 to make regulations prohibiting the compilation of lists of union members or those who have taken part in union activities where these lists are being compiled with a view to their use by employers or employment agencies to discriminate in relation to recruitment or the treatment of workers (although at the time of writing no such regulations have been issued). In addition whether an individual is a union member constitutes 'sensitive personal data' for the purposes of the Data Protection Act 1998, and can be disclosed only in very restricted circumstances.[4] Finally, the Human Rights Act 1998 may be invoked to persuade courts and tribunals towards a more expansive interpretation of the existing legislation, and may in some circumstances give a free-standing right of action to individuals who lie outside the scope of the legislation or whose specific activities are not protected.[5] Article 11 of the ECHR, which guarantees the right to join trade unions, applies to '[e]veryone', as does Article 10, which guarantees the right to freedom of expression, which may also be relevant in this context.

---

1. Police Act 1996, s 64, re-enacting a prohibition in force since 1919. The lower ranks are automatically members of the Police Federation, whose constitution and activities are tightly defined by statute, although it is not compulsory to pay a subscription to the Federation: *ibid.*, s 59; Police Federation Regulations 1969, SI 1969/1789, as amended. *Quaere* whether this is contrary to Article 11 of the ECHR; in *Chassagnon v France* judgment of April 29 1999, the ECtHR held that compulsory membership on the part of landowners of a hunters' association violated Article 11, even though they were not obliged to pay a subscription (para 115). Cf also the ESC jurisprudence relating to this matter, discussed Morris, 1994a, 39 (the Committee of Independent Experts, now called the ECSR, having held that compulsory membership was incompatible with the ESC, decided not to revert to the issue after being informed that there was no obligation to pay a subscription and that failure to do this did not carry any penalty: *Conclusions* X-1, 68). Members of the armed forces may join unions as individuals provided that this does not involve them in activities which would conflict with their military duties, but they have no statutory protection against anti-union discrimination. See paras **1.7** and **1.20** *et seq.* for the exceptions to the right to freedom of association permitted under international conventions.
2. In particular, those who are not 'employees'; see further para **3.3**.
3. Note, however, the restriction of this right by TULRCA 1992, s 148(3)–(5); see further para **3.12**.
4. DPA 1998, ss 2, 4; Scheds 2 and 3.
5. See Chapter 1 for an analysis of the application of the Act.

Protection against Dismissal on Grounds of Trade Union Membership and Activities

Entitlement and procedure

3.3 The protection against dismissal for trade union membership and activities (known in this context as 'inadmissible' reasons) is secured through the unfair dismissal procedure.[1] This remedy is currently confined to 'employees',[2] a restriction which is particularly anomalous in this context given that trade unions are organisations of 'workers'.[3] As we indicated in para **3.2** above, Articles 10 and 11 of the ECHR apply to 'everyone', and in cases where the facts are finely balanced and the decision could go either way, the obligation to read and give effect to legislation in a way which is compatible with Convention rights may be invoked to persuade a tribunal or court to 'construe' the term 'employee' more widely than it may do in other contexts.[4] However there will be many cases where it will not be possible to deem a worker to be an 'employee', in which case individuals will be denied a remedy against dismissal unless they are employed by a 'public authority' against whom proceedings may be brought directly.[5] Curiously, employees who work outside Great Britain are excluded from protection,[6] even though this exclusion has been removed in relation to unfair dismissal based upon other reasons. Thus, an employee who worked outside Great Britain would be able to bring an unfair dismissal claim (assuming that he or she was otherwise qualified to do so), but would be forced to argue that the dismissal was unfair on some other ground. The armed forces and the police are specifically excluded from the statutory protections against dismissal for union membership and activities.[7] In their case Article 11 may not assist, as it expressly permits the imposition of 'lawful restrictions' on the exercise of these rights upon members of these groups (as well as of members of 'the administration of the State').[8] Finally it should be noted that an employment tribunal must dismiss a complaint if it is shown that the action complained of was taken for the purpose of safeguarding national security.[9] No minimum period of employment is required to claim unfair dismissal on grounds of union membership or activities, nor does any maximum age limit apply.[10] However the significance of these differences is modified by the effect of a Court of Appeal decision that when employees are claiming in circumstances where they would not otherwise qualify to do so, it is for them to prove the reason given that they are invoking a jurisdiction which the tribunal would not otherwise have.[11] This may be a difficult burden to satisfy, particularly as employers will generally take care to ensure that other reasons, such as poor work or a disciplinary offence, are attributed to such dismissals.[12] It may be important for the employee to show that non-unionists in a similar position have not been dismissed in order to undermine the credibility of the employer's evidence.[13] The difficulty of the employee's task in discharging the burden of proof may be exacerbated if the decision was taken by a group of persons, as the facts of *Smith v Hayle Town Council*[14] exemplify. The applicant was a town clerk who applied to join a union. He told two councillors that he had done so, and shortly afterwards was dismissed at a council meeting by a vote of six to five. The evidence showed that at least one member of the council had voted for dismissal because of his application to join a union, but there was no evidence to show why the remaining five had voted as they did.[15] The Court of Appeal concluded that, although there was an 'element of [anti-union] prejudice', that had not been shown to be the principal reason behind the thinking of the 'corporate mind'.[16] Once the tribunal finds that the reason for dismissal was based upon an anti-union ground, the dismissal is automatically unfair; the reasonableness of the employer's action is not at issue.

---

1. On 'inadmissible reasons', see TULRCA 1992, s 154(2). See ERA 1996, s 95 for the definition of dismissal. A complaint must be presented to a tribunal before the end of the period of three months beginning with the effective date of termination (defined in ERA 1996, s 97) or within such further period as the tribunal considers reasonable in a case where it is satisfied that it was not reasonably practicable for the complaint to be presented within the three month period: ERA 1996, s 111(2). See App 2 for the meaning of not 'reasonably practicable'.

2. *Ibid.*, s 152; see further App 1. See *O'Kelly v Trusthouse Forte plc* [1983] IRLR 369, CA for an example of the unfortunate consequences of this exclusion. The Secretary of State is empowered to extend protection in this and other contexts to a wider category of individuals under ERA 1999, s 23, but at the time of writing this power has not been exercised.

3. TULRCA 1992, s 1; see further para **2.4**.

4. HRA 1998, s 3; see para **1.14**.

5. *Ibid.*, ss 6, 7; see further Chapter 1 for the definition of a 'public authority' (and the possible distinction between 'pure' public authorities and those with mixed public and private functions, described in para **1.17**) and the scope of Articles 10 and 11. Note also that the restriction to 'employees' does not comply with ILO Convention No 98 on the Right to Organise and Collective Bargaining, which requires protection against acts of anti-union discrimination in respect of their employment for all 'workers', excluding the armed forces and the police.

6. TULRCA 1992, s 285 (although note s 285(2) as regards mariners and s 287 relating to offshore employment). Share fishermen are also excluded: s 284. Prior to ERA 1999 recourse to unfair dismissal protection was excluded in any case where the employee under his or her contract of employment 'ordinarily works outside Great Britain': ERA 1996, s 196(2),(3), repealed by ERA 1999, s 32(3). S 285 uses the term 'works', although in the case of prospective employees it excludes those who *would* ordinarily work outside Great Britain. For the purposes of ERA 1996 s 196(2) the test of what constitutes work 'ordinarily' done within Great Britain was principally regulated by the contract terms, although in case of doubt, such as contracts in which the

employer retained a discretion as to where the work was done, the employee's 'base' or employer's centre of control was regarded as the determining factor: see *Wilson v Maynard Shipbuilding Consultants AB* [1978] ICR 376, CA; *Todd v British Midland Airways Ltd* [1978] ICR 959, CA; *Janata Bank v Ahmed* [1981] IRLR 457, CA; *Carver v Saudi Arabian Airlines* [1999] IRLR 370, CA The courts emphasised in those cases the need to examine the whole contemplated period of the contract. It is submitted that in this context the same test should apply, despite the difference in wording.

7. TULCRA 1992, ss 274, 280.

8. Although note that there is a distinction between the right to belong to a union and the exercise of that right, a distinction overlooked by the EComHR in *CCSU v UK* App No 11603/85, (1987) 50 DR 228. In that case, workers at Government Communications Headquarters were held to be 'members . . . of the administration of the State' because the purpose of GCHQ resembled that of the armed forces and the police in protecting national security. However in the subsequent case of *Vogt v Germany* judgment of 26 September 1995, (1996) 21 EHRR 205, para 67, the ECtHR emphasised that this category should be interpreted narrowly, in the light of the post held by the official concerned. See further para **1.7**.

9. ETA 1996, s 10(1). This provision was substituted by ERA 1999. At the time of writing it has not been brought into force; the equivalent provision in the unamended version is ETA 1996, s 10(4). Note also TULRCA 1992, s 275, which excludes the application of the Act from particular descriptions of Crown employment, or from particular individuals, where a ministerial certificate certifies that this is required for the purpose of safeguarding national security.

10. TULRCA 1992, s 154.

11. *Smith v Hayle Town Council* [1978] ICR 996; see also *Marley Tile Co Ltd v Shaw* [1980] ICR 72, CA. Where an employee would otherwise qualify to claim, the employer must show that the reason for dismissal was one of those specified in ERA 1996, s 98(1),(2) in order to defend the claim: *Maund v Penwith District Council* [1984] IRLR 24, CA. In *Sarker v South Tees Acute Hospitals NHS Trust* [1997] IRLR 328, the EAT held that an employee could claim for unfair dismissal where her contract of employment was terminated for an inadmissible reason before she had taken up her duties.

12. Evans and Lewis, 1987, 95.

13. Employment Tribunals (Constitution and Rules of Procedure) Regulations 1993, SI 1993/2687 Sched 1, para 4. Note that there is no equivalent under TULRCA 1992 to the Sex Discrimination (Questions and Replies) Order 1975, SI 1975/2048 or other such provisions in the areas of race and disability discrimination.

14. Above, note 11.

15. If evidence could not be obtained voluntarily from the five members of the council, it seems surprising that appropriate witness orders were not obtained.

16. Above, note 11, Eveleigh LJ at 1003.

The scope of protection

3.4 Dismissals relating to union membership and activities are automatically unfair where the principal reason for dismissal falls into one of two categories: first, if the employee was, or proposed to become, a member of an independent trade union and, secondly, if the employee had taken part, or proposed to take part, in the activities of an independent trade union at an appropriate time.[1] We discuss the scope of each of these provisions in paras **3.5** and **3.6** *et seq.* respectively. It is also automatically unfair to select an employee for dismissal where the reason for dismissal was that the employee was redundant, but the circumstances surrounding the redundancy applied equally to one or more other employees in the same undertaking who held similar positions to the dismissed employee who were not dismissed, and the reason or principal reason for selection was the employee's union membership or activities.[2] The EAT has held that this provision also allows inquiry into why an employee dismissed for redundancy was not offered alternative employment within the organisation when others were offered such employment; if this was on grounds of union membership or activities it is automatically unfair.[3] There is no requirement to show that the employers were motivated by malice or the deliberate desire to be rid of a union activist in order for an employee to rely upon this protection; it is sufficient for the tribunal to examine the set of facts or beliefs which led to the employee's selection.[4] Thus, in a case where the employee was chosen because the employers considered that he was spending too much time on union duties, this was sufficient to show that the dismissal was unfair.[5] The Court of Appeal has held that in determining whether the dismissed employee and his or her chosen comparator hold similar 'positions', regard should be paid only to their relative positions as *employees*; no account should be paid to what any of them did, or had a contractual right to do, in other capacities, such as a union official. Thus, the fact that a shop steward spent a considerable percentage of his time on union matters was irrelevant in determining his 'position'.[6] In that case the Court relied upon the definition of 'position' in the Employment Protection (Consolidation) Act 1978, in which the protection against dismissal on union grounds was formerly contained. That Act defined position, in relation to an employee, as 'the following matters taken as a whole, that is to say, his status as an employee, the nature of his work and his terms and conditions of employment'.[7] The 1978 Act has been repealed and the definition of 'position' now appears, in substantively identical terms, in the Employment Relations Act 1996[8] (but not in the Trade Union and Labour Relations (Consolidation) Act 1992). However the relevant sections of the 1992 Act are to be construed as one with Part X of the Employment Rights Act 1996, which deals with unfair dismissal, so the definition in that latter Act applies for this purpose.[9] Finally in the context of selection for redundancy, the EAT has emphasised that the protection afforded against dismissal is 'neutral' in the sense that the ways in which employees carry out their union duties should not count either in their favour or against them.[10] Employers may, in practice, be tempted not to select union members or officials for redundancy in order to avoid the dangers of an unfair dismissal claim founded on an inadmissible reason, particularly where other employees lack the one year's continuous employment which is usually required to bring an unfair dismissal claim.[11] However they should also be mindful of the parallel protection afforded to employees against dismissal or selection for redundancy because they are not members of any, or of a particular, union (see further paras **3.17** and **3.18**).

---

1. TULRCA 1992, s 152. See paras **2.6** and **2.7** for the definition of an independent trade union. Note that where s 152 (or 153) is not satisfied, a dismissal on 'anti-union' grounds may still be unfair under the ordinary unfair dismissal provisions.

2. *Ibid.*, s 153. Again the employee must prove that this was the reason for dismissal (see para **3.3**) where he or she would not otherwise qualify to claim and, in practice, the burden of showing unfair selection within the meaning of the statute will rest upon the employee: see *Port of London Authority v Payne* [1992] IRLR 447, EAT. (The Court of Appeal decision in that case ([1994] IRLR 9) was confined to the issue of re-engagement).

3. *Driver v Cleveland Structural Engineering Co Ltd* [1994] IRLR 636, EAT.

4. *Dundon v GPT Ltd* [1995] IRLR 403, EAT, relying upon the oft-cited dictum of Cairns LJ in *Abernathy v Mott, Hay and Anderson* [1974] IRLR 213 at 215.

5. *Ibid.*

6. *O'Dea v ISC Chemicals Ltd t/a Rhône-Poulenc Chemicals* [1995] IRLR 599, CA.

7. S 153.

8. ERA 1996, s 235(1).

9. TULRCA 1992, s 167.

10. *Smiths Industries Aerospace and Defence Systems v Rawlings* [1996] IRLR 656, EAT (a decision relating to a union-selected health and safety representative: see further para **5.32**).

11. Note, however, that there is now a large category of automatically unfair reasons for dismissal, or selection for redundancy, for which no qualifying period of employment is required: ERA 1996, s 108.

3.5 The protection against dismissal for membership or proposed membership of an independent trade union has been held to cover membership of a particular union as well as unions in general, so employees may complain if they are dismissed for joining union X rather than union Y.[1] This prevents employers from inhibiting employees' freedom to join the union of their choice. However the extent to which the concept of union membership goes beyond a bare right to hold a union card is now unclear. In *Discount Tobacco and Confectionary Ltd v Armitage* the EAT considered that it extended also to using the 'essential services' of the union, such as invoking the assistance of a union official to negotiate and elucidate terms of employment, the 'outward and visible manifestation of . . . membership'.[2] It therefore found that an employee who was dismissed after seeking the assistance of her union official to obtain a written statement of her terms and conditions of employment, the employer having failed to reply to her initial personal request, had been dismissed on grounds of union membership. In *Associated Newspapers Ltd v Wilson*; *Associated British Ports v Palmer*, however, the House of Lords held that, although *Armitage* may have been correct on its facts, membership of a union and making use of its services could not be equated.[3] The members of the House who took this view did so in the context of emphasising that collective bargaining was not a union 'service' and that the fact that a union was unrecognised did not render membership of it valueless.[4] In the subsequent case of *Speciality Care plc v Pachela*[5] the EAT took the view that their Lordships' observations on this point were *obiter*. It stated that where a complaint of dismissal by way of union membership was made, it would be for the tribunal to find as a fact whether or not the principal reason for dismissal related to the applicant's trade union membership, not only by reference to whether he or she had simply joined a union, but also by reference to whether the introduction of union representation into the employment relationship had led the employer to dismiss the employee. It urged tribunals to answer this question 'robustly'.[6] This was a bold decision in the light of *Associated Newspapers*, which could be read as effectively overruling *Armitage* and rendering the protection against dismissal for union membership almost nugatory. Given that employers are likely to object not to the mere fact of union membership but to its practical implications, if dismissing an employee because he or she makes use of union facilities is not protected, the scope of the right to join becomes extremely narrow. However it is submitted that the Human Rights Act 1998 lends support to a wider interpretation of union membership than *Associated Newspapers* suggests. Article 11 guarantees everyone the right to join trade unions 'for the protection of his interests'. As we discuss in Chapters 1 and 4, the current jurisprudence of the ECtHR does not support the argument that an individual has the right for his or her union to be recognised by the employer or for an employer to conclude a collective agreement with that union. However, the Court has held that the words 'for the protection of his interests' mean that the article safeguards the freedom to protect the occupational interests of union members by trade union action, and that union members have a right 'that the trade union should be heard', although the state has a free choice of the means to be used towards that end.[7] Once the Human Rights Act 1998 comes fully into force, tribunals and courts will be required to read and give effect to legislation in a way which is compatible with the Convention rights.[8] We consider that there is a strong argument that the concept of union membership should extend at the very least to making use of union services such as clarifying terms of employment, raising grievances and queries with employers, and possibly even negotiating certain terms and conditions of employment on behalf of an individual member even if it does not extend to a right to be represented for collective bargaining purposes.[9] In the event that a 'public authority' (or at least a 'pure' 'public authority') were to dismiss an individual for joining a union for the protection of his interests, he or she would have a free-standing right of action against that authority.[10]

---

1. *Ridgway and Fairbrother v National Coal Board* [1987] IRLR 80, CA. Although *Ridgway* was overruled in *Associated Newspapers Ltd v Wilson*; *Associated British Ports v Palmer* [1995] IRLR 258, HL, this element of the reasoning in that case would appear to remain valid. The employee need not have decided which particular union he or she wishes to join: *Cotter v Lynch Bros* [1972] IRLR 20, NIRC. Membership of a union includes membership of a particular branch or section of that union or one of a number of such branches or sections: TULRCA 1992, s 152(4). See para **2.7** for the definition of an independent trade union.

2. [1990] IRLR 15, EAT, at 16.

3. Above, note 1. See Lord Lloyd at 266, whose judgment on this point was supported by Lords Bridge and Keith (at 263–264 and 260 respectively). Cf. Lord Slynn at 265.

4. See Lord Lloyd at 266. See further paras **3.11**–**3.12**.

5. [1996] IRLR 248.

6. Above at 252. See also the (pre-*Associated Newspapers*) decision of *Overprint Ltd v Malcolm*, EAT 443/92, 1 December 1992 (unreported), where it was held that if the employer dismisses the employee because of what it believes will be the consequences of union membership (for example fears that it will lead to demands to change terms of employment) the reason for dismissal is union membership, regardless of whether such fears are justified.

7. *National Union of Belgian Police v Belgium* judgment of 22 October 1975, (1979–80) 1 EHRR 578, para 39; see also *Swedish Engine Drivers' Union v Sweden* judgment of 6 February 1976, (1979–80) 1 EHRR 617; *Gustafsson v Sweden* judgment of 28 March 1996, (1996) 22 EHRR 409; see further para **1.6**.

8. HRA 1998, s 3; see further para **1.14**.

9. Cf the ILO Committee of Experts on the Application of Conventions and Recommendations, which views collective bargaining as one of the union's essential services which requires protection against anti-union discrimination under Article 4 of Convention 98: Report III (Part 4A), 1996, 225. See also Cases C–193, 194/87 *Maurissen and European Public Service Union v Court of Auditors* [1996] ECR I–95, in which the ECJ held that the right of staff to be members of trade unions under the EU Staff Regulations Article 24(a) prevented Community institutions from prohibiting staff from participating in union activities, or penalising them for doing so, and viewed representational rights as integral to union activity.

10. See further paras **1.16** and **1.17** . Note that Article 11 allows lawful restrictions on the exercise of the right by members of the armed forces, the police, and the administration of the State; see para **3.3**, note 8.

3.6 The narrow protection which appears currently to be afforded in relation to trade union membership makes the scope of the second automatically unfair 'trade union' reason—that the employee had taken part, or proposed to take part in the activities of an independent trade union at an appropriate time[1]— particularly crucial (although if our argument relating to the Human Rights Act 1998 in para **3.5** above is accepted, this issue may become less pressing). We analyse the meaning of 'activities of an independent trade union' in this and the following paragraph, the concept of an 'appropriate time' in para **3.8.** 'Activities' are not defined in the legislation; they clearly include activities connected with internal union organisation and industrial relations, and should, in theory, extend to any activities which a union may lawfully undertake (although in applying this term within the time off provisions, certain political activities have been excluded).[2] The courts have held that, because it is dealt with elsewhere in the legislation, participation in industrial action (as opposed to preparation for it)[3] is not within the scope of protected activities,[4] although, as others have argued, this does not necessary follow:[5] this separate provision generally relates to whether the tribunal has jurisdiction to hear a claim; where it has such jurisdiction, there seems no reason why industrial action should not be a union activity.[6] In practice this debate is largely academic as, to be effective, industrial action is unlikely to be at an 'appropriate time' (see para **3.8** below). It is crucial that the activities should be those *of the union*; it is not sufficient that a union member is taking part in the kind of activities which the union pursues.[7] This appears to require the union in some sense to have 'authorised' the individual to act on its behalf, although such authorisation will rarely be direct and specific; it will usually derive from custom and practice. Thus, union members will generally be protected while participating in internal union affairs, such recruitment and other organisational activities,[8] attending union meetings,[9] and discussing union matters.[10] Contacting a union official for advice in certain circumstances has also been included.[11] However, there is some (questionable) authority for saying that the union should take some action in response to this approach for the employee to be protected,[12] a particularly undesirable approach if the narrow view of membership in *Associated Newspapers* continues (contrary to our argument) to be followed. In this context, as in relation to union membership (see para **3.5** above), we submit that the Human Rights Act 1998 argues for a wider interpretation, based on the argument that that the employee, in contacting the official, is seeking to use the union for the protection of his or her interests, the very purpose for which the guarantee under Article 11 of the ECHR is accorded. Additionally or alternatively, it may be possible to raise arguments based upon the right to freedom of expression guaranteed by Article 10 of the Convention. A further limitation on the existing interpretation of the legislation is that individual union members probably have little or no authority to act on behalf of the union in any dealings with the employer. In *Chant v Aquaboats Ltd*[13] a union member who organised a petition complaining about safety standards in the workplace was found not to have been taking part in the activities 'of the union' in presenting it to the employer, despite the fact that a union official had approved the petition before it was presented; this did not make it a communication of the union given that Mr. Chant was not a shop steward and the petition had been signed by a majority of workers who were not union members. By contrast, union representatives, such as shop stewards, would seem to be 'authorised' to perform a wider range of activities such as taking up members' grievances with management, calling meetings of the workforce[14] and any other activities normally carried out by officials of their grade, provided that they act in accordance with union practice.[15] In their case, therefore, there may be less need to pray in aid the Human Rights Act 1998 unless they do not fall within the category of an employee.[16]

---

1. TULRCA 1992, s 152(1)(b). See paras **2.6** and **2.7** for the definition of an 'independent trade union'. Where the employee is dismissed for proposing to take part in union activities there is no requirement to identify the precise activities: see *Fitzpatrick v British Railways Board* [1991] IRLR 376, CA.

2. See *Luce v London Borough of Bexley* [1990] IRLR 422, EAT, discussed at para **3.32**.

3. *Britool Ltd v Roberts* [1993] IRLR 481, EAT.

4. *Drew v St Edmundsbury Borough Council* [1980] IRLR 459, EAT. See para **6.92** *et seq.* for the relationship between unfair dismissal and industrial action.

5. See, for example, Davies and Freedland, 1984, 191.

6. The strength of this argument may be undermined by the creation of protection against dismissal for taking 'protected industrial action' (see para **6.98** *et seq.*), which could be seen as demonstrating the intention of the legislature that protection against dismissal should be confined to participation only in a restricted form of industrial action.

7. See, for example, *Chant v Aquaboats Ltd* [1978] ICR 643, EAT. See also *Dixon and Shaw v West Ella Developments Ltd* [1978] IRLR 151, EAT, Phillips J at 153 ('trade union' is not 'adjectival').

8. *Lyon v St. James Press* [1976] IRLR 215, EAT. It is irrelevant that these activities are not disclosed to the management. The qualification in this case that 'wholly unreasonable, extraneous or malicious acts' done in support of union activities may not be protected is hard to justify. See, however, the dictum of Pill LJ in *Bass Taverns Ltd v Burgess* [1995] IRLR 596 at 599, where he opined that malicious, untruthful or irrelevant statements at a union recruitment meeting may not fall within the scope of union activities.

9. *Rasool v Hepworth Pipe Co Ltd (No 2)* [1980] IRLR 137, EAT; *British Airways Engine Overhaul Ltd v Francis* [1981] IRLR 9, EAT.

10. *Zucker v Astrid Jewels Ltd* [1978] IRLR 385, EAT.

11. *Brennan and Ging v Ellward (Lancs) Ltd* [1976] IRLR 378, EAT; *Dixon and Shaw v West Ella Developments Ltd*, above, note 7.

12. *Dixon and Shaw v West Ella Developments Ltd*, above, note 7.

13. Above, note 7.

14. Regardless of whether they are critical of more senior officials: *British Airways Engine Overhaul Ltd v Francis*, above note 9.

15. See, for example, *British Airways Engine Overhaul Ltd v Francis*, above note 9; *Marley Tile Co Ltd v Shaw* [1980] IRLR 25, CA.

16. See further para **3.3**. It seems likely that the constraint that the activities be conducted at an 'appropriate time' could be justified under Articles 10(2) and 11(2) as necessary to protect the rights of others (ie the employer): see further para **1.8**.

3.7 As well as differentiating between activities of individual trade unionists and those 'of the union', the courts have also, from the opposite perspective, distinguished between an employer's reactions to an individual employee's activities in a union context and those of a union. In *Therm-A-Stor Ltd v Atkins and Carrington*[1] between 60 and 65 of the company's 70 employees had joined a union, and representatives of those employees asked the union's district secretary to apply to the company for recognition. The company then instructed its chargehands to select 20 employees for dismissal. The employment tribunal found that, although the employers were strongly anti-union and the dismissals were in reaction to the union's letter seeking recognition, the chargehands had not taken account of the actual or proposed union membership or participation in union activities of the employees concerned, and that therefore those employees could not show that this was the reason for their dismissal. The EAT allowed the appeal, but was in turn reversed by the Court of Appeal, which held that the reason for dismissal was not related to anything which the employees personally had done. This interpretation can be criticised as failing to take adequate account of the fact that the union was acting on behalf, and at the request, of individual members. As we discuss in para **4.57** *et seq.*, workers (not just employees) have protection against dismissal or selection for redundancy (or subjection to other detriment) for specified acts relating to the newly-introduced statutory recognition (and derecognition) procedures, including acting with a view to obtaining or preventing recognition or indicating support for recognition.[2] Given that it is government policy to encourage unions and employers to reach voluntary recognition agreements outside this procedure, it is unfortunate that these protections were not extended to the situation where no request for recognition has been made pursuant to the statute.[3] However, an argument in support of such protection may be derived from the Human Rights Act 1998. Article 11 of the ECHR recognises that individuals join trade unions for the protection of their interests. Dismissing those who have sought to obtain recognition for their union (one way in which their union may be 'heard') can be seen as inhibiting the exercise of the right to pursue those interests in the way in which they think best, even though there is no substantive right to have their union recognised. Given that this argument starts from the perspective of the individual rather than of the union, it may be more successfully located in the context of dismissal on the ground of union membership than of union activity (see para **3.5** above). Where a 'public authority' (or at least a 'pure' public authority) interfered with the rights of its workers in this way, they could invoke this argument (and possibly an argument based upon interference with the right to freedom of expression, depending upon the circumstances) to pursue a free-standing claim against it.[4]

---

1. [1983] IRLR 78, CA.
2. TULRCA 1992, Sched A1, paras 156–165.
3. *Quaere* whether an employee who voiced support for voluntary recognition where it was official union policy to seek it could be regarded as 'authorised' by the union.
4. See further paras **1.16** and **1.17**.

3.8 The statutory protection extends only to activities which are carried out at an 'appropriate time', which means a time which is outside the employee's working hours or a time within his or her working hours at which, in accordance with arrangements agreed with or consent given by the employer, participation in the activities of a union is permissible.[1] 'Working hours', in relation to an employee, means any time when, in accordance with his or her contract of employment, he or she is required to be 'at work,[2] and 'at work' has been held to mean when actually working.[3] This means that no permission is required for union activities during recognised breaks or before or after the working day, even if the employee is paid for those times. The House of Lords has inferred from this an entitlement for employees to take part in union activities on the employers' premises, using facilities normally available to the employer's workers, provided that this does not require the employer to incur expense or cause substantial inconvenience either to it or to fellow workers who are not union members.[4] In this respect employers 'must tolerate minor infringements of their strict legal rights which do them no real harm'.[5] Whether activities do cause 'substantial inconvenience' will be a question of fact; thus, a union meeting in the staff canteen at lunchtime may be permissible if all, or a significant majority, of staff are union members but not if only a minority are.[6] Consent to union activities during working hours may be express (an agreement to hold union meetings during working hours, for example)[7] or implied from the circumstances, although consent cannot be implied purely from an employer's silence when the intention to conduct the activity is announced.[8] The principle of implied consent was invoked to mean that employees who were permitted to converse with fellow employees while working could discuss union, as well as other, matters.[9] In relation to union representatives, once an employer has accepted the appointment of an employee as such, or if it is custom and practice for a union to nominate a representative for a particular workgroup, the employer's consent to the employee carrying out the duties of a representative during working hours will probably be implied[10] unless there is an express agreement which limits this.[11] The activities referred to are those in the employment from which the employee has been dismissed.[12] However, this does not necessarily mean that activities in a previous employment are irrelevant if a sufficient link with the current employment can be shown. In *Fitzpatrick v British Railways Board* the Court of Appeal recognised that if 'an employer, having learnt of an employee's previous trade union activities, decides that he wishes to dismiss that employee, that is likely to be a situation where almost inevitably the employer is dismissing . . . because he feels that the employee will indulge in industrial activities of a trade union nature in his current employment'.[13] When the only 'rational explanation' for dismissal is the employer's fear that the employee will 'repeat those . . . activities in [his or] her employment with them' the dismissal will be a breach of the protection.[14] However, if an employee obtains employment by deceit and such deceit was the principal reason for dismissal, then even though the deceit relates to previous union activities he or she will then be outside the scope of the protection.[15] This approach invites employers to frame their reasons for dismissal with care. However, it is submitted that this may depend upon the nature of the deceit. It may conceivably be possible to argue, on the basis of the Human Rights Act 1998, that prospective employees have no obligation to admit to previous union activity if questioned prior to their appointment where this is likely to lead to the employer failing to offer them a job on the ground that this would constitute an interference with their freedom of association or right to respect for private life.[16] However, this is subject to the difficulty that the current jurisprudence of the ECHR does not regard denial of employment as an 'interference' with the exercise of a Convention right, although, for reasons we explain in Chapter 1, we consider that this approach is indefensible.

---

1. TULRCA 1992, s 152(2).
2. *Ibid.*
3. *Post Office v Union of Post Office Workers* [1974] ICR 378, HL (decided under the equivalent provisions of the Industrial Relations Act 1971).
4. *Ibid.*, applied in *Zucker v Astrid Jewels Ltd* [1978] IRLR 385, EAT.
5. *Post Office v Union of Post Office Workers*, Lord Reid at 400. It is unlikely that this principle is open to challenge under the HRA 1998 as interfering with the peaceful enjoyment of possessions under Article 1 of Protocol 1 of the ECHR: see further para **4.63**.

6. Cf, for example, the employment tribunal decision in *Carter v Wiltshire County Council* [1979] IRLR 331 (meeting in a social club where all but one employee a union member).

7. In *Bass Taverns v Burgess* [1995] IRLR 596 the Court of Appeal rejected the suggestion that the employer's consent to the applicant addressing trainee managers to recruit them to the union was subject to the implied limitation that he would not use the occasion to criticise the company. Pill LJ emphasised (at 598) that a consent to recruit 'must include a consent to underline the services which the union can provide. That may reasonably involve a submission to prospective members that in some respects the union will provide a service which the company does not'.

8. *Marley Tile Co Ltd v Shaw* [1980] IRLR 25, CA.

9. *Zucker v Astrid Jewels Ltd*, above note 4.

10. See *Marley Tile Co Ltd v Shaw*, above, note 8.

11. Cf. *Robb v Leon Motor Services Ltd* [1978] ICR 506, EAT (an agreement that the employee could take part in union activities at an 'appropriate time' added nothing to the position where the union was not recognised).

12. *Fitzpatrick v British Railways Board* [1991] IRLR 376, CA.

13. Woolf LJ at 379.

14. *Ibid.* Cf *Port of London Authority v Payne* [1992] IRLR 447, EAT, where the court preferred to rest its conclusion that the reason for selecting the applicants for redundancy was 'past activities' (in their existing employment) rather than 'anticipated future activities', thus avoiding difficult speculation (at 460).

15. *Fitzpatrick v British Railways Board* above, note 12, affirming this aspect of *City of Birmingham District Council v Beyer* [1977] IRLR 211.

16. In *NATFHE v UK* App No 28910/95, the EComHR acknowledged that there may be circumstances where requiring an association to reveal the names of its members to a third party could constitute an unjustified interference with freedom of association. It is submitted that requiring an individual to reveal his or her associations may also be incompatible with Article 11, in addition to constituting an interference with the right to respect for private life under Article 8. If regulations are issued under ERA 1999, s 3, which relates to blacklisting, a greater measure of protection may be afforded to employees in this position: see further para **3.16**.

Remedies

3.9 Detailed consideration of the remedies for unfair dismissal claims lies beyond the scope of this work.[1] In this context we merely highlight the distinctive features of the remedies applicable to dismissals on anti-union grounds (which also apply to dismissals for certain other reasons). First, the dismissed employee may apply for interim relief pending the outcome of the employment tribunal hearing,[2] provided that the application is presented to the tribunal before the end of the period of seven days immediately following the effective date of termination[3] and is supported by a certificate signed by an official of the union authorised to act for this purpose.[4] If a tribunal finds that the employee's claim is 'likely'[5] to succeed at the full hearing, it may order his or her reinstatement or re-engagement pending the determination or settlement of the complaint or, if the employer refuses this, order the continuation of the contract, thus continuing the other benefits of employment until that time.[6] This provision reduces the need for the employee to seek other employment pending the tribunal hearing. Secondly, if the unfair dismissal complaint succeeds a minimum basic award of £3,100 is payable.[7] Prior to the Employment Relations Act 1999, a complainant who sought reinstatement or re-engagement[8] was also entitled to a special award in addition to the basic and compensatory awards. This has now been abolished and in all cases where employers fail to comply with an order to reinstate or re-engage an unfairly dismissed employee an additional award of 26–52 weeks' pay may be awarded unless the employer shows that it was not practicable to comply with the order.[9]

---

1. Note that in deciding whether it would be just and equitable to reduce any part of the award the tribunal must disregard the fact that the employee is in breach of a requirement under the contract or any other agreement not to join a union (or a particular union) or take part in the activities of a union: see TULRCA 1992, s 155. In *TGWU v Howard* [1992] IRLR 170, EAT, a case concerning non-membership, the court distinguished between that which was done by the complainant and the way it was done. 'If the conduct of an employee prior to dismissal deserves to be criticised, the power of reduction is there, but the immediate circumstances giving rise to the finding of the principal reason for dismissal are to be excluded' (at 172).

2. TULRCA 1992, ss 161–166. Note that this right does not apply to selection for redundancy on union grounds.

3. See TULRCA 1992, s 298; ERA 1996, s 97.

4. TULRCA 1992, s 161. 'Official' is defined in s 119: see para **3.27**, note 1; and on authorisation see further *Sulemany v Habib Bank Ltd* [1983] ICR 60, EAT. For the required content of the certificate, see s 161(3) and *Barley v Amey Roadstone Corpn Ltd* [1977] IRLR 299, EAT; *Stone v Charrington and Co Ltd* [1977] ICR 248, EAT; *Bradley v Edward Ryde and Sons* [1979] ICR 488, EAT; *Sulemany v Habib Bank Ltd, above.*

5. 'Likely' means a 'pretty good' chance: *Taplin v C Shippam Ltd* [1978] 1RLR 450, EAT.

6. *Quaere* whether, if a shop steward had a contractual right to be on the premises to exercise his or her functions (see *City and Hackney Health Authority v NUPE* [1985] IRLR 252, CA) this would be covered by TULRCA 1992, s 164(1), which includes 'any . . . benefit derived from the employment . . .'. In practice such circumstances are likely to be rare.

7. TULRCA 1992, s 156; rate as of 1 February 2000. This also applies if an employee has been selected for redundancy on trade union grounds under TULRCA 1992, s 153. However, the award may be reduced on the same ground as in other cases subject to s 156(2) in cases of unfair selection for redundancy.

8. See generally TULRCA 1992, s167; ERA 1996, ss 112–116.

9. ERA 1996, s 117. A 'week's pay' is subject to the statutory maximum of £230 (rate as of I February 2000). In *Port of London Authority v Payne* [1994] IRLR 9, the Court of Appeal emphasised that whilst a tribunal should 'carefully scrutinise' the employer's reasons for failing to comply, it should give 'due weight to the commercial judgment of the management' and the standard should not be set too high: Neill LJ at 16.

Protection Against Subjection to a Detriment Short of Dismissal on Grounds of Trade Union Membership and Activities

Entitlement and the scope of protection

3.10 An employee has the right not to be subjected to any detriment short of dismissal as an individual by any act, or any deliberate failure to act, by his or her employer if the act or failure takes place for the purpose of preventing or deterring him or her from joining, or participating in the activities of, an independent trade union at an appropriate time, or penalising him or her for doing so.[1] In terms of the activities protected, this right parallels the protection afforded against dismissal (with one significant exception, discussed in para **3.12**). Thus, it is unlawful to take action against an employee for joining one union rather than another, for example, and in relation to participation in the 'activities' of a union identical criteria must be satisfied.[2] Once again protection is currently afforded only to employees, and the same groups are excluded from its scope.[3] There is no minimum period of employment required to claim, nor does a maximum age limit apply. Prior to the Employment Relations Act 1999, protection had been afforded against 'action short of dismissal'. The practical effect of this protection had been rendered almost nugatory by the House of Lords decision in *Associated Newspapers Ltd v Wilson; Associated Newspapers v Palmer*[4] that, having regard to the legislative history of this provision, 'action' did not include omissions in this context. The Employment Relations Act 1999 overruled that aspect of that decision in making clear that protection is afforded against both acts and 'deliberate' failures to act; thus a 'deliberate' failure to promote an employee or failure to award a pay rise, for example, would be covered. However, the meaning of 'deliberate' in this context is obscure. A government spokesman indicated that it covered both 'conscious and unconscious failures';[5] if this is right, the term would seem to have little meaning. The notion of subjection to a 'detriment' has been interpreted by the courts in the context of the anti-discrimination legislation,[6] and it is likely that case law deriving from that context will be regarded as heavily persuasive in this. In an early decision on the sex discrimination legislation, the EAT held that a 'detriment' meant something 'serious or important'.[7] However in *Ministry of Defence v Jeremiah* there were indications of a more expansive approach; Brandon LJ considered that it simply meant 'putting under a disadvantage', Brightman LJ thought that a detriment exists if 'a reasonable worker would or might take the view that . . . [a] duty was in all the circumstances to his [or her] detriment'.[8] It was also made clear in that case that it is irrelevant that the complainant receives any financial compensation for the 'detriment'. Transfer to less interesting, responsible and varied work has been held to constitute a detriment.[9] It is unclear whether employees who are threatened with deleterious consequences—for example, dismissal or other disciplinary measures or a promotion block—unless they cease their union activities would be regarded as subjected to a detriment.[10] We would argue strongly that they should be. First, threats of this nature have a serious psychological impact which we submit constitutes a detriment in itself.[11] Secondly, the Human Rights Act 1998, which requires courts and tribunals to read and give effect to legislation in a way which is compatible with the Convention rights, would also argue in favour of such an interpretation.[12] The ECtHR has held in the context of the closed shop that the threat of dismissal involving loss of livelihood is a 'most serious form of compulsion',[13] and it is submitted that the jurisprudence of the Court supports the view that the threat of other forms of disciplinary action should also constitute in itself an interference with the exercise of Convention rights, including the right to join a trade union and the right to freedom of expression.[14]

---

1. TULRCA 1992, s 146(1),(2),(6). Note that this section has been amended by the Employment Relations Act 1999. The definition of 'dismissal' in ERA 1996 (see s 95) applies in this context: TULRCA 1992, s 298. Thus a decision not to renew a fixed-term contract could not be challenged under this provision: *Johnstone v BBC Enterprises Ltd* (22 April 1993, unreported), EAT.
2. See paras **3.5–3.8**.
3. See para **3.3**.
4. [1995] IRLR 258, HL. This was despite the fact that the definition section of the relevant statute (then the Employment Protection (Consolidation) Act 1978) stated that in that Act, except so far as the context otherwise required, 'action' included

'omission'. Their Lordships' opinions were based on a comparison of the comprehensive provisions of the Industrial Relations Act 1971 with those enacted by the Labour Government in 1974.

5. Mr. Michael Wills, Minister for Small Firms, Trade and Industry, Official Report of Standing Committee E, 18 March 1999, 2.30 pm. (refusing an amendment to replace 'deliberate' with 'wilful').

6. SDA 1975, s 6(2)(b); RRA 1976, s 4(2)(b).

7. *Schmidt v Austicks Bookshops Ltd* [1978] ICR 85, EAT.

8. *Ministry of Defence v Jeremiah* [1979] IRLR 436 at 438 and 330 respectively.

9. *Kirby v Manpower Services Commission* [1980] ICR 420, EAT, at 428–429.

10. The EAT had suggested that 'action short of dismissal' could cover threats in *Grogan v British Railways Board*, 19 January 1978, unreported.

11. Support for this view is provided by *Gloucester Working Men's Club and Institute v James* [1986] ICR 603, EAT, at 606.

12. HRA 1998, s 3; see further para **1.14**.

13. *Young, James and Webster v UK* judgment of 13 August 1981, (1982) 4 EHRR 38, para 55.

14. *Dudgeon v UK* judgment of 22 October 1981, (1982) 4 EHRR 149, paras 40, 41; *Ahmed v UK* judgment of 2 September 1998, [1999] IRLR 188.

3.11 The employee must be subjected to a detriment 'as an individual'. This means that the protection cannot be used as a method for unions to claim collective rights; adverse action taken against a union is not, by reason only of the consequential effect it may have on members or officers of the union, to be treated as subjecting individual employees to a detriment.[1] Non-recognition of his or her union by the employer, for example, would not be seen as a detriment to the employee as an individual. By contrast, action against members of a particular union as a group could be protected provided that it affected them as individuals, for example by failing to award them a pay increase agreed with another union (although see now **3.12** below).[2] The Court of Appeal has recently affirmed that the legislation is not confined to the protection of an employee in his or her capacity as such; thus, the derecognition of an employee as a shop steward could constitute action against him 'as an individual', although it was open to the employers to establish that they had taken the action in order to remove an unsuitable individual from that role rather than to prevent or deter him from taking part in union activities.[3] This emphasises another aspect of the protection, which is that the employer's act or failure to act must have taken place for the purpose of preventing or deterring union membership or activities. It is for the employer to show the purpose for which it acted or failed to act,[4] but it remains for the employee to show that this purpose was unlawful. In certain situations, such as a failure to promote, disclosure of information concerning other employees may be important and, if necessary, further particulars and disclosure of documents can be sought from the employment tribunal.[5] However, even if such information is available the employee may face considerable difficulty in the light of the restrictive judicial approach to the interpretation of 'purpose' exemplified by the Court of Appeal decision in *Gallacher v Department of Transport*.[6] In this case a promotions board had recommended that the employee should not be promoted because it was four years since he had held an official job and doubts about his managerial ability and attitude remained. His career development officer advised him that to achieve promotion he would need to acquire more line management experience. This would necessitate him reducing his union activities (which took up 80 per cent to 100 per cent of his time). The tribunal held that these comments were intended to deter the employee from continuing with his union activities. The EAT and Court of Appeal upheld the employer's appeal, the Court of Appeal on the basis that the recommendation was not made 'for the purpose of' deterring him from continuing with his union activities, even if this was its likely effect. Neill LJ averred that 'purpose' denoted an object which the employer desired or sought to achieve which was, on these facts, ensuring that only those with sufficient managerial experience and skill were promoted. In *Associated Newspapers v Wilson; Associated British Ports v Palmer*[7] the House of Lords confirmed that the fact that union membership may become less attractive as a result of an employer's act did not thereby mean that deterring union membership became its purpose. In those cases the employers had each refused a pay increase to employees who refused to transfer to personal contracts, although in *Associated British Ports* the employees had the option of continuing to be represented by the union if they did not transfer. In neither case was the employer found to have been acting with the purpose of deterring union membership. In the case of *Associated Newspapers* the purpose of withholding the pay increase was to encourage as many members as possible to sign up to the new contracts, so obviating any uncertainty or confusion arising out of the termination of collective bargaining and to smooth the transition from the house agreement to the handbook.[8] Even if this was incorrect, there was no evidence that the employer's ultimate purpose was to deter individuals from union membership.[9] In *Associated British Ports* the employer's purpose was to encourage greater flexibility; the fact that if sufficient members opted for personal contracts this might mean that the influence of the union would diminish and membership thereby become less attractive was irrelevant.[10]

---

1. *Ridgway and Fairbrother v National Coal Board* [1987] IRLR 80, CA: these and other cases relate to 'action short of dismissal' prior to the ERA 1999 amendment but the points made remain valid. Cf the Industrial Relations Act 1971, where there was no such limitation, considered by the House of Lords in *Post Office v UPOW* [1974] ICR 378.
2. *Ridgway and Fairbrother v National Coal Board*, above (payment of wage increase to members of the Union of Democratic Mineworkers but not the National Union of

Mineworkers). In *Howle v GEC Power Engineering Ltd* [1974] ICR 13, NIRC, decided under the differently worded Industrial Relations Act 1971, the argument that refusing to allow members of a particular union, unlike members of other unions, to be represented in grievance and disciplinary proceedings should be regarded as discriminating against them rather than as granting different negotiating rights was upheld; (although see now ERA 1999, ss 10–13); see also *Cheall v Vauxhall Motors Ltd* [1979] IRLR 253, where an employment tribunal held that the employers had penalised the employee for being a member of a particular union in not allowing him to be represented in discussions over a shift allowance. It may now be possible to argue that representation is an incident of union membership: see para **3.5** above.

3. *FW Farnsworth Ltd v McCoid* [1999] IRLR 626, CA.

4. TULRCA 1992, s 148(1). No account is to be taken of any pressure exercised on the employer to act or fail to act by calling, organising, procuring or financing industrial action or threatening to do so: s 148(2).

5. Employment Tribunals (Constitution and Rules of Procedure) Regulations 1993, SI 1993/2687 Sched 1, para 4. Note that there is no equivalent under TULRCA 1992 to the Sex Discrimination (Questions and Replies) Order 1975, SI 1975/2048 or similar provisions in the areas of race and disability discrimination.

6. [1994] IRLR 231, CA. See also *Marshall v The Hampshire Probation Service* EAT/1440/98, 29 September 1999 where the distinction was also made between purpose and effect.

7. [1995] IRLR 258, HL; see Lord Lloyd at 267.

8. *Ibid.*, Lord Lloyd at 266. His judgment on this point was approved by Lord Bridge (at 264) and Lord Keith (at 260).

9. *Ibid.*, Lord Lloyd at 266.

10. *Ibid.*

3.12 The decision in *Associated Newspapers v Wilson; Associated British Ports v Palmer* outlined in para **3.11** above was of crucial importance to employers who wished to encourage employees to transfer to personal contracts.[1] The Employment Relations Act 1999 has preserved the distinction between discrimination on grounds of union membership and collective bargaining carved out by that decision (although, as discussed below, it allows the Secretary of State to make specific, but limited, provision to protect workers against dismissal or other detriment for refusing to transfer from an existing collective agreement). In preserving the distinction between union membership and collective bargaining, the government decided to retain in its essentials the notorious 'Ullswater' amendment, introduced as a late amendment to the Trade Union Reform and Employment Rights Act 1993 in response to the Court of Appeal decision in *Associated Newspapers* which had held that the purpose of the respective employers was to penalise or deter union membership.[2] It was designed to ensure that employers may 'offer . . . [employees] an additional pay increase if they will negotiate on an individual basis',[3] but its consequences are more far-reaching. In its amended form it provides that in determining the employer's purpose for its act or failure to act, where (a) there is evidence that the employer's purpose was to further a change in its relationship with all or any class of its employees, and (b) there is also evidence that its purpose was one falling within s 146, (ie to prevent or deter union membership) the employment tribunal must regard the purpose mentioned in paragraph (a) (not the purpose mentioned in paragraph (b)) as the purpose for which the employer acted or failed to act, unless it considers that no reasonable employer would act or fail to act in the way concerned.[4] This means that *any* evidence of purpose (a), regardless of its weight, must be regarded by the tribunal as *the* purpose of the employer's act or failure, even if the predominant, or only real, purpose is clearly to penalise those retaining union membership, unless the tribunal considers that no reasonable employer would act or fail to act in the way concerned, a generous band which it is difficult to envisage an employer exceeding. 'Class' for the purposes of paragraph (a) means 'those employed at a particular place of work, those employees of a particular grade, category or description or those of a particular grade, category or description employed at a particular place of work'.[5] This prevents employers invoking paragraph (a) where the change relates only to a specific individual (unless he or she is the sole member of the 'class'), but it does not limit the criteria according to which the class is formulated; thus, it may consist of members of a particular union who are offered an inducement to accept personal contracts or those based upon negotiations with a different union.[6] The Labour Government justified the retention of this provision, despite opposing it in opposition, on the basis that there may be 'circumstances where employers seek, quite legitimately, to change their bargaining arrangements, for example, following voluntary or statutory derecognition or where the bargaining unit has changed'.[7] However it is unclear why separate provision could not have been made for this eventuality. It is notable that the change in relationship in paragraph (a) is not restricted in its nature, and could cover, for example, the introduction of new appraisal systems or new methods of organising work. It need not be shown that the employer's act or failure will, in fact, produce a change— it is sufficient that its purpose is to further such a change—nor need the change it is sought to further be 'lawful', although employers will need to consider the contractual implications of their actions.[8] Finally, it is provided that where the tribunal determines that the complainant has been subjected to a detriment by an act or failure to act which took place in consequence of a previous act or deliberate failure to act by the employer, paragraph (a) is satisfied 'if the purpose mentioned in that paragraph was the purpose of the previous act or failure'.[9] This provision was inserted to cover the situation where, for example, the employer offered a pay increase to employees who agreed to abandon a contractual right to collective representation by a specified date, and then found that few accepted the offer so decided not to introduce the change but nevertheless gave the increase to those who had indicated their acceptance: there the employer's purpose in not paying the increase to other employees would be to implement the offer rather than to further any change at that time, but nevertheless it will be brought within the scope of paragraph (a).[10] There is no specified period after which 'previous' action may not be relied upon for this purpose. As we indicate earlier in this paragraph, the Employment Relations Act 1999 empowers (but does not require) the Secretary of State to issue regulations protecting workers who refuse to enter into a contract which includes terms which differ from the terms of a collective agreement which applies to him.[11] At the time of writing no regulations have been issued, but we analyse the broad scope of this provision in para **4.72**. For the reasons we set out in that paragraph, the protection which workers may be afforded pursuant to that provision is limited, and even if regulations are eventually issued employers will still be able to discriminate against trade unionists in the circumstances set out in s 148(3) unless their conduct is expressly prohibited by the regulations.

---

1. At the time of writing this decision is the subject of applications to the ECtHR: *Wilson, Palmer and Doolan v UK* Apps 30668/96, 30671/96, 30678/96; the applications were deemed admissible in September 1997. See Ewing, 2000 for a concise history of the case.

2. [1993] IRLR 336, CA.

3. Mr David Hunt, Secretary of State for Employment, HC Debs, Vol 226, col 742, 15 June 1993.

4. TULRCA 1992, s 148(3).

5. *Ibid.*, s 148(5).

6. Viscount Ullswater, HL Debs, Vol 546, col 96, 24 May 1993.

7. Lord McIntosh of Haringey, Deputy Chief Whip, HL Debs Vol 601 , col 1287, 7 June 1999. The Ullswater amendment was condemned both by the ILO (294th Report of the Freedom of Association Committee, paras 192–203; 304th Report para 498; 309th Report, para 342. See also Novitz 2000, 389–393) and the ECSR (formerly the CIE) which supervises the ESC: Conclusions XIII–3, 108–109; see also Conclusions XIV–1. The ILO Committee of Experts on the Application of Conventions and Recommendations has concluded that the 1999 amendments do not prevent TULCRA 1992, s 148(3)–(5) as being tantamount to anti-union discrimination: Report of the Committee of Experts on the Application of Conventions and Recommendations Report III (Part 1A), 2000.

8. The Conservative Government rejected an amendment proposed by Lord Wedderburn, above, note 6, col 46, to require that the change should be effected by lawful means.

9. TULRCA 1992, s 148(4).

10. Viscount Ullswater, above, note 6, at 58.

11. ERA 1999, s 17.

Remedies

3.13 A claim that an employee has been subjected to a detriment on grounds of trade membership or activities must be presented to an employment tribunal before the end of the period of three months beginning with the date of the act or failure to which the complaint relates or, where that act or failure is part of a series of similar acts or failures, the last of them (or where the tribunal is satisfied that it was not reasonably practicable for the complaint to be presented before the end of that period, within such further period as it considers reasonable).[1] Where an act extends over a period, the 'date of the act' refers to the last date of that period.[2] A failure to act is treated as done when it was decided on.[3] In the absence of evidence to the contrary an employer is taken to have decided on a failure to act when it does an act inconsistent with doing the failed act, or, if no such inconsistent act was done, when the period expires when it might reasonably be expected to have done the failed act if it was to be done.[4] The commencement of the time limit from the date when the failure to act was 'decided on' may cause difficulty where the employer can show that it decided upon this course earlier than it might reasonably have been expected to do but that decision was not communicated to the worker. In that event, if the worker could not be expected to have known of the decision, the tribunal may be inclined to use its discretion to extend the time limit for complaining. Where a complaint is upheld, the tribunal must make a declaration to that effect,[5] and may also award compensation, having regard not only to the loss sustained by the employee that is attributable to the act or failure,[6] but also the infringement of the employee's rights,[7] which may include non-pecuniary loss.[8] Unlike the remedies for dismissal, there is no statutory limit on the amount of compensation. The complainant has a duty to mitigate his or her loss,[9] and compensation may be reduced as is considered just and equitable if the tribunal finds that the employee caused or contributed to the act or failure.[10] The tribunal has no power formally to recommend cessation of the unlawful treatment.[11]

---

1. TULRCA 1992, s 147(1). Complaint to an employment tribunal is the exclusive remedy for breach of these provisions: s 151(2). On the circumstances where a tribunal may extend the time limit, see App 2. In *Adlam v Salisbury and Wells Theological College* [1985] ICR 786, the EAT held (under the provisions relating to 'action short of dismissal': see para **3.10**) the date on which an agreement paying the applicants less than other workers was implemented was the date of the 'action', and that each subsequent weekly payment was a continuation of that action and not a 'series of similar actions'; see also *British Airways Board v Clark and Havill* [1982] IRLR 238, EAT, relating to disciplinary proceedings.

2. TULRCA 1992, s 147(2)(a).

3. *Ibid.*, s 147(2)(b).

4. *Ibid.*, s 147(3).

5. *Ibid.*, s 149(1).

6. 'Loss' includes any expenses reasonably incurred by the complainant in consequence of the act or failure complained of and loss of any benefit which he or she might reasonably be expected to have had but for that act or failure: *ibid.*, s 149(3).

7. *Ibid.*, s 149(2)

8. *Brassington v Cauldon Wholesale Ltd* [1978] ICR 405, EAT. Non-pecuniary loss may include, for example, injury to health or frustration of a 'deep and sincere wish to join a union': *ibid.* See also *Ridgway and Fairbrother v National Coal Board* [1987] IRLR 80, CA, and *Cleveland Ambulance NHS Trust v Blane* [1997] IRLR 332, EAT.

9. TULRCA 1992, s 149(4).

10 *Ibid.*, s 149(6).

11 Cf the remedies for sex discrimination (SDA 1975, s 65(1)(c)), race discrimination (RRA 1976, s 56(1)(c)) and disability discrimination (DDA 1995, s 8(2)(c)), and for refusal of employment on grounds of union membership (para **3.15**).

Refusal of Access to Employment

The scope of protection

3.14 It is unlawful to refuse a person employment under a contract of service or apprenticeship because he or she is a member of a trade union or of a particular trade union, or because he or she is unwilling to accept a requirement to cease membership of, or not to join, a union.[1] It is also unlawful for an employment agency to refuse a person any of its services for such a reason.[2] Unlike the protection against dismissal and protection to a detriment, there is no requirement that the union should be 'independent', although breaches of the legislation are more likely to occur where it is.[3] 'Refusal' goes beyond not offering a job; it also extends to refusing or deliberately omitting to entertain and process an application or enquiry (for example failing to respond to telephone calls); causing an individual to withdraw or cease to pursue an application or enquiry (for example saying that there are no vacancies); offering the employment on terms which are such that no reasonable employer who wished to fill the post would offer and which the applicant does not accept (a test which, contemptuous offers apart, may be difficult to satisfy); and withdrawing or causing the individual not to accept an offer previously made.[4] Where employment is offered on condition that the applicant is not a union member, or leaves or agrees not to join a union, and the applicant does not accept the offer because he or she is unwilling to accept that requirement, this is treated as a refusal of employment for that reason.[5] An applicant who did agree to accept such a requirement but, once in employment, contravened it would be protected against dismissal or action short of dismissal, notwithstanding any contractual term, provided that the union he or she joined was independent.[6] It is notable that the protection against refusal of employment extends only to union membership, not to union activities. This was a deliberate decision by the Conservative Government which introduced the protection, on the ground that employers were entitled to protect themselves against 'troublemaker[s]'.[7] This makes the scope of union 'membership' in this context particularly crucial. In para **3.5** we argued for a broad interpretation of this concept, particularly in the light of the Human Rights Act 1998. In that paragraph we focussed on the position of the ordinary union member, given that the position of those participating in union activities is dealt with separately for the purposes of dismissal and action short of dismissal. However it may be possible to argue, on the basis of the ECHR, that a more expansive interpretation still should be accorded in order to protect those who have acted in capacities beyond that of the ordinary member. In *X v Ireland*[8] the EComHR considered that threats of dismissal or other actions intended to make an employee relinquish the office of shop steward could, in certain circumstances, seriously restrict or impede the lawful exercise of freedom of association under Article 11. Moreover, the ECtHR has held that participation in the activities of a political party, including holding party office, may violate Article 10, which guarantees freedom of expression, as well as Article 11.[9] It is conceivable that domestic courts and employment tribunals could be persuaded to interpret 'membership' in the light of these decisions. Alternatively, if the discriminatory employer is a 'public authority' (or at least if it is a 'pure' public authority)[10] an individual may have a free-standing right of action, although this would depend upon acceptance of the arguments which we propound in Chapter 1 that denial of employment should constitute an 'interference' with a Convention right (contrary to the current jurisprudence of the Court).[11] In the light of the power accorded to the Secretary of State in the Employment Relations Act 1999 to issue regulations prohibiting 'blacklisting' of persons who have taken part in the activities of unions, as well as union members (see para **3.16**), it is particularly anomalous that the statutory prohibition on discriminatory hiring continues to be confined to union membership.[12]

---

1. TULRCA 1992, ss 137(1), 143, 295. Membership of a particular branch or section of a trade union is also covered: s 143(3). See para **2.4** for the meaning of 'trade union'. As in the case of dismissal and action short of dismissal, the police and the armed forces are excluded from this right (ss 274, 280), as are those who would ordinarily work outside Great Britain: see further para **3.3**, note 6. However, ETA 1996, s 10(1) does not apply to s 137, nor does its predecessor: see para **3.3** note 9.

2. *Ibid.*, s 138. An 'employment agency' means a person who, for profit or not, provides services for the purpose of finding employment for workers or supplying employers with workers: s 143(1). The definition of 'employment' (see ss 143, 295) means that services in relation to the self-employed are not covered. Services other than those mentioned in the definition are disregarded for the purposes of these provisions: s 143(2). Unions are not regarded as employment agencies by reason of services provided by them only for, or in relation to, their members: *ibid.* Where an employment agency is acting, or purporting to act, on behalf of an employer, it will be covered by s 137.

3. See paras **2.6** and **2.7** for the definition of an 'independent' trade union.

4. TULRCA 1992, s 137(5). s 138(4) defines refusal of service by an employment agency.

5. *Ibid.*, s 137(6).

6. See paras **3.2** *et seq.*; TULRCA 1992, s 288. This would also be the case if the appli-cant had agreed not to take part in union activities.

7. Mr Patrick Nicholls, Parliamentary Under-Secretary of State for Employment, House of Commons, Official Report of Standing Committee D, col 27, 8 February 1990. The protection was originally rooted in the government's desire to prevent the lawful operation of pre-entry closed shops, where only union members could be con-sidered for a job: see para **3.20** and *Removing Barriers to Employment*, Cm 655, 1989, Chapter 2. In *Harrison v Kent County Council* [1995] ICR 434 the EAT held that if a person was refused employment because he or she had been a union activist it would be open to a tribunal to find that this was because of union membership. This reason-ing cannot be reconciled with the House of Lords decision in *Associated Newspapers v Wilson*; *Associated British Ports v Palmer* [1995] IRLR 258; our argument for a wider construction is based upon the HRA 1998.

8. (1971) App. 4125/69.

9. *Vogt v Germany* judgment of 26 September 1995, (1996) 21 EHRR 205; see also *Ahmed v UK* judgment of 2 September 1998, [1999] IRLR 188.

10. See paras **1.16** and **1.17**.

11. See paras **1.10** and **1.11**.

12. Note that Article 1 of ILO Convention No 98 on the Right to Organise and Collective Bargaining requires protection against denial of access to employment on grounds of trade union activity.

Entitlement, procedure and remedies

3.15 A person who is unlawfully refused employment on grounds of trade union membership may complain to an employment tribunal.[1] The complaint must be presented to the tribunal before the end of a three month period beginning with the date of the conduct to which the complaint relates or within such further period as the tribunal considers 'reasonable' where it is satisfied that compliance with the time limit was not 'reasonably practicable'.[2] Where there is a right of complaint against both a prospective employer and an employment agency on the same facts, the complainant may present a complaint against either or both of them, with a right for either the complainant or the respondent to request joinder of the other prospective respondent as a party to the proceedings.[3] In addition, if either the complainant or respondent claims that the respondent was induced to act in the manner complained of by a union or other third party exer-cising pressure by calling, organising, procuring or financing a strike or other industrial action or threatening to do so, then either may request the tribunal to join that third party to the proceedings and where the tribunal upholds the com-plaint and awards the complainant compensation, it may order the third party to pay such part of the compensation as it considers just and equitable.[4] The bur-den of proving that employment was refused for an unlawful reason lies with the complainant, and discovery of information about successful candidates, if any, may be crucial, although there is no need to show that employment was offered to another person.[5] If an advertisement[6] is published which indicates, or might reasonably be understood as indicating, that the employment to which it relates is closed to those who do not satisfy the conditions relating to union membership (such as 'non-union members welcome') a person who does not satisfy any such condition and who seeks and is refused employment is conclusively presumed to have been refused employment for that reason.[7] This means that such a person will succeed in a complaint regardless of his or her suitability or otherwise for the job, although clear lack of suitability may affect the level of compensation awarded. In the absence of such (improbable) evidence, asking questions about union membership should be sufficient to raise a *prima facie* case that this was relevant to the refusal, although it may be displaced by evidence to the contrary, for example, that other members of the union are already employed by the employer. Where a complaint is upheld, the tribunal must make a declaration to that effect and may grant either or both of the following remedies as it considers just and equitable.[8] First, it may order the respondent to pay compensation, up to the limit on the compensatory award for unfair dismissal (at the time of writing, £50,000).[9] Compensation is to be assessed on the same basis as damages for breach of statutory duty and, as in the case of sex, race and disability discrimination, may include compensation for injury to feelings; awards made in those contexts give some guidance here.[10] Where it cannot be said that the complainant would have obtained the employment but for the unlawful discrimination, for example where he or she was one of several rejected applicants, the difficulty in assessing the loss does not mean that compensation will be purely nominal.[11] The second remedy open to the tribunal is to make a recommendation that the respondent takes, within a specified period, action to obviate or reduce the adverse effect on the complainant of any conduct to which the complaint relates, such as recommending that the employer consider the complainant for a job vacancy.[12] If the respondent fails without reasonable justification to comply with a recommendation, the tribunal may increase its award of compensation, subject to the overriding maximum limit or, if it has not made such an award, make one.[13]

---

1. TULRCA 1992, ss 137(2), 138(2). This is an exclusive remedy: s 143(4).
2. *Ibid.*, s 139(1). See App 2 for the meaning of not 'reasonably practicable'. The 'date' of the conduct to which the complaint relates depends upon its nature: for a refusal of employment, or withdrawal of an offer, it is the date of the refusal or withdrawal; for an omission to entertain the application or enquiry or to offer employment, the end of the period within which it was reasonable to expect the employer to act; for conduct causing the complainant to withdraw or cease to pursue the application or inquiry, the date of that conduct; and in any other case where an offer was made but not accepted,

the date on which it was made: s 139(2). In the context of the 'effective date of termination' in ERA 1996, s 97, it has been held that this date cannot be earlier than that on
which the complainant knows that he or she is being dismissed (*McMaster v
Manchester Airport plc* [1998] IRLR 112, EAT), and it is submitted that where the complaint is based upon refusal of employment the date should not be earlier than that on
which the complainant becomes aware of the refusal.

3. *Ibid.*, s 141(1), (2). The request for joinder must be granted if made before the hearing of the complaint begins but may be refused if made after that time. No request can
be made after the tribunal has reached its decision.

4. *Ibid.*, s 142. See note 3 above for the provisions governing the timing of a request
for joinder.

5. On provisions discovery of documents, see Employment Tribunals (Constitution
and Rules of Procedure) Regulations 1993, SI 1993/2687 Sched 1, para 4. Note that
there is no equivalent under TULRCA 1992 to the Sex Discrimination (Questions and
Replies) Order 1975, SI 1975/2048 or other such provisions in the areas of race and disability discrimination. For other points of comparison with the sex and race discrimination legislation, see Townsend-Smith, 1991. On a complaint by the TUC to the ILO
that British law and practice failed to meet the requirements of Article 1 of Convention
No 98 in relation to recruitment, the Committee of Experts concluded that workers
'faced many practical difficulties in proving the real nature of their . . . denial of
employment' and in this respect the UK did not comply with the Convention: Case
1618, 287th Report, paras 224–267.

6. 'Advertisement' includes every form of advertisement or notice, whether to the
public or not: TULRCA 1992, s 143(1).

7. *Ibid.*, ss 137(3), 138(3).

8. TULRCA 1992, s 140(1). Note that in contrast to the SDA 1975, RRA 1976, and
DDA 1995, which explicitly impose liability on employers for persons acting in the
course of employment (subject to a statutory defence) there is no mention of vicarious
liability in relation to this form of discrimination; the common law test would seem to
apply.

9. TULRCA 1992, s 140(4); ERA 1996, s 124(1), as amended by ERA 1999, s 34(4).

10. *Ibid.*, s 140(2).

11. See *Chaplin v Hicks* [1911] 2 KB 786, CA, where it was held that substantial damages could be claimed for loss of a contractual right to belong to a limited class of competitors for a prize; see also *Allied Maples Group Ltd v Simmons and Simmons (a firm)*
[1995] 4 All ER 907, CA.

12. TULRCA 1992, s 140(1)(b).

13. *Ibid.*, s 140(3).

Constraints on the Compilation or Disclosure of Information Relating to Trade Union Membership

3.16 We have discussed in paras **3.3** *et seq.* the protections afforded by legislation
to individuals who are subject to discrimination by employers on grounds of

trade union membership and activities. There are two new provisions which have the potential to combat discrimination at an institutional level, in that they, respectively, impose constraints on the compilation and dissemination of information relating to union membership and activities. First, the Employment Relations Act 1999 empowers the Secretary of State to make regulations prohibiting the compilation of lists which contain details of members of unions or persons who have taken part in the activities of unions with a view to their being used by employers or employment agencies for the purposes of discrimination in relation to recruitment or the treatment of workers.[1] Such regulations may prohibit both the use, and the sale or supply, of such lists. This is designed to outlaw the use of 'blacklists'.[2] The Secretary of State has a wide range of possible remedies at his or her disposal, including the creation of criminal offences punishable by fines (but not by imprisonment), compensatory remedies for individuals who have suffered loss as a result of blacklisting, and enforceable orders to require blacklisting organisations to stop disseminating lists. Interestingly, provision is made to enable unions to bring proceedings on behalf of their members in specified circumstances. At the time of writing no regulations in this area have yet been issued. The second statutory constraint concerns the dissemination of information. Whether an individual is a union member constitutes 'sensitive personal data' for the purposes of the Data Protection Act 1998, and can be disclosed to third parties only in a very limited range of circumstances.[3] It would seem, on the basis of these exceptions, that it would be unlawful for an employer to disclose information about an employee's union membership to any third party, such as a prospective new employer. The Data Protection Act 1998 refers only to whether an individual is a member of a trade union; it does not explicitly cover union activities. However it is submitted that in this context it would not be possible to disclose information about an individual's activities without thereby disclosing that he or she was a union member and thereby contravene the Act.

---

1. ERA 1999, s 3. 'List' includes any index or other set of items whether recorded electronically or by any other means. For further discussion of these provisions, see Ewing 1999, 284–286.

2. The most prominent 'blacklisting' organisation was the Economic League, established in 1919; this was reported to have gone into voluntary liquidation in 1993: Ewing, 1994, para 6.7. Its records were kept on manual files and so were not subject to the Data Protection Act 1984 (now repealed and replaced by the Data Protection Act 1998). See further Evidence by the TUC and the Economic League to the House of Commons Employment Committee Inquiry into Recruitment Practices: House of Commons, Session 1989–90, HC 409–i and iii; Hollingsworth and Tremayne, 1989.

3 Data Protection Act 1998, ss 2, 4(3), Scheds 2 and 3. The full force of this Act does not apply to manually held data until 2007. On the DPA 1998, see further Jay and Hamilton, 1999.

THE RIGHT NOT TO JOIN A TRADE UNION: THE CLOSED SHOP

Sources and General Principles

3.17 The right not to join a trade union has parallel protection in English law to the right to join. The right not to join became an issue because of the practice of the closed shop, 'a situation in which employees come to realise that a particular job is only to be obtained or retained if they become and remain members of one of a number of specified unions'.[1] The closed shop as such is not unlawful but it is now almost impossible in practice to enforce. Individuals who refuse to join a trade union, or a particular union, have statutory protection against the three forms of discrimination by employers. First, the Trade Union and Labour Relations (Consolidation) Act 1992, ss 152 and 153 give employees the right not to be dismissed (or, in specified circumstances, selected for redundancy) for non-membership of a union or a particular union. Secondly, s 146 of that Act gives employees the right not to be subjected to a detriment by any act, or failure to act, to compel them to be or become a member.[2] Lastly, s 137 grants a remedy to any person who is refused employment because he or she is not a member of a trade union. Enforcement of the 'agency shop', requiring a payment equalling the union subscription to the union or to charity to counter the charge that employees may be getting the benefits of collective bargaining without paying for them (and are thus 'free-riders') is also prohibited; there is a right not to comply with a requirement to make a payment, or allow a deduction from remuneration, as an alternative to union membership.[3] The protections are limited to employees or prospective employees, with exceptions which parallel those applicable to the right to join.[4] The Human Rights Act 1998 may give a free-standing right of action against a 'public authority' (or at least a 'pure' public authority), which may be useful to individuals who lie outside the coverage of the statutory protections.[5] Article 11 of the ECHR, which guarantees the right to join trade unions, does not specify a right not to join a union, and the *travaux préparatoires* indicate that it was not intended to be covered. Despite this, the ECtHR has concluded that Article 11 does incorporate a negative right (although it did not determine whether this should be considered on an equal footing with the positive), and closed shops may be difficult to justify under Article 11(2).[6] In practice this seems unlikely to present an issue for domestic courts in the foreseeable future.

---

1. McCarthy, 1964, 9. In 1978, at least 5.2 million workers in Great Britain (23% of workers) were covered by closed shop arrangements: Dunn and Gennard, 1984, 15. In early 1989, the Department of Employment estimated that 2.6 million people were

covered, 1.3 million of whom were in pre-entry closed shops: *Removing Barriers to Employment,* Cm 655 (1989), paras 2.6–2.7. This latter figure was disputed: see Lord McCarthy, HL Debs Vol 521, col 154, 10 July, 1990; see also Dunn and Wright, 1993. The 1998 Workplace Employee Relations Survey found that in 2 per cent of workplaces managers said employees had to be union members to get or keep their jobs, but did not probe further the basis of this compulsion: Cully *et al*, 1999, 89. See also Millward *et al*, 2000, 146–149.

2. Subject to TULRCA 1992, s 148(3)–(5).

3. TULRCA 1992, ss 137(1)(b)(ii), 146(3), 152(3). See Benedictus 1979, 162–163 for the use of such practices in the 1970s.

4. See App 1 for the definition of 'employee', and para **3.3**. Note that in addition to these individual rights, there are other provisions which inhibit the promotion of the closed shop; s 222 removes immunity from industrial action to enforce union membership (see para **6.26**), and under s 145 it is unlawful to make it a requirement of a contract, or of admission to a tender list, that a contractor should employ only union labour (see para **3.22**).

5. See paras **1.16** and **1.17**, but note also paras **1.10** and **1.11**.

6. *Sigurour A Sigurjonsson v Iceland* judgment of 30 June 1993, (1993) 16 EHRR 462, para 35. Cf. *Sibson v UK* judgment of 20 April 1993, (1994) 17 EHRR 193 where the relocation of the applicant at another depot, as permitted by his contract, was found by the ECtHR not to strike at the substance of the freedom. See further Deakin and Morris, 1998, 740–745.

Protection against Dismissal on Grounds of Non-membership

3.18 As in the case of dismissal for trade union membership and activities, dismissal for non-membership is secured through the ordinary unfair dismissal procedure. The qualifications for claiming are identical to those set out in para **3.3**. The dismissal of an employee is automatically unfair if the principal reason for it was that the employee was not a member of any trade union, or a particular union, or one of a number of particular unions, or had refused or proposed to refuse to become or remain a member.[1] Dismissal for refusing, or proposing to refuse, to comply with any requirement to make a payment, or objection to a deduction by the employer from remuneration, in the event of non-membership is also treated as dismissal for non-membership of a union,[2] thus precluding enforcement of the 'agency shop' described in para **3.17** above. In addition, it is automatically unfair to select an employee for redundancy on these grounds where the circumstances described in para **3.3** apply.[3] The remedies for dismissal for non-membership are identical to those discussed in para **3.9**. There are two differences of procedure. First, if interim relief is sought, there is no requirement to obtain a certificate from a union official.[4] Secondly, where either the employer or the complainant claims that the employer was induced to dismiss the complainant by pressure which a union or other person exercised on the employer by calling, organising, procuring or financing a strike or other industrial action (or by threatening to do so) because the complainant was not a union member, either the employer or the complainant may request the employment tribunal to direct that such union or person be joined as a party to the proceedings.[5] That third party may then be made liable to pay all or a proportion of any compensation awarded to the complainant.[6]

---

1. TULRCA 1992, s 152(1)(c). Membership of a union includes membership of a particular branch or section of that union or one of a number of such branches or sections: s 152(4). An employee may still propose to refuse to remain a member even if this proposal is contingent upon some future event: *Crosville Motor Services Ltd v Ashfield* [1986] IRLR 475, EAT.
2. *Ibid.*, s 152(3).
3. *Ibid.*, s 153. Note that where the terms of s 152 or s 153 are not satisfied, a dismissal for non-membership may still be unfair under the ordinary unfair dismissal provisions.
4. *Ibid.*, s 161(3).
5. *Ibid.*, s 160. The request for joinder must be granted if made before the hearing of the complaint begins but may be refused if made after that time. No request can be made after the tribunal has made an award of compensation or ordered reinstatement or re-engagement.
6. *Ibid.*

Protection against Subjection to a Detriment Short of Dismissal to Compel Trade Union Membership

3.19 An employee has the right not to be subjected to any detriment short of dismissal as an individual by any act, or deliberate failure to act, by his or her employer if the act or failure takes place for the purpose of compelling him or her to be or become a member of any, or of a particular, trade union or one of a number of unions.[1] Again, this includes protection against measures to enforce a requirement to make a payment, and any deduction made by an employer from an employee's remuneration attributable to the employee's non-membership is to be treated as itself a detriment.[2] The scope of this protection is analysed in detail in paras **3.10–3.12**. The amended 'Ullswater amendment' described in para **3.12** applies equally in this context.[3] This means that an award of a pay increase or other benefit to union members only could be lawful provided that its purpose was to further a change in the employer's relationship with all or any class of employees; to induce them to accept collectively-agreed terms and conditions, for example. In practice, the only context where one can envisage this provision being relevant in current circumstances is if an employer wishes to encourage employees to adhere to standards agreed in accordance with a single-union deal. The procedure for claiming subjection to a detriment on grounds of non-membership of a union, the procedure, and the remedies available, are identical to those available for infringement of the right to join (see para **3.13**). As in the case of dismissal for non-membership, there is provision for joinder of third parties to the proceedings in the circumstances outlined in para **3.18**.

---

1. TULRCA 1992, s 146(1).
2. *Ibid.*, s 146(3),(4).
3. *Ibid.*, s 148(3)–(5).

Refusal of Access to Employment

3.20 It is unlawful to refuse a person employment under a contract of service or apprenticeship because he or she is not a member of a trade union or of a particular union or because he or she is unwilling to accept a requirement to become or remain a member of a union or to make payments or suffer deductions in the event of non-membership.[1] It is also unlawful for an employment agency to refuse a person any of its services for such a reason.[2] The meaning of 'refusal of employment' is discussed in para **3.14**. These provisions specifically preclude employers relying on unions to supply labour: it is unlawful for an employer (or employment agency) to refuse to employ non-members pursuant to an arrangement or practice whereby employment is offered only to persons put forward or approved by a union where the union does this only in respect of its members (although an affected individual would need to complain for the practice to be challenged).[3] In providing job-finding services, however, unions may legitimately discriminate between members and non-members; they are not regarded as 'employment agencies' by reason of services provided by them only for, or in relation to, their members.[4] Unions may also continue to demand that those applying for union office are members of that union or of a particular branch or section (but not of another union, even if that might be more appropriate to the job in question).[5] The procedure for an applicant to complain that he or she has been refused employment on the grounds of non-membership, and the remedies available, are identical to those relating to complaints based upon union membership, outlined in para **3.15**.[6]

1. TULRCA 1992, ss 137(1),(6), 143, 295. Membership of a particular branch or section of a trade union is also covered: *ibid.*, s 143(3).
2. *Ibid.*,s 138; see further para **3.14** note 2.
3. *Ibid.*, s 137(4).
4. *Ibid.*, s 143(2).
5. *Ibid.*, s 137(7), (8). 'Office' means any position by virtue of which the holder is an 'official' under TULRCA 1992, s 119 or in relation to which the duty to hold elections applies (see para **2.33** *et seq*): *ibid.*
6. The conclusive presumption in relation to advertisements applies in this context where the advertisement indicates, or might reasonably be understood as indicating, that the employment to which it relates is open only to a person who is a union member or who accepts a requirement to become a member or make a payment or suffer a deduction in lieu: TULRCA 1992, s 137(3).

CONTRACT COMPLIANCE

Sources and General Principles

3.21 The term 'contract compliance' is commonly used to describe a strategy whereby the terms of a commercial contract prescribe how the party which is obliged to provide goods or services under that contract behaves towards its workforce. The use of such a strategy in Britain dates back to 1891 when the House of Commons passed the first of three 'Fair Wages Resolutions' requiring government departments to include a term in contracts with private sector employers that contractors should pay their workers the generally accepted rate for the job.[1] Subsequent Resolutions extended these requirements to other conditions of employment and to freedom of association. Although not within the terms of the Resolution, local authorities also applied fair wages polices and later also included other purposes such as the provision of trade union facilities.[2] The Thatcher Conservative Government perceived the Fair Wages Resolution as a damaging anachronism, and it was rescinded with effect from 1983. It also introduced tight statutory controls on the use of contract compliance strategies by all employers in the area of union membership and recognition. Under the Trade Union and Labour Relations (Consolidation) Act 1992, ss 145 and 187 it is unlawful to make it a requirement of a contract, or of admission to a tender list, that a contractor should employ only union or non-union labour or should recognise a union. In addition, the Local Government Act 1988, s 17 makes it unlawful for local authorities and several other public bodies to consider a wide range of 'non-commercial matters' in their choice of, and dealings with, contractors, although the Secretary of State has recently been empowered to remove specified matters from this category.[3] The 1988 Act provides more extensive remedies, and makes it easier to prove an action for non-compliance, than the Trade Union and Labour Relations (Consolidation) Act 1992.[4]

---

1. See generally Bercusson, 1978.
2. Institute of Personnel Management, 1987: ch 2.
3. LGA 1999, s 19. This power applies in relation to 'best value' authorities as defined in s 1; see also s 2.
4. For a detailed examination of this area, see Fredman and Morris, 1989, Chapter 12. For a broader perspective see Turpin, 1989.

The Trade Union and Labour Relations (Consolidation) Act 1992

3.22 A term or condition of a contract for the supply of goods or services (including one entered into by individual householders) is void in so far as it purports to require:

(a) that the whole or part of the work done for the purposes of the contract is done only by persons who are, or are not, members of trade unions or of a particular union,[1] or
(b) a party to the contract to recognise one or more unions (whether or not named in the contract) for the purpose of negotiating on behalf of workers, or any class of worker, employed by it, or to negotiate or consult with an official of one or more unions (whether or not so named).[2]

In addition, there is a statutory duty not to exclude persons from a list of approved suppliers, or to terminate or refuse to consider entering contracts with them, if one of the grounds is that such a requirement is unlikely to be met.[3] The obligation not to refuse to deal with a contractor or potential contractor on one of the prohibited grounds is owed to that person and to 'any other person who may be adversely affected by its contravention', and a breach of that duty is actionable accordingly.[4] However, unlike in the Local Government Act 1988, there is no requirement for persons awarding contracts to provide reasons for their decisions. An employer who was permitted to submit a tender but not selected for a contract might, therefore, find it difficult to show that this exclusion was based upon a prohibited ground. The ban on non-union labour clauses was inserted to demonstrate formal equality between the right to join and the right not to join a union rather than because non-union clauses were perceived as presenting a problem in practice.[5] However, it is notable that there is no reciprocal ban on decisions taken because a contractor recognises, rather than refuses to recognise, a union, a position which the Labour Government has shown no intention of amending. The ban on requirements that the employer should consult with a union or its officials has the anomalous result that it is invalid for a contractor to require compliance even with the statutory consultation duties which we describe in Chapter 5. The Act does not prevent a person awarding a contract only to contractors who observe minimum rates and conditions settled by collective bargaining but it must be careful to ensure that this is not accompanied by a recognition requirement. To date there have been no reported cases on this provision, although there have been occasions when proceedings were commenced.[6]

---

1. See para **2.4**.
2. TULRCA 1992, ss 144 and 186. This provision binds the Crown: s 276(2). See s 178(3), discussed para **4.3** for the meaning of 'recognise'; s 296 (discussed App 1) for 'worker', and s 119 (discussed para **3.27**) for 'official'.
3. *Ibid.*, ss 145 and 187.
4. *Ibid.*, ss 145(5), 187(3). Note also that organising or threatening industrial action to induce a person to include a prohibited term or condition in a contract, or to take a decision in relation to a contract with reference to such a factor, has no immunity in tort: ss 219(4), 222 and 225..
5. See Evans and Lewis, 1988, for the background to these provisions.
6. In one case the Building Employers' Confederation applied for judicial review of the inclusion by Warrington Borough Council in its tender documents of a requirement that the workforce should be members of an appropriate trade union. The council undertook to withdraw this requirement after proceedings were commenced and the action was then dropped. (This case was based on judicial review rather than breach of statutory duty.)

The Local Government Act 1988

3.23 There is a duty on local authorities and several other public bodies, including police and fire authorities and education committees,[1] to exercise their functions in relation to public supply and works contracts without reference to 'non-commercial matters'.[2] These functions cover the inclusion or exclusion of persons from approved or tender lists, the selection of contractors and subcontractors and the termination of contracts.[3] The range of 'non-commercial matters' is currently very extensive, including, as well as clauses referring to freedom of association, the terms and conditions of employment of the contractors' workforce, the legal status of the workers (employees or self-employed), and whether contractors promote equal opportunities policies.[4] However the Secretary of State has recently been empowered to provide by order, in relation to 'best value' authorities, such as local authorities, for any of these matters to cease to be a 'non-commercial matter', either generally or for specified purposes or to a specified extent.[5] At the time of writing no such orders have yet been made. Any person who has suffered loss or damage as a result of an authority breaching its duty to exercise its functions without reference to 'non-commercial matters' may sue the authority for damages.[6] Such persons could probably include the employees of prospective contractors and council tax and rate payers as well as contractors themselves. When an action is brought by a person who merely submitted a tender for a contract, damages are limited to the expenditure reasonably incurred in doing this;[7] in other cases, the liability for damages is unlimited. There are two provisions designed to help potential claimants: an authority is treated as having breached its duty if it asks a question relating to a non-commercial matter or includes such a term in a draft tender or draft contract;[8] and authorities are obliged to tell contractors or potential contractors in writing of the reasons for their decision in relation to a particular contract if this is requested.[9] The Local Government Act 1988 also envisages the remedy of judicial review and provides that potential and former contractors should be among those entitled to institute proceedings.[10]

---

1. LGA 1988, Sch 2.

2. *Ibid.*, s 17(1).

3. *Ibid.*, s 17(4).

4. *Ibid.*, s 17(5). See generally Fredman and Morris, 1989, 464–470 for a more detailed examination of the Act. See also *R v London Borough of Islington, ex p BEC* [1989] IRLR 382, QBD.

5. LGA 1999, s 19. 'Best value' authorities are defined in s 1; see also s 2. In exercising a function with reference to a matter which is the subject of an order, the authority must have regard to any guidance issued by the Secretary of State: s 19(4). At the time of writing a Consultation Paper on draft guidance has been issued by the DETR: *Best Value and Procurement: Handling of Workforce Matters in Contracting*.

6. LGA 1988, s 19(7)(b).

7. *Ibid.*, s 19(8).

8. *Ibid.*, s 19(10).

9. *Ibid.*, s 20.

10. *Ibid.*, s 19(7)(a). A decision based on grounds of union or non-union labour, recognition of unions or adherence to collective agreements could arguably be challenged by judicial review in the absence of legislation: see *Wheeler v Leicester City Council* [1985] AC 1054, HL, discussed Fredman and Morris, 1989, 462–463. In addition, it has been held that a contractor which had been on a local authority's approved list for many years had a legitimate expectation that it would not be removed without being given valid and sufficient reasons and an opportunity to make representations: *R v Enfield*

London Borough Council, ex p TF Unwin (Roydon) Ltd, *Independent*, 21 February 1989. However, in relation to the decisions of public authorities covered by the 1988 Act, that Act offers a much more certain remedy.

RIGHTS OF INDIVIDUAL TRADE UNION MEMBERS

Deduction of Union Subscriptions at Source (the 'Check-off')

3.24 An important way in which employers may show their support for trade union organisation (and also monitor levels of union membership) is by facilitating the collection of union subscriptions. The practice of employers deducting subscriptions directly from workers' pay and passing them to the union concerned, known as the 'check-off', grew substantially from the 1960s onwards. In 1998, two-thirds of unionised workplaces were found to have a check-off system in place.[1] The deduction of subscriptions was always subject to individual workers agreeing to this arrangement as a term of their contract with their employer, either directly or by virtue of a collective agreement incorporated into the contract.[2] However it is now subject to compliance with statutory procedures. The Trade Union and Labour Relations (Consolidation) Act 1992, s 68 provides that where there are arrangements between the employer of a worker and a union for the deduction from workers' wages of the union subscription ('subscription deduction arrangements') the employer must ensure that no such deduction is made from any worker's wages unless the worker has authorised in writing the making of such deductions and this authorisation has not been withdrawn.[3] Arrangements between the parties for deductions from wages of other payments to the union, such as specific levies, are also covered by these provisions. A worker is entitled to withdraw an authorisation at any time by giving notice in writing to the employer; any subsequent deduction will then be unauthorised provided that the employer has received the notice of withdrawal in time for it to be reasonably practicable to secure that no deduction is made.[4] Authorisation by a worker of deductions does not legally oblige the employer to maintain or continue subscription deduction arrangements;[5] these are likely to remain the subject of a collective agreement. If an employer makes a deduction without due authorisation, or after the worker has withdrawn authorisation, the worker may complain to an employment tribunal which may order the employer to repay the amount deducted, less any part which has already been repaid.[6] Where the deduction also contravenes other statutory restrictions relating to deductions from pay[7] the aggregate amount which may be ordered by a tribunal or court (whether on the same or on different occasions) to be paid in respect of these contraventions shall not exceed the greatest amount which may be ordered to be paid in respect of any one of them.[8]

---

1. Cully *et al* 1999, 89. Cf the differing analyses of data in Millward *et al,* 2000, 151.
2. *Williams v Butlers Ltd* [1974] IRLR 253, DC and [1975] IRLR 120, QBD.
3. TULRCA 1992, s 68(1). 'Employer', 'wages' and 'worker' have the same meaning as ERA 1996: s 68(4): see App 1.
4. *Ibid.,* s 68(2). Note that unions may not lawfully discipline members who do not agree to the check-off or withdraw their consent to such arrangements: TULRCA 1992, s 65(2)(f); see further para **2.27**.
5. *Ibid.,* s 68(3).
6. *Ibid.,* s 68A(1), (2). A complaint must be made within three months beginning with the date of the payment of the wages from which the deduction or the last of the deductions was made, or such further period as the tribunal considers reasonable if the tribunal is satisfied that it was not reasonably practicable for the complaint to be presented within that period: see further App 2.
7. *Ibid.,* s 86(1) or s 90(1); ERA 1996, ss 8, 9(1) and 13. Where an employee is entitled to an itemised pay statement, deduction of the union subscription must appear on the statement.
8. *Ibid.,* s 68A(3).

3.25 Where their trade union has established a political fund, members of the union have a statutory right not to contribute to the fund.[1] This has implications for the check-off. Where a member has certified in writing to the employer either that he or she is exempt from contributions to the fund or that the union has been given written notification of his or her objection to contributing to it, the employer must ensure as soon as reasonably practicable that no amount representing the political fund contribution is henceforth deducted from emoluments payable to the member.[2] Any person whose employer fails to do this may complain to an employment tribunal,[3] and if it upholds the complaint the tribunal, as well as granting a declaration to that effect and ordering repayment of the amount unlawfully deducted, may order the employer to take specified steps within a specified period to ensure that the failure is not repeated.[4] Employers cannot avoid the administrative inconvenience of making deductions at differential rates for contributors and non-contributors by withdrawing the check-off facility for non-contributors alone;[5] this may be the subject of an application to the tribunal by a person in respect of whom a refusal to deduct occurs. However, it seems that the difficulty may be circumvented if a union invites non-contributors to consent to deduction of the full subscription but gives them a rebate for the political fund contribution in advance.[6]

1. See para **2.50**.
2. TULRCA 1992, s 86(1), (2).
3. *Ibid.*, s 87(1).
4. *Ibid.*, s 87(4).
5. *Ibid.*, s 86(3). Where there is an issue whether the employer's refusal to deduct is due to the member having certified that he or she is a non-contributor, it is for the employer to prove that it was not: s 87(3).
6. Note that trade unions cannot now make rebates in arrears to non-contributors.

Rights of Trade Unionists to Time Off Work

Sources and general principles

3.26 The rights of trade union members to time off work for union matters divide into two categories. First, employers have a statutory obligation to grant officials of recognised independent trade unions a reasonable amount of paid time off during working hours for specified duties and training.[1] Secondly, members of such unions are also entitled to reasonable time off (which need not be paid) to participate in union activities or to represent the union. The relevant principles are now contained in the Trade Union and Labour Relations (Consolidation) Act 1992, ss 168–173. In addition, an ACAS Code of Practice on Time Off for Trade Union Duties and Activities, revised in 1997, gives practical guidance on when, and under what conditions, time off should be given.[2] Employers and unions are strongly encouraged in the Code to formulate standing agreements for time off which can reflect the needs of the individual enterprise.[3] However, the absence of such an agreement does not prejudice an individual's statutory rights. The right is currently confined to 'employees' rather than the wider category of workers,[4] and employees who work outside Great Britain are excluded.[5] There is a right to take time off only with the employer's permission. Employees who are denied time off may apply to an employment tribunal for a declaration of their rights and an award of compensation.[6] Other worker representatives—'employee representatives', employees' representatives', and 'representatives of employee safety' are also entitled to paid time off work to perform their functions. We discuss their rights in appropriate sections of Chapter 5.

---

1. See para **4.3** for the meaning of 'recognition' and paras **2.6** and **2.7** for the definition of an 'independent trade union'. 'Working hours are defined as 'any time when in accordance with his [or her] contract of employment . . . [the employee] is required to

be at work': TULRCA 1992, s 173(1). In the context of s 152(2), where the definition of 'at work' is identical, this phrase has been held to mean 'while actually working' (*Post Office v UPOW* [1974] IRLR 22, HL), so allowing union activities only during a lunch hour or other break does not constitute 'time off'.

2. A failure to observe the provisions of the Code does not of itself render a party liable to legal proceedings, but the Code is admissible in evidence before an employment tribunal and any provision of the Code which appears to the tribunal to be relevant to any question is to be taken into account in determining that question: TULRCA 1992, s 207(1),(2). On time off for safety representatives, see HSC Code of Practice: Time Off for the Training of Safety Representatives, 1978.

3. Paras 33–37. For the operation of time off in practice by way of agreement, see Cully *et al*, 1999, Chapter 9.

4. The Code of Practice gives guidance not only in relation to employees but also in some contexts in relation to workers: see, for example, paras 25 and 26. Share fishermen, and members of the police and armed forces, have no right to time off: TULRCA 1992, ss 280, 274 and 284. The Secretary of State may extend the application of this right, and other statutory rights to a wider range of individuals, but at the time of writing this power has not been exercised: ERA 1999, s 23.

5. TULRCA 1992, s 285(1), although note s 285(2) relating to persons who work on board ship and s 287 relating to offshore employment. See further para **3.3** note 6.

6. This is the exclusive remedy: *ibid.*, s 173(2).

Trade union officials: rights to paid time off

3.27 Trade union officials (which include any lay representative elected or appointed in accordance with the union rules) are entitled to paid time off for three purposes (although there is nothing to prevent the parties agreeing to such entitlement in a broader range of situations).[1] The first is to carry out any of their duties, as such an official, concerned with negotiations with the employer related to or connected with any matters falling within the statutory definition of collective bargaining in relation to which the union is recognised by the employer. To fall within this category, three conditions must be satisfied. First, the duties must relate to a matter for which the union is recognised by the employer. Recognition may be express or implied from conduct,[2] but in the absence of an agreement specifically relating to time off, a written recognition agreement will help to avoid disputes.[3] The fact that other employers in the same industry, or even an associated employer,[4] may have granted more extensive recognition than the employer in question will be irrelevant; time off rights are determined by the extent of recognition by the official's own employer. Secondly, the matter must be listed in the Trade Union and Labour Relations (Consolidation) Act 1992, s 178(2), which specifies the matters constituting the subject matter of 'collective bargaining'.[5] Lastly, the duties must be 'concerned with negotiations' with the employer. This condition was inserted in the Employment Act 1989 to require proximity to actual negotiations; attending meetings of bodies with no negotiating power to determine national union policies concerned with industrial relations matters, covered under previous legislation,[6] would no longer suffice. Whether sufficient proximity exists will involve examining the facts in each case. In *Adlington v British Bakeries (Northern) Ltd*,[7] decided during the legislative passage of the Employment Act 1989, branch officials of the Bakers, Food and Allied Workers' Union claimed paid time off to attend a union workshop concerning government proposals to repeal the Baking Industry (Hours of Work) Act 1954. The Court of Appeal upheld the claim on the basis that repeal would threaten the continued existence of the industry's National Working Agreement and was thus likely to lead to negotiations between the union and employers, Kerr LJ stressing the 'exceptionally close connection' between the repeal of the legislation and a specific bargaining matter that existed.[8] In drafting the 1989 Act the government sought explicitly to incorporate the concept of proximity propounded in that case. *London Ambulance Service v Charlton*[9] was decided under the new provision. Union officials sought paid time off to attend a union committee to co-ordinate the activities of its district committee within the London Ambulance Service. The EAT affirmed that meetings which were called actively to prepare for negotiations in connection with collective bargaining were covered provided that there was 'sufficient nexus between the collective bargaining and the duty involving preparation for that particular issue'.[10] Moreover, officials of a union which was a member of a multi-union Joint Consultative Committee (JCC) might wish to have their own meeting in the absence of other unions, although the frequency and timing of these separate meetings in relation to those of the JCC might be relevant in considering the issue of reasonableness (see para **3.28** below). The ACAS Code of Practice emphasises that an official's duties must be connected with or related to negotiations or the performance of functions both in time and subject matter. It suggests that reasonable time off may be sought, for example, to prepare for negotiations; inform members of progress; explain outcomes to members; and prepare for meetings with the employer about matters for which the union has only representational rights (although the latter is not strictly speaking within the terms of the legislation).[11] Informing members about the outcome of industry-wide negotiations would seem not to be included,[12] although employers may wish to consider allowing time off for this purpose. The second purpose for which an employer should grant paid time off is to carry out duties concerned with the performance on behalf of its employees of functions related to or connected with 'collective bargaining' matters which the employer has specifically agreed may be performed by the union. The third is to carry out duties concerned with the receipt of information from and consultation with the employer in relation to collective redundancies and a transfer of an undertaking. We discuss those provisions in detail in Chapter 5.

1. TULRCA 1992, s 168(1). 'Official' is defined in s 119 as an officer of the union or of a branch or section of it, or a person elected or appointed in accordance with the union rules to be a representative of its members, or of some of them. 'Officer' *includes* (but is not confined to) any member of the governing body of the union, and any trustee of any fund applicable for the purposes of the union: *ibid*.

2. See para **4.4**.

3. See App 6 for an example of such an agreement.

4. See App 1. Before the Employment Act 1989, duties concerned with industrial relations between the official's 'employer and any associated employer, and their employees' were included.

5. See para **4.3**. See the Code of Practice, para 12 for examples under each heading.

6. *Beal v Beecham Group Ltd* [1982] IRLR 192, CA. Until the Employment Act 1989, the duties for which union officials could claim recognition were not limited by the extent of recognition; the requirement for recognition served only to identify the union whose officials were entitled to claim this right.

7. [1989] IRLR 218, CA; see also the Code of Practice, para 13.

8. *Ibid.*, at 222.

9. [1992] IRLR 510, EAT.

10. *Ibid.*, at 513. Meetings merely to exchange information will not be covered (cf *Sood v GEC Elliott Process Automation Ltd* [1979] IRLR 416, EAT.

11. Para 13.

12. Representation on regional or national bodies negotiating with a range of employers would also not be covered, although officials would be entitled to unpaid time off for this purpose: see para **3.32**.

3.28 In addition to the conduct of the duties specified in para **3.27**, officials are also entitled to paid time off for training relevant to them.[1] Training courses must be approved by the Trades Union Congress or by the official's own union.[2] The kind of training a particular official should have will depend upon the scope of any recognition or other agreement, and his or her position in the union and functions in the workplace.[3] The relationship between training and the scope of recognition may put into question entitlement to attend courses which relate to several topics, not all of which may be covered by the individual recognition agreement.[4] However, the EAT has indicated that the statute should not be given a narrow interpretation,[5] and many contemporary courses focus upon the development of the skills required by officials, such as negotiating and representational skills, rather than substantive topics, and as such are likely to fall within the legislation. The Code of Practice recommends that employers should consider releasing officials for initial training in basic representational skills as soon as possible after their election or appointment. It also recommends consideration of time off for further training where the official has special responsibilities, where there are proposals to change the scope or nature of collective bargaining at the workplace, where significant changes in the organisation of work are being contemplated, or where legislation may affect the conduct of industrial relations at the place of work and may require the reconsideration of existing collective agreements.[6] The EAT relied upon the concept of 'special responsibilities' in holding that a union branch secretary who had been elected to the Management Committee of a pension scheme to represent his members and others, to report back to shop stewards and to advise members in connection with their pensions, was entitled to paid time off to attend a course on pensions.[7] The Code of Practice states that officials should be prepared to provide, on request, a copy of the syllabus or prospectus indicating the contents of a training course and should give at least a few weeks' notice to management of nominations for such courses.[8]

---

1. TULRCA 1992, s 168(2). ERA 1999, s 30 empowers the Secretary of State to spend money or provide money to other persons to encourage and help employers (or their representatives) and employees (or their representatives) to improve the way they work together. It is anomalous that this provision is confined to employees, given that trade unions are organisations of 'workers': TULRCA 1992, s 1, discussed further para **2.4**.
2. *Ibid.*, s 168(2)(b).
3. Code of Practice, para 16.
4. *Menzies v Smith and McLaurin Ltd* [1980] IRLR 180, EAT. The identity of the personnel for whom the course is described as being designed may be a relevant factor: *Ministry of Defence v Crook and Irving* [1982] IRLR 488, EAT.
5. *STC Submarine Systems v Piper* (11 March 1993, unreported), EAT.
6. See para 18.
7. *STC Submarine Systems v Piper,* above, note 5. Although the pension scheme was not directly negotiable, the employment tribunal was justified in concluding that pension rights were relevant to any negotiations over pay and conditions in general, and involved at least in the preparation of matters relevant to collective bargaining.
8. Para 30.

3.29 The amount of time off which an official is to be permitted to take and the purposes for which, occasions on which and conditions subject to which it may be taken, are those which are 'reasonable in all the circumstances'.[1] In determining what is reasonable, which is pre-eminently a question for the employment tribunal as an 'industrial jury' to decide,[2] regard is to be had to the ACAS Code of Practice.[3] Where the employer and union have concluded their own time off agreement, as the Code strongly recommends,[4] its provisions are likely to influence a tribunal considerably in determining what is reasonable in the circumstances.[5] The nature, extent and purpose of time off already taken by the employee in question may be a relevant factor,[6] as may adequate cover for safety, the production process or provision of service.[7] Officials should give management as much notice as possible when time off is sought, giving details of its purpose, the intended location, and its timing and duration.[8] Somewhat curiously, the Code of Practice goes beyond the legislative framework in recommending that management should 'consider making available to officials the facilities necessary for them to perform their duties efficiently and communicate effectively with their members, fellow lay officials and full-time officers'. Where resources permit, such facilities could include accommodation for meetings, access to a telephone and other office equipment, and the use of notice boards and, where the volume of the official's work justifies it, the use of dedicated office space.[9] The provision of these facilities accords with the terms of an ILO convention,[10] but a failure to provide them would not be actionable in English law.[11]

---

1. TULRCA 1992, s 168(3).

2. *Thomas Scott and Sons (Bakers) Ltd v Allen* [1983] IRLR 329, CA; *Wignall v British Gas Corpn* [1984] IRLR 493, EAT.

3. TULRCA 1992, s 168(3); see generally paras 25–32 of the Code. See para **3.26** note 2 for the legal status of the Code.

4. Para 33.

5. An agreement which is less favourable than the legislation ought not to prejudice an employee: see TULRCA 1992, s 288 (cf the discussion in *Ashley v Ministry of Defence* [1984] IRLR 57, where the EAT distinguished between time off pursuant to an internal agreement, which may be in some respects more favourable and in others less favourable than the statute, and time off pursuant to the predecessor of s 168).

6. *Wignall v British Gas Corpn,* above, note 2; and see Code of Practice, para 32.

7. Code of Practice, paras 25 and 31.

8. *Ibid.,* para 29.

9. Para 28.

10. ILO Convention No 135 Concerning the Protection and Facilities to be afforded to Workers' Representatives in the Undertaking provides that 'such facilities shall be afforded to workers' representatives as may be appropriate in order to enable them to carry out their functions promptly and efficiently': see also Recommendation No 143 of the same name.

11. Note that the provision of facilities for a union by an employer could prejudice the union's independent status if the union was dependent on those facilities: see paras **2.6** and **2.7**.

3.30 When time off its granted, the employee should be paid as if he or she had worked.[1] The pre-Employment Act 1989 cases conflict on whether an employer can allow an official time off but argue that it is not reasonable for the official to be paid for that time.[2] Even then it was hard to reconcile such an argument with the statutory language,[3] and the tighter restriction of the duties for which paid time off is due[4] would seem to diminish its chances of success. Where an employee's pay varies with the amount of work done, payment is to be calculated by reference to the average hourly earnings for the work the employee is employed to do.[5] An official who performs the relevant duties outside his or her own 'working hours' (a night worker who attends meetings during the day, for example) has no statutory entitlement to compensating paid time off in lieu.[6] In practice, unions and employers should attempt to reach an agreement to cater for circumstances of this kind.[7] Problems may also arise for employees who do not work full-time who may thereby be disadvantaged if the time they spend on union duties exceeds their working hours. The European Court of Justice has held that compensation received for loss of earnings due to attendance at training courses for staff committees in Germany falls within the definition of 'pay' for the purposes of Article 141 of the EC Treaty (ex Article 119) and the Equal Pay Directive 75/117 because it constitutes a benefit paid by reason of the existence of an employment relationship. Since the members of such committees who are employed part-time are generally women, a legislative provision which results in part-time workers being paid less than full-time workers for attending courses whose length exceeds the number of hours they work constitutes indirect discrimination against women.[8] In *Manor Bakeries v Nazir*[9] the EAT held that this principle did not apply to attendance at a British union conference on the basis that this was not a species of 'work'. However in the later case of *Davies v Neath Port Talbot County Borough Council*[10] a differently-constituted EAT held that *Nazir* should not be followed, affirming that attendance at a union training course, like that of German staff committees, was by reason of the existence of the employment relationship. The European Court of Justice had indicated that it was open to a Member State to justify legislation which limited part-time workers to compensation for their working hours by objective factors unrelated to any discrimination on grounds of sex. In *Davies* the EAT took a robust approach to this issue, affirming that there could not be 'a justifiable policy or aim which maintains the inequality'.[11]

---

1. TULRCA 1992, s 169.
2. In *Beecham Group Ltd v Beal (No 2)* [1983] IRLR 317 the EAT held that the right to payment followed automatically; cf *Thomas Scott and Sons (Bakers) Ltd v Allen* [1983] IRLR 329, where the CA took a different view but did not explain the basis for this conclusion.
3. See Fitzpatrick, 1983, at 260 for further comment.

4. See para **3.27** note 6.

5. TULRCA 1992, s 169(3). If no fair estimate of his or her earnings can be made, the official should be paid at the average hourly earnings of a comparable employee with the same employer or, if there is none, according to a reasonable estimate of earnings: *ibid.* Any contractual remuneration for this period goes towards discharging any statutory entitlement and vice versa: s 169(4).

6. *Hairsine v Kingston upon Hull City Council* [1992] IRLR 211, EAT.

7. Code of Practice, para 35.

8. Case C–360/90 *Arbeiterwohlfahrt der Stadt Berlin eV v Botel* [1992] IRLR 423, ECJ; Case C–457/93 *Kuratorium für dialyse und Nierentransplantation eV v Lewark* [1996] IRLR 637, ECJ.

9. [1996] IRLR 604, EAT.

10. [1999] IRLR 769, EAT.

11. *Ibid.*, at 772.

Remedies if paid time off is refused

3.31 If an official is refused permission to take time off, the sole remedy is to complain to an employment tribunal;[1] there is a right to time off only with permission. (An employee who took time off without permission and was subsequently disciplined for doing so could not claim to have been taking part in a protected union activity because it would not have been at an 'appropriate time'.[2]) An official can also complain if he or she was not paid in accordance with the legislation for time off which was granted.[3] A claim must be presented to the tribunal within three months of the failure to permit time off, or to make the payment, unless the tribunal is satisfied that this was not 'reasonably practicable', in which case it must be presented within such further period as the tribunal considers reasonable.[4] The tribunal must make a declaration and may award compensation, having regard to the employer's default and any loss sustained by the employee because of the failure.[5] There is no upper limit to the amount which may be awarded. By analogy with the provisions relating to subjection to a detriment, it seems likely that 'loss' can include non-pecuniary loss, such as injury to health.[6] Where the complaint concerns a failure to pay the official, the tribunal will order payment by the employer of the amount which is due.[7] The tribunal has no power to impose conditions on the parties as to how time off should be granted in the future.[8]

_____

1. TULRCA 1992, ss 168(4), 173(2). Curiously s 173(2) states that the sole remedy of an employee for infringement of the time off rights is by way of complaint to an employment tribunal under Part III of TULRCA 1992. However, ERA 1996, s 27(1)(e)

includes payment for time off for union duties within the definition of 'wages', so allowing tribunals to treat non-payment as an unlawful deduction from 'wages' under ss 13–27 of that Act. In practice nothing would seem to turn on this in relation to a failure to pay on one occasion, but if the failure related to a series of non-payments the time limit under s ERA 1996, s 23(3)(a) appears to be more generous.

2. See para **3.8**.

3. TULRCA 1992, s 169(5).

4. *Ibid.*, s 171; see further App 2 for the meaning of not 'reasonably practicable'. In *Young, Stewart and Morris v British Airways Board* unreported, EAT 175/83 it was held that the three-month period runs from the date when permission was refused.

5. *Ibid.*, s 172. To establish a right to compensation an employee must establish, on the balance of probabilities, that a request was made for time off, that it came to the notice of the employer's appropriate representative, and that they either refused it, ignored it or failed to respond to it: *Ryford Ltd v Drinkwater* [1996] IRLR 16, EAT.

6. See para **3.13**.

7. TULRCA 1992, s 172(3).

8. *Corner v Buckinghamshire County Council* [1978] IRLR 320, EAT.

Time off for trade union activities

3.32 An employer has an obligation to permit an employee who is a member of an independent trade union which it recognises in respect of that description of employee to take reasonable time off work to take part in 'any activities' of the union and any other activities in relation to which he or she is acting as a representative of it.[1] The need for the union to be recognised in respect of that description of employee is a significant limitation; it means, therefore, that if an employer recognises the X union for clerical staff, managerial grades who belong to the union will not be able to claim time off. There is no requirement that time off for these purposes should be paid, but employers and unions may nevertheless agree that it should be, and the Code of Practice suggests that employers should consider payment in certain circumstances, for example in order to ensure that workplace meetings are fully representative.[2] The scope of union 'activities' is a question of fact for the employment tribunal.[3] The Code of Practice gives as examples of union activities attending workplace meetings to discuss and vote on the outcome of negotiations with the employer, meeting full-time officials to discuss issues relevant to the workplace, and voting in union elections.[4] It is arguable that the right should extend to any activities which the union may lawfully undertake, including those of a political, social or educational nature. Nevertheless, the EAT has said that 'in a broad sense the activity should be one which is in some way linked to [the] . . . employment relationship'.[5] On that basis, the EAT upheld the decision of the tribunal that a teacher was not entitled to time off to attend a TUC lobby of Parliament intended to convey

political or ideological objections to proposed legislation, although it emphasised that not all lobbying would be outside the entitlement. It contrasted lobbying consisting of 'the presentation of arguments intended to persuade a
Member of Parliament to vote in a particular way on a particular issue' with 'an
approach which is in essence based upon mere protest',[6] a distinction whose
logic is hard to discern; even if (contrary to our view) one accepts such a limitation in principle, the subject-matter of the lobby would seem of greater significance than the method of conducting it. Activities where the employee is acting
as a union 'representative'—the second purpose for which time off should be
granted—may include taking part in branch, area or regional meetings of the
union or meetings of official policy-making bodies such as the executive committee or annual conference, or meetings with full-time officials to discuss issues
relevant to the workplace.[7] Thus, union officials who are not entitled to paid
time off for particular duties may qualify under this heading. However it should
be noted that employers must now grant paid time off to any worker (not only
an employee), regardless of whether he or she is a union official, to accompany
a fellow worker who has been required or invited by his or her employer to
attend a disciplinary or grievance hearing at which he or she has reasonably
requested to be accompanied.[8] The statute expressly excludes industrial action
from the right to time off.[9] 'Industrial action' is not defined in this context, nor
is there any case law which serves as a precedent, but decisions arising from other
contexts, in particular that of unfair dismissal, are likely to be heavily persuasive.
In that context, as we discuss in para **6.93**, the purpose of the activity has been
regarded as influential (although as we indicate, that approach is not without its
difficulties). In *Rasool v Hepworth Pipe Co Ltd (No 2)* employees attending an
unauthorised mass meeting during working hours to discuss impending wage
negotiations were found not to be taking industrial action; it was 'more properly
to be regarded as trade union activity, even though a degree of disruption of the
manufacturing process resulted'.[10] In *Faust v Power Packing Casemakers Ltd*[11]
the Court of Appeal considered that whether a refusal to work (voluntary) overtime constituted industrial action depended upon whether it was designed to put
pressure on the employer. It seems likely that a similar approach would be followed in the context of time off (although for the reasons we explain in para **6.93**,
the defining purpose as specified in *Faust* may be regarded as unduly narrow).
Activities connected with the organisation or threat of industrial action, as
opposed to the taking of it, appear not to be excluded from the activities for
which time off should be permitted (although the matter is not wholly free from
doubt),[12] and the Code of Practice emphasises that officials should be given paid
time off (see para **3.27** *et seq.*) to represent members who are taking industrial
action when they are not themselves so doing.[13]

1. TULRCA 1992, s 170. This is a right to be given time off during 'working hours'; see para **3.26** for the definition of 'working hours'.

2. Para 24.

3. *Luce v London Borough of Bexley* [1990] IRLR 422, EAT.

4. Para 21. Note that where union elections are governed by statute (see para **2.33**) voting must be fully postal. Voting in ballots on industrial action must also now be fully postal: see para **6.41**.

5. *Luce v London Borough of Bexley,* above, note 3, at 425.

6. *Ibid.*

7. Para 22. Representing individual members at employment tribunals would probably fall within the category of activities for which time off should be granted by the employer, subject to the general test of reasonableness: see para **3.33**.

8. ERA 1999, s 10. See also ACAS Code of Practice on Disciplinary and Grievance Procedures para 50 *et seq.* 'Worker' is defined in s 13; see further App 1.

9. TULRCA 1992, s 170(2).

10. [1980] IRLR 137 at 140, EAT.

11. *Faust v Power Packing Casemakers Ltd* [1983] IRLR 117, CA.

12. See *Midland Plastics v Till* [1983] IRLR 9, EAT, where for the purposes of TULRCA 1992, s 238, as amended, the threat of taking industrial action was held not to amount to 'industrial action', but cf. *Lewis and Britton v E Mason and Sons* [1994] IRLR 4, where the EAT refused to characterise as perverse the tribunal's finding that the threat of industrial action itself constituted 'industrial action'.

13 Para 39. The Code also emphasises that employers and unions have a responsibility to use agreed procedures to settle problems and avoid industrial action and that time off may be permitted for this purpose, particularly where there is a dispute.

3.33 The amount of time off which an employee is to be permitted to take, and the purposes for which, the occasions on which and any conditions subject to which it may be taken, are those which are 'reasonable in all the circumstances'.[1] The same considerations as apply to time off for union officials, discussed in para **3.29**, apply here. In this context in particular unions are urged to be aware of the desirability of minimising the effect on production and services, which may require consideration to be given to holding workplace meetings towards the end of a shift or the working week or before or after a meal break. Likewise, employers are urged to bear in mind the difficulties for unions in ensuring effective representation and communications with groups such as shift workers, part-timers, individuals employed at dispersed locations and those with domestic commitments.[2] The remedies for unlawful refusal of time off for union activities are identical to those described in para **3.31**, except that in this context there is no statutory requirement that the time off should be paid. In the event that an employer refused to honour a contractual commitment to pay for time off for union activities, employees would be able to complain that this constituted an unlawful deduction from their wages.[3]

---

1. TULRCA 1992, s 170(3).
2. Code of Practice, paras 25–26.
3. ERA 1996, ss 13–27.

4

Trade Union Recognition and Collective Bargaining

INTRODUCTION

4.1 Effective recognition by states of the right to collective bargaining is regarded by the ILO as a fundamental principle.[1] The ESC also commits states to promote, where necessary and appropriate, machinery for voluntary negotiations between employers and workers' organisations with a view to the regulation of terms and conditions of employment by means of collective agreements.[2] For most of the twentieth century UK governments supported collective bargaining as the preferred method of determining terms and conditions of employment, but they did so in the main by example and exhortation rather than by legislation.[3] (Exceptions to this principle included the establishment in 1909 of trade boards (later wages councils) to determine binding terms and conditions of employment in any industry where there was no collective bargaining machinery, with the aim of encouraging such machinery to develop; the post-war nationalisation statutes, which obliged the new public corporations to consult appropriate organisations with a view to establishing joint bargaining machinery; and the House of Commons Fair Wages Resolutions of 1891, 1909 and 1946, which required the government, in concluding contracts, to secure payment for workers of the 'going rate'.[4]) The outcomes of collective bargaining were similarly unregulated; the law did not determine the form of collective agreements, and it was for employers to choose whether to adhere to the standards specified in them.[5] The first break with the predominantly 'collective *laissez-faire*' tradition came with the Industrial Relations Act 1971, introduced by the Conservative Government under the leadership of Mr. Edward Heath. This Act, which attempted to bring British industrial relations within a framework of legal regulation at a stroke, created a complex procedure whereby a trade union (or group of unions) could be designated as the sole bargaining agent for a specified bargaining unit, with the remedy of determination of the contractual terms and conditions of employees in the unit by unilateral arbitration in the event that an employer refused to comply with a recognition order. Although potentially far-reaching, in the event this right had little practical impact because it could be invoked only by unions which were registered under the Act, and TUC policy opposed such registration.[6] The attempt made by the Act to regulate collective bargaining outcomes was also undermined; the Act created the statutory presumption that collective agreements were intended by the parties to be legally enforceable, but this was countered by the widespread and generally consensual use of 'TINALEA' clauses (affirming that 'this is not a legally enforceable agreement').[7] However, despite its failure, the Act heralded a lasting departure from the collective *laissez-faire* tradition in the area of collective labour law. The 'Social Contract' legislation of the Labour Government which came into office in 1974, embodied in the Trade Union and Labour Relations Act 1974 and the Employment Protection Act 1975, brought a much more extensive role for the law in supporting trade unions and collective bargaining than heretofore. The terms of reference of the newly-constituted ACAS explicitly referred to encouraging the extension of collective bargaining, and independent unions could apply to ACAS, under a statutory procedure, for recognition, or further recognition, from employers. Once recognised, such unions had the right to information from employers for collective bargaining purposes, and the results of collective bargaining could be extended by law to other employers who did not pay the going rate. Recognised unions were also granted a range of consultation rights. However, the legislation reflected the collective *laissez-faire* position (and industrial relations practice) by replacing the presumption that collective agreements were intended to be legally enforceable unless otherwise stated with the converse presumption, a principle which remains the case today.

The return to office of a Conservative Government under Mrs Thatcher in 1979 brought a dramatic reversal of this pro-collective bargaining policy. Her government regarded the free market as the most efficient economic principle, and collective bargaining was seen as an undesirable constraint upon a system which required the individualisation of the employment relationship in order to function properly.[8] The repeal of the statutory recognition and extension procedures by the Employment Act 1980 were the first steps in what was to become an incremental programme of reform, the recognition procedure having already been undermined by a series of successful judicial review applications by employers challenging ACAS's use of its statutory discretionary powers.[9] The Employment Act 1982 made it unlawful for persons awarding contracts for the supply of goods or services to make decisions by reference to whether the contractor recognised a union, and made void any contractual specification of this matter. The pursuit of individualism was further facilitated by a provision in the Trade Union Reform and Employment Rights Act 1993 designed to remove any obstacle to employers offering employees inducements to move away from collectively-agreed terms and conditions of employment to personal contracts.

That Act also took the symbolically important step of removing the goal of encouraging the extension of collective bargaining from the terms of reference of ACAS. Hostility to collective bargaining was also mirrored in the Government's role as contractor and employer;[10] the Fair Wages Resolution of 1946 was rescinded, and national collective bargaining structures in public services were undermined by the encouragement of local bargaining, introduction of individualised reward structures, and contracting-out of services. The requirement for employers to disclose information for collective bargaining purposes survived, but this was almost certainly because the statutory exceptions to the requirement rendered it relatively ineffectual in practice.

The advent of a Labour Government in 1997 heralded a more hospitable environment for trade unions with emphasis upon a culture of 'partnership' in the conduct of industrial relations.[11] However the government, under the leadership of Mr. Blair, has not echoed the whole-hearted support for collective bargaining accorded by the Labour Government of 1974–1979. The Employment Relations Act 1999 has re-introduced a procedure for statutory recognition of trade unions, operated by the CAC, whose nature reflects a number of the lessons learned from its predecessor: in particular it specifies the criteria governing determination of an appropriate bargaining unit and the method of assessing support for recognition, and imposes a statutory obligation upon employers to co-operate if a recognition ballot is required, features whose absence from the previous legislation caused considerable difficulty. The procedure is designed to encourage the parties to reach a voluntary agreement, with an opportunity for them to do this incorporated into the appropriate stages of the procedure. If they fail to reach agreement, the CAC determines the bargaining unit, then recognition, and subsequently a method for conducting collective bargaining, but the scope of mandatory recognition is relatively narrow, being limited to 'pay, hours and holidays'. Moreover, if the employer fails to comply with the 'method' of conducting collective bargaining imposed by the CAC, the sanction is restricted to specific performance of that method, whereas its predecessor permitted determination of the terms and conditions of employment of workers in the bargaining unit by unilateral arbitration.[12] The procedure is paralleled by a mechanism for compulsory derecognition of unions which have been recognised via the statutory procedure, and the CAC is required to assist the parties to agree, *inter alia*, to end the bargaining arrangements in the same way as it assists a recognition application. There is thus no policy preference for the maintenance of collective bargaining arrangements. There are other signs that the commitment to collective bargaining is limited. The pre-1993 statutory duty upon ACAS to extend collective bargaining has not been reinstated (although arguably its general duty 'to promote the improvement of industrial relations' can probably embrace this).[13] The capacity of individual employers and workers to negotiate terms and conditions of employment which deviate from those collectively agreed has been explicitly affirmed, although there is an enabling power to introduce a measure of protection for workers who do not wish to move to personal contracts. The prohibition against requiring contractors to recognise trade unions (but not against denying recognition) also remains intact. Thus, whilst there is greater acknowledgement of the legitimacy of collective bargaining as a method of determining terms and conditions of employment than under the 1979–1997 Conservative Government, it is very far from being a fundamental plank of labour relations policy.

We start this chapter by examining the concept and legal significance of recognition of a union by an employer. We then examine in detail the operation and implications of the statutory recognition procedure. The subsequent section explores the position where an employer wishes to derecognise a union, both where recognition has been a voluntary act and otherwise. This is followed by an assessment of the Human Rights Act 1998 for union recognition. The penultimate section analyses the legal provisions relating to collective bargaining and collective agreements, and the final section the effect of a transfer of the undertaking on recognition and collective agreements.

---

1. ILO Convention No 98 on the Right to Organise and Collective Bargaining (1949), Article 4; ILO Declaration on Fundamental Principles and Rights at Work and its Follow-Up, ILO, Geneva, 1998. See further paras **1.19** and **1.20** for ILO Conventions and Recommendations relevant to collective labour law.

2. See further para **1.21**.

3. See Fredman and Morris, 1989, chapter 5.

4. See Davies and Freedland, 1993, chapter 1 for the argument that these measures, taken collectively, made considerable inroads into the collective *laissez-faire* doctrine.

5. An exception was a little-used procedure for enforcing terms and conditions determined in collective bargaining, initially the *quid pro quo* during the Second World War for a ban on strikes, and subsequently continued until it was replaced by the extension procedure contained in the Employment Protection Act 1975: SR&O 1940, No 1305, re-enacted in the Terms and Conditions of Employment Act 1959, s 8.

6. See generally Weekes *et al*, 1975; Davies and Freedland, 1993, chapter 7. The Labour Government, in anticipation of legislation, had established the Commission on Industrial Relations in 1969 on a voluntary basis with the power to hear recognition disputes and make recommendations for their settlement.

7. Weekes *et al*, 1975, 156–161.

8. See Davies and Freedland, 1993, chapter 9 *et seq*; W. Brown *et al*, 1997.

9. See Simpson, 1979; Dickens and Bain, 1986.

10. See generally Fredman and Morris, 1989.

11. See *Fairness at Work*, Cm 3968, 1998. See further W. Brown, 2000.

12. For the use of that sanction, see Doyle, 1980. For assessment of the new procedure, and comparison, variously, with its predecessors and with US and Canadian procedures, see Wood and Godard, 1999; McCarthy, 1999; Towers, 1999; Adams, 1999 and Hepple, 2000.

13. Hepple, 2000.

RECOGNITION OF TRADE UNIONS

Sources and General Principles

4.2 An employer of 21 or more workers can be required to recognise an independent trade union[1] for the purposes of collective bargaining over pay, hours and holidays. In default of agreement between the parties, the 'method' by which collective bargaining is to be conducted can also be specified by the CAC; this has effect as a legally enforceable contract between the parties for which the remedy of specific performance can be granted. The relevant provisions are contained in the Trade Union and Labour Relations (Consolidation) Act 1992, Schedule A1, inserted by the Employment Relations Act 1999, s 1 and Schedule 1. The statutory provisions are supplemented by a Code of Practice, issued by the Secretary of State, on access to workers during recognition (and derecognition) ballots, and by an order of the Secretary of State specifying a method for the conduct of collective bargaining of which the CAC must take account. It remains the case that, with one exception, employers can voluntarily recognise a union of their choice.[2] Doing so prior to a request under the statutory procedure affords the maximum flexibility in varying the scope of recognition, both in terms of the workers covered and the subject-matter. Even a voluntary recognition agreement which follows a statutory request can bind the employer for a minimum of three years unless the parties otherwise agree.[3] 'Recognition' is defined in the Trade Union and Labour Relations (Consolidation) Act 1978, s 178(3).[4] Recognition of an *independent* trade union by an employer, whether voluntary or otherwise, has a number of important legal consequences. First, the employer has an obligation to consult representatives of recognised unions in four situations: in relation to 'collective dismissals' for redundancy; where there is a transfer of the undertaking; on health and safety matters; and before contracting-out of the state earnings related pension scheme. Only if no union is recognised for the employees affected may the employer satisfy its statutory obligation in relation to redundancies or transfers by consulting other 'employee representatives' or (in the case of health and safety matters) employees themselves.[5] These provisions are analysed in detail in Chapter 5. Secondly, recognition entitles the union to claim disclosure of information for collective bargaining purposes.[6] Thirdly, union representatives and members of recognised independent trade unions are entitled to time off work for specified activities.[7] Fourthly, recognition has significant implications for the operation of the statutory recognition procedure: where an employer recognises an independent trade union for a particular group of workers, an application by another union for recognition in respect of a bargaining unit which overlaps to any extent with that group will not be accepted by the CAC; perhaps surprisingly, the same principle generally applies even when a non-independent union is recognised.[8]

Finally, an employer must consult a recognised independent trade union on training matters where that union is recognised in accordance with the statutory procedure and a method for the conduct of collective bargaining has been specified by the CAC and neither its content nor legal effect varied by agreement of the parties.[9] Recognition of unions cannot be promoted by a 'contract compliance strategy'. A term or condition of any contract for the supply of goods or services which requires a party to the contract to recognise a union for any class of worker it employs, or to negotiate or consult with a union official, is void, and there is a statutory duty not to exclude a person from a list of approved suppliers, or to terminate or to refuse to consider entering contracts with them, if one of the grounds is that such a requirement is unlikely to be met.[10] These provisions are discussed in detail in Chapter 3, together with the Local Government Act 1988 which contains additional measures relating to the acts of specified public bodies in this area.

---

1. See paras **2.6** and **2.7** for the definition of an 'independent trade union'.

2. Where an employer recognises a non-independent union, the CAC may issue a declaration that the bargaining arrangements should cease if this represents the wishes of the majority of the bargaining unit: see TULRCA 1992, Sched A1, Part VI, discussed at para **4.53** *et seq.* Re-recognition of such a union within three years will not prevent a recognition application in respect of that bargaining unit being accepted by the CAC: Sched A1, para 35(4).

3. *Ibid.*, para 56. See para **4.32** for the conditions which must be met for this to be the case.

4. The same definition appears to apply in respect of each of the rights 'recognition' brings (other than those applicable under the statutory recognition procedure): *Cleveland County Council v Springett* [1985] IRLR 131 at 136, EAT. Note the differing definitions of 'collective bargaining' used in the context of the statutory recognition provisions: see further para **4.8**.

5. There is no obligation to consult in relation to pensions where no independent trade union is recognised.

6. See para **4.65** *et seq.*

7. See para **3.26** *et seq.*

8. See note 2, above. ILO Convention No. 98, Article 2, states that 'acts which are *designed* to promote the establishment of workers' organisations under the domination of employers' constitute acts of interference with those organisations. *Quaere* whether the implicit encouragement which the procedure gives to employers to establish non-independent unions could be regarded as a violation of the Convention. For discussion of the compatibility of other aspects of the procedure with ILO standards, see Novitz, 2000, 388–389.

9. TULRCA 1992, s70B, inserted by ERA 1999, s 5.

10. *Ibid.*, ss 186–187.

The Definition of Recognition

4.3 'Recognition' in relation to a trade union[1] means 'the recognition of the union by an employer,[2] or two or more associated employers,[3] to any extent, for the purpose of collective bargaining'.[4] 'Collective bargaining' has a uniform statutory definition other than for the purposes of the statutory recognition procedure, which employs two further definitions in addition.[5] In general collective bargaining means 'negotiations relating to or connected with one or more of' the matters specified in the Trade Union and Labour Relations (Consolidation) Act, s 178(2).[6] These matters are:

(a) the terms and conditions of employment, or the physical conditions in which any workers[7] are required to work;
(b) engagement or non-engagement, or termination or suspension of employment or the duties of employment, of one or more workers;
(c) allocation of work or the duties of employment between workers or groups of workers;
(d) matters of discipline;
(e) a worker's membership or non-membership of a trade union;
(f) facilities for officials of trade unions; and
(g) machinery for negotiation or consultation, and other procedures, relating to any of the above matters, including the recognition by employers or employers' associations of the right of a trade union to represent workers in such negotiation or consultation or in the carrying out of such procedures.

The same issues constitute the subject-matter of a 'trade dispute' for the purposes of the statutory immunities relating to industrial action; the scope of 'legitimate' industrial action and that of 'collective bargaining' are therefore co-extensive. Although the legislation does not prevent employers and unions negotiating on matters outside those listed, such as future investment strategy, the list reflects a perception of the issues which are seen as appropriate for joint regulation. The case law relating to the interpretation of the listed matters (holding, for example, that in (a) 'terms of employment' extends beyond contractual terms) has arisen in the industrial action context and we analyse it in greater detail in para **6.21**. The phrase 'to any extent' in the definition of 'recognition' means that it is sufficient that the employer negotiates with a union on any one of these matters for the union to be recognised within the meaning of the statute, although the precise extent of recognition is relevant to the scope of the rights to disclosure of information and time off.

---

1. See para **2.4**.

2. Defined TULRCA 1992, s 295; see further App 1.
3. *Ibid*, s 297; see further App 1.
4. *Ibid.*, s 178(3).
5. '[N]egotiations relating to pay, hours and holidays', or negotiations relating to matters agreed by the parties: *ibid.*, Sched A1, para 3; see further para **4.8**.
6. *Ibid.*, s 178(1).
7. For the definition of 'worker' see TULRCA 1992, s 296; see further App 1.

4.4 The case law on what constitutes 'recognition' has developed mainly in the context of consultation before dismissal for redundancy. The cases turn on their own facts but a number of general principles have emerged. First, there must have been an agreement between the employer and the union to negotiate on one or more of the specified matters,[1] although such agreement may be express or implied. This agreement may be oral, in writing or established by conduct. An express agreement which specifies the range of bargainable issues has advantages for both parties; it puts the fact and extent of recognition beyond doubt and will assist in determining the scope of the rights to disclosure of information and time off for union officials. The courts have adopted a cautious approach towards implying recognition in the light of the legal obligations it entails. In the leading case of *National Union of Gold, Silver and Allied Trades v Albury Bros Ltd* Eveleigh LJ emphasised the need for clear and distinct evidence that the employer had agreed to negotiate with a view to striking a bargain; a willingness merely to discuss would not be enough.[2] Sir David Cairns affirmed previous EAT decisions which had stressed that the acts relied upon 'must be clear and unequivocal and usually involve a course of conduct over a period of time'.[3] On the facts, some correspondence and a single meeting which did not result in agreement was insufficient to constitute recognition (in contrast to an earlier case where recognition was inferred from the cumulative effect of contacts between the employer and union over the period of a year).[4] The court also affirmed that the fact that the employers' federation, of which the employer was a member, recognised the union did not constitute recognition by the employer itself. There is, therefore, no place for the concept of enforced or automatic recognition thrust upon an employer by the act of a third party over which it has no control.[5] It remains unclear whether a disclaimer of recognition can prevent a union being 'recognised' in law. It has been said that recognition cannot be inferred from the negotiation of an agreement which specifically states that there is no intention to recognise for negotiating purposes.[6] However it is strongly arguable that a concerted attempt by an employer to use the services of a union to secure agreements covering the workforce whilst disclaiming any intention to recognise could be challenged as an attempt to exclude entitlement to statutory rights.[7]

---

1. *NUGSAT v Albury Bros Ltd* [1978] IRLR 504, CA; *NUTGW v Charles Ingram and Co Ltd* [1977] IRLR 147, EAT; *TGWU v Andrew Dyer* [1977] IRLR 93, EAT.

2. [1978] IRLR 504 at 506. See also *USDAW v Sketchley Ltd* [1981] IRLR 291, EAT: agreement to provide 'recognition for representation' of members in grievance procedures, together with facilities for appointing shop stewards and collecting union subscriptions, not recognition for the purposes of negotiation.

3. *Ibid.*

4. *Joshua Wilson and Bros Ltd v USDAW* [1978] IRLR 120, EAT.

5. See *Cleveland County Council v Springett* [1985] IRLR 131, EAT: appointment by the Secretary of State of a union to the Burnham Committee, which formerly negotiated teachers' pay at national level, did not bring recognition by an individual local education authority employer.

6. *USDAW v Sketchley Ltd*, above, note 2, at 295.

7. TULRCA 1992, s. 288. Cf, in the context of unfair dismissal, *Igbo v Johnson Matthey Chemicals Ltd* [1986] IRLR 215, CA.

The Statutory Recognition Procedure: Overview and General Principles

4.5 The Trade Union and Labour Relations (Consolidation) Act 1992, Schedule A1 enables an independent trade union (or unions) to make a request for recognition to be entitled to conduct collective bargaining relating to pay, hours and holidays on behalf of a specified group or group of workers (a 'bargaining unit').[1] This is the first stage of complex, multi-step procedure whose stages we list in para **4.8**. A valid request for recognition may be presented only where the employer, together with any associated employer, employs at least 21 workers on the day of the request, or has employed an average of 21 workers in the 13 weeks ending with that day.[2] In the event that the employer refuses to grant the request for recognition, or negotiations between the parties fail, the union or unions may present an application to the CAC to decide whether the proposed, or some other, bargaining unit is appropriate and whether the union has the support of a majority of workers in the appropriate bargaining unit.[3] There are safeguards against disruption of existing bargaining arrangements; an application will not be admissible if the employer already recognises a union in respect of any workers within the proposed bargaining unit, even if such recognition does not cover all (or any) of the areas for which mandatory recognition may be sought (although where an independent union is already recognised, it can use the procedure to extend the scope of recognition to those areas).[4] The procedure also prevents unions making competing applications; joint applications are permitted but only if unions demonstrate that, if recognised, they will co-operate in specified ways.[5] There is a high hurdle to rule out speculative applications; to be admissible, the CAC must find that members of the applicant union (or unions) constitute at least 10 per cent of the workers constituting the proposed bargaining unit, and that a majority of the workers in that bargaining unit would be likely to favour recognition of the union (or unions).[6] Once the application has been deemed admissible, the parties have the opportunity to agree a bargaining unit, in default of which the CAC will decide this according to specified criteria, the primary one of which is 'the need for the unit to be compatible with effective management'.[7] If the bargaining unit agreed by the parties or determined by the CAC differs from the proposed bargaining unit, the CAC must then decide whether the application is valid according to the same criteria which govern its admissibility; thus, if the new bargaining unit overlaps with any existing bargaining unit, for example, the application will not be valid.[8] If the application passes these preliminary tests, there are then two routes to gaining recognition. The first is where the CAC is satisfied that a majority of the workers constituting the bargaining unit are members of the union.[9] The second, applicable where this is not the case, is where a majority of those voting in a ballot, and 40 per cent of those in the bargaining unit, support the union or unions being recognised.[10] However, a ballot may also be required even if a majority of the workers in the bargaining unit are members of the union(s) in specified circumstances, including where the CAC is satisfied that a ballot should be held 'in the interests of good industrial relations'.[11] Employers are under a duty to co-operate with the union(s) and person appointed to conduct the ballot (a 'qualified independent person' appointed by the CAC), in default of which the CAC may ultimately declare the union(s) recognised; the specific duty on employers to allow the union(s) access to the workers is amplified in a Code of Practice.[12] If a union is recognised in consequence of a request which meets the statutory requirements (whether by agreement or otherwise), the CAC may also specify a 'method' by which collective bargaining is to be conducted if the parties cannot reach agreement on this (or if one party defaults on an agreement).[13] In doing so, the CAC must take account of the method contained in an order of the Secretary of State, although it is free to depart from this as it thinks appropriate.[14] The specified method has effect as if it were contained in a legally enforceable contract between the parties unless they agree otherwise in writing, although specific performance is the only remedy available in the event of a failure by either party to comply with its terms.[15] The recognition procedure is designed to promote stable industrial relations, and for that reason a union whose application for recognition is unsuccessful may not reapply for recognition in respect of the same (or substantially the same) bargaining unit within a three year period.[16] Conversely, where a union has been recognised pursuant to a statutory request it may not be derecognised by the employer within three years, although special provision is made if a union loses its certificate of independence or the bargaining unit ceases to exist.[17] Moreover, if recognition is granted pursuant to a finding that a majority of the workers are members of the applicant union(s), or consequent upon a ballot, the employer may derecognise the union only if the requisite support for the termination of the bargaining arrangements has been demonstrated in a ballot.[18] Where recognition results from a declaration of the CAC, the bargaining unit may be varied on application to the CAC but only where the CAC is satisfied that the original bargaining unit has ceased to be appropriate according to specified criteria.[19]

---

1. TULRCA 1999, Sched A1, inserted by ERA 1999, s 1 and Sched 1, paras 1–3.

2. *Ibid.*, para 7. See App 1 for the definition of an 'associated employer'.

3. *Ibid.*, para 11(2);12(2). If the parties have agreed a bargaining unit, only the second of these questions is referred to the CAC: para 12(4).

4. *Ibid.*, para 35. Recognition of a non-independent union also renders an application inadmissible, although if the CAC has issued a declaration that those bargaining arrangements should cease on the basis that this represents the wishes of a majority of the bargaining unit (see Part VI, discussed at para **4.53** *et seq*), re-recognition of such a union within three years will not prevent a recognition application in respect of that bargaining unit being accepted by the CAC: para 35(4).

5. *Ibid.*, paras 37, 51.

6. *Ibid.*, para 36.

7. *Ibid.*, paras 18, 19.

8. *Ibid.*, paras 20, 43–50.

9. *Ibid.*, para 22.

10. *Ibid.*, paras 23, 29.

11. *Ibid.*, para 22.

12. *Ibid.*, paras 26,27.

13. *Ibid.*, paras 30–32; 58–63.

14. *Ibid.*, para 168.

15. *Ibid.*, para 31.

16. *Ibid.*, para 40.

17. *Ibid.*, paras 74–81; 149–155.

18. *Ibid.*, paras 104–133. Where the union was recognised without a ballot, the application is admissible if the CAC is satisfied that fewer than half the workers are members. An employer may also seek to derecognise the union if it, together with any associated employer, employed fewer than 21 workers over a 13-week period provided that three years have passed since the initial declaration.

19. *Ibid.*, Part III.

4.6 The provisions of the Schedule relating to recognition are contained in three Parts: (initial) Recognition (Part I); Voluntary Recognition (Part II); and Changes Affecting Bargaining Unit (Part III). Part IX, which deals with general matters such as the powers of the Secretary of State, is also relevant in this context. Each Part of the Schedule contains its own definition section and we indicate these definitions at the beginning of the section of text which deals with the part in question. In addition, Part IX contains one definition which applies to the Schedule as a whole: a 'working day', crucial to the calculation of time limits, is defined in its application to a part of Great Britain as a day other than a Saturday or Sunday, Christmas Day or Good Friday, or a day which is a bank holiday in that part.[1] Those parts of the Schedule not discussed in this section deal, respectively, with the circumstances in which trade unions may be derecognised, and the protection afforded to workers against dismissal or exposure to other forms of detriment by their employer for stipulated acts relating to the statutory procedures. These are examined in later sections of the chapter, followed by an assessment of the implications of the Human Rights Act 1998 for the recognition and derecognition procedures as a whole.

---

1. TULRCA 1992, Sched A1, para 172. Other definitions are contained in TULRCA 1992, ss 295–298.

The Role and Operation of the CAC

4.7 The operation of the recognition procedure is in the hands of the CAC. The CAC was established by the Employment Protection Act 1975 as a permanent and independent industrial relations arbitration body.[1] It is composed of a chairman, deputy chairmen and other members appointed by the Secretary of State[2] who are recruited for their experience either as representatives of employers or of workers; the chairman is currently a High Court judge. The CAC's other statutory functions relate to the disclosure of information provisions, and the Transnational Information and Consultation of Employees Regulations 1999;[3] it can also serve as a voluntary arbitration body on a reference from ACAS,[4] but it last performed that role in 1989. In all areas of its jurisdiction the CAC seeks to adopt a flexible and problem-solving approach. In the context of the recognition procedure, the CAC consists of a tripartite panel chaired by the chairman or a deputy chairman; a member whose experience is as a representative of employers; and a member whose experience is as a representative of workers.[5] Decisions are reached by a majority; if there is no majority, the chairman of the panel decides.[6] Subject to this, each panel is formally free to regulate its own procedure,[7] although it is to be expected that there will be a measure of consistency between panels.[8] A panel may sit in private at the discretion of its chairman where it appears expedient to do so,[9] for example if particularly confidential matters are to be aired. All applications to the CAC must be made in such form and supported by such documents as the CAC requires; the applicant union(s) must also give notice of and a copy of the application and supporting documents to the employer.[10] The CAC is generally required to consider evidence put to it by the union(s) and employer when deciding particular questions, and the principle of natural justice requires that each side should have the opportunity to comment on the other's case and evidence material to that case. In contrast to its powers under the Transnational Information and Consultation of Employees Regulations, where it must make 'such inquiries as it sees fit',[11] the CAC has no obligation to seek out evidence in this context, nor is it empowered to order disclosure of documents beyond those required for the initial application. If it appears that a hearing will be necessary to determine a particular question the chairman of the panel may hold a preliminary meeting with the parties to set out procedures and identify the issues in dispute. The parties are required to submit and exchange evidence in the form of written submissions prior to the hearing, and new evidence will be admitted at hearings only for good reasons. Each party will be asked at the hearing to comment on and amplify its written statement, to comment on the other's evidence and to answer questions put to them by the panel. The parties are required to specify in advance any speakers proposed for the hearing, who may be cross-questioned where factual issues are in dispute, at the discretion of the panel. Hearings are expected normally to be completed in a day. The parties may appoint representatives, but there is no requirement to use lawyers, and hearings are intended to be held in as informal a way as is consistent with clarity and fairness. The CAC has no power to award costs. It has a range of functions under the recognition procedure. Most notably, once an application has been accepted, it is accorded the role both of conciliator and of adjudicator, a combination which mirrors that of ACAS under the previous procedure. However in trying to help the parties the CAC may suggest that they seek assistance from ACAS. This may be a preferable course of action where a party wishes to communicate confidential information at this stage which it does not wish to be disclosed to the other party at any subsequent hearing; although matters can be discussed in confidence with members of the CAC panel (or with the case manager or ACAS) during the 'conciliation' stage, if information is disclosed that concerns key facts relevant to the panel's decision (for example, impending mergers or take-overs of either businesses or unions) the CAC's Guide to the Parties states that the panel may, after issuing a warning, need to reveal these facts to the other party to enable them to be checked and/or challenged at a hearing. When acting as adjudicator, the scope of the CAC's discretion varies depending upon the context. In some instances—deciding whether an original bargaining unit which is the subject of a recognition declaration continues to be appropriate, for example – it is permitted to have regard exclusively to matters specified in the legislation,[12] although the interpretation of the statutory language may be open to dispute. In others, such as the designation of the original bargaining unit, or the method by which a ballot should be conducted, it has a wider discretion;[13] although the factors which it is required to take into account in reaching its decision are specified, consideration of other matters is not precluded. However, in exercising any of its functions under the Schedule it must always 'have regard to the object of encouraging and promoting fair and efficient practices and arrangements in the workplace, so far as having regard to that object is consistent with applying other provisions of this Schedule in the case concerned'.[14] Tight time limits are laid down for all stages of the procedure, although these may be extended with the consent of the parties and/or the CAC. Where the CAC itself specifies a longer period it must do so by notice to the parties giving reasons for the extension.[15] However there is no general requirement that the CAC should give its decisions in writing; a Government spokesman explained that although it would be expected to do so 'in almost all cases . . . it may be desirable for some minor decisions—for example, on minor procedural matters—to be conveyed orally in the interests of speed and efficiency'.[16] Nor is there is a general statutory requirement for the CAC to give reasons for its decisions; in most areas its duty is confined to notifying the parties of its decision. In recent years the courts have recognised an increasing range of situations in which decision-makers are required to give reasons for their decisions as an element of the duty to act fairly, although this requirement has not, as yet, taken on the character of a general rule.[17] One such class of situation is where the subject matter is an interest so highly regarded by the law—for example personal liberty—that fairness requires that reasons be given as of right.[18] In this context the freedom of an employer to refuse to recognise a union may well be regarded by the judiciary as constituting such an interest, particularly as it can result in the employer becoming party to an obligation—the bargaining 'method'—which is treated as a contract.[19] A further argument, applicable to both unions and employers, lies in the judicial character of the CAC; although the obligation to give reasons is not confined to bodies of this nature, this is a factor which militates in favour of it.[20] It is also strongly arguable that a failure by the CAC to give reasons for its decisions may breach Article 6 of the ECHR, which requires that '[i]n the determination of his civil rights and obligations . . . , everyone is entitled to a fair and public hearing within a reasonable time by an independent and impartial tribunal established by law.'[21] In practice, it is anticipated that in the majority of cases the CAC will give sufficient reasons for its decisions, irrespective of whether it has a statutory duty to do so. The Government recognised that the CAC was more at risk of judicial review if it chose not to give written decisions with reasons, and affirmed that it would normally do so, but concluded that 'it would not be right to oblige it to do so in every case'; there may be situations where the CAC could regard this as 'unnecessary and undesirable', such as where it could damage industrial relations or involve criticism of an individual or the disclosure of commercially sensitive information.[22]

---

1. TULRCA 1992, s 259. See App 5 for details of how to contact the CAC.

2. *Ibid.*, s 260, as amended by ERA 1999, s 24. Members are appointed by the Secretary of State after consultation with ACAS.

3. See paras **4.65** and **5.38**

4. TULRCA 1992, s 212(1).

5. *Ibid.*, s 263A.

6. *Ibid.*, s263A(5),(6).

7. *Ibid.*, s263A(7).

8. The procedures which panels can be expected to follow are detailed in *Statutory Recognition—A Guide for the Parties*, obtainable from the CAC.

9. *Ibid.*, s263A(4). Cf. Article 6(1) of the ECHR, which stipulates when proceedings may be held in private.

10. See TULRCA 1992, Sched A1, paras 33 and 34, for example. There is a standard application form for applications under Part I of the Schedule, obtainable from the CAC. This form requires the union, *inter alia*, to define the bargaining unit by reference to department, location, or trade, function or position in the company; to state the total number of workers, and of union members, in the bargaining unit; and to produce evidence that a majority of workers in the bargaining unit are likely to support recognition.

11. SI 1999/3323, reg 38(2).

12. TULRCA 1992, Sched A1, para 70(3).

13. *Ibid.*, paras 19(3); 25(5).

14. *Ibid.*, para 171.

15. See, for example, *ibid.*, para 14(6)(b).

16. Mr Michael Wills, Minister for Small Firms, Trade and Industry, House of Commons, Official Report of Standing Committee E, 7.15pm, 16 March 1999.

17. In *Stefan v General Medical Council* [1999] 1 WLR 1293 at 1301 the Privy Council acknowledged that there was a 'strong argument for the view that what were once seen as exceptions to a rule may now be becoming examples of the norm, and the cases where reasons are not required may be taking on the appearance of exceptions'.

18. *R v Higher Education Funding Council, ex parte Institute of Dental Surgery* [1994] 1 All ER 651 at 671 (Sedley J), cited with approval in *Stefan*, above. See, for example, *Doody v Secretary of State for the Home Department* [1993] 3 WLR 154, HL.

19. In *Grunwick Processing Laboratories Ltd v ACAS* [1978] ICR 231 Lord Salmon at 268 stressed the 'interference with individual liberty' constituted by the 1975 recognition procedure, in the context of the ultimate sanction of mandatory implication

of contractual terms determined by the CAC (a sanction which remains in the context of the disclosure of information procedure: see para **4.67**).

20. See *Stefan*, above note 12, at 1302. The cases cited in support of this proposition were *R* v *Civil Service Appeal Board, ex parte Cunningham* [1992] ICR 816, CA (board deciding on compensation for dismissal) and *R* v *Ministry of Defence, ex parte Murray* [1998] COD 134, DC (court martial).

21. It seems clear that the recognition procedure involves the determination of 'civil rights and obligations'. For the scope of this concept, which has an autonomous Convention meaning, see Harris *et al*, 1995, 175-192; van Dijk and van Hoof, 1998, 392-406. It seems to be the case that every stage of the procedure will be subject to Article 6. (Cf Harris *et al*, 1995, 191: '[a]ny preliminary decision that is crucial to the applicant's claim is determinative of his civil rights and obligations and hence is subject to Article 6'. *Obermeier* v *Austria* judgment of 22 May 1990 is cited to support this proposition.) The ECtHR has affirmed that it is implicit in the requirement of a fair hearing that courts should give reasons for their judgments: *Ruiz Torija* v *Spain* judgment of 9 December 1994, para 29; *Hiro Balani* v *Spain* judgment of 9 December 1994, para 27. It was emphasised in these cases that what is required in order to fulfil the duty may vary according to the circumstances of the case, but a submission which is decisive to the outcome of the case should be addressed. However there is no need to give a detailed answer to every argument which is raised before them by the parties (*Van de Hurk* v *The Netherlands* judgment of 19 April 1994, (1994) 18 EHRR 481, para 61)

22. Mr. Michael Wills, above note 16; Lord McIntosh of Haringey, Deputy Chief Whip, HL Debs Vol 601, col 1270, 7 June 1999.

The Statutory Recognition Procedure: The Procedure Analysed

Structure and definitions

4.8 A trade union (or unions) seeking recognition to be entitled to conduct collective bargaining on behalf of a group or groups of workers may make a request in accordance with the provisions of Part I of Schedule A1 of the Trade Union and Labour Relations (Consolidation) Act 1992.[1] We discuss the various stages of the procedure under the following headings:

(1) The request to the employer for recognition: conditions of validity;
(2) The implications of the employer's response to the request.
(3) Applying to the CAC: conditions of admissibility and the implications if the CAC accepts the application.
(4) Criteria for determining the appropriate bargaining unit;
(5) The criteria and procedures for determining recognition;
(6) The consequences of recognition.

For the purposes of Part I, 'the bargaining unit' refers to the group of workers concerned (or the groups taken together); 'the proposed bargaining unit' is the bargaining unit proposed in the request for recognition.[2] The 'parties' means 'the union (or unions) and the employer';[3] 'employer' means 'the employer of the workers constituting the bargaining unit concerned'.[4] However there is no correlative definition of 'union' to mean the union which has brought the request for recognition. In some cases it is clear that this is what is intended. However in others, such as the duty by the CAC to consider evidence given by the union(s), it is arguable on the statutory language that it may not be so confined. We indicate at appropriate points in the text the contexts in which we consider this lacuna to be most significant. 'Collective bargaining' is defined distinctively for the purposes of Part I: with the exception of provisions designed to prevent overlap with pre-existing bargaining units, the general meaning of 'collective bargaining' given by section 178 of the Act, which we discussed in para **4.3**, does not apply.[5] Instead, references to 'collective bargaining' are to 'negotiations relating to pay, hours and holidays',[6] although if the parties agree matters as the subject of collective bargaining pursuant to a statutory request the term refers to 'negotiations relating to the agreed matters' (other than in relation to the CAC's power to specify the method by which bargaining is to be conducted in default of agreement between the parties, where the former definition continues to apply).[7] The Act does not define 'pay', 'hours' or 'holidays' and the meaning of 'pay' in particular may give rise to dispute.[8] In view of the fundamental importance of this concept, this seems a surprising omission. It seems tolerably clear that systems for determining pay, such as performance-related pay, will be covered; more questionable is whether it extends to aspects of work organisation that affect pay, or job classification systems.[9] For the purposes of Article 141 EC (previously Article 119 of the EC Treaty), which provides for equal pay for equal work, 'pay' has been accorded a wide definition by the European Court of Justice, extending, *inter alia*, to payments made by an employer under an occupational pension scheme;[10] *ex gratia* payments to employees on termination of employment;[11] and payments in respect of time off to take part in training courses for the purposes of employee representation.[12] There have been a number of cases under the Equal Pay Act 1970 where this approach has been implemented,[13] and it remains to be seen whether domestic courts will apply a similarly broad approach in the context of the recognition procedure. The Government appears to have assumed that where the scope of 'collective bargaining' is defined by reference to the agreement of the parties it will extend beyond pay, hours and holidays, and this is reflected in the explanatory notes to the Employment Relations Act.[14] However there seems nothing on the face of the legislation to prevent such an agreement being more restrictive in its scope, albeit it is difficult to imagine circumstances where a union would agree to this unless it reached such an agreement prior to the CAC deciding on recognition and feared that it would be unable to meet the statutory criteria. There is no requirement that the parties' agreement as to the subject-matter of collective bargaining should be in writing unless it constitutes a variation to a bargaining method specified by the CAC, although it is clearly advisable that it should be.[15] If conduct alone is relied upon in determining the scope of bargaining, the principles discussed in para **4.4** would seem likely to be applied.

---

1. Inserted by ERA 1999, s 1 and Sched 1.
2. TULRCA 1992, Sched A1, para 2(2),(3).
3. *Ibid.*, para 2(5).
4. *Ibid.*, para 2(4).
5. *Ibid.*, para 3(2), (6).
6. *Ibid.*, para 3(3).
7. *Ibid.*, para 3(4), (5).
8. The Government acknowledged that there may have been a case for defining 'pay' when the CAC imposed a bargaining method (Mr. Michael Wills, Minister of State for Small Firms, Trade and Industry, House of Commons, Official Report of Standing Committee E, 11.30am, 16 March 1999) but it did not, in the event, introduce a definition for any purpose.
9. Cf Wood and Godard, 1999, 232.
10. Case 262/88 *Barber v Guardian Royal Exchange Assurance Group* [1990] IRLR 240. The Article itself defines 'pay' as 'the ordinary basic or minimum wage or salary and any other consideration, whether in cash or in kind, which the worker receives directly or indirectly, in respect of his employment, from his employer'.
11. *Barber v Guardian Royal Exchange Assurance Group*, above..
12. Case C–457/93 *Kuratorium für Dialyse und Neirentransplantation eV v Lewark* [1996] IRLR 637.
13. See, for example, *Davies v Neath Port Talbot County Borough Council* [1999] IRLR 769, EAT, discussed at para **3.30**.
14. Para 27. Cf. Lord McIntosh of Haringey, Deputy Chief Whip, HL Debs, Vol 601, col 1147, 7 June 1999, who affirmed that the parties' agreed 'method' of bargaining could include 'dropping' matters from its scope.
15. Para 31(5).

The request to the employer for recognition: conditions of validity

4.9 A trade union (or trade unions) seeking recognition must begin the process by making a request for recognition to the employer.[1] To be valid:

(1) The union (or each of the unions) making the request must have a certificate of independence from the Certification Officer.[2]

(2) The request must be in writing; identify the union or unions and the bargaining unit; and state that it is made under the Schedule.[3]

(3) The request must be received by the employer.[4] There is no statutory mechanism currently laid down for proving that a request has been received, and

we would suggest that all requests should be sent by special delivery post or some other method (including delivery by hand) by which a signature of receipt is obtained. In addition, there seems to be no reason why a further copy of the request should not be sent by fax, particularly as this will constitute evidence of receipt.[5] There was much discussion in Parliament about the position of small employers where the proprietor of the business was away on holiday at the time the request was delivered, given that the time limits for responding (discussed in para **4.10**) begin to run the day after the request is received. It was affirmed by one Government spokesman that time would begin to run on the day after the employer returned.[6] It was further stated that in this context the 'employer' was the person 'with whom the worker has a contract of employment [*sic*]. That will be defined by the company as the person who signs that contract of employment on behalf of the company'.[7] This cannot be right for a variety of reasons, not least because many workers do not have signed contracts. There is no indication on the face of the legislation that the definition of 'employer' given in para **4.8** should not apply for this purpose, and we consider it more appropriate to adopt the test applied for service of legal documents under the Civil Procedure Rules. Where the employer is a company, the request should be served at the last known place of business or at its principal or registered office. Where the employer is a partnership, it would be prudent to serve it on a partner, although service at the last known place of business of the partnership will probably suffice. In the unlikely event of the employer being an individual, the request should be served on that individual personally.

(4) On the day the request is received the employer, together with any associated employer,[8] must employ at least 21 workers,[9] or have employed an average of at least 21 workers in the 13 weeks ending with that day.[10] There is no requirement that workers should have worked a minimum number of hours to be counted for this purpose, nor is there any 'discount' for workers who work below a specified number of hours.[11] The inclusion of 'associated employers' means that employers cannot attempt to circumvent the application of the recognition procedure by dividing their business into separate companies, each employing a small number of workers. Where the average number of workers is being relied upon, this figure should be calculated by taking the number of workers employed in each of the 13 weeks (including those not employed for the whole of the week), aggregating the 13 numbers and dividing this aggregate by 13.[12] In performing this calculation, any worker employed by an associated company incorporated outside Great Britain must be ignored in relation to a week unless the whole or any part of that week fell within a period during which he or she ordinarily worked in Great Britain.[13] Likewise, in deciding whether 21 workers are employed on the day of receipt any worker employed by such a company should be ignored unless that day fell within a period during which the worker

ordinarily worked in Great Britain.[14] Special provision is made for workers employed on ships registered under the Merchant Shipping Act 1995 to be treated as ordinarily working in Great Britain other than in specified circumstances.[15] The Secretary of State may modify the minimum number of workers the employer must employ, and the rules for calculating this number, by order made by statutory instrument subject to approval by resolution of each House of Parliament.[16] The Secretary of State is empowered to prescribe by statutory instrument the form of requests to the employer and the procedure for making them,[17] but at the time of writing this power has not been exercised.

---

1. TULRCA 1992, Sched A 1, inserted by ERA 1999, s1, Sched 1, para 4(1).
2. *Ibid.*, para 6; see further paras **2.6** and **2.7**.
3. *Ibid.*, para 8.
4. *Ibid.*, para 5.
5. Under the CPR Part 6, where the method of service of a document is by first class post, it will be deemed to have been served the second day after it was posted. We recommend service by fax in addition to the post for evidential purposes.
6. Lord McIntosh of Haringey, Deputy Chief Whip, HL Debs Vol 601, col 1180, 7 June 1999
7. *Ibid.*, col 1181.
8. See App 1.
9. See App 1.
10. TULRCA 1992, Sched A1, para 7(1).
11. Cf the Transnational Information and Consultation of Employees Regulations 1999, SI 1999/3323, reg 6(3), discussed in para **5.37** *et seq.*
12. *Ibid.*, para 7(2).
13. *Ibid.*, para 7(4). A number of employment protection rights, including unfair dismissal, were, prior to ERA 1999, excluded in any case where the employee under his or her contract of employment 'ordinarily works outside Great Britain': ERA 1996, s 196(2), (3), repealed by ERA 1999, s 32(3). The test of what constitutes work 'ordinarily' done within Great Britain was principally regulated by the contract terms, although in case of doubt, such as contracts in which the employer retained a discretion as to where the work was done, the employee's 'base' or the employer's centre of control was regarded as the determining factor: see *Wilson v Maynard Shipbuilding Consultants AB* [1978] ICR 376, CA; *Todd v British Midland Airways Ltd* [1978] ICR 959, CA; *Janata Bank v Ahmed* [1981] IRLR 457, CA; *Carver v Saudi Arabian Airlines* [1999] IRLR 370, CA. The courts emphasised in those cases the need to examine the whole contemplated period of the contract. In this context the statute refers to the week falling within a 'period' in which the worker ordinarily worked in Great Britain. It is submitted that the test of 'ordinarily working' specified above should apply.
14. TULRCA 1992, Sched A1, para 7(3).
15. *Ibid.*, para 7(5). The exceptions are if the ship's entry in the register specifies a port outside Great Britain as the port to which the vessel is to be treated as belonging; the

employment is wholly outside Great Britain; or the worker is not ordinary resident in Great Britain.
16. *Ibid.*, paras 6–8.
17. *Ibid.*, para 9.

The implications of the employer's response to the request

4.10 What happens next under the procedure depends upon the employer's response to the request for recognition. If within ten working days[1] starting with the day after the employer receives the recognition request (the 'first period')[2] the parties agree a bargaining unit, and the recognition of the union or unions concerned as entitled to conduct collective bargaining on its behalf, no further steps are to be taken under this Part of the Schedule.[3] This will also be the case if prior to the end of the 'first period' the employer informs the union(s) that it does not accept the request but is willing to negotiate, and the parties agree a bargaining unit and recognition in respect of it before the end of the 'second period'[4]—20 working days starting with the day after that on which the first period ends, or such longer period as the parties may from time to time agree.[5] The employer and the union(s) may request ACAS to assist in conducting the negotiations.[6] It should be noted that an agreement reached during the first or second period will constitute an 'agreement for recognition' and thereby be subject to the provisions of Part II of the Schedule, analysed in paras **4.32** *et seq.* In the event that the employer fails, before the end of the first period, to respond to the request, or rejects it without indicating a willingness to negotiate, the union(s) may apply to the CAC to decide both whether the proposed bargaining unit, or some other bargaining unit, is appropriate and whether the union has (or unions have) the support of a majority of workers constituting the appropriate bargaining unit.[7] It (or they) may also apply to the CAC in the event that no agreement is reached at the end of the 'second period'.[8] (If the parties have agreed on the appropriate bargaining unit, the union(s) may apply to the CAC to decide solely the question of support.[9]) However no application may be made to the CAC if the union(s) concerned rejected the employer's proposal that ACAS be requested to assist in conducting the negotiations, or failed to accept such a proposal within ten working days starting with the day after that on which the proposal was made.[10] The employer must make this proposal within ten working days starting with the day after that on which it informs the union(s) that it is willing to negotiate;[11] it cannot therefore spring it on the union as a last-minute tactic at the end of the second negotiating period.

1. TULRCA 1992, Sched A1, para 172; see further para **4.6**.
2. *Ibid.*, para 10(6).
3. *Ibid.*, para 10(1).
4. *Ibid.*, paras 10(2)–(4).
5. *Ibid.*, para 10(7).
6. *Ibid.*, para 10(5). It is ambiguous whether both parties are required to make the request. The terms of para 12(5), discussed below, suggest that joint consent to the proposal is required, even if the request may be made by one party alone.
7. *Ibid.*, para 11.
8. *Ibid.*, para 12(1), (2).
9. *Ibid.*, para 12(3), (4).
10. *Ibid.*, para 12(5).
11. *Ibid.*

Applying to the CAC: conditions of admissibility and the implications if the CAC accepts an application

4.11 The CAC must notify the parties that it has received an application to decide the appropriate bargaining unit and/or whether support exists for recognition.[1] It must then decide whether the request for recognition is valid in terms of complying with the conditions listed in para **4.9**; made in the circumstances described in para **4.10** (the only circumstances in which an application can be made); and admissible according to the tests set out in paras **4.12** to **4.16** below.[2] This decision must be made within ten working days starting with the day after that on which the CAC receives the application (with provision for extension).[3] The application must be made in such form and supported by such documents as specified by the CAC, and in making its decision the CAC must consider any evidence which it has been given by the employer or union(s).[4] One ground of challenge may be whether the size of the employer's workforce meets the statutory minimum (see para **4.9**). This may cause particular difficulties where an employer uses contract workers on a casual basis, where there may not even be records available.[5] In the event that the CAC decides that the request is not valid or admissible no further steps are to be taken under the procedure;[6] otherwise it must accept the application.[7] Notice of the decision must be given to the parties, but the legislation does not require reasons for that decision to be provided other than where it is based upon the level of existing union membership and potential support for recognition (see para **4.14**).[8]

1. TULRCA 1992, Sched A1, para 13.
2. *Ibid.*, para 15(2).

3. *Ibid.*, para 15(2),(6). 'Working day' is defined in para 172; see further para **4.6**.
4. *Ibid.*, paras 33 and 15(3). There is a standard form for applications, available from the CAC. The union must also give notice and a copy of the application and of supporting documents to the employer: para 34.
5. There may also be difficulties under the DPA 1998 where evidence requires individuals to be identified. One of the permitted purposes for the processing of data is the administration of justice: Sched 2. See further Jay and Hamilton, 1999.
6. *Ibid.*, para 15(4).
7. *Ibid.*, para 15(5)(a).
8. *Ibid.*, paras 15(4)(a), (5)(b); 36(3). However see para **4.7** for the anticipated practice of the CAC.

4.12 *Another recognised trade union.* An application to the CAC will not be admissible if the CAC is satisfied that there is already in force a collective agreement under which a union is (or unions are) recognised as entitled to conduct collective bargaining on behalf of *any* (our italics) workers falling within the proposed or agreed bargaining unit, as appropriate.[1] There are two features of this provision which require particular emphasis. First, in this context the definition of 'collective bargaining' in section 178 of the Trade Union and Labour Relations (Consolidation) Act 1992, described in para **4.3**, and not the more limited definition generally applicable to the Schedule, applies.[2] This means that it is sufficient to bar an application that there is a collective agreement affording recognition in respect of a matter to which the recognition procedure itself does not apply, such as discipline or the allocation of duties. Secondly the definition of a 'collective agreement' has important implications. This means 'any agreement or arrangement made by or on behalf of one or more trade unions and one or more employers or employers' associations' relating to one or more of the matters which constitute the subject-matter of collective bargaining, which include recognition.[3] The inclusion of 'employers' associations' in this context would appear to mean that an application will be barred if any of the workers in the proposed bargaining unit is covered by a national agreement so that a union is recognised to conduct collective bargaining on his or her behalf, even if their own employer does not recognise the union; the legislation notably does not require the collective agreement in question to be made by the employer which is subject to the recognition request. It should also be noted that, as we discuss in para **4.69** *et seq.*, the 'agreement' or 'arrangement' between the parties to the collective agreement need not take any specific form; in particular it need not be in writing. However we would suggest that, to avoid difficulties of proof about the existence and scope of existing recognition agreements, it is preferable (and in the interests of both parties) that these should be reduced to writing, and, should specify precisely which groups of workers are covered by them and the circumstances in which they may be terminated.

1. *Ibid.*, para 35(1); note also para 35(3), which provides that where the CAC has decided that a new bargaining unit is appropriate and has issued a declaration under para 83(2) that the bargaining arrangements for the original unit and those for any 'statutory outside bargaining unit' should cease so far as they relate to workers in the new unit, any declaration of recognition which ceases as a result should be treated in this context as having done so to the extent so specified: see further para **4.40**.
2. *Ibid.*, para 3(6).
3. TULRCA 1992, s 178(1), (2)(g).

4.13 The bar on applications where there is an existing recognition agreement does not apply in two sets of circumstances. The first is where the union(s) making the application and those recognised under the collective agreement in question are the same but the matters in relation to which the union is (or unions are) entitled to conduct collective bargaining do not include pay, hours *or* holidays.[1] This means that the procedure may be used by existing recognised independent unions to extend the scope of recognition to pay, hours and holidays. The term 'or' in the legislation is highly ambiguous; it is probably intended that an application should be admissible if the union is not recognised in respect of only one of these matters, such as pay, rather than requiring it to be unrecognised in relation to all of them, but the matter is not free from doubt. The second situation where the bar does not apply is where the union which is recognised under the agreement does not have a certificate of independence, or *none of the unions has* (our italics) such a certificate; at some time there was an agreement (the 'old agreement') between the employer and the union under which the union (whether alone or with other unions) was recognised as entitled to conduct collective bargaining on behalf of a group of workers which was the same or substantially the same as the group covered by the agreement in question; and the old agreement ceased to have effect in the period of three years ending with the date of the agreement in question.[2] This somewhat tortuous provision means that if there was a recognition agreement with a non-independent union which lapsed and recognition was then revived within a three-year period, that cannot be used to preclude a recognition claim by an independent union or unions.[3] In particular it means that if the CAC has issued a declaration that bargaining arrangements with a non-independent union should cease on the basis that this represents the wishes of the majority of the bargaining unit (see paras **4.53–4.55**) and the employer then re-recognises the non-independent union within three years of the old agreement with it, the new agreement does not constitute a barrier to a recognition claim by an independent union or unions. In this context it is for the CAC to decide whether one group of workers is the same or substantially the same as another, but in so deciding it may take account of the views of any person it believes has an interest in the matter.[4]

---

1. TULRCA 1992, Sched A1, para 35(2).
2. *Ibid.*, para 35(4). See para **2.6** and **2.7** for a certificate of independence.
3. Note that the Explanatory Notes to the Employment Relations Act 1999, para 40, incorrectly state, at the time of writing, that the paragraph applies when the union ceased to be recognised within the three years prior to the application.
4. *Ibid.*, para 35(5).

4.14 *Level of existing union membership and potential support for recognition.* The application will not be admissible unless the CAC decides that members of the applicant union or unions constitute at least 10 per cent of the workers constituting the relevant bargaining unit and a majority of the workers constituting that unit 'would be likely to favour recognition of the union (or unions) as entitled to conduct collective bargaining on behalf of the bargaining unit'.[1] In this context, unusually, the CAC must give reasons for the decision.[2] The first of these tests will be decided on the basis of factual evidence which the applicant union places (or unions place) before the CAC. The CAC does not require the names and addresses of individuals to be disclosed, either in a union's application form or in supporting evidence.[3] However, the union is required to specify the number of its members in the proposed bargaining unit and may provide supporting evidence for this. If the employer provides conflicting evidence to challenge the union's membership figures, there may be an independent check on the level of union membership in the bargaining unit. Investigations of this level may also necessitate inquiry as to the basis upon which a union treats individuals as its 'members'; whether workers who are in arrears with their subscriptions, or who have been offered free or discounted membership, for example, are so regarded.[4] The second test, which measures potential support, could prove particularly contentious, especially as the CAC has to make a positive finding that the majority of workers would be 'likely' to favour recognition. For the purposes of interim relief, in which the term 'likely' also occurs, it has been interpreted as meaning 'pretty good'.[5] Evidence that a majority of workers in the bargaining unit are members of the applicant union(s) would probably suffice; petitions from workers, where available, may also be provided as evidence. However, it cannot be assumed that workers who are not members of the union(s) will not support recognition; indeed, the level of potential support may be greater than that of actual membership.[6] Surveys of the workforce, or of a representative sample, or of evidence of growth in union membership as a result of the recognition campaign, would be further sources of evidence which could be placed before the CAC. The level of potential support is one aspect of the CAC decision-making where the risk of judicial review by employers may be greatest. In theory there appears to be no reason why an employer should not seek an injunction to restrain the CAC from taking further steps under the recognition procedure pending the outcome of a hearing for judicial review.[7] The courts may be wary, however, of employers who seek this as an instrument of delay, given that the level of support for recognition may change, and prejudice the union's application, and that, in any event, the level of actual support for recognition can be determined in a ballot. A practical solution might be for the court to order that the judicial review application be determined with the minimum of delay.

---

1. *Ibid.*, para 36(1),(2).

2. *Ibid.*, para 36(3). It could be argued that reasons need be given only if the CAC rules in favour of admissibility. However we doubt that this reflects the intention of those who drafted the legislation.

3. Unions considering disclosing such information should be aware that whether an individual is a union member constitutes 'sensitive personal data' for the purposes of the DPA 1998, and may not be processed (which includes disclosure: s 1) unless at least one of the conditions in both Sched 2 and Sched 3 to the Act are met. These both include the consent of the data subject (in the case of Sched 3, 'explicit consent') and if such consent could be obtained, this would make the position clear cut. In the absence of such consent, Sched 2 allows processing, *inter alia*, where this is necessary 'for the purposes of legitimate interests pursued by the data controller or by the third party or parties to whom the data are disclosed, except where the processing is unwarranted in any particular case by reason of prejudice to the rights and freedoms or legitimate interests of the data subject'(para 6(1)) and 'for the administration of justice' (para 5(a)). Sched 3 covers, *inter alia*, processing which is 'necessary for the purpose of, or in connection with, any legal proceedings', or 'otherwise necessary for the purposes of establishing, exercising or defending legal rights' or necessary 'for the administration of justice'. It could probably be argued that disclosure of membership records was 'necessary' to establish the legal right to recognition, but clearly unions would wish to consider carefully the implications for their members of such disclosure. On the DPA 1998, see Jay and Hamilton, 1999.

4. See para **2.2** note 2 for further discussion of the concept of a union 'member'.

5. *Taplin* v *C Shippam Ltd* [1978] ICR 1068; see further para **3.9**.

6. Dickens and Bain, 1986, 87.

7. CPR Part 25; Practice Direction – Interim Injunctions.

4.15 *Joint and competing applications.* An application will be inadmissible where more than one union makes an application, unless the unions show that they will co-operate with each other 'in a manner likely to secure and maintain stable and effective collective bargaining arrangements' and that, if the employer wishes, they will enter into arrangements under which collective bargaining is conducted by the unions acting together on behalf of the workers constituting the relevant bargaining unit.[1] This means that the applicant unions would need to agree to single-table bargaining, for example, if the employer wished to conduct bargaining on that basis. The CAC's application form requires unions to provide any available evidence that they will co-operate in the stipulated manner. If the CAC receives an application from more than one union and at least one worker falls within each of their proposed or agreed bargaining units, and neither application has been accepted, the CAC must decide, with regard to each application, whether members of the applicant union or unions constitute at least 10 per cent of the workers in that bargaining unit (the '10 per cent test').[2] If it decides that this test is satisfied in the case of more than one application (or in respect of none), it must accept none of them.[3] However if it decides that the test is satisfied with regard to one application only, it must then decide whether that application is valid and admissible according to the principles set out in paras **4.9–4.16**.[4] An application will be inadmissible if it competes with one which has already been accepted by the CAC.[5] However if at the time that the competing application is ruled inadmissible on this basis the appropriate bargaining unit for the original application has not been agreed by the parties or determined by the CAC, *and* the '10 per cent test' described above is satisfied in relation to the competing application, the CAC must cancel the original application, which is to be treated as if it had never been admissible, and notify the parties of the cancellation.[6] This reduces the possibility that a union which may have less support than the union presenting the competing application will be recognised, although everything depends on whether the bargaining unit has already been agreed or determined. The fact that the application is treated as never having been admissible means that the union(s) party to the original application will not be barred from presenting a fresh application by the 'three-year rule' in para **4.16** below. Clearly, however, it would be desirable for the unions party to both the original and the competing applications to attempt to reach an agreement on the appropriate demarcation line between their desired bargaining units or, if possible, present a joint application, as appropriate. The TUC provides assistance to unions applying to the CAC for recognition and will try to minimise inter-union problems and, where appropriate, facilitate joint applications. Unions preparing applications are required to notify the TUC General Secretary at least two weeks before they submit an application.[7]

---

1. TULRCA 1992, Sched A1, para 37.
2. *Ibid.*, para 14(1)–(6). This must be decided within 10 working days starting with the day after that on which the CAC receives the last relevant application (with provision for extension).
3. *Ibid.*, para 14(7).

4. *Ibid.*, para 14(8).
5. *Ibid.*, para 38. This applies where the first application has not been withdrawn by the union nor have the parties given notice that they want no further steps to be taken; no declaration in favour of or against recognition has been issued by the CAC; and the union(s) or parties to the application have not notified the CAC that they do not wish a ballot to be arranged.
6. *Ibid.*, para 51.
7. *TUC Disputes Principles and Procedures*, TUC, 2000.

4.16 *Application within the previous three years.* An application will be inadmissible if the CAC had previously accepted an application relating to a bargaining unit and the application in question is made by the same union or unions in respect of the same or substantially the same bargaining unit as the previous application within three years, starting with the day after that on which the CAC gave notice of acceptance of the first application.[1] This provision is designed to deter premature applications. The bar applies if the application is made by the 'union (or unions) which made the [first] application'. This clearly would allow a different union to make an application in respect of the bargaining unit within three years; it is less clear whether, in the case of multi-union applications, the bar applies only if *all* such unions were party to the first application or if it is sufficient that any of them were. The three year bar also applies if the CAC 'proceed[ed]' under paragraph 20 with an application.[2] Paragraph 20 applies where the CAC determines that the appropriate bargaining unit is one which differs from that proposed in the request for recognition, or the parties agree such a bargaining unit; before proceeding with the application relating to that unit the CAC must apply most of the tests which it applied to the proposed bargaining unit.[3] If the CAC does so proceed, the three year bar applies both to the 'proposed' and to the 'appropriate' bargaining unit. However, if the union withdraws its application before the CAC applies the requisite tests, or the CAC does not proceed because any of these tests is failed, the bar will (usually) apply only to the proposed bargaining unit.[4] The three-year bar additionally applies where a union has (or unions have) been derecognised following a ballot of the workers in a bargaining unit (see further paras **4.50**–**4.52**); an application by a union which was a party (or unions which were party) to the proceedings leading to the declaration that existing bargaining arrangements should cease is not admissible if made within three years starting with the day after that on which the declaration was issued.[5] In all cases it is for the CAC to decide whether one bargaining unit is the same or substantially the same as another, but in so deciding it may take account of the views of any person it believes has an interest in the matter.[6]

1. *Ibid.*, para 39. If the outcome of the original application was that the CAC issued a declaration that the union was/unions were not entitled to be recognised, the three year period starts with the day after that on which the declaration was issued: para 40.
2. *Ibid.*, para 39.
3. See further para **4.19**.
4. The bar will also apply to the 'appropriate' bargaining unit in the event that it is 'substantially' the same as the proposed bargaining unit.
5. *Ibid.* para 41.
6. *Ibid.*, para 42.

4.17 *Withdrawing an application.* Once an application has been accepted by the CAC the union(s) may not withdraw it after the CAC issues a declaration that it is recognised on the basis of majority membership in the bargaining unit or after the union (or the last of the unions) receives notice that a ballot is to be held to determine whether workers want it to conduct collective bargaining on their behalf.[1] By implication, however, the application may be withdrawn at any time before then. The parties acting jointly may also inform the CAC that they want no further steps to be taken under the procedure provided, again, that they do so before the CAC issues a declaration in favour of recognition on the basis of majority membership in the bargaining unit, or before the period during which they may notify the CAC that they do not wish a ballot to be arranged expires.[2] Given that it is also open to an applicant union (or unions) unilaterally to notify the CAC that they do not wish a ballot to be arranged during this period (which starts when notice of the CAC's intention to arrange a ballot is received) it is anomalous that the union may not 'withdraw' the application during that time, even though the effect in practice in both cases is to halt the procedure. The fact that the 'three-year-bar' discussed in para **4.16** is linked to *acceptance* of the application by the CAC means that a union or unions which withdraws an application after acceptance will not be able to re-apply for recognition in respect of the bargaining unit which was the subject of the application for three years. An application which has been accepted by the CAC may be cancelled only if a competing application is presented which is inadmissible but the appropriate bargaining unit for the original application has not been agreed by the parties or determined by the CAC, *and* the '10 per cent test' described above is satisfied in relation to the competing application (see para **4.15** above).

1. TULRCA 1992, Sched A1, para 16.
2. *Ibid.*, para 17. Notification under this procedure is essential if the parties wish to make an 'agreement for recognition': see para **4.32**.

Determining the appropriate bargaining unit

4.18 If the applicant union(s) and employer agreed a bargaining unit following the request for recognition, the sole question for the CAC will be whether the union has (or unions have) the support of a majority of workers in that unit (see para **4.10** above). In that event the CAC will go straight on to determine whether the union(s) should be recognised according to the procedure in para **4.20** *et seq.* If the parties have failed to reach agreement on this matter, a prior issue will be whether the bargaining unit proposed by the union is appropriate or whether some other bargaining unit is appropriate. Once an application has been accepted the CAC itself must try to 'help' the parties to reach within the 'appropriate period' an agreement as to what the appropriate bargaining unit is.[1] This period is either the period of 20 working days starting with the day after that on which the CAC gives notice of acceptance of the application or such longer period (so starting) as the CAC may specify to the parties by notice containing reasons for the extension.[2] Unlike the 'second period' allowed for negotiations prior to the application to the CAC, therefore, the decision to extend the 'appropriate period' lies solely with the CAC.[3] The Guide for the Parties published by the CAC affirms that where the employer disputes the bargaining unit proposed by the union it should provide the CAC panel with reasons for taking a different view and, if possible, its view of what this bargaining unit should be. If the parties have not agreed the appropriate bargaining unit at the end of the appropriate period, that issue must be determined by the CAC.[4] The CAC must make its decision within ten working days starting with the day after that on which the appropriate period ends (with provision, again, for extension).[5] In deciding the appropriate bargaining unit the CAC must take into account 'the need for the unit to be compatible with effective management'.[6] It must also take five other matters into account, but only 'so far as they do not conflict with' the need for effective management.[7] These matters are the views of the employer and the union(s);[8] existing national and local bargaining arrangements; the desirability of avoiding small fragmented bargaining units within an undertaking; the characteristics of workers falling within the proposed bargaining unit and of any other employees (not workers) of the employer whom the CAC considers relevant; and the location of workers.[9] It is easy to imagine situations where these factors may come into conflict. If a plant consists, say, of production, distribution and managerial workers, each of which belong to separate unions, a 'worker characteristics' approach may suggest separate bargaining units for each group. However, this solution would conflict with the desirability of avoiding fragmentation. The parties are likely to argue tactically here; the union will wish to confine the bargaining unit to groups among which it has the greatest membership, employers will wish to define it more broadly to avoid the prospect of recognition by majority membership or union success in a ballot. It is notable that the views of the parties are subsidiary to the need for 'effective management', an approach which means that the CAC's view, not that of the employer, prevails. In cases where the employer maintains that the bargaining unit should embrace more than one plant, the organisation of the personnel and finance functions may be significant; if, in practice, each plant operates autonomously in these respects it may be difficult to sustain the argument that effective management demands a single unit. The legislation does not prevent the CAC taking into consideration matters additional to those specified in the statute, although its decision could be challenged in judicial review proceedings if these matters were deemed to be irrelevant considerations or to further a purpose which was extraneous to the statutory purpose.[10] The CAC is required to give notice of its decision to the parties, but not its reasons.[11]

---

1. TULRCA 1992, Sched A1, para 18(1). As we indicated in para **4.7**, in trying to 'help' the parties the CAC may suggest that they seek the assistance of ACAS.

2. *Ibid.*, para 18(2). A 'working day' is defined in para 172; see further para **4.6**.

3. *Quaere* whether, once the CAC has given notice of an extension, that period may be extended further. Cf. the definition of the 'second period', which may be 'such longer period . . . as the parties *may from time to time* [our italics] agree': para 10(7)(b).

4. *Ibid.*, para 19.

5. *Ibid.*, para 19(2).

6. *Ibid.*, para 19(3)(a).

7. *Ibid.*, para 19(3)(b).

8. This seems likely to be confined to unions which are party to the application, but the matter is not free from doubt: see para **4.8**.

9. *Ibid.*, para 19(4).

10. *Associated Provincial Picture Houses v Wednesbury Corporation* [1948] 1 KB 223, CA. See generally de Smith, Woolf and Jowell, 1995, as updated, paras 6-059–6-100.

11. TULRCA 1992, Sched A1, para 19(5). See para **4.7** for the anticipated practice of the CAC.

4.19 If the bargaining unit agreed by the parties during the appropriate period, or decided by the CAC, differs from the proposed bargaining unit the CAC must decide within 10 working days starting with the day after the agreement or decision (with provision for extension) whether the application is 'invalid'.[1] This requires the CAC to subject the revised bargaining unit to the same tests which governed the admissibility of the proposed bargaining unit as regards overlap with existing bargaining units (paras **4.12**–**4.13**);[2] the level of existing union membership and potential support for recognition[3] (para **4.14**); competing applications[4] (para **4.15**) and repeat applications within the previous three years[5] (para **4.16**). If it decides that the application is invalid no further steps will be taken under the procedure.[6] It is possible that a union will wish to withdraw an application prior to the ruling by the CAC as to its validity if, for example, it realises that it is unlikely that the CAC will find the requisite level of support for recognition within that unit. It will particularly important for it to do this if it fears that, although the application may not be found invalid, it is nevertheless unlikely to satisfy the criteria for recognition described in para **4.20** below. This is because, as we discussed in para **4.16**, once the CAC proceeds with the application relating to the revised bargaining unit the three year bar on an application relating to that bargaining unit, as well as to the proposed bargaining unit, will apply.

---

1. TULRCA 1992, Sched A1, para 20(1),(2),(6). In reaching its decision it must consider any evidence which it has been given by the employer or union(s): para 20(3). Note that where the parties agreed the bargaining unit during the 'second period', these issues will have been addressed when the CAC decides on the admissibility of the application to determine whether the union has (or unions have) the support of a majority of the workers constituting the bargaining unit.
2. *Ibid.*, paras 43,44.
3. *Ibid.*, paras 43,45.
4. *Ibid.*, paras 43,46,51.
5. *Ibid.*, paras 47–50.
6. *Ibid.*, para 20(4),(5).

The criteria and procedures for determining recognition.

4.20 Once the bargaining unit has been agreed between the parties or determined by the CAC, the CAC must then proceed to determine whether the union should be recognised. If it is satisfied that a majority of the workers constituting the bargaining unit are members of the applicant union or unions, it must issue a declaration that the union is (or unions are) recognised as entitled to conduct collective bargaining on behalf of the workers in the unit.[1] The comments made in para **4.14** about the evidence which should be put before the CAC are equally applicable in this context. Once again, if the union argues (or unions argue) that a majority of workers in the bargaining unit are union members, and the employer provides conflicting evidence to challenge this, the level of membership may be subject to an independent check. However even if the majority of the bargaining unit are members of the applicant union(s), if any of 'three qualifying conditions' is fulfilled, the CAC must instead give notice to the parties that it intends to arrange for the holding of a secret ballot in which the workers constituting the bargaining unit are asked whether they want the union(s) to conduct collective bargaining on their behalf.[2] The 'three qualifying conditions' are:

(1) The CAC is satisfied that a ballot should be held in the interests of good industrial relations.[3]

(2) A significant number of the union members within the bargaining unit inform the CAC (not merely their employer) that they do not want the union(s) to conduct collective bargaining on their behalf.[4] A government spokesman suggested that this may occur in the case of joint applications, if members of union A do not wish to be represented by unions A and B together.[5] What constitutes a 'significant' number of members will probably vary according to the context; the total number of workers in the bargaining unit and the percentage of union members may be relevant factors, for example. As we indicated in para **4.8**, there is no general definition of 'union' in the Schedule to confine the term to the union which has brought the request for recognition. On one view, the reference to 'the' union members makes clear that this is intended in this context. However it is arguable that it could be read to mean *any* union members. If this were to be the case, the CAC may be obliged to hold a ballot if there are significant number of workers who are members of a union which is not party to the application (and which, possibly, does not hold a certificate of independence).

(3) 'Membership evidence' is produced which leads the CAC to conclude that there are doubts whether a significant number of the union members within the bargaining unit want the union(s) to conduct collective bargaining on their behalf.[6] 'Membership evidence' is exhaustively defined for this purpose as:

   (a) evidence about the circumstances in which union members became members, or

   (b) evidence about the length of time for which they have been members, in a case where the CAC is satisfied that such evidence should be taken into account.[7]

A government spokesman suggested that the CAC may be prompted to hold a ballot under this provision if the employer can show that a significant number of union members have recently cancelled their check-off authorisations and appeared to be leaving the union.[8] It is doubtful whether this situation would, in fact, fall within either limb of the definition of 'membership evidence', although it may justify the holding of a ballot 'in the interests of good industrial relations'. Evidence as to the circumstances in which workers joined the union is presumably designed to take account of allegations of undue pressure being placed on them. However, the fact that a substantial number of workers have recently joined the union may be indicative of enthusiasm for recognition, and it is for the CAC to decide on the facts whether it constitutes grounds for the holding of a ballot. In this context the terms on which they joined may be material; whether they were offered free or discounted membership, for example.

The CAC must also notify the parties that it intends to arrange for the holding of a secret ballot if it is not satisfied that a majority of the workers constituting the bargaining unit are members of the union(s).[9] Unlike other stages of the recognition procedure, no time limit is laid down within which the CAC must decide whether a ballot should be held. The legislation does not require the CAC to give reasons for its decision that a ballot should (or should not) be ordered; this is likely to be a contentious issue where a majority of workers in the bargaining unit are union members, and it remains to be seen whether in these circumstances a ballot will be the exception rather than the rule. Where a ballot is ordered, it has cost implications for both parties. The Secretary of State may amend this provision by statutory instrument approved by a resolution of both Houses in the event that the CAC represents to him or her that it has an unsatisfactory effect, although the amendment need not reflect the CAC's proposal.[10] The Secretary of State may issue guidance to the CAC on the way in which it is to exercise its functions in this area, and the CAC must take account of this.[11] At the time of writing no such guidance has been issued.

---

1. TULRCA 1992, Sched A1, para 22(1),(2).
2. *Ibid.*, para 22(3).
3. *Ibid.*, para 22(4)(a).
4. *Ibid.*, para 22(4)(b).
5. Mr. Michael Wills, Minister of State for Small Firms, Trade and Industry, House of Commons, Official Report of Standing Committee E, 11.15 am, 16 March 1999. He described a 'significant number' as 'a number capable of affecting the result'.
6. TULRCA 1992, Sched A1, para 22(4)(c).
7. *Ibid.*, para 22(5).
8. Mr. Michael Wills, above note 5, 4.30pm, 16 March 1999.
9. TULRCA 1992, Sched A1, para 23.
10. *Ibid.*, para 166.
11. *Ibid.*, para 167. The Secretary of State must lay any such guidance before Parliament and arrange for it to be published by such means as appear to him or her to be most appropriate for drawing it to the attention of persons likely to be affected by it.

4.21 If the CAC gives notice to the parties of its intention to arrange for the holding of a ballot, either the union(s) or the parties jointly may, within ten working days[1] starting with the day the notice is received (the 'notification period') notify the CAC that they do not want the CAC to do this, in which case no further steps are to be taken.[2] It is possible that the costs implications of a ballot, which we discuss in para **4.24**, may encourage the parties to settle at this point and, conceivably, may encourage a union to withdraw its application (although it would then be barred from re-applying in respect of that bargaining unit for a further three years: see para **4.16**). If the CAC does not receive any such notification, it must arrange for the holding of the ballot, which must be conducted by a 'qualified independent person' appointed by the CAC.[3] A person constitutes a 'qualified independent person' if he or she:

(a) Satisfies such conditions as may be specified by order of the Secretary of State or who is individually specified;[4] and

(b) there are no grounds for believing either that he or she will carry out any functions conferred on him or her in relation to the ballot otherwise than competently or that his or her independence in relation to the ballot might reasonably be called into question.[5]

The ballot must be conducted within 20 working days starting with the day after that on which such person is appointed or such longer period (so starting) as the CAC may decide.[6] The ballot must be conducted at a workplace or workplaces decided by the CAC; by post; or by a combination of the two, depending on the CAC's preference.[7] In deciding how the ballot is to be conducted the CAC must take into account the likelihood of the ballot being affected by unfairness or malpractice if it were conducted at a workplace or workplaces; costs and practicality; and such other matters as it considers appropriate.[8] Thus the CAC could take into consideration which method is most likely to secure a high participation rate. Where workers are peripatetic, a postal ballot may be most likely to secure a high level of participation; conversely, where workers all work uniform hours at a single site a workplace ballot may be more appropriate, although this may exclude those on holiday, or on sick or maternity leave (but see below for the possibility of 'combination' ballots). Where shift or part-time workers are employed, it would seem appropriate, if a workplace ballot is to be organised, for it to be held over a number of days to ensure that all workers have the opportunity of voting; alternatively the CAC may wish to order a postal ballot in these circumstances. The CAC may not decide upon a combination of a workplace and postal ballot unless there are 'special factors' making such a decision appropriate.[9] Such factors *include* factors arising from the location of workers or the nature of their employment and those put to the CAC by the employer or union(s),[10] but this list is not exhaustive. A government spokesman suggested that the best example of where 'special factors' may exist would be a ballot of the workforce on an oil rig, where one crew is on duty and the other ashore on leave; the on-board crew could be balloted only at the workplace, the crew on shore by post.[11] The CAC Guide to the Parties affirms that a combination ballot may be justified where workers in the bargaining unit are absent, for example on maternity or long-term sick leave. There is no obligation on the CAC to give reasons for its choice of method.[12]

1. TULRCA 1992, Sched A1, para 172; see further para **4.6**.

2. *Ibid.*, para 24. Where more than one union is involved, the period begins with the day on which the last union receives the notice; where the notification is by the parties jointly, that day or (if later) the day the employer receives the notice.

3. *Ibid.*, para 25(1), (2).

4. *Ibid.*, para 25(7)(a). The Recognition and Derecognition (Qualified Persons) Order 2000 SI 2000/1306 specifies six bodies by name: The Association of Electoral Administrators; Election.Com Ltd; Electoral Reform (Ballot Services) Ltd; The Industrial Society; Involvement and Participation Association; and Twenty-First Century Press Ltd. In addition, solicitors who have a current practising certificate and persons eligible for appointment as a company auditor under the Companies Act 1989, s 25 may act.

5. *Ibid.*, para 25(7)(b).

6. *Ibid.*, para 25(3).

7. *Ibid.*, para 25(4).

8. *Ibid.*, para 25(5).

9. *Ibid.*, para 25(6).

10. *Ibid.*

11. Lord McIntosh of Haringey, Deputy Chief Whip, HL Debs Vol 601, col 1196, 7 June 1999.

12. See para **4.7** for the anticipated practice of the CAC.

4.22 As soon as is reasonably practicable after the CAC is required to arrange for the holding of a ballot it must inform the parties that it is so required; the name of the person appointed to conduct it and the date of that appointment; the period within which the ballot must be conducted; whether it is to be conducted by post or at a workplace or workplaces, and, if the latter, at which workplace.[1] An employer which has been so informed must then comply with three duties.[2] The first, and overriding, duty is 'to co-operate generally, in connection with the ballot, with the union (or unions) and the person appointed to conduct the ballot'.[3] The wording here was left deliberately vague on the basis that '[t]he CAC [which is charged with judging non-compliance] must have considerable discretion if it is to deal adequately with non co-operation in a recognition ballot. Rather than having primary legislation describing cunning ways of not co-operating, which, as they have been highlighted, will be circumvented, it is much more satisfactory to give the CAC the power to decide, because it will know non-co-operation when it sees it.'[4] The second duty on the employer is to give to the union(s) 'such access to the workers constituting the bargaining unit as is reasonable to enable the union (or unions) to inform the workers of the object of the ballot and to seek their support and their opinions on the issues involved'.[5] This is the subject of a Code of Practice whose provisions we discuss in para **4.26**

et seq. below. Thirdly the employer must (so far as it is reasonable to expect it to do so) (a) give to the CAC, within ten working days starting with the day after it is informed of the details relating to the ballot,[6] the names and home addresses of the workers constituting the bargaining unit; (b) give the CAC, as soon as is reasonably practicable, the name and home address of any worker who joins the unit after names and addresses were initially supplied; and (c) inform the CAC, as soon as reasonably practicable, of any worker whose name has been given to the CAC who ceases to be within the unit.[7] As soon as reasonably practicable after the CAC receives any such information it must pass it on to the person appointed to conduct the ballot.[8] That person must also, if asked by the union or unions to do so, send to any worker whose name and home address have been provided by the employer and who is still within the bargaining unit (so far as the person so appointed is aware) any information supplied by the union(s) provided that the union(s) bear the cost of sending the information.[9] This affords the union a means of communicating with the workforce without disclosure of workers' names and addresses to it. This may be particularly crucial in the case of workers who are on leave during the period prior to the ballot or who are unable to attend meetings at the workplace; such workers could in the material sent be invited to attend meetings at other times or locations, to contact a union representative by telephone, or to obtain information from the union's web-page, for example. The legislation does not expressly afford the person who conducts the ballot a right of access to the employer's premises, which will be particularly crucial if a workplace ballot is being held. However it is submitted that such a right can be implied from the general duty of co-operation.

---

1. TULRCA 1992, Sched A1, para 25(9).
2. *Ibid.*, para 26(1).
3. *Ibid.*, para 26(2). The second and third duties are not to prejudice the generality of the duty of co-operation.
4. Mr. Michael Wills, Minister of State for Small Firms, Trade and Industry, House of Commons, Official Report of Standing Committee E, 4.30 pm, 16 March 1999.
5. TULRCA 1992, Sched A1, para 26(3).
6. 'Working day' is defined in *ibid.*, para 172; see further para **4.6**. It is unclear whether the phrase 'is informed' refers to the date on which the employer *receives* the information (cf. *ibid.*, para 5, discussed in para **4.9**). This would appear to be the most appropriate interpretation (and see also para **4.9** for the identity of 'the employer').
7. *Ibid.*, para 26(4). *Quaere* whether a worker could challenge this provision before the ECtHR on the basis that it constituted a violation of the right to respect for private life as guaranteed by Article 8 of the ECHR. It is not anticipated that it could constitute a breach of the DPA 1998 because it is contained in a later statute and because disclosure would in any event fall within Sched 2 of that Act.

8. *Ibid.*, para 26(5).
9. *Ibid.*, paras 26(6), (7). The Government considered that disclosure of names and addresses directly to the union could be contrary to Article 8 of the ECHR: Lord McIntosh of Haringey, Deputy Chief Whip, Hl Debs Vol 601, col 1206, 7 June 1999.

4.23 If the CAC is satisfied that the employer has failed to fulfil any of the three duties stipulated in para **4.22** above, and the ballot has not been held, the CAC *may* (our italics) order it to take such steps to remedy the failure as the CAC considers reasonable and specifies in the order, within such specified period as the CAC considers reasonable.[1] The factors which should inform its decision whether or not to make such an order are not specified in the legislation; the Code of Practice on access discussed in para **4.26–4.28** below suggests that minor complaints should not be taken to the CAC before efforts have been made to resolve the matter internally; this suggests that where a union ignores this advice the CAC is unlikely to be inclined to make an order. The law does not provide for employers to complain about the union's behaviour in relation to access, but the Code suggests that, in deciding whether the employer has complied with its duty, the union's behaviour may be a relevant circumstance, thus potentially enabling the CAC to conclude that an employer has acted reasonably in the circumstances where access to the union is denied because the union has acted unreasonably.[2] The Code indicates that if the CAC is asked to make an order very shortly before the access period terminates, and it is impracticable for the CAC to consider the request and for the parties to remedy any failure prior to the ballot, the CAC may extend the access period by ordering the ballot to be rescheduled for a later date to ensure that access is achieved.[3] If an order is made and the CAC is satisfied that the employer has failed to comply with it within the specified period, and the ballot has not been held, it *may* (our italics) issue a declaration that the union is (or unions are) recognised as entitled to conduct collective bargaining for the bargaining unit.[4] If it does so, it must then take steps to cancel the holding of the ballot, and if the ballot is still held it has no effect.[5] There are four features of this provision that should be noted. First, it means that a union may gain recognition even if a majority of the workforce is not in favour of this, regardless of whether a majority are members of the applicant union(s). Secondly, the fact that the declaration may be issued only if the ballot has not been held leaves a lacuna if the employer's non-compliance is not evident before it is held, or if such non-compliance occurs only shortly before the ballot and before the CAC has the opportunity to issue a declaration: in those circumstances there is no provision for any penalty despite the fact that the union(s) may have been disadvantaged in the ballot. Thirdly, in contrast to many other aspects of the procedure, there is no express requirement for the CAC to consider any evidence which the parties may wish to place before it. Fourthly, the fact that it has been left to the discretion of the CAC whether a declaration is issued (with no express requirement to give reasons for its decision) may lead to the penalised employer or disappointed union(s) bringing an application for judicial review. The position of an applicant union will be particularly difficult. Unions are likely to seek judicial review only if the result of the ballot does not favour recognition, an event which may well persuade a court, even if it considers the CAC's decision to have been *Wednesbury* unreasonable, to exercise its discretion not to grant a remedy on the (questionable) assumption that the employer's conduct did not influence the outcome.

---

1. TULRCA 1992, Sched A1, para 27(1). There is no definition of 'held' in this context. It is submitted that it should be construed to mean the conclusion of the ballot, so enabling the CAC to act if the employer refuses to co-operate in appropriate ways with the person who is conducting it, for example by denying him or her access to the premises where a workplace ballot is being held.

2. Para 50

3. Para 48. The legislation does not accord the CAC an express power to reschedule a ballot, but this could probably be derived from its power under TULRCA 1992, Sched A1, para 25(3).

4. *Ibid.*, Sched A1, para 27(2).

5. *Ibid.*, para 27(3).

4.24 If a ballot has been arranged then, regardless of whether it has been cancelled, the gross costs must be divided equally between the employer, on the one hand, and the union or unions on the other.[1] If there is more than one union, they bear their half of the gross costs in such proportions as they jointly indicate to the person appointed to conduct the ballot or, in the absence of such indication, in equal shares.[2] The costs of the ballot cover those costs 'wholly, exclusively and necessarily incurred in connection with the ballot by the person appointed to conduct it', such reasonable amount as that person charges for his or her services, and such other costs as the employer and union agree.[3] The person appointed to conduct the ballot may send to the employer and union(s) a demand stating the gross costs of the ballot and the amount of the gross costs to be borne by the recipient of the demand.[4] This amount must be paid within 15 working days starting with the day after that on which the demand is received; if this is not complied with it will (if a county court so orders) be recoverable by execution issued from that court or otherwise as if it were payable under an order from the county court.[5] This seems to be a somewhat draconian provision, particularly bearing in mind that there is no statutory mechanism for a party to challenge the gross costs. The division of the costs of the ballot equally between employer and union was justified by the government as an incentive to encourage a party which knew its chances of winning were remote to agree recognition or withdraw its application, as appropriate.[6] However, the justification for requiring a union to contribute to a ballot which is cancelled because of the employer's conduct is not apparent.

---

1. TULRCA 1992, Sched A1, para 28(1), (2).
2. *Ibid.*, para 28(3).
3. *Ibid.*, para 28(7).
4. *Ibid.*, para 28(4).
5. *Ibid.*, para 28(5),(6). 'Working day' is defined in para 172; see further para **4.6**.
6. Lord McIntosh of Haringey, Deputy Chief Whip, HL Debs, Vol 601, col 1210, 7 June 1999.

4.25 As soon as reasonably practicable after the CAC is informed of the result of a ballot by the person conducting it, it must take two steps. First it must inform the employer and the union of the result.[1] In contrast to the legislation governing elections to union office,[2] and industrial action ballots,[3] the legislation does not explicitly require a report on the number of votes cast for and against recognition, and it is unclear whether this degree of specificity is required. Secondly, if the union is (or unions are) supported by a majority of the workers voting *and* at least 40 per cent of the workers constituting the bargaining unit, the CAC must issue a declaration that the union is (or unions are) recognised as entitled to conduct collective bargaining on behalf of the bargaining unit.[4] Conversely, if the result is otherwise the CAC must issue a declaration that the union is not entitled to be so recognised.[5]

---

1. TULRCA 1992, Sched A1, para 29(1), (2).
2. See paras **2.33** *et seq.*
3. See paras **6.30** *et seq.*
4. TULRCA 1992, Sched A1, para 29(1),(3). The Secretary of State may amend the degree of support required by order made by statutory instrument, subject to approval by resolution by each House of Parliament: *ibid.*, paras 29(5)–(7).
5. *Ibid.*, para 29(4).

Access to workers and campaigning during recognition ballots

4.26 Practical guidance about access to workers in the bargaining unit by unions seeking recognition (or opposing derecognition) is given in a Code of Practice issued by the Secretary of State.[1] The Code is confined to access to workers at their workplace and/or during their working time;[2] it does not cover other forms of access outside the employer's control, such as the use of local newspapers and media. It aims in the first instance to help the union and employer agree their own arrangements for access, which can take account of individual circumstances.[3] It urges that the parties make full use of the 'notification period' (see para **4.21** above) to prepare for access. The union is encouraged to request an early meeting with the employer during this period to discuss arrangements; the employer, for its part, should arrange the meeting at an early date, at a mutually convenient time, and ensure that those who represent it at the meeting are expressly authorised to take all relevant decisions regarding access, or are authorised to make recommendations directly to those who take such decisions.[4] Where there is more than one applicant union, they should act jointly in preparing and implementing access arrangements which, unless otherwise agreed with the employer, should be common to them.[5] The Code exhorts the parties to reach a written agreement on arrangements, including the union's programme for where and when workers will be accessed on site and/or during their working time and a mechanism for resolving disputes, if any arise, about implementing that programme.[6] It is predicated on the assumption that the union will take the initiative in making proposals, which should be dismissed by the employer only if it considers them to be unreasonable in the circumstances and, if rejected, should be met by alternative proposals at the earliest opportunity, preferably within three days of receiving the union's proposals.[7] It is considered reasonable for the union to request information from the employer to refine its proposals; in particular, the employer should disclose information about its typical methods of communicating with the workforce and 'where relevant' disclose its own plans to put across its views about recognition to the workers, although the names or addresses (postal or e-mail) of those to be balloted should not be disclosed unless the workers concerned have authorised such disclosure.[8] Where changes in access arrangements need to be made (eg. a union official is called away on other urgent business or a selected meeting room is 'unexpectedly and unavoidably' needed for other important business purposes) the union or employer as appropriate should notify the other party at the earliest opportunity and offer alternative suggestions, which should generally be accepted if they are of an equivalent nature to those already agreed.[9] Where the parties fail to agree access arrangements either party, acting separately or together, may ask ACAS to conciliate, and ACAS will aim to do so quickly, preferably within one working day of receiving the request.[10] In a curious provision, the Code suggests that where the process remains deadlocked the CAC may be asked to assist (it is not specified by whom), and could, in appropriate circumstances, consider delaying the ballot for a limited period to give extra time for the parties to settle their difficulties. It is then affirmed that where no agreement is forthcoming, the CAC could be asked to adjudicate and to make an order.[11] However, it should be noted that the employer's duties of co-operation and access take effect only where it has been informed that a ballot is to be arranged, ie. after the expiry of the notification period.[12] Although the legislation itself does not make this explicit, the Code states that the duty to give reasonable access ends when the ballot closes (for postal ballots, the closing date of the balloting period).[13] However, the Code also suggests that where the ballot is to be conducted at the workplace and the union has already had adequate access opportunities, both the employer and union should largely confine their activities during the actual hours of balloting to the encouragement of workers to vote, rather than pursuing other campaigning activities.[14]

---

1. Code of Practice on Access to Workers during Recognition and Derecognition Ballots. A failure to comply with the Code of Practice does not of itself render a person liable to legal proceedings, but the Code is admissible in evidence before a court, employment tribunal, or the CAC, and any provision which appears to any of these bodies to be relevant to any question arising in the proceedings before it must be taken into account in determining that question: TULRCA 1992, s 207.

2. See para **4.22** for the employer's duty to give access to workers, and para **4.23** for the consequences of breaching this duty.

3. Para 9.

4. Para 14.

5. Para 15. The Code states that the amount of time needed for access will normally be the same for single or joint applications.

6. Para 17. It would be good practice for both union and employer to nominate a person to act as a lead contact in the event of questions or disagreements about implementing access arrangements.

7. Para 18.

8. Para 19. There is provision for unions to communicate with workers in the bargaining unit via the qualified independent person who conducts the ballot: see para **4.22**.

9. Para 20.

10. Para 21.

11. Para 22.

12. TULRCA 1992, Sched A1, para 26(1). See para **4.22** note 6 for when an employer 'is informed'.

13. Paras 24, 25.

14. Para 25.

4.27 An access agreement should specify the persons to be given access to the workers in the bargaining unit.[1] The Code states that employers should be prepared to give access to individual union members employed by them who are nominated by the union as the lead representative of their members at workplaces where the bargaining unit is situated; such nominated individuals based at other workplaces provided that it is practicable for them to attend events at workplaces where the bargaining unit is situated; and full time union officials (in respect of whom it is considered reasonable for the employer to wish to give prior permission before allowing them to enter the workplace).[2] The number of representatives entitled to gain access should be proportionate to the scale and nature of the activities or events organised within the agreed access programme.[3] The Code affirms that, where practicable, access should be granted to workers at their actual workplace, but this should reflect local circumstances, in particular the employer's responsibility for health and safety and security issues.[4] Where it is practicable to hold meetings at the workplace, the employer should provide appropriate accommodation, fit for the purpose, which should include adequate heating and lighting, and arrangements to ensure that the meeting is held in private.[5] The employer's typical methods of communicating with its workforce should be used as a benchmark for communication by the union; thus, if the employer generally holds large workforce meetings in a meeting room or canteen the union should be afforded the same facilities. In the exceptional event that the nature of the business or severe space restrictions preclude meetings on-site, the employer should give all reasonable assistance to the union in notifying the workers in advance when such events are to be held and would not normally be expected to hold similar events at the workplace. It is assumed that off-site facilities will be provided at the union's expense unless otherwise agreed with the employer.[6] Access should usually take place during normal working hours, but at times which minimise any possible disruption to the employer's activities. Arrangements should reflect the circumstances of each individual case, but consideration should be given to holding events during rest periods or towards the end of a shift, particularly where a large proportion of workers in the bargaining unit is involved; the employer's custom and practice in communicating with its workforce should serve as a guide to the timing of events. Where access is required to take place away from the workplace, it is recommended that these events should normally occur outside work time unless they are held within reasonable walking distance (a provision likely to be disadvantageous to workers with domestic responsibilities).[7] When meetings have been scheduled, neither side should seek to interfere with that meeting, for example by scheduling competing meetings or events.[8] The Code proposes minimum standards for the frequency and duration of union activities. First, the union should be permitted to hold one meeting of at least 30 minutes in duration for every 10 days of the access period, or part thereof, which all workers or a substantial proportion of them are given the opportunity to attend. However if the employer also organises similar large-scale meetings in work time against the application, it would be reasonable for the union to hold additional meetings, if necessary, to ensure that in total it has the same number of large-scale meetings as the employer and its supporters.[9] Secondly, where they would be appropriate in the circumstances there should be union 'surgeries' at the workplace during working hours, at which each worker would have the opportunity to meet a union representative for fifteen minutes on an individual basis, or in small groups of two or three. The circumstances should include whether there was a demand from the workforce for surgeries; whether they could be arranged off-site as effectively; whether holding surgeries would lead to an unacceptable increase in tension at the workplace; and whether the employer, line managers or others use similar one-to-one or small meetings to put across the employer's case. Where surgeries are held, wherever practicable the union should seek to arrange them during periods of down-time such as rest or meal breaks.[10] The Code states that workers attending meetings or surgeries during periods when they would otherwise have been at work and receiving payment should be paid in full.[11] Workers who are asked by the union to conduct a surgery should also be given time off with pay, subject to exceptional situations where it may be reasonable for the employer to refuse time off, such as lack of adequate cover for the worker or inability if he or she is absent to maintain provision of a service. However before refusing permission the employer should discuss the matter with the union and the worker to explore alternative arrangements.[12] It should be noted that the provisions for time off, and payment for such time, are not reflected in the statutory provisions; they appear only in the Code. It is arguable that permission to take paid time off could be seen as integral to the employer's statutory duty to afford reasonable access, in which case it would be open to the CAC to conclude that in refusing this facility to workers the employer was failing to fulfil that duty and order the employer to remedy its failure by granting time off and/or payment.. However even if that were to be the case, in the event that the employer failed to comply with such an order there is no remedy available to individual workers, although the CAC may issue a declaration that the union has been recognised provided that the ballot has not yet been held.[13] If the employer allowed time off but refused to pay for it, whether a claim for payment could successfully be brought would depend upon the terms of the individual contract. However, *employees* who were prevented or deterred from attending a meeting outside working hours may be able to complain that they had been subjected to a detriment pursuant to the Trade Union and Labour Relations (Consolidation) Act 1992, s 146.[14] Employers are urged, 'where practicable', to provide a notice board for the union's use, in a prominent location, on which the union should be able to display material, including references to off-site meetings, without interference from the employer. The union should also be able to place additional material near to the noticeboard, such as copies of explanatory leaflets.[15] Where a union makes use of its web-site pages on the internet, employers should allow workers access to this material in the same way they are allowed, explicitly or tacitly, to down-load information in connection with activities not related to the performance of their job. Where the employer disallows such internet use, consideration should be given to allowing a nominated union representative to down-load material for dissemination.[16] A nominated representative should also be allowed access to internal electronic communication, such as e-mail or intranets, provided that it is made clear that the advice comes from the union, not from the employer; however, where workers are not allowed to use such systems for matters not directly related to the performance of their job, it would still be reasonable for the representative to use them if the employer uses them to send workers information against the union's case.[17] Finally, employers are urged to bear in mind the difficulties faced by unions in communicating with 'non-typical' workers such as those who work from home, or on a part-time basis, or who are on leave, and to be receptive to a union's suggestions for securing reasonable access to them, such as organising meetings or surgery arrangements on a more flexible basis to secure a broadly equivalent level of access as to typical workers.[18]

----

1. Code of Practice: Access to Workers during Recognition and Derecognition Ballots, para 26.
2. Paras 26 and 16. 'Official' is defined in TULRCA 1992, s 119: see para **3.27**, note 1.
3. Para 26.
4. Para 27.
5. Para 46.
6. Para 28.
7. Para 29. Note that in suggesting that access occurs during rest periods, the Code adopts a different view of 'working hours' to that which applies to the time off provisions: see para **3.26**.
8. Para 45.
9. Para 30.
10. Para 31. Where surgeries do not take place, the Code states that the minimum time allowed for each larger scale meeting should be forty-five minutes.
11. Para 32.
12. Para 33.
13. See further para **4.23**. Note that the statutory rights of employees to time off for trade union duties and activities are confined to members of recognised unions: see para **3.26** *et seq*. An employee who took time off to attend a meeting without an employer's permission who was disciplined or dismissed for so doing would not be able to claim that he or she had been penalised for taking part in union activities under TULRCA 1992 ss 152 or 146 because the activity would not have been at an 'appropriate time': see paras **3.8** and **3.10**.
14. See further para **3.10** *et seq*.
15. Para 34.

16. Para 35.
17. Para 36.
18. Paras 38 and 39. See para **4.22** for the duty of the qualified independent person conducting the ballot to send information supplied by the union to workers within the bargaining unit on request.

4.28 It should be noted that the statutory obligation upon the employer is confined to affording the union reasonable access to the workers in the bargaining unit; although, as we indicate above, the Code urges that the principle of equality of treatment as between union and employer should be applied, the legislation itself does not specifically require this (although this factor may be relevant in determining whether the access afforded to the union is reasonable). Moreover, employers are not prevented from holding 'captive audience' meetings during working hours, nor from bombarding those to be balloted with literature opposing recognition; whilst employers have direct access to such individuals, whose identities will be known to them, unions must either hope that workers will choose to pick up literature which they make available in the workplace or distribute information via the qualified independent person, which will inevitably be a more protracted process, and which may not afford sufficient time for material issued in the closing stages of the campaign to reach its destination. In terms of the content of campaigns, employers are not constrained from threatening that a vote in favour of recognition will bring unfavourable consequences for the workforce as a whole, provided that individual workers are not subjected to any detriment on specified grounds relating to their individual attitude towards, or conduct relating to, the ballot (see further para **4.57** *et seq*).[1] Although the Code counsels against harassment of individuals and behaviour likely to cause unnecessary offence,[2] there is nothing explicit which prevents employers recording the identities of those attending at union meetings or surgeries, although the meetings or surgeries themselves should be held in private. It remains to be seen whether the CAC would regard conduct of this nature by an employer as infringing the duties to afford reasonable access to workers and/or co-operation.

---

1. As we discussed in para **3.10**, it is unclear whether threatening a detriment is covered by these provisions, although we argue strongly that it should be. See *Gloucester Working Men's Club and Institute* v *James* [1996] ICR 603 at 606.
2. Para 43.

The consequences of recognition

4.29 If a declaration in favour of recognition is issued by the CAC, the parties then have the opportunity during the 'negotiation period' (30 working days starting with the day after that on which the parties are notified of the declaration, or such longer period (so starting) as the parties may from time to time agree) to conduct negotiations with a view to agreeing a 'method' by which they will conduct collective bargaining.[1] If no agreement is made during this period either party may apply to the CAC for assistance.[2] An application may also be made by 'the parties' if, following a declaration in favour of recognition, they agree a method by which they will conduct collective bargaining and one or more of them fails to comply with the agreement.[3] In either case the CAC must, following an application, try to help the parties reach an agreement on a method within the 'agreement period': 20 working days starting with the day after that on which the CAC receives the application for assistance, or such longer period (so starting) as the CAC may decide with the parties' consent.[4] If at the end of that period the parties have still not concluded an agreement, the CAC itself must specify to the parties the method by which they are to conduct collective bargaining (unless before that time the parties jointly apply to the CAC requesting it to cease taking any of the steps which follow upon an application for assistance).[5] Any method specified by the CAC is to have effect as if it were contained in a legally enforceable contract made by the parties.[6] However if the parties agree in writing that it should not have this effect, in relation to the whole or any part of the method, or agree to vary or replace the specified method, that written agreement itself has effect as a legally enforceable contract made by the parties.[7] This does not prevent the parties from replacing the method specified by the CAC with an agreement which (like most collective agreements)[8] is not legally enforceable. Where this is the desired result, in order to ensure that the replacement agreement is not itself deemed enforceable it would be preferable for the parties to record their agreement to replace the method (which would be legally enforceable) and the replacement agreement itself in separate documents. The replacement agreement could recite that the CAC-imposed 'method' has been terminated and that the parties have agreed to enter into the replacement agreement. The replacement agreement will be governed by the general statutory presumption that a collective agreement is not a legally enforceable contract.[9] The replacement agreement may change the scope of bargaining as well as the mechanism by which it is to be conducted.

---

1. TULRCA 1992, Sched A1, para 30(1), (2), (4), (5). 'Working day is defined in para 172; see further para **4.6**.

2. *Ibid.*, para 30(3).

3. *Ibid.*, para 32. Note that the parties may apply to the CAC for assistance even if the 'method' goes beyond pay, hours and holidays, but the CAC may only specify a method relating to these matters: para 3(4), (5). The term 'the parties' suggests that any reference to the CAC must be a joint reference. However, as Harvey points out (Division N: Labour Relations, para 960), it is improbable that the defaulting party will co-operate in making a reference. In cases where there are failed procedures following voluntary recognition, a unilateral application is permitted (para 59, discussed at **4.34**). Harvey considers that *either* party should be permitted to apply to the CAC in this context also. We are less sanguine that such an approach could be applied.

4. *Ibid.*, para 31(1) (2), (8). In trying to help the parties the CAC may suggest that they seek assistance from ACAS: see further para **4.7**.

5. *Ibid.*, para 31(3), (7).

6. *Ibid.*, para 31(3).

7. *Ibid.*, para 31(5).

8. See para **4.71**.

9. TULRCA 1992, s 179; see further para **4.70**. There is, in fact, no requirement for the replacement agreement, which is no different from any other collective agreement, to be in writing, but is it usual practice for collective agreements to be in writing.

4.30 The term 'method' is not defined in the legislation and its meaning is obscure. It is clear that it does not impose a substantive obligation to reach agreement, nor even to negotiate with a view to reaching an agreement (a requirement which is imposed on employers in order to fulfil their obligation to *consult* in relation to collective redundancies and transfers of an undertaking).[1] Government spokesmen indicated in the course of parliamentary debate that 'the duty on the parties will be simply to meet and to talk',[2] a result defended as appropriate on the basis that statutory recognition should not deliver more than voluntary recognition, which does not impose any additional obligations as to bargaining conduct unless the parties otherwise agree.[3] Greater clarity has been afforded by the publication of a 'model' which the CAC will be obliged to 'take ... into account', although it may depart from it to such extent as it thinks appropriate in the circumstances.[4] The preamble to the Schedule makes it clear that the specified method is not designed to be applied as a model for voluntary agreements between employers and unions. The CAC Guide to the Parties on Statutory Recognition states that in drawing up the method the CAC will take account of the views of the parties; either party may inform the CAC of the changes it proposes, together with the reasons for those changes. The model method, in outline, provides for the establishment of a single Joint Negotiating Body (JNB), with exclusive bargaining rights to negotiate the pay, hours and holidays of the workers in the bargaining unit unless the employer and union(s) otherwise agree. The membership of the JNB is usually to comprise three employer and three union representatives on each side (subject to a minimum of three), but each recognised union is to have at least one seat. If this means that the Union side exceeds three representatives, the employer may increase its representation by a similar number if it wishes. Representatives on the Employer Side must either be those who take the final decisions in respect of the pay, hours and holidays of workers in the bargaining unit or who are expressly authorised by the employer to make recommendations to such persons, and unless it is unreasonable to do so, the employer should select as a representative the most senior person responsible for employment relations in the bargaining unit. Union representatives must either be employed by the employer or be union 'officials'.[5] The chairmanship of the JNB is to alternate between the two sides on an annual basis. There is provision for union members of the JNB who are employed by the employer to be afforded paid time off to prepare the claim, and to attend the JNB and private union pre-meetings, subject to specified conditions, and for other officials to have access to the employer's premises for these purposes. In addition, facilities for private meetings on company premises with members of the bargaining unit to discuss claims and responses to those claims should be provided where the employer has available premises for meetings on this scale.[6] Where the employer's resources permit, it should make available to the Union side such typing, copying and word-processing facilities as it needs to conduct its business in private, together with a room, with a secure cabinet and a telephone, for its exclusive use. Union proposals for adjustments to pay, hours and holidays are to be dealt with on an annual basis unless the two sides agree a different bargaining period. A six-step bargaining procedure is prescribed, beginning with the union's claim, which should be reasoned and supported by appropriate evidence, and time limits are specified for each step, although these may be varied by agreement of the parties. If the employer does not accept the claim, it should give a written response which sets out all relevant information, including information costing each element of the claim and describing its business consequences, unless such information falls within any of the exceptions to the statutory disclosure of information provisions described in paras **4.65** *et seq.* If no agreement is reached the parties are required to consider, separately or jointly, consulting ACAS to conciliate, but ACAS conciliation is not mandatory. The employer is not permitted to vary the pay, hours or holidays of workers comprising the bargaining unit unless it has first discussed its proposals with the union, although this restriction does not apply to terms in the contract of an individual worker where that worker has agreed that the terms may be altered only by direct negotiation between him or her and the employer. On one view, this provision could be read as requiring the worker and employer to have reached an agreement to this effect which is prior to any agreement on terms departing from those specified in the collective agreement. However the preamble to the Schedule which sets out the specified method affirms that the fact a method has been imposed does not limit the rights of individual workers to agree with their employer terms of their contract of employment, and it is unlikely that a court would construe the provision in a restrictive fashion. The government expressed the hope that the 'model' method would be invoked only rarely, on the basis that employers and unions would prefer to reach a negotiated agreement on a procedure which offered greater flexibility.[6]

---

1 See paras **5.17** and **5.28**

2 Lord McIntosh of Haringey, Deputy Chief Whip, HL Debs Vol 601, col 1275, 7 June 1999; see also Mr. Michael Wills, Minister of State for Small Firms, Trade and Industry, House of Commons, Official Report of Standing Committee E, 10.30 am 16 March 1999.

3 Lord McIntosh, above.

4 TULRCA 1992, Sched A1, para 168; The Trade Union Recognition (Method of Collective Bargaining) Order 2000, SI 2000/1300. The Secretary of State was required to consult ACAS before making the order, which must be made by statutory instrument subject to annulment in pursuance of a resolution by either House of Parliament.

5 Within the meaning of TULRCA 1992, s 119; see para **3.27** note 1.

6 In respect of issues not otherwise specified in the method, the parties are to have regard to the ACAS Code of Practice on Time Off for Trade Union Duties and Activities, discussed at para **3.26** *et seq*. The statutory entitlement of individuals to time off applies regardless of anything specified in the method.

7 Lord McIntosh, above, note 2, col 1159; see also preamble to the Schedule of SI 2000/1300.

4.31 Although the method of bargaining specified by the CAC, and any agreement excluding enforceability or varying or replacing that method, has effect as if contained in a legally enforceable contract, the only remedy available in the event that this 'contract' is breached is specific performance.[1] An order of specific performance requires a defendant to do what he, she or it has promised to do;[2] in this context, for example, ordering the party in default to appoint appropriate representatives to a JNB and attend stipulated meetings on identified dates. It may be sought in either the County Court or the High Court. In practice it is likely that most cases will be instituted in the High Court. The appropriate county court is the court for the district in which the defendant lives or carries on business or for the district where the subject-matter of the claim is situated. Actions for the specific performance of contracts in the High Court are usually commenced in the Chancery Division, but could also be brought in the Queen's Bench Division. They will be commenced by a claim form together with a statement of case. If summary judgment is sought, the claimant may do this at any time after the claim form has been served.[3] Specific performance is an equitable remedy, traditionally confined to situations where damages were regarded as inadequate, although in recent years a more flexible approach has been adopted.[4] In this context consideration of alternative remedies is clearly not an issue. However it is important to emphasise that specific performance is purely discretionary in its nature. It may be refused on grounds which would not justify refusal of a damages award and, importantly 'he who comes to Equity must come with clean hands'. In general, applicants for specific performance must show that they have performed all the contractual obligations which they ought to have performed and are ready and willing to perform future obligations, although breaches of a trivial or non-essential nature may be overlooked.[5] A defendant cannot raise as a defence to an action for specific performance the non-performance of an obligation by the applicant if the defendant has waived performance of that obligation or made it impossible for the claimant to perform it.[6] At one time the courts took the view that there was no power to order specific performance of contracts which involved continuous or successive acts and which consequently required the constant supervision of the court. This position has now been modified, with greater emphasis being placed on whether there is a sufficient definition of what is required to be done to comply with the order of the court.[7] In this context the model procedure would appear to comply with these conditions. The fact that the procedure is limited to an annual round of negotiations (unless the employer wishes to alter terms and conditions at other times) means that the need for supervision is not continuous, and the time limits attached to specified steps make it relatively straightforward to assess whether or not there has been compliance in formal terms.[8] Failure to comply with an order of the Court for specific performance constitutes contempt of court, exposing the party in contempt to an unlimited fine or imprisonment and/or a writ of sequestration against his or her property.[9] Trade unions will be liable for the acts of individuals according to common law principles, ie where they are acting with its express or implied authorisation.[10] In general interim relief may be claimed in a specific performance action, and an interim injunction would be particularly useful to a union claimant in the event that an employer was attempting to vary terms and conditions of employment without going through the requisite procedure.[11] The court is also empowered, in special circumstances, to grant a mandatory interim injunction ordering one party to perform an obligation under the contract, thereby in effect making an order for partial specific performance.[12] Taken literally, the legislation, in stating that '[s]pecific performance shall be the only remedy available', would appear to exclude these forms of interim relief, but the matter is not entirely free from doubt.[13] It remains to be seen how often the CAC's power to specify the 'method' of collective bargaining is exercised, and the consequences which follow where it is deployed. It may well be the case that unions will prefer to concentrate their energies upon enforcing the other rights which accompany recognition (see para **4.2**), where non-compliance carries financial benefits for their members, rather than seeking specific performance of obligations which, even if carried out to the letter, may bring no material improvement in their members' terms and conditions of employment.

1. TULRCA 1992, Sched A1, para 31(6). It is difficult to envisage circumstances where proceedings will arise in relation to the parties' agreement unless the terms of the replacement agreement is covered by the enforceability principle: see para **4.29** above. Failure to comply with the terms of the 'method' may be relevant to the exercise of judicial discretion to grant an interim injunction to halt industrial action (see para **6.54**), and for the length of time that it is automatically unfair to dismiss an employee for taking 'protected industrial action' (see para **6.98** *et seq.*).

2. See generally Jones and Goodhart, 1996, from which the material which follows is taken.

3. CPR Part 24 r 7.

4. Jones and Goodhart, 1996, 1–5.

5. *Ibid.*, 82–85.

6. *Ibid.*, 85–86.

7. *Ibid.*, 44–54.

8. In the event that an employer refused to disclose information which did not appear to be exempted under the statutory procedure, it is probable that this should be enforced by complaint to the CAC: see para **4.65** *et seq.*

9. See further para **6.61** for the procedure for committal, and penalties for, contempt.

10. See further para **6.16** .Note that the statutory regime of liability enshrined in TULRCA 1992, s 20 (see para **6.13** *et seq.*) is confined to liability for specified torts.

11. See para **6.52** *et seq.* for the principles which govern when an interim injunction may be granted.

12. Jones and Goodhart, 1996, 242–246.

13. An attempt by Lord Wedderburn of Charlton to introduce an amendment excluding interim proceedings in this context was rejected by the government: see HL Vol 601, cols 1234–1237, 7 June 1999. The government also rejected a proposed amendment by Lord Wedderburn to exclude liability in tort (or in tort in trade disputes) in this context. For discussion of how such liability may arise, see Wedderburn, 2000, 40–41.

The Effect of Voluntary Recognition Pursuant to a Request under the Statutory Procedure

Overview and definitions

4.32 It is possible that an employer may agree in principle to recognise a trade union but then refuse to implement that agreement in practice, even to the extent of rejecting talks on the procedure by which collective bargaining should be conducted. In relation to a recognition agreement made outside the statutory procedure there is no legal remedy available to the union if the employer fails to comply with its terms (unless—which is unlikely—the recognition agreement is legally enforceable),[1] although the union will be able to claim the statutory rights of 'recognised' trade unions which we outlined in para **4.2**. If the unimplemented agreement covered pay, hours and holidays, the union party to that agreement would need to terminate it in order to invoke the statutory recognition proce-dure which, as we discussed in paras **4.29**, may result in specification by the CAC of the method by which bargaining is to be conducted.[2] Voluntary recognition agreements are in a different position where they are reached pursuant to a (valid) request under the statutory procedure. In this event, the Trade Union and Labour Relations Act 1992, Schedule A1, Part II enables either party to seek the assistance of the CAC in agreeing a bargaining 'method', and if this fails the CAC may specify a method. Such agreements are also protected against unilat-eral termination by the employer for a three year period. These provisions apply only where the agreement (termed 'an agreement for recognition') satisfies three conditions:

(1) It is made between a union (or unions) and an employer during the 'permit-ted period' in consequence of a request made to the employer which satisfies the conditions of validity specified in para **4.9**.[3] The 'permitted period' is the period which begins with the day on which the employer receives the request and ends when the first of one of a number of specified events occurs and whereby the request ceases to be 'live'.[4]

(2) Under the agreement the union is (or unions are) recognised as entitled to conduct collective bargaining on behalf of a group or groups of workers employed by the employer.[5]

(3) If the CAC had received an application in consequence of the request for recognition, and the CAC had either decided it was admissible or had not yet reached a decision on admissibility, the parties must have given notice to the CAC that they wished no further steps to be taken under Part I of the Schedule prior to the 'final event': either the issue by the CAC of a declara-tion in favour of recognition on the basis that the majority of the workers in the bargaining unit are members of the union(s), or the expiry of the last day for the union(s) or employer to notify the CAC that they did not want a ballot to be arranged.[6] It will be important for unions to ensure that the employer gives the requisite notice; it would probably be safest for this to be given in the form of a joint communication to the CAC.

If there is a dispute or uncertainty about whether an agreement constitutes an 'agreement for recognition', one or more of the parties to that agreement may apply to the CAC to decide this.[7] The CAC must give notice of this application to any parties to the agreement who are not parties to the application, and reach its decision within ten working days starting with the day after that on which the application is received (with provision for extension).[8] It must then issue a dec-laration to the effect that the agreement is, or is not, an 'agreement for recogni-tion'.[9] For the purposes of an 'agreement for recognition', 'collective bargaining' refers to negotiations relating to the matters in respect of which the union is (or unions are) recognised as entitled to conduct negotiations under that agree-ment.[10] However in relation to the CAC's duty to specify a bargaining 'method' it is confined to negotiations relating to pay, hours, and holidays.[11] References to the 'bargaining unit' are to the group of workers (or groups taken together) to which the agreement relates; in relation to an agreement for recognition, references to 'the parties' are to the union (or unions) and the employer who are parties to that agreement.[12]

---

1. See further para **4.70**.
2. As a result of TULRCA 1992, Sched A1, para 35(2) an application to the CAC by a union already voluntarily recognised for all these matters would be inadmissible.
3. *Ibid.*, para 52(2)(a).
4. *Ibid.*, para 52(3). The 'permitted period' ends when the first of the following occurs: the union withdraws the request or any application to the CAC in consequence of the request; the CAC gives notice of its decision to reject the request because it competes with another and both or neither meet the '10 per cent' test; the CAC's gives notice of its decision that the request was not valid or the application was not admissible or invalid; the parties notify the CAC that they want no further steps to be taken; the CAC issues a declaration by the CAC in favour of recognition; the union(s) or both parties notify the CAC that they do not want a ballot to be arranged or the period for so notifying the CAC expires; or the CAC is required to cancel an application in circumstances specified in para 51(3) where there is a competing application.
5. *Ibid.*, para 52(2)(b).
6. *Ibid.*, para 52(2)(c)(4), (5).
7. *Ibid.*, para 55.
8. *Ibid.*, para 55(2), (3), (6).
9. *Ibid.*, para 55(4), (5).
10. *Ibid.*, para 54(3).
11. *Ibid.*, para 54(4).
12. *Ibid.*, para 53.

Restrictions on termination

4.33 If an agreement constitutes an 'agreement for recognition' the employer may not terminate it unilaterally before the end of the period of three years starting with the day after the date of the agreement (the 'relevant period').[1] Once the relevant period ends, however, the employer is free to terminate the agreement without union consent,[2] in contrast to the position where recognition follows a declaration by the CAC, where the employer will need to apply to the CAC and ending recognition will usually depend upon the result of a ballot of workers in the bargaining unit.[3] The union (or unions) may terminate the agreement at any time with or without the consent of the employer.[4] If an agreement for recognition is terminated, the agreement and any provisions relating to the collective bargaining method cease to have effect.[5] No sanction is specified if an employer seeks to terminate an agreement for recognition prematurely, nor is it expressly stated that any such attempt would be void, but this can probably be implied from the statutory language (the employer 'may not terminate an agreement for recognition'). On the assumption that the agreement does continue in being, the union could seek specific performance of the bargaining method, if this had been specified by the CAC; alternatively it could apply to the CAC for assistance in agreeing such a method, with specification following in default of an agreement, in accordance with the procedure which we describe in para **4.34** below.[6] The union would also continue to be 'recognised' for the purpose of claiming the other rights which recognised unions are accorded, which we outline in para **4.2**. All the provisions relating to termination of an agreement for recognition 'have effect subject to the terms of the agreement or any other agreement of the parties'.[7] This means that the parties to an agreement for recognition may terminate that agreement at any time. Alternatively, they may maintain that agreement but substitute a specified period of notice (six months, for example) for termination on either side, in which case the three year restriction on the employer will not apply. Conversely, it would seem to be the case that if a term of five years was substituted for three, that would enable the union(s) to seek specific performance of the bargaining method or CAC assistance to agree that method, as appropriate, if the employer sought to terminate the agreement early.

---

1. TULRCA 1992, Sched A1, para 56(1)
2. *Ibid.*, para 56(2).
3. See further para **4.44** *et seq.*
4. TULRCA 1992, Sched A1, para 56(3).
5. *Ibid.*, para 57(1). Provisions relating to the collective bargaining method are either any agreement between the parties as to the method by which bargaining should be conducted with regard to the bargaining unit or any provisions relating to this matter effective as, or as if contained in, a legally enforceable contract: para 57(2).
6. Note, however, that no application will be admissible if the employer has ceased to employ the requisite minimum number of workers or any of the unions party to the agreement no longer has a certificate of independence: see para 60. In that event the 'agreement for recognition' would remain in force, but the union would be unable to take any further steps to require its implementation.
7. *Ibid.*, para 56(4).

Provisions relating to the 'method' of collective bargaining

4.34 The provisions relating to the 'method' of collective bargaining which apply to 'agreements for recognition' mirror those applicable where recognition is consequent upon a declaration by the CAC (see paras **4.29** and **4.30**). Thus, the parties have the opportunity during the 'negotiation period' to conduct negotiations with a view to agreeing a 'method' by which they will conduct collective bargaining.[1] If no agreement is made during this period, either party may apply to the CAC for assistance.[2] An application may also be made by either party if the parties agree a method by which they will conduct collective bargaining but one or more of the parties fails to carry that agreement out.[3] However, unlike the case where recognition is consequent upon a declaration, the CAC must first decide whether the application is admissible, and in doing so consider any evidence which it has been given by the employer or union(s).[4] The substantive conditions of admissibility are two-fold.[5] First, the union (or every union) making an application must have a certificate of independence from the Certification Officer.[6] Secondly, the application will be inadmissible unless on the day that it is made the employer, together with any associated employer, employs at least 21 workers, or has employed an average of at least 21 workers in the 13 weeks ending with that day (see further para **4.9** for the calculation of this number).[7] As these factors are preconditions for the validity of an initial request for recognition, the admissibility stage serves as a check that there was been no change in circumstances between the request and application for assistance. The CAC's decision on admissibility must be made within ten working days starting with the day after that on which the CAC receives the application (with provision for extension)[8], and the parties must be notified of its decision.[9] The CAC must then follow the same procedure described in para **4.29**, which may terminate in specification of the bargaining method by the CAC.[10] There is a conundrum relating to the definition of 'collective bargaining' in this context. As we stated in para **4.32**, 'collective bargaining' in relation to an agreement for recognition means negotiations relating to the matters in respect of which the union is (or unions are) recognised as entitled to conduct negotiations under that agreement.[11] However, for the purposes of the CAC's duty to specify the method by which bargaining is to be conducted, it means 'negotiations relating to pay, hours and holidays'.[12] It is conceivable, however, that the agreement for recognition may not cover all these matters; a union may have agreed to forego recognition over hours in return for recognition over discipline for example. Nevertheless the legislation suggests that the CAC's duty would extend to specification of the bargaining method in relation to hours, so requiring the employer to obtain the consent of the union in order to exclude it.[13] The provisions relating to the legal effect, and enforcement, of the specified method are identical to those which apply where specification follows a declaration in favour of recognition and are analysed in paras **4.29** and **4.31**.

1. TULRCA 1992, Sched A1, para 58. The 'negotiation period' is the period of 30 days starting with the day after the day on which the agreement is made or such longer period (so starting) as the parties may from time to time agree: para 58(4), (5).

2. *Ibid.*, para 58(3).

3. *Ibid.*, para 59.

4. *Ibid.*, para 60(2), 62(2), (3). The CAC must give notice to the parties of receipt of an application: para 62(1).

5. There are also procedural conditions which must be satisfied. First, the application is inadmissible if it is not made in such form, and supported by such documents, as specified by the CAC: *ibid.*, para 61(1). Secondly, if the application is made by a union (or unions), it will be inadmissible if the union fails (or unions fail) to give the employer notice, and a copy of, the application and any supporting documents: para 61(2). If the application is made by an employer, it must give this information to the union, or each of the unions, as appropriate: para 61(3).

6. *Ibid.*, para 60(4).

7. *Ibid.*, para 60(2), (3), (5)–(9).

8. *Ibid.*, para 62(2), (6). 'Working day' is defined in para 172; see further para **4.6**.

9. *Ibid.*, para 62(4), (5).

10. *Ibid.*, para 63. Note that in this context any extension of the 'agreement period' is for the parties to agree; cf para 31(8)(b), where it is CAC to decide subject to the consent of the parties. If the CAC accepts an application, the applicant may not withdraw it unilaterally after the end of the agreement period: para 63(6).

11. *Ibid.*, para 54(3).

12. *Ibid.*, para 54(4).

13. See *ibid.*, para 63(4).

Changes Affecting the Bargaining Unit

Overview and definitions

4.35 Recognition, whether voluntary or otherwise, relates to a specified bargaining unit or units. It is possible that a bargaining unit which was appropriate at the time that the issue of recognition was being determined may cease to be so because of changes in the structure, organisation or nature of the business. Where recognition is the product of voluntary agreement outside the statutory procedure, modification of the bargaining unit is a matter for negotiation between the parties. In the event that the union is unable to secure the employer's agreement to extended recognition, it may ultimately have recourse to the statutory procedure; if an employer wishes to effect a change against the wishes of the recognised union(s), it may derecognise that union or unions in respect of a particular group of workers (subject to the *caveats* discussed in para **4.43)** unless (which is unlikely) the recognition agreement is legally enforceable.[1] In the case of an 'agreement for recognition', which is reached consequent upon a valid request under the statutory procedure (see para **4.32**), varying the scope of recognition also depends upon negotiation between the parties, although if no agreement can be reached the employer may not terminate the agreement unilaterally for three years, unless this restriction has been varied by agreement.[2] A special procedure applies where the CAC has issued a declaration that the union is entitled to be recognised as entitled to conduct collective bargaining on behalf of a bargaining unit and provisions relating to the collective bargaining method (whether derived from the parties' agreement or specified by the CAC) apply in relation to that unit.[3] In this event Part III of Schedule A1 of the Trade Union and Labour Relations (Consolidation) Act 1992 allows either party to apply to the CAC for the bargaining unit to be varied.[4] In order for an application to be admissible, the CAC must decide that it is likely that the original unit is no longer appropriate by reference to specified criteria.[5] The parties then have the opportunity to agree a new bargaining unit, which will replace the old provided that there is no overlap with any existing bargaining unit.[6] If the parties do not reach agreement, the CAC must then decide whether the original unit continues to be appropriate and, if not, what other unit or units is appropriate.[7] There is also provision for an employer to apply to the CAC for the bargaining arrangements to cease altogether if it believes the bargaining unit covered by the declaration imposing recognition has ceased to exist, although this, too, may result in a revised bargaining unit (or maintenance of the original unit) if unsuccessful.[8] If the CAC decides that a new unit is appropriate, it must then decide whether there is any overlap between this unit and any outside bargaining unit. In the event of overlap, the bargaining arrangements for workers in the original unit who are now in the new unit cease (as do those for any 'statutory outside bargaining unit' relating to workers in the new unit).[9] If there is no overlap, the CAC must then decide whether the support for the union in the new bargaining unit needs to be assessed. If it decides it does, it must then determine whether the bargaining unit has the level of actual and potential support required for an initial application.[10] If these tests are passed, the question whether the union should be recognised for the new bargaining unit is determined on an identical basis to the initial application, with identical consequences in the event that recognition is supported.[11] Any applications under this Part will be inadmissible unless made in such form and supported by such documents as the CAC specifies.[12] In addition, an application by a union (or unions) is not admissible unless the union gives (or unions give) to the employer notice, and a copy, of the application and any supporting documents; an employer which makes an application must furnish such documents to each union.[13] Once an application has been accepted by the CAC it may not be withdrawn after the occurrence of one of a number of specified events (but by implication can be withdrawn before that time).[14] In the context of this Part, references to the 'original unit' are to the bargaining unit on whose behalf the union is (or unions are) recognised to conduct collective bargaining; the 'bargaining arrangements' refer to the declaration and the provisions relating to the collective bargaining method which apply in relation to the original unit.[15] With specified exceptions the meaning of collective bargaining in section 178(1) of the 1992 Act does not apply.[16] In relation to a new unit, the term covers negotiations relating to the matters which were the subject of collective bargaining in relation to the corresponding original unit,[17] unless the parties specifically agree such matters in relation to the new unit in which case it refers to those matters.[18] This means that the scope of collective bargaining in the new unit may be wider or narrower than in the old. Other meanings of collective bargaining used in the Part are indicated where appropriate in the text. 'The parties' refers to the employer and union or unions concerned.[19]

----

1. See further para **4.70**. Note that if a union which was recognised for pay, hours and holidays wished to invoke the statutory procedure, it would need first to terminate the voluntary agreement: as a result of TULRCA 1992, Sched A1, para 35(2) an application to the CAC by a union already voluntarily recognised for all these matters would be inadmissible.

2. TULRCA 1992, Sched A1, para 56; see further para **4.33**. The three year period starts with the day after the date of the agreement.

3. *Ibid.*, para 64(1). 'Provisions relating to the collective bargaining method' are defined as (a) the parties' agreement as to the method by which collective bargaining is to be conducted with regard to the original unit; (b) anything effective as, or as if contained in, a legally enforceable contract and relating to the method by which collective bargaining is to be conducted with regard to the original unit; or (c) any provision of this Part of the Schedule that a method of collective bargaining is to have effect with regard to the original unit.

4. *Ibid.*, para 66.

5. *Ibid.*, para 67.

6. *Ibid.*, para 69.

7. *Ibid.*, para 70.

8. *Ibid.*, paras 74–81.

9. *Ibid.*, paras 82–84.

10. *Ibid.*, para 86; see para **4.14**.

11. *Ibid.*, paras 87–89.

12. *Ibid.*, para 92(1).

13. *Ibid.*, paras 92(2), (3).

14. *Ibid.*, para 93. These events are the issue of a declaration by the CAC that the union is recognised in respect of the new bargaining unit(s); the CAC decides that the original unit has (or has not) ceased to exist (and if not, that it continues to be appropriate); the CAC decides that bargaining arrangements for the original unit should cease because of overlap with an existing unit; the union has notified the CAC that it does not wish a ballot to be arranged to assess support within the new unit; or the notification period has ended.

15. *Ibid.*, para 64(2).
16. *Ibid.*, para 94(2).
17. *Ibid.*, para 94(3). The 'corresponding original unit' is the unit which was the subject of the application to the CAC in consequence of which the new unit was agreed by the parties or determined by the CAC.
18. *Ibid.*, paras 94(3), (4). It is irrelevant whether the parties agree matters in relation to the new unit before or after the time the CAC issues a declaration that the union is (or unions are) entitled to conduct collective bargaining on behalf of the new unit.
19. *Ibid.*, para 65.

Either party believes the bargaining unit is no longer appropriate

4.36 If either the employer or the union believes (or unions believe) that the original unit is no longer an appropriate bargaining unit, it (or they) may apply to the CAC to decide what constitutes an appropriate unit.[1] The application is not admissible unless the CAC decides that it is *likely* (our italics) that the original unit is no longer appropriate by reason of one of the following matters:

(1) A change in the organisation or structure of the business carried on by the employer. This could occur if there was a change from centrally to individually managed units, or in the event of geographical reorganisation, for example.
(2) A change in the activities pursued by the employer in the course of the business it carries out.
(3) A substantial change in the number of workers employed in the original unit.[2]

The CAC must give notice to the parties of receipt of an application and decide whether it is admissible within ten working days starting with the day after that on which it receives the application (with provision for extension).[3] In making its decision it must consider any evidence which it has been given by the employer or union(s).[4] The CAC must give notice of its decision to the parties,[5] but is not required by statute to give its reasons.[6]

---

1. TULRCA 1992, Sched A1, para 66.
2. *Ibid.*, para 67. See also para 92, discussed in para **4.35** for the procedural requirements which must be met.
3. *Ibid.*, para 68(1), (2), (6).
4. *Ibid.*, para 68(3).
5. *Ibid.*, para 68(4), (5).
6. However see para **4.7** for the anticipated practice of the CAC.

4.37 If the CAC accepts the application the parties may initially attempt to reach agreement on the issue within the 'first period'—ten working days starting with the day after that on which the CAC gives notice of acceptance of the application or such longer period (so starting) as the parties may from time to time agree and notify to the CAC.[1] If they agree a new bargaining unit or units differing from the original unit within this period the CAC must then consider whether the new unit (or any of such units) contains any worker falling within an 'outside bargaining unit'. This means a unit other than the original unit, in respect of which a union is (or unions are) recognised as entitled to conduct collective bargaining on its behalf, and the union recognised (or at least one of those unions) is not recognised in respect of the original bargaining unit.[2] If the CAC is of the view that at least one worker does fall within an 'outside bargaining unit' (which may be voluntary or statutory in nature), no further steps are to be taken under this Part.[3] This means that the declaration covering the original bargaining unit will remain in place unless and until a fresh application to change it is successfully made, possibly after discussion with the union(s) party to the agreement covering the outside unit. In the definition of an 'outside bargaining unit' 'collective bargaining' has the meaning in s 178(1) of the Trade Union and Labour Relations (Consolidation) Act 1992,[4] so it is sufficient to block a change in bargaining unit that there is recognition in respect of a matter to which the recognition procedure itself does not apply, such as discipline or the allocation of duties. In this respect the provisions mirror those relating to the admissibility of an application for recognition in respect of the original bargaining unit which we discussed in para **4.12**, except that in this context there is no requirement that recognition should be enshrined in a collective agreement, so enabling implied recognition to be considered if the CAC has evidence of this[5] (in addition to recognition pursuant to a CAC declaration). It remains the case, however, that it is sufficient that a union is recognised in *respect of the bargaining unit*; thus, recognition by an employers' association, rather than the employer itself, would appear to suffice. If there is no overlap with an outside bargaining unit the CAC must issue a declaration that the union is (or unions are) recognised as entitled to conduct collective bargaining on behalf of the new unit or units.[6] So far as it affects workers in the new unit(s) who fall within the original unit, the declaration has effect in place of that relating to the original unit.[7] However if any worker falling within the original unit does not fall within the new unit (or any of such units), the CAC must issue a declaration that the bargaining arrangements, so far as they relate to any such worker(s), cease to have effect on a specified date.[8] These workers therefore become 'disenfranchised' regardless of their wishes. The method of collective bargaining relating to the original unit has effect in relation to the new unit(s), with any modification which the CAC considers necessary to take account of the change in the bargaining unit and specifies in the declaration.[9] In relation to the collective bargaining method only, 'collective bargaining' is limited to negotiations relating to pay, hours and holidays.[10] This method has effect as if it were contained in a legally enforceable contract made by the parties (even if the product of agreement for the original unit), but if the parties agree in writing that this provision shall not apply, or shall not apply to particular parts of the method, or agree to vary or replace the specified method, that written agreement itself has effect as a legally enforceable contract between the parties.[11] This is identical to the provision which governs the situation where the CAC specifies a method in relation to the original bargaining unit, which is discussed in detail in para **4.29**, and the points which we make there are equally applicable here. As in that context, specific performance is the only remedy available for breach of anything which is a legally enforceable contract by virtue of these provisions (see further para **4.31**).

---

1. *Ibid.*, para 69(1),(4). 'Working day' is defined in para 172; see further para **4.6**.
2. *Ibid.*, para 69(2),(5).
3. *Ibid.*, para 69(2).
4. *Ibid.*, paras 69(5) and 94(2); see para **4.3**.
5. See para **4.4** for the basis upon which recognition may be implied (and cf. the explanatory notes to the Employment Relations Act 1999, which state incorrectly in para 69 that the test is whether the new unit contains workers covered by a collective agreement with another union). There is no exclusion of agreements satisfying the test in para 35(4) in this context. Thus a bargaining unit may not be varied even if the union recognised for the unit with which it overlaps is non-independent and the CAC has declared that the bargaining arrangements should cease in that unit: cf. para **4.13**.
6. TULRCA 1992, Sched A1, para 69(3)(a). See para 94(3), (4), discussed in para **4.35** for the definition of collective bargaining in this context.
7. *Ibid.*, para 69(3)(b).
8. *Ibid.*, para 73. See para 64(2)(b), discussed in para **4.35** for the definition of 'bargaining arrangements'.
9. *Ibid.*, para 69(3)(c).
10. *Ibid.*,para 94(6).
11. *Ibid.*, para 95.

4.38 If the parties do not inform the CAC before the end of the 'first period' that they have agreed a new bargaining unit or units, the CAC must decide whether or not the original unit continues to be an appropriate bargaining unit and, if not, what other unit or units are appropriate.[1] This decision must be made within the 'second period': ten working days starting with the day after that on which the first period ends (with provision for extension).[2] The CAC must notify the parties of its decision during the 'second period',[3] but need not give any reasons for it.[4] In deciding whether the original unit continues to be appropriate, the CAC must take into account *only* (our italics) those matters which were relevant to its decision as to whether the application to decide the appropriate unit was admissible (see para **4.36**) ie: a change in the organisation or structure of the business carried on by the employer; any change in the activities pursued by the employer in the course of its business; and any substantial change in the number of workers employed in the original unit.[5] It cannot therefore revisit its original decision or take into account subsequent evidence which may have shown that decision to have been misguided. In the event that the CAC decides that the original unit continues to be an appropriate bargaining unit no further steps are to be taken under this Part of the Schedule.[6] Otherwise it must proceed to decide what other bargaining unit or units *are* appropriate, taking into account the same factors which informed its original designation of an appropriate bargaining unit (see para **4.18**).[7] The CAC may decide that two or more bargaining units are appropriate, but if it does so it must ensure that no worker falls within more than one of them.[8] If any worker falling within the original bargaining unit does not fall within the new unit (or any of such units), the CAC must issue a declaration that the bargaining arrangements, so far as they relate to any such worker(s), cease to have effect on a specified date.[9] Having determined the new appropriate unit(s), the CAC must then follow specified procedures in relation to such units which we describe in para **4.40** *et seq.*, after examining the second route by which the CAC may come to make such a determination.

---

1. TULRCA 1992, Sched A1, para 70(1), (2).
2. *Ibid.*, para 70(2), (7). 'Working day' is defined in para 172; see further para **4.6**.
3. *Ibid.*, para 70(2)(c)
4. However see para **4.7** for the anticipated practice of the CAC.
5. *Ibid.*, para 70(3).
6. *Ibid.*, para 71.
7. *Ibid.*, para 70(2)(b), (4).
8. *Ibid.*, para 70(6).
9. *Ibid.*, para 90. See para 64(2)(b), discussed in para **4.35** for the definition of 'bargaining arrangements'.

Employer believes unit has ceased to exist

4.39 If the employer believes that the original bargaining unit has ceased to exist, and wishes the bargaining arrangements to cease to have effect, it must give the union (or each of the unions) notice of specified matters, and give a copy of that notice to the CAC.[1] The method by which such notice should be 'given' to the union is not specified; we would recommend that it should be sent by recorded delivery or otherwise delivered in a form whereby a receipt is obtained. The notice must identify the unit and the bargaining arrangements, and state the date on which it is given; that the unit has ceased to exist; and that the bargaining arrangements are to cease to have effect on a specified date, which must fall after the end of the period of 35 working days starting with the day after that on which the notice is given.[2] The CAC must decide whether the notice complies with these requirements within ten working days starting with the day after that on which it receives a copy of the notice (with provision for extension)[3] and give the parties notice of its decision.[4] If it decides that the employer's notice does not comply with the statutory requirements, it is treated as never having been given.[5] If it decides that it does comply, the bargaining arrangements cease to have effect on the date specified in the notice *unless* the union applies to the CAC to decide whether the original unit *has* ceased to exist and whether the original unit is no longer appropriate by reason of any of the matters specified in the test described in para **4.38**.[6] The union must submit its application within ten working days starting with the day after that on which the notice is *given* (not received).[7] The CAC must give notice to the parties of receipt of such an application and decide within ten working days starting with the day after that on which it receives the application (with provision for extension) whether the application is admissible in that it has been made in the specified form and supported by the requisite documents, and that the employer has been given by the union(s) notice, and a copy of, the application and any supporting documents. [8] In reaching its decision it must consider any evidence which it has been given by the employer and the union(s).[9] If it accepts an application it must then give the employer and the union(s) an opportunity to put their views on whether the bargaining unit has ceased to exist and whether it is no longer appropriate, and give its decision within ten working days starting with the day after that on which the CAC gave notice of acceptance of the application (with provision for extension).[10] There are three possible outcomes of this process. First, the CAC may decide that the original unit has ceased to exist. In that event, it must notify the parties accordingly and the bargaining arrangements cease to have effect on the 'termination date', which is either the date specified in the employer's notice or the day after the last day of the decision period, whichever is the later.[11] Secondly, it may decide that the original unit has not ceased to exist, and has not become inappropriate, in which case the employer's notice is treated as not having been given.[12] Thirdly, it may decide that the original unit has not ceased to exist but that it is no longer appropriate.[13] In that event, the procedure mirrors that which is followed when a union or employer has applied to the CAC to make a decision as to the appropriate bargaining unit, which we describe in paras **4.37** and **4.38** above—ie the parties have the opportunity to agree a new bargaining unit during the 'first period', which must be enshrined in a CAC declaration if there is no overlap with an 'outside bargaining unit'; in default of agreement, the CAC must itself decide what other bargaining unit is appropriate according to the stipulated criteria.[14]

---

1. TULRCA 1992, Sched A1, para 74(1).
2. *Ibid.*, para 74(2).
3. *Ibid.*, para 74(3), (7). 'Working day' is defined in para 172; see further para **4.6**.
4. *Ibid.*, para 74(4)(a); 74(5).
5. *Ibid.*, para 74(4)(b).
6. *Ibid.*, paras 74(6), 75(1)–(3). The bargaining arrangements only cease to have effect if the CAC gives the parties notice of its decision that the employer's notice complies with the statutory requirements.
7. *Ibid.*, para 75(1)(b).
8. *Ibid.*, para 76(1), (2), (6). These requirements are stipulated in para 92.
9. *Ibid.*, para 76(3)–(5).
10. *Ibid.*, para 77(1), (5).
11. *Ibid.*, para 77(2), (6).
12. *Ibid.*, para 77(3).
13. *Ibid.*, para 77(4).
14. *Ibid.*, paras 78–81.

Position where the CAC decides the new bargaining unit

4.40 Where the CAC rather than the parties determines the new appropriate bargaining unit it must then follow specified procedures with regard to that unit, or, if there are two or more new units, with regard to each unit separately.[1] The initial set of procedures are designed to deal with any overlap which may exist between any of the new units and existing bargaining units. First it must consider whether the new unit contains any workers falling within a 'statutory outside bargaining unit'. This is a unit other than the original unit for which a union is (or unions are) recognised as entitled to conduct collective bargaining on its behalf by virtue of a declaration of the CAC, and that union (or at least one of those unions) is not recognised in respect of the original unit.[2] If the CAC is of the view that the new unit does contain at least one worker falling within such a unit, it must issue a declaration that the 'relevant bargaining arrangements', so far as they relate to workers falling within the new unit, cease to have effect on a specified date.[3] The 'relevant bargaining arrangements' are the bargaining arrangements relating to the original unit and those relating to each statutory outside bargaining unit containing workers who fall within the new unit.[4] The specified date must be either the end of the period of 65 working days starting with the day after that on which the declaration is issued (the 'relevant date'), or if the CAC believes that to maintain the relevant bargaining arrangements would be impracticable or contrary to the interests of good industrial relations, the date after the date on which the declaration is issued.[5] The end result of this procedure is that the bargaining arrangements for the original unit will cease without replacement[6] (in contrast to the position where the new unit has been determined by agreement between the parties, where the original bargaining arrangements continue in the event of overlap: see para **4.37**). In addition, any workers within an existing 'statutory outside bargaining unit' who also fall within the new unit will no longer be covered by the recognition declaration for the outside unit.[7] The union(s) will therefore be required to submit a fresh application for recognition in relation to those workers if it wishes to gain statutory recognition in respect of them, although it would be well advised to explore the possibilities of collaboration with the union(s) party to the agreement governing the statutory outside bargaining unit before it does so. A similar procedure must be followed if the CAC's opinion is that the new unit contains at least one worker falling within a 'voluntary outside bargaining unit' (but none within a 'statutory outside bargaining unit').[8] This is a unit other than the original unit for which a union is (or unions are) recognised as entitled to conduct collective bargaining on its behalf by virtue of an agreement with the employer, and that union (or at least one of those unions) is not recognised in respect of the original unit.[9] Once again the bargaining arrangements for the original unit cease without replacement.[10] In this case, however, workers within the new unit who are also within the voluntary bargaining unit do not cease to be covered by the voluntary recognition agreement. Curiously there is no applicable definition of 'collective bargaining' in relation to the definition of an voluntary outside bargaining unit; logic would suggest that it should cover negotiations relating to any matter specified in s 178(1) of the Trade Union and Labour Relations (Consolidation) Act 1992,[11] but this definition is specifically excluded by the statute.[12]

---

1. TULRCA 1992, Sched A1, para 82.
2. *Ibid.*, para 83(7).
3. *Ibid.*, para 83(2).
4. *Ibid.*, para 83(3). The bargaining arrangements relating to the original unit are as defined in para 64: see para 83(4) and see further para **4.35**; those relating to an outside unit are the declaration recognising a union (or unions) as entitled to conduct collective bargaining on behalf of the workers constituting that unit and provisions relating to the collective bargaining method: para 83(5). Provisions relating to the collective bargaining method are any agreement between the employer and unions as to the method by which collective bargaining is to be conducted with regard to the outside unit; anything effective as, or as if contained in a legally enforceable contract relating to this matter; or any Part of this Schedule that a method of collective bargaining is to

have effect with regard to the outside unit: para 83(6). For this purpose, collective bargaining has the same meaning as in TULRCA 1992, s 178(1); see further para **4.3**.

    5. *Ibid.*, para 83(8).

    6. Note that the CAC should have already issued a declaration that the bargaining arrangements for workers in the original unit who do not fall within the new unit cease in compliance with *ibid.*, para 90; see further para **4.38**.

    7. For the position of the remaining workers in the statutory outside bargaining unit, see *ibid.*, para 91, discussed below at para **4.42**.

    8. *Ibid.*, para 84(1). If any workers fall within both a statutory and a voluntary bargaining unit, the procedure relating to statutory outside bargaining units is followed.

    9. *Ibid.*, s 84(4).

    10. *Ibid.*, para 84(2), (5). The 'original bargaining arrangements' are the bargaining arrangements defined in para 64 (see para **4.35**): para 84(3).

    11. See para **4.3**.

    12. TULRCA 1992, Sched A1, para 94(2). None of the other definitions offered in para 94 would appear to be applicable in this context.

4.41 If there is no overlap between a new unit and a statutory or voluntary outside bargaining unit, the CAC must then decide whether the difference between the original unit and the new unit is such that the support of the union (or unions) within the new unit needs to be assessed and inform the parties of its decision.[1] If it decides that such support does not need to be assessed, it must issue a declaration that the union is (or unions are) recognised as entitled to conduct collective bargaining on behalf of the new unit.[2] As in the case of a declaration issued pursuant to the agreement of the parties, this declaration has effect in place of any declaration relating to the original unit so far as it affects workers in the new unit who fell within the original unit, and the method of collective bargaining[3] relating to the original unit has effect in relation to the new unit, with any modifications which the CAC considers necessary to take account of the change of bargaining unit and specifies in the declaration.[4] This method, too, has effect as if it were contained in a legally enforceable contract made between the parties[5] and the comments which we made in para **4.37** apply equally in this context. If the CAC decides that the support for the union or unions within the new unit does need to be assessed, it must first decide whether members of the union or unions constitute at least 10 per cent of the workers constituting the new unit; and whether a majority of the workers constituting the new unit would be likely to favour recognition of the union or unions as entitled to conduct collective bargaining on behalf of the new unit.[6] If it decides one or both of these of these questions in the negative, it must issue a declaration that the bargaining arrangements, so far as they relate to workers in the new unit, are to cease to have effect on a specified date.[7] These questions mirror those relating to the admissibility of applications for initial recognition discussed in para **4.14** and the comments we make there about the interpretation of these criteria are equally applicable in this context. However there are important differences between the two procedures. In this context, there is no explicit requirement for the CAC to take account of any evidence which it has been given by either party, nor is it required on the face of the legislation, to give reasons for its decision.[8] If it decides both questions in the affirmative, and is satisfied that a majority of the workers constituting the new unit are members of the union(s), it must issue a declaration that the union is (or unions are) recognised as entitled to conduct collective bargaining on behalf of the workers constituting the new unit.[9] However, as in the case of the procedure for initial recognition, if any of 'three qualifying conditions' is fulfilled, or if it is not satisfied that a majority of the workers constituting the new unit are members of the union(s), the CAC must again give notice to the parties that it intends to arrange for the holding of a secret ballot (see para **4.20**).[10] Once again the union(s) may notify the CAC within the 'notification period' that it does not want the CAC to arrange for the holding of a ballot; the CAC must then issue a declaration that the bargaining arrangements, so far as they relate to workers falling within the new unit, cease on a specified date.[11] Identical provisions govern the conduct of, and payment for, the ballot, and the employer's duty of co-operation, as apply in relation to the holding of an initial recognition ballot (see paras **4.21–4.28**).[12] If the result of the ballot is that the union is (or unions are) supported by a majority of the workers voting and at least 40 per cent of the workers constituting the new bargaining unit, the CAC must issue a declaration that the union is (or unions are) recognised as entitled to conduct collective bargaining on its behalf.[13] If the CAC issues a declaration that the union is (or unions are) not entitled to be recognised, the bargaining arrangements cease to have effect on the date specified in the declaration.[14]

---

1. TULRCA 1992, Sched A1, para 85.
2. *Ibid.*, para 85(2)(a).
3. For this purpose 'collective bargaining' means negotiations relating to pay, hours and holidays: *ibid.*, para 94(6).
4. *Ibid.*, para 85(2)(b), (c).
5. *Ibid.*, para 95.
6. *Ibid.*, para 86(2).
7. *Ibid.*, para 86(3).
8. See para **4.7** for the anticipated practice of the CAC.
9. TULRCA 1992, Sched A1, para 87(1), (2). See para 64(2)(b), discussed para **4.35**, for the definition of 'bargaining arrangements'.This declaration has effect in place of any declaration relating to the original unit so far as it affects workers in the new unit who fall within the original unit, and the method of collective bargaining relating to the

original unit has effect in relation to the new unit, with any modifications which the CAC considers necessary to take account of the change of bargaining unit and specifies in the declaration. In the context of the latter provision 'collective bargaining' means negotiations relating to pay, hours and holidays: *ibid.*, para 94(6). See para 95, discussed in para **4.37**, for the legal effect of the method of collective bargaining in relation to the new unit.

10. *Ibid.*, paras 87(3), (4), 88. Para 166, which provides for amendment by order of the Secretary of State, applies in this context, as in relation to para 22. The Secretary of State may also issue guidance to the CAC on the way it is to exercise its functions under this provision: para 167.

11. *Ibid.*, para 89. The 'notification period' is the period of 10 working days starting with the day after that on which the union (or last of the unions) receives the CAC's notice that it intends to arrange for the holding of a ballot: para 89(1). Cf. para 24, where the parties jointly may also give such notice.

12. *Ibid.*, para 89(4),(5).

13. *Ibid.*, para 89(5), 29(3). The declaration has the same effect as a declaration issued without the holding of a ballot: *ibid.*, para 89(6): see further note 9 above. These provisions also apply if the CAC issues a declaration under para 27(2) that the union is entitled to be recognised because the employer has failed to comply with an order to remedy a failure to fulfil its duties in connection with the ballot.

14. *Ibid.*, para 89(7).

Residual workers

4.42 The legislation makes special provision for 'residual workers' who are left in a bargaining unit when other workers have been removed from it. There are two situations where this may arise. First, if the CAC determines a new bargaining unit and at least one worker within the original unit (which has been deemed no longer to be an appropriate bargaining unit) does not fall within the new unit (or any of the new units).[1] In those circumstances, as we discussed in para **4.38**, the CAC must issue a declaration that the bargaining arrangements, so far as they relate to such a worker, cease to have effect on a specified date.[2] The second situation is where the CAC has determined a new bargaining unit and issued a declaration pursuant to finding that the new unit overlaps with a statutory outside bargaining unit.[3] The CAC must then, in relation to each declaration issued, identify each statutory outside bargaining unit which contains at least one worker who also falls within the new unit to which the declaration relates.[4] Each unit so identified is referred to as a 'parent unit'.[5] The CAC must then consider each parent unit and in relation to each parent unit identify any workers who fall within the parent unit but who do not fall within the new unit (or any of the new units).[6] The workers so identified are designated the 'residual unit'.[7] In relation to each residual unit the CAC must then issue a declaration that the outside union is (or outside unions are) recognised as entitled to conduct collective bargaining on its behalf, unless the CAC has received an application from either party who believes that the parent unit is no longer an appropriate bargaining unit or from the employer who believes that unit has ceased to exist.[8] This declaration thus confirms that the existing bargaining arrangements with the outside union continue despite the fact workers who fall within the new unit are no longer within the residual unit.

---

1. TULRCA 1992, Sched A1, para 90.
2. *Ibid.*, para 92(2). Similar provision is made where the new unit is determined by agreement between the parties: para 73; see further para **4.37**.
3. *Ibid.*, para 91(1).
4. *Ibid.*, para 91(2).
5. *Ibid.*
6. *Ibid.*, para 91(3).
7. *Ibid.*
8. *Ibid.*, para 91(4), (5). The 'outside union' is the union (or unions) recognised as entitled to conduct collective bargaining on behalf of the parent unit: para 91(6). 'Collective bargaining' in this context means negotiations relating to matters which were the subject of collective bargaining in relation to the corresponding parent unit. This declaration has effect in place of the existing declaration relating to the parent unit, so far as the existing declaration relates to the residual unit: para 91(7)(a). If there is a method of collective bargaining relating to the parent unit, it has effect in relation to the residual unit with any modifications which the CAC considers necessary to take account of the change of bargaining unit and specifies in the declaration: para 91(7)(b).

DERECOGNITION OF TRADE UNIONS

Sources and General Principles

4.43 Where recognition is the product of voluntary agreement between the collective parties, in most cases the employer may derecognise the trade union(s), or vary the scope of recognition, unilaterally.[1] This remains the case even where recognition is express; a recognition agreement falls within the statutory definition of a 'collective agreement' and will thus be covered by the statutory presumption of non-enforceability, displaceable only by a specific statement to the contrary of a kind which is rarely found.[2] Moreover, it is most unlikely that a recognition agreement could be enforced through individual contracts; even if part of a wider collective agreement which is capable of incorporation into individual contracts of employment, terms relating to recognition will almost certainly be regarded by the courts as collective in their nature and thus not appropriate for such incorporation.[3] This does not mean that a decision to derecognise will never have legal implications, however. First, although a commitment to recognise a union is unlikely in itself to be a term of an individual contract, it is possible that some provisions which may be linked to recognition, such as rights to time off for union members, or individual representation in disciplinary and grievance proceedings which exceed the rights specified in statute, may have been incorporated in the employee's contract of employment.[4] If so, any contractual term linked to recognition which the employer wishes to remove following derecognition will require the individual contract to be varied with the consent of the employee.[5] Secondly, derecognition cannot be used to avoid statutory duties which have already become binding; thus, once a union has requested specific information for collective bargaining purposes, for example, the duty to disclose such information survives subsequent derecognition.[6] Finally, in the case of employers which are potentially susceptible to judicial review a decision to derecognise may be open to challenge by this means, at least as regards the procedure which is followed. In *R v Educational Services Committee of Bradford City Metropolitan Council, ex p PAT*[7] the (no-strike) Professional Association of Teachers successfully sought judicial review of the (Labour) Council's decision to rescind a resolution made three months earlier (by its Conservative predecessor) on the ground that it should have been afforded the opportunity to make representations to ensure that the deprivation of the valuable rights thereby occasioned was not unfair. Even this, however, does not ultimately constitute a substantive constraint on the employer's discretion to derecognise. The position is wholly different where recognition follows from a union having invoked the statutory recognition procedure. Where recognition follows a declaration by the CAC that a union is (or unions are) entitled to conduct collective bargaining on behalf of a bargaining unit, recognition may be terminated by the employer only in specified circumstances and in accordance with specified procedures, which we summarise in para **4.44**. Even if recognition is enshrined in an 'agreement for recognition', which has been agreed voluntarily by the employer following a request made under the statutory procedure, the employer may not terminate that agreement unilaterally before the end of a three year period starting with the day after the date of the agreement unless the parties have modified this restriction by agreement (see paras **4.32**–**4.33**).[8] It is conceivable that *workers* may wish their employer to substitute bargaining with one union with another. For recognition agreements reached outside the statutory procedure, there has traditionally been no legal mechanism for achieving this without the consent of the employer. This remains the case in general; the statutory recognition procedure does not permit an application for recognition in respect of a bargaining unit for which there is another recognised union, regardless of the respective levels of membership which each union may have. Thus even if the employer reached a 'single-union' agreement with a union which is unpopular with the workforce there is no legal remedy which workers can invoke. The exception to this principle is where the union recognised by the employer lacks a certificate of independence.[9] It is then open to any worker within the bargaining unit to apply to the CAC to have the bargaining arrangements ended, and the CAC may order that they cease to have effect if this is supported in a ballot by a majority of the workers voting and at least 40 per cent of the workers in the unit. This is likely, in practice, to arise as the first step of an initiative by an independent trade union to gain recognition for the bargaining unit in question; even if the employer were to re-recognise the non-independent union, the recognition agreement, if made within three years of the previous recognition agreement ceasing, would not constitute a barrier to an application by an independent union to the CAC.[10] If that application were successful, the bargaining arrangements with the non-independent union would cease.[11] There is provision in the dercognition procedures for a worker to apply to have a union which was recognised pursuant to a statutory declaration derecognised, but even if he or she is successful in this venture there is nothing to prevent the employer, if it so chooses, re-recognising the union on a voluntary basis.

---

1. On the incidence and areas of derecognition in recent years, see ACAS *Annual Reports*; Gall and McKay, 1994, Claydon, 1996, Brown *et al*, 1998; Cully *et al*, 1999, 238–241; Gall and McKay, 1999; Millward *et al*, 2000.

2. TULRCA 1992, s 179; see further paras **4.70** and **4.71**.

3. *NCB v NUM* [1986] IRLR 439, ChD. Withdrawal of recognition does not, *per se*, amount to subjection to a detriment on grounds of trade union membership or activities: see paras **3.11** and **3.12**.

4. See para **4.69** on incorporation. On the statutory right to individual representation, see ERA 1999, ss 10–15.

5. See Deakin and Morris, 1998, 269–277 on methods of varying contracts of employment when consent cannot be obtained.

6. *Ackrill Newspapers Ltd v NUJ* (CAC, 14 February 1992, unreported).

7. *Independent*, 16 December 1986, discussed Fredman and Morris, 1989, 163.

8. TULRCA 1992, Sched A1, para 56.

9. See paras **2.6** and **2.7**.

10. TULRCA 1992, Sched A1, para 35(4); see para **4.13**.

11. *Ibid.*, para 148.

The Statutory Derecognition Procedure: Overview and General Principles

4.44 The situations in which derecognition may be permitted or required by statute are laid down in Parts IV–VII of Schedule A1 of the Trade Union and Labour Relations (Consolidation) Act 1992. As indicated in para **4.43** above, they are confined to situations where the CAC issued a declaration that the union was entitled to be recognised, with the exception of the case where the recognised union lacks a certificate of independence. Derecognition may be sought only where three years has passed since that declaration, except where the union specified in the declaration loses its certificate of independence. (Derecognition of non-independent unions may also be sought at any time). Part IV of the Schedule (headed 'Derecognition: General) lays down three situations where derecognition may be permitted or required:

(1) If the employer, together with any associated employer, employed fewer than 21 workers over a 13 week period.
(2) At the request of the employer for other reasons.
(3) On application of a worker within the bargaining unit.

For an application to be admissible under (2) or (3), the CAC must first decide that at least 10 per cent of the workers in the bargaining unit favour an end to the bargaining arrangements and a majority of the workers constituting the unit would be likely to favour this. It will *order* derecognition, in default of agreement by the parties, only after the requisite support for the termination of the bargaining arrangements has been demonstrated in a ballot of the workers in the bargaining unit. In the situation where the recognition declaration was issued without a ballot, on the basis that the CAC was satisfied that a majority of the workers in the bargaining unit were members of the applicant union(s), Part V of the Schedule (headed, somewhat confusingly, 'Derecognition where Recognition Automatic') provides a simplified procedure which does not impose the same admissibility test, although approval in a ballot is still required. Applications at the request of the employer (other than those based upon the number employed) or at the request of a worker may be considered by the CAC only if three years have passed since the last application to derecognise. This parallels the restriction on applications for recognition by the same union(s) in respect of a particular bargaining unit, and is designed to ensure an element of industrial relations stability. Part VI deals with mandatory derecognition of non-independent unions, which again is dependent upon approval in a ballot. Part VII covers the (unlikely) situation that a union covered by a recognition declaration loses its certificate of independence. Our discussion of the relevant provisions follows the structure of the legislation. As in the case of the recognition provisions, each Part of the Schedule relating to derecognition contains its own definition section and we indicate these definitions at the beginning of the section of text which deals with the Part in question. Our discussion of the role of the CAC in para **4.7** remains equally applicable in this context.

Derecognition at the Request of Employers or Workers: General

Definitions

4.45 Part IV of Schedule A1 to the Trade Union and Labour Relations (Consolidation) Act 1992 applies if the CAC has issued a declaration that a union is (or unions are) recognised as entitled to conduct collective bargaining on behalf of a bargaining unit.[1] References in this Part to the 'bargaining arrangements' are to the declaration and to provisions relating to the collective bargaining method, which cover the parties' agreement as to the method by which bargaining is to be conducted; anything effective as, or as if contained in, a legally enforceable contract relating to this matter; or any provision that a method of collective bargaining is to 'have effect' following a change in the bargaining unit.[2] The 'relevant date' refers to the date of the expiry of the period of three years starting with the date of the CAC's declaration;[3] 'the parties' refers to the employer and the union (or unions) concerned.[4] The Secretary of State may give the CAC directions as to the order in which it should consider the admissibility of applications under this Part, or Part V, if two or more applications are made in relation to the same bargaining unit.[5]

---

1. TULRCA 1992, Sched A1, para 96(1).
2. *Ibid.*, para 96(2), (3).
3. *Ibid.*, para 97
4. *Ibid.*, para 98.
5. *Ibid.*, para 169.

Employer employs fewer workers

4.46 An employer may seek the termination of the bargaining arrangements if it believes that it, taken with any associated employer or employers, employed an average of fewer than 21 workers in any period of 13 weeks, and that period ends on or after the relevant date.[1] Provided this condition is satisfied the number employed on the date of application itself is irrelevant (although condition 4 below means that an application may be made only where the average has fallen below 21 in the very recent past). The rules for calculating the average, and determining which workers fall within it, are identical to those applicable to a valid recognition request, described in para **4.9**.[2] If it wishes the bargaining arrangements to cease to have effect the employer must give the union (or each of the unions) a notice containing specified information, with a copy to the CAC.[3] The notice must:

(1) Identify the bargaining arrangements;
(2) Specify the period of 13 weeks in question;
(3) State the date on which the notice is given;
(4) Be given within the period of five working days starting with the day after the last day of the specified period of 13 weeks;[4]
(5) State that the employer, taken with any associated employer or employers, employed an average of fewer than 21 workers in the specified period of 13 weeks;
(6) State that the bargaining arrangements are to cease to have effect on a specified date which falls after the end of the period of 35 working days starting with the day after that on which the notice is given. [5]

The CAC must decide within ten working days starting with the day after that on which it receives a copy of the notice (with provision for extension) whether the notice complies with the statutory requirements, and give the parties notice of its decision.[6] If it decides that the notice does not comply, the employer's notice is treated as not having been given.[7] If it decides that it does comply, the bargaining arrangements will cease to have effect on the date specified in the employer's notice unless the union makes an application to the CAC for a decision whether the period of 13 weeks specified in the notice ends on or after the 'relevant date', and whether the statement as to the average number of workers employed is correct.[8] The word 'and' rather than 'or' in this context suggests that the application must require the CAC to decide both these matters, although the employer's notice is ineffective if *either* of these conditions is not satisfied.[9] The application by the union(s) must be made within ten working days starting with the day after that on which the CAC's notice that the employer's notice complies with the prescribed conditions is *given* (not received).[10]

---

1. TULRCA 1992, Sched A1, para 99(1). The 'relevant date' is the date of the expiry of the period of three years starting with the date of the CAC's declaration: para 97.
2. *Ibid.*, para 99(4)–(7).
3. *Ibid.*, para 99(2).
4. 'Working day' is defined in para 172; see further para **4.6**.
5. *Ibid.*, para 99(3).
6. *Ibid.*, para 100(1), (5).
7. *Ibid.*, para 100(2), (3).
8. *Ibid.*, para 101(b).

9. *Ibid.*, para 103(3).
10. *Ibid.*, para 101(1)(b).

4.47 The application by the union or unions to the CAC will not be admissible:

(1) Unless it is made in such form, and supported by such documents, as the CAC specifies.[1]

(2) Unless the union gives (or unions give) the employer notice, and a copy, of the application and any supporting documents.[2]

(3) If a 'relevant application' was made within the period of three years prior to the date of the application; the relevant application and this application relate to the same bargaining unit; and the CAC accepted the relevant application.[3] A 'relevant application' is an application by the union or unions under this procedure; by a worker to have the bargaining arrangements ended where they have been established pursuant to a CAC declaration; or by the employer for a secret ballot of the bargaining unit to decide whether the bargaining arrangements should be ended.[4] The reference to an application by the *union(s)* is highly anomalous in this context. Applications by employers to derecognise for other reasons, and by workers (other than where the recognised union lacks a certificate of independence) may be brought only at three-yearly intervals, and there would be some logic if a similar restriction were imposed on applications by *employers* under this procedure. However to impose such a restriction on a union which wishes to challenge a matter of fact means that an employer which submits one notice which is found after challenge by the union(s) not to satisfy the statutory conditions for derecognition because, for example, the statement made about the average number of workers employed is incorrect, may serve a second notice knowing that it will be immune from challenge provided that the formal requirements for a valid notice stipulated in para **4.46** above have been satisfied.[5] If this were to occur, the union's only option would be to apply once again for recognition under the statutory procedure, assuming that its case was that the employer employed 21 or more workers. If the employer contested this, the union would have the opportunity to put its case before the CAC (see para **4.11**). A union which has been derecognised on the number of workers employed by the employer is not subject to a minimum time limit before it applies for re-recognition; the three-year bar is confined to situations where derecognition follows a ballot of workers in the bargaining unit (see para **4.16**).

The CAC must give notice to the parties of receipt of an application and decide within ten working days starting with the day after that on which it receives the application (with provision for extension) whether is it admissible;[6] in making this decision it must consider any evidence which it has been given by the parties.[7] If it decides that the application is not admissible, it must notify the parties accordingly and the bargaining arrangements will cease to have effect on the date specified by the employer in its notice.[8] If it decides that the application is admissible it must notify the parties and give them an opportunity to put their views on the questions to be decided.[9] These questions must be decided within the 'decision period': ten working days starting with the day after that on which it gave notice of acceptance of the application (with provision for extension).[10] Unusually, the CAC has a statutory obligation to give reasons for its decision in this context.[11] If it decides that the 13 week period ends on or after the 'relevant date' and that the statement in the employer's notice about the number of workers is correct, the bargaining arrangements cease to have effect on the date specified in that notice or the day after the last day of the decision period, whichever is the later.[12] If it decides that either of these tests was not satisfied, the notice is treated as not having been given.[13] As we indicate above, there is nothing to prevent an employer presenting a fresh notice immediately covering another (even if overlapping) 13 week period, which appears to be immune from challenge as to its accuracy by the union(s) if their application to the CAC to decide this on a previous occasion was accepted by the CAC.

---

1. TULRCA 1992, Sched A1, para 101(2).
2. *Ibid.*, para 101(3).
3. *Ibid.*, para 101(4).
4. *Ibid.*, para 101(5).
5. An application by a union under this procedure will, however, block further applications to end the bargaining arrangements by the employer (or by a worker) under any other provisions for a further three year period if those arrangements are maintained and the union's application is successful: *ibid.*, paras 109(2)(a),113(2)(a), 130(2)(a).
6. *Ibid.*, para 102(2), (6). 'Working day' is defined in para 172; see further para **4.6**.
7. *Ibid.*, para102(3).
8. *Ibid.*, para 102(4).
9. *Ibid.*, para 103(1).
10. *Ibid.*, para 103(1)(b), (4).
11. *Ibid.*, para 103(1)(b).
12. *Ibid.*, para 103(2).
13. *Ibid.*, para 103(3).

Employer's request to end arrangements

4.48 After the relevant date an employer may request the union (or each of the unions) to agree to end the bargaining arrangements.[1] To be valid, the request must be in writing; received by the union (or each of the unions); identify the bargaining arrangements; and state that it is made under the Schedule.[2] As in the case of requests for recognition, there is no statutory mechanism currently laid down for proving that a request has been received, and the comments which we made in para **4.9** apply, *mutatis mutandis*, in this context. The procedure which applies in this context also mirrors that applicable to recognition requests. First, there is an opportunity to see whether the union(s) accede to the employer's request. If it does so (or they do so) before the end of the 'first period'—ten working days starting with the day after the day on which the union receives the request or the last day on which any of the unions receives the request—no further steps are to be taken.[3] If before the end of the first period the union informs (or unions inform) the employer that, although the request is not accepted, it or they are willing to negotiate and an agreement is made before the end of the 'second period'—20 working days starting with the day after that on which the first period ends or such longer period (so starting) as the parties may from time to time agree—again no further steps are to be taken.[4] The employer and the union(s) may request ACAS to assist in conducting the negotiations.[5] If, before the end of the first period, the union(s) fail(s) to respond to the request, or inform the employer that they do not accept it (without indicating a willingness to negotiate) the employer may apply to the CAC for the holding of a secret ballot to determine whether the bargaining arrangements should be ended.[6] The employer may also apply for a ballot if the union(s) have indicated a willingness to negotiate but no agreement is made before the end of the second period, although no such application may be made if the employer rejected a proposal by the union(s) that ACAS be requested to assist in negotiations, or failed to accept such a proposal within 10 working days starting with the day after that on which the proposal was made.[7]

---

1. TULRCA 1992, Sched A1, para 104(1).
2. *Ibid.*, para 104(2).
3. *Ibid.*, para 105(1), (6) 'Working day' is defined in para 172; see further para **4.6**.
4. *Ibid.*, para 105(2)–(4), (7).
5. *Ibid.*, para 105(5).
6. *Ibid.*, para 106(2).
7. *Ibid.*, para 107. The union(s) must make the proposal within 10 working days, starting with the day after that on which it or they informed the employer of their willingness to negotiate.

4.49 An application to the CAC for the holding of a ballot is not admissible:

(1) If it is not made in such form, and supported by such documents, as specified by the CAC.[1]
(2) If the employer fails to give to the union (or each of the unions) notice, and a copy, of the application and any supporting documents.[2]
(3) If a 'relevant application' was made within the period of three years prior to the date of the application; the relevant application and this application relate to the same bargaining unit; and the CAC accepted the relevant application.[3] A 'relevant application' is an application by the union or unions under the procedure we described in para **4.47**; by a worker to have the bargaining arrangements ended where these have been established pursuant to a CAC declaration; or any other application by the employer for a secret ballot of the bargaining unit to decide whether the bargaining arrangements should be ended.[4]
(4) Unless the CAC decides that at least 10 per cent of the workers constituting the bargaining unit favour an end to the bargaining arrangements and a majority of the workers constituting the bargaining unit would be *likely* to favour an end to the bargaining arrangements.[5] The CAC must give reasons for its decision whether these tests are met.[6] The first of these criteria will require factual evidence in the form of a petition or some other document which confirms that 10 per cent of the workers are of this view. As in the context of the procedure for recognition, which this provision mirrors, the second criterion is likely to be more contentious and the comments which we made in para **4.14** about the standard and difficulties of proof apply *a fortiori* in this context. The presentation of a petition or other document signed by a majority of workers in the unit seems to be the only method by which an employer could be assured of surmounting this hurdle. Evidence of support for recognition of another union would also be material, although recruitment to TUC-affiliated unions is constrained by the Bridlington Principles which we describe in para **2.26**. Evidence of falling union membership within the bargaining unit would be persuasive, but this may be hard to obtain, given that the recognised union, not being the applicant, cannot under this procedure be required to disclose information such as membership figures. Where the employer operates a check-off system, evidence of a decline in the numbers using this facility would be relevant but given that there are other means of paying union subscriptions could not be regarded as conclusive.

---

1. TULRCA 1992, Sched A1, para 108(1).
2. *Ibid.*, para 108(2).
3. *Ibid.*, para 109(1).

4. *Ibid.*, para 109(2).
5. *Ibid.*, para 110(1).
6. *Ibid.*, para 110(2).

4.50 The CAC must give notice to the parties of receipt of an application to hold a ballot and decide within ten working days starting with the day after that on which it receives the application (with provision for extension)[1] whether the request is valid; follows the events described in para **4.48**; and admissible.[2] In deciding these questions it must consider any evidence it has been given by the employer or union(s), and must notify the parties of its decision.[3] If the CAC accepts the application, it must then arrange for the holding of a secret ballot in which the workers constituting the bargaining unit are asked whether the bargaining arrangements should be ended.[4] The same provisions govern the conduct of, and payment for, the ballot and the employer's duty of co-operation as apply to the holding of a recognition ballot: these are analysed in detail in paras **4.21–4.28**.[5] (Note, however, that there is no equivalent provision for the employer or parties jointly to notify the CAC that they do not wish a ballot to be arranged.) If an employer fails to comply with an order of the CAC to remedy a failure to comply with any of its duties in connection with the ballot (such as affording the union(s) access to the workers in the bargaining unit) and the ballot has not been held the CAC *may* refuse the application.[6] The same comments which we made in para **4.23** about the discretionary nature of this sanction, and the lacuna if non-compliance is not discovered in time, apply *mutatis mutandis* in this situation. In this context a union may be more likely to succeed in a judicial review application if the CAC decided not to refuse the application because it would have lost a benefit which it previously held (although, once again, a court may be persuaded that if the workforce had shown support for the termination of the bargaining arrangements it should exercise its discretion not to grant a remedy). If the result of the ballot is that a majority of the workers voting and at least 40 per cent of the workers constituting the bargaining unit favour termination of the bargaining arrangements, the CAC must issue a declaration stating that the bargaining arrangements are to cease to have effect on a specified date; otherwise the application must be refused.[7]

---

1. TULRCA 1992, Sched A1, para 111(6). 'Working day' is defined in para 172; see further para **4.6**.
2. *Ibid.*, para 111(1),(2).
3. *Ibid.*, para 111(3)–(5).

4. *Ibid.*, para 117(1)–(3).
5. *Ibid.*, paras 117–121.
6. *Ibid.*, para 119(2). If the CAC refuses an application it must take steps to cancel the holding of the ballot; if held, it is of no effect: para 119(4).
7. *Ibid.*, para 121(3)–(5). The Secretary of State may amend the degree of support required by order made by statutory instrument, subject to approval by resolution by each House of Parliament: para 121(6)–(8).

Workers' application to end arrangements

4.51 A worker or workers falling within the bargaining unit may after the relevant date apply to the CAC to have the bargaining arrangements ended.[1] All four criteria for admissibility described in para **4.49**, and the comments which we made thereon, apply equally in this context.[2] In deciding upon admissibility, the CAC must take account of any evidence which it has been given by any of the workers within the bargaining unit as well as by the employer and union(s).[3] If it accepts the application, during the 'negotiation period' it must 'help' the employer, union(s) and worker(s) with a view to the employer and the union(s) agreeing to end the bargaining arrangements or the worker(s) withdrawing the application.[4] The 'negotiation period' is the period of 20 working days starting with the day after that on which the CAC gives notice of acceptance of the application, or such longer period (so starting) as the CAC may decide with the consent of the worker (or workers), the employer and the union(s).[5] If there is no such agreement or withdrawal the CAC must arrange for the holding of a secret ballot in which the workers constituting the bargaining unit are asked whether the bargaining arrangements should be ended.[6] Identical provisions govern the conduct of the ballot to those which apply where the employer requests an end to the arrangements[7] (see para **4.50**) with one exception. If the employer fails to comply with an order by the CAC to remedy its failure to fulfil any of its duties in connection with the holding of the ballot, and the ballot has not been held, that order, on being recorded in the county court, may be enforced in the same way as an order of that court.[8] This may involve specific performance or a mandatory injunction, backed up by proceedings for contempt of court in the event of disobedience by the employer. This means that the application by the worker(s) is not prejudiced by the employer's failure. In the light of our earlier comments about the difficulty of challenging the CAC's decision in the event that it decides not to refuse a employer's application where an order has been violated, this sanction may come to seem the preferable one from the point of view of unions. However it should be noted that no express provision is made for the ballot to be delayed pending the recording of the order[9] nor, indeed, is it expressly stated that it is the duty of the CAC to enforce it. Whilst it is open to the court to make an order for commital of its own motion, in practice it is unlikely to do so in these circumstances. As we indicated in para **4.43**, if dere-cognition occurs contrary to the wishes of the employer, there is nothing to prevent it entering a voluntary recognition agreement, although clearly this may pose industrial relations problems if the majority of the workforce has voted against continued bargaining with the union.

---

1. TULRCA 1992, Sched A1, para 112(1).
2. *Ibid.*, para 112(2)–(3), 113, 114.
3. *Ibid.*, para 115(3). If the CAC specifies a period for making its decision which exceeds 10 working days starting with the day after that on which it receives the application, it must do so to the worker (or workers), the employer and the union (or unions) by notice containing reasons for the extension: para 115(6).
4. *Ibid.*, para 116(1). In helping, the CAC may suggest that assistance is sought from ACAS: see para **4.7**.
5. *Ibid.*, para 116(2).
6. *Ibid.*, para 117(3).
7. *Ibid.*, para 117–121.
8. *Ibid.*, para 119(3).
9. The ballot must be conducted within 20 working days starting with the day after that on which the qualified independent person who conducts the ballot is appointed or such longer period (so starting) as the CAC may decide: *ibid.*, para 117(5). The Code of Practice on Access to Workers during Recognition and Derecognition Ballots assumes that the CAC is empowered to reschedule a ballot whose date has been announced (para 48), presumably on the assumption that this can be derived from para 25(3), which is identical to para 117(5).

Derecognition where No Ballot was Held Prior to Recognition

4.52 Distinctive provision is made in Part V of Schedule A1 of the Trade Union and Labour Relations (Consolidation) Act 1992 for termination of bargaining arrangements where the CAC has issued a declaration that a union is (or unions are) recognised without holding a ballot because it has been satisfied a majority of the workers constituting the bargaining unit are members of the applicant union(s). These provisions apply both where recognition followed an initial application and where there has been a change in the bargaining unit.[1] In these circumstances, rather than requiring the CAC to be satisfied that it is likely that a majority of the workers in the bargaining unit would be likely to favour termination before arranging for a ballot (see para **4.49**), it is sufficient that it is satisfied that fewer than half the workers are members of the union(s). This avenue is open only to derecognition applications by employers, however, not by workers. The employer starts the procedure by making a request (after the relevant date) to the union (or unions) to agree to end the bargaining arrangements.[2] To be valid, the request must be in writing; be received by the union or each of the unions; identify the bargaining arrangements; state that it is made under the Schedule; and state that fewer than half of the workers constituting the bargaining unit are members of the union (or unions).[3] As in the case of requests for recognition, there is no statutory mechanism currently laid down for proving that a request has been received, and the comments which we made in para **4.9** apply, *mutatis mutandis*, in this context. No further steps are to be taken under this Part of the Schedule if before the end of the period of ten working days starting with the day after the last day on which any of the unions receives the request, or such longer period (so starting) as the parties may from time to time agree, the parties agree to end the bargaining arrangements.[4] In the absence of such agreement, the employer may apply to the CAC for the holding of a secret ballot to decide whether the bargaining arrangements should be ended.[5] The conditions of admissibility of such an application are identical to those described in para **4.49** except that point (4) is not applicable; rather the CAC must be satisfied that fewer than half of the workers constituting the bargaining unit are members of the union or unions, a decision for which it must give reasons.[6] Although intended to parallel the test employed for initial recognition in this context, it may be a more difficult test to satisfy, given that there is no power to compel the recognised union or unions, not being the applicants, to reveal membership figures. As we discussed in para **4.49** where the employer provides a check-off facility for the payment of union subscriptions, evidence of a declining use of this facility may be relevant but, given that there are alternative ways of making payment, not conclusive. In deciding whether the application is admissible, which it must do within ten working days starting with the day after that on which it receives the application (with provision for extension),[7] the CAC must consider any evidence which it has been given by the parties and must notify them of its decision.[8] If it accepts the application the CAC must arrange for the holding of a secret ballot in which the workers constituting the bargaining unit are asked whether the bargaining arrangements should be ended.[9] The principles governing matters relating to the ballot are identical to those described in para **4.50**.

---

1. TULRCA 1992, Sched A1, Part V. Note that there is nothing in the provisions of Part IV of the Schedule, discussed in paras **4.45**–**4.50**, to prevent applications in these circumstances being dealt with under Part IV and it is conceivable (albeit unlikely) that an employer would be able to satisfy the admissibility criteria under Part IV more easily than under Part V.

2. *Ibid.*, para 127(1). The 'relevant date' is the date of the expiry of three years starting with the date of the CAC's declaration: para 125. Where the parties have agreed a method by which they will conduct collective bargaining, ' bargaining arrangements' mean the declaration and the parties' agreement; where the CAC has specified a method, the declaration and anything effective, or as if contained in, a legally enforceable contract; where a bargaining unit has been changed and the method for the original bargaining unit has effect for the new unit, the declaration which gives that effect: paras 122–124.

3. *Ibid.*, para 127(2).

4. *Ibid.*, para 128(1). 'Working day' is defined in para 172; see further para **4.6**. 'The parties' are the employer and the union (or unions) concerned: para 126.

5. *Ibid.*, para 128(2).

6. *Ibid.*, paras 129–131.

7. Para 132(6). 'Working day' is defined in para 172; see further para **4.6**.

8. *Ibid.*, paras 132(3)–(5).

9. *Ibid.*, para 133.

Derecognition where the Recognised Union is not Independent

4.53 The derecognition procedures which we examined in paras **4.45**–**4.52** apply only where the CAC has issued a declaration that the union was recognised. Separate provision is made in Part VI of Schedule A1 of the Trade Union and Labour Relations (Consolidation) Act 1992 where an employer and union(s) have agreed that the union is (or unions are) recognised as entitled to conduct collective bargaining on behalf of a groups of workers and the union does not have (*or none of the unions has*) a certificate of independence.[1] As we explained in para **4.43**, this is the only situation in which workers can force derecognition of a union voluntarily recognised by the employer and, if successful, it can open the way to a recognition claim in respect of the bargaining unit in question by an independent union.[2] In this context the 'bargaining arrangements' refer to the parties' agreement that the union is (or unions are) recognised as entitled to conduct collective bargaining on behalf of a group or groups of workers, and any agreement between the parties as to the method by which they will conduct collective bargaining.[3] It is notable that the definition of 'collective bargaining' in s 178(1) of the Trade Union and Labour Relations Act 1992, is excluded, but no other definition is given.[4] It seems, therefore, as if agreements to bargain on any issue, even if exclusively outside the scope of s 178(1), must be included. Unlike other contexts where derecognition may be called for there is no requirement that the union should have been recognised for a minimum three-year period, nor is there any restriction on the frequency with which applications may be brought.[5]

1. TULRCA 1992, Sched A1, para 134(1); for the concept of an independent trade union see further paras **2.6** and **2.7**.
2. Re-recognition of the union within three years of the previous recognition agreement will not constitute a barrier to such an application: *ibid.*, para 35(4). In the event that the independent union's application for recognition is successful, the revived bargaining arrangements with the non-independent union will be required to cease: para 148.
3. TULRCA 1992, Sched A1, para 134(2).
4. *Ibid.*, para 136; see para **4.3** for discussion of section 178(1).
5. This restriction does not apply to applications by employers based on the number of workers they employ: see para **4.47**.

Workers' application to end bargaining arrangements

4.54 An application to the CAC to have the bargaining arrangements ended may be brought by a worker or workers falling within the bargaining unit.[1] The application is not admissible:

(1) Unless it is made in such form, and supported by such documents, as the CAC specifies.[2]
(2) The worker gives (or workers give) to the employer and the union (or each of the unions) notice, and a copy, of the application and any documents supporting it.[3]
(3) If the CAC is satisfied that *any* of the unions has a certificate of independence.[4]
(4) Unless the CAC decides that at least 10 per cent of the workers constituting the bargaining unit favour an end to the bargaining arrangements and a majority of the workers constituting the bargaining unit would be likely to favour an end to the arrangements.[5] The CAC must give reasons for its decision.[6] The comments which we made in para **4.49** are equally applicable in this context. However the difficulties of proof which workers face in relation to the second criterion are likely to even more substantial than those of employers, given that in this situation neither the employer nor the union are likely to co-operate with the applicant or applicants. It may also be particularly difficult in this context to satisfy the first criterion by persuading workers to sign a petition or other document indicating that they favour an end to the bargaining arrangements; they may fear that this document will come into the hands of the employer and lead to reprisals, despite the formal protection against dismissal or other detriment for such acts.[7]
(5) If the CAC is satisfied that the union (or *any* of the unions) has made an application to the Certification Officer for a certificate of independence and the Certification Officer has not come to a decision on the application (or each of the applications).[8] This clearly requires the application to the

Certification Officer to have been made prior to the worker's application to the CAC. It is conceivable, however, that a union or unions could engage in a continuous round of applications to the Certification Officer, given that there is no limit on the number of times a union can apply for a certificate, nor is it required to wait for a specified period for re-applying if rejected.[9]

The CAC must give notice to the worker (or workers), the employer and the union (or unions) of receipt of an application and of its decision as to its admissibility; this decision must be made within the period of ten working days starting with the day after that on which the CAC receives the application (with provision for extension).[10] In making its decision the CAC must consider any evidence which it has been given by the employer, the union(s) or any of the workers falling within the bargaining unit.[11]

-----

1. TULRCA 1992, Sched A1, para 137(1).
2. *Ibid.*, para 137(2).
3. *Ibid.*, para 137(3).
4. *Ibid.*, para 138.
5. *Ibid.*, para 139(1).
6. *Ibid.*, para 139(2).
7. *Ibid.*, paras 156–161; see further para **4.58** *et seq.*
8. *Ibid.*, para 140.
9. See further paras **2.6** and **2.7**.
10. *Ibid.*, paras 141, 141(6). 'Working day' is defined in para 172; see further para **4.6**.
11. *Ibid.*, para 141(3).

4.55 If the CAC accepts a worker's application, there follows a 'negotiation period'[1] during which it must help the employer, the union(s) and the worker(s) with a view to the employer and the union(s) agreeing to end the bargaining arrangements or the worker(s) withdrawing the application.[2] This is subject to a curious proviso. If during the negotiation period the CAC becomes aware that the union (or each of the unions) has applied to the Certification Officer for a certificate of independence; any such application was made before the application for derecognition by the worker; and the Certification Officer has not come to a decision on the application(s), the CAC's obligation to 'help' immediately ceases to apply.[3] It is very unclear why this provision is required, given that it seems improbable, to say the least, that the union(s) resisting derecognition would not have informed the CAC that it or they had made an application (a matter which could easily be verified), so rendering the worker's application inadmissible (see para **4.54** above). Moreover, it applies only when each of the unions has made an application, whereas an application is inadmissible if any of them has done so. When the CAC learns the Certification Officer's decision, it must inform the worker(s), union(s) and employer accordingly.[4] If the decision is that the union (or *any* of the unions) is independent, the worker's application is treated as not having been made;[5] otherwise a 'new negotiation period' begins during which the CAC must again 'help' the worker (or workers) employer, and union(s) with the same objectives as before.[6] If there is no agreement or withdrawal in either the negotiation period or the new negotiation period, as applicable, the CAC must arrange for the holding of a secret ballot in which the workers constituting the bargaining unit are asked whether the bargaining arrangements should be ended.[7] Identical provisions apply to those applicable to a worker's request to end bargaining arrangements established pursuant to a CAC declaration, which we described in para **4.51**. However even after a ballot has been arranged the application may be treated as if it had never been made if a certificate of independence is issued to the union (or any of the unions) during the 'relevant period'[8], which starts with the first day of the 'negotiation period' or the 'new negotiation period' as applicable and ends with the *first of the following to occur:*

(a) any agreement by the employer and union(s) to end the bargaining arrangements;
(b) any withdrawal of the application by the worker(s);
(c) the CAC being informed of the result of a ballot held under the Schedule by the person conducting it.[9]

This provision applies even if the application for a certificate of independence is made after the worker has applied to terminate the bargaining arrangements.[10]

---

1. The period of 20 working days starting with the day after that on which the CAC gives notice of acceptance of the application, or such longer period (so starting) as the CAC may decide with the consent of the worker (or workers), the employer and the union (or unions): TULRCA 1992, Sched A1, para 142(2).
2. *Ibid.*, para 142(1). In helping, the CAC may suggest that assistance is sought from ACAS: see para **4.7**.
3. *Ibid.*, para 143.
4. *Ibid.*, paras144, 145.
5. *Ibid.*, para 144.
6. *Ibid.*, para 145(3). The 'new negotiation period' is defined identically to the 'negotiation period': para 145(4). It is also possible for the CAC to be required to cease to help during this period where a union has applied to the Certification Officer for a certificate of independence and the other conditions described above are satisfied: para 143(1).
7. *Ibid.*, para 147.
8. *Ibid.*, para 146(1),(5).

9. *Ibid.*, para 146(2)–(4).

10. It is expressly stated to apply only where para 143, which requires the application to the Certification Officer to have been made prior to the application by the worker, does *not* apply.

Effect of Loss of Certificate of Independence by a Recognised Union

4.56 Part VII of Schedule A1 of the Trade Union and Labour Relations (Consolidation) Act 1992 provides that if an independent trade union which has been recognised pursuant a request for recognition loses its certificate of independence, it is treated as being recognised on a purely voluntary basis (unless there are other unions recognised for the bargaining unit which retain their certificates).[1] It would thus be susceptible to an application for derecognition by a worker under the procedure we described in paras **4.53–4.55**. There appears to be no precedent for an independent union losing its certificate, and it is unlikely, therefore, that this procedure will need to be invoked.

------

1. TULRCA 1992, Sched A1, paras 149–154. Where recognition resulted from agreement between the parties, Part VII applies only where the CAC specified the method by which they are to conduct collective bargaining and the parties have not agreed in writing to replace that method or agreed that the method should not have effect as if it were contained in a legally enforceable contract made between the parties: para 150. In the event of a successful appeal against the Certification Officer's decision to withdraw the certificate, the bargaining arrangements have effect again: para 153(4).

PROTECTION AGAINST DISMISSAL OR OTHER DETRIMENT FOR ACTS RELATING TO THE RECOGNITION PROCEDURE

Overview

4.57 Part VIII of Schedule A1 to the Trade Union and Labour Relations (Consolidation) Act 1992[1] provides protection for workers against dismissal or subjection to other forms of detriment by their employer for specified acts relating to the statutory recognition and derecognition procedures. In the event that the detriment amounts to dismissal within the meaning of the Employment

Rights Act 1996 and the worker is an employee, the employee is accorded specific protection under the unfair dismissal provisions of that Act. It should be noted that these protections do not apply where the worker is exposed to a detriment because of his or her support for voluntary recognition of a union by the employer where no request for recognition has been made pursuant to the statute. He or she may be able to bring proceedings under s 146 of the Trade Union and Labour Relations (Consolidation) Act 1992 or s 94 of the Employment Rights Act 1996 on the ground that the acts in question are regarded as 'taking part in the activities of an independent trade union'.[2] However at the time of writing those protections are confined to employees. Moreover, as we indicate in para **3.6** *et seq.*, the courts have to date adopted a restrictive approach in deciding when employees fall within their scope. However, where it is official union policy to seek recognition in the enterprise it is possible that an employee may be treated as being 'authorised' to perform the acts in question. It is also arguable that where the employee's act constitutes the exercise of freedom of expression, dismissal or subjection to other detriment for its exercise could give a right of action where the employer is a 'public authority' for the purposes of the Human Rights Act 1998, and may also be relevant in a claim for unfair dismissal or breach of contract.[3] As we discuss in para **3.5** *et seq.*, arguments based upon freedom of association and freedom of expression may also justify a broader interpretation of the scope of statutory protection accorded to union members than has heretofore been the case.

----

1. Inserted by ERA 1999, s 1 and Sched 1.
2. See paras **3.6** *et seq.* See also TULCRA 1992, s 152.
3. See further para **1.13** *et seq.*

Protection against Detriment

4.58 A worker has a right not to be subjected to any detriment by any act, or any deliberate failure to act, by his employer if the act or failure takes place on any of a number of specified grounds.[1] The protection against 'being subjected to any detriment' was also accorded by the Employment Rights Act 1999 in relation to trade union membership and activities (replacing the pre-existing protection against 'action short of dismissal'), and our discussion of the ambit of this phrase in para **3.10** is equally applicable in this context. In this area, in particular, workers may be subject to threats of detrimental consequences if they lend their support to union recognition; as we argued in para **3.10**, we consider that workers have been 'subjected to a detriment' if they cease activities they wish to carry out because of intimidation, the 'threat' here constituting the employer's 'act'. However the employer's act will still need to be attributable to the action of the individual worker. Thus a warning to the workforce in general that terms and conditions of employment will be less favourable, or that redundancies will follow, if a union is accorded recognition would not suffice. Action taken against the workforce as a whole following a declaration in favour of recognition, such as withdrawal of *ex gratia* benefits or facilities, would also seem not to be protected; although it may be a consequence of workers having participated in activities which are protected, such as voting in a ballot, again there would be an insufficient nexus between the employer's act and that of the individual worker . The grounds to which protection pertains under paragraph 156 of the Schedule are that:

(a) the worker acted with a view to obtaining or preventing recognition of a union (or unions) by the employer under this Schedule.
(b) the worker indicated that he or she supported or did not support recognition of a union (or unions) by the employer under this Schedule.
(c) the worker acted with a view to securing or preventing the ending under this Schedule of bargaining arrangements;
(d) the worker indicated that he or she supported or did not support the ending under this Schedule of bargaining arrangements;
(e) the worker influenced or sought to influence the way in which votes were to be cast by other workers in a ballot arranged under this Schedule.
(f) the worker influenced or sought to influence other workers to vote or to abstain from voting in such a ballot.
(g) the worker voted in such a ballot.
(h) the worker proposed or failed to do, or proposed to decline to do, any of the things referred to in (a)–(g) above.[2]

A ground does not fall within (a)–(h) above 'if it constitutes an unreasonable act or omission by the worker'.[3] An example of an act which would seem to fall within this category would be canvassing other workers during working hours to vote in favour of recognition instead of performing normal duties. Clearly, however, there may be scope for argument whether a worker's act falls within this proviso. In the light of this, where the complainant is an employee it would be prudent to include, in appropriate circumstances, an additional complaint that he or she has been subjected to a detriment for taking part in union activities, where no qualification of this nature applies (although the activities must be at an 'appropriate time', which means that the employer's consent is required where they are performed during working hours).[4]

1. TULRCA 1992, Sched A1, para 156(1).
2. *Ibid.*, para 156(2).
3. *Ibid.*, para 156(3). Originally the Bill also excluded protection where the worker's act constituted a breach of contract. This exclusion was removed to prevent employers inserting into contracts a requirement not to campaign against recognition, and to bring it into line with other provisions relating to detriment and dismissal: Lord McIntosh of Haringey, Deputy Chief Whip, HL Debs Vol 603, col 1072, 8 July 1999.
4. TULRCA 1992, s146(2); see further para **3.8**.

4.59 A worker may present a complaint to an employment tribunal on the ground that he or she has been subjected to a detriment in contravention of the provisions in para **4.58** above.[1] This is stated to be the only remedy for 'infringement of the right conferred on him' by the Trade Union and Labour Relations (Consolidation) Act 1992, Schedule A1 paragraph 156.[2] This excludes workers from claiming injunctive or other relief for breach.[3] However it does not mean that other relief may not be sought if these acts additionally constitute a violation of other statutory or common law rights. Thus, for example, if the employer is a public authority and its action interferes with the worker's freedom of expression it remains open to the worker to seek other forms of remedy under the Human Rights Act 1998.[4] If the worker concerned is an employee and the detriment amounts to a dismissal within the Employment Rights Act 1996, he or she is required to seek a remedy under the unfair dismissal protection (see para **4.60**).[5] This has the advantage of enabling the employee to seek interim relief, which is extended to dismissals for these reasons; workers other than employees have no such remedy. The complaint under paragraph 156 must be presented before the end of the period of three months starting with the date of the act or failure to which the complaint relates or, if that act or failure is part of a series of similar acts or failures (or both), the last of them.[6] For these purposes, where an act extends over a period, the 'date of the act' refers to the last day of that period, and a failure to act is treated as done when it was decided on.[7] In the absence of evidence to the contrary, an employer must be taken to decide on a failure to act when it does an act inconsistent with doing the failed act, or if it has done no such inconsistent act, when the period expires within which it might reasonably have been expected to do the failed act if it was to be done.[8] This provision is identical to that applicable to detriments on grounds of union membership or activities. As we discussed in para **3.13**, to start the time limit running from the date when the failure to act was 'decided on' may cause difficulty where the employer can show it decided upon this course earlier than it might reasonably have been expected to do the failed act but that decision was not communicated to the worker. In that event, if the worker could not be expected to have known of the decision, the tribunal may use its discretion to extend the time limit for complaining.[9] It is for the employer to show the ground on which it acted or failed to act,[10] but it will still be for the worker to show that the employer's ground breached the statute. Where a complaint is upheld the tribunal must make a declaration to that effect and may also award such compensation as it considers 'just and equitable in all the circumstances having regard to the infringement complained of and to any loss sustained by the complainant which is attributable to the act or failure which infringed his [or her] right'.[11] The loss is to be taken to include any expenses reasonably incurred by the complainant in consequence of the act or failure complained of, and loss of any benefit which he or she might reasonably be expected otherwise to have had.[12] By analogy with the protection against detriment on union grounds, compensation may be awarded for injury to feelings.[13] There is a duty on complainants to mitigate their loss, and the tribunal must reduce the compensation by such proportion as it considers just and equitable if it finds that the act or failure was to any extent caused or contributed to by the action of the complainant.[14] There is no upper limit on the total amount which may be awarded, except that if the detriment consists of termination of the worker's contract, and that contract was not a contract of employment, compensation is limited to the total of the basic and compensatory awards for unfair dismissal, the basic award to be calculated as if the worker had been an employee.[15] In theory, therefore, a worker could be awarded more for suffering a detriment short of dismissal than for dismissal itself.

---

1. TULRCA 1992, Sched A1, para 156(5).
2. *Ibid.*, para 156(6).
3. Cf *Griffin v South West Water Services Ltd* [1995] IRLR 15, where Blackburn J refused an injunction restraining dismissals for redundancy pending conclusion of the redundancy procedure on the ground, inter alia, that the protective award was stated to be the exclusive remedy: see further para **5.22**.
4. See further para **1.13** *et seq.*
5. TULRCA 1992, Sched A1, 156(4). See App 1 for the definition of 'employee'. See ERA 1996, s 95 for the definition of dismissal.
6. *Ibid.*, para 157(1). The usual provision for extension to such further period as the tribunal considers 'reasonable' applies where the tribunal is satisfied that it was not 'reasonably practicable' for the complaint to be presented before the end of that period: para 157(1)(a); see further App 2.
7. *Ibid.*, para 157(2).
8. *Ibid.*, para 157(3).
9. See note 6, above.
10. TULRCA 1992, Sched A1, para 158.
11. *Ibid.*, para 159(1), (2).
12. *Ibid.*, para 159(3).

13. *Cleveland Ambulance NHS Trust v Blane* [1997] IRLR 332 (although *quaere* whether the decision will be different in the light of the abolition of the special award; see also *Brassington v Cauldon Wholesale Ltd* [1978] ICR 405 and the discussion in para **3.13**.

14. TULRCA 1992, Sched A1, para 159(4), (5).

15. *Ibid.*, para 160; see also para 165. Note that the limit on the compensatory award now stands at £50,000; ERA 1996, s 124.

Protection against Dismissal of Employees

4.60 The dismissal of an employee will be automatically unfair if the reason, or main reason, is one of those listed in para **4.58** above.[1] Dismissal for redundancy will also be automatically unfair where this was the reason, or principal reason, why the employee was selected for redundancy, provided that the circumstances constituting the redundancy applied equally to one or more other employees in the same undertaking who held positions similar to that held by the dismissed employee and who were not dismissed.[2] There is no qualifying period, or upper age limit, applicable to dismissals which are unfair under either of these provisions.[3] However where the employee would not otherwise qualify to claim, he or she will be required to prove that the reason for dismissal was one of those specified.[4] As in the case of subjection to a detriment, a reason will not fall within those specified if it constitutes an 'unreasonable act or omission' by the employee.[5] However it is conceivable that the employee's dismissal could still be unfair on general principles if, for example, the employer did not follow a fair procedure. In such a case, however, the employee would need to meet the normal qualifications to claim. As we indicated in para **4.58** it would be prudent to include a complaint that the employee had been dismissed for taking part in union activities in addition to a complaint under this provision. The remedy of interim relief is available for complaints under both provisions, although where the employee alleges that the reason for dismissal is participation in union activities an authorised official of the union in question must confirm that there appear to be reasonable grounds to suppose that this was indeed the case.[6] We discuss the procedure for applying for interim relief and the nature of the remedies in para **3.9**. This remedy may be particularly significant where the employer has dismissed employees prior to the ballot in the hope that they will thereby be excluded from participation in it. It is a moot point, however, whether all the remedies available on an application for interim relief would ensure that the dismissed employees could participate in the ballot. Reinstatement requires the employer to treat the employee in all respects as if he or she had not been dismissed.[7] This, if granted, would seem clearly to imply continued membership of the bargaining unit. However it can be ordered only with the consent of the employer. Re-engagement also requires the employer's consent. This remedy provides that the employee is re-engaged in another job 'on terms and conditions not less favourable than those which would have been applicable had he or she not been dismissed', which, for this purpose, means 'as regards seniority, pension rights and other similar rights, that the period prior to the dismissal should be regarded as continuous with the employment following the dismissal'.[8] It is unclear whether this would cover entitlement to vote in a ballot which had been held prior to the order of re-engagement being made. If the employer refuses to accept either of these remedies, the employment tribunal must make an order for continuation of the contract, which provides that the contract of employment continues in force for the purposes of pay or any other benefit derived from the employment, seniority, pension rights and other similar matters, and for the purpose of determining the period of continuity of employment, from the date of its termination until the determination or settlement of the complaint.[9] It would need to be argued in this context that membership of the bargaining unit, and entitlement to vote in the ballot, was a 'benefit derived from the employment'. Even if the granting of interim relief does render an employee a member of the bargaining unit, there could be difficulties if the ballot had been held after the dismissal and prior to the tribunal's order. It is submitted that an applicant union should ensure that the CAC is made immediately aware of any dismissal for a 'protected reason' and that the CAC would be justified in these circumstances in postponing the ballot pending the tribunal hearing on the employee's interim relief application.[10]

---

1. TULRCA 1992, Sched A1, para 161.
2. *Ibid.*, para 162.
3. *Ibid.*, para 164.
4. See para **3.3**.
5. TULRCA 1992, Sched A1, para 161(3).
6. ERA 1999, s 6, which inserts this into ERA 1996, ss 128 and 129; see further para **3.9** for the procedure for claiming interim relief.
7. TULRCA 1992, s 163(2)(a); ERA 1996, s 129(3)(a).
8. TULRCA 1992, ss 163(2)(b), (3); ERA 1996, ss 129(3)(b), (4).
9. TULRCA 1992, ss 163(6), 164; ERA 1996, ss 129(9), 130.
10. TULRCA 1992, Sched A1, para 25(3)(b); see para **4.23**, note 3. This need not lead to substantial delay. The tribunal has no jurisdiction to hear an application for interim relief unless it is presented before the end of the period of seven days immediately following the effective date of termination (whether before, on or after that date). The tribunal must determine the application for interim relief as soon as practicable after receiving the application: TULRCA 1992, ss 161(2), 162; ERA 1996, s128(2), (3).

THE HUMAN RIGHTS ACT 1998 AND RECOGNITION

4.61 We discuss the operation of the Human Rights Act 1998, and its general relevance to collective labour law in Chapter 1. In this section we highlight some of the issues which may arise specifically in relation to the statutory recognition and derecognition procedures, in addition to those to which we have already drawn attention at appropriate points in the text.[1] We first examine to what extent, if any, a union may invoke the Human Rights Act to claim recognition from employers. We then consider the aspects of the recognition and derecognition procedures which may raise issues under that Act, in particular the employer's duty to allow the union access to its premises prior to ballots and to provide facilities for meetings, and constraints on the conduct of campaigns.

---

1. On the issues raised for the role of the CAC by the HRA 1998, see para **4.7**; on workers' freedom of expression during recognition campaigns, see para **4.57**.

The Human Rights Act 1998 and Recognition

4.62 Article 11 of the ECHR guarantees to everyone the right to form and to join trade unions for the protection of his interests. As we discussed in para **1.6**, the ECtHR has refused to hold that this implies a right for individual trade union members that their union should be recognised for collective bargaining purposes. However the Court has held that the words 'for the protection of his interests' mean that the article safeguards the freedom to protect the occupational interests of trade union members by trade union action and that union members have a right 'that the trade union should be heard', although the state has a free choice of the means to be used towards that end.[1] This right does not depend upon the level of support among the workforce for the union in question. Thus the fact that the union fails to have a specified percentage of workers within the bargaining unit as members, as required by the statutory procedure, is irrelevant. On this basis, 'public authorities' (or at least some 'public authorities') would seem obliged to ensure that they allow some means by which unions which they do not currently recognise can be 'heard'.[2] Moreover, the right guaranteed by Article 11 applies irrespective of the size of the employer, in contrast to the statutory procedure which has a 21-worker threshold. The issue of whether non-independent, as well as independent, unions may claim the right to be heard has not arisen before the ECtHR. The text of Article 11 does not draw any distinction between these categories; it may be possible to argue, drawing upon ILO Convention No 98,[3] that a non-independent union cannot adequately fulfil the objective of protecting its members' interests, but this could be regarded as a matter for the individual to decide. In practice it is unlikely that a non-independent union which, by definition, has the support or endorsement of the employer, will be denied the right to be heard. It is notable that the right under Article 11 applies irrespective of whether another union is recognised or otherwise 'heard' by the employer. This means that even if a union (or group of unions) has been accorded exclusive recognition, the employer should still provide a channel for the views of members of non-recognised unions to be heard.[4] This does not mean that all unions have to be treated equally, however; because of the choice of means afforded to the state, Article 11 allows that some unions may be recognised for collective bargaining purposes whereas others may have only rights of consultation. Potentially differences in treatment could violate Articles 11 and 14 together: Article 14 provides that the rights and freedoms set forth in the Convention should be secured without discrimination, and the ECtHR has held that, although Article 11 does not afford unions or their members a right to be recognised or consulted, where this means of making the Article 11 right 'possible and effective' has been chosen it must be implemented without discrimination.[5] However, if the employer can demonstrate a legitimate aim, such as the desire to avoid a large number of bargaining partners, previous case law of the ECtHR suggests that this will justify the differential treatment;[6] by contrast, the desire to marginalise a militant union would be more difficult to justify. As well as affecting employers for which state responsibility is engaged, Article 11 has been found in other contexts to require the state to take positive measures to secure the exercise of the rights it guarantees as between private individuals, and it is strongly arguable that it should do so in this context too.[7] There is no liability under the Human Rights Act for a failure to legislate,[8] and it is difficult to see how a right for unions to be heard could be created from existing common law forms of action. It appears, therefore, that a union which was denied a right to be 'heard' by a private sector employer would need to apply to the ECtHR to complain that the UK had violated Article 11 by not providing a means by which this right is secured.

---

1. *National Union of Belgian Police v Belgium* judgment of 22 October 1975, (1979-80) 1 EHRR 578, para 39; see also *Swedish Engine Drivers' Union* v *Sweden* judgment of 6 February 1976, (1979-80) 1 EHRR 617; *Gustafsson* v *Sweden* judgment of 28 March 1996, (1996) 22 EHRR 409.
2. See para **1.17** for the definition of 'public authority' and the distinction between 'pure' public authorities and those with mixed public and private functions.
3. Article 1; see further para **1.20**.
4. *Swedish Engine Drivers' Union* v *Sweden*, above, note 1. In this case, although it was not incompatible with Article 11 for the Swedish National Collective Bargaining Office

to restrict the number of organisations with which collective agreements were concluded, it was material that the applicant union was still able to make representations to the Government for the protection of its members' interests.

5. *National Union of Belgian Police* v *Belgium*, above note 1, paras 44–45.

6. *National Union of Belgian Police* v *Belgium*, above, note 1, para 48; *Swedish Engine Drivers' Union* v *Sweden*, above, note 1, para 42.

7. See *Young, James and* W*ebster* v *UK* judgment of 13 August 1981, (1982) 4 EHRR 38, para 49; *Platfform "Ärtzte für das Leben"* v *Austria*, judgment of June 21 1988, (1991) 13 EHRR 204, paras 32-34.

8. HRA 1998, s 6(6).

4.63 The Code of Practice on access to workers during recognition and derecognition ballots provides that, where practicable, employers should allow specified union representatives access to workers at their workplace and should provide appropriate accommodation for this purpose.[1] It may be thought possible to argue that these requirements constitute an interference with an employer's right to the peaceful enjoyment of its possessions, contrary to Article 1 of the First Protocol of the ECHR. However the Convention jurisprudence to date does not support such a conclusion. Until recently it appeared to be the case that responsibility for a violation of the article would be engaged only where the economic value of a right or interest was affected,[2] which clearly would not be the case in this context. However in *Chassagnou* v *France*[3] the ECtHR found that the compulsory transfer of hunting rights over land belonging to landowners opposed to hunting constituted an interference with their enjoyment of their rights as owners of the property even though they were not deprived of their right to use or sell their property (and its market value did not appear to be affected). It is submitted, however, that the level of access to premises required under the Code is of a very different nature and should be regarded as *de minimis* in this context; it may also be seen as relevant that the duty arises in the context of a process designed to establish or maintain the right of unions to be 'heard', an objective compatible with Article 11 of the ECHR.[4] Even if, contrary to this view, a domestic court were to conclude that the requirements of the Code could constitute an interference, it would be open to the state to justify the interference as 'lawful', and striking a fair balance between the demands of the general interest of the community and the requirements of the protection of the individual's fundamental rights.[5] Employers may also seek to argue that the Code interferes with their right to freedom of expression in specifying that the level of access that it is reasonable for union representatives to have to their workers should be related to their own, at least as far as addressing large-scale gatherings and the use of internal electronic communication are concerned, thereby constituting a disincentive to such communication if not an impediment as such. In this context we would submit that this principle of reciprocity does not constitute an interference with the employer's right. However, even if it were to be so regarded, there is a strong argument to say that any restriction on the exercise of the right is justified as necessary for the protection of the rights of others.[6] The same argument can be made in relation to the circulation of provocative propaganda or threatening material by employers, contrary to the provisions of the Code, particularly as the exercise of the right to freedom of expression, unlike other Convention rights, explicitly carries with it 'duties and responsibilities'.

1. See paras **4.26-4.28**.
2. *Rayner* v *UK* App No 9310/81 (1986) 47 DR 5; *S* v *France* App No 13728/88 (1990) 65 DR 250.
3. Judgment of 29 April 1999.
4. See *Van der Mussele* v *Belgium* judgment of 23 November 1983, (1984) 6 EHRR 163, para 49 (expenses incurred acting for *pro bono* clients as required for entry on the register of *avocats* relatively small and resulted from the obligation to perform work compatible with Article 4).
5. *James* v *UK* judgment of 21 February 1986, (1986) 8 EHRRR 123; *Iatridis* v *Greece*, judgment of March 25 1999; *Sporring and Lonnroth* v *Sweden* judgment of 23 September 1982, (1983) 5 EHRR 35, para 69. 'Lawful' in this context, like other areas of the Convention, extends to the quality of law: *James* v *UK*, para 67; see further para **1.8**. The Code of Practice would appear to be sufficiently clear and precise to satisfy the requisite criteria.
6. See further para **1.8** for the principles which apply in this context.

COLLECTIVE BARGAINING AND COLLECTIVE AGREEMENTS

Sources and General Principles

4.64 Where a trade union is recognised pursuant to a statutory request for recognition, the CAC may specify, at the request of the union or employer and in default of an agreement between them, the 'method' by which collective bargaining is to be conducted.[1] Other than in these circumstances, the conduct of the collective bargaining process is left entirely to the discretion of the parties, with the exception of a limited statutory duty on any employer which recognises an independent trade union to disclose to union representatives on request information for the purposes of collective bargaining on matters, and in relation to workers, for which the union is recognised. This duty is contained in the Trade Union and Labour Relations (Consolidation) Act 1992, ss 181–185. In addition, an ACAS Code of Practice gives further guidance on when information should be disclosed. There is a complex enforcement procedure where an employer fails to comply with the duty to disclose, culminating in compulsory arbitration. The legal status of collective agreements (the product of collective bargaining) is governed by the Trade Union and Labour Relations (Consolidation) Act 1992, s 179, which lays down a conclusive presumption that collective agreements as therein defined are not legally enforceable contracts. This means that recognition or 'no-strike' agreements between unions and employers, for example, will be enforceable only if they are specifically stated to be so.[2] The terms of collective agreements will have legal effect if they become terms of individual contracts of employment, but there is no provision for this to happen automatically: even where a union is recognised pursuant to the statutory procedure, there is no obligation for employers to offer contracts of employment which incorporate collective agreements with the recognised union. However, the Secretary of State is empowered to make regulations protecting workers against dismissal or subjection to a detriment where they refuse to enter into a contract which includes terms which differ from the terms of a collective agreement which applies to them.[3] Collective agreements between an employer and an independent trade union may exclude or modify specified provisions of the Working Time Regulations 1998, as amended,[4] and may also regulate the terms upon which parental leave is taken under the Maternity and Parental Leave etc. Regulations 1999.[5] This role may also be fulfilled by 'workforce agreements' between the employer and elected members of the workforce.

---

1. See paras **4.29** *et seq.*
2. Note the statutory restrictions on 'agreements for recognition', however: see para **4.32** *et seq.*
3. ERA 1999, s 17. At the time of writing no regulations implementing this provision have yet been issued.
4. SI 1998/1833, as amended by SI 1999/3372.
5. SI 1999/3312.

The Duty to Disclose Information

4.65 The duty of employers to disclose information about the undertaking to representatives of recognised independent trade unions on request applies to all stages of collective bargaining about matters, and in relation to descriptions of workers, for which the union is recognised.[1] 'Representative' means an official or other person authorised by the union to carry on such collective bargaining.[2] Both the request and the information sought should be in writing or confirmed in writing if the employer or union representatives, as appropriate, so request.[3] The information to be disclosed may be in the possession of the employer in question or that of an associated employer.[4] It must satisfy two tests. First, it must be information without which the union representatives would be to a 'material extent' impeded in carrying out collective bargaining with the employer.[5] This test, in addressing the importance rather than the relevance of the information, 'focuses attention not on the nature of the bargaining that disclosure might facilitate but, rather, on whether bargaining can take place at all without disclosure'.[6] It is difficult for a union to argue that bargaining is impossible if it has managed without such information in the past; the difference which access to the information would have made can be a matter of speculation only. 'Many employers have successfully objected that there was no impediment and unions are severely disadvantaged in arguing the need for information, which they do not have'.[7] Secondly, it must be information which the employer should disclose in accordance with good industrial relations practice, on which regard is to be had, *inter alia*, to the ACAS Code of Practice.[8] The Code is not particularly helpful on this matter, however. It does not attempt to give an exhaustive, or 'check', list of items which should be disclosed on the ground that this will vary according to factors such as the subject-matter, level of negotiations and size of the company and business in which it is engaged.[9] Rather, it confines itself to giving examples of information which it suggests could be relevant in certain situations which it divides into five broad headings: pay and benefits; conditions of service; manpower [*sic*]; performance (eg productivity and efficiency data, savings from increased productivity and output, return on capital invested, sales and state of the order book) and financial matters (eg. profits, assets, loans to parent or subsidiary companies, and liabilities).[10] This list does, at least, make clear that subjects which are not themselves within the statutory definition of 'collective bargaining' are nevertheless potentially within the duty. Moreover, the CAC has held that information about workers who are outside the union's sphere of recognition may nevertheless be relevant to bargaining about those who are within it.[11] However, it is clear that the information need be disclosed only for the *purpose* of collective bargaining, and, depending on its nature, it is conceivable that an employer could restrain its use in any other context on the basis that this would constitute a breach of confidence.[12]

---

1. TULRCA 1992, s 181(1). For the definition of 'worker' see *ibid.*, s 296 (discussed App 1). The CAC, which adjudicates upon this procedure, has held that provided the union is recognised at the time of the request for information, subsequent derecognition is irrelevant: *Ackrill Newspapers Ltd v NUJ*, judgment of 14 February 1992, unreported. It has also held that the procedure's application to 'all stages' of collective bargaining means that there is no need for negotiations to have started before disclosure is sought, and unions may wish to request information in order to decide where to

pitch a claim, an approach approved by Forbes J in *R v Central Arbitration Committee ex parte BTP Tioxide Ltd* [1982] IRLR 60, 67. An employer cannot avoid the obligation to supply information by announcing in a given situation that it has decided not to negotiate: *HM Prison Service v POA* (CAC, 27 March 1995, unreported) IRLB No 523, 9.

2. *Ibid.* 'Official' is defined in s119 and includes shop stewards elected or appointed in accordance with the rules of the union and other staff representatives as well as branch and other union officers. See para **4.3** for the definition of collective bargaining. Note that providing information which is confidential under the contract of employment to union representatives will be a breach of contract on the part of individual employees and seeking it may constitute the tort of inducing breach of contract: *Bent's Brewery Co Ltd v Hogan* [1945] 2 All ER 570, Liverpool Spring Assizes.

3. *Ibid.*, s 181(3), (5).

4. *Ibid.*, s 181(2). See s 297 and App 1 for the meaning of 'associated employer'.

5. *Ibid.*, para 181(2).

6. Dickens and Bain, 1986, 98.

7. Gospel and Lockwood, 1999, 244. However the CAC has emphasised that 'collective bargaining must be looked at more widely than simply relating to a process in which two parties are clearly agreed that they are negotiating to reach a mutually acceptable solution. The term "collective bargaining" refers to the continuing relationship between an employer and a trade union, not simply the nature of the interaction on one particular occasion': *Annual Report*, 1995, para 2.17.

8. TULRCA 1992, s 181(2)(b). ACAS Code No. 2: *Disclosure of Information to Trade Unions for Collective Bargaining Purposes* (1997). This Code, which came into force on 5 February 1998, replaces the original version published in 1977. Failure to comply with the Code does not render an individual liable to any proceedings, but the Code is admissible in evidence before the CAC, and any provision which appears to the CAC to be relevant to any question arising in the proceedings must be taken into account in determining that question: TULRCA 1992, s 207(1), (2). Other evidence of good industrial relations practice may also be adduced: s 181(4). The CAC Annual Reports are a more useful source of guidance in this area.

9. ACAS Code No 2, paras 11, 12.

10. *Ibid.*, para 11.

11. See, for example, CAC *Annual Report* 1993, para 2.6, which recognises the interest of unions in knowing the level of pay increases, including those of senior managers, throughout a company.

12. I. Smith and G. Thomas, 1996, 52. On the factors which determine whether an action for breach of confidence can succeed, apart from contract, see Toulson and Phipps, 1996, Chapter III.

4.66 The duty to disclose is subject to significant limitations. First, there is a list of six categories of information which need not be disclosed. The most wide-ranging are any information 'which has been communicated to . . . [the employer] in confidence'[1] and information whose disclosure 'would cause substantial injury to . . . [the employer's] undertaking for reasons other than its effect on collective bargaining'.[2] For the latter category the Code gives as examples cost information on individual products; detailed analysis of proposed investment, marketing or pricing policies; and price quotas or the make-up of tender prices.[3] 'Substantial injury may occur if, for example, certain customers would be lost to competitors, or suppliers would refuse to supply necessary materials, or the ability to raise funds to finance the company would be seriously impaired as a result of disclosing certain information'.[4] A further exempted category—information relating specifically to an individual without that individual's consent[5]—has assumed greater practical significance with the spread of performance-related pay and management-only grading schemes. The CAC has acknowledged unions' interests in having the information necessary to monitor the operation of such schemes and has reconciled this with respect for individual confidentiality by awarding that particular breakdowns of annual salary increases should be provided, for example, by age groups, sex and by functional area.[6] The second important limitation is that employers are not obliged to produce, or allow inspection of, any document, or to compile or assemble any information where this would involve an amount of work or expenditure 'out of reasonable proportion to the value of the information in the conduct of collective bargaining'.[7] This exception assumes both that the value of information can be objectively assessed and, moreover, that it can be assessed before disclosure. The Code goes beyond the statute in recommending that employers should present information in a form or style which recipients can reasonably be expected to understand,[8] and clearly it may be in the interests of employers to sustain any additional costs involved in doing this. More generally, the Code also recommends that employers and unions should endeavour to arrive at a joint understanding on how the disclosure provisions can be implemented most effectively, and should agree the procedures for resolving potential disputes in this area, where possible relating these to existing arrangements within the undertaking or industry.[9]

---

1. TULRCA 1992, 182(1)(c). In *Civil Service Union v Central Arbitration Committee* [1980] IRLR 274, it was held by Forbes J that the Ministry of Defence could rely on this defence in refusing to disclose to the Civil Service Union information as to the number of cleaners and their hours of work supplied in a tender from private contractors. Several cases before the CAC in recent years have concerned market-testing and contracting-out, including the information given to potential bidders. The CAC has urged upon those conducting the process the benefits of involving staff and their representatives at an early stage: see, for example, *Annual Report*, 1996, para 2.8. The legislation does not provide for union representatives receiving access to information on

a privileged basis, subject to a duty of confidentiality; (cf TICER 1999, discussed at para **5.56**). However in its *Annual Report*, 1996 para 2.7, the CAC referred cryptically to the possibility of an employer 'negotiating some understanding with a trade union officer over a wider release of confidential information' relating to a job evaluation exercise.

2. *Ibid.*, s 182(1)(e). In relation to Crown employment the reference to the employer's undertaking is to be construed as a reference to the national interest: *ibid.*, s 273(4)(d).
3. ACAS Code No 2, para 14.
4. *Ibid.*, para 15.
5. TULRCA 1992, s 182(1)(d).
6. See, for example, *Annual Reports* for 1991, 1992 and 1993.
7. TULRCA 1992, s 182(2)(b).
8. ACAS Code No 2, para 21.
9. *Ibid.*, paras 22 and 23.

4.67 Where an employer fails to disclose information which it is required to disclose, or fails to confirm such information in writing, the union may complain in writing to the CAC, which may refer the complaint to ACAS for conciliation if it considers that this is reasonably likely to produce a settlement.[1] The CAC also seeks to encourage the parties to resolve their differences jointly. It is CAC practice to hold an informal meeting involving a chairman, both parties, and usually an ACAS conciliator as the first stage of the procedure. This may result in the union withdrawing the complaint, if the employer concedes disclosure or there seems no prospect of success. If a conciliated settlement seems likely, arrangements are made for the parties to meet with ACAS. Alternatively (or if conciliation fails) the case proceeds to a full hearing, at which the parties are sometimes legally represented, following which the CAC makes a declaration on whether it finds the complaint well-founded, giving reasons.[2] If the declaration requires the employer to disclose information and this is not done within the specified period, the union may present a further complaint to the CAC.[3] It may at the same time or subsequently present a claim that the contracts of particular descriptions of employees should include specified terms and conditions.[4] The CAC, if it upholds the complaint, may, after hearing the parties, make an award (either in the terms sought by the union or otherwise) which takes effect as a term in the contracts of the employees affected, and may be superseded or varied only by a subsequent award under this procedure, a collective agreement between the employer and the union representing those employees, or by express or implied agreement between the employer and individual employees if that agreement improves upon the terms specified in the award.[5] This sanction therefore constitutes a rare example of statutory intervention in the contract. It has significant weaknesses, however. First, it means that the duty to disclose cannot, ultimately, be enforced.[6] Secondly, although the duty is framed in terms of 'workers', only 'employees' may be the subject of a claim for improved terms and conditions. Thirdly, although the duty covers information in the possession of an associated employer, there is no provision for a remedy against an associated employer who refuses to comply. Lastly, the CAC is not empowered to prescribe the information which should be disclosed on future occasions,[7] although clearly the parties may be guided in their behaviour by the outcome of previous complaints. However the fact that the CAC may adjudicate only upon a past failure to disclose means that 'the matter in dispute has to be capable of being pursued over a considerable length of time. Otherwise it will mean the employer can delay disclosure of the information until its usefulness is limited or has passed'.[8]

---

1. TULRCA 1992, s183(1), (2).

2. *Ibid.*, s 183(3). Four of the CAC's decisions have been the subject of judicial review: Gospel and Lockwood, 1999, 238.

3. *Ibid.*, s 184. This section and s 185 do not have effect in relation to Crown employment or parliamentary staff: ss 273(2), 278(2), 277(1A).

4. *Ibid*, s 185(1). The CAC makes an award only in respect of employees, and comprising only terms and conditions relating to matters in respect of which the union making the claim is recognised by the employer. See App 1 for the definition of 'employee'.

5. *Ibid.*, para 185(5).

6. *Quaere* whether the CAC could award any of the information sought as part of the contracts of employment. In *Holokrome Ltd v ASTMS* (CAC, 6 August 1979, unreported) the CAC did not accept the employer's argument that it could not award any of the information sought; the test was whether what was claimed was appropriate as a term or condition of an individual contract. In its judgment the CAC thought that individual contracts could contain a term requiring information about salary ranges and increments within the grade in which an employee fell. However the actual award does not appear to mention 'information'; the CAC awarded that the salary ranges and increments should have effect as part of the contracts of employment.

7. *R v Central Arbitration Committee ex parte BTP Tioxide Ltd* [1982] IRLR 60 at 67 (Forbes J).

8. Gospel and Lockwood, 1999, 245.

4.68 Relatively little use has been made of the enforcement provisions of the disclosure procedure. Between February 1977 (when these provisions came into force) and the end of 1999, 476 complaints had been received, of which less than 13.7 per cent went to a full hearing.[1] The majority of the balance were withdrawn after a settlement had been reached, a tribute to the success of the CAC's proce-dures which favours the avoidance of 'win/lose scenarios'.[2] The highest number of complaints in any year was 62 (in 1978), and in many there have been consid-erably fewer.[3] This does not of itself indicate that the disclosure provisions have little impact; their existence may have an indirect effect in influencing voluntary behaviour, a view endorsed by the CAC itself.[4] However, it seems to be gener-ally accepted that the limited scope of the information of which disclosure may be ordered has contributed to the low level of recourse to this provision.[5]

---

1. Information supplied by the CAC; CAC *Annual Report* 1999–2000.

2. CAC *Annual Report* 1998, para 2.3. There have been only two cases to date where the CAC has had to issue a second award after an employer's failure to honour the first declaration.

3. Information supplied by the CAC. In 1998 there were six complaints, in the period 1 January 1999–31 March 2000, 11: *Annual Report* 1999/2000.

4. *Annual Report* 1993, para 3.4.

5. For an analysis of the matters in relation to which information has been sought, and CAC decisions up to the time of their respective publication, see Gospel and Willman, 1981; Dickens and Bain, 1986, 94–101; Gospel and Willman 1999, and CAC Annual Reports. In recent years information has been sought on a wide range of issues includ-ing staffing, grading and pay distribution; pensions; financial information; market-test-ing and contracting-out; and redundancy plans and selection procedures.

Collective Agreements

The function of collective agreements

4.69 Collective agreements fulfil two main purposes. First, they regulate rela-tions between employers or employers' associations and trade unions (the pro-cedural or contractual function). These arrangements are usually of a procedural or constitutional nature (generically called procedural agreements) and can take a variety of forms. Thus they may, for example, establish perma-nent joint machinery for the negotiation of terms and conditions of employment or specify the procedural stages to be followed for the resolution of disputes, possibly limiting industrial action until the procedure has been exhausted. The second function of collective agreements is to regulate the terms of individual contracts of employment (the normative function).[1] These 'substantive' terms may cover pay scales, working hours, holidays, shift work, and overtime, and many other areas. These terms may become terms of individual contracts of employment by means of the doctrine of incorporation; once incorporated, they may be enforced like any other contractual term.[2] Incorporation may be express (the contract may state that the individual contract is subject to a particular collective agreement or agreements, or the collective agreement for the time being in force between the employer and a specified trade union or unions)[3] or implied, often on the basis of evidence that it is the acknowledged custom or practice of the particular enterprise or industry to follow the agreement in question.[4] Importantly, however, unlike some other systems, whether incorporation occurs is a matter entirely for the individual parties.[5] The written statement of employment terms which employers must give their new employees must contain particulars of any collective agreements which directly affect the terms and conditions of employment including, where the employer is not a party, the persons by whom they were made.[6] In practice both procedural and substantive terms may frequently be found in the same collective agreement. There may also be terms which cannot be classified in either category, such as an obligation on every employer belonging to an employers' association which is party to an agreement to provide copies of the agreement to its employees.

---

1. In 1998 it was estimated that 41 per cent of employees were covered by collective agreements: Cully *et al*, 1999, 242.

2. It is possible for a union to negotiate with the employer as agent for each individual union member as principal. However this view has been confined to exceptional cases (see, for example, *Edwards v Skyways Ltd* [1964] 1 All ER 494, QBD; cf *The Burton Group v Smith* [1977] IRLR 351) and would present a host of practical difficulties: see Deakin and Morris, 1998, 261–262. The mere existence of the contract of membership does not authorise the union to act as the agent of the member: *Boxfoldia Ltd v NGA (1982)* [1988] IRLR 383; see further para **6.82**.

3. *National Coal Board v Galley* [1958] 1 WLR 16, CA. Note that not all clauses of a collective agreement will be appropriate for incorporation: see *National Coal Board v NUM* [1986] IRLR 439, ChD and para **6.84**.

4. *Hill v Levey* (1858) 157 ER 366; *MacLea v Essex Lines* (1933) 45 Ll L Rep 254, KBD; cf. *Associated Newspapers Group Ltd v Wade* [1979] IRLR 201, CA.

5. See further Deakin and Morris, 1998, 78–80 and 258–261; Wedderburn, 1992a.

6. ERA 1996, s 1(4)(j).

The legal status of collective agreements

4.70 Collective agreements between employers and trade unions fall into three categories, each governed by distinctive legal provisions. The first category is by far the most common. These are agreements which fall within the statutory definition of a 'collective agreement' and which were made before 1 December 1971 and after 31 July 1974. A 'collective agreement' means 'any agreement[1] or arrangement made by or on behalf of one or more trade unions[2] and one or more employers or employers' associations,[3] and relating to one or more of the matters specified' in the Trade Union and Labour Relations (Consolidation) Act 1992, s 178(2).[4] These matters constitute the subject-matter of 'collective bargaining' (for purposes other than the statutory recognition procedure, where a more limited definition usually applies)[5] and are listed in para **4.3**. The agreement need not be in any particular form. Such an agreement is conclusively presumed not to have been intended by the parties to be a legally enforceable contract unless the agreement is in writing and contains a provision which (however expressed) states that the parties intend the agreement to be a legally enforceable contract.[6] To demonstrate the requisite intention, the agreement must contain a statement which demonstrates that the parties have directed their minds to the question of legal enforceability and have decided in favour of it; a statement merely that the parties intend to be 'bound' will not suffice as this could mean 'binding in honour only'.[7] It does not follow that an agreement which clearly shows that legal enforceability is intended will necessarily constitute a contract because it may still be expressed in language which is too uncertain to be interpreted, or void as in restraint of trade, or for some other reason not a contract. The second category of collective agreements are those which were made between 1 December 1971 and 31 July 1974. These agreements were conclusively presumed to be legally enforceable unless they contained an express exclusion clause.[8] Most agreements made during that period did, in fact, contain such a clause.[9] The third category is those agreements which are not 'collective agreements' within the statutory definition. Examples would include those concerning union involvement in future investment decisions or product development relating to the undertaking. These agreements are governed by the common law, which offers no clear guidance. It would be open to the parties to stipulate that they intended their agreement to constitute a contract and provided that the terms were sufficiently clear to be capable of enforcement by the courts, there would seem to be no barrier to this. If the agreement were silent on the question of intention the courts would probably conclude that the parties had not intended to create legal relations. In *Ford v AEU*, where this situation arose, the court concluded that the 'climate of opinion was almost unanimous to the effect that no legally enforceable contracts resulted from . . . collective agreements'[10] and held that the parties to the Ford agreement must be credited with knowledge of these sources which also provided evidence of their state of mind at the time. The court reached the same conclusion applying an objective test, maintaining that 'the fact that the agreements *prima facie* deal with commercial relationships is outweighed by the other considerations, by the wording of the agreements, by the nature of the agreements, and by the climate of opinion voiced and evidenced by the extra-judicial authorities.'[11] It is, of course conceivable (if unlikely) that the 'climate of opinion' may change in the future so as to provide a different answer to that given in the *Ford* case.[12]

---

1. It is irrelevant how the agreement was achieved, and the fact that it may require endorsement from another body makes no difference to its status: *Edinburgh Council v Brown* [1999] IRLR 208, EAT. In *Burke v Royal Liverpool University Hospital NHS Trust* [1997] ICR 730, the EAT held that an exchange of letters between the employer and union as to future terms of employment could constitute a 'collective agreement', although it was also stated (at 738) that there needed to be 'a mutual intention on the part of employers and employees' bargaining agents to enter into a collective bargain, the effect of which will be to modify the contracts of employment between employer and employee'. The latter constitutes a gloss on the statute, and does not cater for procedural agreements or other agreements not dealing with substantive terms and conditions of employment.

2. See para **2.4**.

3. See App 1.

4. TULRCA 1992, s 178(1).

5. See para **4.8**.

6. TULRCA 1992, s 179(1), (2). Parts only of the agreement may be specified as intended to be enforceable; the presumption against enforceability will then apply to the remainder: s 179(3).

7. *National Coal Board v NUM* [1986] IRLR 439, Scott J at 449. See also *Monterosso Shipping Co Ltd v ITWF* [1982] IRLR 468, CA.

8. Industrial Relations Act 1971, ss 34 and 35 (now repealed); TULRCA 1992, Sched 3, para 5.

9. Weekes et al, 1975, 156–161.

10. [1969] 2 All ER 481, Lane J at 494.

11. *Ibid.*, at 496. See Hepple, 1970 and Selwyn, 1969 for critiques of this decision.

12. Lewis, 1979.

4.71 The vast majority of current collective agreements fall into the first category. In practice it is very rare for the collective parties to attempt to make their collective agreements legally enforceable,[1] which means that their status is governed by the presumption that they are not contracts. This means that procedural agreements between employers and unions cannot be enforced directly at collective level, nor can unions enforce terms governing their members' employment against recalcitrant employers. Where a term of a collective agreement becomes a term of the individual contract of employment, however, it is then enforceable between employer and employee in the normal way.[2] The legal status of a collective agreement is entirely irrelevant to the question of enforceability of the terms of the agreement between the employer and individual workers,[3] although the courts have, on occasion, confused the two.[4] Once incorporated into the individual contract, the terms of the collective agreement remain binding regardless of whether the collective agreement itself remains in existence.[5]

---

1. The collective agreement to ensure staff relations are conducted peacefully and without disruption to operations at GCHQ, 3 September 1997, is a notable exception to this. Stringent statutory conditions must be met for restrictions on industrial action contained in collective agreements to take effect as terms of individual contracts: see TULRCA 1992, s 180, discussed at para **6.84**.

2. See para **4.69**.

3. *Marley v Forward Trust Group Ltd* [1986] IRLR 369, CA.

4. *Loman and Henderson v Merseyside Transport Services Ltd* (1968) 3 ITR 108, CA; *Gascol Conversions Ltd v Mercer* [1974] ICR 420, CA.

5. *Morris v CH Bailey Ltd* [1969] 2 Lloyds Rep 215, CA; *Robertson and Jackson v British Gas Corporation* [1983] IRLR 302, CA; *Gibbons v Associated British Ports* [1985] IRLR 376, QBD; *Lee v GEC Plessey Communications* [1993] IRLR 383, QBD.

Collective agreements: protection against detriment and dismissal

4.72 As we indicated in para **4.69** whether the terms of collective agreements become terms of individual contracts of employment depends upon whether the parties choose to incorporate the terms of those agreements; there is no obligation to incorporate them. Moreover, even if employees' contracts initially incorporate such terms, the parties are free to depart from them by agreement. Employers may wish to take steps to encourage their employees to agree to such a course. As we discuss in paras **3.11** and **3.12**, a distinction has been drawn between acts by employers which are done for the purpose of deterring union membership, which are unlawful, and those which are designed to encourage employees to move away from terms which have been collectively-agreed. In the combined appeals in *Associated Newspapers v Wilson* and *Associated British Ports v Palmer*[1] the House of Lords held that offering an inducement to employees to transfer from collectively-agreed terms and conditions of employment to 'personal' contracts was not unlawful on the ground, *inter alia*, that neither employer had as its purpose the deterrence of union membership. The Employment Relations Act 1999 has preserved the distinction between discrimination on grounds of union membership and collective bargaining: that aspect of the *Wilson* and *Palmer* judgment has not been overturned,[2] and the facility for employers to defend claims of anti-union discrimination by providing evidence that they wish to further a change in their relationship with all or any class of their employees remains.[3] However, a new provision has been introduced empowering (although not requiring) the Secretary of State to make regulations about cases where a worker is dismissed or subject to detriment by his or her employer 'on the grounds that he [or she] refuses to enter into a contract which includes terms which differ from the terms of a collective agreement which applies to him' or her.[4] As a government spokesman indicated,

> Detriment could take several forms—perhaps a block on promotion for those who refuse to give up the terms of a collective agreement, the withholding of discretionary benefits if the employer chooses to award such benefits to those who have accepted contracts differing from the collective agreement, or the allocation of workers who refuse to give up the terms of collective agreement [*sic*] to less favourable duties or locations. However, the mere fact that the terms of the collective agreement differ from those of individual contracts will not obviously [*sic*] constitute detriment.[5]

At the time of writing, no such regulations have been issued, so any discussion of the use of this power is inevitably incomplete. Nevertheless some points about its scope can be noted. First, it appears to be confined to cases where the worker is employed under a contract which already incorporates the terms of a collective agreement, rather than extending to cases where the worker falls within a bargaining unit which is subject to terms which have been collectively agreed but where his or her own contract does not currently incorporate such terms.[6] Secondly, although the meaning of 'subjected to detriment' is not wholly clear, it is submitted that threats of detrimental action should themselves be regarded as 'subjection to detriment'.[7] Thirdly, the statute itself provides that:

> [t]he payment of higher wages or higher rates of pay or overtime or the payment of any signing on or other bonuses or the provision of other benefits having a monetary value to other workers employed by the same employer shall not constitute a detriment to any worker not receiving the same or similar payments or benefits . . . so long as—
> (a) there is no inhibition in the contract of employment of the worker receiving the same from being the member of any trade union, and
> (b) the said payments of higher wages or rates of pay or overtime or bonuses or the provision of other benefits are in accordance with the terms of a contract of employment and reasonably relate to the services provided by the worker under that contract.

It is notable that this proviso does not on the face of it prevent the employer linking acceptance of personal contracts with the opportunity to provide services which differ from those provided by workers whose terms continue to reflect those collectively agreed; indeed, it seems to be a requirement of it that such a linkage should be made. Thus, an employer could offer those on personal contracts the opportunity to work on different shifts or a wider range of tasks, and on the basis that these 'reasonably relate' to the services provided under the contract this will not constitute a detriment to other workers. It is unclear how the line would be drawn between the offer of such opportunities and the offer of some form of promotion, a distinction which will be required if the government's intention of outlawing promotion blocks on those who do not agree to transfer is to be achieved. The reference in the statute to services 'provided' suggests that it will not suffice to have a notional obligation to undertake such work which is not exercised in practice, although there is no specific obligation to have regard to the frequency with which they are performed.[8]

---

1. [1995] IRLR 258, HL.

2. However the prohibition against 'action short of dismissal', which was held by their Lordships not to cover omissions, has been replaced: see further para **3.10**.

3. TULRCA 1992, s 148(3)–(5); see further para **3.12**.

4. ERA 1999, s 17. 'Collective agreement' has the same meaning as in TULRCA 1992, s 178(1) (see further para **4.70**), 'employer' and 'worker' the meaning given by s 296 (see App 1).

5. Mr. Michael Wills, Minister for Small Firms, Trade and Industry, Official Report of Standing Committee E, 18 March 1999, 5 pm.

6. Although the words 'which applies to him' are ambiguous, it is submitted that this is the more likely construction. Ministerial language also supports this construction (see, for example, Mr. Wills, above, who spoke of employees 'giv[ing] up' the terms of a collective agreement.

7. See further para **3.10**, and see *Gloucester Working Men's Club and Institute v James* [1986] ICR 603 at 606.

8. Cf the Equal Pay Act 1970, s 1(4).

Collective agreements and workforce agreements: working time and parental leave

4.73 Specified provisions of the Working Time Regulations 1998 may be excluded or modified by collective agreements and 'workforce agreements'.[1] These instruments may also determine the terms upon which parental leave is taken under the Maternity and Parental Leave etc. Regulations 1999.[2] This substantive law of both these regulations, which were introduced to comply with EU Directives,[3] lies beyond the scope of this work. However there are a number of points which are noteworthy in the context of collective labour law. First, a collective agreement is defined in these contexts as an agreement within the meaning of s 178 of the Trade Union and Labour Relations (Consolidation) Act 1992, the trade union parties to which are *independent*.[4] This reflects the significance of the role of such agreements in modifying (and, in the case of working time, excluding) statutory rights. However no such condition is placed upon the worker parties to a 'workforce agreement', a novel statutory concept designed to provide for the flexibility in the application of standards permitted by the Directive in the situation where the employer does not recognise trade unions.[5] A 'workforce agreement' means an agreement between an employer and its workers or their representatives which satisfies prescribed conditions. It must be in writing; last for a specified period of no more than five years; apply to all the 'relevant members of the workforce' or all the relevant members of a particular group; be signed by representatives of the workforce or of the group to which the agreement applies (with a modification for small employers); and prior to being available for signature, have been provided by the employer to all workers to whom it was intended to apply with such guidance as they may reasonably require to understand it fully.[6] 'Relevant members of the workforce' are 'all of the workers employed by a particular employer, excluding any worker whose terms and conditions of employment are provided for, wholly or in part, in a collective agreement'.[7] This means that the employer cannot negotiate a workforce agreement where it has negotiated a collective agreement with an independent trade union, at least where the terms of that agreement have been incorporated into individual workers' contracts.[8] Workers representatives must be elected, and although statutory requirements govern their election these leave the employer considerable discretion.[9] The number of representatives is determined by the employer, as is the mode of conduct of the election, subject to the requirements that the election must be conducted so as to secure that, so far as practicable, those voting do so in secret and the votes are fairly and accurately counted. Other conditions are that the candidates must themselves be relevant members of the workforce or group in question; no worker who is eligible to be a candidate should be unreasonably excluded from standing; and all relevant members of the workforce or the group should be permitted to vote, for as many candidates as there are representatives to be elected. These requirements (whilst less prescriptive in some respects) reflect those governing the election of 'employee representatives' in the context of collective redundancies and transfers of undertakings, and the comments which we make in paras **5.11** *et seq.* are equally applicable in this context. Here, however, there are no provisions enabling workers to challenge whether the election of representatives complied with the statutory requirements; it would seem that such a challenge could occur only in the context of a claim by a worker to enforce a statutory right which he or she alleged had not been modified or excluded by a valid 'workforce agreement'.

---

1. SI 1998/1833, as amended by SI 1999/3372, reg 23. The provisions which may be modified or excluded relate to night work, daily and weekly rest, and in-work rest breaks. In addition the reference period over which working time is calculated may, for specified reasons, be increased from 17 to up to 52 weeks.

2. SI 1999/3312, reg. 16. Default provisions apply in the case of employees whose contract of employment does not confer an entitlement to absence from work for the purpose of caring for a child, and incorporates or operates by reference to all or part of a collective agreement or workforce agreement.

3. Council Directive 93/104/EC (working time) and Council Directive 96/34/EC, extended to the UK by Council Directive 97/75/EC (parental leave).

4. SI 1998/1833, as amended, reg 2; SI 1999/3312, reg 2. See paras **2.6** and **2.7** for the definition of an 'independent trade union'.

5. See Council Directive 93/104/EC, article 17(3); Council Directive 96/34/EC, Annex clause 4.

6. SI 1998/1833, as amended, reg 2, Sched 1; SI 1999/3312, reg 2, Sched 1. If the employer employed 20 or fewer workers on the date on which the agreement was first made available for signature, the agreement may be signed either by the appropriate representatives or by the majority of workers employed by the employer. It is questionable whether this complies with Article 17(3) of Council Directive 93/104/EC; see Barnard, 1999, 69. Parental leave applies only to *employees* (see App 1) and the definition of a 'workforce agreement' in that context reflects this.

7. *Ibid.*, Sched 1, para 2.

8. *Quaere* whether 'provided for' could extend to situations where terms have not been so incorporated.

9. SI 1998/1833, as amended, Sched 1, paras 2, 3; SI 1999/3312, Sched 1, paras 2, 3.

THE EFFECT OF A TRANSFER OF THE UNDERTAKING ON RECOGNITION AND COLLECTIVE AGREEMENTS

Effect on Recognition

4.74 Where an undertaking is transferred and the transferor employer recognised an independent trade union in respect of the employees transferred, the transferee is deemed to recognise the union to the same extent provided that the undertaking or part transferred 'maintains an identity distinct from the remainder of the transferee's undertaking'.[1] This means that all rights which are dependent upon recognition, such as rights to time off for union members and officials,[2] will apply in the transferred undertaking. In the light of the fact that recognition may be implied from conduct (see para **4.4**), transferees cannot simply rely on the absence of a formal agreement to indicate lack of recognition; they should also establish whether there is a course of dealing which could imply it. Having said that, the requirement that a distinct identity is maintained may be difficult to show when the transferee already operates an undertaking of its own; it is common in such circumstances for trading methods etc. as well as employee terms and conditions to be harmonised.[3] The practical effect of the provisions is also weakened considerably by the fact that where the transferor employer has recognised the union voluntarily (and not pursuant to a statutory request for recognition)[4] there is nothing in the Regulations to prevent the transferee employer varying recognition or derecognising the union after the transfer,[5] subject to the existence of contractual obligations consequent upon recognition and any obligations relating to disclosure of information or consultation which may already have arisen (see para **4.43**). However, if a transferor employer were to derecognise the union prior to the transfer at the insistence of the transferee it may be possible to argue that recognition should continue to the point of transfer.[6] Where the transferor recognised the union pursuant to a CAC declaration or an 'agreement for recognition' it would seem to be the case that the transferee employer will be bound by the same obligations as the transferor if the undertaking or part transferred maintains a distinct identity, given that the union is 'deemed to have been recognised by the transferee to the same extent' in respect of the employees in respect of whom it was recognised by the transferor. Thus, the transferee would be unable, for example, unilaterally to terminate an agreement for recognition before the end of the period of three years starting with the date of the agreement (see para **4.33**). However the Regulations apply only to recognition in respect of 'employees', not, like the recognition procedure, 'workers'. Thus if the transferor's workers who comprised the bargaining unit were not 'employees', recognition would not transfer; if only some were employees and recognition was pursuant to a CAC declaration, the transferee employer would be able to invoke the statutory procedure applicable to changes in the bargaining unit discussed at para **4.35** *et seq*.

---

1. TUPE 1981, reg 9. On TUPE, see generally Bowers *et al*, 1998 as updated, McMullen, 1998 as updated.
2. See para **4.2**.
3. The precise meaning of 'distinct identity' has not, to date, been clarified: it could require a separate legal structure or merely a separate management structure.
4. See para **4.9** *et seq*.
5. This is expressly stated in reg 9(2)(b), but would in any event be the position under the general law: see para **4.43**.
6. By analogy with *Litster v Forth Dry Dock and Engineering Co Ltd* [1989] IRLR 161, HL.

Effect on Collective Agreements

4.75 Regulation 6 of the Transfer of Undertakings (Protection of Employment) Regulations provide that any 'collective agreement'[1] made by the transferor employer with a union recognised in respect of an employee whose contract is preserved by regulation 5(1) applies to that employee as if made by the transferee.[2] In the light of the presumption that collective agreements are not intended to be legally enforceable contracts (a presumption expressly preserved by the regulation)[3] this provision is of limited significance, although it may be relevant in contexts in which regard is paid to the terms of collective agreements in determining the scope of individual employees' rights, such as whether it was reasonable for a trade union official or member to claim time off for union duties or activities.[4] Extra-contractual disciplinary and redundancy procedures may also be relevant to unfair dismissal claims. The Regulations will also be important where employees have a contractual entitlement to have their terms and conditions of employment determined by reference to the collective agreement from time to time negotiated between the transferor employer and a specific union or unions. In *Whent v T Cartledge Ltd*[5] the applicant employees had been employed until 1994 by the London Borough of Brent and their contracts specified that their terms of employment would be in accordance with the agreement made by a specific National Joint Council (NJC) agreement. In 1994 the activities of the borough which the applicants were employed to fulfil were taken over by a private contractor which, after the transfer, wrote to their union withdrawing recognition and stating that any collective agreements which may have been in force covering the transferred employees no longer had effect. The applicants sued for the benefit of new pay rates agreed by the NJC, and the EAT held that their contracts of employment continued, by virtue of regulation 5, to provide that their terms were determined by reference to the NJC agreement and it was irrelevant that their employer was not party to that agreement. The Regulations also state that 'anything done under or in connection with' the collective agreement by or in relation to the transferor before the transfer shall, after the transfer, be deemed to have been done by or in relation to the transferee. The meaning of this is obscure. It has been suggested that it includes commitments or offers made by the transferor during negotiations which have not yet been formalised in an agreement;[6] if so, in the light of the opening words of the regulation, it can cover only changes to an existing agreement.

---

1. This has the same meaning as in TULRCA 1992, s178(1); see para **4.70**.

2. Note that recognition may transfer under this provision free from the restrictions in reg 9 (see para **4.74** above). Agreements relating to occupational pension schemes within the meaning of the Social Security Pensions Act 1975 are excluded: reg 7(1). Provisions of such a scheme which do not relate to benefits for old age, invalidity or survivors are treated as not being part of the scheme: reg 7(2).

3. *Ibid.*, s 179.

4. See para **3.26** *et seq.*

5. [1997] IRLR 153, EAT. Cf *William West and Sons (Ilkeston) Ltd v Fairgieve and*

EXEL/BRS Ltd, IRLB January 2000, Vol 632, 15, where the EAT held that on the proper construction of the contract of employment the name of the transferee was to be substituted for that of the transferor, and the transferred employees were not, therefore, subject to an agreement between the transferor and the recognised trade union negotiated after the date of the transfer.

6. Younson, 1989, 115.

4.76 It is debatable whether the UK complies with the Acquired Rights Directive in relation to collective agreements. The Directive provides that following a transfer 'the transferee shall continue to observe the terms and conditions agreed in any collective agreement on the same terms applicable to the transferor under that agreement, until the date of termination or expiry of the collective agreement or the entry into force or application of another collective agreement'.[1] Member States may limit the period for observing such terms and conditions, subject to a minimum period of a year.[2] In the UK, unless the terms of a collective agreement have been incorporated into individual contracts of employment (and some terms are not appropriate for incorporation) there is nothing to prevent the transferee departing from them.[3] In 1989 the European Commission gave notice to the UK government that it had failed to comply with its obligations under the Directive in a number of respects,[4] including the absence of an obligation on the transferee to continue to observe the terms and conditions agreed in any collective agreement on the same terms applicable to the transferor, but did not, in the event, proceed with this complaint.

---

1. Council Directive 77/187, as amended by Council Directive 98/50, Article 3(3). This provision applies only in respect of employees already employed by the undertaking at the time of transfer and excludes those who were recruited after that date: *Landsorganisationen i Danmark v Ny Mølle Kro* [1989] IRLR 37, ECJ.

2. *Ibid.*

3. In the case of employers whose decisions are potentially subject to judicial review, it is conceivable that a public law remedy may be sought but the circumstances would probably need to be unusual and this is not a remedy of general application.

4. See para **5.1**.

5

Statutory Rights of Collective Representation and Consultation other than Collective Bargaining

INTRODUCTION

5.1 In Chapter 4 we analysed the law relating to collective bargaining. In this chapter we examine the rights which legislation affords to workers to be represented and consulted on a collective basis by methods other than collective bargaining. In formal terms, there is a fundamental distinction between collective bargaining and consultation; whereas collective bargaining connotes joint regulation of a particular area, in the case of consultation the right to decide remains ultimately with the employer. However this does not mean that consultation is a mere formality; serious consequences may ensue if an employer fails to meet its obligations. Moreover, 'consultation' does not have a uniform meaning; for example, in the context of European Works Councils it means 'the exchange of views and establishment of dialogue', whereas in relation to redundancies the employer must consult 'with a view to reaching agreement' a requirement which takes it close to negotiation.

In the UK legislation relating to consultation is of comparatively recent origin, and in most cases derives from obligations undertaken under EU law.[1] There are now four contexts in which all employers are required to consult employee representatives: in relation to dismissals for redundancy; where there is a transfer of the undertaking; on health and safety matters; and (where the employer recognises an independent trade union) before contracting out of the state earnings-related pensions scheme. Employers must also consult on training matters if they recognise a trade union in accordance with the statutory recognition procedure (see Chapter 4), and a method of collective bargaining has been specified by the CAC and the parties have not varied either its legal effect or content. Finally, a limited class of employers is subject to transnational consultation obligations: the central management of a 'Community-scale undertaking' or

'Community-scale group of undertakings' which is situated in the UK (or treated as such) must initiate negotiations to establish a European Works Council or information and consultation procedure if a specified number of employees or their representatives drawn from at least two Member States so request.

There is, as yet, no general obligation for employers to inform and consult worker representatives in areas not covered by these measures. However, it is conceivable that the Human Rights Act 1998 may grant unions the right to be consulted on a more extensive basis by at least some 'public authorities'; as we discussed in Chapters 1 and 4,[2] Article 11 of the ECHR has been interpreted to mean that union members have the right that their union should be 'heard', a concept which may embrace the right to be consulted on matters affecting their members' interests. Moreover, the European Commission has proposed the establishment of an EU-wide framework of minimum standards of information and consultation at national level in undertakings where 50 or more workers are employed, covering, *inter alia*, the development of employment within the undertaking and decisions likely to lead to substantial changes in work organisation or in contractual relations.[3] However this proposal is being vehemently resisted by the UK Government, which prefers any such arrangements to be adopted on a purely voluntary basis.

The provisions relating to consultation on redundancies and transfers of the undertaking have undergone considerable amendment since their initial introduction into domestic law. The Directive on Collective Redundancies[4] and the Acquired Rights Directive[5] require the provision of information to, and consultation with, the 'worker' or 'employee' representatives respectively provided for by the law or practice of the Member States. The redundancy procedure was initially enacted in the Employment Protection Act 1975, the transfer consultation provisions in the Transfer of Undertakings (Protection of Employment) Regulations 1981.[6] In both cases the duty to consult arose only where the employer recognised a union for the category of employees affected. From an early stage commentators had questioned whether either of these provisions met the requirements of the respective Directives, and in 1992 the European Commission instigated infringement proceedings citing a number of deficiencies. Most of these had been admitted by the UK Government by the time the matter came before the ECJ, and important amendments were introduced in the Trade Union Reform and Employment Rights Act 1993 to correct them (although it is arguable that other deficiencies, which were not grounds of complaint in these proceedings, remain: see paras **5.2** and **5.19** below). The major outstanding issue from the infringement proceedings was the lack of any provision in UK law for the designation of worker representatives where the employer failed to recognise a union. The Court affirmed, on the basis of its previous decisions, that national legislation which made it possible to impede protection unconditionally guaranteed to workers was contrary to EC law, and that whilst the Directive left to

Member States the task of determining the arrangements for designating representatives, they could not fail to have any system of designation whatsoever.[7] As a result of this decision the Conservative Government introduced the Collective Redundancies and Transfer of Undertakings (Protection of Employment) (Amendment) Regulations 1995[8] which required employers to consult, at their choice, either a recognised trade union or elected 'employee representatives' of any of their employees who might be dismissed. This marked the first breach in UK legislation of the principle of 'single channel' representation through unions, and the ECJ decision was criticised by one commentator for permitting a reduction in the degree of legal support for an independent and effective representation of employees' interests: a 'triumph for the form of consultation over its substance'.[9] Further amending Regulations were introduced in 1999, following a fresh complaint by the European Commission to the UK Government that the Directives had not been properly implemented;[10] major changes included more detailed regulation of the election of employee representatives and the requirement that, if the employer recognised an independent trade union, its representatives should be consulted. They also increased the limit on compensation which could be awarded to employees if an employer failed to comply with its statutory obligations to consult in relation to a transfer of the undertaking. However the requirement to consult in relation to redundancies only where 20 or more employees were to be dismissed at one establishment over 90 days or less, introduced in 1995, was not, despite earlier indications to the contrary,[11] removed.

In the area of health and safety, provision for employee representation was initially made in the Health and Safety at Work etc Act 1974. As originally formulated, this legislation envisaged the appointment of safety representatives by either trade union appointment or workforce election. However the latter option was quickly repealed (partly on the ground that non-union representatives would lack the resources to put pressure on employers) and the Safety Representatives and Safety Committees Regulations 1977[12] were promulgated, giving recognised independent trade unions the right to appoint employees as safety representatives with a wide range of duties. In 1989 a EC Framework Directive on the working environment was adopted,[13] following which the Management of Health and Safety at Work Regulations 1992[14] amended the 1977 Regulations to require employers to consult safety representatives 'in good time' on specified matters. Following the infringement proceedings brought against the UK in the context of redundancies and transfers, the Health and Safety (Consultation with Employees) Regulations 1996[15] provided for consultation where there was no recognised independent trade union, although in this case they operated purely as a back-up measure. Following the apparent scope of the 1989 Directive they gave employers the choice of consulting employees directly or of consulting elected 'representatives of employee safety'. These provisions remain in force unamended; the absence of any specified procedure for electing 'representatives of employee safety' now constitutes a marked contrast to the provisions governing redundancies and transfers.

Consultation of worker representatives in relation to the contracting-out of pensions is purely a domestic law requirement; in the event that no independent trade union is recognised there is no alternative provision for consultation of other worker representatives. The current requirements are contained in the Occupational Pension Schemes (Contracting Out) Regulations 1996.[16]

The Transnational Information and Consultation of Employees Regulations 1999[17] are designed to implement the European Works Council Directive,[18] which was adopted under the Agreement on Social Policy from which the UK had initially opted out. Following the election of the Labour Government in 1997, the UK opted in to this Agreement, and a Directive extending the original Directive to the UK, with an implementation date of 15 December 1999, was agreed.[19] These Regulations present some interesting contrasts to the obligations which apply to purely national employers; elections to the body which negotiates the consultative procedure must be supervised by an independent ballot supervisor and employers are explicitly permitted to disclose information on confidential terms, with provision for this restriction to be challenged before the CAC. This legislation introduces yet another term for worker representatives, that of the 'employees' representative', which is distinctively defined and applicable only in this context.

As this brief overview makes clear, UK law is now characterised by a heterogeneous collection of provisions relating to worker representation and consultation. In a short period, the system has shifted from 'single-channel' to 'multi-channel' forms of representation,[20] although employers who recognise an independent trade union are spared the difficulty of organising the selection of appropriate representatives for each occasion (other than in relation to the transnational procedure). Moreover the concept of 'consultation' differs materially depending upon the context, as do the consequences of failing to comply with the respective statutory obligations. We indicate at appropriate points in the text where comparisons between these various provisions can usefully be made.

---

1. For a discussion of voluntary consultation in the post-War period, see MacInnes, 1985. For a recent analysis of the incidence of consultation in British workplaces, see Cully *et al*, 1999, 98–112. Strikingly, workplaces with recognised unions had a much higher incidence of joint consultative committees than those without: *ibid.*, 100. See also Millward *et al*, 2000.

2. See paras **1.6** and **4.62**.

3. Proposal for a Council Directive establishing a general framework for informing and consulting employees in the European Community, COM(98)612 final.

4. Council Directive 75/129/EEC, subsequently amended by Council Directive 92/56/EEC, and now consolidated in Council Directive 98/59/EC.

5. Council Directive 77/187/EEC. This Directive has been amended by Council Directive 98/50/EC, which must be implemented by 17 July 2001.

6. SI 1981/1794.

7. Case C–382/92 *EC Commission v United Kingdom* [1994] IRLR 392 (transfers) and Case C–383/92 [1994] IRLR 412 (collective redundancies).

8. SI 1995/2587.

9. Davies, 1996, 123. On the 1995 Regulations see Hall, 1996, and Wedderburn, 1997, and for discussion of their operation in practice J. Smith, P. Edwards and M. Hall, 1999, and Hall and Edwards, 1999. Interestingly, hardly any employers which recognised trade unions took the 'non-union' option: Hall and Edwards, 306–308.

10. SI 1999/1925. The Commission was reported to have questioned in particular whether the Regulations adequately reflected the ECJ's views on procedures for designating employee representatives, and expressed concern about the effectiveness of the purely monetary sanctions provided for: *Industrial Relations Law Bulletin* Vol. 560, January 1997, 16.

11. *Employees' Information and Consultation Rights on Transfers of Undertakings and Collective Redundancies*, DTI, URN 97/988, February 1998, paras 37–40. This restriction is permitted by the Directive.

12. SI 1977/500.

13. Council Directive 89/391/EEC.

14. SI 1992/2051. These Regulations have now been revoked and replaced by the Management of Health and Safety at Work Regulations 1999, SI 1999/3242.

15. SI 1996/1513.

16. SI 1996/1172.

17. SI 1999/3323.

18. Council Directive 94/45/EC.

19. Council Directive 97/75/EC.

20. See also the concept of 'workforce agreements' discussed in para **4.73**. See generally Millward *et al*, 2000, chapter 4.

THE DUTY TO CONSULT ON REDUNDANCIES

Sources and General Principles

5.2 An employer which is proposing to dismiss as redundant 20 or more employees at one establishment within a period of 90 days or less has a duty to consult about the dismissals 'all the persons who are appropriate representatives of any of the employees who may be affected by the proposed dismissals or may be affected by measures taken in connection with those dismissals'.[1] This process must include consultation about ways of avoiding the dismissals, reducing the number of employees to be dismissed, and mitigating the consequences of dismissals, and must be undertaken by the employer with a view to reaching agreement.[2] If the employees concerned are of a description in respect of which the employer recognises an independent trade union,[3] representatives of that union (or those unions) must be consulted.[4] If no independent trade union is recognised, the employer must consult 'employee representatives': either (at the employer's option) representatives elected specifically by the employees affected for that purpose, or those elected or appointed for other purposes but which have the employees' authority to be consulted about the proposed dismissals on their behalf.[5] Where affected employees who have been invited to elect representatives fail to do so within a reasonable time the employer must give specified information to the employees individually, but has no obligation to consult them on its proposals.[6] If an employer fails to comply with any of its statutory obligations, a complaint may be presented to an employment tribunal by, variously, a trade union; an employee representative; or any affected employee or employee dismissed as redundant, depending upon the nature of the alleged default.[7] Employers covered by the duty to consult must also notify the Department of Trade and Industry of specified matters; failure to do so is a criminal offence.[8] The relevant principles are currently contained in the Trade Union and Labour Relations (Consolidation) Act 1992, ss 188–198, as amended by the Trade Union Reform and Employment Rights Act 1993, and the Collective Redundancies and Transfer of Undertakings (Protection of Employment) (Amendment) Regulations of 1995 and 1999.[9] The 1999 Regulations came into force on 28 July 1999 and apply to dismissals which took effect on or after 1 November 1999. As we stated in para **5.1** it had long been doubted whether the provisions in their original form adequately implemented the Collective Redundancies Directive, and the successive amendments have been introduced for the purpose of effecting compliance with both the original and subsequent amending Directives.[10] However it is strongly arguable that this legislation continues to fall short of the current Directive's stipulations in important respects which we indicate at appropriate points in the text (one striking example being the employer's defence in domestic law that it was unable to meet its obligations due to 'special circumstances', which has no counterpart in the Directive).[11] In the event that there is a continuing failure to comply with the requirements of EU law, it is conceivable that the *Francovich* principle could be invoked by those affected, although this requires proof that the Member State manifestly and gravely disregarded the limits on its discretion.[12] It may also be difficult in this context to satisfy the condition that quantifiable loss was caused by the failure to comply. There has been no ruling by the ECJ on whether the consultation provisions of the Collective Redundancies Directive have direct effect, and may thus be relied upon against an organ of the state. However in *Griffin v South West Water Services Ltd* the High Court has expressed the view that because it gives the Member States such a wide discretion in designating worker representatives, Article 2 of that Directive is not directly effective because it is not unconditional and sufficiently precise.[13] The exclusion of workers employed by public administrative bodies or establishments governed by public law from the Directive would, in any event, reduce the impact of direct effect,[14] although the court in *Griffin* did not accept that such bodies were coincident with those which are subject to this doctrine.

1. TULRCA 1992, s 188(1). Note that 'redundant' has a broad definition in this context; see para **5.3**.
2. *Ibid.*, s 188(2).
3. See paras **2.6** and **2.7** for the definition of an 'independent trade union and **4.3** for the definition of recognition.
4. TULRCA 1992, s 188(1B).
5. *Ibid.*
6. *Ibid.*, s 188(7B).
7. *Ibid.*, s 189(1).
8. *Ibid.*, ss 193–194.
9. SI 1995/ 2587 and SI 1999/ 1925.
10. Council Directive 75/129/EEC, amended by Council Directive 92/56/EEC and replaced by (the essentially consolidating) Council Directive 98/59/EC. For the evolution of domestic provisions, see Hall and Edwards, 1999.
11. TULRCA 1992, ss 188(7), 189(6).
12. Joined cases C–46/93 and C–48/93, *Brasserie du Pêcheur SA v Federal Republic of Germany*; *R v Secretary of State for Transport, ex parte Factortame Ltd (No.3)*, [1996] IRLR 267.
13. [1995] IRLR 15, ChD, at 30–32. The provisions of Article 2 are unchanged in the 1998 Directive.
14. Council Directive 98/59, Article 1(2)(b).

Proposed Dismissals Covered by the Duty to Consult

The meaning of 'redundant'

5.3 An employee is 'redundant' for the purposes of the consultation procedure when the dismissal is 'for a reason not related to the individual concerned or for a number of reasons all of which are not so related'.[1] By contrast, for the purposes of entitlement to a statutory redundancy payment an employee is 'redundant' where the employer has ceased, or intends to cease, to carry on the business for the purposes of which the employee was employed or the requirements of that business for employees 'to carry out work of a particular kind' have ceased or diminished or are expected to cease or diminish.[2] The definition for the purposes of the consultation procedure is considerably wider, and applies to dismissals arising from reorganisation or restructuring of a business, for example, as well as those arising from closure or slimming down of the workforce. Thus, if an employer dismisses employees and offers re-engagement on different terms and conditions (usually after failing to secure changes by agreement) it must comply with the duty to consult. As we indicate in para **5.8** it may not be easy to determine the point in time at which the duty to consult arises in relation to proposed dismissals in the context of restructuring or reorganisation. A potential difficulty with the definition is that it requires 'all' the reasons for dismissal not to relate to the individual concerned. Taken literally this could narrow the application of the duty considerably, given that selection for redundancy, in the sense used in relation to individual payments, is usually based upon factors relating to the individual such as performance, attendance or, at the very least, length of service. Such an interpretation would not comply with the intention of the government department which introduced the legislation,[3] and were that argument to be raised a court or tribunal should have regard to the less ambiguous wording of the Directive,[4] which refers to 'dismissals effected by an employer for one or more reasons not related to the individual workers concerned.[5] There is a statutory presumption that an employee is or is proposed to be dismissed as redundant unless the contrary is proved.[6]

---

1. TULRCA 1992, s 195(1). This definition was introduced by TURERA 1993. Prior to that time the definition applicable to statutory redundancy payments applied also in this context. However the obligation to consult has always applied irrespective of the individual employee's right to a statutory redundancy payment. Thus, even if employees are subsequently offered suitable alternative employment which they unreasonably refuse the obligation to consult remains, although this offer may be relevant to the amount of remuneration to which an employee is entitled under a protective award: see para **5.21**. It is also irrelevant to the duty to consult that the employee has waived his or her statutory rights: *AUT v University of Newcastle upon Tyne* [1987] ICR 317, EAT.
2. ERA 1996, s 139(1). The definition also applies where the employer ceases to carry on business in the place where the employee was employed or the requirement for work of a particular kind has ceased or diminished in that place: *ibid.*
3. At that time the Employment Department, which in its summary of TURERA 1993, which extended the definition beyond 'redundancy' in the narrow sense (see note 1), stated that the definition 'is now widened' (press notice 2 July 1993, 19).
4. Case C–14/83 *Von Colson and Kamann v Land Nordrhein-Westfalen* [1984] ECR 1891; Case C–106/89 *Marleasing SA v La Comercial Internacional de Alimentation SA* [1990] ECR I–4135; *Pickstone v Freemans plc* [1988] IRLR 357, HL; *Litster v Forth Dry Dock and Engineering Co Ltd* [1989] IRLR 161, HL.
5. Council Directive 98/59, Article 1(1)(a).
6. TULRCA 1992, s 195(2).

Groups covered by the duty

5.4 The duty to consult is currently confined to the proposed dismissal of employees.[1] It applies irrespective of employees' period of service or hours worked. However, it does not apply to employment under a contract for a fixed term of three months or less, or under a contract made in contemplation of the performance of a specific task which is not expected to last for more than three months, and in either case the employee has not been continuously employed for a period of more than three months.[2] Crown servants, the armed forces, the police, parliamentary staff and share fishermen are excluded from these provisions.[3] However it should be noted that the provisions requiring disclosure of information for collective bargaining purposes may be relevant in the context of redundancies. These cover a wider group of 'workers' (not just employees), and notably extend to Crown employment,[4] although they apply only where an independent trade union is recognised for the description of workers in question. The CAC has taken the view that recognised unions may have a right under these provisions to information relating to the decision to reduce a level of activity, close a site or restructure an organisation.[5]

---

1. See App 1. Note that the Secretary of State may apply this provision by order to a wider group of workers: ERA 1999, s 23; see also TULRCA 1992, s 286.

2. TULRCA 1992, s 282(1). Council Directive 98/59 provides that collective redundancies effected under contracts of employment concluded for limited periods of time or for specific tasks are excluded from its scope *except where such redundancies take place prior to the date of expiry or the completion of such contracts*: Article 1(2)(a). There is no such exception in TULRCA 1992, s 282(1).

3. TULRCA 1992, s 273(1), (2), 274, 277, 278, 280, and 284. Note that the exclusion of those who under their contracts of employment work outside Great Britain has been removed by ERA 1999, s 32 although the notification requirements described in para **5.22** do not apply to such employees: TULRCA 1992, s 285, as amended by ERA 1999.

4. TULRCA 1992, s 273; see further para **4.65** *et seq*.

5. CAC *Annual Report* 1993, paras 2.3–2.5. See also CAC *Annual Reports* 1994, para 2.8, 1996, para 2.9 and 1997, para 2.13.

A minimum of 20 employees at one establishment

5.5 The duty to consult applies only where the employer is proposing to dismiss as redundant 20 or more employees at one establishment within a period of 90 days or less.[1] In determining how many employees an employer is proposing to dismiss, no account is to be taken of any employees in respect of whom it has already begun consulting.[2] This limitation means that if an employer proposes 20 dismissals, begins consultations, and then decides that a further ten are necessary there is no duty to consult about the additional ten because the original 20 are discounted. However if the employer begins with ten and subsequently adds 20 (within 90 days) there will be a duty to consult about all 30; the original ten will not be discounted unless the employer has begun consulting about them.[3] Clearly employers may be tempted to try and avoid their statutory obligation by dividing a large group of redundancies into small successive groups. In cases where this may have happened, employment tribunals can be expected to scrutinise the evidence carefully in order to ensure that the employer acted in good faith.[4] Thus if it can be shown by disclosure of documents or otherwise that the employer intended to dismiss the total number of employees eventually dismissed from the outset, its compliance with the duty to consult should be measured by reference to that number. It should also be remembered that even where the employer proposes to dismiss fewer than 20 employees, if those employees qualify to claim unfair dismissal, procedural fairness will generally require consultation with them and/or their representatives.[5] In addition, the right of independent recognised unions to information for collective bargaining purposes, noted in para **5.4** above, may be particularly important where there are fewer than 20 employees involved.

---

1. TULRCA 1992, s 188(1). Although this limitation accords with the Directive, prior to SI 1995/2587 the UK provisions had required consultation even if only one employee was affected. The Government estimated that the amendment would remove the statutory obligation to consult from 96% of UK businesses: DTI press notice 5 October 1995.
2. *Ibid.*, para 188(3).
3. Harvey, paras 2505 and 2506.
4. *Ibid.*, para 2507, citing the tribunal decision in *Transport and General Workers' Union v Nationwide Haulage Ltd* [1978] IRLR 143 as an example.
5. See, for example, *King v Eaton Ltd* [1996] IRLR 199, Ct of Session.

5.6 In calculating the number of employees the employer is proposing to dismiss, account is taken only of those working at one 'establishment'. There is no statutory definition of 'establishment', even though this concept occurs in a variety of contexts. In domestic law a fairly wide view of its meaning has been taken. Thus, although the case law has not produced a comprehensive test, '[a]mong the relevant factors in determining the scope of an establishment may be the geographical separation of the premises from other premises owned by the employer, the separation of financial accounting, the separation of services, and the separation of profits'.[1] In addition, an 'establishment' has been said to require some degree of permanence or stability.[2] Using these guidelines a court or tribunal could hold that a number of different sites could together constitute an 'establishment'. Thus, 14 building sites administered from a company's head-quarters were not treated as separate establishments,[3] nor were 28 retail shops, a factory and a bakery.[4] In 1995, however, the European Court of Justice held that for the purposes of the Collective Redundancies Directive the term 'establishment' should

> be interpreted as designating, depending on the circumstances, the unit to which the workers made redundant are assigned to carry out their duties. It is not essential in order for there to be an 'establishment' for the unit in question to be endowed with a management which can independently effect collective redundancies.[5]

In the context in which this decision was given the ECJ intended to maximise the application of the duty to consult.[6] However when applied in the British context it may considerably reduce the occasions when the 20-employee threshold is crossed. The scope of protection is further narrowed by the fact that the duty to consult is confined to a single employer; thus, even if associated employers operate from the same establishment each set of redundancies must be considered separately.[7]

---

1. Hepple, 1981, 10. See generally *Barratt Developments (Bradford) Ltd v UCATT* [1978] ICR 319, EAT; *Bakers' Union v Clarks of Hove Ltd* [1977] IRLR 167, IT, accepted on this point by the EAT [1977] IRLR 264 and CA [1978] IRLR 366; and for cases on the old selective employment tax relevant to this issue see *Secretary of State for Employment and Productivity v Vic Hallam Ltd* (1969) 5 ITR 108, HL; *Lord Advocate v Babcock and Wilcox (Operations) Ltd.* [1972] ITR 168, HL; *May and Robertson Ltd v Ministry of Labour* (1967) 2 ITR 607, IT.

2. *Ibid.*

3. *Barratt Developments (Bradford) Ltd v UCATT*, above, note 1; see also *Barley v Amey Roadstone Corporation Ltd (No 2)* [1978] ICR 190, EAT.

4. *Bakers' Union v Clarks of Hove*, above, note 1. Where the work is not done 'at' an establishment, it is treated for relevant purposes as done at the establishment *from* which it is done: *Gardner Merchant v Catering Industry Training Board* (1969) 4 ITR 60, IAT (employees of a company operating canteens at various factory premises employed from the company's establishment for the purposes of a training board levy). Cf also SDA 1975, 10(4) and RRA 1976, s 8(4).

5. Case C–449/93 *Rockfon A/S v Specialarbejderforbundet i Danmark, acting for Nielsen* [1996] IRLR 168 at 175.

6. Danish law had adopted the alternative 'threshold' formulation for the duty to consult under the Directive, which comes into play where, *inter alia*, redundancies affect at least 10 per cent of workers in establishments employing at least 100 but fewer than 300 workers: Article 1(1)(a). According to this formulation, it benefits employees if the 'establishment' is defined as narrowly as possible.

7. *E Green and Son (Castings) Ltd v ASTMS* [1984] IRLR 135, EAT. See App 1 for the definition of 'associated employer'.

When Consultation Must Begin

5.7 The duty to consult arises as soon as the employer is 'proposing' to dismiss employees for redundancy.[1] 'Dismiss' in this context means giving notice (or intending to dismiss without notice), so consultation with the union after dismissal notices have been issued is not sufficient and, indeed, would negate the very purpose of the procedure.[2] The courts have held that 'proposing' goes beyond the mere contemplation of a possible event or 'the diagnosis of a problem and appreciation that at least one way of dealing with it would be by declaring redundancies'; rather, the employer must have formed some view of how many employees are to be dismissed, when this is to take place, and how it is to be arranged.[3] By contrast, Article 2(1) of Directive 98/59 requires consultations to begin where the employer is 'contemplating' redundancies. In *R v British Coal Corporation ex parte Vardy* Glidewell LJ pointed out the significance of this difference in wording.

> The verb 'proposes' in its ordinary usage relates to a state of mind which is much more certain and further along the decision-making process than the verb 'contemplate'; in order words, the Directive envisages consultation at an early stage when the employer is first envisaging the possibility that he may have to make employees redundant.[4]

It is strongly arguable that in the light of this discrepancy the courts should interpret domestic legislation in conformity with EU law and read 'proposing' in the sense of 'contemplating'.[5] However the meaning given to 'contemplating' by Glidewell LJ has not been universally accepted; in *Griffin v South West Water Services Ltd* Blackburne J considered that the obligation under Article 2 arose only when 'the employer's contemplation of redundancies has reached the point where he is able to identify the workers likely to be affected and can supply the information which the Article requires him to supply'.[6] There is no decision of the European Court of Justice on this point, (although Advocate General Lenz has opined that the fact that there is an obligation under the Directive to notify the public authorities of 'planned' collective redundancies suggests, by contrast, that workers' representatives must be consulted at an earlier stage).[7] In response to Blackburne J, whom we consider to be mistaken on this point, it should be noted that the Directive merely requires the employer to identify the number and categories of workers who may be made redundant, not to identify them individually. Moreover, the information specified in Article 2(3) of the Directive is required to be supplied *in good time during the course of the consultations.* This suggests that it may not be essential to supply all the information at the outset, although as we discuss in para **5.17** in relation to domestic law, where information is supplied in stages it may not be easy to determine when sufficient detail has been given for meaningful consultations to be said to have begun. We would suggest that the interpretation of 'contemplating' accorded by Glidewell LJ sits more easily with the primary purpose of the consultation, which is attempting to avoid redundancies rather than merely to consider the ways in which those already decided upon should be implemented.[8] Thus consultations should begin as soon as redundancies are envisaged as a possibility. Regardless of the precise moment at which the legal requirement bites, there is clearly nothing to prevent an employer consulting before that time, and particularly where there are appropriate representatives already in place there may be considerable industrial relations advantages in doing so.

---

1. TULRCA 1992, s 188(1).

2. *NUT v Avon County Council* [1978] ICR 626, EAT.

3. *Hough v Leyland DAF Ltd* [1991] IRLR 194, EAT at 198; see also *Association of Pattern Makers and Allied Craftsmen v Kirvin Ltd* [1978] IRLR 318, EAT. As Harvey notes at paras 2435 and 2451 these decisions should be treated with some caution because they were reached under unamended provisions. For reasons we discuss below, we consider a wider interpretation to be appropriate. However these decisions have yet to be overruled. Note also the relevance of the disclosure of information provisions in this context: see para **5.4** above, and generally para **4.65** *et seq.*

4. [1993] IRLR 104 at 116.

5. See Case C–106/89 *Marleasing SA v La Comercial Internacional de Alimentacion SA* [1990] ECR I–4135, ECJ. Cf the unhelpful approach in *Re Hartlebury Printers Ltd (in Liquidation)* [1992] IRLR 516, ChD.

6. [1995] IRLR 15 at 23.

7. Case C–284/83 *Dansk Metalarbejderforbund and Specialarbejderforbundet i Danmark v H Nielsen and Son Maskinfabrik A/S (in liquidation)* [1985] ECR 553 Second Question, para 2. In *Dansk* the ECJ held that Article 2(1) does not apply where, because of the financial state of the undertaking, the employer ought to have contemplated redundancies but did not in fact do so. *Quaere* whether the obligation on employers under Article 2(1) to begin consultations 'in good time' obliges an employer to start consultations before the financial state of the undertaking becomes so bad that any consultation is otiose.

8. Cf also the dictum of Glidewell LJ in *R v British Coal Corporation and Secretary of State for Trade and Industry, ex parte Price* [1994] IRLR 72 at 75 (fair consultation means consultation 'when the proposals are still at a formative stage'), cited with approval by the Court of Session in *King v Eaton Ltd* [1996] IRLR 199 at 202. The explicit requirement to attempt to avoid redundancies was introduced by TURERA 1993.

5.8 Additional difficulties may arise in determining the point of time at which the duty to consult arises in relation to dismissals in the context of reorganisation or restructuring. On the one hand it may be argued that where an employer has attempted to implement these changes by voluntary agreement, it did not 'propose' to dismiss employees until these attempts had failed. Conversely, it could be argued that where it has adopted a fall-back strategy of dismissing and offering re-engagement from the outset, on the basis that opposition to its proposals from 20 or more employees was predictable, the duty to consult arises from the time at which that strategy was adopted. Although the latter view would not accord with the interpretation of 'proposing' adopted by domestic courts, it would accord more closely with the concept of 'contemplating' redundancies articulated in the Directive, discussed in para **5.7** above. In the light of these uncertainties it would be advisable for employers to involve unions or employee representatives in restructuring proposals at the earliest possible stage. Even more complex problems are presented by the application of these principles to 'constructive dismissals', which may arise where an employer imposes changes to the contract of employment which an employee finds unacceptable and as a consequence resigns.[1] Although, here, the employer may not have 'proposed' the dismissals, it has nevertheless acted in a way which risks provoking this response and thus, again, could be said at the least to have the dismissals within its contemplation. If there is also a 'relevant transfer' for the purposes of TUPE 1981, separate requirements to inform and consult must be met in addition: see further para **5.24** *et seq.*

---

1. Constructive dismissal constitutes 'dismissal' in this context: TULRCA 1992, s 298; see also *Pearl Assurance Plc v MSF* 26 February 1997, EAT 1162/96, *Industrial Relations Law Bulletin* Vol 572, July 1997, 15. Constructive dismissal seems not to be covered by Directive 98/59/EC. Article 1(1) refers to 'terminations of an employment contract which occur on the employer's initiative', but it is questionable whether this is wide enough to cover such dismissals. Case C–284/83 *Dansk Metalarbejderforbund and Specialarbejderforbundet i Danmark v H Nielsen and Son Maskinfabrik A/S (in liquidation)* [1985] ECR 553, in which the ECJ held that termination by workers of their contracts following an announcement by the employer that he was suspending payment of his debts did not constitute dismissal, was decided prior to the amendment of the Directive in 1992.

5.9 Once the employer is 'proposing to dismiss', consultation with 'appropriate representatives' must begin 'in good time', and in any event at least 90 days before the first dismissal takes effect where the employer plans to dismiss 100 or more employees at one establishment within a period of 90 days or less; otherwise at least 30 days before the first of the dismissals takes effect.[1] The fact that these periods are calculated back from the date when the first dismissal 'takes effect' may appear problematic in that this date cannot be known at the time when the dismissals are initially proposed, and, indeed, it is one of the purposes of the consultation procedure to avoid any dismissals whatsoever. The better view is that it means the requisite period before the date which the employer *proposes* for the first dismissal.[2] Employers should avoid the temptation to issue dismissal notices in advance of consultation for employees whose notice periods exceed 90 or 30 days, as applicable, a course which again would negate the purpose of the exercise. In circumstances where employee representatives need to be elected prior to the consultation process, it is sufficient for employers to comply with the statutory requirements as soon as reasonably practicable after the election provided that they have invited any of the affected employees to elect employee representatives long enough before consultation is required to begin to allow for an election to take place.[3] If elections are required, this may substantially delay the implementation of the redundancy programme. It is suggested in the DTI guidance on redundancy consultation that employers should also allow time for representatives to undertake appropriate training, if necessary.[4] This would certainly seem to be good practice, although the legislation does not specifically provide for this, nor does it accord representatives a right to training, merely a right to time off work for this purpose (see para **5.15**).

---

1. TULRCA 1992, s 188(1A).
2. *Transport and General Workers' Union v RA Lister and Co Ltd* [1986] IRLIB, 21 May 1989, 11.
3. TULRCA 1992, s 188(7A).
4. Redundancy Consultation and Notification PL833, Section 2.

The Persons who Must be Consulted

5.10 The employer must consult all 'appropriate representatives' of *any* of the employees who may be affected by the proposed dismissals or *may* be affected by measures taken in connection with those dismissals.[1] Prior to the entry into force of the 1999 amending regulations, the duty was confined to consultation with representatives of the employees whom it was proposed to dismiss. This wider formulation, which echoes the duty to consult in the event of a transfer of the undertaking,[2] would seem to cover all those whose terms and conditions of employment or working conditions may be affected by the proposed dismissals which could mean much, if not all, of the workforce. In case of doubt, employers should err in the direction of an inclusive approach, given that a mere possibility that employees will be affected will suffice. It is not clear that this amendment was required by the Directive; whereas the Acquired Rights Directive specifies consultation of representatives of employees affected by a transfer,[3] the Collective Redundancies Directive merely requires an employer who is contemplating collective redundancies to begin consultation with 'the workers' representatives'.[4] The wider formulation may make it easier to find employees who are willing to stand for election as representatives, and they are less likely to be demoralised than those representing only those whose jobs are at risk.[5] However it may not always benefit those whom it is proposed to dismiss; it is conceivable that representatives who are answerable to a broader, and possibly much more numerous, constituency may be less willing to fight hard for the specific interests of the target group for redundancy if, in return, they receive assurances regarding other employees.

---

1. TULRCA 1992, s 188(1).
2. See para **5.24** *et seq.*
3. Council Directive 77/187 EEC, Article 6.
4. Council Directive 98/59/EC, Article 2(1).
5. Cf the findings of J. Smith, P. Edwards and M. Hall, 1999

5.11 There are three possible sources from which 'appropriate representatives' of any affected employees may be drawn. First, if the employees are of a description in respect of which an independent trade union is recognised by the employer, the employer *must* consult representatives of that union.[1] This applies irrespective of whether the affected employees are union members. Where more than one union is recognised for a particular description of employees, it follows from the obligation to consult *all* the appropriate representatives that all such unions must be consulted about the dismissals of all employees in that group.[2] 'Representatives of a trade union' are defined in this context as 'officials or other persons authorised by the trade union to carry on collective bargaining with the employer'.[3] If there is no independent recognised trade union, the employer must consult 'employee representatives'. In this event, the employer may choose either to consult persons elected specifically for the purposes of the consultation exercise in question in accordance with prescribed procedures, or persons appointed or elected by the affected employees for another purpose who (having regard to the purposes for and the method by which they were appointed or elected) have authority from those employees to receive information and to be consulted about the proposed dismissals on their behalf.[4] In either case such representatives must be employed by the employer at the time when they are elected or appointed (although not necessarily thereafter),[5] thus excluding external professional advisers. Where an independent trade union is recognised only for some categories of affected employees, the employer will be required to consult employee representatives for the remaining categories; it cannot choose to consult union representatives for categories of employee outside the scope of recognition. No guidance is given about a minimum (or maximum) number of representatives to be consulted, beyond the stipulation that the employer must consult *all* 'appropriate representatives' of any affected employees. However, the use of the plural in the legislation strongly suggests that there must be more than one representative. Moreover, although a union, in order to be consulted, must be independent of the employer, there is no requirement that employee representatives should be so; thus they may be members of a body, such as a works council or staff consultative committee, which is dependent on the employer financially or otherwise.[6] In its 1998 consultation document which preceded the 1999 Regulations the government claimed that independence would be secured if representatives were required to be properly elected, protected against dismissal or other detriment for acting as such, and with time off and the necessary training to fulfil their role.[7] This contention, however, takes no account of the other pressures, such as the threat to financial support of, or promise of future favours to, compliant representatives which may result from a relationship of dependence (and which takes no account of the fact that representatives may have obtained their position by appointment, as well as by election). It may be possible for affected employees to argue that dependence on the employer means that such a body would not have the requisite implied authority to be consulted about the proposed dismissals on their behalf, but much may depend upon that body's terms of reference. An affected or redundant employee may complain to an employment tribunal that the employer has failed to meet its statutory obligations because any one of the employee representatives consulted was not 'appropriate'.[8] In the event of a complaint of this nature being made, it is for the employer to show that the individual concerned did, in fact, have the authority to represent the affected employees.[9] Where employers wish to consult a standing body, they may find it advisable to include specifically within the terms of reference of that body consultation on redundancies. The officers of a non-independent union, such as a staff association, may not be 'appropriate representatives', unless, possibly, the union had universal membership among affected employees. It is possible that employee representatives may ask the employer to indemnify them against any potential claims from those whom they represent as a result of their activities.[10] We suggest that one method of dealing with this difficulty would be for the employer to pay for representatives to receive advice from an independent source of their choice, a course of action which would also go some way to meeting allegations that the representatives themselves may not be sufficiently independent of the employer.

1. TULRCA 1992, s 188(1B)(a). 'Recognition' is defined in s 178(3); see further para **4.3**.

2. This view, which seems clear from the wording of the legislation, was confirmed by the Northern Ireland Court of Appeal in *Governing Body of the Northern Ireland Hotel and Catering College and North Eastern Education and Library Board v NATFHE* [1995] IRLR 83.

3. TULRCA 1992, s 196(2). 'Collective bargaining' is defined in s.178(1),(2); see further para **4.3**. 'Official' is defined in s 119. The term includes shop stewards and other staff representatives as well as branch and other union officers: see para **3.27** note 1.

4. *Ibid.*, s 188(1B)(b). Note that in Case 382/92 *EC Commission v United Kingdom* [1994] IRLR 392 (transfers) and Case C–383/92 [1994] IRLR 412 (collective redundancies) the Advocate General considered that the *ad hoc* designation of worker representatives would meet the requirements of the Directive. The ECJ was silent on this point.

5. *Ibid.*, s 196.

6. See paras **2.6** and **2.7** for the criteria of trade union independence. The lack of any requirement for representatives to be independent would appear to allow employers even now to frustrate the protection for workers provided by the Directive: Case C–383/92, *EC Commission v UK* [1994] IRLR 412, ECJ, paras 16–27.

7. *Employees' Information and Consultation Rights on Transfers of Undertakings and Collective Redundancies*, DTI, URN 97/988, February 1998.

8. TULRCA 1992, s 189(1),(1A).

9. *Ibid.*, s 189(1A). In the case of representatives elected for another purpose, the DTI booklet on redundancy consultation and notification suggests that where redundancies are to take place amongst sales staff, for example, it would not be sufficient to consult a committee of managers set up to consider the operation of a staff canteen, but it may well be appropriate to consult a committee which is regularly informed or consulted more generally about the business's financial position and personnel matters.

10. See para **2.22** for the possibility of trade unions being liable in negligence to their members.

5.12 Where an employer chooses to consult specially elected representatives, it must invite affected employees to hold an election.[1] The provisions relating to the election of employee representatives also raise some difficult issues. The employer has a duty to determine the number of representatives to be elected 'so that there are sufficient representatives to represent the interests of all the affected employees having regard to the number and classes of those employees'.[2] The employer may also determine whether employees should be represented by representatives of all the affected employees or by representatives of particular classes;[3] in this context no criteria are prescribed to inform the employer's choice. It is conceivable therefore that where both managerial staff and those below them are 'affected employees', representatives may be elected by the workforce as a whole who are derived solely from the managerial group; the requirement that there be 'sufficient representatives' to represent the interests of all affected employees could conceivably be construed as imposing a purely numerical requirement. A more appropriate view (where those other than employees with managerial status are threatened with redundancy) is that 'anyone holding a significant managerial role is not properly independent from management and should not take part in consultations affecting other employees',[4] even if this may not necessarily be demanded by the legislation. The employer must, prior to the election, stipulate employee representatives' term of office, ensuring that it is of sufficient length to enable the consultative process to be completed.[5] Clearly this would be a matter on which it would be preferable to err on the side of caution. Candidates for election must themselves be affected employees on the date of the election, and no affected employee may be 'unreasonably excluded' from standing.[6] There is nothing to prevent the employer itself nominating candidates, but ACAS advised under the pre-1999 Regulations that the nomination process should be independent of management,[7] and this would clearly be good industrial relations practice. In determining what constitutes 'unreasonable exclusion' the decisions of the Certification Officer in relation to standing for union office, although of no precedent value, may be a useful source of guidance.[8]

---

1. This is not directly stated in the legislation but is implicit from s 188(7A); see also *R v Secretary of State for Trade and Industry ex parte Unison* [1996] IRLR 438, QBD, at 445.
2. TULRCA 1992, s 188A(1)(b).
3. *Ibid.*, s 188A(1)(c)
4. Hall and Edwards, 1999, 310.
5. *Ibid.*, s 188A(1)(d).
6. *Ibid.*, s 188A(1)(e) and (f).
7. J. Smith *et al*, 1999, 19.
8. See para **2.37**.

5.13 All affected employees on the date of the election must be entitled to vote in the election, and to vote for as many candidates as there are representatives to be elected to represent them, or their particular class of employee.[1] The election must be conducted so as to secure that, so far as is reasonably practicable, those voting do so in secret and the votes given are accurately counted.[2] As in the case of 'unreasonable exclusion' of candidates discussed in para **5.12** above, these

provisions echo the requirements of elections to union office. There is no equivalent requirement that the ballot be conducted by the marking of a voting paper
(see para **2.42**), but this would seem to be the most effective way of satisfying the
statutory conditions, and of showing that those conditions have been satisfied.
The condition that votes be accurately counted is absolute; it is irrelevant that
any inaccuracy would be immaterial to the outcome.[3] The requirement that the
voting be in secret means that there should be no identifying mark on the voting
paper, nor should individuals be required to sign for a voting paper against a
particular serial number. The employer has a general duty to 'make such
arrangements as are reasonably practical to ensure that the election is fair'.[4] A
purposive construction of this duty would require the employer to give appropriate publicity to the election to ensure that all affected employees are informed
that it is taking place. It may also entail ensuring that the election is held over a
number of days if the workforce is peripatetic, or if shift and part-time workers
are employed, although the statutory language, which refers to 'the date of the
election', with no further definition, presents a difficulty in this respect.[5] Where
the workforce is not based at the workplace, or does not work according to a regular pattern, consideration should be given to a postal ballot, although there is
no statutory requirement for this. In contrast to elections for a special negotiating body (discussed at para **5.47** *et seq.*), there is no requirement for employers
to employ an independent person or body to conduct the election and count the
votes (although this would be the safest course of action), but it would be advisable to publicise the voting figures and to allow employees who wish to check
those figures to do so. The legislation does not prohibit the employer or third
parties attempting to put pressure on employees to vote a certain way; it is questionable whether conduct of this nature would violate the duty to make
'arrangements' to ensure that the election is fair.[6] The legislation does not explicitly make compliance with the other specified matters, such as voting entitlement
and a secret ballot, the employer's direct responsibility. However if the election
does not satisfy all the statutory requirements listed, those elected will not be
'appropriate representatives' for consultation and it is therefore in the
employer's interest to ensure compliance with them. A further contrast with
the elections to a special negotiating body is that there is no requirement for the
employer to underwrite the cost of the election.. However it would be in its interests to do so in order to ensure that the statutory requirements are met. An
affected or redundant employee may complain to an employment tribunal that
there has been a failure relating to the election of employee representatives, and
in this event it is for the employer to show that the statutory requirements have
been satisfied.[7] This reinforces the importance of employers constructing and
retaining complete and proper written records of all stages of the election
process. However unless a defect in the electoral process can be shown, individual employees would seem to have no recourse in the event that they think their
interests have not been, or will not be, properly represented by the employee rep-

resentatives who have been elected.[8] If an elected employee representative ceases to act as such, and any affected employee is consequently no longer represented, those left unrepresented must elect another representative in an election satisfying the statutory requirements.[9]

---

1. TULRCA 1992, s 188A(1)(g), (h). Employees are protected against dismissal, selection for redundancy, or subjection to a 'detriment' for taking part in elections: see para **5.16** below.

2. *Ibid.*, para 188A(1)(i).

3. Cf. *ibid.*, s 51(5)(b), discussed para **2.43**.

4. *Ibid.*, s 188A(1)(a).

5. See *ibid.*, s 188(1A)(e) and (g). In the context of industrial action ballots, the term 'date of the ballot' is used, and defined, in the case of a ballot on which votes may be cast on more than one day, as the last of those days: s 246. Employees are entitled to vote for a special negotiating body if they are employed on the day on which votes may be cast, or if votes may be cast on more than one day, on the first of those days: TICER 1999, reg 13(3)(b). It is submitted that it would be unduly restrictive to require the election for employee representatives to be held on a single day. However s 188(1A)(e), which requires candidates to be affected employees 'on the date of the election', and s 188(1A)(g), which requires all affected employees 'on the date of the election' to be entitled to vote, creates difficulties in this respect. There is no explicit requirement that those entitled to vote be given the opportunity to do so (cf. TICER 1999, reg 14(2)(c)(i)).

6. The protection against dismissal and subjection to a detriment extends only to taking part in an election and not to the way the employee votes: see para **5.16**.

7. TULRCA 1992, s 189(1), (1B). See para **5.18** for remedies in general.

8. Cf *Keane v Clerical Medical Investment Group Ltd*, Industrial Tribunal Case No 2900491/97, IDS Brief 595, August 1997 where an employment tribunal held (in the context of consultation under TUPE) that once there are employee representatives and consultation has taken place with them, only those representatives can pursue a claim that the statutory duties have not been complied with. *Quaere* whether disgruntled employees could sue representatives in negligence: see further para **2.22**.

9. TULRCA 1992, s 188A(2).

5.14 In the event that the employer invites affected employees to elect representatives and they fail to do so, it will be treated as having satisfied its statutory obligation to consult provided that the invitation was issued long enough before the time when consultations were required to begin to enable the election to take place.[1] However if, pursuant to an invitation, the affected employees fail to elect representatives within a reasonable time (for example, because no employee comes forward for election) the employer must give each affected employee individually the information which it is required to give to appropriate representatives.[2] However there is no requirement to consult such employees. The Collective Redundancies Directive appears to envisage consultation only through the medium of workers' representatives,[3] although the European Court of Justice, in somewhat ambiguous terms, affirmed that the Directive required that Member States should take 'all measures necessary to ensure that workers are informed, consulted and in a position to intervene through their representatives in the event of collective redundancies'.[4] If there are already potentially appropriate representatives in existence (eg a works council) it is strongly arguable that the employer should, in default of an election being held, consult those persons.

---

1. This is the implication of TULRCA 1992, s 188(7A), which treats the employer as complying with the requirements to inform and consult if this is done as soon as reasonably practicable after the representatives are elected. If no representatives are elected, the employer cannot take these steps.
2. TULRCA 1992, s 188(7B).
3. Cf. Council Directive 89/391 on health and safety, discussed at para **5.33**.
4. Case 383/92. *EC Commission v United Kingdom* [1994] IRLR 412, ECJ, para 23.

The Rights of Appropriate Representatives

5.15 Employee representatives, and candidates for this position, are entitled to be permitted by the employer to take 'reasonable' paid time off during working hours to perform their functions or in order to undergo training to perform such functions.[1] This provision is identical, *mutatis mutandis*, to that governing time off for trade union duties, discussed at para **3.27**; thus it is a right to time off only with the employer's permission, with recourse to an employment tribunal if time off or payment for that time is unreasonably refused, and payment need be made only for duties performed during working hours.[2] In contrast to time off for trade union duties, however, there is no reference to a Code of Practice to determine what is reasonable, although the parties may find some assistance from the ACAS Code governing that area. However, it is strongly arguable that in the context of redundancies priority should be given to ensuring that employee representatives have all the time off which they reasonably need to carry out their functions, so that considerations such as the amount of time off which the employee has been granted for other purposes, referred to in that Code,[3] should not be relevant in this context. The 'functions' for which time off must be permitted are not specified. The right to time off for training was added by the 1999 Regulations.[4] Notably, however, they do not give a right to training,[5] so that representatives who are not members of or otherwise associated with an independent trade union may find it difficult to get access to the requisite assistance, particularly as time will be of the essence. Moreover they are likely to be financially dependent on the employer for any training which they receive. They have no right to call in experts to assist them; although the Collective Redundancies Directive permits Member States to provide for such assistance, this is not obligatory.[6] However there is nothing to prevent an employer offering to pay for representatives to receive such advice, and as we indicated in para **5.11** it would be good industrial relations practice to do so. Where representatives of a recognised independent union are being consulted, their rights to time off for this purpose and for relevant training are governed by the provisions relating to trade union duties.[7] In this case, therefore, the ACAS Code of Practice will apply in determining the amount of time off which may be taken and any conditions applicable to it. All 'appropriate representatives' ('employee' or union) must be allowed access to the affected employees by the employer and must be given such accommodation and other facilities as may be appropriate;[8] this would probably include meeting rooms and a telephone, for example. The amount and timing of such access is not stipulated, but would probably be regarded by employment tribunals as subject to a test of reasonableness. In this connection it may be helpful to refer to the Code of Practice relating to recognition ballots discussed at para **4.26** *et seq.*, although clearly it will have no statutory authority in this context. If a tribunal finds that the employer has failed to allow employee representatives reasonable access or appropriate facilities, it must make a declaration to that effect and may make a protective award of compensation to the employees dismissed as redundant or whose dismissal was proposed.[9] By contrast, if appropriate representatives are denied time off to perform their functions, which is potentially of equal or greater significance for affected employees, the remedy, as we indicate above, is confined to a claim by individual representatives on their own behalf.

---

1. ERA 1996, s 61.

2. *Ibid.*, ss 61–63. Note that the provisions governing the calculation of payment are more detailed than those in TULRCA 1992, s 169 relating to payment for trade union duties.

3. ACAS Code of Practice on Time Off for Trade Union Duties and Activities, para 32.

4. Collective Redundancies and Transfer of Undertakings (Protection of Employment) (Amendment) Regulations 1999, SI 1999/1925.

5. Cf the Health and Safety (Consultation with Employees) Regulations 1996, reg 7; see further para **5.33**.
6. Council Directive 98/59, Article 2(2).
7. TULRCA 1992, s 168(1)(c). See s 196(2) for the definition of representatives of a trade union, discussed in para **5.11** above.
8. *Ibid.*, s 188(5A). The section requires access to 'the affected employees' rather than *all* affected employees, but the latter can probably be implied.
9. *Ibid.*, s 189. This would seem to be a failure relating to employee representatives for the purpose of s 189(1)(b), but *quaere* whether a complaint could also be brought by affected employees or those dismissed.

5.16 It is automatically unfair to dismiss, or to select for redundancy, an employee for performing or proposing to perform the functions or activities of an employee representative or of a candidate in an election for such a position, or for taking part in an election of employee representatives.[1] An employee who is dismissed on any such ground may apply for interim relief (see further para **3.9**).[2] The minimum basic award applicable to dismissals and selection for redundancy for 'trade union reasons' applies in this context.[3] Employees also have the right not to be subjected to any detriment by any act, or deliberate failure to act, by their employer on any of these grounds; where this right is infringed an employment tribunal may award such compensation as it considers just and equitable in the circumstances, having regard to the infringement of the right and to any loss attributable to the employer's act or failure.[4] The employer must show the ground on which any act, or deliberate failure to act, was done.[5] This provision mirrors the protection against detriment on grounds of trade union membership or non-membership, and the discussion in para **3.10** is relevant in this context. There is nothing specific in the legislation to prevent employers from according employee representatives more favourable treatment than those whom they represent, and where dismissals are selective and representatives are members of the 'target group' employers may be tempted to err on the side of caution by not dismissing them. This must be read in the light of general principles governing selection for redundancy. Thus, if an employer selected employees according to specified criteria such as last in first out, or performance record, and did not apply those to employee representatives, those dismissed in their stead may have a claim for unfair dismissal. The capacity of employers to accord more favourable treatment to employee representatives throws a further question-mark over the efficacy of the legislation in protecting employees' rights.

1. ERA 1996, ss 103, 105(1), (6). Where the principal reason for dismissal is redundancy it must be shown that the circumstances constituting the redundancy applied equally to one or more employees in the same undertaking who held similar positions and who were not dismissed: s 105(1)(b). Employees who are being consulted in their capacity as union officials will be covered by the protections afforded to those dismissed, or subjected to a detriment, for anti-union reasons: see para **3.3** *et seq.*

2. *Ibid.*, s 128.

3. *Ibid.*, s 120.

4. *Ibid.*, ss 47–49; see further para **3.13**. Once again there is no upper limit on the amount which may be awarded. This provision does not apply where the detriment amounts to dismissal; in that event the provisions relating to compensation for unfair dismissal apply.

5. *Ibid.*, s 48(2).

What is Meant by 'Consultation'?

5.17 For the purposes of consultation the employer must disclose in writing to the appropriate representatives a number of specified matters: the reasons for its proposals; the numbers and descriptions of employees whom it is proposed to dismiss as redundant; the total number of employees of any such description employed by the employer at the establishment in question; the proposed method of selecting the employees who may be dismissed; the proposed method of carrying out the dismissals, with due regard to any agreed procedure, including the period over which the dismissals are to take effect; and the proposed method of calculating the amount of any redundancy payments to be made to employees who may be dismissed, other than those required by statute.[1] The information must be delivered to the appropriate representatives or sent by post[2] to an address notified by them to the employer, or in the case of union representatives, sent by post to the union at the address of its head or main office.[3] However it has been suggested that it may not be essential for the employer to provide full and specific information under all these headings before consultation can begin,[4] and that where information is made available over a period it is a question of fact and circumstance at what point it is regarded as sufficiently detailed for meaningful consultation to be deemed to have started.[5] However employers would be well advised to attempt to provide the maximum possible information in their possession at the outset in order to avoid disputes over this issue. The process must include consultation about ways of avoiding the dismissals, reducing the number of employees to be dismissed and mitigating the consequences of the dismissals.[6] The first two categories may include consideration, for example, of alternative strategies such as reallocating work, reducing overtime, or giving employees the opportunity to work more flexible hours or to job share. Where appropriate the possibility of redeployment elsewhere in the organisation, possibly after retraining, should also be explored. Where dismissals are inevitable, mitigating action may include the provision of counselling and outplacements for employees and information as to retraining schemes, to maximise their prospects of obtaining fresh employment elsewhere.[7] The employer must undertake the consultation 'with a view to reaching agreement' with the appropriate representatives,[8] and must, therefore, be able to demonstrate that it took seriously the points which they made, and that it made reasonable efforts to reach accommodation with them. Employers should, therefore, keep a written record of all discussions; ideally minutes should be prepared of all meetings and signed as agreed by both parties as being an accurate record. Whilst ultimately employers retain the right to decide upon the implementation of redundancies, this procedure requires them to do more than merely go through the motions of listening to what representatives have to say. For this reason it would be unwise for employers to issue dismissal notices during the consultation period; although the legislation does not specifically forbid this, it may undermine the argument that there was a genuine attempt to reach agreement.[9] It may also undermine an argument that consultation had begun 'in good time'.

---

1. TULRCA 1992, s 188(4).

2. Defined *ibid.*, s 298 as a postal service which is provided by the Post Office or under a licence granted under the British Telecommunications Act 1981, s 68, or which does not infringe the exclusive privilege of the Post Office by virtue of an order made under s 69 of that Act. It thus excludes delivery by internal mail or private courier. Cf *NALGO v London Borough of Bromley* (11 January 1993, unreported), EAT, 671/91.

3. *Ibid.*, s 188(5). See s 196(2), discussed in para **5.11** above, for the definition of 'representatives of a trade union'.

4. *MSF v GEC Ferranti (Defence Systems) Ltd (No 2)* [1994] IRLR 113, EAT, at 116.

5. *GEC Ferranti Defence Systems Ltd v MSF* [1993] IRLR 101, EAT, at 103. Cf *E Green and Son (Casting) Ltd v ASTMS* [1984] IRLR 135, EAT.

6. TULRCA 1992, s 188(2).

7. There is an obligation on employers to give certain employees who have been given notice of dismissal for redundancy reasonable paid time off work to look for new employment or to make arrangements for training for future employment: ERA 1996, ss 52–54.

8. TULRCA 1992, s 188(2).

9. For cases on this point decided prior to the introduction of this requirement in TURERA 1993, see *NUT v Avon County Council* [1978] IRLR 55, EAT; *TGWU v Ledbury Preserves (1928) Ltd* [1985] IRLR 412, EAT; *Sovereign Distribution Services Ltd v TGWU* [1989] IRLR 334, EAT. Cf *R v British Coal Corporation and the Secretary of State for Trade and Industry ex parte Price* [1994] IRLR 72, where the Queen's Bench Division held that the payment of voluntary redundancy payments before the termination of the consultation process did not make that process a sham.

Remedies

5.18 If an employer fails to fulfil any of the statutory requirements a complaint may be made to an employment tribunal. If the failure relates to trade union or employee representatives, it may be made by the union or any of the employee representatives to whom the failure relates respectively; in any other case, including, specifically, a failure relating to the election of employee representatives, it may be made by any of the affected employees or any of the employees who have been dismissed as redundant.[1] However it seems that the scope for individual employees or ex-employees to complain about matters other than the conduct of an election may be confined to situations where the employer fails to issue an invitation to elect employee representatives; chooses to consult a body which does not have the authority of employees to consult on their behalf; or fails, in the event that there is no response to the invitation to elect representatives, to provide individual employees with the requisite information.[2] This is because, if appropriate representatives (employee or union) are in place, the employer's duty to provide information or engage in proper consultations is owed to them rather than individual employees, and if such representatives are unwilling to complain to an employment tribunal there would seem to be nothing that individual employees could then do.[3] Where an employer has voluntarily recognised a trade union it is possible to imagine circumstances where it may choose not to bring proceedings in order to safeguard its relationship with the employer, particularly if those dismissed are not union members.[4] Likewise employee representatives may lack the will, or the resources, to bring a claim on behalf of others. The complaint to a tribunal must be presented before the date on which the last of the dismissals to which it relates takes effect or during the three month period beginning with that date except where the tribunal is satisfied that compliance with the three-month period was not 'reasonably practicable', in which case claims must be brought within a 'reasonable' period.[5]

---

1. TULRCA 1992, s 189(1). It is for the employer to show that the requirements for the election of employee representatives have been met: s 189(1B).
2. See **5.10** *et seq.* The employer must show that an employee representative had the authority to represent the affected employees: *ibid.*, s 189(1A).
3. In *Kerry Foods Ltd v Creber* [2000] IRLR 10, EAT, Morison P opined that in Case C–383/92 *EC Commission v UK* [1994] IRLR 412 the ECJ had made clear that the Collective Redundancies Directive was designed to protect the rights of workers as individuals. On this view it may be possible to argue that workers should not be obstructed from pursuing an effective remedy. However we do not read the ECJ judgment as giving sufficient support to that proposition.

4. It is unlikely that a term requiring a union to bring proceedings on behalf of a member could be implied into the contract of membership: see further para **2.15**.

5. *Ibid.*, s 189(5). For the interpretation of not 'reasonably practicable' see App 2.

5.19 The employer may defend the complaint by showing that there were 'special circumstances' which rendered it not reasonably practicable for it to comply with the requirements to disclose the requisite information to appropriate representatives and consult them about the specified matters within the prescribed time limits, and that it took all such steps towards compliance with the requirement(s) as were reasonably practicable in the circumstances.[1] This defence has been construed narrowly by the courts; to be 'special' circumstances must be uncommon or out of the ordinary—a sudden and unexpected, rather than a predictable, disaster.[2] Insolvency may or may not be a special circumstance, depending on its cause; a gradual rundown which made insolvency foreseeable would not fall within this category,[3] nor would shedding workers to make the purchase of the business more attractive to a potential purchaser,[4] or the fact that the company is in administration.[5] However other factors, such as a sudden withdrawal of further credit facilities and appointment of a receiver,[6] or continued trading despite adverse economic pointers in the reasonable expectation of avoiding redundancies (provided that the employer is not merely shutting its eyes to the obvious)[7] may lead to a different result depending on the facts. At one time it was thought that a failure to consult prior to the public announcement of a merger could be justified on the ground that this was necessitated by Stock Exchange rules.[8] However the Director-General of the Takeover Panel has confirmed that Stock Exchange rules do not preclude representatives being informed and consulted in advance where collective redundancies are planned in connection with a takeover. The DTI guidance on consultation suggests that in these circumstances representatives can be made subject to confidentiality constraints for a specified period, but at the same time be sufficiently informed to hold meaningful consultations with the employer.[9] However this may be more difficult to implement where there are no appropriate representatives in place and employers are required to invite affected employees to hold an election. More broadly, the position is uncertain if the union or employee representatives refused to accept the information subject to such confidentiality constraints; logically, the employer should not then be able to rely on the special circumstances defence. Finally, the statute provides that where the decision leading to the dismissals was taken by a person controlling the employer (directly or indirectly) rather than the employer itself, a failure by that person to provide information to the immediate employer cannot constitute the 'special circumstances' defence.[10] Thus a subsidiary of a transnational company, for example, cannot argue that it was unable to meet its obligations because its parent company, which took the decision to reduce the workforce, was unwilling to disclose the requisite information to it. The 'special circumstances' defence does not appear in the Collective Redundancies Directive, and it is curious that its presence in the legislation was not a ground for complaint by the Commission in the infringement proceedings referred to in para **5.1** above. In the light of the principle that national legislation should be interpreted to conform with EU law[11] it would seem open to a complainant to argue that an employer should not be able to rely upon the 'special circumstances' defence.

---

1. *Ibid.*, ss 188(7), 189(6).

2. *Clarks of Hove Ltd v Bakers' Union* [1978] IRLR 366, CA. The tribunal must indicate what it regards about the circumstances as 'special': *GMB v Messrs Rankin and Harrison (as joint administrative receivers of Lawtex plc and Lawtex Babywear Ltd)* [1992] IRLR 514, EAT. Ignorance of a requirement to consult is not a 'special circumstance': *UCATT v Rooke and Son (Cambridge) Ltd* [1978] IRLR 204, EAT.

3. *Clarks of Hove v Bakers' Union*, above.

4. *GMB v Messrs Rankin and Harrison*, above, note 2.

5. The duty to consult applies where the employer is a company in administration and the administrator proposes the dismissals: *Re Hartlebury Printers Ltd (in liquidation)* [1992] IRLR 516, ChD. Remuneration due under a protective award constitutes a preferential debt under the Insolvency Act 1986, Sched 6, para 13(2)(d).

6. *USDAW v Leancut Bacon Ltd (in liquidation)* [1981] IRLR 295, EAT. See also *Hamish Armour v ASTMS* [1979] IRLR 24, EAT (application for a further government loan pending).

7. *APAC v Kirvin Ltd* [1978] IRLR 318, EAT.

8. See the *Financial Times*, 26/27 June 1999, reporting the employment tribunal decision in *MSF v Refuge Assurance* to this effect.

9. *Redundancy Consultation and Notification* PL833, Section 2.

10. TULRCA 1992, s 188(7).

11. See Case C–106/89 *Marleasing SA v La Comercial Internacional de Alimentation SA* [1990] ECR I–4135, ECJ.

5.20 If an employment tribunal upholds a complaint it must make a declaration to that effect and may also make a 'protective award' in respect of employees who have been dismissed as redundant or whom it is proposed to dismiss as redundant and in respect of whose dismissal or proposed dismissal the employer has failed to comply with a statutory requirement.[1] The award entitles the employees subject to it to receive their normal pay for the period of the award (the 'protected period').[2] Although the rate of remuneration is required to be calculated in accordance with Chapter II of Part XIV, of the Employment Rights Act 1996, the statutory maximum of a 'week's pay' stipulated in s 227 does not appear to be applicable in this context.[3] An employee to whom a protective award relates may complain to a tribunal if the employer fails to pay him or her any of the remuneration due under the award.[4] The length of the protected period is at the discretion of the tribunal, but may not exceed 90 days.[5] Its length is such as the tribunal 'determines to be just and equitable in all the circumstances, having regard to the seriousness of the employer's default in complying with any [statutory] requirement . . .'.[6] The interpretation of this provision—and, in particular, deciding whether the award was designed to compensate the employees affected, penalise the employer, or both—caused the courts and tribunals considerable difficulty in the legislation's early years. However in a widely-cited judgment Slynn J emphasised that the question to be examined was not the loss or potential loss of actual remuneration to the employee during the relevant period; rather:

> It is to consider the loss of days of consultation which have occurred. The Tribunal will have to consider, how serious was the breach on the part of the employer? It may be that the employer has done everything that he can possibly do to ensure that his employees are found other employment. If that happens, a Tribunal may well take the view that either there should be no award or, if there is an award, it should be nominal. . . .[7]

On this basis it was irrelevant that the dismissed employees had suffered no financial loss because they had immediately found alternative employment. Slynn J also pointed out that there could be

> defaults of different gravity. For example, one requirement of the Act is that the necessary information shall be disclosed in writing. It might be that if all the information had been given orally to a trade union [or employee] representative, a Tribunal would not take a very serious view of that as a failure to comply with a requirement. On the other hand, failure to give reasons at all . . . might be more serious. A failure to consult at all, or consultation only at the last minute, might be taken to be even more serious.[8]

Determining when the protected period should begin also proved a source of difficulty. The statute states that the award begins with the date on which the first of the dismissals to which the complaint relates 'takes effect' or the date of the award, whichever is the earlier.[9] After conflicting decisions, the date on which the first of the dismissals 'takes effect' has most recently been interpreted by the EAT as the date on which it was originally proposed that the first of the dismissals should take effect, rather than the actual date.[10]

---

1. TULRCA 1992, s 189(2),(3).
2. The calculation date for computing payments is the date on which the protective award was made, or, in the case of an employee who had been dismissed before that

time, the date which under ERA 1996 s 226(5) is the calculation date for the purpose of computing a redundancy payment in relation to that dismissal (whether it not the employee is entitled to such a payment): s 190(5).

3. Cf. TULRCA 1992, s 70C(5B), and note also that there is no reference to protective awards in the Employment Rights (Increase of Limits) Order 1999, SI 1999/3375.

4. *Ibid.*, s 192(1). Such a complaint must be brought within three months of the last of the days in respect of which the complaint of failure to pay is made, except where the tribunal is satisfied that compliance with the three month period was not 'reasonably practicable', in which case claims must be brought within a 'reasonable' period: *ibid.*, s 192(2); see App 2 for the meaning of not 'reasonably practicable'. This can cause a difficulty where a tribunal holds that an employee is entitled to a protective award long after the protected period has ended; the employee may then be out of time to present a claim under s 192 in the event that the employer refuses to pay. In *Bolam v Howlett Marine* an employment tribunal in Newcastle held that in these circumstances it was not 'reasonably practicable' for the employee to have presented a claim within the three month time limit: 10 June 1999, reported ELA Briefing Vol. 6 No. 10 October 1999, 284.

5. *Ibid.*, s 189(4).

6. *Ibid.*

7. *Spillers-French (Holdings) Ltd v USDAW* [1979] IRLR 339 at 342. See also *Sovereign Distribution Services Ltd v TGWU* [1989] IRLR 334, EAT.

8. *Ibid.*, at 341. In *Purssord v Essex Furniture Plc* EAT/557/99, 25 November 1999, the EAT emphasised that the fact that it was very unlikely that consultation would have altered matters was not a ground for not making a protective award.

9. TULRCA 1992, s 189(4).

10. *TGWU v Ledbury Preserves (1928) Ltd* [1986] IRLR 492, EAT, following *E Green and Son (Castings) Ltd v ASTMS* [1984] IRLR 135, EAT, on this point in preference to *GKN Sankey Ltd v NSMM* [1980] IRLR 8, EAT. The determination of this date was more significant before TURERA 1993 removed the provision requiring a protective award to be set off against payments under the contract of employment or damages for breach of contract.

5.21 The protective award is payable regardless of whether employees are working during the protected period. However employees who are still employed during any part of the protected period will be entitled to payments under the protected award only if they would be entitled to payment under their contract of employment or under their statutory rights during a period of notice;[1] thus employees who take unpaid leave or time off pursuant to a statutory rather than a contractual right, for example, would not be so entitled. Employees lose the right to remuneration under a protected award if they are fairly dismissed for reasons other than redundancy,[2] or unreasonably terminate the contract of employment, in respect of any period during which they would otherwise have been employed.[3] They also lose this right for the period when they would otherwise have been employed if, in circumstances where they are entitled to a statutory redundancy payment, they unreasonably refuse an offer of suitable employment from the employer (or new or renewed employment on the same terms) to take effect before or during the protective period.[4] If the purpose of the award is to compensate for the loss of period of consultation, as Slynn J suggested, it is not clear why any of these events should be relevant: the loss has occurred regardless of subsequent events. The fact that the basis for determining the length of a protective award is so unclear, and in particular the fact that an employment tribunal may make only a nominal—or even no—award for reasons which have only partial relevance to the subject-matter of the consultation process (such as attempting to find workers alternative employment) makes it extremely doubtful that in its present form the legislation complies with the requirements of EU law that there be an 'effective, proportionate and dissuasive' penalty for breach of the duty to consult.[5] Employees who are unemployed and in receipt of a protective award may not claim a Jobseeker's Allowance for this period.[6] If an employee has already claimed the Jobseeker's Allowance (or income support) and a protective award is subsequently made in respect of that period the employer must deduct that amount from the award and repay it to the DSS.[7] The tribunal, when it makes the protective award, will inform the employer of the appropriate procedure.[8]

---

1. TULRCA 1992, s 190(4).
2. Note that the wider meaning of redundancy defined in s 195(1) applies in this context.
3. TULCRA 1992, s 191. As Harvey, para 2673 points out, if the employment would have ended before the end of the protected period in any case, the employee is entitled to payment under the award for any period during which he or she would not in any event have been employed by the employer.
4. TULRCA 1992, s 191. There is provision for a trial period where the terms and conditions of employment differ from the previous contract: s 191(4)–(7).
5. See Case C–68/88 *EC Commission v Greece* [1989] ECR 2965 and Case C–7/90 *Belgium v Vandevenne* [1991] ECR I–4371.
6. The Employment Protection (Recoupment of Jobseeker's Allowance and Income Support) Regulations 1996, SI 1996/2349, para 8.
7. *Ibid.*
8. *Ibid.*, para 5.

5.22 The sanction of a protective award is stated in the statute to be the exclusive remedy for a failure to follow the statutory requirements in respect of information and consultation on redundancies.[1] On this basis an application for an injunction restraining dismissals for redundancy pending conclusion of the consultation procedure was unsuccessful.[2] However where the employer is a body whose decisions are susceptible to judicial review and there are consultation procedures particular to the industry or service in question the position may be different. In 1992 decisions by British Coal and the Secretary of State to close collieries without any consultation, in breach of the Coal Industry Nationalisation Act 1946 and machinery established thereunder, were deemed to be a matter of public law, and a declaration was granted that no decision should be made on the closure of any collieries until the stipulated procedure had been followed.[3] Where, however, there is no special procedure and such an employer has failed merely to consult in accordance with the general law the statutory provision for exclusivity presents obstacles to a claim for any additional remedy.[4] Nevertheless, in principle, there seems no reason why, in an application for an interim injunction for breach of contract, the court cannot at least take into account an employer's breach of its statutory obligations to consult when exercising its discretion as to whether or not to make an order. Equally, the fact that the employer has breached these obligations may render the dismissal unfair.[5]

---

1. TULRCA 1992, s 188(8).
2. *Griffin v South West Water Services Ltd* [1995] IRLR 15, Blackburne J.
3. *R v British Coal Corporation and Secretary of State for Trade and Industry, ex parte Vardy* [1993] IRLR 104, QBD. Note that the concept of consultation in this context may not be identical to the statutory formulation: see *R v British Coal Corporation and Secretary of State for Trade and Industry, ex parte Price* [1994] IRLR 72, Glidewell LJ at 75. The employer returned to the court at a later date to determine whether it had done what was necessary in order to comply with the order.
4. See *Vardy*, above, at 116; *Griffin*, above, note 2.
5. See *King v Eaton Ltd* [1996] IRLR 199, CS.

Notification to the Department of Trade and Industry

5.23 In addition to the obligation to consult appropriate representatives, employers proposing to dismiss for redundancy 20 or more employees within a period of 90 days or less must notify the Department of Trade and Industry (DTI) in writing within the same time limits applicable to consultation—ie at least 90 days before the first dismissal takes effect where they propose to dismiss 100 or more employees within 90 days or less; otherwise, at least 30 days before.[1] The notification must identify the appropriate representatives and state when consultation with them began (although the general duty to notify exists even if there were no 'appropriate representatives' because, for example, there were no candidates for an election).[2] The employer must also supply any additional information which the DTI requires.[3] A copy of the notice given to the DTI must also be given to appropriate representatives.[4] An employer who fails to comply with the obligation to notify the DTI risks criminal prosecution and a fine of up to level 5 on the standard scale.[5] Where the employer is a limited company. a director, manager, secretary or other similar officer, or any person who was purporting to act in any such capacity, who fails to notify the Department may incur personal liability if the offence is shown to have been committed with his or her consent, or connivance, or attributable to his or her neglect.[6] The same 'special circumstances' defence as applies to the failure to consult, described in para **5.19**, applies also in this context.[7] Prosecutions may be instituted only by the Secretary of State or by an officer authorised for that purpose.[8] There is no record of any prosecutions for this offence.

---

1. TULRCA 1992, s 193(1), (2). In determining the number to be dismissed, no account is to be taken of employees in respect of whose dismissal notice has already been given to the Secretary of State. See further para **5.5**. This duty is subject to the same exceptions as the duty to consult. Article 4 of Council Directive 98/59 states that the projective collective redundancies notified to the competent public authority shall take effect not earlier than 30 days after notification (although Member States may grant the authority power to reduce this period). This period is to be 'used by the competent public authority to seek solutions to the problems raised by the projected collective redundancies'. There are no equivalent provisions in domestic legislation. Article 4 need not be applied to collective redundancies arising from termination of the establishment's activities where this is the result of a judicial decision.

2. *Ibid.*, s 193(4)(b). See para **5.11** *et seq.* for the meaning of 'appropriate representative'.

3. *Ibid.*, s 193(4)(c), (5).

4. *Ibid.*, s 193(6). The copy must be delivered to them or sent by post to a notified address or, in the case of trade union representatives, sent by post to the union at its head or main office. There is no sanction for breach of this obligation.

5. *Ibid.*, s194(1). At the time of writing level 5 stands at £5,000: Criminal Justice Act 1982, s 37(2), as substituted by the Criminal Justice Act 1991, s 17(1).

6. *Ibid.*, s 194(3).

7. *Ibid.*, s 193(7). Again, ignorance on the part of an employer of the obligation to notify is no defence: *Secretary of State for Employment v Helitron Ltd* [1980] ICR 523, EAT.

8. *Ibid.*, s 194(2).

THE DUTY TO CONSULT ON A TRANSFER OF THE UNDERTAKING

Sources and General Principles

5.24 When an undertaking is being transferred,[1] both transferor and transferee employers have a duty to inform and consult 'appropriate representatives' of any 'affected employees'.[2] Unlike in the context of redundancies, the duties to inform and consult are separate: the duty to consult applies only where the employer envisages that it will, in connection with the transfer, be 'taking measures' in relation to affected employees, whereas information must be provided to appropriate representatives regardless of whether any measures will be taken. In practice the two duties are likely in most cases to be coincident. No minimum number of employees need be affected before the duties to inform and consult apply. If the employees concerned are of a description in respect of which the employer recognises an independent trade union, representatives of that union (or those unions) must be informed and consulted.[3] If no independent trade union is recognised, the employer must inform and consult 'employee representatives'. These are described in the regulations as either (at the employer's option) representatives elected specifically by the employees affected for that purpose, or those elected or appointed for other purposes but which have the employees' authority to receive information and to be consulted about the transfer on their behalf.[4] Where affected employees who have been invited to elect representatives fail to do so within a reasonable time, the employer must give specified information to each affected employee individually,[5] but has no obligation to consult them on its proposals. If an employer fails to comply with any of its statutory obligations, a complaint may be presented to an employment tribunal by, variously, a trade union; an employee representative; or any affected employee, depending upon the nature of the alleged default.[6] The relevant principles are currently contained in the Transfer of Undertakings (Protection of Employment) Regulations 1981, as amended by the Trade Union Reform and Employment Rights Act 1993, and the Collective Redundancies and Transfer of Undertakings (Protection of Employment) (Amendment) Regulations of 1995 and 1999.[7] The 1999 Regulations came into force on 28 July 1999 and apply to transfers taking effect after 31 October 1999. The duties to inform and consult were introduced to give effect to the EC Directive on Transfers, often referred to as the Acquired Rights Directive.[8] As we stated in para **5.1** it had long been doubted whether these provisions, like those relating to collective redundancies, adequately implemented the Directive, and the successive amendments were introduced for the purpose of effecting compliance with it. However, as in the case of collective redundancies, it is strongly arguable that the current provisions continue to fall short of the Directive, for example in allowing a defence of 'special circumstances'. In the event that there is a continuing failure to comply with the requirements of EU law, it is conceivable that the *Francovich* principle could be invoked by those affected, although as in relation to redundancies it may be difficult to show that quantifiable loss was caused by that failure.[9] To date there has been no ruling by the European Court of Justice on whether the consultation provisions of the Acquired Rights Directive have direct effect and may thus be relied upon against an organ of the state. However the High Court has expressed the view that the consultation provision in the Collective Redundancies Directive[10] is not directly effective because it gives Member States such a wide discretion in designating who the workers' representatives are to be, and does not, therefore, meet the conditions of being unconditional and sufficiently precise.[11] Where a transfer may give rise to collective redundancies, the employer proposing the dismissals of its employees must also comply with the separate duty imposed under the Trade Union and Labour Relations (Consolidation) Act 1992, ss 188–198, as amended, analysed in paras **5.2** *et seq.*

---

1. See TUPE 1981, reg 3.

2. *Ibid.*, regs 10–11A.

3. *Ibid.*, reg 10(2A)(a). See paras **2.6** and **2.7** for the definition of an 'independent trade union'.

4. *Ibid.*, reg 10(2A)(b), as amended by SI 1999/2402.

5. *Ibid.*, reg 10(8A).

6. *Ibid.*, reg 11(1).

7. SI 1995/ 2587 and SI 1999/ 1925.

8. Council Directive 77/187/EEC. This Directive has been amended by Council Directive 98/50/EC, which must be implemented by 17 July 2001. At the time of writing no amending legislation has been enacted. We indicate the additional requirements of the amending Directive in relation to information and consultation at appropriate points in the text.

9. See para **5.2**.

10. Council Directive 75/129/EEC, subsequently amended by Council Directive 92/56/EEC, and now consolidated in Council Directive 98/59/EC.

11. *Griffin v South West Water Services Ltd* [1995] IRLR 15, ChD, at 30–32.

The Persons who Must be Informed and Consulted and Their Rights

5.25 The transferor and transferee employers must inform and consult appropriate representatives of 'affected employees'. 'Affected employees' are defined as 'any employees of the transferor or transferee (whether or not employed in the undertaking or part of the undertaking to be transferred) who *may* [our italics] be affected by the transfer or may be affected by measures taken in connection with it';[1] thus a mere possibility of being affected is sufficient. In many cases much of, if not the entire, workforce of both transferee and transferor employer are likely to fall within this category; in case of doubt, employers should err on the side of inclusiveness. Employees of 'associated employers'[2] of the transferor or transferee are not included within the obligation, however, even though they may well be 'affected' by the transfer. 'Appropriate representatives' are defined in identical terms as in the context of collective redundancies,[3] and the same comments as to their designation, and provision for election, as were made there apply, *mutatis mutandis*, in relation to transfers of the undertaking (see paras **5.10–5.13**). They have identical rights to time off,[4] access to affected employees and facilities,[5] and protection against dismissal, selection for redundancy, or subjection to any other detriment.[6] These rights are discussed in paras **5.15–5.16.**

---

1. TUPE 1981, reg 10(1). See App 1 for the definition of 'employee'. Note that the definition of employee in this context extends to 'any individual who works for another person whether under a contract of service or apprenticeship or otherwise but does not include anyone who provides services under a contract for services': reg 2(1). Anomalously, regs 10 and 11 (and 8) do not apply to employment where under his or her contract of employment the employee ordinarily works outside the UK (certain mariners excepted): reg 13(1), (2): see further para **3.3** note 6. This exclusion has been removed by ERA 1999, s 32 in relation to the duty to consult on collective redundancies.
2. See App 1.
3. TUPE 1981, reg 10(2A), reg 11A.
4. ERA 1996, s 61.
5. TUPE 1981, reg 10(6A).
6. ERA 1996, ss 103, 105(1), (6), 47–49.

The Duties to Inform and to Consult: Scope and Timing

5.26 Appropriate representatives of affected employees must be informed of specified matters '[l]ong enough before a relevant transfer to enable the employer of any affected employees to consult all the persons who are appropriate representatives of any of those affected employees'.[1] This is a vague and anomalous test, given that the duty to consult does not apply in every case, but only where the employer 'envisages that . . . [it] will, in connection with the transfer, be taking measures' in relation to those employees.[2] As formulated, it would allow an employer who envisages no 'measures' being taken in relation to affected employees to comply with the duty to inform immediately before the transfer.[3] Although the EAT has held that the duty to consult applies to a proposed transfer which does not, in the event, take place,[4] this does not overcome the difficulty because of the specific link which is made between the time limit for the transmission of information and the consultation. In practice, the situations where an employer can be said not to envisage 'measures' are likely to be rare. 'Measures' are not defined, but would certainly include changes to working practices and working conditions,[5] and it is

> not altogether clear when employees may be said to be affected by a transfer without measures being taken. On a broad view, virtually all workers will be affected by a transfer, if only because the merging of workforces is likely to have some further consequences—whether beneficial or not—for the workers of both transferor and transferee.[6]

It has been suggested that an employer 'envisages' measures when it has 'formulated some definite plan or proposal which it has in mind to implement', so excluding mere hopes or possibilities.[7] The requirement that the measures be envisaged 'in connection with the transfer' has been said to exclude measures which would have taken place irrespective of the transfer.[8] The adoption of a wide interpretation of 'measures' does not solve the difficulty of estimating the appropriate time to be allowed for consultation, which may vary greatly depending upon the number of employees affected and the nature of the changes envisaged. At a minimum, employers should allow time for the representatives to present their views and for a reasoned response to be made to them.[9] The position is further complicated where the employer has invited any of the affected employees to elect employee representatives. Here, provided that the employer issued the invitation long enough before the time when it is required to give information to the representatives to allow them to elect representatives by that time, the employer is treated as complying with the regulations if it complies with those requirements as soon as reasonably practicable after the election.[10] In this context, where an employer wishes to keep the transfer secret for as long as possible, it may be tempted not to create suspicions by inviting an election but, rather, to consult with union representatives or persons already elected for some other purpose, where these exist, at the latest possible time.

---

1. TUPE 1981, reg 10(2). It is unclear whether the 'relevant transfer' refers to the moment of exchange of contracts or completion. There is authority to support the latter (*IPCS v Secretary of State for Defence* [1987] IRLR 373, ChD, at 377) but the decision in *BIFU v Barclays Bank Plc* [1987] ICR 495, EAT, which allows a complaint to be presented even if a proposed transfer never takes place, suggests otherwise. The text of this provision could be read to require employers to inform and consult with representatives other than those of its own employees, but it seems highly unlikely that this effect was intended: Elias and Bowers, no date of publication given, 96–97. Reg 10(2)(d) also argues against such an interpretation.

2. *Ibid.*, reg 10(5). Further difficulty is caused by the fact that the duty to inform covers a much wider range of matters than the duty to consult. In *IPCS v Secretary of State for Defence* above at 376 Millett J sought to reconcile this apparent inconsistency on the basis that (the equivalent of) this provision was referring to voluntary consultations 'which the unions may seek on any topic once they have the requisite information, but which the . . . employer is not compelled to grant if it chooses not to do so'. In practice, even when there is no legal duty to consult it will be good industrial relations practice to discuss the implications of the transfer with appropriate representatives.

3. Hepple, 1982, 32.

4. *BIFU v Barclays Bank*, above, note 1. Cf the view of Millett J in *IPCS v Secretary of State for Defence* above note 1 at 377 that 'transfer' means the date of actual transfer.

5. See *IPCS v Secretary of State for Defence*, above, note 1, where Millett J opined at 376 that 'measures' included 'any action, step or arrangement'. It is suggested in Harvey that by transferring employees to the transferor along with its business the transferor thereby 'takes measures' in respect of them (transfer of undertakings, para 281).

6. Elias and Bowers, no date given, 93.

7. *IPCS v Secretary of State for Defence*, above, note 1, at 376.

8. *Ibid.* However as Harvey states, if the transferee intends to introduce changes for its existing workforce for reasons unconnected with the transfer, these changes will be connected with the transfer as far as employees of the transferor are concerned, given that they would not affect them but for the transfer: Transfer of Undertakings, para 286.

9. See TUPE 1981, reg 10(6).

10. TUPE 1981, reg 10(8).

5.27 The information which must be provided to appropriate representatives of affected employees must be delivered to them, or sent by post to an address notified by them to the employer, or in the case of union representatives, sent by post to the union at its head or main office.[1] There is no obligation to give the information in any particular form (although the references to its being delivered and posted implies that it should be in writing) and representatives cannot demand to see specific documents.[2] If the employer invited affected employees to elect representatives and they failed to do so within a reasonable time, the employer must give the information directly to each affected employee.[3] The information to be supplied falls into four categories[4]:

(1) the fact that the transfer is to take place, when approximately, it is to take place and the reasons for it;[5]
(2) the legal, economic and social implications of the transfer for the affected employees;[6]
(3) the measures which the employer envisages it will, in connection with the transfer, take in relation to affected employees or, if it envisages that no measures will be taken, that fact;
(4) in the case of the transferor, the measures which the transferee envisages it will take in connection with the transfer in relation to those employees who will transfer to its employment by virtue of the regulations (or, if no measures are envisaged, that fact).

In relation to category (4) the transferee has an obligation to give the transferor the requisite information 'at such a time as will enable the transferor to perform the duty imposed on' it.[7] On the wording of the legislation, this would seem to imply that the information should be supplied in time for consultation to take place on those measures (although as we discuss in para **5.28** below, the transferor does not have to consult about measures which the transferee envisages taking). However in *IPCS v Secretary of State for Defence* Millett J pointed out that there was no obligation upon the transferee to envisage measures at any particular time and, indeed, that 'measures' may be developed or changed once consultation with the transferee's own [representatives] has begun. He suggested that there was a duty for the transferee to supply the information ' as soon as measures are envisaged and if possible long enough before the transfer' for consultations to take place.[8] As we indicate in para **5.28** below, the suggestion that consultations should only take place if possible is not, in its unadulterated form, compatible with the statutory regime.

---

1. TUPE 1981, reg 10(4).
2. *ICPS v Secretary of State for Defence* [1987] IRLR 373 at 378, Millett J.
3. TUPE 1981, reg 10(8A). Specific provision for this eventuality is made in Council Directive 77/187/EC, as amended by Council Directive 98/50 EC Article 6(6) (and a more limited obligation is placed on the employer under the unamended Directive); cf

in the context of collective redundancies (discussed in para **5.14**) where no equivalent provision is made in the Collective Redundancies Directive.

4. TUPE 1981, reg 10(2).

5. Council Directive 98/50, which amends Council Directive 77/187 requires the 'date or proposed date' of the transfer to be given. This suggests that the precise date, if known, should be given.

6. This phrase appears in Article 6 of Council Directive 77/187. 'Legal' implications would seem to cover employees' statutory and contractual rights; 'economic and social implications' are delphic phrases which may cover matters such as the economic prospects of employees, job security implications etc., but this awaits clarification from the courts.

7. TUPE 1981, reg 10(3). Information may not be supplied under the cloak of commercial confidentiality: *IPCS v Secretary of State for Defence*, above, note 2, at 375.

8. Above, note 2, at 376.

5.28 As stated in para **5.26** above, the duty to consult arises only where the transferor or transferee employer 'envisages that . . . [it] will, in connection with the transfer, be taking measures in relation to any [affected] employees'; the employer must then consult all appropriate representatives of any of the employees in respect of whom measures are envisaged.[1] The ambit of 'envisages . . . taking measures' was discussed in para **5.26**. The duty applies only to measures which the employer itself envisages taking; the transferor does not have to consult about measures which the transferee may envisage (although it is required to inform representatives of such measures). Moreover, the duty does not extend to measures which may be envisaged by an associated employer,[2] so excluding those of a parent company or another company in the same group. In contrast to the provisions relating to collective redundancies, the duty to consult is much less specifically defined. The regulations merely state that the employer must consider any representations made by the representatives, reply to them and give reasons if those representations are rejected.[3] However there is an analogous (although not identical) duty to enter the consultations with a view to seeking agreement.[4] As in that context, we would advise employers to keep appropriate records enabling them to demonstrate that they took seriously the points made to them by union representatives and made all reasonable attempts to reach an accommodation with them. Representatives should be given sufficient time to enable them properly to consider the proposals which are being put to them. We would respectfully suggest that the dictum of Millett J referred to in para **5.27** above, which suggests that if 'measures' are not envisaged at the outset, information about their nature should be supplied *if possible* long enough before the transfer' for consultations to take place, should not be followed. Employers have the choice of postponing a transfer to enable consultations to occur;

alternatively they may attempt to bring themselves within the defence of 'special circumstances' (see para **5.29** below).

---

1. TUPE 1981, reg 10(5).
2. See App 1.
3. TUPE 1981, reg 10(6). See also the definition of consultation propounded by Glidewell LJ in *R v British Coal Corporation and the Secretary of State for Trade and Industry, ex parte Price* [1994] IRLR 72 at 75.
4. *Ibid.*, reg 10(5). In the context of collective redundancies, consultation must be undertaken with a view to *reaching* agreement: TULRCA 1992, s 188(2). Note that there is no requirement in either context to *reach* agreement.

Remedies

5.29 If an employer fails to fulfil any of its statutory duties, a complaint may be presented to an employment tribunal.[1] If the complaint relates to trade union or employee representatives, it may be made by the union or any of the employee representatives respectively; in any other case, including, specifically, a failure relating to the election of employee representatives, it may be made by any of the affected employees.[2] However, as in the case of redundancy consultation, it seems that the scope for individual employees to complain about matters other than the conduct of the election will be confined to situations where the employer fails to issue an invitation to elect employee representatives; chooses to inform or consult a body which it is not appropriate for it to inform or consult; or fails, in the event that there is no response to the invitation to elect representatives, to provide individual employees with the requisite information (see further para **5.18**). The complaint must be presented within three months of the date on which the relevant transfer is completed, except where the tribunal is satisfied that it was not 'reasonably practicable' for the complaint to be presented within this period, in which case it must be presented within a 'reasonable' period.[3] The employer can defend the complaint by showing that there were 'special circumstances which rendered it not reasonably practicable' for it to perform the duty in question, and that it took all reasonable steps towards its performance as were reasonably practicable in the circumstances.[4] The case law in the context of redundancies, where a similar defence appears, is likely to be relevant here (see para **5.19**): this stresses the need for circumstances to be out of the ordinary and not foreseeable. It is possible that the defence will be applied more willingly in a transfer situation due to the speed with which a transfer can take place and because of the fact that, often, its occurrence is surrounded in secrecy.[5] Clearly allowing secrecy *per se* to operate as a defence could effectively nullify the duty, although it is possible that if an exchange of contracts and completion took place on the same day, and a tribunal were persuaded that the sale would not otherwise have occurred, these may be regarded as 'special circumstances', although the defence is still subject to the requirement to take such steps as were reasonably practicable. The 'special circumstances' defence does not appear in the EC Directive, and it would seem open to a complainant to argue that an employer should not be able to invoke it.[6] If a transferor wishes to defend a claim that it did not inform representatives of measures which the transferee envisaged taking because it was not supplied with the requisite information, it must give the transferee notice of that fact, whereupon the transferee becomes a party to the proceedings.[7] However the complainant has no right to seek the joinder of the transferee on his or her own initiative. At one time this presented the possibility that employees could be left at risk of awards payable by an insolvent transferor.[8] However in 1999 the EAT held in *Kerry Foods Ltd v Creber* that liability for a failure to consult passes automatically, on a transfer, to the transferee under regulation 5 of the transfer regulations.[9] This decision, however desirable from one perspective, is difficult to reconcile with the statutory regime, which clearly envisages claims being brought against either the transferor or transferee (although it could be argued that it is not left empty of purpose as it allows for claims where a proposed transfer does not proceed). Where the transfer is effected by direct sale, transferee employers will wish to safeguard their position by ensuring that appropriate indemnities and warranties are inserted in the contract of sale.

---

1. TUPE 1981, reg 11(1).

2. *Ibid.*

3. *Ibid.*, reg 11(8). See App 2 for the meaning of not 'reasonably practicable'. This does not prevent a complaint being presented before completion of the transfer: *BIFU v Barclays Bank Plc* [1987] ICR 495, EAT; *South Durham Health Authority v UNISON* [1995] IRLR 407, EAT.

4. *Ibid.*, reg 11(2).

5. Note, however, the statement of the Director General of the Takeover Panel, referred to in para **5.19**, that Stock Exchange rules do not preclude representatives being informed and consulted in advance where collective redundancies are planned in connection with a takeover. The DTI guidance in that context, which suggests that in these circumstances representatives can be made subject to confidentiality constraints for a specified period, and our comments thereon, are equally applicable here.

6. Council Directive 98/50/EC, which amends Council Directive 77/187/EEC, stipulates that the obligations of informing and consulting apply irrespective of whether the decision resulting in the transfer is taken by the employer or an undertaking controlling the employer, and the argument that a breach occurred because the information

was not provided by an undertaking controlling the employer shall not be accepted as an excuse: Article 6(4) as amended.

7. TUPE 1981, reg 11(3). An employment tribunal has held that this provision does not apply where the complaint is one of a failure to consult: *Unison v P.B. Kennedy and Donkin Ltd* and *Unicorn Consultancy Services Ltd*, Liverpool ET, Case No 2101746/99, 21 October 1999: ELA Briefing Vol 7 No 2, 14. However we do not think that reg 11(3) should be regarded as prejudicing the transferor's right to argue the defence of 'special circumstances' in relation to the duty to consult.

8. It has been argued that where a transferor fails to exercise the right to join the transferee, courts and tribunals may be persuaded to read into the regulation a right for the union (or employee representatives) to do so in order to ensure that employees are not deprived of compensation in these circumstances: see Hepple and Byre, 1989, 141, based upon *Von Colson and Kamann v Land Nordrhein-Westfalen* [1984] ECR 1891, ECJ and *Litster v Forth Dry Dock and Engineering Co Ltd* [1989] IRLR 161, HL.

9. [2000] IRLR 10, not following *Angus Jowett and Co Ltd v NUTGW* [1985] IRLR 326, EAT. The EAT considered that liability was apt to transfer under both reg 5(2)(a) or (b).

5.30 If an employment tribunal upholds a complaint, it must make a declaration to this effect and may also order the employer to pay 'appropriate compensation' to such descriptions of affected employees as are specified in the award.[1] 'Appropriate compensation' means such a sum not exceeding 13 weeks' pay for the employee in question 'as the tribunal considers just and equitable having regard to the seriousness of the failure of the employer to comply with . . . [its] duty'.[2] Where the transferee has been joined to proceedings, as described in para **5.29**, compensation may be awarded against the transferee,[3] although if the decision in *Kerry Foods Ltd v Creber*[4] that liability passes in any event to the transferee continues to stand, this may occur in practice only where the transfer does not proceed. Prior to the implementation of the 1999 amending regulations, compensation for breach of the duties in this context was limited to a maximum of four weeks' pay. It was strongly arguable that this did not meet the EU law requirement that a penalty should be 'effective, proportionate and dissuasive';[5] it could still be argued, albeit with less force, that the revised figure fails to meet these conditions. An employee who does not receive the compensation due to him or her under an award may complain to a tribunal, which will order the employer to pay the amount awarded.[6] The complaint must be presented within three months of the award being made by the tribunal except where the tribunal is satisfied that compliance with the three month period was not 'reasonably practicable', in which case it should be presented within a 'reasonable' period.[7]

1. TUPE 1981, reg 11(4)(a).
2. *Ibid.*, reg 11(11). There is little guidance in the case law on the appropriate amount to be awarded; see the discussion in para **5.20** relating to compensation for non-compliance with the obligation to consult on redundancies. Although the rate of remuneration is required to be calculated in accordance with Chapter II of Part XIV of the Employment Rights Act 1996 (reg 11(12)), the statutory maximum of a week's pay does not appear to be applicable in this context. Cf. TULRCA 1992, s 70C(5B), and note also that there is no reference to such awards in the Employment Rights (Increase of Limits) Order 1999, SI 1999/3375. The calculation date is the date of the transfer, unless the employee has been dismissed, in which case it is the calculation date for the purposes of entitlement to a redundancy payment, if the employee has been dismissed for redundancy (or the date which would be the calculation date if the employee was so entitled), or the effective date of termination of his or her contract of employment: reg 11(2).
3. *Ibid.*, reg 11(4)(b).
4. [2000] IRLR 10.
5. Case C–14/83 *Von Colson v Land Nordrhein-Westfalen* [1984] ECR 1891, ECJ; Case C–68/88 *EC Commission v Greece* [1989] ECR 2965; Case C–7/90 *Belgium v Vandevenne* [1991] ECR I–4371.
6. TUPE 1981, reg 11(5), (6).
7. *Ibid.*, reg 11(8). See App 2 for the meaning of not 'reasonably practicable'.

HEALTH AND SAFETY

Sources and General Principles

5.31 There are two sets of regulations of general application which govern consultation of employee representatives in the area of health and safety. The Safety Representatives and Safety Committees Regulations 1977, made under the Health and Safety at Work etc. Act 1974, apply where the employer recognises an independent trade union.[1] These Regulations have been amended on a number of occasions, including in 1992[2] to comply with the requirements of EC Directive 89/391 on the introduction of measures to encourage improvements in the health and safety of workers. The Health and Safety Commission has issued Codes of Practice which respectively amplify the duties of safety representatives and time off for their training.[3] The Health and Safety (Consultation with Employees) Regulations 1996[4] were made under the European Communities Act 1972 in response to concern that the UK was in breach of the 1989 Directive because provision for consultation under the 1977 Regulations rested upon the will of the employer.[5] These give employers the choice of consulting employees directly or of consulting elected 'representatives of employee safety'. Both the 1977 and the 1996 Regulations are enforced by health and safety inspectors. Some industries are also governed by specific regulations which impose rights and obligations which exceed those of the general law.[6]

---

1. SI 1977/500, amended by SI 1992/2051; SI 1996/1513; SI 1997/1840; SI 1999/860. See paras **2.6** and **2.7** for the definition of an 'independent trade union' and para **4.3** for the definition of recognition.

2. The Management of Health and Safety at Work Regulations 1992, SI 1992/2051. These Regulations have now been revoked and replaced by the Management of Health and Safety at Work Regulations 1999, SI 1999/3242, but the amendments made by the 1992 Regulations to the 1977 Regulations remain in force subject to a minor amendment made by the 1999 Regulations: SI 1999/3242, reg 29, Schedule 2.

3. Safety Representatives and Safety Committees (1978) and Time Off for the Training of Safety Representatives (1978). A failure to observe a provision of a Code of Practice does not of itself render the individual liable to any civil or criminal proceedings, but where in any criminal proceedings a party is alleged to have committed an offence by reason of a contravention of any requirement or prohibition imposed by or under the HSWA 1974 or health and safety regulations, a provision of the code appearing to the court to be relevant to the requirement or prohibition alleged to have been contravened is admissible in evidence: HSWA 1974, s 17. See s 16(2) for the effect of a failure to observe the code on the proceedings.

4. SI 1996/1513.

5. See Case C–382/92 *EC Commission v United Kingdom* [1994] IRLR 392 (transfers) and Case C–383/92 [1994] IRLR 412 (collective redundancies).

6. The Mines and Quarries Act 1954, s 123; the Construction (Design and Management) Regulations 1994, SI 1994/3140, amended by SI 1996/1592; the Railway (Safety Case) Regulations 1994, SI 1994/237, amended by SI 1996/1592; the Offshore Installations (Safety Representatives and Safety Committees) Regulations 1989, SI 1989/971, amended by SI 1992/2885; SI 1993/1823; SI 1995/738; SI 1995/743; and SI 1995/3163; and the Quarries Regulations 1999, SI 1999/2024.

5.32 The Safety Representatives and Safety Committees Regulations 1977 enable independent trade unions to appoint safety representatives from among the employees of any employer by whom they are recognised.[1] Representatives may, but need not, be union officials; if reasonably practicable they should either have been employed by the employer for at least two years or have had two years' experience in similar employment.[2] The detailed functions of safety representatives are beyond the scope of this work.[3] In broad terms, they include investigating potential hazards and employees' complaints, and conducting regular inspections of the workplace.[4] Employers have a general obligation to consult them on arrangements for co-operating with employees in promoting and developing health and safety matters and in checking their effectiveness,[5] and to provide them with such facilities and assistance as they reasonably require,[6] and with the information and documents they require (with specified exceptions), to carry out their functions.[7] In addition employers have a specific obligation to consult safety representatives 'in good time' on certain matters: the introduction of any measure at the workplace which may substantially affect the health and safety of the employees whom they represent; the arrangements for appointing or nominating individuals with specified health and functions under the regulations; the provision of information to employees; the planning and organisation of training in health and safety; and the consequences of introducing new technologies.[8] Safety representatives are entitled to be given such paid time off during working hours as is necessary to perform their functions and to undergo reasonable training, with a right to complain to an employment tribunal if time off or payment is refused.[9] The Health and Safety Commission Code of Practice on Time Off for the Training of Safety Representatives states that such training should be approved by the TUC or the union(s) which appointed the safety representative;[10] unlike 'representatives of employee safety' they have no right to training at the employer's expense (see para **5.33** below), although the preface to the Code suggests that employers should provide training on hazards and arrangements specific to the workplace. If at least two safety representatives so request in writing, the employer must establish a 'safety committee' within two months of the request with the function of 'keeping under review the measures taken to ensure the health and safety at work of [the] employees and such other functions as may be prescribed'.[11] The structure of the safety committee is a matter for management and union(s) to decide. The employer must post a notice informing employees of its composition and the workplaces covered by it.[12] It is automatically unfair for an employer to dismiss an employee (or select an employee for dismissal in a 'redundancy case') in connection with being a safety representative or member of a safety committee, and such employees have the right not to be 'subjected to 'any detriment by any act, or any deliberate failure to act, by the employer'.[13]

---

1 SI 1977/500, reg 3(1); see also the Code of Practice issued by the Health and Safety Commission on Safety Representatives and Safety Committees (1978) See paras **2.6** and **2.7** for the definition of an 'independent trade union' and para **4.3** for the definition of recognition. The Police (Health and Safety) Regulations 1999, SI 1999/860 require police organisations, such as the Police Federation of England and Wales, to be treated as recognised trade unions in this context: SI 1997/500, reg 2A, Schedule 1. In *Costain Building and Civil Engineering Ltd v Smith* [2000] ICR 215, EAT

the appointment of a safety representative was ineffective because at the time of the purported appointment he was not an employee.

2. SI 1977/500, reg 3(4).

3. See further Redgrave, Hendy and Ford, 1998.

4. SI 1977/500, regs 4–6.

5. Health and Safety at Work etc Act 1974, s 2(6).

6. SI 1977/500, reg 4A(2).

7. *Ibid.*, reg 7.

8. *Ibid.*, reg 4A.

9. *Ibid.*, reg 4(2), 11 and Schedule 2. See also the Code of Practice issued by the Health and Safety Commission on Time Off for the Training of Safety Representatives (1978).

10. Para 3.

11. Health and Safety at Work etc Act 1974, s 2(7); SI 1977/500, reg 9.

12. SI 1977/500, reg 9(2)(b).

13. ERA 1996, ss 100, 105, 44. There is no qualifying period of employment applicable to such claims, nor is there an upper age limit: ss 108, 109. Note that there is no statutory limit to the compensatory award if an employee is unfairly dismissed for health and safety reasons: ERA 1996, s 124(1A). See para **3.10** for analysis of the scope of subjection to a detriment. In *Shillito v Van Leer (UK) Ltd* [1997] IRLR 495, the EAT stated, obiter, that it was no defence to a complaint under s 44 that the safety representative intended to embarass the employer in front of external safety authorities or that he performed these duties in an unreasonable way, unacceptable to the employer (see also *Bass Taverns Ltd v Burgess* [1995] IRLR 596, discussed at para **3.6**). In *Shillito* the complaint was dismissed because it was found that the representative's purpose was not to pursue a genuine health and safety matter but to pursue a personal agenda to embarrass the company. In a redundancy selection case, the EAT has emphasised that the way in which employees carry out their health and safety duties should not count either in their favour or against them: *Smith Industries Aerospace and Defence Systems v Rawlings* [1996] IRLR 656, EAT; on selection for redundancy, see further para **3.4**.

5.33 The Health and Safety (Consultation with Employees) Regulations 1996 apply only where groups of employees are not covered by union safety representatives appointed under the 1977 Regulations.[1] They permit employers to choose between consulting employees directly or, in respect of any group of employees, to consult one or more persons in that group, referred to as 'representatives of employee safety', who were elected by employees in the group at the time of the election, to represent them for the purposes of such consultation.[2] No procedures are stipulated for the conduct of such elections, in marked contrast to the provisions which now govern the election of 'employee representatives' in the context of collective redundancies and transfers of the undertaking. Employees or their representatives must be consulted 'in good time' about matters relating to their health and safety at work, and in particular about the specified matters listed in para **5.32** above.[3] Employers have a duty to ensure that representatives of employee safety receive reasonable training for the performance of their statutory functions (at the employer's expense), and representatives have a right to paid time off during working hours for such training and to perform their functions.[4] A representative may complain to an employment tribunal if time off, or payment for that time, is not granted (but not if there is a refusal or failure to prove training).[5] Employers are required to provide representatives of employee safety with such facilities as they may reasonably require, and such information as is necessary to enable them to participate fully and effectively in consultations on the matters specified in the legislation and to carry out their functions of making representations on various health and safety matters.[6] However their functions are less extensive than those of safety representatives; they do not, for example, have the right to conduct workplace inspections or the investigation of employee complaints, nor are they entitled to require the establishment of safety committees. It is automatically unfair for an employer to dismiss an employee (or select an employee for redundancy in a 'redundancy case') for taking part or proposing to take part in consultations under the Regulations or in the election of representatives of employee safety, and such employees have the right not to be 'subjected to 'any detriment by any act, or any deliberate failure to act, by the employer'.[7]

---

1. SI 1996/1513, reg 3.

2. *Ibid.*, reg 4. Council Directive 89/391, which the Regulations are designed to implement, requires provides that '[e]mployers shall consult workers and/or their representatives and allow them to take part in discussions on all questions relating to safety and health at work. This presupposes the consultation of workers, the right of workers and/or their representatives to make proposals, [and] balanced participation in accordance with national laws and/or practices'. The meaning of 'balanced participation' is unclear; see Nielsen and Szyszczak, 1997, 308; Neal, 1990, 97–98. Weiss, 1996, 219, suggests that given that it is to be something other than the consultation mentioned in the same paragraph 'it can only be interpreted as providing a stronger degree of influence'.

3. SI 1996/1513, reg 3.

4. *Ibid.*, reg 7, Sched 1. Candidates for election also have a right to reasonable paid time off.

5. *Ibid.*, reg 7, Sched 2.

6. *Ibid.*, regs 7(4), 5 and 6.

7. ERA 1996, s 100(ba),105 and 44 (ba); see further para **5.32** note 13. See para **3.10** for analysis of the scope of subjection to a detriment.

5.34 Identical procedures apply to the enforcement of the 1977 and the 1996 Regulations. Health and safety inspectors are statutorily empowered to issue an 'improvement notice' which requires any person contravening the legislation to remedy the breach within a specified period; non-compliance with the regulations also constitutes a criminal offence.[1] However from the outset the Health and Safety Commission resolved to try and avoid inspector involvement in industrial relations issues and stressed that enforcement action should not be considered unless inspectors were satisfied that all voluntary means of resolving a dispute, including resort to ACAS, had been exhausted.[2] Even in that eventuality the Commission suggested that the issuing of an improvement notice, rather than prosecution, would normally be the most appropriate first step. This reflects the emphasis of the Health and Safety Commission Code of Practice on Safety Representatives and Safety Committees which urges the employer, unions and safety representatives to make 'full and proper use of the existing agreed industrial relations machinery to reach the degree of agreement necessary to achieve the purpose of the Regulations and in order to resolve any differences'.[3] At the time of writing the Health and Safety Commission has recently consulted on a range of issues relating to employee consultation and involvement in health and safety, including how greater publicity can be given to the statutory obligations and the possibility of greater use of enforcement action by inspectors.[4]

---

1. Health and Safety at Work etc Act 1974, ss 21 and 33(3); SI 1996/1513, reg 10.
2. HSC guidance issued October 1978.
3. Safety Representatives and Safety Committees (1978), para 3.
4. *Employee Consultation and Involvement in Health and Safety*, Health and Safety Commission Discussion Document, 2000, para 64. For discussion of possible reforms in this area see James, 1992; for discussion of the wider issues raised by the Regulations see James and Walters, 1997 and Gunningham and Johnstone, 1999; for useful background, see Beck and Woolfson, 2000.

OCCUPATIONAL PENSIONS

5.35 The law of occupational pensions lies outside the scope of this work, but we indicate briefly the obligation in this area to consult trade unions. If an employer wishes its employees to be contracted out of the state earnings-related pension scheme, it must consult any independent trade union it recognises in respect of the earners concerned.[1] In order to apply for a contracting-out certificate, the employer must give written notice to the Commissioners of Inland Revenue. In practice, the Contributions Agency in Newcastle-upon-Tyne deals with such matters. The notice must contain specified information, including a statement that the Commissioners of Inland Revenue have power to refuse to give effect to the election to contract out if they are not satisfied that the employer has undertaken consultations about the matters covered by the notice with all independent trade unions recognised in relation to the relevant earners. There is no definition of 'consultation' in this context.[2] Any question whether an organisation is an independent trade union recognised in relation to earners may be referred to an employment tribunal by the employer or by the organisation itself, as may any question whether the employer has complied with the consultation requirements.[3] Where an employer has established a contracted-out scheme, unions also have the right to receive on request specified information relating to the scheme so far as it relates to the earners concerned, including basic information about membership, contributions and benefits; the constitution of the scheme; and audited accounts and an actuarial statement.[4] Unlike the provisions relating to redundancies, transfers and health and safety, there is no provision for consultation of any other employees' representatives if no recognised trade union exists.

---

1. The Occupational Pension Schemes (Contracting Out) Regulations 1996, SI 1996/1172, reg 4, as amended by the Social Security Contributions (Transfer of Functions) Act 1999. Curiously, the regulations define an 'independent trade union' as 'an independent trade union recognised to any extent for collective bargaining': reg 1(2) See paras **2.6** and **2.7** for the definition of an independent trade union, and para **4.3** for the definition of recognition in other contexts. Similar consultation takes place on variation or surrender of a contracting-out certificate.

2. In an oft-quoted dictum in *R v British Coal Corporation and the Secretary of State for Trade and Industry, ex parte* Price [1994] IRLR 72, Glildewell LJ (at 75) suggested that consultation involved 'giving the body consulted a fair and proper opportunity to understand fully the matters about which it is being consulted, and to express its views on those subjects, with the consultor thereafter considering those views properly and genuinely'.

3. *Ibid*, reg 4(2). Note. however, TULRCA 1992, s 8(4) which requires the tribunal to stay proceedings until the Certification Officer has reached a decision on the matter. The tribunal itself may make a reference to the Certification Officer: s 8(5).

4. See generally the Occupational Pension Schemes (Disclosure of Information) Regulations SI 1996/1655, as amended by SI 1997/786; SI 1997/819; SI 1997/3038; and SI 1999/3198.

TRAINING

5.36 An employer must consult an independent trade union about training matters where two conditions are satisfied.[1] First, the union must be recognised in accordance with the statutory recognition procedure as entitled to conduct collective bargaining on behalf of a bargaining unit.[2] Secondly, a method for the conduct of collective bargaining must have been specified by the CAC, and neither its legal effect nor its content subject to variation by the parties.[3] The employer must then 'from time to time' invite the union to send representatives to a meeting for the purpose of consulting about the employer's policy on training for workers within the bargaining unit; consulting about its plans for training for those workers during the six months starting with the day of the meeting; and reporting about training provided for those workers since the previous meeting.[4] The first meeting must take place within six months of the obligation applying in relation to a bargaining unit; each subsequent meeting must take place within six months of the last.[5] The employer must provide to the union any information without which its representatives would be to a material extent impeded in participating in the meeting, and which it would be in accordance with good industrial relations practice to disclose, prior to the period of two weeks ending with the date of a meeting.[6] This obligation echoes that imposed in relation to the disclosure of information for collective bargaining purposes discussed in Chapter 4, and the same restrictions on the general duty to disclose are applicable.[7] These are analysed in detail in para **4.65** *et seq.* Unlike in that context there is no Code of Practice to give guidance on what it is good industrial relations practice to disclose, although as we indicated in para **4.65**, that Code has been of limited use. The employer is required to 'take account of any written representations about matters raised at a meeting which . . . [it] receives from the trade union' within four weeks starting with the date of the meeting.[8] It is unclear what this duty entails. On one view, an employer would satisfy the obligation merely by taking such representations into account in its own mental deliberations on training. However we would suggest that the more appropriate course would be for employers to write to the union indicating their response to the representations which have been made. If an employer fails to comply with its statutory obligations a union may complain to an employment tribunal which, if it finds the complaint to be well founded, must make a declaration to that effect and may make an award of compensation, not exceeding two weeks' pay, to each person who was, at the time of the failure, a member of the bargaining unit.[9] Any proceedings for enforcement of the award of compensation must be brought by the individual and not by his or her trade union.[10] The provision for recourse to an employment tribunal rather than the CAC, which adjudicates upon failure to disclose information for the purposes of collective bargaining, means that divergent lines of practice may develop in relation to the restrictions on the obligation to disclose. However if the Government's aspiration that the CAC will rarely impose a method of collective bargaining is fulfilled, this may be more of theoretical than practical concern.

---

1. See paras **2.6** and **2.7** for the definition of 'independent trade union'. The requirement for the union to be independent is not explicitly stated, but follows from the condition that it has been recognised pursuant to the statutory procedure.

2. TULRCA 1992, s 70B(1)(a), inserted by ERA 1999, s 5. See paras **4.5** *et seq.*

3. *Ibid.*, s 70B(1)(b); see further para **4.29**.

4. *Ibid.*, s 70B(2). There is no definition in this context of the term 'representative' (cf TULRCA 1992, s 181(1)). A government spokesman stated that unions could send their full-time officials, or other experts or consultants, to attend as their representatives: Mr. Michael Wills, Minister for Small Firms, Trade and Industry, Official Report of Standing Committee E, 18 March 1999, 4.45 pm. There is no specific requirement for an employer to grant its employees time off for this purpose. However, it would almost certainly constitute an activity of the union; whether it would fall within the provisions for paid time off is much less certain: see paras **3.26** *et seq.*

5. *Ibid.*, s 70B(3).

6. *Ibid.*, s 70B(4).

7. *Ibid.*, s 70B(5).

8. *Ibid.*, s 70B(6)

9. *Ibid.*, s 70C. Such a complaint must be presented within three months of the alleged failure, except where the tribunal is satisfied that compliance with the three month period was not 'reasonably practicable', in which case complaints must be presented within a 'reasonable' period: s 70C(2). See App 2 on the meaning of not 'reasonably practicable'. A week's pay is calculated according to Chapter II of Part XIV of ERA 1996 (taking the date of the employer's failure as the calculation date), and is subject to the statutory maximum of a week's pay, which at the time of writing stands at £230: s 70C(5).

10. *Ibid.*, s 70C(6).

EUROPEAN WORKS COUNCILS

Sources and General Principles

5.37 The central management of a 'Community-scale undertaking' or 'Community-scale group of undertakings' which is situated in the UK (or treated as such) is required to initiate negotiations to establish a European Works Council (EWC) or information and consultation procedure (ICP) at the request of a specified number of 'employees' (not workers), or their 'employees' representatives', drawn from at least two Member States.[1] The central management may also initiate negotiations in the absence of any such request. An employee or employees' representative can request information from the management of an establishment or undertaking in the UK (even if it is not the central management) to determine whether an establishment or undertaking is covered by the obligation to initiate negotiations, with provision for complaint to the CAC in the event of a failure to comply.[2] A UK-situated central management may also ask the CAC to determine whether the criteria which oblige it to initiate negotiations are met.[3] The scope, composition, functions, and term of office of a EWC or the arrangements for implementing an ICP, are determined by a 'special negotiating body' (SNB) in conjunction with central management.[4] The composition of the SNB is tightly specified, and its UK members must be elected by a ballot of UK employees, supervised by an 'independent ballot supervisor', except where there is an elected 'consultative committee' representing all the UK employees which may nominate SNB members from among its number.[5] The SNB and central management may decide to establish either an ICP or a EWC.[6] It is also open to the SNB to decide, by a two-thirds majority, not to open negotiations or to terminate negotiations.[7] Assuming this does not occur, but the parties have failed to reach agreement on information and consultation arrangements within three years of the date of the initial request to initiate negotiations, or management has refused to commence negotiations within six months of a valid request, an EWC established according to a statutory model comes into being.[8] A failure by a UK central management to establish a EWC or ICP in accordance with the parties' agreement or the statutory model, as applicable, is punishable on complaint to the EAT by a maximum penalty of £75,000.[9] Information or documents may be disclosed by central management to members of an SNB or EWC, or to information and consultation representatives, in confidence, although the necessity for confidentiality can be challenged (where central management is in the UK) by the recipient before the CAC.[10] Management may also refuse to disclose information or documents which would seriously harm the functioning of, or be prejudicial to, the undertaking or group of undertakings, with provision for the CAC to determine if it falls within this category.[11] Members of an SNB or EWC, and information or consultation representatives, have the right to reasonable paid time off from work to perform their functions; they and other employees are also protected against dismissal or subjection to other forms of detriment for specified activities relating to the establishment and operation of the relevant bodies or procedures. These rights are enforced by complaining to an employment tribunal.[12] The relevant provisions are laid down in the Transnational Information and Consultation of Employees Regulations 1999,[13] which came into force on 15 January 2000. The Regulations, which were made under s 2(2) of the European Communities Act 1972, are designed to implement the European Works Councils Directive (styled in the Regulations as the Transnational Information and Consultation

Directive).[14] This Directive was adopted in September 1994 under the Agreement on Social Policy (the 'Social Chapter' of the Maastricht Treaty), with a deadline for implementation of 22 September 1996. It did not initially apply to the UK, which had 'opted out' of the Agreement on Social Policy. This meant that employees of UK undertakings were not counted for the purpose of determining whether an undertaking constituted a 'Community-scale undertaking' or group of undertakings,[15] and there was no requirement to include UK representatives in EWCs or ICPs established in other Member States (although in the vast majority of cases they were included).[16] The Directive was extended to cover the three other Member States of the European Economic Area (Norway, Liechtenstein and Iceland) in June 1995. Following the election of a Labour Government in 1997 and the UK's 'opt-in' to the Social Chapter, a Directive extending the European Works Council Directive to include the UK (the 'Extension Directive') was agreed, with an implementation deadline of 15 December 1999.[17] This meant that UK employees were required to be included in existing EWCs and ICPs, as well as subjecting an estimated 200 additional undertakings to the Directive's requirements.[18] The obligations imposed by the Regulations do not apply in two situations (reflecting the exceptions permitted by the respective Directives). The first is where undertakings have in place an 'Article 13' agreement providing for the transnational information and consultation of employees which covers the entire workforce and which was in force immediately before 23 September 1996 or the day after the date when the national law of the Member State (other than the UK) giving effect to the Directive came into force.[19] The second is where undertakings which became subject to the obligation to initiate negotiations for a EWC or ICP solely as a result of the Extension Directive have in place an 'Article 3' agreement which was in force immediately before 16 December 1999 and which, again, provides for the transnational information and consultation of employees and covers the entire workforce.[20] The application of the Regulations is modified where the central management is in the UK but at the time the Regulations came into force a EWC or ICP had been established under the law or practice of another Member State.[21]

---

1. TICER 1999, reg 9.
2. *Ibid.*, regs 7 and 8.
3. *Ibid.* reg 10.
4. *Ibid.*, regs 16 and 17.
5. *Ibid.*, regs 11–15.
6. *Ibid.*, reg 17.
7. *Ibid.*, reg 16.
8. *Ibid.*, reg 18; Schedule.
9. *Ibid.*, regs 20–22.
10. *Ibid.*, reg 23.

11. *Ibid.*, reg 24.

12. *Ibid.*, regs 25–33.

13. SI 1999 No 3323.

14. Council Directive 94/45/EC of 22 September 1994. On the background to the Directive see Gold and Hall, 1994, Barnard, 1996, 422 *et seq.*, and Bellace, 1997; for a comparative overview of the implementation of the Directive including TICER 1999, see Carley and Hall, 2000.

15. However some 120 UK-based undertakings were subject to the Directive because their non-UK employees took them over the threshold: *Implementation in the UK of the European Works Council Directive*, URN 99/926, DTI, 1999, para 7.

16. *Implementation of the Regulations on European Works Councils—Regulatory Impact Assessment*, DTI, 1999, para 42.

17. Council Directive 97/74/EC of 15 December 1997.

18. *Implementation in the UK of the European Works Council Directive*, URN 99/926, DTI, 1999, para 8.

19. TICER 1999, reg 45. See further Marginson *et al*, 1998; see also Marginson, 2000.

20. *Ibid.*, reg 44.

21. *Ibid.*, regs 42–43.

Bodies Concerned with the Enforcement of the Regulations

5.38 As we indicate in para **5.37** above, enforcement of the Regulations is entrusted, variously to the EAT, the CAC and employment tribunals. The procedure of the EAT in this area, as in others, is governed by the Employment Tribunals Act 1996. The normal rules on costs apply in this context. The composition of the CAC is described in para **4.7**. The Regulations specifically provide that where a complaint or application is made to the CAC it must be in writing and in such form as the CAC requires.[2] In considering a complaint or application the CAC must make such enquiries as it sees fit and give any person whom it considers has a proper interest in the application or complaint an opportunity to be heard.[3] A declaration or order made by the CAC following a complaint or application must be in writing and state the reasons for its findings.[4] It may be relied upon as if it were a declaration or order made by the High Court in England and Wales, and an order may be enforced in the same way as a High Court order.[5] Thus breach of an order will constitute contempt of court.[6] Unusually, an appeal lies to the EAT on any question of law arising from any declaration or order of, or arising in any proceedings before, the CAC under the Regulations.[7] If either the CAC or EAT, on receipt of an application or complaint, considers that it is reasonably likely to be settled by conciliation it must refer the matter to ACAS.[8] If the application or complaint is not settled or withdrawn and ACAS considers that further attempts at conciliation are unlikely to result in a settlement, the matter is referred back to the CAC or EAT, as the case may be, for hearing and determination.[9] Rights to time off, and protection against detriment and dismissal are enforced in the employment tribunals, which operate in this area in accordance with their usual procedures (see para **5.58** *et seq.*).

---

1. TICER 1999 reg 35 amends the ETA 1996 to bring the Regulations within its scope. Note reg 34, which deals with the geographical location of proceedings.
2. *Ibid.*, reg 38(1).
3. *Ibid.*, reg 38(2).
4. *Ibid.*, reg 38(7).
5. *Ibid.*, reg 38(3). This is the case where the central management is situated in England and Wales, separate provision is made for Scotland. See *ibid.*, reg 5, discussed in para **5.41**, for the rules determining when the central management is treated as situated in the UK. See also regs 38(5) and(6).
6. See further para **6.61** *et seq.* for the penalties for contempt of court.
7. *Ibid.*, reg. 38(8). Usually the only remedy is judicial review.
8. *Ibid.*, reg 39(1). If a settlement is made under the auspices of a conciliation officer and recorded in the appropriate form it may not proceed to a hearing: reg 41(1); ETA 1996, s 18. There is also provision for complaints to be settled by compromise agreements: reg 41(2)–(8).
9. *Ibid.*, reg 39(2), (3).

The Meaning of 'Employees' Representatives'

5.39 An 'employees' representative', a term exclusive to the Regulations, is empowered to make a request to initiate negotiations for the establishment of a EWC or ICP and to request information from the management of an establishment or undertaking in the UK about the number of employees employed in the undertaking or group of undertakings.[1] Employees' representatives may also, if they represent all UK employees, choose the UK representatives for a EWC established on the basis of the statutory (default) model.[2] There are two distinct groups of 'employees' representatives' for the purposes of the Regulations. First, if the employees are of a description in respect of which an independent trade union is recognised by their employer for the purpose of collective bargaining, 'employees' representatives' are the representatives of the union who normally take part as negotiators in the collective bargaining process.[3] In multi-union environments representatives of more than one union may fall within this category. Secondly, the term covers 'any other representatives elected or appointed by employees to positions in which they are expected to receive, on behalf of the employees, information (i) which is relevant to the terms and conditions of employment of the employees, or (ii) about the activities of the undertaking which may significantly affect the interests of the employees'. However it expressly excludes representatives who are expected to receive information relevant only to a specific aspect of the terms and conditions or interests of the employees, such as health and safety or collective redundancies.[4] Unlike in the context of health and safety, redundancies, and transfers of the undertaking, a trade union, where recognised, is not the exclusive channel; even where there is such a union, other employee representatives may also act.

---

1. TICER 1999, regs 7 and 9.
2. *Ibid.*, Schedule, para 3.
3. *Ibid.*, reg 2. 'Independent trade union' has the same meaning as in TULRCA 1992; see paras **2.6** and **2.7**. There is no definition of 'recognition' or 'collective bargaining' in this context; cf TULRCA 1992, s 178 (see para **4.3**). The Regulations state that in the absence of a definition contained within them, words and expressions used in particular regulations and paragraphs of the Schedule which are used also in the Directive or the Extension Directive to which they are designed to give effect have the same meaning as they have in those provisions: TICER 1999, reg 2(5). The terms 'recognition' and 'collective bargaining' do not appear in the Directive; 'employees' representatives' are those representatives provided for by national law and/or practice: Council Directive 94/45 of 22 September 1994, Article 2(d). In practice, pan-European federations of unions may make a request. Strictly speaking, these are outside the terms of the Regulations, but if there is an independent trade union recognised in this country there may be no point in the employer challenging this as the request could be re-presented by that union.
4. *Ibid.*, reg 2. Note that, unlike a trade union, 'employees' representatives' are defined in terms of their relationships with 'employees' (see reg 2(1)) and not 'workers'.

The Application of the Regulations

Community-scale undertakings or Community-scale group of undertakings

5.40 Only Community-scale undertakings or Community-scale groups of undertakings are required to make provision for a EWC or ICP. There is no definition of an 'undertaking' in either the Regulations or the Directive. However jurisprudence of the European Court of Justice relating to Article 81 EC, which prohibits anti-competitive behaviour, has made clear that the term covers any natural or legal person carrying on activities of an economic or commercial nature,[1] including for example limited companies, partnerships, trade associations, sole traders, and state corporations.[2] The fact that the body is engaged in non-profit-making activities does not, of itself, suffice to deprive its activities of their economic character.[3] In the context of the Acquired Rights Directive it has been held by the Court to be irrelevant that an undertaking does not receive remuneration for its services,[4] a position confirmed in the amending Directive, which states that it applies to 'public and private undertakings engaged in economic activities whether or not they are operating for gain'.[5] This approach means that charities and public sector bodies also constitute 'undertakings' where they are carrying out an economic activity. A 'Community-scale undertaking' is defined as an undertaking with at least 1,000 employees within the Member States and at least 150 employees in each of at least two Member States.[6] A 'Community-scale group of undertakings' means a group of undertakings which has at least 1,000 employees within the Member States; at least two group undertakings in different Member States; and at least one group undertaking with at least 150 employees in one Member State and at least one other group undertaking with at least 150 employees in another Member State.[7] A 'group of undertakings' means a controlling undertaking and its controlled undertakings; a 'group undertaking' an undertaking which is part of a Community-scale group of undertakings.[8] A 'controlling undertaking' is an undertaking which can exercise a dominant influence over another undertaking by virtue, for example, of ownership, financial participation, or the rules which govern it.[9] A 'controlled undertaking' means an undertaking over which such a dominant influence can be exercised.[10] The ability of an undertaking to exercise a dominant influence over another undertaking is presumed, unless the contrary is proved, when in relation to another undertaking it directly or indirectly can appoint more than half of the members of that undertaking's administrative, management or supervisory body; controls a majority of the votes attached to that undertaking's issued share capital; or holds a majority of that undertaking's subscribed capital.[11] However a dominant influence is not presumed solely by virtue of the fact that an office holder is exercising functions, according to the law of a Member State, relating to liquidation, winding-up, insolvency, cessation of payments, composition of creditors or analogous proceedings.[12] Where the law governing an undertaking is that of a Member State, the law applicable to determine whether an undertaking is a controlling undertaking is that of the Member State.[13] Where the law governing an undertaking is not that of a Member State, the law applicable is that of the Member State within whose territory the representative of the undertaking is situated or, in the absence of such a representative, the Member State within whose territory the management of the group undertaking which employs the greatest number of employees is situated.[14] No provision is made in the Regulations (or the Directive) for the situation where two or more undertakings are equal partners in a joint venture such that none exercises a 'dominant influence'. It is possible that the joint venture may constitute a Community-scale undertaking in its own right, depending on its legal form, but there will be no 'controlling' or 'controlled' undertaking if dominant influence cannot be shown. Franchises under franchise agreements will normally fall within the definition of 'controlled undertakings' given that there will normally be an undertaking with a dominant influence.

---

1. Case 170/83 *Hydrotherm Geratebau GmbH v Compact del Dott. Ing. Mario Andreoli and C. sas* [1984] ECR 2999, paras 10–12.

2. Barnard, 1996, 356–357.

3. Case C–382/92 *Commission v UK* [1994] IRLR 392 at 411.

4. Case C–29/91 *Dr Sophie Redmond Stichting v Bartol* [1992] IRLR 366.

5. Council Directive 98/50 EC of 29 June 1998, amending Council Directive 77/187/EEC of 14 February 1977, Article 1(c).

6. TICER 1999, reg 2(1).

7. *Ibid.*

8. *Ibid.*

9. *Ibid.*, reg. 3(1).

10. *Ibid.* The provisions for determining whether a dominant influence can be exercised are in material respects identical to Article 3 of Council Directive 94/45.

11. *Ibid.*, reg 3(2). This is subject to reg 3(4), which provides that an undertaking is not to be regarded as a controlling undertaking where the first undertaking is a company referred to in Article 3(5)(a) or (c) of Council Regulation 4064/89 of 21 December 1989 on the control of concentrations between undertakings. In applying the criteria listed in reg 3(2), a controlling undertaking's rights as regards voting and appointment include the rights of its other controlled undertakings, and the rights of any person or body acting in his, her or its own name but on behalf of the controlling undertaking or of any other of the controlling undertaking's controlled undertakings: reg 3(3). If two or more undertakings meet one or more of the criteria in relation to another undertaking, the criteria are to be applied in the order listed in relation to each undertaking and that which meets the criterion that is highest in the order listed is presumed, unless the contrary is proved, to exercise a dominant influence over the undertaking in question: reg 3(8); cf. Article 3(7), which refers only to the first criterion.

12. *Ibid.*, reg 3(5).

13. *Ibid.*, reg 3(6).

14. *Ibid.*, reg 3(7).

The location of central management

5.41 The responsibility for creating the conditions and means necessary for setting up a EWC or ICP rests on 'central management' (defined as the central management of a Community-scale undertaking or, in the case of a Community-scale group of undertakings, the central management of the controlling undertaking), where the central management initiates, or is required to initiate, negotiations for a EWC or ICP.[1] Responsibility under the Regulations for this, and other duties, applies only where central management is situated in the UK or is treated as being situated in the UK.[2] However some provisions of the Regulations, such as the obligation to arrange a ballot to elect members of the SNB, apply regardless of the location of the central management; we indicate where this is the case at appropriate points in the text.[3] The central management is treated as situated in the UK (and thereby as 'the central management' for the purposes of the Regulations) in two situations.[4] The first is where the central management is not situated in any Member State (for example, it is in Japan) but the 'representative agent' of the central management (to be designated if necessary) is situated in the UK. The term 'representative agent' is not defined in either the Regulations or the Directive. There is no obligation upon an undertaking to designate a 'representative agent', but it may wish to do so if it has a preference about the Member State whose laws govern its conduct in this area. However, it should be noted that the designation of a representative agent may have wider implications including, for example, residence for tax purposes. The second situation is where neither the central management nor a representative agent is situated in a Member State, and

(a) in the case of a Community-scale undertaking there are employed in an establishment, which is situated in the UK, more employees than are employed in any other establishment which is situated in a Member State, or

(b) in the case of a Community-scale group of undertakings, there are employed in a group undertaking, which is situated in the UK, more employees than are employed in any other group undertaking which is situated in a Member State.

It is notable that in the case of (a) above, the crucial issue is not the total number of employees employed in the UK but the total number employed *in an establishment* situated in the UK. Thus, if a Japanese group of companies owns fifty establishments in the UK, each employing 100 employees, and a single establishment in France employing 300, the central management will not, according to this provision, be treated as situated in the UK. In this respect the Regulations reflect the language of Article 4(2) of the Directive. There is no definition of 'establishment' in either the Directive or the Regulations; in the context of redundancy consultation, where the concept is also used, domestic courts have taken a fairly wide view of the term, whereas the ECJ has interpreted it as designating, depending on the circumstances, 'the unit to which the workers made redundant are assigned to carry out their duties',[5] a much narrower interpretation (see further para **5.6**). It remains to be seen how the term will be interpreted in this context. There may be a further difficulty in determining the number of employees employed at an establishment where employees are contractually bound to work in more than one Member State.

1. TICER 1999, reg 5. See reg 2 for the definition of 'central management' and para **5.40** above for the definition of controlling undertaking.
2. *Ibid.*, regs 4,5(1).
3. These are listed in *ibid.*, reg 4(2).
4. *Ibid.*, reg 5(1),(2).
5. Case C-449/93 *Rockfon A/S* v *Specialarbejderforbundet i Danmark, acting for Nielsen* [1996] IRLR 168 at 175.

Minimum number of employees

5.42 It is integral to the definition of a 'Community-scale undertaking' and 'Community-scale group of undertakings' that the undertaking employs a minimum number of employees. It should be noted that the Regulations apply only to *employees*, not workers; this may lead to practical difficulties in determining workers' status, particularly where they are no longer with the organisation. An 'employee' in the context of the Regulations means 'an individual who has entered into or works under a contract of employment'; and 'contract of employment' means 'a contract of service or apprenticeship, whether express or implied and (if it is express) whether oral or in writing'.[1] In the case of UK employees, the number employed is determined by ascertaining the average number of employees employed during a two year period.[2] This number is calculated by determining the number of UK employees employed in each month in the two year period preceding the 'relevant date' (whether they were employed throughout the month or not), adding these numbers together and dividing the number so determined by 24.[3] There is no requirement that employees should have worked a minimum number of hours in order to be counted. However, if the UK management[4] so decides, an employee may be counted as half a person for any particular month within the two year period in which he or she, for the whole of that month, worked under a contract by virtue of which he or she would have worked for 75 hours or less within that month were the month to have contained 21 working days; were the employee to have had no absences from work; and were the employee to have worked no overtime.[5] In the case of employees in another Member State, the number employed is to be determined by ascertaining the average number of employees employed during a two year period, calculated in accordance with the provisions of the law or practice of the Member State which is intended to give effect to the Directive.[6]

1. TICER 1999, reg 2; see further App 1. ERA 1999, s23 empowers the Secretary of State to apply this provision to a wider category of individuals.
2. *Ibid.*, reg 6(1)(a).

3. *Ibid.*, reg 6(2). The meaning of 'relevant date' depends upon whether a valid request has been made to the central management to initiate negotiations for the establishment of a EWC or ICP under Regulation 9(1). Where such a request is made, the 'relevant date' is the last day of the month preceding the month in which the request is made; where a request for information under regulation 7 is made (and no valid request under regulation 9) it means the last day of the month preceding the month in which the request under regulation 7 is made: reg 6(4).

4. Either the central or the local management in the UK: *ibid.*, reg 2. 'Local management' means the management of one or more establishments in a Community-scale undertaking or of one or more undertakings in a Community-scale group of undertakings which is not the central management: *ibid.*

5. *Ibid.*, reg 6(3). The Directive states that prescribed thresholds shall be based on the average number of employees, including part-time employees, employed during the previous two years calculated according to national law and/or practice: Council Directive 94/45, Article 2(2). Governments in this country have been happily assessing animals by half since at least the Norman Conquest: see, for example, Domesday Book i 218b; ii 287. The reduction of people to fractions appears to be novel, at least in the employment law sphere.

6. *Ibid.*, reg 6(1)(b).

Establishing the number of employees

5.43 An employee or an employees' representative may request information from the management of an establishment or undertaking in the UK to determine whether it is, respectively, part of a Community-scale undertaking or group of undertakings, or a Community-scale undertaking or group of undertakings.[1] The recipient of the request must, in response, provide information on the average number of employees employed by the undertaking or group of undertakings in the UK and in each of the other Member States in the last two years.[2] This obligation applies irrespective of whether the central management is situated in the UK.[3] The employee or employees' representative making the request may present a complaint to the CAC that the recipient has failed to provide the information, or the information provided is false or incomplete in a material particular.[4] The CAC will not consider a complaint unless it is made after the expiry of a one month period beginning on the date on which the complainant made his or her request for information.[5] This is a tortuous way of saying that the recipient must be allowed a minimum of one month to reply. Unusually, however, there is no time limit beyond which a complaint may not be presented. However it is clearly advantageous for a timely application to be made, as there may be evidential difficulties in establishing the number of employees, particularly if there have been changes in the numerical composition of the workforce since the 'relevant date'. Where the CAC upholds the complaint it must make an order requiring the recipient to disclose information to the complainant which specifies the information to be disclosed; the date (or, if more than one, the earliest date) on which the recipient failed to disclose the information, or disclosed false or incomplete information; and a date (not being less than one week from the date of the order) by which the recipient must disclose the information.[6] If the CAC considers that, from the information it has obtained in considering the complaint, it is 'beyond doubt' that the undertaking is, or the establishment is part of, a Community-scale undertaking, or that the establishment or undertaking is part of a Community-scale group of undertakings, it may make a declaration to that effect.[7] Given that the CAC's finding must be made from the information it has obtained in considering the complaint, rather than its general knowledge, there may be limited circumstances where it will make a declaration of this nature.

---

1. TICER 1999, reg 7(1). See reg 2, discussed in para **5.39**, for the definition of employees' representative.
2. *Ibid.*, reg 7(2), (3).
3. *Ibid.*, reg 4(2)(a).
4. *Ibid.*, reg 8(1).
5. *Ibid.*, reg 8(4).
6. *Ibid.*, reg 8(2). See para **5.38** for the effect of such an order; in particular, note that failure to comply with it is a contempt of court.
7. *Ibid.*, reg 8(3).

The Obligation to Negotiate an Agreement for a European Works Council (EWC) or Information and Consultation Procedure (ICP)

5.44 The central management must initiate negotiations for the establishment of a EWC or ICP where a valid request has been made by employees or employees' representatives and on the relevant date the undertaking is a Community-scale undertaking or the group is a Community-scale group of undertakings.[1] It may also initiate negotiations on its own initiative.[2] A valid request may be in one of two forms. First it may consist of a single request made by at least 100 employees, or employees' representatives who represent at least that number, in at least two undertakings or establishments in at least two different Member States.[3] There is no requirement that a given percentage should come from each undertaking or establishment. As we indicated in para **5.41** above, there is no definition of 'establishment' for the purposes of the Regulations (or the

Directive), although case law derived from the context of collective redundancies may be relevant in this context. Secondly, the request may consist of a number of separate requests made on the same or different days by employees, or employees' representatives, which when taken together mean that at least 100 employees, or employees' representatives who represent at least that number, in at least two undertakings or establishments in at least two Member States have made requests.[4] No time limit is specified within which separate requests must be made. In either case the request (or each request) must be in writing; be sent to the central or local management and specify the date on which it was sent.[5] If a special negotiating body has previously decided not to open negotiations with central management or to terminate negotiations, a request which is made before two years have expired since such a decision will not be valid unless the special negotiating body and central management have agreed otherwise.[6]

---

1. TICER 1999, reg 9(1),(5). See reg 6(4), set out in note 3 of para **5.42**, above, for the meaning of 'relevant date'.
2. *Ibid.*, reg 9(5).
3. *Ibid.*, reg 9(2)(a).
4. *Ibid.*, reg 9(2)(b).
5. *Ibid.*, reg 9(3)(a)–(c). 'Local management' means the management of one or more establishments in a Community-scale undertaking or of one or more undertakings in a Community-scale group of undertakings which is not the central management: reg 2.
6. *Ibid.*, reg 9(3)(d).

5.45 If the central management considers that the obligation to initiate negotiations did not apply to it on the relevant date (for example, because the undertaking does not employ the requisite number of employees or it already has a valid 'Article 13' or 'Article 3' agreement) it may, within a period of three months starting on the date on which a valid request was made, apply to the CAC for a declaration whether the obligation did apply to it on the relevant date.[1] It may also apply to the CAC for a declaration if it considers that a request (or separate request) did not satisfy the statutory requirements for validity.[2] The CAC may only consider such an application if it is:

(a) made within a three month period beginning with the date when a request, or the first request, was made;
(b) made before the central management takes any step to initiate negotiations for the establishment of a EWC or ICP; and
(c) the central management had not already made an application for a declaration that it was not covered by the obligation discussed above to initiate negotiations.[3]

1. *Ibid.*, reg 10(3). See reg 6(4), set out in note 3 of para **5.42**, above, for the meaning of 'relevant date'. Where the request consisted of a single request or separate requests made on the same day, a valid request is 'made' on the date on which the request is or requests are sent; where it consists of separate requests made on different days, it is 'made' on the date of the sending of the request which resulted in at least 100 employees (or their representatives) in at least two undertakings or establishments in at least two Member States having made requests: reg 9(4). See further para **5.60** for discussion of Article 13 agreements.

2. *Ibid.*, reg 10(1).

3. *Ibid.*, para 10(2). Note in relation to the time limit that this appears to be absolute, with no exceptions for a late application.

The Establishment of a Special Negotiating Body (SNB)

The composition of a SNB

5.46 The scope, composition, functions, and term of office of a EWC or the arrangements for implementing an ICP are to determined, by written agreement, by a 'special negotiating body' (SNB) in conjunction with the central management of the undertaking or controlling undertaking.[1] This means that the central management cannot unilaterally foist a procedure on its workforce once it becomes subject to the statutory procedure (although the scope for this to happen in relation to 'Article 13' or 'Article 3' agreements was clearly greater: see further para **5.60**). The composition of the special negotiating body where the central management is situated in the UK is tightly specified in the Regulations.[2] It must contain at least one member representing each Member State in which the Community-scale undertaking has one or more establishments, or in which the Community-scale group of undertakings has its controlling undertaking or one or more controlled undertakings.[3] It must also contain one additional member from each Member State in which there are employed 25 per cent or more but less than 50 per cent of the employees of the undertakings or group of undertakings who are employed in the Member States; two additional members from a Member State in which there are employed 50 per cent but less than 75 per cent of such employees; and three additional members from a Member State in which there are employed 75 per cent or more of such employees.[4] It may thus contain a maximum of four members from an individual state. The SNB must inform the central management and local managements of its composition.[5] The Directive leaves it to Member States to determine the method to be used for the election or appointment of the members of the SNB in their territories. However it requires Member States to ensure that employees in undertakings and/or establishments where there are no employees' representatives 'through no fault of their own' have the right to elect or appoint such members.[6] The Regulations implement this requirement by providing that the UK members of the SNB shall be elected by a ballot of the UK employees except where a 'consultative committee' (described in para **5.50** below) exists.[7] These provisions apply regardless of whether the central management is in the UK. Thus, if the central management is in France but there is an establishment of the undertaking in the UK, the UK members of the SNB must be chosen in accordance with the Regulations.

---

1. TICER 1999, reg 11.
2. *Ibid.*, reg. 12. The Directive states only that the SNB shall have a minimum of three and maximum of 18 members, that each relevant Member State is represented by one member, and that 'there are supplementary members in proportion to the number of employees working in the establishments, the controlling undertaking or the controlled undertakings as laid down by the legislation of the Member State within the territory of which the central management is situated': Council Directive 94/45, Article 5(2)(c) as amended. It does not, therefore, stipulate a universal formula to be adopted by every Member State; the composition of the SNB will depend upon the law of the state in which the central management is located.
3. TICER 1999, reg 12(1), (2). See para **5.41** for discussion of the meaning of 'establishment'.
4. *Ibid.*, reg 12(3).
5. *Ibid.*, reg 12(4).
6. Council Directive 94/45, Article 5(2)(a).
7. TICER 1999, reg 13(1).

Arrangements for a ballot

5.47 Where a ballot of UK employees is required, it is for the UK management to arrange for such a ballot, complying with specified conditions, to be held.[1] In general the ballot should be a single ballot of all UK employees.[2] However it may consist of separate ballots of such constituencies as the UK management may determine if more than one UK member is to be elected to the SNB and management considers that if separate ballots were held for those constituencies the UK members to be elected would better reflect the interests of the UK employees as a whole.[3] All UK employees of the Community-scale undertaking or group of undertakings on the day on which votes may be cast in the ballot (or, if more than one, the first of those days) are entitled to vote in the ballot.[4] Any UK employee, or UK employees' representative, who has this status in the undertaking or group of undertakings immediately before the latest time at which a person may become a candidate in the ballot is entitled to stand as a candidate for election.[5] This means that where there is a recognised trade union, representatives of that union who normally take part in the negotiating process may stand;[6] there is no requirement for them to be employed by the employer. An 'independent ballot supervisor' must be appointed on specified terms to supervise the conduct of the ballot.[7] Unlike the tests of eligibility to supervise recognition ballots or ballots of trade union members, which we discuss in paras **4.21** and **2.39** respectively, the designation of such individuals or categories of individuals is not a matter for ministerial order. Rather, a person constitutes an 'independent ballot supervisor'

> if the UK management reasonably believes that he will carry out any functions conferred on him in relation to the ballot competently and has no reasonable grounds for believing that his independence in relation to the ballot might reasonably be called into question.[8]

Where there are to be separate ballots, more than one independent ballot supervisor may be appointed, each of whom must supervise a specified ballot or ballots.[9] The UK management must publish the final arrangements for the ballot in such a manner as to bring them to the attention of, so far as reasonably practicable, the UK employees and UK employees' representatives.[10] The safest way of doing this would be to send each employee and employees' representative an individual copy of the arrangements, but employers may also wish to use other means of communication such as notice boards or e-mail in addition. 'Final arrangements' are not defined; although the matter is not free from doubt, we would suggest that they should include the identity of the independent ballot supervisor.[11] Before publishing these arrangements the management must, so far as reasonably practicable, consult with the UK employees' representatives (if such exist) on its proposals.[12] Any UK employee or UK employees' representative who believes that the arrangements for the ballot of UK employees are defective may, within a period of 21 days beginning with the date on which the UK management published those arrangements, present a complaint to the CAC.[13] The arrangements are 'defective' for this purpose if any of the statutory requirements are not satisfied, or, in a case where the ballot is to comprise separate ballots, the constituencies determined by the UK management do not reflect adequately the interests of the UK employees as a whole.[14] Where the CAC upholds the complaint it must make a declaration to that effect and may make an order requiring the UK management to modify the arrangements it has made for the ballot or to satisfy the statutory requirements, specifying the modifications and requirements in question.[15]

---

1. TICER 1999, regs 13(2), 4(2)(b). The UK management is either the central management or the local management in the UK: reg 2. 'Local management' means the management of one or more establishments in a Community-scale undertaking or of one or more undertakings in a Community-scale group of undertakings which is not

the central management: *ibid.* See para **5.41** for discussion of the meaning of 'establishment'.

2. *Ibid.*, reg 13(3)

3. *Ibid.* These constituencies may be divided along geographical or occupational lines, for example.

4. *Ibid.*, reg 13(3)(b).

5. *Ibid.*, reg 13(3)(c). There is an exception in the case of a 'long haul crew member': a member of a merchant navy crew other than a ferry worker or a person who normally works on voyages of less than 48 hours' duration. Such persons may not be members of an SNB. EWC or an information or consultation representative, or stand for election as such, without the consent of the central management (reg 46) but are entitled to vote. Cf the wide exemption in Article 1(5) of the Directive.

6. See *ibid.*, reg 2, discussed at para **5.39**, for the definition of employees' representative.

7. *Ibid.*, regs 13(3)(d), 14(2).

8. *Ibid.*, reg 13(7).

9. *Ibid.*, reg 13(3)(d).

10. *Ibid.*, reg 13(3)(f).

11. Cf, for example, TULRCA 1992, s 49(5), which specifically requires trade unions to notify all union members of the identity of an independent scrutineer of election ballots.

12. *Ibid.*, ref 13(3)(e). There is no definition of 'consult' in this context (the definition of 'consultation' in reg 2 being appropriate only in relation to an EWC or ICP). In an oft-quoted dictum in *R v British Coal Corporation and the Secretary of State for Trade and Industry, ex parte Price* [1994] IRLR 72, QBD, Glidewell LJ (at 75) suggested that consultation involved 'giving the body consulted a fair and proper opportunity to understand fully the matters about which it is being consulted, and to express its views on those subjects, with the consultor thereafter considering those views properly and genuinely'.

13. *Ibid.*, reg 13(4). Taken in isolation, the linking of the time limit with an event whose non-occurrence can, of itself, be a cause for complaint appears to present a conundrum; if the results are not published no complaint can be made. However, as we indicate in para **5.48** below, the ballot supervisor may not conduct the ballot before the expiry of a period of 21 days beginning on the date when the arrangements were published. If no ballot is conducted the SNB would not be properly constituted and, ultimately the statutory EWC model would be imposed, although *quaere* whether it would be imposed under reg 18(1)(b) or 18(1)(c); see para **5.52** below.

14. *Ibid.*, reg 13(8)(a) and (b).

15. *Ibid.*, reg 13(5), (6).

The role of the independent ballot supervisor

5.48 The UK management must ensure that a ballot supervisor carries out his or her functions, and that there is no interference with the carrying out of those functions from the UK management or the central management (where it is not the UK management).[1] It is possible to envisage situations where these two duties may conflict, although this is less likely to happen if an experienced ballot supervisor is selected. There is no provision which expressly permits the management to replace an unsatisfactory supervisor, and the position if it wished to do so mid-way through the election is unclear.[2] The management has a duty to comply with all reasonable requests by the ballot supervisor for the purposes of, or in connection with, the carrying out of those functions.[3] This probably entails allowing the supervisor to look at records, obtain relevant information and visit premises, for example. The ballot supervisor's terms of appointment must require that he or she:

(a) supervises the conduct of the ballot, or the separate ballots he or she is being appointed to supervise, in accordance with the arrangements published by the UK management or, where appropriate, the arrangements as required to be modified by order of the CAC;

(b) does not conduct the ballot or any of the ballots before the UK management has consulted with the UK employees' representatives (if any) , or before a 21 day period has expired beginning with the date on which the UK management published its arrangements, if no complaint about those arrangements has been presented to the CAC, or, if such a complaint has been presented, before the complaint has been determined and, where appropriate, the arrangements modified by order;

(c) conducts the ballot, or each separate ballot, so as to secure that, so far as reasonably practicable, those entitled to vote are given the opportunity to do so; those entitled to stand are given the opportunity to do so; and those voting are able to do so in secret. He or she must also conduct the ballot so as to secure that votes are fairly and accurately counted.[4] Unlike the provisions relating to elections for union office, for example, the Regulations do not state that the ballot should be conducted by the marking of a voting paper (cf para **2.42**) but this would seem to be the most effective way of satisfying the statutory conditions. The obligation to ensure that those entitled to vote are given the opportunity to do so may require the ballot to be held over more than one day to ensure that shift and part-time employees have the opportunity to participate in it; indeed, it could be said to require a postal ballot to ensure that those who are absent due to illness or on leave have the requisite opportunity. It will be particularly important to have a postal ballot where there is a peripatetic workforce, and to allow an appropriate amount of time for the return of voting papers. The need for the ballot to be secret means that there should be no identifying mark on the voting paper, nor should employees be required to sign for a voting paper against a particular serial number.

Notably there is nothing to prevent the employer or third parties attempting to put pressure on employees to vote in a particular way (although employees are protected against dismissal, selection for redundancy or subjection to other detriment on specified grounds, which we discuss in para **5.59**.)

---

1. TICER 1999, reg 14(1)(a).
2. Unlike in the context of trade union elections (see TULRCA 1992, s 49(1)), the Regulations do not expressly state that the supervisor must be appointed prior to the election. It is conceivable therefore that there may be more scope for appointing a substitute than in that context: cf. para **2.40**.
3. *Ibid.*, reg 14(1)(b).
4. *Ibid.*, reg 14(2).

5.49 As soon as reasonably practicable after the holding of a ballot, the ballot supervisor must publish the results of the ballot in such a manner as to make them available to the UK management and, so far as reasonably practicable, the UK employees entitled to vote in the ballot and the persons who stood as candidates in the ballot.[1] There is no statutory requirement for the supervisor to make a full report on the conduct of the election.[2] However, if he or she considers that any of the requirements listed in para **5.48** (a)–(c) above was not met, with the result that the outcome of the ballot would have been different, he or she must publish 'an ineffective ballot report'.[3] Such a report must also be published if the ballot supervisor considers that there was interference with the carrying out of his or her functions, or failure by management to comply with all reasonable requests made by him or her, with the result that he or she was unable to form a proper judgment as to whether each of the requirements listed was satisfied.[4] An ineffective ballot report must be published within one month of the date on which the ballot result is published, and made available to the UK management and, so far as reasonably practicable, the UK employees entitled to vote in the ballot and the candidates.[5] If there has been a single ballot, or a number of separate ballots each of which has been the subject of an ineffective ballot report, the outcome of the ballot(s) has no effect and the UK management is obliged to arrange for the holding of another ballot.[6] Alternatively, if the ineffective ballot report relates only to one of a number of ballots, the separate ballot(s) in respect of which the report has been issued must be reheld.[7] All costs relating to the holding of a ballot, including payments made to the ballot supervisor, must be borne by central management (regardless of whether an ineffective ballot report has been made).[8] The Regulations do not explicitly require the UK management to pay the costs of postage of employees returning their votes in a postal ballot,[9] but we would suggest that this is a cost 'relating to the holding of the ballot' which central management should meet.

1. TICER 1999, reg 14(3).
2. Cf. the duty of the independent scrutineer in relation to trade union elections, discussed at paras **2.39** and **2.40**.
3. TICER 1999, reg 14(4).
4. *Ibid.*
5. *Ibid.*, reg 14(5),(6).
6. *Ibid.*, reg 14(7).
7. *Ibid.*
8. *Ibid.*, reg 14(8).
9. Cf TULRCA 1992, s 51(3)(b), which requires voters in ballots for union elections, for example, to be enabled to vote without incurring any direct cost to themselves.

Position where a consultative committee exists

5.50 Where a 'consultative committee' exists, that committee is entitled to nominate from its number the UK members of the SNB.[1] However if it fails to nominate such persons, or nominates the wrong number of members, a ballot meeting the requirements described above must be held.[2] A 'consultative committee' means a body of persons:

(a) whose normal functions include or comprise the carrying out of an information and consultation function;
(b) which is able to carry out its information and consultation function without interference from the UK management, or from the central management (where it is not also the UK management);
(c) which, in carrying out its information and consultation function, represents all the UK employees; and
(d) which consists wholly of persons who were elected by a ballot (which may have consisted of a number of separate ballots) in which all the employees who, at the time, were UK employees were entitled to vote.[3]

'Information and consultation function' for this purpose means the function of receiving, on behalf of all the UK employees, information which may significantly affect the interests of UK employees (but excluding information which is relevant only to a specific aspect of their interests, such as health and safety or collective redundancies) and being consulted by the UK management or the central management (where it is not the UK management) on that information.[4] The requirement that the committee must be *able* to carry out its function without management interference is reminiscent of the test of trade union independence, discussed in paras **2.6** and **2.7**. The absence of any statutory protection for members of such a committee against dismissal or subjection to any other detriment would make it particularly important to inquire whether any members of the committee have been subject to any attempts by management to influence their conduct.[5] In addition we would suggest that there should also be enquiry into whether the committee has the wherewithal in terms of financial and material resources to function without interference in the event, for example, that management were to withdraw the provision of accommodation or any other facilities. The consultative committee is required to publish the names of the persons it has nominated to be UK members of the SNB in such a manner as to bring them to the attention of the UK management and, so far as reasonably practicable, the UK employees and employees' representatives.[6] The safest course would be to bring attention of employees and employees' representatives individually. Where the management or an employee or employees' representative believes that the 'consultative committee' does not satisfy the statutory definition, or any of the persons it nominates is not entitled to be nominated, a complaint may be made to the CAC within 21 days beginning with the date on which the names were published.[7] If the CAC upholds the complaint, it must make a declaration to this effect, whereupon the nomination is ineffective and all the UK members of the SNB must be elected by a ballot conducted in accordance with the statutory requirements described in paras **5.48** and **5.49** above.[8] Once the 21-day period for making a complaint to the CAC has passed, or a complaint is made but not upheld, the consultative committee's nomination has effect.[9] This means that, although there is no direct sanction if the committee fails to publish names in accordance with the statutory requirement, the nominations cannot have effect until it has done so. However, there is no provision for challenging whether the committee has done everything practicable to bring the names to the attention of UK employees and their representatives. This appears to be a gap in the Regulations.

---

1. TICER 1999, reg 15(1).
2. *Ibid.*, reg 15(2), (3).
3. *Ibid.*, reg 15(4).
4. *Ibid.*, reg 15(5).
5. 'Employee representatives' elected for the purposes of consultation on redundancies and transfers of the undertaking, and 'representatives of employee safety' who are consulted on health and safety matters, are protected, and individuals are protected against detriment on grounds of trade union activity, but there is no specific protection for members of consultative committees.
6. TICER 1999, reg 15(6).
7. *Ibid.*, reg 15(7).
8. *Ibid.*, reg 15(8), (9).
9. *Ibid.*, reg 15(10).

European Works Council (EWC) and Information and Consultation Procedure (ICP)

The roles of management and the SNB and the options available to them

5.51 The central management of the undertaking or group of undertakings must convene a meeting with the SNB with a view to reaching a written agreement on the detailed arrangements for the information and consultation of employees, and inform local managements accordingly.[1] 'Consultation' means the 'exchange of views and establishment of dialogue' between members of a EWC, or ICP representatives, and central management or any more appropriate level of management.[2] It is notable that this definition of the concept of consultation (which reflects that in the Directive) says nothing about the stage of any decision-making process at which consultation must take place, or even whether it must take place before any decision is taken.[3] The SNB itself may decide, by two-thirds of the votes cast, not to open negotiations with central management or to terminate negotiations.[4] If it does so, the negotiating procedure ceases from the date of that decision, and a purported request by employees or their representatives to establish a EWC or ICP less than two years after that date must be disregarded unless both the SNB and central management agree otherwise.[5] Any other decisions of the SNB must be taken by a majority vote of its members and each member has one vote.[6] For the purpose of its negotiations the SNB may be assisted by experts of its choice.[7] The central management must pay for any reasonable expenses relating to the negotiations that are necessary to enable the SNB to carry out its functions in an appropriate manner, but is required to pay the expenses of one expert only.[8] The parties must 'negotiate in a spirit of co-operation'.[9] They may decide to establish an ICP instead of a EWC;[10] if so, the resulting agreement must specify a method by which the information and consultation representatives[11] are to enjoy the right to meet to discuss the information conveyed to them, and the information so conveyed must relate in particular to transnational questions which significantly affect the interests of the employees.[12] Thus the procedure is not designed to be used to convey information relating purely to national or sub-national issues. The powers and competence of the EWC, or scope of an ICP, must in the case of a Community-scale undertaking, cover all the establishments located within the Member States and, in the case of Community-scale group of undertakings, all group undertakings within the Member States unless the parties' written agreement provides for it to have a wider scope.[13]

---

1. TICER 1999, reg 16(1).
2. *Ibid.*, reg 2.
3. Lecher and Rüb, 1999, 10.

4. *Ibid.*, reg 16(3).
5. *Ibid.*, reg 16(4).
6. *Ibid.*, reg 16(2).
7. *Ibid.*, reg 16(5).
8. *Ibid.*, reg 16(6).
9. *Ibid.*, reg 17(1).
10. *Ibid.*, reg 17(3). Reg 2 defines an ICP as one or more information and consultation procedures agreed under reg 17, or where appropriate, the provisions of the law or practice of a Member State other than the UK which are designed to give effect to give effect to Article 6(3) of Council Directive 94/45. See text above note 2 for the definition of 'consultation'.
11. Such a representative is defined as a person 'who represents employees in the context of an information and consultation procedure': TICER 1999, reg 2.
12. *Ibid.*, reg 17(5). See also reg 19(2), discussed in para **5.52** below.
13. *Ibid.*, reg 17(8).

Content and scope of a EWC agreement

5.52   Where the parties decide to proceed with the establishment of a EWC, their agreement must determine the undertakings of the Community-scale group of undertakings or the establishments of the Community-scale undertaking which are covered by that agreement;[1] the composition of the EWC, the number and term of office of members, and the allocation of seats; the functions and procedure for informing and consulting it; the venue, frequency and duration of its meetings; the financial and material resources to be allocated to it; and the duration of the agreement and procedure for its renegotiation.[2] The parties may agree, in relation to any of these matters, to apply the 'statutory model' (labelled in the Regulations and the Schedule the 'Subsidiary Requirements').[3] The statutory model also applies if the UK central management refuses to commence negotiations within the period of six months beginning with the date on which a valid request was made by employees or their representatives; or if after the expiry of a three year period beginning with the date on which a valid request was made the parties have failed to conclude an agreement on the detailed arrangements for the information and consultation of employees (assuming that the SNB has not decided not to open, or to terminate, negotiations with central management).[4] This would appear to enable an employer to delay the establishment of a EWC or ICP by up to three years provided that its conduct falls short of an outright refusal to commence negotiations. The model, which we outline in para **5.53** below, provides for the composition of a EWC; the appointment or election of its UK members;[5] the competence of the EWC; the frequency of its meetings; and its procedures. Regardless of whether the EWC is constituted by agreement or otherwise, it and the central management are under a duty 'to work in a spirit of co-operation with due regard to their reciprocal rights and obligations'.[6] This duty also applies to central management and information and consultation representatives.[7]

---

1. Where a Community-scale group of undertakings comprises one or more undertakings or groups of undertakings which are themselves Community-wide undertakings or groups of undertakings, the EWC is to be established at the level of the former Community-scale group of undertakings unless the parties' agreement provides otherwise: TICER 1999, reg 17(7).

2. *Ibid.*, reg 17(4). For information on the forms of agreements which have been negotiated throughout the EEA, see the *European Works Council Bulletin*; a useful summary of agreements prior to the Regulations coming into force is given in the *European Industrial Relations Review* June 1999, 25–28.

3. *Ibid.*, reg 18(1)(a). Where the parties have agreed to establish a EWC or ICP, these provisions apply only with the parties' express agreement: reg 17(6).

4. *Ibid.*, reg 18(1)(b), (c). *Quaere* whether ignoring a request constitutes a refusal to commence negotiations. In our view, it does. Note that if the central management applies to the CAC for a declaration under regulation 10 and a valid request was made prior to the date of any declaration made pursuant to such an application, the operation of these periods of time are suspended between the date of the application and the date of the declaration unless the CAC considers that the central management has, in making the application or conducting the proceedings, acted frivolously, vexatiously, or otherwise unreasonably, and does not make any declaration in its favour: reg 10(4),(5). It is difficult to see why the latter condition has been inserted given that, by definition, the central management's application will not have been successful; if it had been, it would not be covered by the obligation to establish a EWC or ICP.

5. Note that the provisions relating to the appointment or election of UK members, unlike other provisions of the Schedule, apply even if the central management is not situated in the UK: *ibid.*, reg 4(2).

6. *Ibid.*, reg 19(1).

7. *Ibid*, reg 19(2).

The 'statutory model' (or 'Subsidiary Requirements')

5.53 An EWC established according to the statutory model must comprise a minimum of three, and a maximum of 30, members.[1] Subject to this, its composition is determined according to the formula applicable to the representation of members of the SNB described in para **5.46**.[2] If the EWC decides that its size so warrants, it must elect from its members a 'select committee' with a maximum of three members to act on its behalf.[3] All UK members of the EWC must be UK employees (in contrast to members of the SNB), thus excluding union representatives who are not so employed.[4] Where *all* UK employees are represented by UK employees' representatives, the UK members of the EWC are chosen by those representatives by whatever method they decide; otherwise they must be elected by a ballot of employees which complies with the same conditions, *mutatis mutandis*, as apply to the election of members of the SNB (see paras **5.47** and **5.48**), with identical provisions for complaint to the CAC if the requisite procedures are not followed.[5] UK employees are 'represented by employees' representatives' if there is an independent trade union recognised by the employer for the purpose of collective bargaining in respect of each employee, or if each employee has elected or appointed an employees' representative for the purpose of receiving, on his or her behalf, information which is relevant to his or her terms and conditions of employment or about the activities of the undertaking which may significantly affect the employee's interests.[6]

---

1. TICER 1999, Sched, para 2(1).
2. *Ibid.*, para 2(2)–4).
3. *Ibid.*, para 2(6).
4. *Ibid.*, para 3(1). This is required by the Annex to Council Directive 98/45, para 1(b).
5. TICER 1999, Sched, paras 4 and 5.
6. *Ibid.*, para 3(2). The definition of an independent trade union in TULRCA 1992, s 5, applies in this context: reg 2; see further paras **2.6** and **2.7**. There is no statutory definition of 'recognition' or 'collective bargaining' in this context: see para **5.39** note 3. Representatives who are expected to receive information relevant only to a specific aspect of the terms or conditions or interests of the employee, such as health and safety or redundancy, are excluded.

5.54 The competence of the EWC is to be limited to information and consultation on the matters which concern the Community-scale undertaking or Community-scale group of undertakings as a whole, or at least two of its establishments or group undertakings situated in different Member States.[1] It cannot, therefore, be used as a vehicle to deal with national or local concerns. However, this is subject to the proviso that decisions taken in relation to employees in one Member State may impact on employees in another Member State, for example in relation to redundancies where a redundancy programme in one Member State may result in the preservation of jobs in another Member State. It is free to adopt its own rules of procedure;[2] thus, the chairing of the EWC, for example, is a matter for determination by its members. The EWC has the right to meet with central management once a year in an information and consultation meeting, to be informed and consulted, on the basis of a report drawn up by the central management, on the progress and prospects of the undertaking or the group.[3] The meeting must relate in particular 'to the structure, economic and financial situation, the probable development of the business and of production and sales, the situation and probable trend of employment, investments, and substantial changes concerning organisation, introduction of new working methods or production processes, transfers of production, mergers, cut-backs or closures of undertakings, establishments or important parts thereof, and collective redundancies'.[4] In addition, whenever there are 'exceptional circumstances affecting the employees' interests to a considerable extent, particularly in the event of relocations, the closure of establishments or undertakings or collective redundancies', the select committee, or, where none exists, the EWC, has the right to be informed, and the right to meet, at its request, the central management, or any other more appropriate level of management within the undertaking or group having its own power of decision, so as to be informed and consulted on measures significantly affecting employees' interests.[5] If the meeting is held with the select committee, those members of the EWC elected or appointed by the establishments or undertakings which are directly concerned by the measures in question also have the right to participate in this 'exceptional information and consultation meeting'.[6] Such a meeting is to take place as soon as possible on the basis of a report drawn up by the central management, or other appropriate level of management, on which an opinion may be delivered at the end of the meeting or within a reasonable time.[7] It is explicitly affirmed in the Schedule (and in the Directive) that an exceptional meeting does not affect the prerogatives of the central management.[8] Before either a routine or exceptional information and consultation meeting with the central management, the EWC or select committee is entitled to meet without the management concerned being present.[9] The operating expenses of the EWC must be borne by central management.[10] In common with the SNB, the EWC or the select committee may be assisted by experts of its choice, in so far as this is necessary for it to carry out its tasks, but the central management is not required to pay expenses in respect of more than one such expert.[11] The central management must provide the EWC members with the financial and material resources to enable them to perform their duties in an appropriate manner; in particular, the cost of organising meetings and arranging for interpretation facilities, and accommodation and travelling expenses, must be paid for unless the central management and the EWC, or select committee, as appropriate, otherwise agree.[12] Subject to the duty not to disclose any information which has been given in confidence, the EWC members have a duty to inform the employees' representatives in the relevant establishments or undertakings or, to the extent that they are not represented by such representatives, the employees themselves, of the content and outcome of the information and consultation procedure.[13] Four years after being established according to the 'statutory model', the EWC is required to examine whether to continue to operate according to the statutory model or whether to open negotiations with central management to reach an agreement on arrangements for the information and consultation of employees.[14] If it decides to negotiate an agreement, it must notify the central management in writing and such notification is to be treated as a valid request.[15] It then assumes the role taken by the SNB in relation to any subsequent negotiations to establish information and consultation arrangements.[16] Research published in June 2000 indicated that, at the time of writing, there had been no known case in which a company had been required to establish a EWC according to the Directive's subsidiary requirements but that these provisions had strongly influenced arrangements introduced by agreement.[17]

---

1. TICER 1999, Sched, para 6(1). Where the central management is not situated in a Member State but is treated by the Regulations as situated in the UK (see para **5.41**) the competence of the EWC is limited to those matters concerning all of its establishments or group undertakings situated within the Member States or concerning at least two of its establishments or group undertakings situated in different Member States: para 6(2).

2. *Ibid.*, para 9(3).

3. *Ibid.*, para 7(1). See para **5.51** for the meaning of 'consultation' in this context.

4. *Ibid.*, para 7(3).

5. *Ibid.*, para 8(1).

6. *Ibid.*, para 8(2).

7. *Ibid.*, para 8(3). In the event of management failing to issue a report, or issuing a report which is inadequate, the sole remedy is complaint to the EAT: see para **5.55**.

8. *Ibid.*, para 8(4). In contrast to the consultation obligations relating to collective redundancies (para **5.17**) and transfers of the undertaking (para **5.28**), there is no requirement in this or any other context to consult with a view to reaching (or seeking) agreement.

9. *Ibid.*, para 9(1). Representatives of establishments or undertaking directly concerned when there are exceptional circumstances also have the right to join such a meeting. On a literal interpretation, this right does not apply where the meeting is with a lower tier of management.

10. *Ibid.*, para 9(5).

11. *Ibid.*, paras 9(4), 9(5).

12. *Ibid.*, para 9(6).

13. *Ibid.*, para 9(2). See para **5.56** for the consequences of information having been given in confidence.

14. *Ibid.* para 10(1).

15. *Ibid.*, para 10(2).

16. *Ibid.*; see further para **5.51**.

17. Carley and Hall, 2000, 105.

Failure to Establish an EWC or ICP or Comply with an Agreement or the Statutory Model

5.55 If the parties agreed to establish an EWC or ICP, or the statutory EWC model became applicable, but, due to a failure of central management, no EWC or ICP has been established (fully or at all), the SNB or, where none exists, an employee, employees' representative, or former member of the SNB, may complain to the EAT.[1] There is also provision for the central management, EWC or any information or consultation representative to complain to the EAT that the terms of the parties' agreement or the statutory model have not been complied with because of the failure of the other party.[2] If the EAT finds the complaint well-founded, it must make a decision to that effect and make an order requiring the central management to take specified steps to establish the EWC or ICP, or the defaulter to take such steps as are necessary to comply with the agreement or statutory model, as appropriate.[3] Where the central management has failed to establish the EWC or ICP, or is the defaulting party in a case of non-compliance with the agreement or statutory model, the EAT must also issue a written penalty notice requiring it to pay a penalty to the Secretary of State in respect of the failure, unless it is satisfied, on hearing the representations of central management, that the failure resulted from a reason beyond its control or that it has some other reasonable excuse for the failure.[4] The maximum penalty is £75,000.[5] When determining the penalty the EAT must take into account the gravity of the failure, the period of time over which it occurred, the reason for it, the number of employees affected, and the total number of employees of the Community-scale undertaking or Community-scale group of undertakings in the Member States.[6] There is provision for appeal on a question of law to the Court of Appeal against a decision or order made by the EAT, with permission of the EAT or Court of Appeal.[7] The date set for payment of the penalty must not fall before the end of the period within which an appeal may be made (currently four weeks).[8] Once the specified date in a penalty notice has passed and the period for appeal has expired, or an appeal has been made and determined, the Secretary of State may recover from the central management, as a civil debt, any amount payable under the penalty notice which remains outstanding.[9]

---

1. TICER 1999, reg. 20(1)–(3). 'Failure' in this context means 'act or omission', and a failure by the local management is treated as a failure by the central management: reg 20(2).
2. *Ibid.*, reg 21(1)–(3). An agreement may provide an internal mechanism for resolving disputes prior to taking the matter to the EAT.
3. *Ibid.*, regs 20(4), (6); 21(4), (5). No such order can have the effect of suspending or

altering the effect of any act done or agreement made by the central or local management: regs 20(10), 21(9).

4. *Ibid.*, regs 20(7), (8); 21(6), (7).

5. *Ibid.*, reg 22(2). This figure was chosen on the basis that the average cost of holding a EWC had been estimated at around £60,000: *Implementation in the UK of the European Works Council Directive*, URN 99/926, July 1999, 37.

6. *Ibid.*, reg 22(3).

7. ETA 1996, s 37.

8. TICER 1999, reg 22(4).

9. *Ibid.*, reg 22(5). The making of an appeal suspends the effect of a penalty notice: reg 22(6).

Confidential Information

5.56 The Regulations (reflecting the requirements of the Directive) make special provision for the protection of information and documents disclosed in confidence by central management.[1] In this respect they contrast with other provisions in domestic law relating to the disclosure of information, such as information disclosed for collective bargaining purposes, where no express statutory provision is made (although as we indicated in para **5.19** the DTI is of the view that information may be given in confidence to representatives in the context of redundancies and transfers of the undertaking where this in necessary in respect of takeovers) . Members of an SNB or EWC, information or consultation representatives, or experts assisting them (collectively termed 'recipients'), owe a duty to the central management (UK or otherwise) not to disclose any information or document which is or has been in their possession by virtue of their position as such which the central management has entrusted to them on terms requiring it to be held in confidence.[2] The duty is a permanent one, continuing after the expiry of the recipient's term of office. Disclosure constitutes breach of a statutory duty, without prejudice to any other liability, such as breach of confidence, which the recipient may incur.[3] There is an exception where the recipient reasonably believed the disclosure to be a 'protected disclosure' under the 'whistleblowing' provisions of the Employment Relations Act 1996; in that event, the disclosure is stated not to be a breach of statutory duty.[4] Where central management is situated in the UK, a recipient may apply to the CAC for a declaration as to whether it was reasonable for it to require that information or documents be held in confidence.[5] If the CAC considers that the disclosure of the information or document would not, or would not be likely to, prejudice or cause serious harm to the undertaking it must grant a declaration that the requirement was not reasonable, whereupon the document or information is not thereafter regarded as having been entrusted to any recipient in confidence.[6] The CAC will need to examine each case on its merits; the Code of Practice on Disclosure of Information to Trade Unions for Collective Bargaining purposes, which provides examples of information whose disclosure would cause 'substantial injury' to the employer's undertaking,[7] may provide some persuasive guidance but it will have no statutory authority in this context. The Government suggested that

> harm or prejudice could arise in a range of areas, provided that they are capable of objective assessment. They might for example include, but not be limited to, damage to the company's financial or commercial position, or its reputation and general prospects, or on a more specific level, its employment prospects or compliance with regulatory or statutory rules. . . . [I]t is clear [however] that management may not withhold information on arbitrary grounds, or where disclosure would have trivial consequences.[8]

This extract emphasises the important point that the CAC is powerless if the information reveals wrongdoing or a threat to the environment, for example, given that revelation of such information would almost certainly cause serious harm to the undertaking. The protection afforded to individuals against dismissal or other forms of detriment for performing their functions or activities, which we describe in para **5.59** below, does not apply where such action was taken because they disclosed information given in confidence (other than where the individual reasonably believed the disclosure to be 'protected').[9] Recipients who do not consider that information entrusted to them is properly impressed with confidence would, therefore, be well advised to seek a declaration from the CAC. However if they believe that the information tends to show any of the activities which qualify for protection under the 'whistleblowing' provisions, such as danger to health and safety, and they consider that this information should be disclosed, they will have to act in accordance with the statutory procedure and hope that their belief that the disclosure was 'protected' is vindicated in any proceedings which may ensue.

---

1. TICER 1999, reg 23; Council Directive 94/45/EC, Article 8.
2. TICER 1999, reg 23(1), (2).
3. *Ibid.*, reg 23(3), (4). There appears to be no reason why this could not be heard in a UK court even if central management was non-UK and disclosure took place outside the jurisdiction.
4. *Ibid.*, reg 23(5); see ERA 1996, s 43A–L and see generally Bowers, Mitchell and Lewis, 1999. Technically the central management could still pursue other forms of action. However an act which was 'protected' under ERA 1996 would almost certainly fall within the 'public interest' defence to breach of confidence (see generally Toulson and Phipps, 1996, Chapter VI) and the standards set in ERA 1996 may themselves influence judges in applying the public interest defence.
5. TICER 1999, reg 23(6).

6. *Ibid.*, reg 23(7), (8).
7. See para **4.65** *et seq.*
8. *Implementation in the UK of the European Works Council Directive*, URN 99/926, July 1999, 34.
9. TICER 1999, regs 28(4) and 31(4).

5.57 In addition to affording specific protection to information transmitted in confidence, the Regulations (once again reflecting the Directive) also provide that the central management is not required to disclose any information or document to a recipient when its nature is such that, 'according to objective criteria', this would 'seriously harm the functioning of, or would be prejudicial to, the undertaking or group of undertakings concerned'.[1] This provision applies only where central management is situated in the UK; compliance with the Directive requires other Member States to apply the same dispensation where central management is located there.[2] Where there is a dispute between the central management and the recipient about whether the nature of the information or document which central management has failed to provide falls within the scope of the exception, either party may apply to the CAC for a declaration.[3] If the CAC makes a declaration that disclosure would not be harmful or prejudicial, it must order the central management to disclose the information or document to specified recipients by a specified date.[4] The order must also specify the terms on which it is to be disclosed.[5] Information which is the subject of an order should not *per se* be impressed with the duty of confidence described in para **5.56** above; if management has been unable to satisfy the CAC that it is protected from disclosure then equally it will not be reasonable for it to be disclosed on confidential terms. However there appears nothing to prevent the CAC from ordering disclosure on terms which require the information or document to be disclosed subject to its contents being anonymised or particular statistics removed, for example. The Directive enables Member States to make management's dispensation from disclosing information subject to prior administrative or judicial authorisation.[6] The Regulations put the onus on the 'recipients' of information to challenge non-disclosure. The former method relies on management acknowledging that specified documents or information exists; for the latter, recipients will need to be aware that the information to which access is being withheld has been compiled. It is notable that there is nothing in the statutory model which entitles members of a EWC or information or consultation representatives to have sight of original documents, although agreements reached between the SNB and central management (or 'Article 3' or 'Article 13 agreements') may make provision for this.

1. TICER 1999, reg 24(1).
2. *Ibid.*, reg 4; Council Directive 94/45/EC, Article 8.
3. *Ibid.*, reg 24(2).
4. *Ibid.*, reg 24(3).
5. *Ibid.*, reg 24(4).
6. Council Directive 94/45/EC, Article 8(2).

Rights of Individuals in Relation to EWCs and ICPs

Rights to time off

5.58 Employees who are members of an SNB or EWC, an information and consultation representative, or candidates in an election for any of these positions, are entitled to be permitted by their employer to take reasonable paid time off during the employee's working hours to perform their functions as such.[1] These rights apply regardless of the location of central management.[2] The rules for calculating payment are identical to those which apply in relation to time off for employee representatives, discussed in para **5.15**; 'working hours' are also identically defined. As in that context, it is a right to time off only with permission; the sole recourse for an employee who is refused time off, or payment for that time, is to complain to an employment tribunal.[3] Unlike in relation to trade union activities, there is no further guidance on what constitutes 'reasonable' time off; however, the cycle of activities which the employee is required to undertake should make this easier to determine. Controversially, there is no provision for time off for training for any of these activities (or, *a fortiori*, for employer-provided training), despite the fact that participation in a EWC or ICP is likely to require skills which national representatives are unlikely to have acquired to date.[4] Clearly, however, it is open to the parties to agree that time off should be permitted for this purpose.

1. TICER 1999, regs. 25 and 26.
2. *Ibid.*, reg 4(2).
3. *Ibid.*, reg 27.
4. These include reading company accounts in a transnational dimension; interaction with works councillors from other countries, the management of meetings in a mutlicultural context and language training: Miller and Stirling, 1998, 37. It may be possible to argue that the requirement in the statutory model for central management to provide EWC members with the material resources to enable them to perform their duties in an appropriate manner should extend to training: Schedule, para 9(6), discussed above para **5.54**.

Protection against dismissal and other detriment

5.59 It is automatically unfair to dismiss an employee who is a member of an SNB or EWC, an information or consultation representative, or a candidate in an election for any of these positions, for performing any functions or activities as such, for requesting time off for the purposes described in para **5.58** or payment for that time, or for proposing to do any of these things.[1] No minimum period of employment is required for this protection to apply, nor is there any upper age limit.[2] Employees also have the right not to be 'subjected to any detriment by any act, or deliberate failure to act' by their employer for such a reason.[3] As we indicated in para **5.56** above, those who disclose information or documents which were entrusted on terms of confidence are outside this protection unless they reasonably believe the disclosure to be a 'protected disclosure'.[4] However employees who had been dismissed would still be able to claim unfair dismissal in the normal way (if, for example, the employer failed to follow a fair procedure), although they would need to meet the usual qualifications to claim. In addition to the protection specifically afforded to office-holders and candidates, it is also automatically unfair to dismiss any employee for a range of reasons relating to the establishment or operation of a EWC or ICP.[5] There is parallel protection against being subjected to a detriment for such a reason.[6] These reasons are that the employee:

(a) took, or proposed to take, any proceedings before an employment tribunal to enforce a right or secure an entitlement conferred on him or her by the Regulations. It is immaterial for this purpose whether the employee had the right or whether the right had been infringed, but the claim to the right and, if applicable, the claim that it has been infringed must be made in good faith.

(b) exercised, or proposed to exercise, any entitlement to apply or complain to the EAT or the CAC conferred by the Regulations;

(c) requested, or proposed to request, information to establish whether an undertaking constitutes a Community-scale undertaking or group of undertakings (see para **5.43**);

(d) acted with a view to securing that a SNB, EWC or ICP did or did not come into existence;

(e) indicated that he or she supported or did not support the coming into existence of a SNB, EWC or ICP;

(f) stood as a candidate in an election in which any person would, on being elected, be a member of an SNB or EWC or an information and consultation representative;

(g) influenced or sought to influence the way in which votes were to be cast by other employees in a ballot arranged under the Regulations.

(h) voted in such a ballot;

(i)   expressed doubts, whether to a ballot supervisor or otherwise, whether such a ballot had been properly conducted; or

(j)   proposed to do, failed to do, or proposed to decline to do, any of the things mentioned in (d)–(i)

It is notable that, in contrast to the analogous protections for workers in relation to recognition and derecognition of trade unions discussed in para **4.58**, acts which constitute 'an unreasonable act or omission' are not excluded. This may be particularly significant in relation to (g), where there is no restriction on the form of 'influence' which an employee may seek to exercise. The protections against dismissal and subjection to a detriment apply irrespective of where the central management is located.[7]

---

1. TICER 1999, reg 28(1)–(3). It is also automatically unfair to select an employee for redundancy on any of these grounds in a 'redundancy case': reg 29(1).
2. *Ibid.*, reg 29(2), (3).
3. *Ibid.*, reg 31. See further para **3.10** for what is meant by subjection to a detriment.
4. *Ibid.*, regs 28(4); 31(4).
5. TICER 1999, reg 28(6), (7). It is also automatically unfair to select an employee for redundancy on any of these grounds in a 'redundancy case': reg 29(1).
6. *Ibid.*, regs 31(5)–(7).
7. *Ibid.*, reg 4(2).

Situations where the Regulations do Not Apply Wholly or in Part

5.60 There are four situations where, even though the central management is located in the UK, the application of the Regulations is modified. First, there are two situations where none of the obligations specified in the Regulations applies.[1] These are:

(a)   *Article 13 agreements.* Article 13 of the Directive provided that its obligations did not apply to Community-scale undertakings or groups of undertakings in which a voluntary agreement providing for the transnational information and consultation of employees, covering the entire workforce, was in force on 22 September 1996 (the date for implementation of the Directive) or the date of the Directive's transposition into the national law in question.[2] The Regulations reflect this exemption.[3]

(b)   *Article 3 agreements.* Article 3 of the Extension Directive afforded a similar exemption in the case of undertakings or groups of undertakings which became subject to the obligation to initiate negotiations for the establishment of a EWC or ICP solely as a result of this 'Extension Directive'.[4] The agreement in question was required to be in force immediately before 16 December 1999.[5]

The facility to establish EWCs outside the regime set by the Directive 'meant that the specific framework of each EWC derived from a complex bargaining process reflecting the relative power of employee representatives, unions and employers'.[6] Where an Article 13 or Article 3 agreement expires, the parties may jointly decide that it should be renewed. If they fail to do so, employees or employees' representatives may request that negotiations be initiated to establish a EWC or ICP, or the management may decide to initiate such negotiations, in the normal way (see para **5.44**). Where such a request is made and the central management considers that the obligation to initiate negotiations does not apply because an 'Article 13' or 'Article 3' agreement remains in force, the CAC may be required to decide the validity of such an agreement (see para **5.45**). However, neither the EAT nor the CAC have a role in resolving disputes about the operation of Article 13 or Article 3 agreements, the legal status of which is for the parties to decide.[7]

---

1. Note that although Council Directive 94/95 EC, Article 1(5) permits Member States to exclude merchant navy crews from its provisions, the Regulations provide a much narrower exclusion for such workers: see para **5.47**, note 5.

2. Council Directive 94/45/EC, Article 13. It has been estimated that around 450 Article 13 agreements were concluded prior to September 1996: Carley and Hall, 2000, 107. See Marginson *et al*, 1998, for the content of such agreements. Many of these took the form of joint management–employee bodies.

3. TICER 1999, reg 45. The Regulations do not specify who the parties to such an agreement representing the employees should be; the Government took the view that given the variety of such signatories it would be undesirable to limit the flexibility of the parties on this matter: *Implementation in the UK of the European Works Council Directive*, URN 99/926, July 1999, 19.

4. Council Directive 97/74/EC, Article 3.

5. *Ibid.* See TICER 1999, reg. 44.

6. Royle, 1999, 330. Royle provides a fascinating account of the McDonald's Article 13 EWC.

7. *Outcome of the Public Consultation on Implementation of the European Works Councils Directive*, DTI, 1999.

5.61 There are two further situations where only those obligations imposed by the Regulations which apply regardless of the location of central management, such as those relating to the protection of employees, are applicable. These are as follows:

(a) *Existing Article 6 agreements.* Where the central management is in the UK and immediately before the Regulations came into force an agreement between the SNB and central management for the establishment of a EWC or ICP had been made under the law or practice of a Member State other than the UK to give effect to Article 6 of the Directive, the full Regulations apply only if the parties agree at any stage that the provisions which would have governed the agreement had it been made under the Regulations should apply, or if the Article 6 agreement ceases to have effect.[1] This leaves it essentially to the parties to decide whether they wish to come under UK jurisdiction.

(b) *Existing Article 7 EWCs.* Where the central management is in the UK and immediately before the Regulations came into force an EWC was established under the law or practice of a Member State designed to give effect to Article 7 of, and the Annex to, the Directive (the 'subsidiary requirements'), the Regulations apply only if the EWC and central management agree at any stage that the 'statutory model' prescribed in the Regulations should apply, or if the EWC decides to negotiate an agreement for a EWC or ICP.[2]

---

1. TICER 1999, reg 42.

2. *Ibid.*, reg 43. Note that there is no provision for the 'repatriation' of Article 13 agreements, consistent with the government's approach that they are private agreements which are not subject to the Regulations: *Outcome of the Public Consultation on Implementation of the European Works Councils Directive*, DTI, 1999.

Transitional Provisions

5.62 The Regulations contain transitional provisions to deal with, respectively, the composition and selection of members of an SNB which had been validly requested or established under the law or practice of a Member State other than the UK before the time the Regulations came into force,[1] and the composition and selection of UK members of an 'Article 7' EWC established under the law or practice of another Member State prior to the Regulations coming into force.[2]

1. TICER 1999, reg 47.
2. *Ibid.*, reg 48.

6

Industrial Action

INTRODUCTION

6.1 Industrial action can take a wide variety of forms, ranging from a strike, which involves a complete withdrawal of labour, to a work-to-rule, go-slow, overtime ban, or ban on particular duties. As we discussed in Chapter 1, the right of workers to withdraw their labour is guaranteed by a number of international treaties, although it is recognised that the exercise of this right may be subject to conditions, such as those relating to the object of a strike (excluding those which are purely political in their nature, for example) or the procedures to be followed (which may include balloting the workforce or giving reasonable prior notice to employers). Developed legal systems vary greatly in how they treat the right to strike, even within the European Union.[1] However, Britain is relatively unusual in not according workers any positive right to organise or participate in industrial action, nor, indeed, in having any principled concept of the boundary between what is 'lawful' and 'unlawful' in this area. At the collective level, whether industrial action attracts legal liability depends upon a complex and not always predictable interplay between common law and statute. In relation to the individual worker hardly any kind of action is fully 'protected' against all forms of liability because participation in industrial action almost always constitutes a breach of the employment contract, as well as having implications for employees' statutory rights.

At the collective level, industrial action is likely to be unlawful at common law because those who organise it almost invariably commit at least one tort.[2] This exposes them to claims for damages from employers and others who have suffered loss and, more importantly in practice, to an application for an interim injunction to halt the action. In addition, there is a statutory right for individuals to seek an order to halt industrial action regardless of whether they have suffered loss. Hearings for interim injunctions can take place at very short notice and are usually decided on the basis of witness statements or affidavit evidence only. If the injunction is granted, it requires the organisers to withdraw the industrial action pending the full hearing of the case. Given that a case may take months or even years to come to trial, effectively the interim stage decides the issue. Non-compliance with an injunction constitutes contempt of court, which is punishable by an unlimited fine, imprisonment and/or sequestration of assets. Both trade unions and individual dispute organisers can be sued in tort for organising industrial action; whether or not a trade union is liable for the acts of its officials or members is determined according to statutory or common law principles, depending upon the tort in question.

The emphasis upon civil liability in relation to industrial action is a relatively recent phenomenon; historically, the criminal law was the most important constraint upon the withdrawal of labour.[3] In 1875, however, the Conspiracy and Protection of Property Act abolished many of the offences relating to industrial action, and since that time the legal focus has shifted to the civil law other than in the area of picketing. The period following the 1875 Act saw the protections it provided against criminal liability effectively outflanked by the expansion by the courts of the scope of tortious liability. A new tort of conspiracy to injure was developed, and the tort of inducing breach of contract applied to industrial action, for which the furtherance of union objectives was no defence. Moreover, in 1901 the House of Lords decided that a trade union registered under the Trade Union Act 1871, although not a corporate body, could nevertheless be sued for the torts of its officials, so exposing union funds to damages claims for loss caused by industrial action.[4] The encroachment of the civil law was partially impeded in 1906 when a Liberal Government, elected with Labour support, enacted the Trade Disputes Act of that year. This Act, which remained in force until 1971, accorded comprehensive immunity to trade unions against tortious liability. It also gave immunity to any person who 'in contemplation or furtherance of a trade dispute' committed the new tort of conspiracy, induced some other person to breach a contract of employment, or interfered with the trade, business or employment of another. A 'trade dispute' was defined as 'any dispute between employers and workmen, or between workmen and workmen, which is connected with the employment or non-employment, or the terms of the employment, or with the conditions of labour, of any person. . .'.

The 'immunities' approach to industrial action adopted in the Trade Disputes Act 1906, which defines 'lawfulness' in negative rather than positive terms, has remained to this day, although the scope of the immunities has varied greatly. Regardless of their scope, however, this approach has always been a fragile base upon which to rest the freedom to organise industrial action for two important reasons. The first is because it specifies the individual torts against which immunity is granted. In a common law system, this means that it is always possible that new forms of liability may be developed by the courts which lie outside the scope of these immunities, either in relation to industrial disputes or in wholly different contexts, such as commercial litigation, where the relevant 'economic torts' are at issue. If this does occur, it is entirely a matter of political will whether the resulting gap in protection which is opened up will be closed. Thus, when in

1965 the House of Lords applied for the first time the tort of 'intimidation' to industrial action,[5] the Labour Government then in power quickly introduced legislation to extend immunity to this tort. However, there was no equivalent response by the 1979–1997 Conservative governments when new forms of liability emerged during their period in office. There is no guarantee that a positive 'right' to strike would, of itself, confer greater substantive freedom,[6] but it would probably be less vulnerable to circumvention of this tangential nature. The second respect in which those organising industrial action remain vulnerable to legal liability lies in the failure to remove the overriding discretion of the courts to grant interim injunctions to restrain industrial action. In theory, this discretion allows the courts to grant an injunction even if the action appears to be protected under statute. In practice, the main importance of this discretion has lain in the application of the legal tests for obtaining an injunction (since 1975, the requirement only to show that there is a 'serious question to be tried', whereupon the issue is decided upon the 'balance of convenience'), which have favoured employer claimants who can persuade the courts that the dispute is excluded from the statutory immunities or that a wrong may have been committed which lies outside their scope.

Between 1906 and 1971 the scope of the immunities remained essentially unchanged. Since 1971, however, they have been subject to radical reformulation according to the political complexion of the government in power. In 1971 the Heath Conservative Government replaced them with an entirely new framework of liability under the Industrial Relations Act 1971; in 1974 the Labour Government restored the 1906 structure but expanded the scope of protection against liability in tort and extended the definition of a trade dispute. In 1979, the Thatcher Conservative Government was returned to office in the wake of a 'winter of discontent' of high profile strikes in both the public and the private sectors. In 1980 it began a process of restriction and regulation which, by degrees, narrowed considerably the scope for organising industrial action within the scope of the immunities.[7] The ambit of a trade dispute and the scope for lawful picketing were considerably reduced, and immunity was withdrawn altogether for 'secondary' industrial action (a technical exception apart); industrial action to enforce the closed shop and to enforce 'union-only' or 'recognition-only' practices in contracts with suppliers to the employer; and action in response to the dismissal of participants in unofficial industrial action. The traditional immunity of unions from liability in tort was removed, subject to statutory limits on the amount of damages which could be awarded against them in a single set of proceedings in tort. In addition, industrial action for which a trade union was legally liable was required to be supported by a ballot conducted in accordance with detailed statutory requirements. Immunity was also lost in relation to particular claimants (the employer in respect of whom the default occurred and those exercising the 'statutory right of action') where the union failed to provide specified information to the employer or appropriate notice before the industrial action started.

A number of aspects of this legislation were criticised as incompatible with international legal standards to which the UK had agreed to conform; we indicate the findings of the appropriate supervisory bodies at relevant points in the text. Despite this, the Blair Labour Government has left the key elements of the law which it inherited unchanged; there have been minor amendments to the balloting and notification requirements, but it is not regarded as a matter of apology by the government that UK law remains more restrictive than that of comparable systems. Constraints introduced by its predecessor on unions' ability to secure compliance by their members with a call to take industrial action (even though this has been approved by a majority in a ballot), and restrictions on the use of union property, have also remained in place. Despite statutory clarification in some areas, the law also remains extremely complex, and it is still difficult for any union to organise industrial action confident in the knowledge that it will be free from legal liability. In outline, the decision whether a specific dispute involves civil liability at common law entails examination of the following issues:

(1) Does the industrial action give rise to civil liability at common law? In nearly all cases the answer to this will be 'yes'. (Note: for the statutory right of action it is sufficient that the industrial action is actionable in tort by *any* person.)

(2) If there is liability at common law, is this liability removed because the tortious act is protected by the statutory immunities? This requires two elements to be satisfied: first, the statute must extend protection to the tort in question (there are some torts against which no protection is afforded); and, secondly, the act must have been done in contemplation or furtherance of a trade dispute.

(3) Is the act excluded from statutory protection for any reason? An act may be excluded for one of six reasons: if its purpose is to enforce trade union membership; if it is a response to the dismissal of participants in unofficial industrial action; if it constitutes unlawful secondary action; if its purpose is to require the employer to pursue a 'union-only' or 'recognition-only' practice in a supply contract; if it constitutes unlawful picketing; or, where applicable, if the requisite balloting requirements have not been met. In addition, a trade union has no immunity in relation to an employer to whom the requisite information prior and subsequent to a ballot, and pre-industrial action notice, has not been provided (or in relation to an individual exercising the statutory right of action).

In addition, the residual discretion of the courts to grant an interim injunction to restrain industrial action regardless of whether it appears to be lawful under statute should always be remembered. Members of the House of Lords have suggested that this may be done where the consequences of industrial action appear to be particularly disastrous, although to date no injunction has been granted on this basis where the immunities appear likely to apply. For the reasons we explain in Chapter 1, the Human Rights Act 1998 is unlikely to affect the way in which the courts approach the liability of dispute organisers, other than (possibly) in the area of picketing; indeed, the Act may furnish an additional weapon to the armoury of employer claimants if industrial action interferes with the exercise of a Convention right such as freedom of expression or even, conceivably, the right to life.

The position of individual workers who take industrial action is even less protected. Any form of industrial action, other than (possibly) a ban on voluntary overtime, constitutes a breach of the employment contract. A strike has been generally regarded by the courts as a breach regardless of the circumstances which provoked it, and this usually remains the case even where strike notice has been given (unless it took the form of collective resignation, which would be unwise, or the contract provides for suspension, which is unlikely). Giving notice of other forms of industrial action merely constitutes notice of intended breach. The remedies open to the employer are the same as in any other context: damages; withholding of some or all of workers' salary or wages; and, where the breach is sufficiently serious, dismissal without notice. The courts are prohibited by statute from ordering an employee to work normally by way of an order for specific performance of the contract, or an injunction restraining a breach or threatened breach, but this restriction applies generally, not only in connection with industrial action. Participation in industrial action also affects a panoply of employees' statutory rights (the broader category of 'workers' currently has hardly any employment rights in this area to lose). In the context of this introduction, we confine ourselves to unfair dismissal. Here, the general principle is that tribunals have no jurisdiction to determine fairness where at the date of dismissal the applicant was taking part in a strike or other industrial action. There is no requirement for the industrial action to constitute a breach of contract. There is a limited measure of protection against victimisation of particular employees in the case only of industrial action which is not deemed 'unofficial'; jurisdiction is restored to the tribunal if it is shown that the employer did not dismiss all the participants at the establishment taking part in the action on a particular day, or re-engaged one or more such employees within a three month period. (The pool for determining victimisation was narrowed considerably in 1982, and this provision has been left untouched). The only significant reform which has been made is that it is now automatically unfair for an employer to dismiss an employee for taking 'protected industrial action' (loosely speaking, action which is protected by the statutory immunities) during the first eight weeks of his or her participation, or later in some circumstances. There is also a limited class of other reasons for which it is also unfair to dismiss participants in both 'non-unofficial' and 'unofficial' action; however, these, notably, do not include trade union activities. Ironically, workers who are locked out by their employer have no greater protection under statute, even though this may constitute a breach of contract entitling them to sue for loss of wages and other contractual benefits. An 'even-handed' approach under statute serves to deprive employees of unfair dismissal rights in an analogous way to when they themselves are taking industrial action, with the exception now that there is no equivalent of the remedy accorded to those dismissed for taking protected industrial action.

In addition to civil liability, industrial action may also involve workers in committing criminal offences. For most workers, withdrawing labour in itself is not an offence, but there is a wide range of offences which may be committed in the course of picketing. In addition, there are specific groups (the police, armed forces, merchant seamen and postal and, possibly, telecommunications workers) for whom industrial action is restricted by the criminal law, and any group which takes industrial action in breach of contract which puts at risk life, health or property may commit an offence.[8] However, the criminal law has not been invoked against such groups in recent times and the likelihood of prosecution for participation in industrial action, without more, would seem remote. Traditional British practice has centred upon invoking emergency powers to lessen the consequences of industrial action once it has been taken, either by introducing substitute labour or by taking more extensive measures, rather than by relying upon the criminal law to forestall it in the first place.[9]

---

1. See Wedderburn 1991; Ben-Israel 1994; Jacobs, 1998, and for an overview of the areas in which legal systems may differ, Deakin and Morris, 1998, 858–862.

2. This section is designed merely to provide a framework for the detailed analysis which follows. Full references to the current law are provided later in the text.

3. See Jacobs, 1986.

4. *Taff Vale Railway Co v ASRS* [1901] AC 436.

5. *Rookes v Barnard* [1964] AC 1129.

6. Wedderburn, 1991, 314–316; Davies and Freedland, 1984, 786–787.

7. For detailed analyses of the policy background to, and legislative history of, these provisions up to their respective times of writing, see Auerbach, 1990, and Davies and Freedland, 1993, Chapter 9 *et seq.*

8. See generally Morris, 1986 and 1991, and for an overview, Deakin and Morris, 1998, 933–937.

9. See *ibid.*

LIABILITY FOR INDUSTRIAL ACTION

Liability in Tort

Sources and general principles

6.2 In almost every case, those who organise industrial action will commit at least one common law 'economic tort', which may or may not be protected by the statutory immunities described in para **6.17** *et seq*. There are four major torts which are relevant in this context: inducing breach of contract, intimidation, interference with trade or business by unlawful means, and conspiracy. The purpose of the 'economic torts' is to protect interests in trade, business or livelihood. The principles which govern them have been laid down in a series of decisions dating from the turn of the twentieth century. One fundamental principle is that an intention to harm another will not of itself give rise to liability without an additional element of unlawfulness,[1] which may take the form of either interference with a pre-existing right of the claimant, such as performance of a contract, or the use of some independently unlawful means. The exception to this principle is the tort of conspiracy to injure, where the act of combination or association between the defendants, when coupled with an intention to harm the claimant, is sufficient for liability even though otherwise lawful means are used. The 'economic' torts have been developed and extended by the courts in a piecemeal fashion, often in the context of liability for industrial action, and there is continuing uncertainty about their scope in crucial areas such as the requisite element of intention and, indeed, in some cases, their very existence.[2] Moreover, judicial responses given in relation to one tort are not always consistent with those given in relation to another. The difficulties of developing a coherent framework of liability are exacerbated by the fact that many pivotal decisions have arisen out of applications for interim injunctions to prevent the commission or continuance of alleged torts, where the court is concerned only with whether there is a serious question to be tried and does not explore in detail the relevant facts and legal principles.[3] This has been a particular feature of industrial action cases because of the interest of employer claimants in arguing that wrongs have been committed which are outside the protection of the statutory immunities, such as inducing breach of a statutory duty.[4] Convincing the court that such a wrong may exist can be sufficient, whereupon it can be added to the legal armoury of employers even though questions may remain about its key elements. Moreover, a decision in a completely different context, such as litigation between two companies, can have fundamental consequences for the law of industrial action. Even if a tort is within the scope of the statutory immunities, staying within those immunities can be a difficult task for dispute organisers, particularly given that in interim proceedings it is sufficient to persuade the court that there is a 'serious question' whether the requisite conditions for doing so have been met. Finally, it is notable that the constraints upon the right to bring proceedings contained in the economic torts are circumvented entirely by the statutory right of individuals to seek injunctive relief in specified circumstances: see para **6.11**.

---

1. *Allen v Flood* [1898] AC 1, HL.
2. In this section we outline the elements of these torts, and focus upon the implications of major current controversies for those involved in industrial action. For the most detailed consideration of the economic torts, see Clerk and Lindsell, 1995, as updated, Chapter 15. Also useful are Elias and Ewing, 1982; Carty, 1988; Weir, 1997; and Markesinis and Deakin 1999, Part 5, Chapter 5.
3. See para **6.52** *et seq.*
4. See para **6.6**.

Inducing breach of contract or interfering with performance of a contract by unlawful means

6.3 There are two forms of this tort: direct and indirect. Direct inducement occurs if A intentionally induces B to breach a contract between B and C; C may then sue A.[1] Although the defendant must intend to interfere with the claimant's contractual rights, he or she need not intend to cause the claimant harm.[2] A defendant cannot intend to induce the breach of a contract of which he or she is unaware.[3] However there is also authority to the effect that a defendant may, in some circumstances, be deemed to have knowledge of the almost certain existence of contracts,[4] although the court will not invent hypothetical contracts which might be breached were they to exist.[5] It is clear that A need not know the precise terms of the contract provided that the requisite intent is present, and it seems that mere recklessness whether or not a breach occurs will suffice.[6] Despite a suggestion to the contrary by Lord Denning,[7] it seems that for the direct form of the tort (in contrast to the indirect), bare interference with a contract which does not amount to a breach (where there is a *force majeure* clause in operation, for example) will not suffice.[8] 'Inducement' will normally consist of a direct approach, but less direct methods may also constitute inducement, including passing on information that a given company is being boycotted by a union, which leads the recipient to act in breach of contract with it,[9] and 'direct prevention' of performance, such as hiding an employee's tools.[10] In the context of picketing the concept has been taken even wider, to include the mere presence of pickets where it was clear that their presence was intended to induce, and was successful in its object of inducing, breach of contract.[11] It is crucial, however, to the direct form of the tort that the inducement is directed to a party to the contract.[12] Participation in industrial action nearly always constitutes a breach of contract, and therefore dispute organisers will generally commit the direct form of the tort in persuading workers to take industrial action.[13] It may also be committed if, for example, a dispute organiser approaches a supplier of the employer in dispute and persuades it not to deliver supplies in breach of an existing contract.[14] There is a defence of justification available for this tort but it has been very narrowly construed; the rejection by the House of Lords of the argument that a union could be justified in organising industrial action where it was in the economic interests of its members[15] has rendered it virtually meaningless in the industrial action context. It is strongly arguable that inducing employees to stop work in specified circumstances for health and safety reasons should be covered, given that employees are protected against dismissal or other detriment both for stopping work themselves and for taking 'appropriate steps' to protect themselves and others from the danger,[16] either on the basis that the duty to obey lawful and reasonable orders should be subject to this right or on the basis of the justification defence. However this point has yet to be tested in the courts. In general, it is crucial for dispute organisers to attempt to ensure that they can bring themselves within the statutory immunity for this tort provided by the Trade Union and Labour Relations (Consolidation) Act 1992, s 219(1)(a) (see further para **6.18**).

---

1. *Lumley v Gye* (1853) 2 E and B 216, QB; *Allen v Flood* [1898] AC 1; *South Wales Miners' Federation v Glamorgan Coal Co Ltd* [1905] AC 239, HL.
2. *Smithies v NATSOPA* [1909] 1 KB 310, at 316; *DC Thomson and Co v Deakin* [1952] Ch 646, Jenkins LJ at 696–697 and Morris LJ at 702; *Edwin Hill and Partners (a firm) v First National Finance Corpn plc* [1988] 3 All ER 801, CA. On the requisite intention, cf *Millar v Bassey* [1994] EMLR 44 (and Weir, 1997, App 1) where the Court of Appeal refused to strike out a claim based on the allegation that the defendant had refused to perform her own contract knowing that such refusal would make it impossible for the other party to fulfil its contractual obligations to the claimant. It was not pleaded that the defendant intended this result. See Weir, 1997, 18–19 and 38–39 for a stringent critique of this decision.
3. See *Timeplan Education Group Ltd v NUT* [1997] IRLR 457, CA.
4. See *Merkur Island Shipping Corpn v Laughton* [1983] 2 AC 570, HL (dictum of Sir John Donaldson MR approved); *Union Traffic Ltd v TGWU* [1989] IRLR 127, CA.
5. *Middlebrook Mushrooms Ltd v TGWU* [1993] IRLR 232, CA.
6. *JT Stratford and Son Ltd v Lindley* [1965] AC 269, HL; *Emerald Construction Co Ltd v Lothian* [1966] 1 WLR 691, CA; see also *Grieg v Insole* [1978] 3 All ER 449 at 488, ChD; *Metropolitan Borough of Solihull v NUT* [1985] IRLR 211, ChD.
7. *Torquay Hotel Co Ltd v Cousins* [1969] 2 Ch 106 at 137–138.
8. See Clerk and Lindsell, 1995, as updated, para 23-19. See also Lord Diplock in *Merkur Island Shipping Corpn v Laughton*, above, note 4: it is unclear whether or not

he was referring to the direct as well as the indirect form of the tort in this judgment. *Falconer v ASLEF and NUR*, discussed in para **6.5**, appears to be a case of indirect, not direct, interference.

9. *JT Stratford and Son Ltd v Lindley*, above, note 6, at 333. In *DC Thomson and Co v Deakin*, above, note 2, the communication was found to fall short of an inducement.

10. *DC Thomson and Co v Deakin*, above, note 2 Jenkins LJ at 696.

11. See *Union Traffic Ltd v TGWU*, above, note 4. Cf the stricter approach to inducement to procure the infringement of copyright by Lord Templeman in *CBS Songs Ltd v Amstrad Consumer Electronic plc* [1988] 2 All ER 484 at 496–497, HL: 'generally speaking, inducement, incitement or persuasion to infringe must be by a defendant to an individual infringer and must identifiably procure a particular infringement in order to make the defendant liable as a joint infringer'.

12. *Middlebrook Mushrooms Ltd v TGWU* [1993] IRLR 232, CA.

13. See para **6.82** *et seq*. Note TULRCA 1992, s 245, which states that where any person 'holds any office or employment under the Crown on terms which do not constitute a contract of employment', those terms shall nevertheless be deemed to constitute such a contract for the purpose of the torts based upon inducing breach of, or interference with, a contract. Note that where there is an element of doubt whether the action does constitute a breach of contract, this in itself may constitute a 'serious question to be tried': see for example *Metropolitan Borough of Solihull v NUT*, above, note 6.

14. It remains lawful to persuade a person not to make a contract: *Midland Cold Storage Ltd v Steer* [1972] Ch 630. However the courts have been prepared to countenance granting injunctions (formerly known as *quia timet* injunctions) to prevent respondents from inducing breach of a future contract: see *JT Stratford and Son Ltd v Lindley* , above, note 6, Lord Upjohn at 339; *Union Traffic Ltd v TGWU* above, note 4.

15. *South Wales Miners' Federation v Glamorgan Coal Co Ltd*, above, note 1. The defence has succeeded only once in England in an industrial action context: *Brimelow v Casson* [1924] 1 Ch 302, ChD, where the facts were highly unusual (duty to prevent payment of insufficient wages to chorus girls because this led them to resort to prostitution), approved in *Pritchard v Briggs* [1980] 1 All ER 294, CA. Cf the New Zealand case of *Pete's Towing Services v Northern Industrial Union* [1970] NZLR 32. On general principles, see *Edwin Hill and Partners (a firm) v First National Finance Corpn plc*, above, note 2, and the useful discussion by O'Dair, 1991. See also *SOS Kinderdorf International v Bittaye* [1996] 1 WLR 987, PC (circumstances such as to justify an employer in dismissing an employee cannot, except perhaps in exceptional circumstances, constitute justification for a third party interfering with the contract).

16. ERA 1996, ss 44(1)(d), 100(1)(d). For the relationship between this provision and 'industrial action', see para **6.93**.

6.4 Liability for the indirect form of the tort of inducing breach of contract occurs where, rather than directly inducing a breach of contract between B and C, A uses unlawful means which produce this result. In relation to industrial disputes, a common situation is where A persuades B's employees to take industrial action in breach of their contracts of employment and by these unlawful means produces the result that B is unable to fulfil a commercial contract with C. This form of liability was first recognised in *DC Thomson and Co v Deakin*, where Jenkins LJ stated that the elements of the tort were:

> first that the person charged with actionable interference knew of the existence of the contract and intended to procure its breach; secondly, that the person so charged did definitely and unequivocally persuade, induce or procure the employees concerned to break their contracts of employment with the intent I have mentioned; thirdly, that the employees so persuaded, induced or procured did in fact break their contracts of employment; and fourthly, that breach of the contract forming the alleged subject of the interference ensued as a necessary consequence of the breaches by the employees concerned of their contracts of employment.[1]

The indirect form of the tort, unlike the direct, has been extended to cover the situation where the interference with the contract falls short of actual breach, although it may be argued that this conflicts with the principle laid down in *Allen v Flood*[2] that no liability should lie in the absence of independent unlawfulness. This first occurred in *Torquay Hotel Co Ltd v Cousins*,[3] where a contract for the supply of oil between Esso and the hotel provided that Esso was not to be liable for any failure to fulfil the agreement if it was prevented from doing so by labour disputes. Although, strictly speaking, there was no breach of contract when industrial action prevented deliveries, Lord Denning MR held that there could still be liability for preventing or hindering performance of the contract.[4] In 1983 the House of Lords approved this extension of the tort, Lord Diplock stating that in the elements of the tort articulated by Jenkins LJ in *DC Thomson and Co v Deakin* the term 'interference with performance' should be substituted for 'breach' (except in relation to the breaking by employees of their own contracts of employment).[5] He denied that this involved any extension of the decision in the latter case; although Jenkins LJ had confined himself to breach of contractual rights because that was the form of interference at issue, '[a]ll prevention of due performance of a primary obligation under a contract was intended to be included even though no secondary obligation to make monetary compensation thereupon came into existence, because the second obligation was excluded by some form of force majeure clause'.[6] Logically, however, if this argument holds good in this context, interference with performance should also suffice for the direct form of the tort. In *Dimbleby and Sons Ltd v NUJ* Sir John Donaldson MR affirmed that 'interference' meant 'hindrance as well as prevention'.[7] Here the NUJ was conducting a boycott of a third-party company, TBF Ltd, in pursuance of a trade dispute. Dimbleby had a contract for some printing to be carried out by another company in the TBF group, TBF Printers Ltd. The union called on its members employed by Dimbleby to refuse to supply copy to Dimbleby for printing by TBF. Dimbleby sought an injunction against the union on the basis that it had thereby interfered with the contract between

Dimbleby and TBF Printers. The Court of Appeal upheld this argument and granted Dimbleby the injunction even though it had, in the event, managed to produce newspapers by finding copy from other sources; the 'loss of services of staff journalists was quite clearly a hindrance to the performance by the . . . [claimants] . . . of their contractual obligations towards TBF Printers Ltd'.[8] It is also notable that in this case the claimant invoked the tort as the party whose performance was being interfered with not, as in *Torquay Hotel*, the party to whom performance was owed.

---

1. *DC Thomson and Co v Deakin* [1952] Ch 646, CA, at 697; see also *JT Stratford and Son Ltd v Lindley* [1965] AC 269. For a discussion of the distinction between the direct and indirect form of the tort, see *Middlebrook Mushrooms Ltd v TGWU* [1993] IRLR 232, CA. Note that an act which is not actionable in itself by virtue of the immunities bestowed by TULRCA 1992, s 219 (see para **6.18**) may not constitute 'unlawful means' for the purpose of those torts where unlawful means is a requirement: *Hadmor Productions Ltd v Hamilton* [1982] IRLR 102, HL.

2. [1898] AC 1.

3. [1969] 2 Ch 106, CA.

4. Russell LJ preferred to ground his decision on the basis that the clause was 'an exception from liability for non-performance rather than an exception from obligation to perform' (at 143); Winn LJ said that it was actionable if the normal course of dealing between the parties had led the parties to expect performance (at 147).

5. *Merkur Island Shipping Corpn v Laughton* [1983] ICR 490, HL, at 506.

6. *Ibid.*, at 506. This reasoning was developed in Lord Diplock's own judgment in *Photo Production Ltd v Securicor Transport Ltd* [1980] AC 827.

7. [1984] IRLR 67, CA, at 73. This point was not at issue in the subsequent appeal to the House of Lords.

8. *Ibid.*

6.5 The nature of the intent required on the part of the defendant to constitute the indirect form of the tort is not entirely clear. In *DC Thomson and Co v Deakin* Jenkins LJ made clear that the defendant must have intended to procure the breach of contract by the use of unlawful means.[1] On one view, this can be equated with an intention by the defendant to harm the claimant.[2] However, it seems that liability is not confined to situations where the defendant so intended; rather, the courts have permitted proceedings to be brought by claimants who are not the direct target of the defendant's action.[3] An indication of the implications of allowing the tort to be widened in this way is provided by the county court decision of *Falconer v ASLEF and NUR*.[4] In this case industrial action by British Rail employees prevented the claimant from using his return train ticket from London to the north of England on the day he had intended and he stayed in a hotel in London for the next two days. He successfully sued the rail unions for damages representing his expenses on the basis that they had interfered with the contractual obligation of British Rail to provide carriage by train. The court allowed this claim despite a clause in the conditions of carriage enabling British Rail to withdraw all services on any day or suspend the running of trains without being liable for any loss thereby occasioned.[5] The judge held that this did not remove or exclude the primary obligation of British Rail to provide carriage, but merely limited its liability and, moreover, the unions could not rely on an exclusion clause when their own actions had caused the breach. He also accepted the claimant's argument that it was sufficient to show that the defendants knew that there were existing contracts between the Board and the group or class of persons (passengers) of which the claimant was one; it was irrelevant that his actual name and description were unknown to them at the time. He rejected the unions' argument that the claimant was not the object of the action when the strike was called. To suggest that harm to passengers was merely a consequence of, rather than an intended object of, their action was 'naive and divorced from reality'.[6] In any event, he was willing to hold that the 'reckless' imposition of harm was sufficient for the tort. This decision has not been tested in a higher court; were it to be upheld it would expand enormously the range of potential claimants at common law in relation to industrial action which is not protected by the statutory immunities.

---

1. See para **6.4** above.
2. Sales and Stilitz, 1999, 434. In *Barretts and Baird (Wholesale) Ltd v IPCS* [1987] IRLR 3, Henry J assumed (at 11) that the defendant's predominant purpose must be injury to the claimant.
3. *Dimbleby and Sons Ltd v NUJ* [1984] IRLR 67, CA.
4. [1986] IRLR 331.
5. Relying upon *DC Thomson and Co v Deakin* [19521 Ch 646, CA; see para **6.4**.
6. [1986] IRLR 331, at 334.

Liability for inducement to breach, or interference with, other legal rights

6.6 Liability for inducing breach of contracts rests upon the ground that 'a violation of a legal right committed knowingly is a cause of action'.[1] In recent years this form of liability has been extended to inducement to breach a statutory duty[2] and inducement to breach an equitable obligation,[3] both wrongs which lie outside the scope of the statutory immunities. Inducing breach of a statutory duty is potentially of great significance in public services, where many workers perform duties which their employer is obliged by statute to carry out.[4] The potential for this form of liability was first suggested by the Court of Appeal in *Meade v Haringey London Borough Council*.[5] Here the claimant parents argued that, by closing its schools during a strike by school caretakers, the authority was breaching its statutory duty to provide education. The majority of the court refused to decide this issue conclusively in interim proceedings, but it was suggested that if the authority was in breach, the unions, by calling on the employer to close the schools, could be inducing the authority to breach its statutory duty. The application of this tort in its direct form is circumscribed by the general principle that the statutory duty which is obstructed must be independently actionable at the suit of the claimant (a point not addressed in *Meade*).[6] Whether or not a claimant has an independent right of action depends entirely upon the language and purpose of the statute in question; usually it involves showing that the duty was imposed for the benefit of a particular class of persons to which the claimant belongs,[7] but whether this requirement will be met is often unpredictable.[8] However it has been suggested that a non-actionable breach of statutory duty may constitute the requisite 'unlawful means' for the purpose of the tort of interference with trade or business by unlawful means,[9] an approach which widens considerably the scope of potential liability. Where the inducement is indirect rather than direct, analogy with the indirect form of inducing breach of contract suggests that unlawful means should be required, but this has yet to be decided.[10] If unlawful means were not required, there would be little scope for any form of industrial action in the public sector.[11]

---

1. *Quinn v Leathem* [1901] AC 495, per Lord Macnaghten at 510.

2. *Meade v Haringey LBC* [1979] ICR 494, CA; *Associated Newspapers Group Ltd v Wade* [1979] IRLR 201, CA; *Associated British Ports v TGWU* [1989] IRLR 305, CA (reversed by the House of Lords at [1989] IRLR 399 on the point that there was no statutory duty in those circumstances).

3. *Prudential Assurance Co Ltd v Lorenz* [1971] 11 KIR 78, ChD (inducement of breach of the obligation to account); *Boulting v ACTT* [1963] 2 QB 606, CA (breach of fiduciary duty); although cf. *Metall und Rohstoff AG v Donaldson Lufkin & Jenrette Inc* [1990] 1 QB 391; see also *Crawley Borough Council v Ure* [1996] QB 13. In *Wilson v Housing Corporation* [1997] IRLR 346, Dyson J held that the tort of inducing unfair dismissal did not exist.

4. Note that in some contexts liability for inducement to breach a statutory duty has been incorporated in statute: see the Telecommunications Act 1984, s 18. For possible liability under analogous provisions in the gas, electricity and water industries, see Morris, 1991, 96. Note also the statutory duty owed to the Secretary of State not to induce a prison officer to withhold his services as such an officer or to commit a breach

of discipline: Criminal Justice and Public Order Act 1994, s 127(1),(2); see further Morris, 1994b, 328–329.

5. Above note 2.

6. *Associated British Ports v TGWU*, above, note 2.

7. The other circumstance is where the statute creates a public right and a particular member of the public suffers special damage peculiar to himself. see *Lonrho Ltd v Shell Petroleum Co Ltd (No 2)* [1981] 2 All ER 456, HL, Lord Diplock at 461–462.

8. See generally Clerk and Lindsell, 1995, as updated, Chapter 11. Note also in this context *Barretts and Baird (Wholesale) Ltd v IPCS* [1987] IRLR 3, discussed Fredman 1987; Simpson 1987, where the scope of the statutory duty was at issue.

9. *Associated British Ports v TGWU*, above, note 2; see also *Surzor Overseas Ltd v Koros* [1999] 2 Lloyd's Rep 611, CA, Waller LJ at 616–617; see also para **6.10**.

10. *In Barretts and Baird (Wholesale) Ltd*, above note 8, Henry J was sympathetic to this argument (which would seem also to apply by analogy to inducing breach of an equitable obligation).

11. Napier, 1987.

Interference with trade or business by unlawful means

6.7 The tort of interference with trade or business by unlawful means occurs where A intentionally uses unlawful means with the purpose and effect of causing damage to B in B's trade or business. This 'genus' tort is of potentially wide application. There are two crucial questions in relation to it. The first is the acts which are capable of constituting 'unlawful means' for this purpose. The second is the nature of the intention on the part of the defendant which must be shown. We examine these issues insofar as they relate to industrial action in para **6.8**. In the remainder of this paragraph we discuss the 'species' tort of intimidation, which is particularly important in the context of industrial action and which raises questions material to analysis of the broader tort. The tort of intimidation is committed when A threatens B that he or she will commit an act or use means which are unlawful as against B with the intention of causing B to do or refrain from doing something which B is at liberty to do, so causing damage either to B (two-party intimidation) or to C (three-party intimidation).[1] For the purposes of this tort it has long been clear that the application of physical force or violence or the threat of such violence constitutes unlawful means.[2] Thus, a threat of violence by a picket against a worker who crossed a picket-line would fall within this category, for example.[3] However the wider relevance of this tort to industrial action was made clear by the landmark case of *Rookes v Barnard*,[4] where the House of Lords accepted that a threat to breach a contract could constitute the requisite unlawful means for the purposes of this tort. Here, two shop stewards and a union official threatened an employer, called BOAC, with a strike unless a non-unionist, Rookes, was dismissed. The employers terminated Rookes's contract lawfully and with due notice. Rookes then sued the union officers. It was conceded (most unusually) that a no-strike clause in a collective agreement was incorporated as a term in the employees' contracts of employment.[5] The court held that, even though Rookes could not have sued BOAC for breach of contract, this did not rule out his claim for the tort of intimidation given that BOAC had responded to pressure of an unlawful kind from the union officials who were intending to injure Rookes. The threat to breach the contract of employment constituted intimidation; in Lord Reid's words, Rookes was suing for 'loss caused to him by the use of an unlawful weapon against him— intimidation of another person by unlawful means'.[6] This tort is likely to be committed whenever industrial action is threatened provided that the industrial action constitutes a breach of contract,[7] and it is therefore crucial for potential defendants to ensure that they are protected by the statutory immunity against this tort provided by TULRCA 1992, s 219(1)(b) (see further para **6.18**). It seems unlikely that there is a defence of justification to this tort; if there is, the circumstances where it could apply would probably be rare.[8] It has been argued that where a breach of contract constitutes the threat in the context of intimidation, it would be inappropriate to extend the doctrine of *Rookes v Barnard* (a case of three-party intimidation) to two-party intimidation, where both claimant and defendant are parties to the same contract, on the ground that this would enable circumvention of rules of contract law, such as remoteness and mitigation, which limit the extent of contract damages in comparison with tort.[9] In practice this may be a less important issue in the light of the development of the doctrine of economic duress, which gives rise to a remedy in restitution. We discuss this remedy further in para **6.66**.

---

1. It is almost certainly the case that the claimant must be a person whom A intended to injure: see Clerk and Lindsell, 1995, and supplement, para 23–38, note 59, where the view is expressed that A will not be liable to C without such intention even if reckless as to the effect of the threat to B upon C.
2. *Tarleton v McGawley* (1793) Peake 270.
3. See *Messenger Newspapers Group Ltd v NGA* [1984] ICR 345, CA.
4. [1964] AC 1129, HL.
5. See para **6.84** for the current position. Note TULRCA 1992, s 245, discussed in para **6.3**, note 13, in this context.
6. [1964] AC 1129, 1168. The basis of liability of one of the union officials has always been puzzling, given that he was not employed by the employers and therefore had no contract he could threaten to break. In *Morgan v Fry* [1968] 2 QB 710 at 729 Lord Denning suggested that he not only threatened to induce a breach of contracts of employment (which would have been within the immunities as they then existed) but was also party to the conspiracy of the others to break contracts. However, as Kidner, 1983, 133, note 85, states, this explanation is not entirely satisfactory as he would not have been directly liable for conspiracy to injure by unlawful means, but could only be liable for conspiring with others to use the unlawful means of the others.

7. In *Morgan v Fry*, above, it was suggested by Russell LJ (at 737–739) that the breach of contract should be more than a minor one, but it is unlikely, even if that argument were accepted, that in interim proceedings the nature of the breach would be investigated unless it were possible to argue that it was too minor to cause damage: Hepple and Matthews, 1991, 723.

8. The possibility of a justification defence was rejected by the House of Lords in *Rookes v Barnard*, above, note 4; see also Lord Denning in *Cory Lighterage Ltd v TGWU* [1973] ICR 339 at 357. It is suggested in Markesinis and Deakin, 1999, 486, that there may be a limited justification defence that the defendant was asserting a pre-existing legal right which was at least the equivalent of the right he was interfering with.

9. See Carty, 1988, 260–262; cf Sales and Stilitz 1999, 422–425.

6.8 In relation to the wider tort, the requirement of 'unlawful means' delimits what conduct by the defendant will be regarded as illegitimate; the dividing line is between 'doing what you have a legal right to do and doing what you have no legal right to do . . .'[1] The categories of unlawful means are now very wide.[2] Threats of unlawful action, as well as constituting the tort of intimidation, may also constitute 'unlawful means' for the purposes of this tort.[3] It seems that the torts of nuisance (for example, blocking the entrance to an employer's premises) or trespass will suffice.[4] In *Associated British Ports v TGWU* the majority of the Court of Appeal considered that inducing breach of a statutory duty may also constitute unlawful means, regardless of whether the duty is independently actionable by the claimant,[5] in contrast to the direct form of the tort where independent actionability is required. If this view prevails, it is capable of having widespread implications for industrial action in public services whose provision is subject to statutory duties, particularly if, as has been suggested,[6] an employer upon whom the statutory duty has been placed could invoke the tort. It could also have implications if the unlawful means which it is sought to invoke consists of breach of a penal statute, although there is weighty authority to the effect that breach of a penal statute should not amount to unlawful means for the purposes of this tort.[7] Finally, it has been suggested that breach of contract *per se* may constitute unlawful means for the purposes of the wider tort as it may for the tort of intimidation.[8] If accepted, this view would mean that individual participants in industrial action could be personally liable in tort to third parties whose businesses were interfered with by the action merely by breaching their own contracts of employment. This would be particularly significant in view of the fact that there is no statutory immunity against breach of contract *simpliciter* and claimants would be able to claim damages from individual workers in circumstances where the dispute organisers were immune from liability.[9] The potentially wide application of this tort makes the test of intention particularly crucial. It is generally accepted that it needs to be shown that the unlawful act was directed against the claimant or intended to harm him or her.[10] There is also authority for the view that this need not be the defendant's predominant purpose.[11] However, at the time of writing there is no clear line of authority on the requisite mental element,[12] a matter which awaits clarification by the House of Lords.

---

1. See *Rookes v Barnard* [1964] AC 1129, Lord Reid at 1168–1169; see also Lord Pearce at 1234; Lord Devlin at 1207, 1209; *DC Thomson and Co Ltd v Deakin* [1952] Ch 646, Lord Evershed MR at 679–682; *Torquay Hotel Co Ltd v Cousins* [1969] 2 Ch 106, Lord Denning MR at 139. Note that acts which are afforded immunity under TULRCA 1992, s 219 cannot constitute 'unlawful means' for this purpose: *Hadmor Productions Ltd v Hamilton* [1982] IRLR 102, HL.

2. Here we mention only those most material to industrial action. For a wider discussion see Markesinis and Deakin, 1999, 480–485; Sales and Stilitz, 1999; also useful (although not entirely up to date) is Carty, 1988.

3. *Hadmor Productions Ltd v Hamilton*, above, note 1.

4. See *Norbrook Laboratories Ltd v King* [1984] IRLR 200, NI CA; *Messenger Newspapers Group Ltd v NGA (1982)* [1984] IRLR 397, QBD; see further paras **6.68** and **6.69**.

5. [1989] IRLR 305; Butler-Sloss LJ at 314; Stuart-Smith LJ at 316; cf the reservations expressed by Neill LJ at 311. The House of Lords reversed the decision on the ground that the obligation of a registered dock worker to work for his employer was essentially a contractual obligation, and the statutory scheme did not impose a statutory obligation to work independent of, and additional to, this obligation. The case was therefore one of inducing dockworkers to break their contracts of employment: [1989] IRLR 399, HL. See also para **6.10**.

6. Markesinis and Deakin, 1999, 484. This is by analogy with *Dimbleby and Sons v NUJ* [1984] IRLR 67, CA; see para **6.4** above.

7. *Lonrho Ltd v Shell Petroleum Co Ltd (No 2)* [1981] 2 All ER 456, HL; *RCA Corporation v Pollard* [1982] 3 All ER 771, CA; *Lonrho plc v Fayed*, [1989] 2 All ER 65, CA. Cf Sales and Stilitz, 1999, 416, and authorities therein, where it is argued that this should not be a barrier if the requisite intention is shown.

8. *Barretts and Baird (Wholesale) Ltd v IPCS* [1987] IRLR 3, QBD.

9. For further discussion of this case, see Fredman, 1987; Simpson, 1987, 506. Because of TULRCA 1992, s 236 the claimant's remedy in such a case would probably be limited to damages: see para **6.81** and *Barretts and Baird (Wholesale) Ltd v IPCS*, above, Henry J at 10.

10. *Allen v Flood* [1898] AC 1, Lord Watson at 96, 98. Cf. *Lonrho plc v Fayed* [1989] 2 All ER 65, Woolf LJ at 73, who considered that the tort could be committed if a defendant deliberately embarked upon a course of conduct the probable consequence of which on the claimant he appreciated (but cf. again *Associated British Ports v TGWU*, above note 5, where intent to injure was treated as the essence of the tort, although without explaining fully the nature of the requisite intent).

11. *Lonrho plc v Fayed*, above. The ingredients of the tort of interference with business by unlawful means were not discussed in the judgments on appeal to the House of Lords [1991] 3 All ER 303 (although see Lord Bridge at 312).

12. See further Clerk and Linsell, 1995, with supplement, paras 23–56 *et seq.*; Sales and Stilitz, 1999, 425–430.

Conspiracy to injure (or 'simple' conspiracy)

6.9 The tort of conspiracy to injure is committed where two or more persons combine with the predominant purpose of injuring a third party rather than serving their own *bona fide* and legitimate interests.[1] Thus action which would not be unlawful if taken by one person can become so by the element of combination. This tort has been of little importance in the context of industrial disputes since *Crofter Hand Woven Harris Tweed Co v Veitch*,[2] in which the House of Lords recognised the legitimacy of trade union interests (in that case, to achieve 100 per cent union membership). It was also emphasised in that case that the court would not make its own assessment of whether the action was, in objective terms, likely to achieve the combiners' goal; it was sufficient that the object was the 'legitimate benefit of the combiners' rather than 'deliberate damage without any such just cause'.[3] The anomalous nature of this tort has been acknowledged in a number of cases, particularly given the establishment of large corporations which, although legally single individuals, may wield extensive power.[4] Despite this, the House of Lords has affirmed that it is 'too well-established' to be discarded.[5]

---

1. *Quinn v Leathem* [1901] AC 495, HL. The predominant purpose requirement was emphasised in *Crofter Hand Woven Harris Tweed Co Ltd v Veitch* [1942] 1 All ER 142, HL; *Lonrho Ltd v Shell Petroleum Ltd (No 2)* [1981] 2 All ER 456, HL; *Allied Arab Bank Ltd v Hajjar (No 2)* [1988] 3 All ER 103, QBD; *Lonrho plc v Fayed* [1991] 3 All ER 303, HL.
2. Above, note 1.
3. Lord Wright at 161. In *Scala Ballroom (Wolverhampton) Ltd v Ratcliffe* [1958] 3 All ER 220, CA a boycott by the Musicians' Union of the claimant's ballroom to get a colour bar lifted was found to be legitimate. Cf *Huntley v Thornton* [1957] 1 All ER 234, *per* Harman J (union district committee thinking only of their 'ruffled dignity' and not the interests of the union in continued victimisation of an individual member). Note the immunity afforded by TULRCA 1992, s 219(2); see para **6.18**.
4. *Crofter Hand Woven Harris Tweed Co Ltd v Veitch*, above, note 1, Lord Wright at 162; *Lonrho Ltd v Shell Petroleum Ltd (No 2)*, above note 1; *Lonrho plc v Fayed*, above, note 1.
5. Above, note 1, Lord Diplock at 464.

Conspiracy to commit an unlawful act or use unlawful means

6.10 Where two or more persons combine to commit an unlawful act or use unlawful means, they may commit the tort of conspiracy to commit an unlawful act or use unlawful means. For this tort, unlike simple conspiracy, it need not be shown that the sole or predominant purpose of the defendants' agreement was to injure the claimant's interests; it is sufficient to make their action tortious that the means used were unlawful. The precise nature of the intent required awaits clarification; consistency with the intent required for the tort of interfering with business by unlawful means would seem desirable.[1] The allegation of conspiracy makes it possible to impose liability on a person who cannot himself or herself commit the tort in question, for example a union official who supports employees who threaten to break their contracts of employment.[2] It is unclear whether the tort extends beyond combinations to commit a tort[3] and, in particular, whether there can be an actionable conspiracy to break contracts *simpliciter*[4] (an open question in relation to the tort of interference with trade or business by unlawful means: see para **6.8** above) If such an argument were to be upheld, this would mean that any two or more workers who agreed to take industrial action in breach of contract could be liable for conspiracy and would not be protected by the statutory immunities.[5]

---

1. *Lonrho plc v Fayed* [1991] 3 All ER 303, HL, overruling *Metall und Rohstoff AG v Donaldson, Lufkin and Jenrette Inc* [1989] 3 All ER 14, CA on this point; *Kuwait Oil Tanker Co Sak v Abdul Fattah Sulaiman Khalad Al Badar*, CA, 18 May 2000, para 118. In *Lonrho plc v Fayed* the House of Lords affirmed that the two causes of action in that case should stand or fall together.

2. As in *Rookes v Barnard* [1964] AC 1129, HL, para **6.7**. Note, however, that acts which are afforded immunity under TULRCA 1992, s 219 cannot constitute the requisite 'unlawful act' or 'unlawful means' for the purposes of this tort: *Hadmor Productions Ltd v Hamilton* [1982] IRLR 102, HL.

3. In *Lonrho Ltd v Shell Petroleum Co Ltd* [1981] 2 All ER 456 the House of Lords held that there could not be liability based upon the commission of criminal acts which did not also constitute torts. In this context, as in the context of interference with trade or business by unlawful means, it has been suggested that the unlawful means may not have to be actionable at the suit of the claimant: see *Surzur Overseas Ltd v Koros* [1999] 2 Lloyd's Rep 611, CA, Waller LJ at 616–617; *Kuwait Oil Tanker Co Sak*, above note 1.

4. This point was left open in *Rookes v Barnard*, above, note 2. In *Barretts and Baird (Wholesale) Ltd v IPCS* [1987] IRLR 3, Henry J thought that there was an arguable case that a breach of contract was unlawful means for the purposes of the tort of interference with business: see para **6.8**.

5. But see para **6.8**, note 9.

The Statutory Right of Action

6.11 The Trade Union Reform and Employment Rights Act 1993 introduced a new statutory right of action which circumvents entirely the restrictions on the categories of potential claimants erected by the courts at common law.[1] It enables any 'individual' who claims that a 'trade union or other person has done, or is likely to do, an unlawful act to induce any person to take part, or to continue to take part, in industrial action' where 'an effect, or a likely effect, . . . is or will be' to 'prevent or delay the supply of goods or services', or to reduce the quality of those supplied, to him or her to apply to the High Court for an order.[2] The right applies irrespective of whether the individual is entitled to be supplied with the goods or services in question;[3] although, in theory, in the absence of a contract or other document specifying standards it may be hard to measure precisely the reduction in quality which may occur, the courts would probably not examine this question too closely. There is no requirement to demonstrate that material loss or damage, or even inconvenience, has been, or would be, suffered as a result of the disruption, so that non-collection of refuse on a particular day, for example, would suffice. An act to induce any person to take part, or continue to take part, in industrial action is unlawful for this purpose in two contexts.[4] The first is where it is actionable in tort *by any person* (our italics). Thus, even if at common law the only claimant would be the employer in dispute, any 'individual' who meets the statutory conditions may apply; there is no requirement to show any intent towards him or her. Moreover, the individual is able to bring proceedings even if the protection of the statutory immunities in relation to the act in question is otherwise lost only in relation to the employer in dispute because the union has failed to comply with the requisite information and notification requirements (see para **6.30** *et seq.*). The second context in which an act is unlawful is if it is attributed by statute to a trade union and could form the basis of an application by a union member under the Trade Union and Labour Relations (Consolidation) Act 1992, s 62 that he or she has been, or is likely to be, induced by the union to take part in industrial action which lacks the support of a valid ballot.[5] The second category will normally overlap with the first but its inclusion means that there will be an individual right to bring proceedings in relation to industrial action which does not constitute a breach of contract on the part of those participating in it and which may not, therefore, attract liability in tort. Where the argument is based upon a defect in the ballot this second category of unlawfulness will be the simplest line of argument as there will be no need to demonstrate that any tort has been committed. Where the court finds the claim 'well-founded' it must make an order requiring the person by whom the act or inducement has been, or is likely to be, done to take steps to ensure that no (or no further) act is done by him or her to induce any persons to take (or to continue to take) part in the industrial action and that no person takes industrial action as a result of any prior inducement.[6] Interim relief may be granted for this purpose,[7] and in practice most applications will be dealt with in this way. Until 1999 where the actual or prospective defendant was a trade union, the individual could seek assistance from the Commissioner for Protection Against Unlawful Industrial Action, but this office was abolished by the Employment Relations Act 1999.[8] Perhaps surprisingly, at the time of writing no applications under this provision have yet reached the courts.

---

1. This right took effect as TULRCA 1992, s 235A. For a detailed discussion of the right, see Morris, 1993.
2. *Ibid.*, s 235A(1). The normal statutory principles apply in determining whether an act of inducement is done by a union. Modern drafting practice treats 'individual' as excluding corporations (see, for example, the Company Securities (Insider Dealing) Act 1985), and in debates on TURERA 1993 it was assumed that it did not include a corporate body: HL Debs, Vol 545, cols 97–103, esp 100–101, 26 April 1993 (cf *Great Northern Rly v Great Central Rly* (1899) 10 Ry and Can Tfc Cas 275, where Wright J opined that 'individual' 'included a company or corporation, ie any legal person').
3. *Ibid.*, s 235A(3).
4. *Ibid.*, s 235A(2).
5. See further para **6.114**. See para **6.13** for the basis upon which action is attributed by statute to a union.
6. TULRCA 1992, s 235A(4).
7. *Ibid.*, s 235A(5). For the principles governing the granting of interim injunctions, see paras **6.52** *et seq.*
8. ERA 1999, s 28. The office was established by TURERA 1993. It supported only one application in its history, which did not proceed to court: Mr. Michael Wills, Minister of State for Small Firms, Trade and Industry, Official Report of Standing Committee E, 4 March 1999, 4.15 pm.

When is a Trade Union Liable in Tort?

Sources and general principles

6.12 Whether and on what basis trade unions have legal liability for the tortious acts of their members and officials is determined according to statutory or common law principles, depending upon the tort in question. The Trade Union and Labour Relations (Consolidation) Act 1992, s 20 governs union liability for the torts of inducing breach of contract or interfering with the performance of a contract, intimidation, or conspiracy to commit one of these torts, and for proceedings for failure to comply with an injunction imposed to restrain further commission of these torts. Organisers of industrial action generally commit the torts of inducing breach of contract and intimidation,[1] so the statutory principles, which make unions liable for the acts of a wide range of persons, are very likely to be relevant in this context. It is important to know in advance of any dispute whether the union will be liable because in that event the action must be preceded by a ballot; if it is not, then statutory immunity will automatically be lost (unless the union takes advantage of the limited opportunity to repudiate the act in question) and the union will be vulnerable to an application for an interim injunction and/or a claim for damages.[2] It is notable that the legislation brings within the scope of industrial action requiring approval in a ballot that which, under the rules of many unions, would probably not be classified as 'official' industrial action.[3] The union may repudiate the acts of persons other than the president, general secretary or principal executive committee, or persons empowered by the union rules to authorise or endorse industrial action, provided that a specified procedure is followed. This means that the union will not be legally liable for those acts. However, it should be noted that repudiation, which makes the industrial action 'unofficial', means that participants will be exposed to selective dismissal (other than for a limited range of automatically unfair reasons) within a short time of repudiation taking place.[4] Union liability is determined according to common law principles for torts other than those specified in the Trade Union and Labour Relations (Consolidation) Act 1992, s 20, such as nuisance,[5] and in proceedings for contempt of court not arising from breach of an injunction imposed in relation to a tort covered by s 20. These common law principles dictate that the union is liable for the acts of individuals acting with its express or implied authorisation, concepts which have been given a broad interpretation in the case law. Liability on the part of unions for the activities of individuals does not absolve those individuals of personal liability,[6] but proceedings are likely to be brought against the union where this is possible, although individuals may be joined as co-defendants.

---

1. See paras **6.3** and **6.7**.
2. See para **6.52** *et seq*. Note the statutory limit on the damages in actions in tort which may be awarded against trade unions under TULRCA 1992, s 22. See also s 20(6) which states, *inter alia*, that the statutory rules on union liability will apply in proceedings arising from breach of injunctions imposed in relation to the torts specified in s 20.
3. Research has shown that up to 1992 union rule books tended to remain unchanged in the area of industrial action, but there was much greater centralisation in practice over the authorisation of industrial action: see Undy *et al*, 1996, Chapter 6.
4. See paras **6.103** *et seq*.
5. See para **6.69**.
6. This is made explicit in TULRCA 1992, s 20(5).

Determining liability under statute

6.13 In relation to the torts specified in para **6.12** above, an act is taken to have been authorised or endorsed by a trade union if (but only if) it was done, or authorised or endorsed by, one of three categories of persons.[1] The first is any person empowered by the union rules to do, authorise or endorse acts of the kind in question. The term 'rules' is defined to mean both the written rules of the union and any other written provision forming part of the contract of membership.[2] Custom and practice in the union which has not been reduced to writing is therefore excluded in this context.[3] The second category is the principal executive committee,[4] president or general secretary.[5] The third is 'any other committee of the union or any other [union] official', whether employed by it or not. 'Official' is widely defined, covering an officer of the union, or of a branch or section, or a person elected or appointed in accordance with the union rules to be a representative of some or all of the members, including an employee of the same employer as the members (or one or more of them) whom he or she represents.[6] Shop stewards and other lay officials are therefore among those whose actions bind the union provided that their election or appointment is in accordance with the union rules. It is notable that liability for the acts of the second and third categories of persons applies notwithstanding anything in the union rules, or in any contract or rule of law.[7] This means that action which is 'unofficial' in terms of the union's own rules may not be viewed as such by the statute, a product of a deliberate strategy by the Conservative Government (which introduced this regime) of encouraging greater control by unions over their officials' actions.[8] In relation to the third category any group of persons constituted in accordance with the union rules is a 'committee' of the union; and an act is attributable to an official if it was done, authorised or endorsed by, or by any member of, any group of persons of which he or she was at the material time a member whose purposes included organising or co-ordinating industrial action.[9] This means that the official need not have approved of, or even been involved in taking, the decision to call for industrial action; it is sufficient that he or she was a member of the group at the 'material time'.[10] It is possible that mere attendance at a meeting to obtain information, or even to discourage industrial action, could constitute 'membership'; the Conservative Government denied that this would happen but it is not precluded by the statute.[11] There have been no cases on this point to date. The 'group' need not be a standing body; it may have been constituted on an *ad hoc* basis, and it is sufficient that its purposes include the organisation or co-ordination of industrial action; these need not be its principal purposes. In proceedings arising out of an act which is taken to have been done by a trade union under the statutory regime, the power of the court to grant injunctive relief includes power to require the union to take such steps as the court considers appropriate for ensuring that there is no, or no further, inducement of persons to take part or to continue to take part in industrial action, and that no person engages in any conduct after the granting of the injunction by virtue of a prior inducement to participate in industrial action.[12] This provision also applies to proceedings for contempt.[13] It was inserted because of doubt whether the union could be required to control persons who were not its servants or agents under common law principles of vicarious liability.[14]

---

1. TULRCA 1992, s 20(1)–(4). There is no statutory definition of 'authorised' or 'endorsed'. The term 'authorisation' is generally used when industrial action is approved before it commences; endorsement when it is authorised after commencement. In the event that industrial action begins spontaneously among a workforce, it is unclear whether mere participation by an official could imply 'authorisation'. However, it should be noted that in order for the union to be liable under the statutory regime, the official must have induced other workers to break their contracts of employment or committed some other tort covered by the statute. Cf *Express and Star Ltd v NGA (1982)* [1985] IRLR 455, QBD, where Skinner J made clear (at 459) that 'nods, winks, turning of blind eyes and similar clandestine methods of approval, which do not appear in records or minutes or circulars,' could amount to authorisation.

2. *Ibid.*, s 20(7).

3. See *British Railways Board v RMT* (17 September 1992, unreported), QBD. Cf the position at common law: see para **6.16**.

4. Curiously TULRCA 1992, s 20(2) keeps this term (used in the Employment Act 1982) although elsewhere in the legislation (including s 21) the term 'executive' (which has the same meaning) is used. 'Executive' is defined as 'the principal committee of the union exercising executive functions, by whatever name it is called' (TULRCA 1992, s 119).

5. In each case, where there is no such office, the term covers the person who holds the nearest equivalent office: *ibid.*, s 119.

6. *Ibid.* 'Officer' includes any member of the union's governing body and any trustee of any fund applicable for the purposes of the union (*ibid.*), but it is not confined to these categories. In *British Railways Board v RMT*, above, note 3, Laws J considered that the definition of rules in s 20(7) applied also in this context, despite the fact the definition in s 20(7) is prefaced by the words '[i]n this section'.

7. TULRCA 1992, s 20(4).

8. Research showed that unions were exercising a greater degree of centralised control over members' actions even before the scope of potential liability was widened: see Martin *et al*, 1991; Undy *et al*, 1996, Chapter 6.

9. TULRCA 1992, s 20(3).

10. Lord Strathclyde defined 'material time' as 'when the act for which the union is potentially liable was done': HL Debs, Vol 521, col 1250, 23 July 1990. However, as Lord Wedderburn pointed out (at col 1252) by the time the act for which liability arises—calling out the workforce—is done, the group may well have dispersed. It is unlikely that a court would take a restrictive view of this question.

11. Lord Strathclyde (*ibid.*, at 1251).

12. TULRCA 1992, s 20(6).

13. *Ibid.* Cf the common law principles of liability for contempt, outlined in paras **6.61** *et seq.*

14. Mr Patrick Nicholls, Parliamentary Under-Secretary of State for Employment, House of Commons, Official Report of Standing Committee D, col 312, 8 March 1990.

6.14 In relation to an act by the third category of persons only, the union can avoid liability if the act is repudiated by the executive, president or general secretary as soon as reasonably practicable after coming to the knowledge of any of them.[1] It is unclear whether the term 'executive' in relation to the acquisition of knowledge means the whole committee or merely an individual member of it; the fact that only the committee as a whole can effect a valid repudiation suggests the former. Whether the repudiation takes place 'as soon as reasonably practicable' will be a question of fact; where the executive is geographically scattered but a meeting is scheduled for a few days' time, that may not be sufficient in an age of the telephone, fax machine and e-mail. Given that many disputes organised at local level begin and end very rapidly, it is possible that the dispute may be over by the time that repudiation takes place. Repudiation involves an 'open disavowal and disowning of the acts of the officials concerned'.[2] Where an act is repudiated, a specified procedure must be followed or the repudiation will be ineffective. First, written notice of the repudiation must be given 'without delay' to the committee or official whose act is attributable to the union.[3] Secondly, the union must 'do its best' to give individual written notice of the fact and date of repudiation, without delay, to every member of the union whom the union has reason to believe is taking part, or might otherwise take part, in industrial action as a result of the act, and to the employer of every such member.[4] This obligation may be far reaching given that there is no need to show that it is probable, or even likely, that a member may otherwise take part in industrial action; a mere possibility appears to suffice. In relation to a strike call by a relatively junior official, deciding which members may be likely to respond may be problematic. The statute seems to require separate communication with each relevant member and their employer. It would be safest to send the notice by first class post; it is unclear whether using second-class post would be sufficient to satisfy the requirement that communication must be 'without delay'. The notice given to members must contain the following statement:

> Your union has repudiated the call (or calls) for industrial action to which this notice relates and will give no support to unofficial industrial action taken in response to it (or them). If you are dismissed while taking unofficial industrial action, you will have no right to complain of unfair dismissal.[5]

It appears that the prescribed wording must be followed to the letter. However, there is nothing to prevent the union including any additional message if it so wishes provided that this does not contradict the specified statement, or make its text ambiguous; indeed, the use of the word 'contain' seems to presuppose that the notice may contain other statements. Unions must also ensure that they are vigilant about their subsequent activities in relation to the industrial action; an act will not be treated as repudiated if *at any time* subsequently the executive, president or general secretary behaves in a manner which is inconsistent with the purported repudiation.[6] They will be treated as so behaving if they fail to confirm the repudiation in writing 'forthwith' on a request made within three months of the purported repudiation by a party to a commercial contract whose performance was at risk of interference from the act in question who has not already received written notice of this.[7] It seems that this eventuality may expose the union to liability at the instance not only of the person making the request but also of any other person who would have had a claim against the union in the absence of repudiation.

---

1. TULRCA 1992, s 21(1).
2. *Express and Star Ltd v NGA (1982)* [1985] IRLR 455 at 459, QBD.
3. TULRCA 1992, s 21(2)(a).
4. *Ibid.*, s 21(2)(b).
5. *Ibid.*, s 21(3). See para **6.103** *et seq.* for the withdrawal of protection against selective dismissal for those participating in unofficial industrial action.
6. *Ibid.*, s 21(5).
7. *Ibid.*, s 21(6). 'Commercial contract' means any contract other than a contract of employment or any other contract under which a person agrees personally to do work or perform services for another: *ibid.*, s 21(7). Lord Strathclyde considered that a union would be entitled to expect the request to be made in appropriate terms which would enable the union to identify the inducement which the customer wished to know about: HL Debs, Vol 521, col 1270, 23 July 1990.

6.15 The effect of a union repudiating liability is to make the industrial action 'unofficial' as from the end of the next working day after the day on which repudiation takes place.[1] In the event that the act of the committee or official was not preceded by a ballot in accordance with the statutory requirements (see para **6.30** *et seq.*), it would be open to the union to repudiate but then immediately hold a ballot on the issue. If this course were pursued, it would be advisable for the union to broaden the scope of the dispute, so rendering it a different dispute, to avoid the difficulty that immunity could be lost because it had 'called' the action before the date of the ballot (albeit that the call had subsequently been repudiated).[2] It is also uncertain what effect a repudiation which is deemed subsequently to be ineffective will have on the position of an employee who becomes liable to selective dismissal once an act has been repudiated. Under the Trade Union and Labour Relations (Consolidation) Act 1992, s 237 an employee has no right to complain of unfair dismissal if at the time of dismissal he or she was taking part in 'unofficial' industrial action, unless the dismissal is for one of a very limited range of automatically unfair reasons (see further para **6.103** *et seq.*). It could be argued that if an act is not, after all, to be treated as repudiated, the industrial action remains 'non-unofficial' in this context also and thus employees retain the protection against selective dismissal. It is conceivable that employees could also then come under the protection against automatically unfair dismissal where they have been dismissed for taking 'protected industrial action',[3] but in practice it is difficult to imagine circumstances where a union would wish to repudiate action which is protected in a ballot or, indeed, that it would be possible for it to do so, given that the action would probably have been authorised or endorsed by a person empowered by the rules or by the principal executive committee, president, or general secretary. The relationship between these provisions still awaits clarification by the courts and tribunals.

---

1. See further TULRCA 1992, s 237(4).

2. *Ibid.*, s 233(3). Note that s 20(2)–(4) applies for the purpose of determining whether a call has been authorised or endorsed by a union; s 20(4) makes liability subject to s 21, which provides for repudiation. However, in case the validity of repudiation were jeopardised by any subsequent conduct the safest course would be to proceed as suggested in the text. See further para **6.48** for the position of a 'call' by an unspecified person following a ballot.

3. TULRCA 1992, s 238A; see para **6.98** *et seq.* Provision is made for repudiation in s 238A(8).

Liability at common law

6.16 The liability of trade unions for tortious acts other than those specified in the Trade Union and Labour Relations (Consolidation) Act 1992, s 20, such as nuisance, is determined according to principles established by the common law. The union is liable for the acts of persons acting with its express or implied authorisation, regardless of whether they are its employees. A wide view of the concept of authorisation in this context was taken by the House of Lords in *Heatons Transport (St Helens) Ltd v TGWU.*[1] In this case the union was held liable for the acts of unofficial committees of shop stewards which were not provided for in the union rule book and had been set up solely on the initiative of the stewards themselves, on the basis that the stewards had general implied authority and discretion to act on the union's behalf in protecting members' wages and working conditions by industrial action in the circumstances in question and they were promoting general union policy in doing this. The court emphasised that in determining the scope of the authority of an official to bind the union regard must be had both to the written rule book and to custom and practice, which could have the effect of modifying the union's rules as they operated in practice or compensate for the absence of formal rules. To avoid liability in this situation the union would have needed to withdraw the authority of the stewards to continue organising the industrial action 'in terms which would be reasonably understood by them as forbidding them to continue',[2] possibly by withdrawing their credentials and, if necessary, taking disciplinary action. This broad-brush approach to liability, to the extent that it pays regard to the wider circumstances, and in particular whether officials are acting in accordance with union policy,[3] accords greater respect to internal union practices than the statutory approach (see para **6.13**). However it may require unions to go to extreme lengths to disassociate themselves from the acts of their members. The measures which the courts may require to avoid liability for the acts of members and officials who commit a tort in the course of picketing was considered in *News Group Newspapers Ltd v SOGAT 82 (No 2)*,[4] where liability for, *inter alia*, the torts of public and private nuisance was at issue. Stuart-Smith J accepted the view that unions are not liable merely by organising a march or picketing during the course of which tortious acts are committed by third parties even though such acts can be foreseen. However, he held that unions may be taken to have authorised the commission of a nuisance or other tort or to have continued a nuisance[5] where they continue to organise events which in the light of experience constitute a tort, in the knowledge or presumed knowledge that such torts are being committed by those whom they organise. In this case the conduct of the pickets had been repeated regularly and must have been well known to the unions. The court rejected the argument that the unions lacked sufficient control over their members to restrain the commission of the torts in question; they had failed to discipline or threaten to discipline those who persistently flouted union instructions that picketing was to be peaceful, nor had they forbidden them to act as official pickets. If the unions could not exercise sufficient control, they might have to desist from organising the picketing altogether or organise it elsewhere. On the basis of this reasoning, therefore, unions may have to curtail or abandon picketing entirely, and have evidence that they have done so, in order to avoid liability for their members' acts.

1. [1972] ICR 308, HL.
2. *Ibid.*, Lord Wilberforce at 404.
3. On the importance of this element, see *General Aviation Services (UK) Ltd v TGWU* [1976] IRLR 224, HL.
4. [1986] IRLR 337, QBD.
5. The concept of 'continuing' a nuisance, developed in the context of private nuisance *in Sedleigh-Denfield v O'Callaghan* [1940] AC 880, HL was applied by Stuart-Smith J also to public nuisance.

THE SCOPE OF STATUTORY IMMUNITY

Sources and General Principles

6.17 As we discussed in paras **6.2** *et seq.*, the organisation of industrial action will almost invariably give rise to civil liability at common law. It then becomes necessary to ask whether that liability is removed because the tortious act in question is protected by the statutory immunities.[1] This is also crucial to the (limited) protection against unfair dismissal afforded to employees who are dismissed for taking industrial action.[2] Protection by the statutory immunities requires two elements to be satisfied. First, there must be statutory protection for the tortious act in question. The protected torts are specified in the Trade Union and Labour Relations (Consolidation) Act 1992, s 219(1) and are discussed in para **6.18** below. Secondly, the act must fall within the formula which sets the boundary of legitimate industrial action: it must have been done 'in contemplation or furtherance of a trade dispute'.[3] We analyse the scope of this formula in paras **6.19** *et seq.* Even if the act satisfies these two requirements, however, it may still be excluded from the statutory protection for one of six reasons. These are, in outline,

(a) if the action constitutes unlawful picketing (s 219(3));
(b) if the purpose of the action is to enforce trade union membership (s 222);
(c) if the reason for the action is the fact or belief that an employer has dismissed one or more employees in connection with unofficial industrial action who thereby have no right to complain of unfair dismissal (s 223);
(d) if the action constitutes unlawful secondary action (defined in s 224);
(e) if the purpose of the action is to require the employer to pursue a 'union only' (or 'non-union only') or 'recognition-only' practice in supply contracts (ss 222(3), 225);
(f) if a trade union is legally responsible for the action and the statutory balloting requirements have not been followed (s 226(1)).[4]

In addition, protection is excluded in relation to the employer in respect of whom the default occurs (and in relation to an individual exercising the statutory right of action[5]) when a union fails to provide specified pre-ballot information, notify it of the ballot result or give notice before industrial action starts.[6] In assessing whether a given campaign of industrial action is vulnerable to challenge in the courts, the principles governing the grant of interim injunctions (discussed in para **6.52** *et seq.*) should always be borne in mind.

---

1. Note that industrial action by the police and armed forces is excluded from this protection (TULRCA 1992, ss 274 and 280), and it is a breach of statutory duty to induce prison officers to withhold their services or commit a breach of discipline: see para **6.6**.
2. TULRCA 1992, s 238A(1); see further paras **6.98** *et seq.*
3. TULRCA 1992, s 219(1). 'Trade dispute' is defined in s 244.
4. *Ibid.*, s 219(4).
5. *Ibid.*, s 235A(2); see further para **6.11**.
6. *Ibid.*, s 226(1)(b),(3A), 234A(1).

Torts which are Granted Immunity

6.18 The legislation provides that an act done by a person in contemplation or furtherance of a trade dispute[1] is not actionable in tort on the ground only (a) that it induces another person to break a contract or interferes or induces another person to interfere with its performance; or (b) that it consists in his or her threatening that a contract (whether one to which he is a party or not) will be broken or its performance interfered with, or that he will induce another person to break a contract or to interfere with its performance.[2] In addition, an agreement or combination by two or more persons to do or procure the doing of an act in contemplation or furtherance of a trade dispute is not actionable in tort if the act is one which, if done without any such agreement or combination, would not be actionable in tort.[3] This means that there is statutory immunity for the torts of inducing breach of contract;[4] 'simple' conspiracy; and intimidation based upon the threat to break (or induce the breach of) a contract.[5] In addition, an act which is not actionable in itself by virtue of the statute may not constitute the requisite 'unlawful means' for torts such as interfering with trade or business by unlawful means or conspiracy to use unlawful means.[6] However, other torts which may be committed in the course of taking industrial action, such as nuisance and torts based on breach of statutory duty, have no immunity.[7] This method of listing torts, rather than of giving a comprehensive immunity against civil liability, means that those organising industrial action have always been vulnerable to new nominate torts being created. This vulnerability is increased by the fact that in interim proceedings it is sufficient to show that there is a serious question to be tried.[8] Thus, if the claimant persuades the court that there is a serious question whether a wrong has been committed which lies outside the scope of the statutory immunities, the issue will shift to the balance of convenience.

---

1. See para **6.19** *et seq.* for the meaning of this concept.

2. TULRCA 1992, s 219(1).

3. *Ibid.*, s 219(2).

4. Protection against possible liability for bare interference with performance of a contract short of breach was included to guard against the adoption of the liability suggested by Lord Denning in *Torquay Hotel Co Ltd v Cousins* [1969] 2 Ch 106, CA, although there appears to be no case in which the defendant has been made liable for interference with a contract, short of causing a breach, unaccompanied by unlawful means: Clerk and Lindsell, 1995, and supplement, para 23-19; see further para **6.3**.

5. See paras **6.7** and **6.9** for the elements of these torts. Note that the immunity means that these torts are not then actionable by anyone: *Hadmor Productions Ltd v Hamilton* [1982] IRLR 102, HL.

6. *Ibid.* Before 1980, this was specifically stated in the legislation (Trade Union and Labour Relations Act 1974, s 13(3), repealed by the Employment Act 1980). *Quaere*, however, whether there may be liability against which there is no statutory immunity based upon breach of contract *simpliciter* as unlawful means: *Barretts and Baird (Wholesale) Ltd v IPCS* [1987] IRLR 3, QBD: see further para **6.8**.

7. See paras **6.69**, and **6.6** and **6.7**, respectively for discussion of these torts, and see para **6.64** for the position where the defendant has committed both torts which are protected and those which are not.

8. See paras **6.53** *et seq.*

In Contemplation or Furtherance of a Trade Dispute

The definition of a trade dispute

6.19 A 'trade dispute' means 'a dispute between workers and their employer which relates wholly or mainly' to one or more of a number of specified matters.[1] This involves considering both the parties to the dispute and its purpose. We discuss the parties in this and the following paragraph, and the purpose in paras **6.21** *et seq.* It is consistent with the definition of a 'trade union' as an organisation of 'workers'[2] that 'workers', not merely 'employees', may be a party to a trade dispute (although only employees have any chance of being protected against unfair dismissal). Moreover, in this context the term 'worker' has an extended meaning. It covers both workers employed by the employer at the time of the dispute and also former workers whose employment was terminated in connection with the dispute or where the termination was one of the circumstances giving rise to it.[3] It is unclear whether a union as an organisation of 'workers' may stand in the shoes of a worker for this purpose. At one time there was specific statutory provision that a dispute involving a union was to be treated as one to which workers were a party.[4] This provision was repealed,[5] but earlier cases pre-dating its enactment allowed a union to be a party to a dispute along with its members as long as it was representing those members.[6] It is not entirely clear whether there needs to be a pre-existing dispute between the workers and their employer, although this seems to be a distinction without a difference.[7] What is clear is that a union which had no members employed by a specific employer, or which acted entirely independently of those members, would now have no protection.

---

1. TULRCA 1992, s 244(1).
2. *Ibid.*, s 1. For the definition of 'worker' see App 1.
3. *Ibid.*, s 244(5).'Employment' is defined as including 'any relationship whereby one person personally does work or performs services for another': *ibid.*
4. Trade Union and Labour Relations Act 1974, s29(4).
5. By the Employment Act 1982.
6. *NALGO v Bolton Corpn* [1943] AC 166 at 189, HL. Lord Wright thought that it would be 'strangely out of date to hold . . . that a trade union cannot act on behalf of its members in a trade dispute, or that a difference between a trade union acting for its members and their employer cannot be a trade dispute'.
7. This point was left open in the *NALGO* case (above) : see Lord Simonds at 176. In *Associated British Ports v TGWU* [1989] IRLR 291, Millett J stated (at 300) that given that the union had 'authority to negotiate' on behalf of its members, 'if it fails to achieve a resolution of its demands, then there is a dispute not only between the union and the employers but between its members and the employers'. In addition, if workers take industrial action in response to their union's call, they adopt the dispute as their own (*ibid.*). See also Kidner, 1983, 146 (a pre-existing dispute should not be necessary, although it would be open to those workers specifically to withdraw the authority of the union to conduct a dispute on their behalf).

6.20 The need for a dispute to be between 'workers and their employer' excludes the following types of dispute:

(a) cases where workers are employed through an intermediary company, which is not their true 'employer', To date the courts have refused to 'lift the corporate veil' and look at where power is centred in reality in the context of industrial action;[1]

(b) cases where the employer's own workers are not in dispute with it, for example if picketing is organised at an employer's premises because that employer employs low-paid foreign workers who are not themselves objecting to their conditions;[2]

(c) cases where the dispute is characterised as being with an employer to whom workers may at some future date transfer. In *University College London Hospital NHS Trust v UNISON*[3] the Court of Appeal rejected the argument that the refusal by the employer to guarantee that employees transferred to a private sector consortium would have equivalent terms and conditions to those not transferred could be regarded as a dispute with their current, rather than their so-far-unidentified new, employer;[4]

(d) disputes between workers and workers, such as demarcation or inter-union disputes, although circumstances where this does not spill into a dispute with the employer may be rare;

(e) industrial action against the government, unless the government is the direct employer. There are two statutory exceptions to this principle.[5] The first is where the dispute relates to matters which have been referred for consideration by a joint body on which there is statutory provision for a government minister to be represented. The second is where the dispute relates to matters which cannot be settled without a Minister of the Crown exercising a statutory power (such as the powers of the Secretary of State to make orders relating to teachers' statutory conditions of employment)[6]. In situations not failing within these exceptions, the line between strikes against the government and strikes against an individual employer may sometimes be hard to draw given the close relationship between industry and the labour market, on the one hand, and government economic policies on the other. As Otto Kahn-Freund stated some years ago:

> Is it not true that, not only in publicly owned industries, governmental decisions on wages policies—whether statutory or not—on credits and on subsidies, on the distribution of industry . . . and on a thousand other things, affect the terms and conditions of employment at least as much as the decisions of individual firms. Where is the line between a strike to induce an employer to raise, or not to reduce, wages and a strike to press the government for measures which would enable the employer to do?[7]

To date, the courts have not been faced with this argument in this form,[8] although, as we indicate in para **6.22**, related problems may arise in relation to the predominant purpose of a dispute.

---

1. *Dimbleby and Sons Ltd v NUJ* [1984] IRLR 161, HL.

2. Cf *NWL Ltd v Woods* [1979] IRLR 478, HL. Before 1982, defendants could claim immunity in disputes between workers and any employer. At that time, also, a dispute to which a union was a party was treated as a dispute to which 'workers' were a party: see para **6.19** above. This meant that in *NWL* a dispute between a trade union (the ITF) and shipowners over the terms of employment of a foreign crew who themselves were content, despite being paid below ITF rates, was a trade dispute.

3. [1999] IRLR 31, CA.

4. In our view, this decision can be criticised as not giving due weight to the fact that the current employer had the power to specify in the commercial contract the terms and conditions which would apply to the employees with their new employer. On current government policy where staff transfer from the public to the private sector, see *Staff Transfers in the Public Sector*, Cabinet Office, January 2000.

5. TULRCA 1992, s 244(2).

6. These powers are contained in the School Teachers' Pay and Conditions Act 1991: see *London Borough of Wandsworth v NAS/UWT* [1993] IRLR 344, CA.

7. Davies and Freedland, 1983, 317.

8. However, see *Associated British Ports v TGWU* [1989] IRLR 291, ChD for a related discussion. In *Associated Newspapers Ltd v Flynn* (1970) KIR 17, ChD, a one-day strike against the Industrial Relations Bill was held not to be a trade dispute. Union leaders did not even try to argue that a national strike called in 1980 to protest against the government's economic policies attracted immunity: *Express Newspapers Ltd v Keys* [1980] IRLR 247, QBD.

6.21 As far as subject matter is concerned, a 'trade dispute' must relate 'wholly or mainly' to one or more of a list of specified matters. These matters are identical to those which constitute the statutory subject matter of 'collective bargaining'.[1] They are as follows.

(1) *Terms and conditions of employment,*[2] *or the physical conditions in which any workers are required to work.* The phrase 'terms of employment' extends beyond contractual terms, but its precise ambit is uncertain. In *British Broadcasting Corpn v Hearn*[3] Lord Denning MR stated that it could also cover those terms used and applied by the parties in practice or habitually or by common consent without ever being incorporated into the contract, and this interpretation was approved by Lord Diplock in *Hadmor Productions Ltd v Hamilton.*[4] However, the phrase does not cover terms which regulate a relationship between an employer and a third party acting as principal rather than as agent for the employee and for which no provision is made in the terms under which the employee works for the employer, such as the clauses of a collective agreement which relate solely to the relationship between a trade union and employer.[5] It cannot extend to the terms and conditions of employment of employees of a third party who have never been employed by

the employer in dispute. On this basis industrial action to secure a guarantee, *inter alia*, that employees engaged by a private consortium would be employed on terms and conditions no less favourable than their public sector counterparts was found to be outside the scope of the immunities.[6]

(2) *Engagement or non-engagement, or termination or suspension of employment or the duties of employment, of one or more workers.* This may include fear of future redundancies, and there is no need for dismissal notices to have been issued.[7]

(3) *Allocation of work or the duties of employment between workers or groups of workers.* This is limited to demarcation disputes between workers or groups of workers employed by the same employer.[8]

(4) *Matters of discipline.*

(5) *A worker's membership or non-membership of a trade union.*[9]

(6) *Facilities for officials of trade unions.*[10]

(7) *Machinery for negotiation or consultation, and other procedures, relating to any of the above matters.* This includes the recognition by employers or employers' associations of the right of a trade union to represent workers in such negotiation or consultation or in the carrying out of such procedures.

A dispute relating to matters occurring outside the United Kingdom is capable of constituting a 'trade dispute', but only if the person(s) whose actions in the United Kingdom are said to be in contemplation or furtherance of a trade dispute relating to matters occurring outside the United Kingdom are likely to be affected by the outcome of the dispute in respect of one or more matters specified in the Trade Union and Labour Relations (Consolidation) Act 1992, s 244(1).[11] This prevents the organisation of any form of solidarity action with workers overseas where there is no immediate connection between the outcome of that dispute and UK workers. It also overlooks the fact that transnational companies may now be organised in such a way that decisions taken in relation to workers in another country (for example, in relation to working conditions or redundancies) may have considerable repercussions in the UK.[12]

---

1. See para **4.3**.
2. See TULRCA, s 244(5) (set out in para **6.19,** note 3, above).
3. [1977] IRLR 273, CA.
4. [1982] IRLR 102 at 108, HL.
5. Per Lord Diplock in *Universe Tankships Inc of Monrovia v ITWF* [1982] IRLR 200 at 206.
6. *University College London Hospital NHS Trust v UNISON* [1999] IRLR 31, CA; see further para **6.20** above. This decision is the subject of an application to the European Court of Human Rights. At the time of writing, no decision on admissibility has been made. See Hendy, 2000, 58, who argues that the case may be authority for the propo-

sition that industrial action may not be called or supported by unions save where the dispute is in relation to *existing* terms and conditions, as well as with an existing employer, thus removing the immunities from any worker seeking any change to existing terms and conditions, for example by pursuing a simple wage claim. We doubt if this view is correct; in any event, a dispute over higher wages could be regarded as a dispute over the unsatisfactory nature of existing terms and conditions of employment. In our view, there is a clear distinction between the issue in dispute (for example, current wage levels) and the consequences which may arise from that dispute (for example, increased wages).

7. *Hadmor Productions,* above, note 4; *General Aviation Services (UK) Ltd v TGWU* [1975] ICR 276, CA; *Health Computing Ltd v Meek* [1980] IRLR 437, ChD.

8. *Dimbleby and Sons Lid v NUJ* [1984] IRLR 161, HL.

9. This must now be considered in the light of TULRCA 1992, s 222; see para **6.26** below.

10. See TULRCA 1992, s 119, set out in para **3.27**, for the definition of 'official' and para **2.4** for the definition of 'trade union'.

11. TULRCA 1992, s 244(3).

12. See Wedderburn, 2000, 28–33.

6.22 The statutory requirement that the dispute must relate 'wholly or mainly' to one of the matters specified in para **6.21** means that the court must look at its predominant purpose.[1] Disputes which are judged to be furthering a 'political' or other non-industrial purpose, such as a personal feud or grudge,[2] will have no immunity. In this context, as in relation to determining the parties to a dispute, the borderline between the political and the 'trade' dispute may be hard to discern. Particular problems may arise in public services; for example, disputes over matters such as wages or job cuts, which are clearly within the definition of a trade dispute, often involve challenging broader government policies, such as incomes policies, reductions in public spending or privatisation. At the time the predominant purpose test was introduced, ministers maintained that they did not intend to jeopardise the lawfulness of public service disputes concerning pay, conditions or jobs, even if they did challenge government policies. However, in interim proceedings, doubt about the predominant purpose of a dispute may be sufficient to persuade a court to grant an interim injunction (see para **6.53** *et seq.*). To date, there have been four decisions where the predominant purpose of a dispute has been at issue.[3] In *Mercury Communications Ltd v Scott-Garner and the POEU*[4] the union argued that it had instructed its members not to connect Mercury, a private company, to the British Telecommunications (BT) network in furtherance of a dispute with BT over employees' job security which, the union claimed, would be put at risk if Mercury was connected.[5] The Court of Appeal rejected this argument and held that the dispute was primarily concerned with the union's opposition to government policies of liberalisation and privatisation of the telecommunications industry. In reaching its decision, the court was influenced heavily by evidence of a Job Security Agreement between the union and the employer which the union had not sought to invoke, a fact which pointed away from concern about jobs. This decision does not mean, therefore, that all industrial action relating to the consequences of privatisation will be unlawful, but unions need to be careful to ensure that it is linked sufficiently closely with one of the matters which characterise a trade dispute. Thus, *Mercury* was distinguished in *Associated British Ports Ltd v TGWU*,[6] where the union called a strike in furtherance of its demand from port employers for new national conditions in the docks after the Conservative Government had announced the introduction of legislation to abolish the National Dock Labour Scheme. Millett J rejected the employers' argument that this was not a 'trade dispute'; whereas in *Mercury*, the matters of genuine industrial concern were only aspects of a 'wider political dispute', in this case 'the union's concern for the future employment conditions of former registered dock workers' could not be so characterised.[7] He also roundly rejected the contention that the dispute with the employers was manufactured as a spurious pretext for a dispute with the government; this was a 'serious calumny', 'wholly without substance'.[8] The link between the legislation abolishing the scheme and dockers' terms and conditions of employment was inextricable, and given that the employers had made clear their intention to deprive dockers of valued features of their employment relationship which the scheme had bestowed, there was a genuine dispute between them. The employers did not seek to raise the 'trade dispute' argument on appeal.[9] Although the decision may give some reassurance to unions involved in disputes which are linked to government policies, the unions' success 'was secured only by very deliberate action' to secure the necessary evidence to substantiate its case.[10] Thirdly, in *London Borough of Wandsworth v NAS/UWT*[11] the union had instructed its members to boycott 'all the unreasonable and unnecessary elements of assessment connected with the national curriculum'. The Court of Appeal dismissed the employers' argument that this was a dispute about the content of work which the national curriculum required teachers to undertake; rather it was about teachers' working time, and therefore mainly related to terms and conditions of employment. In reaching this conclusion the court attached 'considerable importance'[12] to the wording of the question put to members in the ballot which preceded the industrial action, which asked them whether they were willing to take action 'to protest against the excessive workload and unreasonable imposition made upon teachers, as a consequence of national curriculum assessment and testing'. Finally, in *University College London Hospital NHS Trust v UNISON*[13] the employer sought to argue that industrial action over its refusal to guarantee that staff transferred to a private consortium, and those subsequently employed by the consortium, would be at least as favourable as those applicable to staff it continued to employ, had a political objective. This argument was rejected by the Court of Appeal, although the more limited objective ascribed to the union of alleviating the adverse consequences of the Private Finance Initiative did not, on the facts, fall within the terms of s 244(1) (see paras **6.20** and **6.21** above).

---

1. TULRCA 1992, s 244(1). *Mercury Communications Ltd v Scott-Garner and the POEU* [1983] IRLR 494, CA. The Employment Act 1982 amended the Trade Union and Labour Relations Act 1974 (now repealed), which provided that the dispute had only to be 'connected with' a collective bargaining matter and a court had only to be satisfied that a collective bargaining matter was genuinely at issue: see *NWL Ltd v Woods* [1979] IRLR 478, HL.
   2. See, for example, *Huntley v Thornton* [1957] 1 WLR 321. For a method of bringing political disputes within s 244, and limitations thereon, see para **6.24**.
   3. In 1987, the Department of Employment secured an injunction against an officer of the Civil and Public Services Association who organised a strike in opposition to an ethnic monitoring exercise in unemployment benefit offices on the ground that this was a 'political' issue, but no full judgment was given.
   4. [1983] IRLR 494, CA.
   5. This is protected under TULRCA 1992, s 244(1)(b); see para **6.21**.
   6. [1989] IRLR 291, ChD.
   7. At 301.
   8. At 299.
   9. [1989] IRLR 305, CA; [1989] IRLR 399, HL.
   10. Simpson, 1989, 237.
   11. [1993] IRLR 344, CA.
   12. *Ibid.*, at 350.
   13. [1999] IRLR 31, CA.

'In contemplation or furtherance' of a trade dispute

6.23 To decide whether a defendant is acting 'in contemplation or furtherance' of a trade dispute, both the time of the action and its purpose are relevant. As far as time is concerned, 'either a dispute is imminent and the act is done in expectation of and with a view to it, or . . . the dispute is already existing and the act is done in support of one side to it'.[1] When a dispute is not in existence, whether or not it is sufficiently imminent is a question of degree. In one case the union sought information from its pub-manager members, including their takings, trade, and total wages bill, prior to formulating a wage claim.[2] Giving the union this information would have involved members breaking their contracts of employment. On an application for a declaration by the employers that their employees were not entitled to provide this information, the court rejected the argument that the union was acting in contemplation of a trade dispute; such a dispute was neither in being nor imminent. The most that could be said was that the union had sent out documents which, after consideration of the information obtained, might lead to a request which, if not granted, might lead to a dispute. By contrast, a health service union was held to be acting in contemplation of a trade dispute in sending out a circular instructing its NHS members not to co-operate with the claimants, a private contractor which specialised in computer systems for medical services which was seeking to do business with health authorities.[3] The purpose of the circular, according to the union's general secretary, was to pre-empt the disputes which would inevitably arise in the event that health authorities did do business with them. The evidence showed that some health authorities, at least, would be likely to say that they reserved the right to use the contractor's services and it was reasonable to foresee that the enforcement of the union's policy of banning it from the NHS might lead to disputes with those authorities.[4] Thus, the circular had been distributed in contemplation of those disputes. From the other end of the spectrum, there may be scope for argument whether a dispute has ended or still remains in being, a particularly significant question when a union is organising the action as the preceding ballot will cover only the action to which that ballot relates, not a fresh campaign. Again it will be a question of scrutinising the facts to establish whether the original dispute remains 'real or live'.[5] The test of a dispute organiser's purpose in acting is a subjective one; it is sufficient that he or she honestly thinks at the time that the action may help one of the parties to the trade dispute to achieve its objective, and it is done for that reason.[6] It is immaterial, therefore, that the belief was unreasonable, that the action did not, in fact, assist the dispute, or that the action taken was disproportionate to the grievance to be settled. However, evidence that no reasonable person could have thought the action may have this result may be relevant to the credibility of the defendant's evidence that the belief was honestly held, a matter upon which he or she will need to satisfy the court.[7] In practice, this issue is unlikely to be contentious now that virtually all forms of secondary action have no protection under the immunities (see para **6.28** below).

---

1. Lord Loreburn in *Conway v Wade* [1909] AC 506 at 512, HL. See also *JT Stratford and Son Ltd v Lindley* [1965] AC 269, HL.
2. *Bent's Brewery Co Ltd v Hogan* [1945] 2 All ER 570, Liverpool Spring Assizes.
3. *Health Computing Ltd v Meek* [1980] IRLR 437, ChD.
4. The dispute was motivated by fear of future redundancies, protected under TUL-RCA 1992, s 244(1)(b) (see para **6.21**).
5. *London Borough of Newham v NALGO* [1993] IRLR 83, CA, at 87. The suggestion that for a dispute to continue it is sufficient if the side which still regards itself as being in dispute 'honestly and genuinely believes this is the position' (at 87) is contrary to

authority (see note 6, below) and, indeed, the court went on to affirm that there had to be a 'real or live dispute' which, on the evidence, there was.

6. Note, however, that the 'trade dispute' itself must exist or be imminent as an objective fact: Lord Diplock in *Express Newspapers Ltd v MacShane and Ashton* [1980] IRLR 35, HL at 39.

7. *Express Newspapers*, above; see also *Duport Steels Ltd v Sirs* [1980] IRLR 116, HL. In *Associated British Ports v TGWU* [1989] IRLR 291, Millett J emphasised that purpose must not be confused with motive and that there is no requirement that the union should be acting exclusively in furtherance of a trade dispute.

6.24 A dispute may be prevented from coming into being if an employer accedes to a trade union's demand under the threat of industrial action, which usually constitutes the tort of intimidation.[1] The legislation provides that an act, threat or demand which, if resisted, would have led to a trade dispute, shall be treated as being done or made in contemplation of it even though no dispute arises because the other person submits.[2] It is crucial, however, that the demand is made in a form which is sufficiently closely related to the matters listed in the Trade Union and Labour Relations (Consolidation) Act 1992, s 244(1). In *BBC v Hearn*[3] a union asked its members not to transmit the Cup Final after the BBC refused to take steps to ensure that the broadcast was not transmitted to South Africa where the policy of apartheid, to which the union was opposed, was still in force. The Court of Appeal held that there was no trade dispute in existence. However, Lord Denning MR suggested that it could have become one had the union asked the BBC to insert a clause in its members' contracts, or for a condition to be understood, that they would not be asked to participate in any broadcasts to South Africa whilst there was a policy of apartheid. This suggestion received support from Lord Diplock in *NWL Ltd v Woods*.[4] However, its possibilities are not unlimited. In a later case Lord Cross emphasised that a union cannot turn a dispute which in reality has no connection with terms and conditions of employment (in that case a demand that the employer made a payment to the union welfare fund) into a trade dispute by insisting that the employer inserts appropriate terms into the contracts of employment.[5] This approach allows the courts discretion to decide whether the dispute has the appropriate connection.[6]

---

1. See para **6.7**.
2. TULRCA 1992, s 244(4).
3. [1977] IRLR 273, CA (Lord Denning MR at 275).
4. [1979] IRLR 478 at 483, HL.

5. *Universe Tankships Inc of Monrovia v ITWF* [1982] IRLR 200, HL, at 208.
6. See, for example, Griffiths LJ at 71, Lord Donaldson MR at 73 in *Dimbleby and Sons Ltd v NUJ* [1984] IRLR 67 (decision affirmed [1984] IRLR 161, HL).

Exclusions from Protection of the Statutory Immunities

6.25 The grounds for excluding protection were summarised in para **6.17**. They can be divided into four broad categories. First where the requisite balloting and information procedures are not followed in relation to industrial action organised by a trade union. We discuss these in detail in para **6.30** *et seq*. Second, where the action constitutes unlawful picketing. We discuss this in para **6.67** *et seq*; see, in particular, para **6.72**. Third, where the action is taken for a proscribed purpose: to enforce trade union membership or in relation to the dismissal of participants in 'unofficial' industrial action. We discuss this in paras **6.26** and **6.27** below. Finally, where industrial action constitutes unlawful 'secondary' action. We discuss this in paras **6.28** and **6.29**.

Action relating to union membership and to recognition and collective consultation

6.26 Industrial action (or the threat of such action) is excluded from the protection of the statutory immunities if one of the reasons for it is the fact or belief that a particular employer is employing, has employed or might employ a person who is not a member of a trade union,[1] or of a particular union, or is failing, has failed, or might fail to discriminate against any such person.[2] In this context, discrimination means treating workers or job applicants differently according to whether or not they are union members, or members of a particular union, and according more favourable treatment to those who are members.[3] It is significant that the employer's failure to discriminate need be only one of the reasons for the action. Thus, a union cannot take industrial action to enforce a demand that only union members should be accorded the benefit of a wage increase or other award secured by collective bargaining, or that union members should be accorded preferential treatment in the allocation of jobs. However, industrial action would not lose immunity if taken where an employer was favouring non-unionists, provided that the union was arguing only for equal, and not more favourable, treatment for its members. Acts to induce or attempt to induce an employer to incorporate into a contract for the supply of goods or services a term which is or would be void under the Trade Union and Labour Relations (Consolidation) Act 1992, s 144 or 186 are also unprotected.[4] These sections respectively provide that a term or condition in such a contract is void insofar as it purports to require the work (or part of it) to be carried out by union (or non-union) labour, or by members or non-members of a particular union, or because it requires a party to the contract to recognise or consult with a union official.[5] Protection is also excluded for action to induce, or attempt to induce the employer to refuse to deal with another party who does not comply with such requirements.[6] This means that industrial action cannot be used as a means of helping workers employed by another employer to get voluntary recognition, or even consultation rights from their employer. It is also unlawful for a union to organise industrial action by employees to persuade their employer's supplier to recognise a union or negotiate or consult with a union official.[7] Thus, while it may be lawful for a union to organise industrial action by employees of A to persuade A to recognise a union or consult with union officials, if the purpose of the action is to persuade employer B, a supplier of employer A, to do likewise, it will have no immunity.

---

1. See para **2.4**.
2. TULRCA 1992, ss 219(4), 222. References to not being a member of a union include not being a member of a particular branch or section or one of a number of such branches or sections: s 222(5). References to an employer employing a person are references to a person acting in the capacity of the person for whom a worker (see App 1) works or normally works: s 222(4).
3. *Ibid.*, s 222(2). For individual remedies for persons discriminated against for not joining a union, or a particular union, see para **3.2** *et seq.*
4. *Ibid.*, ss 219(4), 222(3), 225. For further discussion of the prohibition of union-only (or non-union only) labour and recognition requirements in contracts, see para **3.22**, *ibid.*, ss 222(3)(b), 225(1)(b).
5. See *ibid.*, s 119, set out in para **3.27**, for the definition of 'official'.
6. *Ibid.*, s 222(3)(b), 225(1)(b).
7. *Ibid.*, 225(2). The exclusion of immunity applies if the act interferes with the supply (whether or not under a contract) or goods and services (or can reasonably be expected to have that effect) and one of the facts relied upon to establish liability is inducement of breach (including inducement to interfere with) a contract, or intimidation, in respect of a contract of employment (see paras **6.3** and **6.7** respectively) where the supplier of the goods or services is not the employer under the contract of employment and the reason, or one of the reasons, for the act is the fact or belief that the supplier does not, or might not, recognise one or more unions or negotiate or consult with a union official.

Action in response to dismissal of participants in unofficial industrial action

6.27 Industrial action (or the threat of such action) is excluded from the protection of the statutory immunities if the reason, or one of the reasons, for it is the fact or belief that an employer has dismissed one or more employees in circumstances such that by virtue of the Trade Union and Labour Relations (Consolidation) Act 1992, s 237[1] (dismissal in connection with unofficial industrial action) they have no right to complain of unfair dismissal.[2] It is notable that this fact or belief need be only one of the reasons for the action; it need not be the main, or even a substantial, reason. This means that where an employer has dismissed an employee in such circumstances in the recent past and the union wishes to organise industrial action on a separate matter, it will have to ensure that the dismissal is dissociated entirely from the industrial action.

---

1. See further para **6.103** *et seq.*
2. TULRCA 1992, ss 219(4), 223. In *British Railways Board v RMT* (17 September 1992, unreported), QBD, industrial action had no immunity on this basis.

Secondary industrial action

6.28 Industrial action (or the threat of such action) is excluded from the statutory immunities if one of the facts relied on for the purpose of establishing liability is that there has been secondary action.[1] This reflects the concept of 'enterprise confinement';[2] the idea that industrial action is legitimate, if at all, only at the level of the enterprise. 'Secondary action' occurs when there is inducement to breach, or interference with the performance of a contract of employment[3] (or the threat of such inducement or interference), and the employer under the contract of employment is not party to the trade dispute.[4] By contrast, 'primary action' is where there is action of this nature and the employer under the contract of employment is party to the dispute.[5] Exclusion of secondary action means, for example, that if employees of employer X are in dispute with X, and the union calls on employees of employer Y, who supplies goods to X, not to deliver those supplies in breach of their contracts of employment, it will thereby have induced them to breach their contracts, an act for which it will have no immunity in tort. An employer may not be treated as party to a dispute between another employer and its workers[6], and where more than one employer is in dispute with its workers, each dispute is to be treated separately.[7] This means that it is impossible to organise national industrial action against more than one employer unless a dispute with each individual employer can be shown; a dispute with an employer as a member of an employers' association with which the union is in dispute, for example, will not suffice. However, an act in contemplation or furtherance of a trade dispute which is primary action in relation to that dispute may not be relied on as secondary action in relation to another trade dispute.[8] Thus, even if industrial action taken against one employer assists workers in dispute with another employer, it does not thereby constitute secondary action unless it could not be said, in reality, to have been taken to further a dispute with the first employer.[9] The only exception to the ban on 'secondary action' is where there is an inducement, or threatened inducement, to breach a contract of employment of an employee of another employer in the course of otherwise lawful picketing.[10] We analyse this exception further in para **6.72**.

---

1. TULRCA 1992, ss 219(4), 224(1).
2. Wedderburn 1989, 27–30.
3. Defined for the purposes of TULRCA 1992, s 224 as including 'any contract under which one person personally does work or performs services for another': s 224(6).
4. *Ibid.*, s 224(2).
5. *Ibid*, s 224(5). Note, however, that the definition of 'primary action' does not cover the (probably rare) situation where these torts are not committed but others are: see Lord Wedderburn, HL Debs, Vol 521, col 1240, 23 July 1990. In relation to education, the Education (Modification of Enactments Relating to Employment) Order 1998, SI 1998/218, Article 5 renders industrial action by teachers in schools with delegated budgets in support of colleagues in other schools secondary action in certain circumstances, notwithstanding that those employees may share a common employer.
6. As defined in *ibid.*, s 244; see para **6.19**.
7. *Ibid.*, s 224(4).
8. *Ibid.*, s 224(5). *Quaere* whether it could be relied upon as secondary action in relation to a non-'trade dispute'?
9. See para **6.23** for the meaning of 'in furtherance'.
10. TULRCA 1992, s 224(1),(3).

6.29 The withdrawal of immunity for secondary action applies even where employers have parallel shareholdings; the courts will not 'lift the corporate veil' in this context.[1] Thus, the scope of lawful industrial action is defined entirely by the legal scope of the employment unit; even if a dispute between one company and its employees in a group directly affects workers in another company within the same group, the workers in the second company cannot take supportive industrial action. The same point holds if workers are employed by a subsidiary company which is technically their employer but which lacks the decision-making capacity to resolve the dispute. Nor can workers organise industrial action against another employer to whom the manufacture or supply of goods or services has been diverted by the employer in dispute, even if that employer is 'associated' with the first employer.[2] However, the workers employed by the second employer could take industrial action against their own employer as a result of the transfer of work provided that they could bring it within the scope of the Trade Union and Labour Relations (Consolidation) Act 1992, s 244(1), possibly by asking for a clause in their contracts that they should not be required to handle such work.[3] If such action was 'official', it would require the support of a validly conducted ballot. However, the union would need to ensure that the action was 'related wholly or mainly' to one of the matters listed in s 244 and that it was being taken genuinely to further that dispute and not, in reality, to further the first dispute.[4] The restriction on secondary action contravenes ILO standards on freedom of association; the Committee of Experts has held that action against an employer not directly involved in a given dispute should be regarded as a legitimate exercise of the right to strike where it 'relates directly to the social and economic interests of the workers involved in either or both of the original dispute and the secondary action' provided that the original dispute and the secondary action are not unlawful in themselves.[5] The fact that unions cannot take action against a company which is the 'true' employer but which may hire workers through an intermediary company has also been criticised by the CIE (now the ECSR) which supervises compliance with the ESC.[6] Nevertheless there is no indication that the Labour Government has any intention of changing the position. As we indicated in para **1.6**, the European Court of Human Rights has, to date, refused to imply a right to strike from the right of individuals to join trade unions for the protection of their interests, and it is unlikely, therefore, that any arguments could be successfully made on the basis of the Human Rights Act 1998.

---

1. *Dimbleby and Sons Ltd v NUJ* [1984] IRLR 161, HL.
2. See App 1 for the definition of 'associated employer'.
3. See Lord Denning MR in *BBC v Hearn* [1977] IRLR 273, CA and Lord Diplock in *NWL Ltd v Woods* [1979] IRLR 478, HL; these, and other cases on this point, are discussed at para **6.24**.
4. See para **6.23**.
5. *Report of the Committee of Experts on the Application of Conventions and Recommendations*, 1989, Report III (Part 4A), 1989, 238.
6. See, for example, comments on the UK's compliance with Article 6(4) in the XIV-I supervision cycle

INDUSTRIAL ACTION BALLOTS AND NOTICE TO EMPLOYERS

Sources and General Principles

6.30 An act done by a trade union to induce[1] a person to take part, or continue to take part, in industrial action[2] is not protected by the statutory immunities unless the industrial action has the support of a majority of those voting in a postal ballot.[3] The ballot must be conducted in accordance with complex statutory requirements laid down in the Trade Union and Labour Relations (Consolidation) Act 1992, ss 226–235, as amended by the Trade Union Reform and Employment Rights Act 1993 and the Employment Relations Act 1999. Where more than 50 workers are to be balloted, the ballot must be supervised by an independent scrutineer.[4] Unions are also required to give employers of those entitled to vote in the ballot specified information both before and after the ballot takes place.[5] In addition, employers of persons whom the union intends to induce to take part in the industrial action should receive a minimum of seven days' notice of the action, including specified details of its scope, before the action starts.[6] The consequences of failing to comply with the balloting requirements vary. In general, if industrial action lacks the support of a ballot the union has no immunity against liability in tort, regardless of the identity of the claimant.[7] However, where the union fails to comply with its obligations to provide pre-ballot information, notify a relevant employer of the ballot result, or give notice before industrial action starts, protection is excluded only in relation to the employer in respect of whom the default occurs.[8] Anomalously, however, although the union could continue to invoke the statutory immunities in relation to other employers involved in the dispute or otherwise harmed by the action, they are excluded also for the purposes of the statutory right of action described in para **6.11**.[9] Given that dispute organisers almost invariably commit at least one tort, a union which fails to hold a valid ballot or provide employers with the requisite information will be exposed to an application for an interim injunction and/or a claim for damages.[10] Such a failure also means that an employment tribunal will be unable to determine a claim for unfair dismissal by any employee who is dismissed for taking part in the unprotected action, even during the first eight weeks of his or her participation, unless that dismissal is 'selective' within the terms of the legislation.[11] Finally, failure to comply with the balloting requirements also entitles individual union members to apply to the High Court for an order requiring their union to take steps to ensure that there is no further inducement of members to take part in the action and that no members continue to participate as a result of a prior inducement.[12] A Code of Practice on Industrial Action Ballots and Notice to Employers, issued by the Secretary of State, amplifies the statutory requirements. This Code was first issued in 1990 and revised in 1991, 1995 and 2000 . Although, like other Codes, it does not impose obligations which are legally enforceable,[13] non-compliance with its pro-visions may be influential when a court is deciding whether to grant an applica-tion for an interim injunction to halt the industrial action. As we describe in para **6.51**, the 2000 version of the Code, like its predecessors, does not forbear from making recommendations which go beyond the limits of the legislation. Despite greater clarity in some areas as a result of amendments made by the Employment Relations Act 1999,[14] there remain many points of uncertainty relating to the balloting and notification requirements and, as in relation to all areas of the law concerning collective industrial action, it should be borne in mind that argument as to their interpretation is most likely to arise in the context of interim pro-ceedings where the relevant principles tend not to favour union defendants.[15]

---

1. This includes an inducement which is or would be ineffective, because the person is unwilling to be influenced by it or for any other reason: TULRCA 1992, s 226(4).

2. See para **6.31** for the meaning of 'industrial action'.

3. TULRCA 1992, ss 219(4). For the circumstances in which unions are deemed to be legally liable for such acts, see para **6.13** *et seq.* Special provisions apply to merchant seamen: s230(2A),(2B); see further para **6.41**

4. *Ibid.*, ss 226(2), 226B, 226C.

5. *Ibid.*, ss 226(1), 226A.

6. *Ibid.*, ss 219(4), 234A.

7. *Ibid.*, ss 219(4), 226(2)(a).

8. *Ibid.*, ss 219(4), 226(1)(b), 226(3A), 234A(1).

9. *Ibid*, ss 219(4); 226(1)(b). The definition of unlawful in s 235A(2) includes acts actionable in tort *by one or more persons.* For debate on the issues raised by this, see HL Debs, Vol 546, cols 103–109, 24 May 1993.

10. See para **6.52** *et seq.*

11. See para **6.92** *et seq.*

12. TULRCA 1992, s 62; see further para **6.114**. It is possible that a union's own rules will require a higher majority than the statute, in which case an individual member could challenge the lawfulness of industrial action organised with a smaller majority: see para **6.110**.

13. TULRCA 1992, s 207(1). However the Code is admissible in evidence in any pro-ceedings before a court or employment tribunal, and any provision which appears to the court or tribunal to be relevant to any question arising in the proceedings must be taken into account in determining that question: s 207(3). At the time of writing the draft 2000 Code has been laid before Parliament. References in the text are to that Code.

14. ERA 1999, s 4 and Sched 3.

15. See para **6.53** *et seq.* for the criteria governing the decision to grant or refuse an interim injunction.

When Must a Ballot be Held?

6.31 Industrial action must be preceded by a ballot if a trade union is legally responsible for organising it. As we explained in para **6.12** *et seq.*, unions are legally liable for the acts of an extensive range of persons; in certain circumstances they may repudiate those acts but the price of doing so is to expose the employees participating in the action to selective dismissal within a short time of repudiation taking place.[1] The obligation to hold a ballot applies in relation both to employees and those working under 'any contract under which one person personally does work or performs services for another';[2] it thus includes those working under a contract for services. There is no requirement that the action should involve a breach of contract on the part of those participating in it. In the great majority of cases, industrial action does constitute such a breach;[3] in the rare event that it does not, organising the action may not attract liability in tort. However, the union would still be liable to an application by a union member to halt the action; 'industrial action' in that context is defined as 'a strike or other industrial action by persons employed under contracts of employment'.[4] It would remain liable to an individual exercising the statutory right to seek injunctive relief (see para **6.11**); industrial action is 'unlawful' for that purpose both where it is actionable in tort by any person *and* where it could form the basis of a statutory application by a union member.[5] It is crucial to the validity of a ballot that there should have been no call by the trade union to take part or continue to take part in industrial action, or any authorisation or endorsement by the union of any such action, before the date of the ballot.[6] We discuss the meaning and implications of this provision in para **6.48**.

---

1. See para **6.103** *et seq.*
2. TULRCA 1992, s 235. Ballots must also be held in respect of industrial action by civil servants and others holding 'any office or employment under the Crown': TULRCA 1992, s 245 (see further para **6.3,** note 13).
3. See para **6.81** *et seq.*
4. TULRCA 1992, s 62(6). 'Contracts of employment' have the same definition as in relation to the balloting provisions: see s 62(8), (7).
5. TULRCA 1992, s 235A(2).
6. TULRCA 1992, s 233(3)(a).

Independent Scrutiny of Ballots

6.32 Before an industrial action ballot is held, the trade union must appoint an independent scrutineer.[1] Only persons specified in regulations issued by the Secretary of State are potentially qualified to act as scrutineers;[2] in addition the union must have no grounds for believing either that the person will carry out the statutory functions otherwise than competently or that his or her independence in relation to the union, or the ballot, might reasonably be called into question.[3] Three bodies are specified by name: Electoral Reform Ballot Services Ltd; The Industrial Society; and Union Security Balloting Services Ltd, now called Election.Com Ltd. In addition, solicitors who have a current practising certificate and accountants who are qualified as auditors are potentially qualified to act, although specified connections with the union, or previous activities, may disqualify them.[4] Unions may appoint their own choice of scrutineer from among those qualified. The name of the independent scrutineer must appear on the voting paper.[5] There is no provision for replacement of a scrutineer or appointment of a deputy if the named scrutineer becomes indisposed, so unions would be best advised to choose a qualified partnership or one of the three named organisations rather than a single individual. Payment of the scrutineer must be met in full by the union. The statutory obligation to appoint a scrutineer does not apply unless the number of persons entitled to vote in the ballot (or, where separate workplace ballots are held, the aggregate number entitled to vote in each) exceeds 50.[6] There is nothing to prevent a union appointing a scrutineer where the number involved is less than this as an additional safeguard against the ballot being susceptible to legal challenge, but clearly the costs of doing this will need to be considered.[7]

---

1. TULRCA 1992, s 226B.
2. *Ibid*, s 226B(2)(a); the Trade Union Ballots and Elections (Independent Scrutineer Qualifications) Order 1993, SI 1993/1909.
3. *Ibid.*, s 226B(2)(b).
4. SI 1993/1909, regs 3–6. Such persons are disqualified if, *inter alia*, they, or any present partner of theirs, has during the preceding 12 months been a member, officer (other than an auditor) or employee of the union concerned.
5. *Ibid.*, s 229(1A)(a).
6. TULRCA 1992, s 226C.
7. The Code of Practice on Industrial Action Ballots and Notice to Employers (like its predecessors) urges unions to consider whether the appointment of a scrutineer would still be of benefit in enabling it to demonstrate compliance with the statutory requirements more easily even where fewer than 50 members are involved (para 13).

6.33 The terms of appointment must require the scrutineer to make a report to the union covering specified matters as soon as reasonably practicable after the date of the ballot and, in any event, not later than the end of the period of four weeks beginning with the date of the ballot, and to take any steps which he or she considers appropriate to enable such a report to be made.[1] Trade unions have a duty to ensure that the scrutineer duly carries out his or her functions, but this must be done without any interference from the union or any of its members, officials or employees.[2] It is possible to envisage situations where these two duties may conflict, although this is less likely to happen if the union selects an experienced scrutineer who requires little supervision. There is no provision which expressly allows a union to replace an unsatisfactory scrutineer, and the position if the union sought to do this mid-way through the balloting process is unclear; at the very least it would present a substantial risk of the validity of the ballot being challenged.[3] The union must comply with all reasonable requests by the scrutineer connected with the performance of his or her functions;[4] this probably entails, for example, allowing the scrutineer to look at records, obtain relevant information and visit any premises as appropriate.[5] In contrast to the functions of an independent scrutineer in relation to union election and political fund ballots, the scrutineer of an industrial action ballot has no statutory right of access to the union's membership register.[6] Taken together with the absence of any related duty on the union to impose a duty of confidentiality in relation to the register,[7] this would strongly suggest that no such right of access should be implied from the general duty of the union to comply with reasonable requests.[8] Given the possibility that the ballot process may not be completed, by order of the court or otherwise, unions would be prudent to make provision for this eventuality in the terms of appointment of the scrutineer, and to limit their costs accordingly. We discuss the scrutineer's report in greater detail in para **6.43**.

---

1. TULRCA 1992, s 226B(1).
2. *Ibid.*, s 226B(3).
3. On the one hand replacement could be seen as failing to comply with the duty to appoint a scrutineer before a ballot is held; on the other it could be argued that, by appointing a scrutineer before that time, albeit an unsatisfactory one, the union had discharged its obligation. A union would be unwise to risk putting this question to the test in interim proceedings: see para **6.53** *et seq*.
4. TULRCA 1992, s 226B(4).
5. See para **2.40** in relation to an identically-worded provision in relation to election ballots.
6. See para **2.40**.
7. *Ibid.*
8. See also Viscount Ullswater, Parliamentary Under-Secretary of State, Department

of Employment, HL Debs, Vol 545, col 93, 26 April 1993: 'So far as the industrial action balloting requirements are concerned, the Government recognise that the nature of the process means that a union's membership register may not have the significance which applies in respect of other kinds of union ballot. So, for example, the scrutineeer for an industrial action ballot will not have the same rights of access to a union's membership register as is to be available to scrutineers of other ballots.'

The Balloting Constituency

6.34 The principles which govern the determination of the balloting constituency are complex. They involve consideration of two interlocking questions: which trade union members should be granted a vote, and how should the general scope of the balloting constituency be defined? Although the Employment Relations Act 1999 has simplified the position somewhat, difficulties still remain. In relation to the first question, the legislation requires that entitlement to vote in the ballot must be accorded equally to all members whom it is reasonable 'at the time of the ballot' for the union to believe will be induced to take part (or, as the case may be, to continue to take part) in the industrial action in question, and to no others.[1] However, if there is an accidental failure to comply with this requirement which is on a scale which is unlikely to affect the ballot result, that failure can be disregarded.[2] This may be a particularly useful provision for unions where some of those voting are workers under contracts of services, whose whereabouts may not always be known or who may be difficult to contact. 'Time of the ballot' is not defined; it is unclear whether it can be equated with 'date of the ballot', which does have a statutory definition.[3] A union which has overseas members[4] may choose whether or not to grant any of those members a vote.[5] There are special provisions governing the position of members who, throughout the period during which votes may be cast, are in Northern Ireland.[6] The Employment Relations Act 1999 has established (by implication) that industrial action is not regarded as failing to have the support of a ballot because individuals who take up employment or join the union after the ballot has been held (or, indeed, non-members) participate in it (giving statutory force to an earlier Court of Appeal decision to that effect).[7] This is the outcomeof the provision that action is not regarded as having the support of a ballot if *any union member at the time the ballot was held* (our italics) whom it was reasonable at that time for the union to believe would be induced to take part in the action was not accorded entitlement to vote in the ballot and was induced to take part in it.[8] This provision is not subject to the exception for 'accidental failures' specified above, and unions will need to be careful that they do not induce persons who were not accorded entitlement to vote, for example if groups of workers are called out in rotation.

1. TULRCA 1992, s 227(1).

2. *Ibid.*, s 232B, inserted by ERA 1999, s 4, Sched 3, paras 1, 9.

3. In the case of a ballot in which votes may be cast on more than one day, the last of those days: TULRCA 1992, s 246.

4. A 'member (other than a merchant seaman or offshore worker) who is outside Great Britain throughout the period during which votes may be cast': *ibid.*, s 232(3). An 'offshore worker' is a person in offshore employment (defined s 287) other than one who is in such employment in an area where the law of Northern Ireland applies; *ibid.*, s 232(3).

5. *Ibid.*, s 232(1). Nothing in ss 226B–230 and 231B applies in relation to an overseas member or a vote cast by such a member: *ibid.*

6. *Ibid.*, s 232(4): such a person shall not be treated as an overseas member if the union has a reasonable belief that all those members have the same workplace, and his or her place of work is in Great Britain, or, where there is an 'aggregated' ballot (see para **6.36** and **6.37**) which relates to industrial action involving members both in Great Britain and in Northern Ireland. In relation to offshore employment the references in ss 232(4) to Northern Ireland include any area where the law of Northern Ireland applies and the references to Great Britain include any area where the law of England, Wales or Scotland applies; *ibid.*, s 232(5).

7. *London Underground Ltd v RMT* [1995] IRLR 636, CA.

8. TULRCA 1992, s 232A, inserted by ERA 1999, s 4, Sched 3, paras 1,8. Prior to ERA 1999, the requirement in s 227(1) was taken not to be satisfied if any member was *denied* entitlement to vote. There was some authority to suggest that this required a deliberate decision by the union rather than mere oversight: *British Railways Board v NUR* [1989] IRLR 349 at 351 (Lord Donaldson MR). In *RJB Mining (UK) Ltd v NUM* [1997] IRLR 621, Maurice Kay J held that it was highly arguable that the errors and omissions in the ballot in question were of such an extent as to contravene the statute.

6.35 In general, the constituency for a ballot is a 'workplace'. Where the members entitled to vote in a ballot have separate workplaces, there must be a separate ballot for each workplace, and entitlement to vote must be accorded equally to, and restricted to, union members who have that workplace and who it is reasonable at the time of the ballot to believe will be induced to take part in the action.[1] A separate majority must be obtained in each workplace and all the other statutory requirements must be satisfied for industrial action therein to be lawful.[2] 'Workplace' in relation to a person who is employed means '(a) if the person works at or from a single set of premises, those premises' and (b) in any other case, the premises with which the person's employment has the closest connection'.[3] (Prior to the Employment Relations Act 1999 the equivalent definition (of a 'place of work') required the premises to be 'occupied' by the employer, a requirement which created difficulties where it was unclear when parts of premises used by a variety of employers, such as a railway station, were 'occupied' by them.[4]) The 'closest connection' provision means that everyone has a place of work; for delivery drivers, for example, their place of work will be the depot from which they set out; for homeworkers most probably the administrative office of the employer with which they deal.[5] There is no statutory definition of 'premises'.[6] It seems clear that different sites of the same undertaking would require a separate ballot; for a single site containing a number of buildings, it is possible that a separate ballot may be required for each building, but the matter is not free from doubt.[7] The 'workplace' of a worker who is employed to work in one place but temporarily moved to another is also unclear. However, some assistance is given by the provision that the requirement to hold a separate ballot for each workplace does not apply if the union reasonably believes that the members accorded entitlement to vote have the same workplace.[8] Thus, even if a court subsequently decides that the union was incorrect in its conclusion, the ballot remains valid provided that the union was 'reasonable' in forming its belief at the relevant time.

---

1. TULRCA 1992, s 228(1). Ss 228(1) and 228A were substituted by ERA 1999, s 4, Sched 3, paras 1, 5.

2. TULRCA 1992, s 226(3).

3. *Ibid.*, s 228(4).

4. This problem arose in *Intercity West Coast Ltd v RMT* [1996] IRLR 583, where the majority of the Court of Appeal held that the concept of 'occupied' should be construed in the context of industrial relations and the conduct of unions. In this case it was immaterial that the rail operating companies did not have a lease on the railway station which the union claimed constituted its members' 'place of work'; the claimants had a licence to use the operating part of the station for the purposes of their business and therefore 'occupied it'.

5. Examples given in relation to the original provision by Mr Patrick Nicholls, Parliamentary Under-Secretary of State for Employment, House of Commons, Official Report of Standing Committee F, col 523, 19 January 1988.

6. Cf the Health and Safety at Work etc Act 1974, s 53 where 'premises' are defined broadly as including 'any place', including any vehicle, vessel, aircraft, hovercraft, offshore installation or other installation, and any tent, or moveable structure.

7. Cf the definition of 'establishment' for the purposes of consultation on redundancies: see para **5.6**. Under those provisions 14 building sites were held to be one establishment; *Barratt Developments (Bradford) Ltd v UCATT* [1978] ICR 319, EAT.

8. TULRCA 1992, s 228(2).

6.36 The restriction of ballots to a 'place of work' was originally designed to ensure that unions could not achieve a majority in favour of industrial action by aggregating votes at 'militant' and 'moderate' workplaces.[1] Votes could be aggregated in specified circumstances,[2] but the statutory language governing these was complex, to the extent of bordering on the incomprehensible. The Labour Government considered that there was little or no evidence that unions had attempted to obtain majorities by illegitimate means,[3] and the Employment Relations Act 1999 introduced a simplified (albeit still complex) provision which allows aggregate ballots instead of separate workplace ballots in three sets of circumstances,[4] based, loosely speaking, on a common interest in the subject-matter of the dispute; common occupation(s); or a common employer or employers.

(a) *Common interest*: aggregation is permitted where the workplace of each member of the union entitled to vote is the workplace of at least one member who is affected by the dispute.[5] Those 'affected' fall into four categories, divided according to the subject-matter of the dispute. The first applies where the dispute relates wholly or partly to a decision which the union reasonably believes that the employer has made or will make concerning terms and conditions of employment or the physical conditions in which workers are required to work; engagement or non-engagement or termination or suspension of employment or the duties of employment of one or more workers; or the allocation of work or the duties of employment between workers or groups of workers. Here the term 'affected' means members whom the decision directly affects.[6] The second is if the dispute relates wholly or mainly to matters of discipline. Here, again, it means members whom the matter directly affects.[7] It is particularly important to emphasise in these first two contexts that it is sufficient that only one member needs to be directly affected. This reflects the Government's recognition that '[w]here one or more workers are directly involved, it will normally be the case that others at the same workplace, sometimes many others, will rightly feel themselves to be indirectly involved by an employers' handling of an issue . . . [which] may set a precedent in relation to other workers'.[8] It may not always be clear, however, when a worker is 'directly affected'. In the context of unfair dismissal and lock-outs 'relevant employees' are defined as employees 'directly interested' in a dispute, a term which has been interpreted to cover anyone whose terms of employment are likely to be immediately and automatically affected by the outcome of the dispute.[9] However, this approach does not cater for forms of trade dispute, such as those motivated by fear of future redundancies, where employees are potentially, but not automatically, at risk. The requirement that the decision 'directly affect' the members in question is not judged by reference to the union's 'reasonable belief' that they are so affected, and in cases where this question is unclear unions may be best advised to hold separate workplace ballots. The third 'common interest' category is if a dispute relates (wholly or party) to a worker's membership or non-membership of a union. Here an 'affected' member means one whose membership or non-membership is in dispute.[10] The final category is where the dispute relates wholly or partly to the facilities for union officials. Here, officials of the union who have used or would use the facilities concerned in the dispute are 'affected members'.[11] The fact that the workplace of each member entitled to vote must be that of at least one member who is affected by the dispute means that a ballot cannot be aggregated across workplaces if the dispute concerns facilities for full-time officials who, by definition, are not attached to any individual workplace.

(b) *Common occupation(s) and employer(s)*: aggregation is permitted where entitlement to vote is accorded to, and limited to, all the union's members who according to the union's reasonable belief have an occupation of a particular kind, or any of a number of particular kinds of occupation, and are employed by a particular employer or any number of particular employers with whom the union is in dispute.[12] Thus aggregation is permitted across different employers provided that the workers concerned share a common occupation or occupations and the union is not selective in according entitlement to vote. To take a practical example, it would be legitimate for a civil service union to ballot all its computer-operator members together, but if it wished to ballot operators at only two out of many workplaces, separate ballots would be required for each workplace. The meaning of 'occupation' is unclear; it could be seen in terms of broad job specification or function, grade, qualifications, or a combination of those factors.[13] Whilst the union need only have a 'reasonable belief' that the members have an occupation of a particular kind, the 'reasonableness' of that belief will be a matter for the courts (or, in the context of an unfair dismissal claim, employment tribunals).

(c) *Common employers*: aggregation is permitted where entitlement to vote is accorded to, and limited to, all the members of the union who are employed by a particular employer, or by any of a number of employers, with which the union is in dispute.[14] Again it is crucial that the union is not selective in according entitlement to vote. Thus, if the union does not wish to ballot all its members at all workplaces, it must either do so on the basis of (a) or (b) above or organise separate workplace ballots.

---

1. See Mr Patrick Nicholls, House of Commons, Official Report of Standing Committee F, col 494, 14 January 1988.

2. The circumstances when votes could be aggregated were, very broadly speaking, where members had a factor or factors in common relating to their terms or conditions of employment or occupational description.

3. Lord McIntosh of Haringey, Deputy Chief Whip, HL Debs Vol 604, col 576, 15 July 1999.

4. TULRCA 1992, s 228A(1). The Code of Practice on Industrial Action Ballots and

Notice to Employers makes clear that it is possible for a union to hold more than one ballot on a dispute at a single workplace: para 25.

5. *Ibid.*, s 228A(2).

6. *Ibid.*, s 228A(5)(a).

7. *Ibid.*, s 228A(5)(b).

8. Lord McIntosh of Haringey, Deputy Chief Whip, HL Debs Vol 604, col 576, 15 July 1999.

9. TULRCA 1992, s 238(3)(a); *Presho v Department of Health and Social Security (Insurance Officer)* [1984] IRLR 74, HL. See further para **6.95**.

10. TULRCA 1992, s 228A(5)(c).

11. *Ibid.*, s 228A(5)(d).

12. *Ibid.*, s 228A(3).

13. Cf *ibid.*, s 174(3)(b), where 'occupational description' is said to include 'grade, level or category of appointment'.

14. *Ibid.*, s 228A(4). Note that there is no 'reasonable belief' exception under this provision. This may create difficulties where what appears to be a single employer may in fact be a group of companies.

6.37 Of these three tests for aggregation, the 'common interest' tests accords unions the greatest flexibility in that it does not require the inclusion of *all* workplaces at which the common interest applies. This means that a union may choose to exclude particular workplaces from the aggregated ballot, even if they are part of the same bargaining unit as those which are balloted together. Conversely, it means that if responsibility for industrial relations matters within a national employer is devolved to regional management or regional centres of operation, those workplaces within the region may be balloted together. The need to ballot on a non-selective basis where a ballot is aggregated on the common occupation and common employer tests may create difficulties for unions which wish to maintain emergency cover during disputes. As we stated in para **6.34**, a union must ballot only those whom it is reasonable for it to believe will be induced to take part in the industrial action. This suggests that members involved in maintaining emergency cover should not be balloted. However, the union cannot exclude them if it wishes to aggregate the ballot (unless it is aggregating on the basis of a common occupation and all those furnishing emergency cover fall within a distinctive occupation). In this situation, a union would probably be best advised, if this is feasible, to ballot all the workers in dispute and then rotate those who provide emergency cover so that all the members balloted are called upon at some stage to participate in the industrial action.

The Content of the Voting Paper

6.38 The legislation requires a voting paper for the ballot to contain four sets of provisions.[1] We discuss the first three in this paragraph and the fourth (relating to the voting questions) in para **6.39** below. The first set covers matters relevant to the conduct of the ballot. Each voting paper must clearly specify the address to which, and the date by which, it is to be returned, and there are statutory requirements as to the numbering of voting papers.[2] The voting paper must also contain the name of the independent scrutineer of the ballot where applicable.[3] Secondly, the voting paper for the ballot must specify who, in the event of a vote in favour of industrial action, is authorised to call upon members to take part or continue to take part in industrial action.[4] Only a person who is so specified will be able to claim the support of a ballot in making such a call.[5] Persons may be specified individually or by description; members of the executive or regional officers, for example.[6] The person or description of persons so specified need not be authorised under the union rules to call industrial action but must be within the categories specified in the statute as those whose authorisation or endorsement binds the union (in the absence of a valid repudiation).[7] The reason for extending the category of permissible specified persons beyond the scope of the union rules is unclear. Thirdly, the voting paper for the ballot must contain the statement:

> If you take part in a strike or other industrial action, you may be in breach of your contract of employment.[8] However, if you are dismissed for taking part in strike [*sic*] or other industrial action which is called officially and is otherwise lawful, the dismissal will be unfair if it takes place fewer than eight weeks after you started taking part in the action, and depending on the circumstances may be unfair if it takes place later.[9]

This statement must not be 'qualified or commented upon by anything else on the voting paper'.[10] Thus, even if industrial action, such as a ban on voluntary overtime, is (probably) not a breach of contract, a union cannot say this on the voting paper. There is nothing to prevent the union commenting on the statement elsewhere, but such material should not be attached to the voting paper in any way (for example, by staple or paper-clip) as this could be seen as appearing 'on' it.[11] It is unclear whether it is permissible to enclose unattached material in the same envelope as the voting paper;[12] to put the matter beyond challenge a union which had sufficient resources would be best advised to issue any commentary under separate cover. The sentence in the statement relating to unfair dismissal was added by the Employment Relations Act 1999, which introduced this limited protection (see para **6.98** *et seq.*). It is notable that it talks of industrial action which is called 'officially', a term which is not defined and not used elsewhere in the legislation. We prefer to use the term 'not unofficial', given that 'unofficial' does have a statutory meaning,[13] albeit the line which the legislation draws between the two forms of action is not necessarily coincident with the understanding which members would have of this boundary on the basis of their union's rules.

1. TULRCA 1992, s 229.

2. *Ibid.*, s 229(1A). The paper must be given one of a series of consecutive whole numbers every one of which is used in giving a different number in that series to each voting paper produced for the purposes of the ballot and each paper must be marked with its number: *ibid*. In relation to a ballot in which merchant seamen to whom s 230(2A) applies are entitled to vote (see para **6.34**) a reference to the ship to which the seamen belong is substituted for the address to which the paper is to be returned: *ibid.*

3. *Ibid.*, see further paras **6.32–6.33**.

4. TULRCA 1992, s 229(3).

5. *Ibid.*, s 233(1), (2). In *Tanks and Drums Ltd v TGWU* [1991] IRLR 372, CA, it was held to be permissible for a specified person to authorise a subordinate union official to call a strike should further negotiations with the employers prove unsuccessful, although a very close link in time between the strike and the event, such as an unsuccessful meeting, precipitating the final action was required; whether the link was sufficiently close was a question of fact and degree. The court also recognised that it would be impractical to leave matters so that no discretion could be exercised by local officials as to how a call for industrial action was to be put into operation.

6. This derives by implication from TULRCA 1992, s 229(3).

7. *Ibid.*; see para **6.13** *et seq.*

8. Note the extended definition of 'contract of employment': TULRCA 1992, s 235; see para **6.31,** note 2.

9. TULRCA 1992, s 229(4). It is notable that the Code of Practice on Industrial Action Ballots and Notice to Employers para 32 refers to 'a' strike, unlike the statute.

10. *Ibid.*

11. Lord Trefgarne, HL Debs, Vol 486, cols 57–85, 25 April 1988.

12. This point was left open during parliamentary debate: *ibid.*, cols 58–59. In *Blue Circle v TGWU* (7 July 1989, unreported), Alliott J held that a statement defining the nature of industrial action which appeared in a circular accompanying a voting paper should be treated in the same way as if it had appeared on the ballot paper itself (see para **6.39** below). It is conceivable that the same reasoning may be applied in this context, although we consider that it would be incorrect to do so because a statement in any accompanying circular would not be 'on' the voting paper. The Code of Practice on Industrial Action Ballots and Notice to Employers recommends that unions should give members specified additional information: para 36.

13. See para **6.104**.

6.39 The fourth requirement for the voting paper is that it must contain at least one of the following questions:

(a) a question (however framed) which requires the person answering it to say, by answering 'Yes' or 'No', whether he is prepared to take part or, as the case may be, to continue to take part in a strike;

(b) a question (however framed) which requires the person answering to say, by answering 'Yes' or 'No', whether he is prepared to take part or as the case may be, to continue to take part in industrial action short of a strike.[1]

In the context of the balloting provisions in general, a 'strike' is defined as 'any concerted stoppage of work'.[2] However, in response to a Court of Appeal decision which held that a ban on overtime and rest-day working fell within this definition,[3] the Employment Relations Act 1999 specifically excludes it in this context.[4] It also states that for the purposes of this provision (only) an overtime ban and a call-out ban constitute industrial action short of a strike.[5] Whilst clarifying the position in relation to these two forms of action, the Act leaves uncertain the position of other forms of action which may, in practice, involve stoppages for specific periods, such as a ban on lunch-time cover or on duties which take place only at specified times of day. The dividing line between a strike and industrial action short of a strike is crucial because a union must acquire separate approval from members for each form of action; it cannot assume that those who have voted for a strike would necessarily approve of industrial action short of a strike on the basis that the greater implies the lesser.[6] *A fortiori*, a 'rolled-up' question in the form 'are you willing to take industrial action up to and including strike action?' is invalid.[7] However it is sufficient for the union to obtain a majority on an individual question, and not the voting process as a whole, in order for that action to be approved.[8] The need for separate approval may mean holding more than one ballot during the course of a dispute; because the mandate provided by a ballot lapses after four weeks (unless extended by agreement between the union and employer),[9] a union cannot rely on strike action as a 'fall-back' beyond that time if industrial action short of a strike fails to produce a settlement. It is advisable for a trade union not to specify the form or scope of the industrial action to a greater extent than the legislation requires in order to allow itself maximum room for manoeuvre. In *Blue Circle v TGWU*[10] Alliott J held that the extent of the immunity conferred by the ballot was limited by qualifications both on the voting paper itself and in the accompanying literature, which was treated as if it had appeared on the voting paper. This led the court into construing the precise extent of the ballot mandate: on the facts, withdrawal of shift cover was held to come within the scope of an overtime ban but general exhortations for a 'yes' vote to enable the union to respond to countermeasures taken by the employers were insufficient to authorise more than the one 24-hour strike per week for which support was specifically requested. Alliott J affirmed, however, that other oral or written statements by union officials could not be used to limit the extent of the action which the union was authorised by the ballot to take.

---

1. TULRCA 1992, s 229(2).
2. *Ibid.*, s 246.

3. *Connex South Eastern Ltd v RMT* [1999] IRLR 249, CA.

4. TULRCA 1992, s246.

5. *Ibid.*, s 229(2A).

6. *Post Office v UPW* [1990] IRLR 143, CA.

7. *Ibid.*

8. *West Midlands Travel Ltd v TGWU* [1994] IRLR 578, CA (majority in favour of strike action, but not in favour of industrial action short of a strike).

9. See para **6.49**.

10. 7 July 1989, unreported.

6.40 Apart from requiring the four matters discussed in paras **6.38** and **6.39** to be addressed, the legislation says nothing further about the content of voting papers, and it is open to a trade union to include additional material as long as this does not infringe the limitation set out in para **6.38**. However, in *London Underground Ltd v NUR*[1] Simon Brown J propounded a further restriction, suggesting that the legislation would not be satisfied where the ballot posed a question which, either wholly or in part, asked whether the member was prepared to participate in a strike by reference to matters which were not existing matters in dispute. In that case the ballot asked: 'Do you agree to support the executive committee in their fight to maintain the current agreement on seniority and to resist the imposition of organisational changes [unsatisfactory attendance procedures and competitive tendering] by taking strike action?' The employers argued that, at the time of the ballot, there was no 'genuine, definite, substantial dispute' between the parties, either actual or reasonably foreseeable, on any of the issues other than seniority and the court considered that there were 'powerful arguments' to support this contention.[2] There seems no justification for the insertion of a restriction of this nature, which 'confuses the conditions for a valid ballot with the need for a union to prove that it was acting in contemplation or furtherance of a trade dispute . . . a separate prerequisite for the protection of the immunities . . .'.[3] Nevertheless, the same approach was adopted by the Court of Appeal in *University College London Hospital NHS Trust v UNISON*.[4] In this case, the ballot asked members whether they were prepared to take strike action, *inter alia*, because the employer had failed to guarantee that staff who were employed by a private sector consortium in the future (and who had never been employed by the Trust) would receive the same terms and conditions of employment as those whom the Trust continued to employ. Having held that this demand could not constitute the subject-matter of a 'trade dispute', the court went on to hold that it was therefore 'an impermissible subject for the ballot' and, although it was only one of the issues identified on the ballot paper, nullified the ballot which had taken place.[5] A first instance court has held that there is no requirement for a union to define or describe every issue with which a dispute is concerned in the information supplied to members taking part in the ballot; it is sufficient that there was evidence to identify the strike which had been approved in the ballot.[6] Where there are a number of different issues, not all of which fall squarely within the 'trade dispute' definition, it may be wise not to detail those over which there is uncertainty. However, where there is some contention as to whether the central issue constitutes a 'trade dispute', spelling it out on the ballot paper in appropriately-drafted terms may help to substantiate the union's case. In *London Borough of Wandsworth v NAS/UWT*,[7] where it was argued for the employers that the dispute in question was about the content of the work which the national curriculum required schoolteachers to undertake, in finding that there was a 'trade dispute', the Court of Appeal attached 'considerable importance'[8] to the wording on the ballot paper which asked teachers whether they were willing to take action '[i]n order to protest against the excessive workload and unreasonable imposition made upon teachers, as a consequence of national curriculum assessment and testing . . .'.[9] As discussed in para **6.49**, it is also important for unions to ensure that the terms of the ballot cover any matters which might arise out of and in consequence of the dispute in question.

---

1. [1989] IRLR 341, QBD.
2. *Ibid.*, at 342.
3. Simpson, 1989, 235.
4. [1999] IRLR 31, CA; see further paras **6.20** and **6.21**.
5. *Ibid.*, Lord Woolf MR at 35.
6. *Associated British Ports v TGWU* [1989] IRLR 291, ChD. This case went on appeal to the Court of Appeal ([1989] IRLR 305) and to the House of Lords ([1989] IRLR 399).
7. [1993] IRLR 344; see para **6.22**.
8. *Ibid.*, at 350.
9. *Ibid.*, at 348. Although the union was successful in resisting the employer's application for an interim injunction in this case, we would counsel that the wording on the ballot paper should relate solely to the matters in dispute, for example terms and conditions of employment, rather than their causes, particularly where these are politically controversial.

The Conduct of the Ballot

6.41 The method of voting in a ballot must be by the marking of a voting paper by the person voting.[1] The ballot must be fully postal; so far as is 'reasonably practicable' every person who is entitled to vote must have sent to him or her by post a voting paper and be given a convenient opportunity to vote by post.[2] The definition of 'post' excludes delivery by hand, internal mail, or private courier.[3]

The concept of 'reasonable practicability' recognises that it is unrealistic to expect a trade union to guarantee delivery to every member who is entitled to vote. In *British Railways Board v NUR*[4] the Court of Appeal acknowledged that in a large-scale national ballot it is inevitable that some members may be omitted through factors such as changes of address or job,[5] but emphasised that it is not necessary to show that the number of members who were not supplied with a ballot paper was sufficiently great to have affected the result of the ballot before it becomes invalid.[6] The Employment Relations Act 1999 introduced a more generous approach to this question, providing that an accidental failure which is on a scale which is unlikely to affect the result of the ballot should be disregarded.[7]

---

1. TULRCA 1992, s 229(1).

2. *Ibid.*, s 230(2). The voting paper must be sent to the individual's home address or any other address which he or she has requested the union in writing to treat as his or her postal address: *ibid*. Special provision is made for 'merchant seamen' (defined as persons whose employment, or the greater part of it, is carried out on board seagoing ships: *ibid.*, s 230(2C)). Where the union reasonably believes that a merchant seaman will be employed in a ship either at sea or at a place outside Great Britain at some time in the period during which votes may be cast, and that it will be convenient for him to receive a voting paper and to vote while on the ship or while at a place where the ship is rather than having it sent to his postal address and voting by post, he shall, if it is reasonably practicable, have a voting paper made available to him, and be given an opportunity to vote, while on the ship or at a place where the ship is: *ibid.*, s 230(2A),(2B). Prior to the ERA 1999, this method of balloting could be used only where the merchant seaman was at sea or at a foreign port for the entire period of the ballot.

3. 'Post' means a postal service which is provided by the Post Office or under a licence granted under the British Telecommunications Act 1981, s 68, or which does not by virtue of an order made under s 69 of that Act infringe the exclusive privilege of the Post Office: *ibid.*, s 298.

4. [1989] IRLR 349, CA.

5. *Ibid.*, Lord Donaldson MR at 351. Lord Donaldson stated that had the union 'claimed to produce evidence that every one of the entitled members had received a ballot paper and returned it, I think that the court would have been justified in looking very carefully at the evidence to see whether something had not been fiddled'. 63,719 ballot papers were issued, of which 51,628 were returned.

6. *Ibid.*, at 352. For the approach of the Certification Officer in relation to union elections, see para **2.42**.

7. TULRCA 1992, s 232B.

6.42 The ballot must be conducted so as to secure that, so far as reasonably practicable, those voting do so in secret.[1] Every person who is entitled to vote in the ballot must be allowed to vote without interference from, or constraint imposed by, the union or any of its members, officials or employees.[2] The Court of Appeal has affirmed that the union is 'perfectly entitled to be partisan' and to campaign for a 'yes' vote,[3] although when such conduct will cross the line into unlawful interference is not readily apparent.[4] So far as is reasonably practicable, voters must be enabled to vote without incurring any direct cost to themselves.[5] In the context of union elections, the Certification Officer has held that this requires the cost of return postage to be borne by the union.[6] There is a duty to ensure that votes are fairly and accurately counted but any inaccuracy which is accidental and on a scale which could not affect the result of the ballot may be disregarded.[7] Unlike union election and political fund ballots, there is no statutory requirement for an independent person to count the votes, but the scrutineer (where applicable)[8] is required specifically to state in his or her report to the union whether he or she was satisfied that the counting arrangements included all such security arrangements as were reasonably practicable to minimise the risk of unfairness or malpractice, as well as commenting more broadly on whether any of the statutory requirements were contravened (see further para **6.43**). As soon as reasonably practicable after the ballot has been held, the union must take such steps as are reasonably necessary to ensure that all those entitled to vote in the ballot are informed of the number of votes cast, the number voting 'yes' (to each question if more than one was put), the number voting 'no', and the number of spoiled ballot papers.[9] The statute requires the union to obtain the support of the majority of those voting in the ballot to the question applicable to the industrial action of the kind to which any act of inducement relates.[10] For the obligation to inform relevant employers of the ballot result, see para **6.44** *et seq.*

---

1. TULRCA 1992, s 230(4)(a). Thus, there should be no identifying mark on the voting paper which can link it with a particular individual.
2. *Ibid.*, s 230(1)(a). Interference from a third party, such as an employer or another union, has no invalidating effect.
3. *London Borough of Newham v NALGO* [1993] IRLR 83, CA.
4. In relation to union elections, the Certification Officer has held that this excludes 'such conduct as would intimidate or put a member in fear of voting, or amount to physical interference' (*Rey v Film Artistes' Association* (11 April 1986, unreported; see further para **2.42**) and this approach may be echoed by the courts. See para **2.2** for the role and status of the Certification Officer.
5. TULRCA 1992, s 230(1)(b).
6. *Paul v NALGO* [1987] IRLR 43. The simplest way of effecting this would be by including a stamped addressed envelope. The Certification Officer regards it as a 'cost'

to a union member to pay and reclaim the cost of a stamp. If overseas members are to be included in the ballot, they should be sent an international reply coupon or some other mechanism should be arranged which enables them to vote without any prior expenditure on their part.

7. TULRCA 1992, s 230(4).

8. See para **6.32**.

9. TULRCA 1992, s 231. Where overseas members have voted in the ballot (see para **6.34**), there is no obligation to supply them with this information. However, the information required to be supplied must distinguish between overseas and other members: *ibid*, s 232(2).

10. *Ibid*., s 226(2)(a)(ii); *West Midlands Travel Ltd v TGWU* [1994] IRLR 578, CA, above para **6.39**. It is not entirely clear whether spoiled papers count for this purpose, but the wording would suggest the need for a majority of 'yes' over 'no' votes and spoiled papers taken together.

The Independent Scrutineer's Report

6.43 The terms of appointment of the independent scrutineer must require him or her to make a report to the union on the ballot as soon as reasonably practicable after the date of the ballot[1] and, in any event, no later than the end of the period of four weeks beginning with that date.[2] The report must state whether the scrutineer is satisfied of specified matters (with reasons if he or she is not so satisfied): that there are no reasonable grounds for believing that there was any contravention of a statutory requirement in relation to the ballot; that the arrangements made for producing, storing, distributing, returning and other handling of the voting papers, and the arrangements for counting votes, included all such security arrangements as were reasonably practicable to minimise the risk of any unfairness or malpractice; and that he or she has been able to carry out the requisite functions without any interference from the union or any of its members, officials or employees.[3] Unlike the provisions governing union electoral and political fund ballots, there is no obligation on the scrutineer to indicate the number of voting papers distributed for the purposes of the ballot. If at any time within six months of the date of the ballot any person entitled to vote in the ballot or the employer of such a person requests a copy of the scrutineer's report, the union must, as soon as practicable, provide a copy either free of charge or on payment of a reasonable fee specified by the union.[4] A critical report will not of itself invalidate the ballot but it will draw the attention of members and employers to the existence of possible grounds on which they may seek to argue that the industrial action is not protected by the statutory immunities (although proceedings may be commenced before that time).[5] It is possible that the industrial action will begin before the scrutineer's report has been received.[6]

If the report provides ammunition to challenge the validity of the ballot, unions may be exposed both to an application for an interim injunction to halt any further action and to a claim in damages for any unprotected action which had been undertaken before that date.[7] In addition, the employment tribunal will not be able to assess the fairness of the dismissal of any employees dismissed for taking industrial action during that period unless the dismissals were 'selective' within the meaning of the legislation.[8]

---

1. In the case of a ballot in which votes may be cast on more than one day, the last of those days: TULRCA 1992, s 246.
2. *Ibid.*, s 226B(1)(b).
3. *Ibid.*, s 231B(1).
4. *Ibid.*, s 231B(2).
5. Where proceedings have been commenced before the scrutineer's report is published, the industrial action is deemed to have the support of a ballot provided that such of the requirements of ss 226B and 231B as have fallen to be satisfied at the time at which proceedings are commenced have been so satisfied: TULRCA 1992, s 226(1), (2)(b).
6. Given that the ballot ceases to be effective at the end of a period of four weeks beginning with the date of the ballot (unless otherwise agreed between union and employer: see para **6.49**), the same date as the deadline for presentation of the scrutineer's report, this is not improbable. To that extent the advice in the Code of Practice on Industrial Ballots and Notice to Employers that unions may wish to delay any call until receiving the scrutineer's report (para 49) seems unrealistic.
7. See para **6.52** *et seq.*
8. See para **6.92** *et seq.*

Information and Notice to Employers

6.44 There are three sets of requirements which unions must satisfy in relation to employers in order for industrial action to be protected by the statutory immunities. First, notice of the ballot and a sample voting paper must be received by employers of persons entitled to vote in the ballot. Secondly, such employers should be informed of the result of the ballot. Thirdly, employers of persons whom the trade union intends to induce to take part in industrial action must be given due notice. We discuss the details of these requirements below. The consequences of failing to comply with any of these obligations is that protection is excluded only in relation to the employer in respect of whom the default occurs and (anomalously) for the purposes of the statutory right of action described in para **6.11**.[1] In the event of non-compliance with the pre-ballot obligations, (or a challenge based upon the content of the voting paper) it is not wholly clear at what point an injunction could be sought. On the one hand it could be argued that it is inappropriate to grant what was formerly called a *quia timet* injunction (or a remedy under the statute) until, at the earliest, it becomes clear that there is a majority in favour of industrial action on the basis that an unlawful act is not, at that stage, sufficiently likely.[2] On the other hand, experience suggests that the courts may be persuaded to grant a remedy even at this stage.[3]

---

1. TULRCA 1992, ss 219(4), 226(1)(b), 226(3A). The definition of 'unlawful' in s 235A(2), which includes acts which are actionable in tort *by any one or more persons* (our italics) means that the statutory right is available when the statutory immunities may still apply as regards third-party claimants at common law. See HL Debs, Vol 546, cols 103–109, 24 May 1993.

2. See Spry, 1997, 377–382, 468–470 on the principles governing *quia timet* injunctions. As Auerbach (1988b) points out (229), at the most there can only be a 'conditional' inducement of industrial action at the point when the ballot is proposed. TULRCA 1992, s 235A(1) requires the individual to claim that an unlawful act was, at the very least, 'likely': see para **6.11**.

3. See Auerbach (1988b) on proceedings during the 1988 seafarers' dispute, where employers obtained an injunction restraining the union from conducting a ballot of the workforce (a lawful activity) on the basis that the proposed action would be unprotected secondary action. Support for industrial action in a ballot can be an important tactical weapon for unions: see Elgar and Simpson, 1992; Martin *et al*, 1991; Undy *et al*, 1996.

6.45 The requirements relating to pre-ballot information fall into two categories. First, the trade union must take such steps as are 'reasonably necessary' to ensure that, not later that the seventh day before the opening day of the ballot,[1] written notice of intention to hold the ballot is received by every person who it is reasonable for the union to believe (at the latest time when steps could be taken to comply with this requirement[2]) will be the employer of persons entitled to vote in the ballot.[3] Secondly, the union must take such steps to ensure that not later than the third day before the opening day of the ballot each such person receives a sample of the form of voting paper to be sent to those of its own employees whom it is reasonable for the union to believe will be entitled to vote in the ballot.[4] This will enable the employer to learn whether a strike and/or industrial action short of a strike is contemplated. In the light of the specification that the information must be 'received' rather than given, we would suggest that all requests should be sent by special delivery post or some other method by which a signature of receipt is obtained (including delivery by hand). By analogy with High Court proceedings, it would seem prudent for the union to post any first-class letters in a post box rather than arranging for them to be dispatched following an internal collection. In addition, there seems to be no reason why a further copy of the notice and sample voting paper should not be sent by fax, particularly as this will constitute evidence of receipt. Under the Civil Procedure Rules, Part 6, where the method of service of a document is by first class post it will be deemed to have been served the second day after it was posted. We recommend service by fax in addition to the post for evidential purposes. Where the employer is a company, the material should be sent to the last known place of business or its principal or registered office. Where it is a partnership, it would be prudent to serve it on a partner, although sending it to the last known place of business of the firm would probably suffice. In the event that the employer is an individual, the documentation should be sent or delivered to that individual personally. The pre-ballot notice must state that the union intends to hold the ballot; specify the date which the union reasonably believes will be the opening date of the ballot; and contain 'such information in the union's possession as would help the employer to make plans and bring information to the attention of those of his employees who it is reasonable for the union to believe' (at the time when steps to ensure the notice is received are taken) will be entitled to vote in the ballot.[5] In satisfying the third of these requirements, if the union possesses information about the number, category or workplace of the employees concerned, a notice must contain that information (at least).[6] It would seem that if the union has already decided upon the form of industrial action (for example, a go-slow or overtime ban) that information should be communicated; equally, if a rolling strike is planned, the order in which employees are to be called out. However, given that the obligation is limited to information in the union's possession, unions may consider it prudent not to formulate specific proposals at this stage. It cannot be a ground of non-compliance that the notice does not name any employees.[7] Prior to the Employment Relations Act 1999, the union was required to describe those employees who it was reasonable for it to believe would be entitled to vote in the ballot so that the employer could 'readily ascertain them', a requirement which the Court of Appeal held, on the facts of the case before it, could be satisfied only if the union named individual staff.[8] A Labour Government spokesman claimed that the amendment would protect workers against having their union membership disclosed to their employer against their will.[9] However it is far from clear that this is the case. He gave the example of a number of lecturers being called out on strike on a certain day.

> The management knows that a number of lecturers will be called out on strike on a certain day. Unless the union provides the information, the management has no way of knowing which lecturers or where. So they cannot warn students whose classes will be cancelled. But unless the union tell the management, 'We are calling out 50 lecturers in the English department and 30 in chemistry' or 'There will be 200 lectures at site A and

100 at site B', the college cannot give its students some warning of the scale of the action.

It may be the case that if a notice in this form were challenged, a court would conclude that information of this nature met the requirements of the statute in indicating the number and categories of lecturers.[10] However, one purpose of providing the information to the employer is to enable it to 'make plans'. If the employer wished to ensure that students were provided with lectures on the days that industrial action was contemplated, if need be by replacement staff, it would need first to know which lectures would otherwise be cancelled if industrial action took place. Specifying the 'Shakespeare' or the 'Chaucer' lecture would usually identify the individual who normally took those lectures as precisely as naming them. It is submitted that where this would be the outcome, the court should construe the union's obligation in the light of the right to respect for private life, protected by Article 8 of the ECHR, and not require this degree of specificity.[11] It should be emphasised that the obligation is limited to information in the union's possession; the union may think it prudent to limit the knowledge which it seeks of the detailed organisation of the enterprise, for example, by not obtaining a copy of the college lecture timetable. However the position if the employer serves the information on the union is uncertain. It is notable that there is no requirement for the employer to notify its plans, such as bringing in contractors or replacement labour, to the union, despite the Government's emphasis upon a 'long-term partnership approach'.[12] The second explicit objective behind the pre-ballot notice is to enable the employer to bring information to the attention of those of its employees who will be entitled to vote in the ballot, and enables the employer to target material presenting its side of the dispute more precisely. There is no specific protection against dismissal or other forms of detriment for taking part in an industrial action ballot (in contrast, for example, to ballots relating to recognition or derecognition).[13] It is arguable that were an employer to take such measures, or, possibly, threaten them, this would infringe the protection against taking part in union activities at an appropriate time.[14] However no such constraint applies to those threatened with a detriment were they to participate in the industrial action itself, which would not be at an appropriate time, although there is protection in specified circumstances against dismissal.[15]

---

1. The first day when a voting paper is sent to any person entitled to vote in the ballot: TULRCA 1992, s 226A(4).

2. *Quaere* whether the onus is on unions to inquire whether what may appear to be a monolithic employer is, in reality, divided into separate companies.

3. TULRCA 1992, s 226A(1), (2).

4. *Ibid.*, s 226(3)(a), 3B. Where not all its employees will be sent the same voting paper, a sample of each form of voting paper which is to be sent to any of them must be sent

to the employer: s 226A(3)(b), 3B. Prior to ERA 1999, samples of all the different voting papers had to be sent to all the employers involved in the dispute, even if they were not being used in relation to its own employees. See the Code of Practice on Industrial Action Ballots and Notice to Employers, para 15.

5. *Ibid.*, s 226A(2). The Code of Practice gives as examples of 'making plans' warning customers of the possibility of disruption, taking steps to ensure health and safety and safeguarding equipment: para 14.

6. *Ibid.*, s 226A(3A)(a).

7. *Ibid.*, s 226A(3A),(b).

8. *Blackpool and Fylde College v NATFHE* [1994] IRLR 227, CA. Here the union specified 'all our members in your institution'. The college had been told by the union branch secretary some months previously that around one-third of its staff (288) were union members but only 109 had their dues debited directly from their salaries. The court concluded that the employer had not received adequate information. The CIE (now called the ECSR) which supervises the ESC considered that this was a threat to the right to organise as guaranteed by Article 5: Conclusions XIII–3, 109; Conclusions XIV–I. An application alleging that the requirement to reveal names violated Article 11 of the ECHR was ruled inadmissible by the EComHR: *NATFHE v UK*, App No 28910/95. The Commission acknowledged that there may be circumstances where requiring an association to reveal the names of its members to a third party could constitute an unjustified interference with freedom of association, but did not consider that there was anything inherently secret about union membership, nor was there any evidence to suggest that the obligation adversely affected the union's right to protect its members' interests.

9. Lord McIntosh of Haringey, HL Debs Vol 602, col 300, 16 June 1999.

10. Lord McIntosh seemed to equate 'category' with 'broad occupational characteristic' (*ibid.*, col 298). However he indicated that if only train drivers on the Central Line were to be called out in an underground strike, this should be specified. See also the Code of Practice, para 18.

11. Human Rights 1998, s 3. Violation of Article 8 was not argued in *NATFHE v UK*, above, note 8. *Quaere* whether such disclosure would violate the DPA 1998. Whether an individual is a union member constitutes 'sensitive personal data': s2(d). Schedule 2 permits disclosure, *inter alia*, where the processing 'is necessary for the purposes of legitimate interests pursued . . . by the third party or parties to whom the data are disclosed, except where the processing is unwarranted in any particular case by reason of prejudice to the rights and freedoms or legitimate interests of the data subject'. We would submit that disclosure of union membership would be unwarranted, and none of the other provisions of Schedule 2 appears applicable in this case. Schedule 3 allows disclosure where the 'processing is necessary for the purposes of exercising or performing any right or obligation which is conferred or imposed by law on the data controller in connection with employment'. There is no definition of 'employment' in the Act.

12. Lord McIntosh of Haringey, HL Debs Vol 602, col 300, 16 June 1999. He considered that the *quid pro quo* for the union's obligation was that of the employer to disclose information to recognised unions for the purposes of collective bargaining: col 301.

13. See para **4.57** *et seq.*

14. See para **3.6** *et seq.*

15. See para **6.98** *et seq.*

6.46 As soon as reasonably practicable after the holding of the ballot the trade union must take such steps as are reasonably necessary to ensure that every 'relevant employer' of persons entitled to vote in the ballot is informed of the number of votes cast in the ballot, the number voting 'yes' (to each question if more than one was put), the number voting 'no' and the number of spoiled ballot papers.[1] A 'relevant employer' is a person who it is reasonable for the union to believe (at the time when steps are taken) was at the time of the ballot the employer of any persons entitled to vote.[2] It has been suggested (and would seem to be the case) that where separate workplace ballots are required,[3] results must be notified for each ballot; otherwise employers should receive notification of the overall result.[4] Employers of those entitled to vote in the ballot are also entitled to a copy of the scrutineer's report when it becomes available, on request, either free of charge or on payment of a reasonable fee specified by the union.[5]

---

1. TULRCA 1992, s 231A(1).
2. *Ibid.*, s 231A(2).
3. See para **6.35**.
4. See Mr Patrick McLoughlin, House of Commons, Official Report of Standing Committee F, col 254, 15 December 1992.
5. *Ibid*, s 231B(2).

6.47 Before inducing a person to take part (or continue to take part) in industrial action the union must take such steps as are 'reasonably necessary' to ensure that the person's employer[1] receives within the 'appropriate period' a relevant notice.[2] The 'appropriate period' begins when the union satisfies its obligation to supply relevant employers with information about the result of the ballot and ends with the seventh day before the day specified in the notice for the industrial action to begin.[3] The need to commence the industrial action within four weeks of the date of the ballot (unless extended by agreement between union and employer), discussed in para **6.49**, should be borne in mind here. The notice, which must be in writing, must:

(a) Contain such information in the union's possession as would help the employer to make plans and bring information to the attention of those of his employees whom the union intends to induce or has induced to take part, or continue to take part, in the industrial action (the 'affected employees').[4] The discussion in para **6.45** about what this requires applies also in this context. By this time, however, the information in the union's possession about the form and scope of industrial action is likely to be much more specific, although once again the union may wish to limit the information it seeks about the tasks which individual members undertake. Thus, to return to the example of the college lecturers given in that paragraph, it would be advisable for the union not to seek a copy of the lecture timetable. Unions should be aware that any documents which are in their possession may be susceptible to an order for disclosure from the court. Similarly a union official could be ordered to depose by way of witness statement or affidavit the extent of the information which is in the union's possession.

(b) State whether industrial action is intended to be continuous or discontinuous. Industrial action is 'discontinuous' where the union intends it to take place only on some days on which there is an opportunity to take it; where not so restricted it is deemed to be 'continuous'.[5] For continuous action, the notice must specify when any of the affected employees will begin to take part in it; for discontinuous, the intended dates for any of the affected employees to take part.[6] If both continuous and discontinuous action are intended (eg a continuous overtime ban coupled with a series of one-day strikes), notice of both must be given.[7]

(c) State that it is given for the purposes of the section.[8]

Having given such a notice, the union will not lose the protection of the immunities in inducing an affected employee to take part in the action provided that any participation accords with the terms of the notice given (and, in particular, that in the case of discontinuous action participation has not been induced on an unspecified day).[9] Where continuous industrial action is called off or suspended, a fresh notice must be given if industrial action (whether continuous or discontinuous in nature) is resumed at a later date.[10] This is subject to two exceptions. The first is where the industrial action is called off or suspended by the union in order to enable it to comply with a court order or an undertaking to the court.[11] This could occur if industrial action were the subject of an interim injunction at first instance but the injunction were lifted on appeal. The second (a new exception introduced by the Employment Relations Act 1999) is where the union agrees with the employer that the industrial action will be suspended with effect from a specified date ('the suspension date') and that it may be resumed from a date not earlier than another specified date ('the resumption date'). This agreement must be reached before the industrial action is suspended. If the action is then suspended in accordance with the terms of the agreement, it will be covered by the earlier notice provided that it is not authorised or endorsed by the union prior to the resumption date or such later date as the union and employer may agree.[12] This may make unions more willing to allow a breathing space for negotiations. A union will need to ensure, however, that in a dispute involving more than one employer (in local government or the National Health Service, for example), agreement is reached with each of them; a failure to do this will mean that any unnotified resumed action will be unprotected in relation to the employer in respect of whom the default occurs (and for the purposes of the statutory right of action described in para **6.11**). The legislation does not specify that the agreement between the union and employer(s) should be in writing, but it would be highly advisable for unions to ensure that it is reduced to writing and signed by all the parties. In the case of discontinuous industrial action there is no obligation upon the union to take action on any of the notified days; it seems that failing to do so would not prejudice the lawfulness of subsequent previously notified action.

---

1. The section covers any employer it is reasonable for the union to believe, at the latest time when steps could be taken to ensure that it receives such a notice, that it is the employer of persons who will be or have been induced to take part or to continue to take part in the industrial action: TULRCA 1992, s 234A(2). The statutory principles governing the persons whose actions are attributable to the union apply in this context (see para **6.13** *et seq.*): *ibid.*, s 234A(8),(9). Thus, the notice may be furnished to the employer(s) by any such persons.

2. TULRCA 1992, s 234A(1). See para **6.45** for discussion of the methods which unions should use to ensure that information is received and they have adequate evidence of this.

3. *Ibid.*, s 234A(4).

4. *Ibid.*, s 234A(3)(a), (5A).

5. *Ibid.*, s 234A(6).

6. *Ibid.*, s 234A(3)(b). See para **6.94** for the difficulties which may arise in determining when individuals 'begin' and cease to take part in industrial action.

7. This was the view of Mr. Michael Forsyth, House of Commons, Official Report of Standing Committee F, col 260, 15 December 1992, and would seem to be correct.

8. TULRCA 1992, s 234A(3)(c).

9. *Ibid.*, s 234A(5).

10. *Ibid.*, s 234A(7).

11. *Ibid.*, s 234A(7A).

12. *Ibid.*, s 234A(7B). For discussion of the separate but crucial question whether the original *ballot* will cover resumed industrial action, see para **6.49** below. The Code of Practice on Industrial Action Ballots and Notice to Employers emphasises the need for the resumed industrial action to be of the same kind as that covered in the original notice: para 52. This presumably is based upon the interpretation of 'it' in TULRCA 1992 s 234A(7B)(a).

Call by a Specified Person

6.48 Industrial action may be validly called only by a person specified (either individually or by description) on the voting paper.[1] As we discussed in para **6.38**, such a person need not be authorised under the union rules to call industrial action; it is sufficient that he or she belongs to a category of persons speci-fied in the statute as those whose authorisation or endorsement binds the union (in the absence of a valid repudiation). The Court of Appeal has allowed some flexibility in this area when it held that it was permissible for a specified person to authorise a subordinate union official to call a strike should further negotia-tions with the employers prove unsuccessful, although it emphasised that a very close link in time between the strike and the event precipitating the final action, such as an unsuccessful meeting, would be required, such closeness to be a mat-ter of fact and degree.[2] The court also recognised in that case that it would be impractical to leave matters so that no discretion could be exercised by local offi-cials as to how a call for industrial action was to be put into operation. The call must be made, and the industrial action to which it relates must take place, before the expiry of the ballot mandate (see para **6.49**).[3] It is crucial to the law-fulness of industrial action approved in a ballot that there should have been no call by the trade union to take part (or continue to take part) in the action to which the ballot relates, or any authorisation or endorsement of such industrial action, before the date of the ballot.[4] The meaning of 'call' here is obscure, but it appears to refer to a specific event rather than a prevailing attitude towards prospective action; the Court of Appeal has affirmed that a union is not required to adopt a neutral stance before that time on whether industrial action should be taken; rather, it is 'perfectly entitled to be partisan'.[5] The implications of a non-specified person whose actions are attributable to the union (see para **6.13** *et seq.*) making a call depend upon the timing. A call made before the date of the ballot cannot be endorsed; the union then will have to choose between repudia-tion (where this is possible) or accepting liability. If a non-specified person makes a call after the date of the ballot, it is possible that the union will not be liable provided that a specified person endorses it,[6] although this is not free from doubt, nor is it clear whether the union can repudiate the unauthorised call (where it is open to it to do so) and still rely on the ballot to make a valid call thereafter, although the Code of Practice on Industrial Action Ballots and Notice to Employers suggests that it can.[7] If an unauthorised call is made sub-sequently to a call by a specified person, the unauthorised call will be irrelevant.

---

1. TULRCA 1992, s 233(1), (2).
2. *Tanks and Drums Ltd v TGWU* [1991] IRLR 372, CA; see further para **6.38** note 5.
3. TULRCA 1992, s 233(3)(b).
4. *Ibid*, s 233(3)(a). A call is made by a union if 'authorised or endorsed' by the union (s 233(4)); the statutory principles of liability (see para **6.13** *et seq.*) apply in this con-text. 'Date of the ballot' means, in the case of a ballot in which votes may be cast on more than one day, the last of those days: s 246. The fact that the restriction is limited to industrial action to which the ballot relates means that a union can hold a fresh bal-lot to broaden the scope of existing industrial action without first repudiating any call

for that first action, and it is irrelevant that the earlier action would be subsumed in the later: *London Borough of Newham v NALGO* [1993] IRLR 83, CA.

5. *Ibid.*,at 86.

6. This argument is based on the fact that the statute merely requires that there should have been no call prior to the date of the ballot (s 233(3)(a)) and that the call should be made by a specified person: it is silent on the question posed in the text.

7. See footnote 10 in the Code.

The Expiry Date on the Ballot Mandate

6.49 A ballot in favour of industrial action ceases to be effective at the end of a period of four weeks beginning with the date of the ballot or a period 'of such longer duration not exceeding eight weeks as is agreed between the union and the members' employer'.[1] This latter option, introduced by the Employment Relations Act 1999, means that a union is not obliged to commence industrial action within the four week period where, for example, the parties consider that a settlement could be achieved by negotiation. Although the legislation does not require that any provision for extension should be in writing, it would be highly advisable for unions to ensure that it is reduced to writing and signed by all parties. It will also be important to ensure that, in a dispute involving more than one employer, an agreement for extension is reached with each of them; the four-week deadline must be kept in relation to any employer with whom there is no such agreement. It is possible that industrial action may start and then be suspended for further negotiations to take place, only to be followed by the re-imposition of industrial action if these negotiations are not successful. As we indicated in para **6.47**, the legislation now provides that where this is done by agreement between the parties no fresh notice need be issued in respect of resumed industrial action. However there is also the additional question whether or not a further ballot is required for the second period of industrial action. This depends upon whether it can be viewed as sufficiently connected with the first to be seen as a continuation of it or whether the first was deemed to have terminated, in which case a fresh ballot will be required. In *Monsanto plc v TGWU*[2] union members voted in favour of industrial action 'in pursuit of a settlement of the dispute with Monsanto Ltd [*sic*] over the employment of Temporary Labour'. The company responded with counter-sanctions, including suspension of sick pay, guaranteed week and early retirement schemes. The union suspended the industrial action pending further negotiations but re-imposed it two weeks later after negotiations broke down over the counter-sanctions. The Court of Appeal held that there was no need for a further ballot; the industrial action had not been discontinued but merely suspended temporarily for the purposes of negotiation with the intention that it would be resumed should negotiations fail. The court also rejected the employer's argument that the re-imposed action was outside the terms of the ballot; these terms were sufficiently wide to encompass any matters within the scope of settlement of the original dispute. This case shows the necessity for unions to ensure that the terms of the questions on the ballot paper are sufficiently broad to cover any matters which may arise out of and in consequence of the dispute at issue (although note the dangers, discussed in para **6.40**, of including issues which do not relate to the central matter in dispute). *Monsanto* was distinguished by the Court of Appeal in *Post Office v UCW*.[3] In September 1988 postal officers and assistants voted in favour of industrial action in support of the union's opposition to the Post Office's plans to close up to 750 post offices, and between October and December there was a series of selective 24-hour strikes, culminating in a national one-day strike on 12 December. Between January and April 1989 there was no industrial action, although the union mounted a public relations campaign in opposition to the Post Office's policy, but in May the union's Assistant General Secretary told the annual conference that industrial action would continue. There were two brief local strikes in the autumn, and in January 1990 the union gave instructions for a 24-hour strike in London and the South-East. The Post Office successfully applied for an interim injunction to halt this strike. The ground for the decision was that the form of question on the ballot paper did not meet the statutory requirements discussed in para **6.39**. However, the Court of Appeal also held that the campaign of industrial action authorised by the ballot had terminated with the national strike in December 1988 and industrial action subsequent to that required the support of a fresh ballot. According to Lord Donaldson MR, it was implicit that industrial action, once begun, should continue without 'substantial interruption' if reliance were to continue to be placed upon the verdict of the initial ballot. This was a question of fact and degree, but:

> the question which the Court has to ask itself is whether the average reasonable trade union member, looking at the matter at or shortly after any interruption in the industrial action, would say to himself, 'the industrial action has now come to an end', even if he might also say 'the union may want to call us out again if the dispute continues.[4]

Whereas in *Monsanto* the action was suspended for a short period to enable active negotiations to take place, in this case after 12 December there had been a complete change of tactics, with reversion to a tactic of industrial action over nine months later. Unions must ensure, therefore, that when they suspend industrial action, they make clear to members that this is contingent upon a successful outcome to negotiations and they should not delay its resumption for an extended period.[5] Where industrial action is resumed then unless suspension was the product of a prior agreement with the employer as described in para **6.47**, the notice requirements discussed in that paragraph must be complied with once again.

1. TULRCA 1992, s 234(1). Where votes may be cast on more than one day, the 'date of the ballot' is the last of those days: *ibid.*, s 246. The period of four weeks ends at the stroke of midnight on the last day of the fourth week, so where a ballot ceased to be effective on 12 June at the stroke of midnight, action called for 13 June was outside the period of the ballot mandate: *RJB Mining (UK) Ltd v NUM* [1995] IRLR 556, CA.

2. [19861 IRLR 406, CA.

3. [1990] IRLR 143, CA.

4. *Ibid.*, at 147; see also Butler-Sloss LJ at 147–148. It is unclear why the test should depend on the views of a trade union member (or, indeed, an employer) rather than a court's objective assessment of the facts before it.

5. See also *London Underground Ltd v RMT*, QBD, 22 December 1998 (unreported), where, in interim proceedings, Sullivan J thought it 'quite unrealistic' that in a fast-moving situation a campaign of industrial action could have been suspended for a five-month period. He also found that the nature of the issues had changed; the material leading to the ballot which gave authority for the earlier strikes showed that their primary objective had been that employees working on the underground should remain employees of London Transport, whereas the later strikes concerned ensuring that those who were being transferred to infrastructure companies received the best possible deal.

6.50 Initially, the legislation made no provision for the situation where industrial action was halted temporarily by legal proceedings, and during a docks dispute in 1989 the ballot mandate expired by the time an interim injunction granted by the Court of Appeal was discharged by the House of Lords. It is now provided that where for the whole or part of the four-week period the calling or organising of industrial action is prohibited by virtue of a court order which subsequently lapses or is discharged, recalled or set aside (or by an undertaking given to a court by any person from which he or she is subsequently released or by which he or she ceases to be bound), the trade union may apply to the court for an order that the period during which the prohibition had effect shall not count towards the four weeks.[1] The application must be made to the court whose decision led to the cessation 'forthwith' upon the prohibition ceasing to have effect.[2] Where an order lapses or an undertaking ceases to bind without any such decision, application must be made to the court by which the order was made or to which the undertaking was given.[3] No such application may be made after the end of an eight week period beginning with the date of the ballot.[4] The period between the making of an application and its determination does not count towards the four-week period,[5] but in no circumstances may a ballot be regarded as effective later than 12 weeks after the date of the ballot.[6] The making of an order is entirely at the discretion of the court and no appeal lies from its decision.[7] However, the court must not make an order if it considers that the result of the ballot no longer represents the views of the union members concerned[8] or that an event is likely to occur as a result of which those members would vote against industrial action if another ballot were to be held.[9] This second factor, in particular, may present difficulties for a union, given its highly speculative nature. Ultimately, most disputes end in a compromise solution being reached so that one could argue that in most cases an 'event' of the kind specified is likely to occur at some stage. Where an extension is refused a union will have to incur all the trouble and expense of a fresh ballot, even though its actions may have been fully vindicated in the legal proceedings in which the employers sought to halt the industrial action.

---

1. TULRCA 1992, s 234(2). This provision has not been amended in the light of the provision for a longer ballot mandate by agreement between the parties described in para **6.49** except as indicated in note 5 below; in practice, it is probably unlikely that such an agreement could be reached if the employer is bringing legal proceedings in respect of the action.
2. *Ibid.*, s 234(3)(a).
3. *Ibid.*, s 234(3)(b).
4. *Ibid.*, s 234(3). Where votes may be cast on more than one day, the 'date of the ballot' is the last of those days: s 246.
5. *Ibid.*, s 234(6). The same principle applies to any longer period agreed by the parties.
6. *Ibid.*
7. *Ibid.*, s 234(5). Whilst this provision prevents delay, it is curious that there should be no right of appeal, regardless of the circumstances.
8. Evidential problems may be overcome by the production of newspapers, television reports or evidence that some of the union members had ceased to participate in the industrial action.
9. *Ibid.*, s 234(4).

The Code of Practice on Industrial Action Ballots and Notice to Employers

6.51 As we indicated in para **6.30**, the Code of Practice, now in its fourth version, includes provisions which exceed the requirements of the legislation.[1] Particularly significant is the statement that a ballot should not take place until any agreed procedures, whether formal or otherwise, which might lead to a resolution of the dispute without the need for industrial action have been completed and consideration has been given to resolving the dispute by other means, including seeking assistance from ACAS.[2] This seems somewhat anomalous in the light of the fact that collective agreements are not, in general, legally enforceable and there is no equivalent exhortation when employers break agreements.

There could also be scope for argument as to whether procedures have been exhausted in any given case. Another notable provision is that unions should consider delaying any call for industrial action following a ballot until the scrutineer's report has been received, which could create considerable difficulties given the tight time limits which apply.[3] Although neither these nor other provisions of the Code are directly enforceable, it is conceivable that non-observance of them, particularly the first, may be influential when a court is deciding whether to grant an interim injunction to halt the action.

---

1 This was also a feature of earlier Codes; see Simpson, 1995.

2 Para 6.

3 Para 49.

CIVIL LAW REMEDIES

Injunctions

Sources and general principles

6.52 Injunctions are by far the most important remedy in industrial disputes; for those affected by industrial action usually the main priority is to restrain the action in the first place rather than to claim damages for consequent economic loss. The High Court has a wide discretionary power to order injunctions at any time, including before the claim form is issued and after judgment has been given.[1] Claimants in industrial action cases will generally seek an interim injunction, issued pending a full trial, and most cases do not proceed beyond the interim stage. In this context, granting an interim injunction does not fulfil the usual purpose of preserving the *status quo* until full trial; rather, it effectively decides the issue, given that timing is crucial and matters do not remain 'on ice'. In exercising its discretion, the Trade Union and Labour Relations (Consolidation) Act 1992, s 221, requires the court to have regard to the likelihood of the industrial action being protected by the statutory immunities, where this defence is claimed.[2] The section also qualifies the power of the court to grant injunctions in the respondent's absence.[3] In contrast to the position prior to the introduction of the Civil Procedure Rules in 1999, there is no right to appeal without permission against the decision of a judge to grant or refuse an interim injunction.[4] Flouting an injunction constitutes contempt of court, rendering the respondent liable to an unlimited fine and, where appropriate, imprisonment. It may also lead to sequestration of a respondent's assets. The Trade Union and Labour Relations (Consolidation) 1992, s 236 prevents a court from ordering an employee to work by way of an order for specific performance of the contract of employment or an injunction restraining a breach or threatened breach. Where an applicant relies solely upon the statutory right of action relating to industrial action affecting the supply of goods or services to an individual (see para **6.11**), an order to halt industrial action (or threatened industrial action) is the only form of relief available.[5] The statute states that where the court finds the claim 'well founded' it 'shall' grant an order in specified terms, thus seeming to leave no room for the exercise of discretion.[6] It also indicates that, without prejudice to any other power of the court, interim relief may be granted for this purpose[7] and we would argue that where, as will generally be the case, applications are dealt with in interim proceedings, without full trial of the issues, the decision as to whether or not to grant a remedy remains one for the discretion of the court.

---

1. CPR Part 25.2
2. TULRCA 1992, s 221(2) makes specific reference to the defences specified in TUL-RCA 1992, s 219 (protection from certain tort liabilities) or s 220 (peaceful picketing): see further paras **6.17** and **6.72**.
3. *Ibid.*, s 221(1).
4. CPR, r 52.3.
5. TULRCA 1992, s 235A.
6. *Ibid.*, s 235A(4). See Spry, 1997, 444–446 for the principles governing the granting of injunctions by virtue of a specific statutory power.
7. *Ibid.*, s 235A(5).

Applications for interim injunctions: the courts' approach

6.53 The granting of an interim injunction, which is an equitable remedy, is always at the discretion of the court. In general, however, as a first step the court must be satisfied that there is a 'serious question to be tried'.[1] This may not be difficult in relation to industrial action, where the facts may be complex and disputed and the applicant may allege the commission of several torts, the boundaries of which are sometimes uncertain.[2] If an applicant suggests some novel head of liability the courts may be reluctant to dismiss the suggestion out of hand.[3] Where the evidence before the court[4] is insufficient to decide a disputed matter, the court is likely to conclude that there is a serious issue.[5] Once the applicant has passed this hurdle, the court then considers whether the 'balance of convenience' lies in granting or refusing the injunction. (Where the defence of statutory immunity is claimed, this too must be considered: see para **6.17** *et seq.*) Basically, the 'balance of convenience' test requires the court to consider whether damages would be an adequate remedy for either side if their position were vindicated at the trial.[6] If damages would be an adequate remedy, an injunction should not be granted. Damages will rarely be a sufficient remedy if the respondent is unable or unlikely to pay them. Damages may also not be sufficient if the alleged wrong is regarded by the court as irreparable, incapable of pecuniary compensation or if damages would be very difficult to assess.[7] If damages are not regarded as a sufficient remedy the court will then consider whether more harm will be done by granting or refusing the injunction. To quote Lord Diplock in the leading case of *American Cyanamid Co v Ethicon Ltd.*:

> The object of the . . . [interim] injunction is to protect the . . . [applicant] against injury by violation of his right for which he could not be adequately compensated in damages recoverable in the action if the uncertainty were resolved in his favour at the trial; but the . . . [applicant's] need for such protection must be weighed against the corresponding need of the . . . [respondent] to be protected against injury resulting from his having been prevented from exercising his own legal rights for which he could not be adequately compensated under the . . . [applicant's] undertaking in damages if the uncertainty were resolved in the . . . [respondent's] favour at the trial. The court must weigh one need against another. . . .[8]

---

1. *American Cyanamid Co v Ethicon Ltd* [1975] 1 All ER 504 at 510, HL. Another way of expressing it was that the claim should not be 'frivolous or vexatious' (*ibid.*) or to put it another way, that the applicant has a good arguable claim to the right he or she seeks to protect. It is interesting to note that some decisions in other contexts 'have sidestepped the *American Cyanamid* advice and . . . recognised the importance of a test of merits' (Zuckerman, 1993, 328): see, for example, *Lansing Linde Ltd v Kerr* [1991] 1 All ER 418, CA; *Cambridge Nutrition Ltd v BBC* [1990] 3 All ER 523, CA. It seems unlikely that the line of argument which succeeded in the latter case would persuade a court not to halt industrial action, and for the reasons we explain in para **1.6**, interference with taking industrial action is unlikely to be seen as interference with a Convention right for the purposes of the HRA 1998. However, where industrial action itself interferes with a Convention right, such as freedom of expression, this may be an additional factor which persuades a court to grant an interim injunction: see further para **1.18**,
2. See paras **6.2** *et seq.*
3. *Ibid.*
4. See para **6.57** for the form of evidence.
5. See for example *Metropolitan Borough of Solihull v NUT* [1985] IRLR 211, ChD, where there was a conflict of affidavit evidence on the question whether teachers were contractually obliged to perform a particular task.
6. Where an individual is relying upon the statutory right of action under TULRCA 1992, s 235A damages may very well not be available to him or her as a remedy because he or she would not have any right of action beyond the statute, and so the union will be denied the opportunity of arguing that damages would be adequate compensation.
7. *Merchant Adventurers Ltd v Grew and Co Ltd* [1972] Ch 242, ChD.
8. Above, note 1, at 509.

6.54 In *American Cyanamid*, the House of Lords warned against attempts to specify exhaustively the matters which the courts should take into account in assessing the 'balance of convenience'. With that warning in mind, some factors can be isolated which have proved influential in the industrial action context. One consistently weighty factor is the extent of the loss which the employer would suffer if the action was not restrained. This was a particularly powerful argument before 1982, when trade unions could not be sued in tort and employers could proceed only against individual dispute organisers, who were unlikely to have the means to pay substantial damages and costs.[1] In 1984, the House of Lords stated that the repeal of this immunity by the 1982 Employment Act, which thenceforth exposed unions to claims for damages, meant that there was no reason for judges to assume that a case would never come to trial where the defendant was the union itself.[2] In practice, this change does not appear to have made judges less willing to grant interim injunctions, although it seems to have made employers more willing to apply for them.[3] Moreover, the statutory limit upon the amount which may be claimed in damages against a union[4] has been used against them in some cases, where the court has found that the losses which the employer would incur were the action not injuncted would exceed this sum.[5] It has proved much more difficult for unions to persuade the courts that they and/or their members will sustain irrecoverable losses if an injunction is imposed; admittedly the losses which may arise from the inability lawfully to pursue industrial action are less tangible and less easy to quantify.[6] However, the difficulty of quantifying loss, which on occasion has swayed the issue in favour of an employer,[7] has traditionally met with less success when used by unions, and the courts have tended not to accord great weight to the argument that industrial action, once postponed, may not be easily revived.[8] However in the light of the statutory requirements for a postal ballot and (usually) independent scrutiny of industrial action ballots, both of which impose considerable costs on unions (see para **6.30** *et seq.* and para **6.32**), the position may be different: these costs are quantifiable and, where pleaded, will need to be taken into account by the court in exercising its discretion whether the injunction should be granted. Where an interim injunction has been granted unions may be more inclined to take a case to full trial to recover these amounts. A further factor, whose weight remains untested, is that of the damage to the 'public interest', which was propounded by the Court of Appeal as a factor for consideration during the 1989 docks dispute.[9] In 1998, a court took into account in granting an interim injunction to restrain strikes on the London underground the public disruption which the strikes would occasion, particularly if they were to take place on New Year's Eve, when the large number of people wishing to travel into London would also raise issues of public safety.[10] The notion of the 'public interest', an undefined and malleable concept, could be of overwhelming impact; indeed '[i]n major disputes it could turn the balance of convenience into a mere formality'.[11] Another consideration of uncertain significance and scope is non-compliance with the extra-statutory requirements of the Code of Practice on Industrial Action Ballots and Notice to Employers, such as those provisions which direct that industrial action should be taken only after all other avenues have been explored.[12] The fact that industrial action is interfering with a right guaranteed by the ECHR, such as freedom of expression, or, possibly, the right to life, may also influence a court in favour of granting an injunction once the Human Rights Act 1998 comes fully into force, and, indeed, in relation to some of the Convention rights, at least, there may be a positive obligation for the court to grant the order.[13] However, for the reasons we explained in para **1.18**, the fact that an injunction interferes with the taking of industrial action is unlikely to be a material consideration because the ECtHR has not regarded the right to strike as an essential element of freedom of association. Lastly, where the balance of convenience does not weigh decisively one way or another, the court has regard to the desirability of preserving the status quo.[14] Where industrial action has not yet started, this means preventing it occurring.[15] Where the discretion is being exercised pursuant to an application under the statutory right of action (see para **6.11**), it remains to be seen whether courts may be persuaded to have regard to factors such as the wishes of the parties, the imminence of a settlement, the position of the supplier of goods and services in the marketplace and the ease with which alternative supplies may be obtained.[16]

---

1. Trade Disputes Act 1906, s 4, repealed by the Industrial Relations Act 1971; Trade Union and Labour Relations Act 1974, s 14 (now repealed).

2. *Dimbleby and Sons v NUJ* [1984] IRLR 161, HL.

3. For an early survey see Evans, 1987.

4. TULRCA 1992, s 22; see further para **6.64**.

5. See, for example, *Mercury Communications Ltd v Scott-Garner and the POEU* [1983] IRLR 494, CA; *News Group Newspapers Ltd v SOGAT 82 (No 2)* [1986] IRLR 337, QBD (expenses incurred in busing employees and providing extra security staff already beyond the statutory limit).

6. For an example of judicial acknowledgment of this, see Henry J in *Barretts and Baird (Wholesale) Ltd v IPCS* [1987] IRLR 3 at 11.

7. See *News Group Newspapers Ltd*, above, note 5 (value of loss of key staff could not be quantified).

8. See, for example, May LJ in *Mercury Communications Ltd v Scott-Garner and the POEU*, above, note 5, at 504; *Metropolitan Borough of Solihull v NUT* [1985] IRLR 211, ChD (only loss choosing between holding a ballot and accepting arbitration); *Associated British Ports v TGWU* [1989] IRLR 305, CA; cf. recognition by Lord Diplock in *NWL Ltd v Woods* [1979] IRLR 478 at 484 of the need for unions to 'strike while the iron is still hot', and *Cambridge Nutrition Ltd v BBC* [1990] 3 All ER 523, CA (damages not an adequate remedy for the BBC if an action to restrain the broadcast of a television programme failed at full trial because it would have been deprived of the opportunity to broadcast on a matter of public interest in the form and manner of its choice). See also the HRA 1998, s 12.

9. *Associated British Ports v TGWU*, above. The relevance and significance of this factor was not discussed by the House of Lords: [1989] IRLR 399.

10. *London Underground Ltd v RMT*, 22 December 1998, QBD (unreported).

11. Simpson, 1989 at 240. A more specific version of this has been freedom of the press: see *Beaverbrook Newspapers Ltd v Keys* [1978] IRLR 34, CA. *Quaere* whether one could argue for the public interest in securing the freedom to withdraw labour: cf *Cambridge Nutrition Ltd v BBC*, above, note 8.

12. Para 6; see para **6.51**.

13. See para **1.18**. The scope of the right to life in ECHR jurisprudence is uncertain: see Harris *et al*, 1995, Chapter 2; McBride, 1999.

14. *American Cyanamid Co v Ethicon Ltd* [1975] 1 All ER 504 at 511.

15. See, for example, *Associated British Ports v TGWU*, CA, above, note 8; *London Underground Ltd v NUR* [1989] IRLR 341, QBD.

16. See further Morris, 1993. Lord Mottistone sought unsuccessfully to introduce amendments put forward by the CBI which were designed to limit the discretion of the courts in this context, such as a requirement to have regard to representations by the parties and to prevent an injunction being granted where the court was satisfied there was a reasonable prospect of a settlement.

6.55 Taken alone, the criteria by which the courts decide whether or not to grant interim injunctions could clearly set at nought the protection for industrial action afforded by the statutory immunities. In an attempt to avoid this situation, the Trade Union and Labour Relations (Consolidation) Act 1992 states that where a respondent claims to have acted in contemplation or furtherance of a trade dispute:

> the court shall, in exercising its discretion whether or not to grant the injunction, have regard to the likelihood of that party's succeeding at the trial of the action in establishing any matter which would afford a defence to the action under section 219 (protection from certain tort liabilities) or section 220 (peaceful picketing).[1]

In *NWL Ltd v Woods* in 1979[2] the House of Lords stated that this provision required the court to put into the balance of convenience the degree of likelihood of the defence succeeding; the greater the degree of likelihood, the greater the weight to be given to it.[3] However, the impact of this provision is restricted in three different ways. First, it refers only to the likelihood of the respondent successfully arguing that the industrial action is protected by the immunities; it does not cover situations where the applicant suggests heads of liability which are outside the immunities altogether, such as those based on breach of statutory duty. In that situation, the test in *American Cyanamid alone* applies. Secondly, considerable uncertainty surrounds elements of the statutory immunity defence and, in particular, the balloting requirements, non-compliance with which will remove immunity for 'non-unofficial' disputes.[4] In cases of doubt, other factors are likely to sway the 'balance of convenience' in favour of an injunction.[5] Lastly, the courts have continued to affirm their residual discretion to grant an injunction irrespective of the likelihood of the immunities applying where the consequences of disruptive action for the employer or the public may be particularly 'disastrous'.[6] According to Lord Fraser, 'if the probable result of the threatened act would be to cause immediate serious danger to public safety or health and if no other means seemed to be available for averting the danger in time', it would not be wrong to grant an injunction.[7] This position means that even industrial action which is clearly protected by the statutory immunities may nevertheless be enjoined by an injunction if the court considers that the circumstances warrant it. There have been no cases as yet where this has occurred,[8] and it is arguable that the statutory requirement for unions to notify the employer of information in their possession which will help the employer to 'make plans' (see para **6.47**) may obviate the need for judicial discretion to be exercised in this manner.

---

1. TULRCA 1992, s 221(2).
2. [1979] IRLR 478, HL.
3. Lord Diplock considered that 'in the normal way' the injunction should be refused where it was 'more likely than not' that the defence would succeed: *ibid.*, at 484.
4. See para **6.30** *et seq.*
5. See, for example, *London Underground Ltd v NUR* [1989] IRLR 341, QBD.
6. Lord Diplock in *NWL*, above, note 2, at 430 (as amended [1980] ICR 167).
7. *Duport Steels Ltd v Sirs* [1980] ICR 161 at 187. See also *London Underground Ltd v RMT*, 22 December 1998, QBD (unreported).
8. In *Associated British Ports v TGWU*, discussed in para **6.54**, the allegedly wrongful act was not protected by the immunities and the CA did not, therefore, consider the effect of TULRCA 1992, s 221(2).

6.56 Applications for an interim injunction in industrial relations disputes are made either to the Chancery Division or to the Queen's Bench Division of the High Court of Justice.[1] An application in the Chancery Division is normally heard in open court. An application in the Queen's Bench Division is heard in chambers, although the judge has discretion to hear the application and/or give judgment in open court. A number of cases relating to industrial disputes have been commenced in the Chancery Division. In some cases, however, claimants have preferred to institute proceedings in the Queen's Bench Division because of the privacy afforded by a hearing in chambers, which the press and public are not permitted to attend. Normally applicants for an interim injunction must serve on the respondent the application notice as soon as practicable after issue at the court, together with evidence in support. At the outside this should be not less than three days before the court is due to hear the application, and the hearing will then take place with all the parties to the proceedings being present before the court.[2] However, where a matter is sufficiently urgent, the application may be made to the court even more speedily, even before a claim form is issued, without notice to the respondent.[3] Applications can be made at weekends and public holidays; there are duty judges who are available to deal with emergency applications. Due to the fact that imminent industrial action will generally be deemed sufficiently urgent to justify an application without notice (formerly known as an *ex parte* application),[4] the Trade Union and Labour Relations (Consolidation) Act 1992 attempts to provide some rudimentary protection for respondents. It states that where a party against whom an injunction without notice is sought claims, or in the opinion of the court would be likely to claim, that he or she acted in contemplation or furtherance of a trade dispute (see para **6.19** *et seq.*) the court shall not grant the injunction unless satisfied that all steps which in the circumstances were reasonable have been taken with a view to securing that notice of the application and an opportunity of being heard with respect to the application have been given to him or her.[5] There is an important obligation on an applicant to give full and frank disclosure of all material facts to the court, but nevertheless the absent respondent may still be at risk of losing the benefit afforded by the legislation since it will be for the applicant to explain to the court why better notice could not have been given, an explanation which, by definition, the respondent cannot challenge. It is notable that only the steps, not the notice itself, need be reasonable; the trade union which receives notice which is inadequate but nevertheless sufficient to enable it to appear in court, albeit unprepared, may be unable to rely on the statutory protection.[6] Although the court will appreciate that the union will inevitably be advancing contentions at short notice,[7] in these circumstances a respondent may often be better advised to seek an adjournment. The statutory requirement to take 'reasonable steps' to give the respondent notice has been liberally interpreted, being often by telex, fax or telegram and sometimes even by a telephone call to the union headquarters, provided that it is supported by a witness statement, verified by a statement of truth or by affidavit. With the extensive use of fax machines and e-mail today, we suggest an abortive communication by telephone cannot be safely regarded as 'reasonable steps' save in exceptional circumstances. In practice, applicants would be better advised to use fax or e-mail in any event because they will then have evidence of the fact and time of their communication. In *Barretts & Baird (Wholesale) Ltd v IPCS*[8] the applicants left a message on the union's telephone answering machine after 5 pm on a Friday afternoon. They then obtained an injunction without notice over the telephone on the following Sunday afternoon. This seems at odds with the intention of the statute. Under the Civil Procedure Rules it is normal for a court officer to prepare and seal any order made.[9] Normally the terms of the injunction will grant the respondent the right to apply to the court to discharge or vary an injunction without notice on giving notice of a specified number of hours or days (often 24 or 48 hours) to the applicants. Applications to discharge or vary an interim injunction are, however, not always afforded the expeditious treatment received by the original application,[10] and the court may be reluctant to disturb the *status quo* which has been achieved by the granting of an injunction without notice. It may also decline to consider detailed evidence on an application to vary or discharge unless the facts are very clear, preferring to leave conflicts of evidence to be determined at the main trial.

---

1. For more detailed guidance on procedure see CPR Part 25, CPR Practice Direction 25. Claim forms can be issued either in the Royal Courts of Justice in London or in one of the district registries throughout England and Wales. The county court may grant an injunction if it is ancillary to a claim for money or other relief within its substantive jurisdiction (County Courts Act 1984, s 38). In practice, few cases relating to industrial action are brought before the county court.

2. CPR Practice Direction 25—Interim Injunctions. Whenever possible a draft of the order sought should be filed with the application notice. The application notice must state the order sought and the date, time and place of the hearing: para 2.1.

3. *Ibid.*, para 4.3. Where an application is made before the application notice has been issued, a draft order should be provided at the hearing or faxed to the judge, and the application notice and evidence in support must be filed with the court on the same or next working day or as ordered by the court and, except where secrecy is essential, the applicant should take steps to notify the respondent informally of the application. Where the claim form has not been issued, the applicant must undertake to issue a claim form immediately or in accordance with directions given by the court.

4. There are two forms of applications without notice, one without formal notice to the respondent, the other without *formal* notice but where the applicant notifies the respondent in advance that the application was being made.

5. TULRCA 1992, s 221(1).

6. Although note the approach of Turner J in *Post Office v UCW* [1990] IRLR 143, CA, who refused to grant an injunction on the grounds, *inter alia*, that TULRCA 1992, s 221(1) had not been complied with, despite the attendance of the union at the hearing which had refused the offer of an adjournment.

7. *Pickwick International Inc (GB) Ltd v Multiple Sound Distributors* Ltd [1972] 1 WLR 1213, ChD.

8. See [1987] IRLR 3, QBD for the discharge of the injunction.

9. Together with a draft of the order sought, a disc containing the draft should also be made available to the court.

10. In *Barretts & Baird Wholesale Ltd v IPCS*, above, note 8, the hearing with notice (formerly known as the *inter partes* hearing) of the respondent's application for discharge of the injunction made two days after it was granted was adjourned for a week because of pressure of business, then a further two days passed before judgment was given and the injunction discharged (Simpson, 1987). Delay of this length may mean that a union loses the protection provided by a ballot if the industrial action has not already started; see paras **6.49** and **6.50**.

6.57 The decision whether to grant or refuse an interim injunction is normally made on the evidence set out in a witness statement.[1] In cases of urgency, however, the court will be prepared to grant an interim injunction where there are no statements after hearing oral evidence from the applicant either at a hearing or even on the telephone.[2] The applicant's witness statement must set out all the relevant facts on which the applicant relies and of which the court should be made aware.[3] The witness statement should cover the relevant background facts including the conduct of the trade union or other dispute organiser, as much information as possible concerning the employees involved, the urgency and importance of the matter and the likely loss and damage to the applicant. Although there is power to cross-examine the deponent of a witness statement, this is very rarely done in industrial dispute cases at the interim stage.[4] The interim procedure often gives respondents very little time to respond to the application, and unions which anticipate the possibility of legal challenge would therefore be well advised to prepare their evidence and defence in advance. A respondent cannot serve a 'holding' witness statement in an application without notice without the risk of later being refused an application to discharge or vary the injunction on the evidence of more detailed witness statements; the parties will not be allowed 'two bites at the first instance cherry merely because the first bite was hurried'.[5] An interim injunction will not normally be granted unless the applicant gives an undertaking to the court to pay any damages which reflect the loss which the respondents (or any party served with or notified of the order) may sustain which the court considers the applicant should pay. In some cases, the applicant may be ordered to provide a bank guarantee where, for example, it is a company outside the jurisdiction with limited assets within it, or to pay a sum into court or into the joint names of the solicitors for each party.[6] It is important for claimants, therefore, to appreciate from the outset of proceedings that they may be liable to the defendants if their claim fails at main trial, or in the unlikely event that they succeed at trial but it is nevertheless held that they should not have succeeded in obtaining an interim injunction.[7] In the past, in industrial action cases, the financial risks to claimants were usually more theoretical than real; employees and unions have had serious difficulty in proving that they have suffered financial loss,[8] and few cases relating to industrial action ever reached the stage of main trial, as was often acknowledged by the court at the interim stage.[9] This is likely to remain the case in general. However, the statutory requirements to conduct a postal ballot and (usually) to appoint an independent scrutineer where industrial action is organised by a union (see para **6.30** *et seq.* and **6.32**) impose quantifiable costs on unions, and it is possible that where significant costs have been incurred before industrial action was injuncted unions may be more inclined to take a case to full trial to recover these amounts.

1. CPR Practice Direction 25—Interim Injunctions paras 3.1 and 3.2. Applications for interim injunctions must be supported by evidence set out in either a witness statement or a statement of case, provided in each cases that they are verified by a statement of truth.

Applications for search orders (formerly known as Anton Piller orders) and freezing injunctions (formerly known as Mareva injunctions) must be supported by affidavit evidence.

2. *Ibid.*, para 4.2.

3. *Ibid.*, para 3.3. References may, in appropriate cases, be made to newspaper cuttings and reports on radio and television.

4. But note the cross-examination of Mr Ron Todd, General Secretary of the TGWU and other TGWU officials in *Associated British Ports v TGWU* [1989] IRLR 291, ChD.

5. *London Underground Lid v NUR (No 2)* [1989] IRLR 343, QBD.

6. *Baxter v Claydon* [1952] WN 376, ChD.

7. *Barclays Bank Ltd v Rosenberg* [1985] 135 NLJ 633, *Financial Times*, 12 June 1985, QBD.

8. *Metropolitan Borough of Solihull v NUT* [1985] IRLR 211, ChD.

9. See, for example, *Thomas v National Union of Mineworkers (South Wales Area)* [1985] IRLR 136, ChD; *Cayne v Global Natural Resources plc* [1984] 1 All ER 225, CA.

6.58 The award of costs in High Court proceedings is always at the discretion of the court, and this discretion should be exercised with reason and justice.[1] It is possible, therefore, for no award of costs to be made; more usually, however, some order for costs is made. A common order which is made on an application for an interim injunction is 'costs in the case',[2] which means that the party in whose favour an order for costs is made at the end of the proceedings is entitled to his or her costs in respect of the interim injunction. This is because the judge, when deciding whether or not an interim injunction should be granted, has usually only read evidence in a witness statement or affidavit at that stage, and thus the facts of the dispute have yet to be determined and the legal issues fully argued. It follows, therefore, that in many industrial action cases in which an interim injunction is sought, costs are not paid by one party to another unless a settlement involving costs is agreed between the parties. This is because the action never reaches the trial stage where an award of costs against a party would be made. If, however, the action reaches the trial stage, the party who succeeds is usually awarded his or her costs of the whole action. The rules on costs are complicated. Unless an order for indemnity costs is made, a party to a High Court action will normally be entitled only to receive from the other side his or her costs on a standard basis,[3] which means a reasonable amount in respect of all costs reasonably incurred. In practice, this means that the successful party will not recover all costs payable to his or her solicitors and barristers, as the total amount of costs incurred invariably exceeds the costs recoverable on a standard basis. If there is no agreement between the parties about the amount of costs to be paid, the costs will be taxed by a Costs Judge of the Supreme Court.[4]

---

1. CPR Part 44. For guidance on the court's discretion and circumstances to be taken into account when exercising its discretion as to costs, see CPR Part 44.3 and 44.5 See also *Aiden Shipping Ltd v Interbulk Ltd* [1986] AC 965, HL, Lord Goff at 981.
2. For other orders on costs which can be made, see Table under CPR Part 44.3.
3. On the standard basis, the additional test of proportionality is imposed, and the court will only allow costs which are proportionate to the matter at issue. See CPR Part 44.5.
4. A Costs Judge of the Supreme Court is a barrister or solicitor of not less than ten years' standing (Supreme Court Act 1981, Sched 2, Part 11). Although his or her title is new, the Costs Judge is still addressed at a hearing as 'Master'.

6.59 An appeal can only be made with permission against the decision of a judge to grant or refuse an interim injunction.[1] The general approach of an appeal court (ie. the court hearing the first appeal from a decision) will be only to allow an appeal where the decision of the lower court was wrong, or where it was unjust because of a serious procedural or other irregularity in the proceedings.[2] Notices of appeal must be filed at the appeal court within 14 days after the date of the decision of the lower court which is being appealed or within such period as may be directed by the lower court.[3] Thereafter the notice of appeal must be served on all parties, not later than seven days after it is filed.[4] In practice, many appeals in the industrial action context proceed to the Court of Appeal and even to the House of Lords very swiftly under an expedited procedure. Following the introduction of the Civil Procedure Rules, every appeal is now limited to a review of the decision of the lower court. This general rule applies unless a practice direction makes different provision for a particular category of appeal, or the Court considers that in the circumstances of an individual appeal it would be in the interests of justice to hold a re-hearing.[5] It follows, therefore, that the decision of the lower court will attract much greater significance as an appeal will no longer generally take the form of a re-hearing. A decision of a lower court may, however, be set aside on the grounds that there has been a change of circumstances after the judge made the order that would have justified his or her acceding to an application to vary it.[6] There may be greater scope for appeal under the Human Rights Act 1998; failure to take appropriate account of the requirements of that Act will constitute a misunderstanding of the law. The impact of legal proceedings upon the duration of a ballot mandate where a union is liable for industrial action are discussed in para **6.50**.

---

1 CPR, r 52.3. For a discussion of when it is appropriate to seek the discharge of an injunction from the High Court, rather than an appeal, see *London Underground Ltd v NUR (No 2)* [1989] IRLR 343, QBD. An appeal does not operate as a stay of execution; an application for a stay should be made if a stay is desired: CPR, r 52.7.

2 CPR, r 52.11(3). See also *Tanfern Ltd* v *Cameron-MacDonald* [2000] 2 All ER 801, CA.

3 CPR, r 52.4(2) and 52.5(4).

4 CPR, r 52.4(3) and 52.5(6).

5 CPR, r 52.11(1).

6 *Union Traffic Ltd v TGWU* [1989] IRLR 127, CA. For an example of important new evidence being introduced at the appeal stage, see *Mercury Communications Ltd v Scott-Garner and the POEU* [1983] IRLR 494, CA. Under CPR, r 52.11(5), however, a party may not rely on a matter not contained in its appeal notice unless the appeal court gives permission.

The forms and scope of interim injunctions

6.60 Many injunctions are prohibitory in form, ordering the respondent not to do something, for example restraining a trade union from inducing breach of contract. To obtain a mandatory injunction, which orders the respondent to take steps to undo the wrong (for example, to withdraw instructions to take industrial action) the applicant must show, as a general rule, that grave damage would accrue if the injunction were not granted and that damages would not be an adequate remedy.[1] However, in recent decades there has been a tendency for the courts to grant mandatory injunctions in strike cases in support of prohibitory orders.[2] An injunction may be granted to prevent an apprehended legal wrong (formerly known as a *quia timet* injunction), even though none has yet occurred, provided that the applicant can provide adequate evidence of the fear that the wrong is likely otherwise to be committed. The courts have granted such an injunction to prevent a respondent from inducing the breach of a future contract,[3] and in 1988 such an order was even granted to prevent a union conducting a (lawful) ballot on the basis that the proposed industrial action would be unlawful.[4] Injunctions cannot be used to force individual employees to return to work; by statute, no court may compel an employee to work or attend at any place to work by way of an injunction restraining a breach or threatened breach of a contract of employment.[5] A court can only make orders which bind the party or parties to the proceedings; where a union is a named respondent, the principle of vicarious liability (which may be determined according to common law or statutory criteria, depending upon the context) governs whether the union will be legally responsible for its servants or agents who act in defiance of an injunction.[6] However, this rule does not necessarily mean that only those named in an injunction are affected by it. First, the court has a discretion to allow a representative action against (or by) individuals who represent a class of persons with coincident interest in any proceedings.[7] In reliance on this rule, the Court of Appeal issued an injunction restraining picketing by individual respondents on their own behalf and on behalf of all other members of the organisation to which they belonged (Animal Aid).[8] In the context of industrial disputes, this concept may be useful in cases of unofficial picketing or sit-ins, where the applicant is unlikely to know the names of all the individuals involved, provided that the relevant criteria can be satisfied.[9] Secondly, as we indicate in para **6.62**, non-parties to the litigation with knowledge of the injunction who breach its terms, or who aid and abet those named to do so, may find themselves in contempt of court.

---

1. *Redland Bricks Ltd v Morris* [1970] AC 652, HL.

2. See also TULRCA 1992, s 235A(4). Where an applicant seeks a mandatory injunction to compel an employer whose workers have taken industrial action to perform a service, the court is very unlikely to grant such an order; see *Harold Stephen Ltd v Post Office* [1978] 1 All ER 939, CA, esp Geoffrey Lane LJ at 944. For a rare case where a mandatory injunction was granted in these circumstances, see *Parker v Camden London Borough Council* [1985] 2 All ER 141, CA.

3. *JT Stratford & Son v Lindley* [1965] AC 269, HL, per Lord Upjohn at 339; *Union Traffic Ltd v TGWU* [1989] IRLR 127, CA. Cf Auerbach, 1989, 170, who argues that given that it remains lawful to persuade a person not to make a contract *(Midland Cold Storage Ltd v Steer* [1972] Ch 630, ChD) and if in fact the applicant has no long-term contract, this 'comes perilously close to protecting the . . . [applicant's] expectations, and not merely rights'. See Spry, 1997, 377–382, 468–470 on the principles governing injunctions formerly known as *quia timet* injunctions.

4. See Auerbach, 1988, 229.

5. TULRCA 1992, s 236 but note that, in certain circumstances, an employer may be able to obtain an injunction to restrain the employee from working for a competitor (*Evening Standard v Henderson* [1987] IRLR 64, CA).

6. See para **6.61**. For the tests as to when a union is liable for the commission of a tort, see para **6.12** *et seq*.

7. CPR, r 19.6.

8. *Michaels (Furriers) Ltd v Askew* (1983) 127 Sol Jo 597, CA.

9. *Ibid.* See *United Kingdom Nirex Ltd v Barton, The Times,* 14 October 1986, QBD, and see also *Huntingdon Life Science Ltd v Curtin and 10 other respondents,* 15 October 1997, unreported.

Contempt of Court

6.61 Failure to comply with an injunction constitutes contempt of court. Once an injunction has been obtained, it is for the applicant to arrange for personal service on the respondent of a copy of the court's order, which must bear the court's seal. It is the responsibility of the applicant to endorse a penal notice on the copy of the order; if a penal notice is not so endorsed, a respondent cannot later be imprisoned or fined for contempt for breach of the order. Committal is at the behest of the applicant, who can waive a civil contempt. It is possible that the court may also act of its own motion against a person guilty of a civil contempt.[1] In practice this rarely happens. 'Civil' contempt is punishable by way of a fine or imprisonment and/or a writ of sequestration against the property of the person in contempt. In the case of a body corporate it is necessary to serve personally the officer against whose property leave is sought to issue a writ of sequestration with a copy of the order endorsed with a penal notice. In the context of industrial action, fines and/or sequestration of union property are now the most likely penalties to be imposed.[2] It is provided by statute that 'punishment for contempt' may be enforced against any property held in trust for a trade union 'to the same extent and in the same manner as if it were a body corporate',[3] and the limit on the amount of damages which may be awarded against a union,[4] and protection of specified property from certain other awards,[5] do not apply to fines for contempt. The basis for determining whether a union is liable for the acts of its officials or members depends upon the torts in relation to which the injunction has been imposed. The statutory rules on union liability discussed in paras **6.12** *et seq.* apply to contempt proceedings arising from breaches of injunctions imposed in relation to the torts specified in the Trade Union and Labour Relations (Consolidation) Act 1992, s 20.[6] In relation to other torts, the liability of a union will be determined according to common law principles of vicarious liability, so that it will be liable for persons acting within the scope of their express or implied authority. If a union knows that such persons are breaching the law, it must take active steps to require them to comply with it.[7] In the leading case of *Heatons Transport (St Helens) Ltd v TGWU*,[8] the union was advised to withdraw the authority of shop stewards to continue organising industrial action in unequivocal terms, possibly by withdrawing their credentials.

---

1. CPR Sched 1 RSC Ord 52, r 5. See also *Re Supply of Ready Mixed Concrete* [1992] ICR 229, CA, per Lord Donaldson MR at 248; for a critique see Wedderburn, 1992b. For the relationship between motions for contempt and dispute settlement, see Auerbach, 1988, 232–234. For a detailed account of the law of contempt, see Arlidge,

Eady and Smith, 1999. For the operation of contempt during the 1984–1985 miners' strike, see Lightman, 1987. For the procedure for applications for committal for contempt, see CPR Sched 1 RSC Ord 52, r 4.

2. In industrial disputes, imprisonment is generally recognised to create martyrs. If made, a committal order must be for a fixed term not exceeding two years (Contempt of Court Act 1981, s 14(1)) although an imprisoned individual may be discharged on application at any time: CPR Sched 1 RSC Ord 52, r 8. In 1984 the NUM President Mr Arthur Scargill was judged guilty of 'wilful and repeated disobedience' of a court order but the penalty was a fine of £1,000 rather than imprisonment.

3. TULRCA 1992 s 12(2).

4. *Ibid.*, s 22; see further para **6.64**.

5. *Ibid.*, s 23.

6. *Ibid.*, s 20(6) Cf *Express and Star Ltd v NGA (1982)* [1986] IRLR 222, CA, which defined the position before the Employment Act 1990. These principles also apply in relation to proceedings for failure to comply with an order made under the statutory right of action: s 235A(6): see para **6.11**.

7. *UKAPE and Newall v AUEW (Technical and Supervisory Section)* [1972] ICR 151, *NIRC*; *Heatons Transport (St Helens) Ltd v TGWU* [1972] IRLR 25, HL. See also *Richard Read Transport Ltd v NUM (South Wales Area)* [1985] IRLR 67, QBD. The NGA was in contempt when two branch officials indicated to members 'by nods and winks' that they should disobey an injunction whilst the union was putting up a 'humbugging pretence' of complying with the law: *Express and Star Ltd v NGA*, above.

8. Above; see paras **6.16**. See also *Re Supply of Ready Mixed Concrete*, above, note 1, where it was suggested that if X which is subject to a restraining order should have appreciated that its servant or agent would be likely to do the prohibited act unless dissuaded by X, the act will then be regarded as within the mandate of the servant or agent if X has not taken all reasonable steps to prevent it. Such steps may in appropriate cases involve far more than express prohibition and extend to elaborate monitoring and compliance machinery and procedures and the creation of positive incentives designed to dissuade the servant or agent (Lord Donaldson MR at 258).

6.62 In addition to the respondents to an injunction, third parties may also be held to be in contempt of the order if they knowingly act in breach of its terms. Thus, for example, it seems likely that in the context of industrial disputes if an employer obtains an injunction to restrain one group of pickets and another replaces them, knowing of the terms of the injunction, the second group will be liable for contempt. It has been suggested that a solicitor may be liable if he or she advises a course of conduct to thwart orders which it is anticipated a court might make in the future,[1] a principle which, if adopted, could have widespread implications. Third parties may also be liable if they 'aid and abet' a respondent to commit a breach. It was once assumed that third parties could not be liable for aiding and abetting in the absence of a breach by the respondent, there being no 'primary' breach to aid or abet.[2] However, in an action brought against three newspapers which had published material deriving from the memoirs of Mr Peter Wright, a former member of the security service, when two other newspapers had been injuncted from publishing such material, the House of Lords held that the three newspapers could be liable for contempt on the grounds that they had knowingly interfered with the administration of justice.[3] The scope for applying this principle in contexts other than breach of confidence is unclear. The court emphasised that the third party must have, by his or her conduct, knowingly have interfered with the administration of justice by the court in the action between the parties.

---

1. *Taylor v National Union of Mineworkers (Yorkshire Area)*, *The Times*, 20 November 1985, ChD. In his judgment Nicholls J stated: 'Those who give professional or other advice to a person against whom an injunction has been granted . . . must be vigilant to see that they are not assisting in a breach of the injunction. . . . Solicitors as officers of this court have a particularly heavy responsibility in this regard. Giving advice on the legal implications of particular conduct is one thing. Assisting in a course of conduct which they know is or may be a contempt of court is altogether different. Further, those who assist others to take steps intended to thwart orders which it is anticipated that a court may thereafter make should not regard themselves as necessarily unassailable.' The possibility of pre-emptive action constituting contempt appears to be a significant extension of the law.

2. See, for example, *Thorne RDC v Bunting (No 2)* [1972] 3 All ER 1084, CA.

3. *A-G v Times Newspapers Ltd* [1991] 2 All ER 398, HL. This is a criminal contempt but the distinction between criminal and civil contempt seems in many respects hard to discern: see *Re Supply of Ready Mixed Concrete* [1992] ICR 229, CA, where the duty on every citizen not to interfere with the administration of justice was affirmed without qualification to its context (Lord Donaldson MR at 249). See also *M v Home Office* [1993] 3 All ER 537, esp Lord Woolf at 568.

6.63 The penalties are aimed at coercing the contemnors to 'purge' their contempt and to accept the authority of the court. The courts recognise that contempt may take various forms, ranging from 'flat defiance' at the top end of the scale, to a 'half-hearted or, perhaps, colourable attempt' to comply with the court's order, down to a 'genuine, wholehearted' use of best endeavours to comply with the order which nevertheless has been unsuccessful.[1] 'Flat defiance' is likely to attract a greater fine than a more minor or technical breach.[2] Whether or not the contemnor displays contrition may also be a relevant factor.[3] The statutory limit on the damages which may be awarded against a union[4] does not apply to fines for contempt. The fine may be paid by someone other than a contemnor; it may even be paid without his or her consent.[5] However, where an individual union member or officer for whom the union is not legally liable is found to be in contempt, it is unlawful for union property to be used to pay the fine; if this were to happen, it would be open to any union member, as well as the union itself, to recover from the individual the amount applied for this purpose.[6] Sequestration of a contemnor's assets as a further remedy may be ordered in addition to, or instead of, other penalties. Its aim is to compel obedience to the injunction or to enforce a fine,[7] and the property sequestrated will be returned when the contemnor is released from the contempt, less any fines (which may be deducted from the property) or costs incurred (the sequestrator's bill is likely to be large). The writ of sequestration charges up to four commissioners, at least two of whom must act, to seize the defendant's property until the contempt is purged to the satisfaction of the court.[8] Third parties have a duty not to obstruct the sequestrators in carrying out their duties, and it has been held that a union's banks and auditors must co-operate with them by accounting for whatever property they hold and responding to inquiries about the whereabouts of property, whether or not they hold property themselves.[9] A possible result of being held in contempt is that the courts may refuse to hear an application at the suit of the contemnor in either the pending or any other proceedings until the contempt has been purged.[10] What is sufficient to purge contempt depends on the attitude of the judge; in some cases, rigorous action by the union to repudiate the unlawful action, together with an apology in open court, has been required; in others, the judge has not insisted upon a formal apology if satisfied that the union has otherwise recognised the authority of the court.[11] A court may order the removal of the trustees of the union's assets and the appointment of a receiver of the income and assets of the union. In *Clarke v Heathfield*[12] 16 members of the National Union of Mineworkers instituted proceedings against the trustees and various officers of the union on the ground that the assets of the union were in jeopardy in their hands[13] since the union had already been fined for contempt and was likely to incur further fines. A receiver was appointed, initially on an application without notice (formerly known as an *ex parte* application) and then after a hearing with notice (formerly known as an *inter partes* hearing) pending the appointment of new trustees or, on a change of heart, the restoration of the removed trustees. A receiver has no legal title to the union's assets; his or hers is a custodial role to collect and take possession of the union's assets, including property abroad. Although the receiver is appointed by the court, it is unclear whether the union has the right to object to his or her identity or whether anyone approached by the receiver is under a duty to assist or co-operate with him or her as an officer of the court.[14] The receiver may at any time request the court to give him or her directions and this request must state in writing the matters with regard to which directions are required.[15] Parties may not interfere with the assets of the union once they have knowledge of the appointment of the receiver. It is open to the union at any time to apply to the court for the discharge of the receivership but such an application may have little chance of success if the union continues to be in contempt, even where new trustees have been appointed who have satisfied the court as to their fitness and independence.[16]

---

1. *Howitt Transport Ltd and Howitt Bros Ltd v TGWU* [1973] IRLR 25, NIRC at 26. In *Guildford Borough Council v Valler, The Times*, 18 May 1993, QBD, Sedley J held that, although any conscious non-compliance with an order of the court was a contempt, only deliberate or wilful contempt could be visited with imprisonment or sequestration of assets; in other cases the court's power was limited to the award of costs and possibly to fines. On the requisite intention which needs to be shown, see *Re Supply of Ready Mixed Concrete* [1992] 2 QB 213, CA; *P v P* [1999] 3 FCR 547, CA.

2. In *Austin Rover Group Ltd v AUEW (Technical and Supervisory Section)* [1985] IRLR 162, QBD no penalty was imposed because the contempt was not serious and the union might have taken sufficiently vigorous steps to dissociate itself from the industrial action had it taken legal advice at an early stage. Cf *Richard Read (Transport) Ltd v NUM (South Wales Area)* [1985] IRLR 67, QBD (deliberate defiance); *Kent Free Press v NGA* [1987] IRLR 267, QBD (union taking as long as possible to withdraw instructions). Note that a requirement to comply with the terms of an injunction 'forthwith' means forthwith from proper notice of the order's terms rather than from personal service of the order. In 1983, fines of £525,000 were imposed upon the NGA. Note the restrictions upon unions paying fines imposed upon individuals: see para **6.116**.

3. See, for example, *Sealink UK Ltd v NUS, Independent*, 12 February 1988, QBD.

4. See para **6.64**.

5. Wedderburn, 1986, 715.

6. TULRCA 1992, s 15. This restriction does not cover payment of the expenses of defending the contempt proceedings. See further para **6.116**.

7. See, for example, *Con-Mech (Engineers) Ltd v AUEW (Engineering Section) (No 2)* [1974] ICR 332, NIRC; *Messenger Newspapers Group Ltd v NGA (1982)* [1984] ICR 345, CA. For a discussion of the use of sequestration orders during the 1984–1985 miners' strike, see Lightman, 1987.

8. The writ may limit the total amount and the funds to be seized. In *News Group Newspapers Ltd v SOGAT 1982* [1986] IRLR 227, CA it was held that the sequestrators could not seize the funds of local branches, which were the property solely of the branch and vested in trustees who had to comply with the decisions of the branch committee. Note also TULRCA 1992, s 23.

9. *Eckman v Midland Bank Ltd* [1973] 1 All ER 609, NIRC; *Messenger Newspapers Group Ltd*, above, note 7. The position where the banks and others comply with their client's instructions to take pre-emptive action to mitigate the effects of a feared sequestration order is unclear: see Auerbach, 1988, 231. In 1988 the NUS's bank obtained an injunction restraining its client from transferring assets abroad when Sealink was pursuing a writ of sequestration against it—*Midland Bank plc v NUS* (28 April 1988, unreported); see also *Taylor v NUM (Yorkshire Area), The Times*, 20 November 1985, and para **6.62**. Nicholls J's dictum also extended to sequestration orders. In *Clarke v*

Heathfield (No 2) [1985] ICR 606, ChD, the court removed the trustees of the NUM who had sought to frustrate the efforts of the sequestrators by sending money abroad. In *Sealink UK Ltd v NUS*, above, note 3, and *P & O European Ferries (Dover) Ltd v NUS* (24 May 1988, unreported), QBD a sequestration order was 'transferred' from one employer to another: see Auerbach, 1988, 234.

10. *Clarke v Heathfield* [1985] ICR 203, CA; *ibid. (No 2)*, above. See also X *Ltd v Morgan-Grampian Publishers Ltd* [1990] 2 All ER 1, HL.

11. *Richard Read (Transport) Ltd v NUM (South Wales Area)* [1985] IRLR 67, QBD.

12. See *Clarke v Heathfield* (above, note 9) and *Clarke v Heathfield (No 2)* (above, note 10).

13. See Lightman, 1987 for a discussion of the legal constraints of receivership and sequestration in relation to the 1984–1985 miners' strike on which this paragraph has largely been based. For the statutory powers of union members in relation to trustees' use of union property contained in TULRCA 1992, see para **6.117**.

14. See *Halsbury's Laws of England*, vol 47, para 1514.

15. CPR Sched 1 RSC Order 30 r 8.

16. See Lightman, 1987, 48.

Damages

Sources and general principles

6.64 Persons suffering loss as a result of unlawful industrial action may claim damages in tort against the organisers.[1] Claims for more than £15,000 can be brought in the High Court; those for less than that normally in the county court.[2] Before 1982, claims for damages were very rare because they could be brought only against individual trade union officers and not against unions.[3] The Employment Act 1982 removed this immunity and trade unions may now be sued,[4] although the Trade Union and Labour Relations (Consolidation) Act 1992, s 22 imposes limits on the amount of damages which may be awarded against them in any proceedings in tort (with specified exceptions not relevant in the industrial action context). In practice, interim injunctions remain the more common remedy, although there have been examples of employers threatening to bring substantial damages claims if industrial action does take place. Employers considering such claims, however, should bear in mind the long-term impact upon industrial relations if the dispute has been settled by that time. Damages are awarded according to the general principles applicable to the law of tort, aiming to put the claimant in the position he or she would have been in had the tort not been committed.[5] The claimant must prove that the amount claimed arises from the defendant's wrongful act. Difficulty may arise where a defendant has committed various torts, all of which contributed to the claimant's loss but some of which are protected by the statutory immunity.[6]

There have been no reported cases on this point as yet in English law, but the Northern Ireland Court of Appeal has held that damages must be limited to loss attributable to the non-protected torts.[7] Claims by public service employers, who frequently do not suffer direct financial loss when services are disrupted, may be difficult to quantify.[8] It may be possible for employers to claim compensation for expenditure incurred in anticipation of the defendants committing unlawful acts, provided that the torts do, in the event, take place.[9] It is conceivable that exemplary or aggravated, as well as compensatory, damages may be awarded if the court considers that the defendant's conduct warrants this,[10] although the circumstances where exemplary damages may be awarded have been restricted by the courts.[11]

---

1. See para **6.86** for damages claims against individual participants. If *Barretts and Baird (Wholesale) Ltd v IPCS* [1987] IRLR 3, QBD, were to be followed, individual workers could be sued in tort (see further para **6.8**). There have been no cases where this has been attempted. Note that the statutory right of action does not give a right to sue for damages: see para **6.11**.

2. CPR Part 7 Practice Direction para 2.1 and the High Court and County Court Jurisdiction (Amendment) Order 1999, SI 1999/1014. For a rare example of a county court case, see *Falconer v NUR* [1986] IRLR 331 (see para **6.5**).

3. Trade Disputes Act 1906, s 4; repealed by the Industrial Relations Act 1971; Trade Union and Labour Relations Act 1974, s 14.

4. See TULRCA 1992, s 20 (discussed in para **6.12** *et seq.*) for the circumstances when a union is deemed liable under statute.

5. See McGregor, 1997.

6. Wedderburn, 1986, 682.

7. *Norbrook Laboratories Ltd v King* [1984] IRLR 200, NI CA.

8. *Cf Hereford and Worcester County Council v NAS/UWT*, *The Times*, 26 March 1988, QBD, where the claim arising out of a half-day teachers' strike included 'waste of services'. The council was granted summary judgment against the union, which admitted liability. The claim was settled out of court.

9. See *Messenger Newspapers Group Ltd v NGA (1982)* [1984] IRLR 397, QBD. See M. Jones and A. Morris, 1985, for a critique of this and other aspects of the decision.

10. *Messenger Newspapers Group Ltd v NGA (1982)*, above.

11. *AB v South West Water Services Ltd* [1993] 1 All ER 609, CA, for the basis of recoverability of exemplary damages.

Limits on damages against a trade union

6.65 The maximum amount of damages which may be awarded against a trade union in any proceedings in tort depends upon the size of the union. There is a maximum of £10,000 if the union has fewer than 5,000 members; £50,000 if it has 5,000 or more but fewer than 25,000 members; £125,000 if it has 25,000 or more but fewer than 100,000 members; and £250,000 if it has 100,000 or more members.[1] For federated trade unions,[2] the members of such of its constituent or affiliated organisations as have their head or main office in Great Britain are treated as members of the union.[3] The relevant time for counting the number of members is not specified, nor is the method of determining the number in cases of dispute.[4] Where there is more than one claimant, the union may be made liable up to the limit in each case. It is less clear whether a single claimant could issue several claim forms for different torts, or in respect of different acts, arising from the same industrial action and claim the maximum in each; it is suggested that a court is unlikely to be sympathetic to any such approach, and in any event the union could ask the court for an order for consolidation of the proceedings into one action. Under the Supreme Court Act 1981, s 35A interest may be awarded on the damages and this may take the total amount awarded over the statutory maximum.[5] The statutory limits do not apply to fines imposed for contempt of court, nor do they include the legal costs which a union may have to pay.[6] Also excepted are damages for personal injury resulting from negligence, nuisance or breach of duty, or a breach of duty in connection with the ownership, occupation, possession, control or use of property or proceedings relating to product liability.[7] Remedies based on restitution, not being proceedings in tort, are not subject to the limits.[8] It is provided by statute that any 'judgment, order or award' made in any proceedings against a union shall be enforceable 'against any property held in trust for it to the same extent and in the same manner as if it were a body corporate'.[9] However, certain property held by or on behalf of a union is protected against the enforcement of any part of an award of damages, costs or expenses.[10] This protection is not restricted to proceedings in tort, and covers any award, whether against the union itself, trustees (otherwise than in respect of a breach of trust) or members or officials in a representative capacity. It does not, however, include fines for contempt of court. 'Protected property' means any property belonging to the trustees concerned otherwise than in their capacity as such; belonging to any member of the union 'otherwise than jointly or in common with the other members'; belonging to an official who is neither a member nor a trustee; comprised in a political fund;[11] or comprised in a provident benefits fund.[12]

---

1 TULRCA 1992, s 22(2). The Secretary of State may vary these sums by order: s 22(3), (4).

2 Trade unions consisting wholly or mainly of constituent or affiliated organisations, or representatives of such organisations: *ibid.*, s 118(1).

3 *Ibid.*, s 118(3).

4. As Wedderburn, 1986, 682, points out, the time could be the date of the judgment, of the writ or of the commission of the tort. Records of union membership kept by the Certification Officer are inevitably out of date, as may be the register kept by the union itself under TULRCA 1992, s 24: see para **2.31**.

5. *Boxfoldia Ltd v NGA (1982)* [1988] IRLR 383, QBD (award of interest not an award 'by way of damages').

6. Contempt fines of £675,000 were awarded against the NGA in 1983: see further M. Jones and A. Morris, 1985.

7. TULRCA 1992, s 22(1). 'Breach of duty' means breach of a duty imposed by any rule of law or by or under any enactment; 'personal injury' includes any disease and any impairment of a person's physical or mental condition; 'property' means any property, whether real or personal: s 22(5). Proceedings relating to product liability are those under Pt 1 of the Consumer Protection Act 1987: s 22(1)(c).

8. See further paras **6.66**.

9. TULRCA 1992, s 12(2).

10. *Ibid.*, s 23. Property held by an 'employers' association' (see App 1) is similarly protected: s 130.

11. Provided the fund is, and was at the time the act in respect of which proceedings are brought was done, prevented by the rules from being used to finance industrial action, *ibid.*, s 23(2)(d). See para **2.46** *et seq.* for the provisions relating to union political funds.

12. *Ibid.*, s 23(2). See ICTA 1988, s 467(2) for the definition of 'provident benefits'.

Restitution

Sources and general principles

6.66 A remedy based on restitution may exist independently of any alternative remedy in tort and it is not subject to the statutory limits which govern trade union liability in tort.[1] In the industrial action context, the relevant restitutionary remedy is that of 'economic duress', which enables a party to a transaction who enters it under 'economic duress' to claim later that the transaction is invalid because he or she did not truly consent to it and to recover any money paid to the other party.[2] To establish 'economic duress' it must be shown that the victim has been placed in a situation where he or she is deemed to have no practical alternative to agreeing to the demand made by the other party by pressure which the law does not regard as legitimate. The form of the duress may constitute intimidation (or some other tort), but its scope may be wider, in that the action threatened need not always be unlawful.[3] The doctrine was applied to industrial disputes in *Universe Tankships Inc of Monrovia v ITWF*[4] where the owners of a ship flying a 'flag of convenience' were able to recover from the International Transport Workers' Federation payments of back pay to the crew and a contribution to the Seafarers' Welfare Fund which they had previously agreed to make under threat of blacking. In the House of Lords it was conceded by the ITWF that the consequences to the shipowners of the blacking continuing were sufficiently catastrophic to constitute economic duress. It was also conceded that guidance could be found on the boundary between legitimate and illegitimate pressure from examining whether or not the action was within the statutory immunities as being 'in contemplation or furtherance of a trade dispute'.[5] This meant that the court did not hear arguments on either of these points, leaving open the possibility that a remedy based on 'economic duress' may be granted even if the action would be granted immunity in tort,[6] although there are highly persuasive dicta that such an approach would be contrary to legislative policy.[7]

---

1. See para **6.65**. Where the form the duress takes is tortious, the restitutional remedy will be an alternative to an action for damages in tort: see *Universe Tankships Inc of Monrovia v ITWF* [1982] IRLR 200, HL, Lord Diplock at 205, HL.
2. For a detailed discussion, see Goff and Jones, 1998. For recent analysis of the doctrine of economic duress, see Beatson, 1991, chapter 5; Burrows, 1993, 174–185; Birks and Yin, 1995.
3. In *Universe Tankships Inc of Monrovia v ITWF*, above note 1, Lord Scarman appeared to suggest that economic duress could be actionable as a tort *per se*. If this were to be the case the principle of *Allen v Flood* requiring independent unlawfulness would be further undermined: see para **6.2**.
4. Above, note 1. See also *Dimskal Shipping Co SA v ITF* [1992] IRLR 78, HL.
5. See para **6.19** *et seq.*
6. Above, note 3, Lord Diplock at 205, Lord Brandon at 214; cf Lord Scarman at 212 who considered it would be 'inconsistent with legislative policy' to say that acts which were protected by statute from liability in tort could nevertheless amount to duress. See also *Dimskal Shipping Co SA v ITWF* [1992] IRLR 78, HL, per Lord Goff at 82.
7. See Lords Scarman and Goff, above.

PICKETING

Civil Liability

Sources and general principles

6.67 There is no statutory definition of picketing, but it is commonly understood to mean persons, either singly or in groups, attending at or near premises connected with an industrial dispute.[1] Usually the object of pickets is to persuade non-strikers or substitute workers not to continue working or to persuade suppliers not to furnish goods or services to the employer in dispute.[2] Pickets are likely to commit the tort of inducing a breach of contract,[3] and they may also commit other torts outlined in para **6.2** *et seq.* The statutory immunities afford protection for the torts specified in the Trade Union and Labour Relations (Consolidation) Act 1992, s 219 on condition that pickets do not exceed the terms of s 220 of that Act[4] and they satisfy the general requirement of acting 'in contemplation or furtherance of a trade dispute'.[5] However, they (and/or where applicable, their trade union)[6] can lose that protection for any of the reasons listed in para **6.17** *et seq.* (with a narrow exception for certain secondary action as specified in s 224(3)). In addition to the torts generally relevant to industrial action, pickets may commit the torts of trespass to the highway, private nuisance and public nuisance.[7] Guidance on the conduct of picketing is provided by a Code of Practice, initially issued by the Secretary of State for Employment in 1980 and revised in 1992. Although there have been major changes to the law governing industrial action since 1992, those amendments did not directly affect the law of picketing. The statement in paragraph 51 of the Code that the number of pickets at any entrance to or exit from a workplace should not generally exceed six has influenced the courts in deciding whether, and in what form, to grant interim injunctions to restrain picketing.[8] As with industrial action in general an interim injunction is the usual remedy sought by employers who are subject to picketing; here, again, satisfying the hurdle that there is a serious question to be tried is not generally an onerous task.[9] Under the Human Rights Act 1998, however, the courts will be required to consider the implications of the ECHR for the law on picketing. Both Article 10, which guarantees the right to freedom of expression, and Article 11, which guarantees the right to freedom of peaceful assembly, are material in this context; in practice cases are likely to turn on whether interferences with the exercise of the respective rights can be justified. The principle of proportionality may require the courts to look more carefully at the terms in which interim injunctions are framed, and to pay closer attention to the individual circumstances rather than relying upon the Code of Practice. Moreover, where injunctions are sought to constrain the provision of information (to other workers or to consumers, for example), they should be subject to particularly careful scrutiny because of their nature as a form of prior restraint,[10] a view reflected in a weaker form in the Human Rights Act 1998, s 12(3).[11] Finally, state action which has an impact upon the free movement of goods when this process is disrupted by the activities of pickets may raise issues under EU law.[12] Consideration of that area lies outside the scope of this work.

1. Hepple, 1981b, para 89.
2. See further Bercusson, 1977, for other activities in which pickets may engage.
3. See paras **6.3** *et seq.*
4. TULRCA 1992, s 219(3).
5. See paras **6.19** *et seq.*
6. Note in particular that the union will lose the protection against any liability in tort afforded by s 219 where (*inter alia*) what is done in the course of picketing amounts to a call to take part in industrial action for which the union is legally responsible and the action has not been preceded by a properly-conducted ballot: see further para **6.30** *et seq.*
7. TULRCA 1992, s 220 is of little practical significance in this context because pickets who commit those torts (other than trespass to the highway) are likely to exceed the terms of s 220.
8. See *Thomas v NUM (South Wales Area)* [1985] IRLR 136, ChD; *News Group Newspapers Ltd v SOGAT 82 (No 2)* [1986] IRLR 337, QBD. A failure to comply with a provision of the Code of Practice does not of itself render a person liable to legal proceedings, but the Code is admissible in evidence before a court or employment tribunal and any provision which appears to a court or tribunal to be relevant to any question arising in the proceedings before it must be taken into account in determining that question: TULRCA 1992, s 207. The Code states that frequently a smaller number than six will be appropriate: para 51.
9. See para **6.52** *et seq.* for a discussion of the principles governing interim injunctions.
10. *Observer and Guardian v UK* judgment of 26 November 1991, (1992) 14 EHRR 153; *Open Door Counselling and Well Women v Ireland* judgment of 29 October 1992, (1993) 15 EHRR 244; see also *Hertel v Switzerland* judgment of 25 August 1998, (1999) 28 EHRR 534. See further para **6.80**.
11. Note also the Human Rights Act 1998, s 12(1),(2) on the granting of injunctions without notice, formerly known as *ex parte* injunctions.
12. Case C–265/95 *Commission v France* [1997] ECR I–6959; *R v Chief Constable of Sussex, ex parte International Trader's Ferry Ltd* [1999] 1 All ER 129. See generally Barnard and Hare, 2000. Note also in this context Council Regulation 2696/98, [1998] OJ L337/8, designed to set up an intervention mechanism to safeguard free trade in the single market, Article 2 of which provides that '[t]his Regulation may not be interpreted as affecting in any way the exercise of fundamental rights, as recognised in Member States, including the right or freedom to strike': see Barnard and Hare, 2000.

The torts in outline

6.68 Pickets may commit any of the torts outlined in para **6.2** et seq. In particular, they frequently commit the tort of inducing a breach of contract, the contracts being either the employment contracts of the workers they seek to persuade not to work or commercial contracts between an employer and its customers or suppliers. In *Union Traffic Ltd v TGWU*[1] the Court of Appeal held that the mere presence of pickets may be deemed sufficient to constitute an 'inducement' if it is clear that their presence is intended to induce breach of a contract and it is successful in this object. However, it is important to note that persuasion must be directed at one of the parties to the contract for the direct form of the tort. In *Middlebrook Mushrooms Ltd v TGWU*[2] the claimants failed to obtain an injunction to prevent union members handing leaflets to customers of a supermarket to which they supplied their produce, one ground being that, even assuming the existence of a contract between the supermarket and the claimants, there was no direct pressure on the supermarket to breach it. There are four other forms of tortious liability to which picketing may give rise: trespass to the highway, private nuisance, public nuisance, and liability under the Protection from Harassment Act 1997. Trespass to the highway can be dealt with briefly. Until recently it appeared that this tort was committed by using the highway for purposes not reasonably incidental to passage.[3] However in *Jones v DPP*[4] the House of Lords held that this view was unduly narrow, and that reasonable user of the highway could extend to peaceful and non-obstructive assembly. In practice this tort has been a dead letter in the context of industrial action. Only the owner of the subsoil—normally the highway authority[5]—may sue for trespass to the highway, and it is unlikely that a highway authority would take this step. The torts of public and private nuisance and the Protection from Harasssment Act 1997, however, constitute greater threats to pickets.

---

1. [1989] IRLR 127, CA. In this case the picketing was outside the predecessor to s 220.
2. [1993] IRLR 232, CA.
3. *Harrison v Duke of Rutland* [1893] 1 QB 142; *Hickman v Maisey* [1900] 1 QB 752, CA; *Hubbard v Pitt* [1975] ICR 77, QBD.
4. [1999] 2 All ER 257, HL.
5. In the case of a private road, the soil of the highway is presumed to belong, up to the middle of the highway, to the owner of land on either side.

6.69 Private nuisance consists of an unlawful interference with a person's use or enjoyment of land, or some right over or in connection with it.[1] There has been judicial controversy whether picketing *per se* can constitute private nuisance. In 1899 the Court of Appeal considered that picketing may of itself amount to nuisance simply because of the attempt to persuade and regardless of any obstruction caused.[2] Seven years later, however, a different Court of Appeal reached the opposite conclusion,[3] and this latter view was echoed by Lord Denning in a widely-quoted dissenting judgment in *Hubbard v Pitt* when he stated that:

> . . . [p]icketing is not a nuisance in itself. Nor is it a nuisance for a group of people to attend at or near the . . . [claimant's] . . . premises in order to obtain or to communicate information or in order peacefully to persuade. It does not become a nuisance unless it is associated with obstruction, violence, intimidation, molestation or threats.[4]

In *Mersey Dock and Harbour Co v Verrinder*,[5] however, the High Court held that putting what was perceived as improper pressure on employers could constitute nuisance, thus relating liability to the motive for the pickets' action rather than the nature of that action. The aim of the pickets, who stood at the entrance to two container terminals, was to protest at the use of 'cowboy' haulage contractors who undercut established operators. They brought the terminals to a virtual standstill because drivers refused to cross the picket line but there were no allegation of violence. The court found that the intention of the pickets was to ensure that only established operators were employed to the exclusion of others not acceptable to them, not merely to obtain or communicate information, and that this was capable of amounting to a private nuisance. In *Thomas v NUM (South Wales Area)*[6] Scott J sought to extend the application of the tort in a number of respects. As well as affirming that mass picketing was in itself an actionable nuisance, a view supported by authority, he also considered that regular picketing outside the home of an individual non-striker could constitute the tort regardless of the number of those involved and however peaceful their conduct. Even more controversially, he also held that unreasonable interference by way of harassment of workers who wished to use the highway to go to work could constitute a tort, which could be described as a species of private nuisance, despite the absence of any interference with the enjoyment of land. On this basis, he held that the daily presence of between 50 and 70 men hurling abuse, in circumstances requiring a police presence and the use of vehicles to transport the workers into work, was sufficient to constitute this wrong. In *News Group Newspapers Ltd v SOGAT 82 (No 2)*[7] Stuart-Smith J acknowledged the substance of the defendants' criticisms of such an extension of the tort, especially given that it did not appear that damage was a necessary ingredient of it. In the light of the House of Lords decision in *Hunter v Canary Wharf Ltd*,[8] affirming the nature of private nuisance as a tort based upon the enjoyment of land, it would be difficult to argue that harassment can *per se* constitute a nuisance. However the wider question whether there was a separate tort of harassment was not considered,[9] although this is a now less pressing question in the light of the enactment of the Protection from Harassment Act 1997.

---

1 In *Hunter v Canary Wharf Ltd* [1997] 2 All ER 426 the House of Lords affirmed the need for the claimant to have a right to the land affected. Ordinarily this requires

a right to exclusive possession of the land. A mere licensee on the land has no right to sue.

2. *J Lyons and Sons v Wilkins (No 2)* [1899] 1 Ch 255, CA.
3. *Ward, Lock and Co Ltd v OPAS* (1906) 22 TLR 327, CA.
4. [1975] ICR 308 at 317.
5. [1982] IRLR 152, ChD.
6. [1985] IRLR 136, ChD.
7. [1986] IRLR 337 at 348.
8. [1997] 2 All ER 426, HL.
9. See *Khorasandjian v Bush* [1993] 3 All ER 669, CA; Hepple, forthcoming.

6.70 The tort of public nuisance is less frequently relied upon by claimants. It consists of an act or omission which obstructs or causes inconvenience or damage to the public in the exercise of rights common to all Her Majesty's subjects. It is a flexible wrong which covers 'a multitude of sins, great and small'[1] which interfere with the rights of the public at large. (It is also a common law crime.) In order to sue for public nuisance, an individual must show particular damage greater than that suffered by the public at large,[2] although this loss need not be of a pecuniary nature; inconvenience or delay may be sufficient.[3] Obstruction of the highway can amount to public nuisance provided that the use of the highway by the defendants is 'unreasonable'.[4] In *News Group Newspapers Ltd v SOGAT 82 (No 2)*[5] the conduct of pickets was held to constitute unreasonable use, and daily demonstrators and various claimants were found to have suffered special damage, including *The Times* newspaper which had lost journalists because of the demonstrations, and an individual worker who could not leave the plant during the day and felt drained by the constant pressure of having to come to work through the picket line.

---

1. *Southport Corporation v Esso Petroleum Co Ltd* [1954] 2 QB 182, Lord Denning MR at 196.
2. The meaning of particular damage is obscure; see generally Spencer, 1989, especially 74–75.
3. See, for example, *Halsey v Esso Petroleum Co* [1961] 2 All ER 145, Veale J.
4. *R v Clark (No 2)* [1964] 2 QB 315; *News Group Newspapers Ltd v SOGAT 82* [1986] IRLR 337, QBD.
5. Above.

The Protection from Harassment Act 1997

6.71   The Protection from Harassment Act 1997 introduced a new statutory tort which, although aimed at stalkers, pickets may commit. The Act makes it an offence to pursue a 'course of conduct' (defined as involving conduct 'on at least two occasions')[1] which amounts to harassment of another and which he or she knows or ought to know amounts to harassment of the other (the latter element to be tested by reference to whether a reasonable person in possession of the same information would think this).[2] 'Conduct' in this context includes speech.[3] In addition, a person who is or may be the victim of such conduct may seek an injunction to restrain it, and it is an offence, punishable by up to five years' imprisonment, to breach that injunction without reasonable excuse.[4] Damages may also be awarded in respect of harassment, including for any anxiety caused by it.[5] References to harassing a person include 'alarming the person or causing the person distress',[6] but the concept is not confined to this. The wrong is not committed, *inter alia*, if the person who pursued the conduct shows that 'in the particular circumstances the pursuit of the course of conduct was reasonable'.[7] Previous judicial attitudes do not suggest that pickets are likely to be able successfully to invoke this defence. It has been held that it is difficult, if not impossible, to imagine circumstances in which the pursuit of a course of conduct amounting to harassment in breach of an injunction could be 'reasonable', though an isolated act in exceptional circumstances, such as rescuing someone in danger, may be defended on that basis.[8]

---

1. S 7(3).
2. S 1(2),(2). See further para **6.79** for the penalties which may be imposed for this offence. A person also commits an offence under the Act if he or she knows or ought to know that their course of conduct will cause another to fear, on at least two occasions, that violence will be used against them: s 4. In the case of both offences a court sentencing or otherwise dealing with a defendant may make an order prohibiting specified behaviour in order to protect the victim or any other person mentioned in the order from the offending conduct: s 5.
3. S 7(4).
4. S 3. In *Huntingdon Life Science Ltd v Curtin* and 10 other respondents, CA, 15 October 1997, unreported, the Court of Appeal held that an injunction could be granted against a corporate body. On the facts, it was difficult to pin down responsibility on anybody, and the court ordered substituted service by fixing notices in the appropriate places so that any potential demonstrator could see it and know what he or she could or could not do.
5. *Ibid.*
6. S 7(2).
7. S1(3)(c).
8. *R v DPP ex parte Moseley*, QBD, 9 June 1999 (unreported).

The scope of statutory immunity

6.72 As we indicated in para **6.67**, there are two provisions relating to statutory immunity in the context of picketing. First, there is a specific (but limited) immunity contained in the Trade Union and Labour Relations (Consolidation) Act 1992, s 220. Secondly, the general immunities which afford protection against certain of the economic torts may also be applicable. However this itself depends upon two requirements being met. First, the usual requirements for their application must be satisfied, and the general exclusions from their scope apply (see para **6.17** *et seq.*). Secondly, the conduct of the pickets must stay within the boundaries of s 220; s 219(3) provides that nothing in s 219(1) or (2) prevents an act done in the course of picketing from being actionable in tort unless it is done in the course of attendance declared lawful by s 220.[1] Thus, if pickets who are seeking to persuade other workers not to enter a workplace exceed the terms of s 220, they will have no protection against the tort of inducing breach of contract.[2] S 220(1) provides that it is 'lawful for a person in contemplation or furtherance of a trade dispute'[3] to attend at or near his own place of work for the purpose *only* of 'peacefully obtaining or communicating information, or peacefully persuading any person to work or abstain from working'. A trade union official may also attend for that purpose at or near the place of work of a member of that union whom he is accompanying and whom he represents. The term 'official' covers union officers and also any other person elected or appointed in accordance with the union rules to be a representative of the members or some of them;[4] it thus includes shop stewards and other staff representatives as well as branch and other union officers. However, a person who has been elected or appointed to represent a portion of the membership (eg those at a particular workplace or in a particular region) may attend to represent those members only.[5] It is important to stress that s 220 gives merely a limited immunity to attend for the specified purposes,[6] the terms of which are easily exceeded (see para **6.74**). *A fortiori*, pickets have no right to require others to listen to their case.[7] This lack of any positive right has been particularly significant in the light of the broad discretionary powers of the police to control picketing, which we discuss in para **6.78**. However as we indicate in that paragraph, greater weight may need to be accorded to the Convention rights of pickets under the Human Rights Act 1998.[8] Section 220 does not give any right to attend on land against the will of its owner (or the person to whom the owner has granted exclusive occupation), nor does it affect the operation of any byelaws by which the use and operation of land may be regulated.[9] It may afford protection against the torts of trespass to the highway and nuisance,[10] but this is of little real importance: the former is irrelevant in practice, and where there is an actionable nuisance it is unlikely that the conduct will fall within the section. The main significance of s 220 is in relation to the protection which it affords against the economic torts, provided, as we explained above, that the usual conditions governing their application are met. The withdrawal of immunity for secondary industrial action is particularly significant in this context. There is one very narrow exception applicable to pickets; immunity is retained if the secondary action is done in the course of attendance which is lawful under s 220 by a worker employed (or, in the case of a worker not in employment, last employed) by the employer party to the dispute, or by a union official whose attendance is lawful under the section.[11] This means that protection is afforded if the pickets interfere with the contract of employment of a worker employed by another employer (for example, if they attempt to persuade a driver employed by a customer or supplier not to remove goods from, or deliver them to, the premises).

---

1. Note, however, that the immunity is displaced by an act done 'in the course of picketing', not, for example, an act inducing a union to organise picketing in breach of its rules: see *Thomas v NUM (South Wales Area)* [1985] IRLR 136 at 155, ChD.

2. It is possible that liability for conspiracy to use unlawful means may arise if pickets who are lawfully attending actively associate with others from whom the protection of the immunities has been removed by s 219(3). The Code of Practice (para 57) states that a picket organiser should ensure that workers from other places of work do not join the picket line and that any offers of support on the picket line from outsiders are refused. However, it is unclear that lawful pickets need go that far to refute an allegation of 'combination' with the illicit pickets.

3. Defined *ibid.*, s 244; see further para **6.19** *et seq*.

4. TULRCA 1992, s 119; an 'officer' includes any member of the union governing body or any trustee of any fund applicable for the purposes of the union: *ibid*.

5. *Ibid.*, s 220(4). Thus a shop steward for a particular workplace may accompany only those members who work at the workplace., conversely a national official who represents the whole union may accompany any member: see the Code of Practice, para 23.

6. *Broome v DPP* [1974] ICR 84, HL; *Kavanagh v Hiscock* [1974] ICR 282, DC.

7. *Broome v DPP*, above, Lord Reid at 89–90.

8. See para **1.13** *et seq*.

9. *British Airports Authority v Ashton* [1983] IRLR 287, QBD. On the issues posed by the use of 'quasi-public' spaces see Gray and Gray, 1999.

10. See paras **6.68** and **6.69**. The Code of Practice oversimplifies the position in para 5 by stating that the immunities afford no protection in relation to any civil wrong not specified in s 219; the examples given in para 27 of the Code are more appropriate.

11. TULRCA 1992, s 224(3).

6.73 There is no statutory definition of 'place of work' for the purposes of s 220, in comparison with industrial action ballots where the equivalent term 'workplace' is defined. The Code of Practice indicates that the restriction means that 'lawful picketing must be limited to attendance at, or near, an entrance to or exit from the factory, site or office at which the picket works'.[1] On this basis the immunity would not cover those picketing other premises of their own employer in a multi-plant group. If the picket works at an establishment composed of a large number of buildings on a single site (a university or a hospital, for example), on a narrow view this restriction could imply that the immunity extends only to the individual building in which the worker's office is located. It is submitted that this would be too narrow an interpretation, and would not reflect the understanding of either the worker or the employer on the location of the employment. As we indicated in para **6.72** above, there is an exception to the 'place of work' requirement in relation to union officials. There are also two further qualifications to it. First, a worker who is 'not in employment' whose last employment was terminated in connection with a trade dispute, or the termination of whose employment was one of the circumstances giving rise to a trade dispute, can attend at his or her former place of work.[2] However the exclusion of those 'not in employment' means that a worker who had found even a part-time job elsewhere would not qualify under this provision. Secondly, where a person does not normally work at any one place, or the location of the place makes it impractical to attend there for the protected purposes, the place of work is 'any premises of his employer from which he works or from which his work is administered'.[3] A lorry driver or a travelling service engineer would come into the first category, an oil-rig worker into the second. Notably, however, there is no express provision for picketing by dismissed workers whose former place of work has closed down. In *News Group Newspapers Ltd v SOGAT 82 (No 2)*[4] the court held that dismissed workers who had formerly worked in central London were outside the immunity when they picketed the employers' new premises in Wapping, given that they had never worked there. A similar result was reached in *Union Traffic Ltd v TGWU*,[5] where the claimants had decided to close down one of their transport depots in Liverpool and make a number of drivers redundant. The drivers picketed another depot in Liverpool, where the employers carried on a container repair business, and a transport depot 13 miles away. The Court of Appeal held that, although these places had been ports of call, neither had been the 'base' from which the defendants worked and so could not be deemed their 'place of work'. This reasoning leaves workers in this situation with no premises which they can effectively picket.[6] It may be possible to argue that attendance at the empty site at which the pickets previously worked is 'impracticable' and they should therefore be able to picket the new premises of the employer,[7] but this approach has yet to be accepted by the courts. By contrast, a more purposive approach has been taken to the construction of the phrase 'at or near'. In *Rayware Ltd v TGWU*[8] the Court of Appeal held that the phrase had to be considered in a geographical sense in the light of the purpose of the legislation, which was to grant a freedom peacefully to persuade, and that 'near' should be seen as an 'expanding' word.[9] Here, the claimant's factory was on a private trading estate on a private road some seven-tenths of a mile away from the entrance to the estate from the highway. The employees in dispute had established a picket at a gate leading from the highway onto the estate as being the nearest practicable point at which to picket without committing a trespass. The court held that they were within s 220. Whether a particular spot will be deemed 'near' is a question of fact, but two members of the court indicated that if their decision 'established a precedent for other comparable industrial and commercial developments' they would 'not flinch from that result in an area of the law where it is especially desirable that rights and duties should be certain'.[10]

---

1. Para 17.

2. TULRCA 1992, s 220(3). See para **6.21** *et seq.* for the definition of trade dispute' and App 1 for the definition of 'worker'.

3. *Ibid.*, s 220(2). 'Any' in this context would appear not to limit the worker to one set of premises, although cf Lloyd LJ in *Union Traffic Ltd v TGWU* [1989] IRLR 127 at 133, CA, who limited 'place of work' to the worker's 'principal place of work' or 'base'. By definition, however this interpretation cannot apply in the case of those for whom picketing their place of work is impractical. See also note 6, below.

4. [1986] IRLR 337, QBD, at 350.

5. [1989] IRLR 127, CA.

6. Lloyd LJ assumed that a person could have only one 'place of work' his 'principal place of work' or 'base' (at 133) and Bingham LJ too spoke of the 'base' (at 131). However, there is nothing in the section to prevent a person within s 220(2) having both a place 'at' which and a place 'from which' he works; the lorry drivers in *Union Traffic Ltd v TGWU*, above, note 3, may have come into this category.

7. Auerbach 1989, 168–169. This argument involves arguing that s 220(2) and (3) may apply simultaneously, a proposition not ruled out by the statute. Lloyd LJ left this point open in *Union Traffic Ltd v TGWU*, above, note 3 (at 133).

8. [1989] IRLR 134, CA. See also the Code of Practice, para 17.

9. The court adopted the dictum of Byles J in *Tyne Keelman v Davison* (1864) 16 CBNS 612 at 622, Ct of Common Pleas.

10. Above, note 8, at 137. In *Timex Electronics Corpn v AEU* (26 March 1993, unreported) the First Division of the Court of Session in Scotland held that the words 'at or near' were not too imprecise for an interdict (injunction) against unlawful picketing.

6.74 In general terms the ambit of s 220(1) and its predecessors[1] has been interpreted very restrictively by the courts, so rendering pickets likely to be liable in tort (although note that picketing outside the scope of s 220 is not *per se* unlawful). In particular, the courts have been ready to infer that the conduct of pickets has gone beyond that of communicating information or peacefully persuading. In *Tynan v Balmer*[2] the Divisional Court held that 40 pickets who were walking in a circle which spilt onto the public highway at the entrance to a factory had no immunity because one of their objects was to seal off the highway. In *Broome v DPP*[3] Lord Reid suggested that if pickets assembled in 'unreasonably large numbers' it 'would not be difficult to infer' that they were doing this to prevent the passage of others. In more recent cases the courts have been influenced by the Code of Practice on picketing, which suggests a limit of six pickets at any entrance to a workplace.[4] Thus, in *Thomas v NUM (South Wales Area)*[5] Scott J found that the 50–70 pickets who assembled daily at the entrance to a workplace could not be protected by the immunity.

> It may be that the six persons who are selected to stand close to the gates could bring themselves within the provision, but the many others who are present cannot do so. What is their purpose in attending? It is obviously not to obtain or communicate information. Is it peacefully to persuade the working miners to abstain from working? If that is the case what is the need for vehicles to bring the working miners safely into the collieries?[6]

It seems, therefore, that mere attendance in sufficient numbers may, without more, take pickets outside s 220. Under the Human Rights Act 1998, however, it is submitted that the courts will need to pay closer regard to the exigencies of the particular situation rather than merely relying upon the provisions of the Code.

---

1. Trade Disputes Act 1906, s 2, continued in a modified form by the Industrial Relations Act 1971, s 134, substantially re-enacted by the Trade Union and Labour Relations Act 1974, s 15 and amended substantially by the Employment Act 1980.
2. [1967] 1 QB 91, DC.
3. [1974] ICR 84, HL, at 90.
4. Para 51. See para **6.67** for the influence of the Code on the terms of injunctions.
5. [1985] IRLR 136, ChD.
6. *Ibid.*, at 148. See also *News Group Newspapers Ltd v SOGAT 82 (No 2)* [1986] IRLR 337, QBD. Note, however, that this dictum arose from a case concerning mass picketing; it should not be taken to mean that picketing by more than six persons will be unlawful *per se*.

Criminal Liability

Sources and general principles

6.75 There is a multiplicity of criminal offences which pickets may commit in the course of their activities. Here we give an outline of the major ones.[1] Unlike liability in civil law, criminal liability falls wholly on the individuals concerned. It is unlawful for union property to be used to pay a fine, nor may individuals be indemnified by the union for any liability they may incur,[2] although this restriction does not extend to the payment of the expenses of defending a prosecution if the union rules permit this.[3] The major offences are, first, those specified in the Trade Union and Labour Relations (Consolidation) Act 1992, s 241; secondly, obstruction of the highway under the Highways Act 1980, s 137; thirdly, obstruction of a constable in the execution of his duty under the Police Act 1996, s 89(2) (most commonly in relation to an anticipated breach of the peace); fourthly, offences under the Public Order Act 1986; and fifthly, offences under the Protection from Harassment Act 1997.[4] This range of offences gives the police a broad discretion to control picketing behaviour, although, as we discuss in para **6.78**, the exercise of their discretion to prevent a breach of the peace may be more vulnerable to challenge under the Human Rights Act 1998 than previously. In particular the adoption of the six-picket guideline suggested by paragraph 51 of the Code of Practice, which has influenced the exercise of police as well as judicial discretion in the past, is likely to be questioned. The immunity afforded by the Trade Union and Labour Relations (Consolidation) Act 1992, s 220 (see para **6.72**) is negligible in relation to criminal liability;[5] in any case, as we described in para **6.74**, the courts readily infer that pickets have exceeded the terms of s 220, in which case the protection it gives is lost entirely.

---

1. For further details of the elements of these offences, see J C Smith, 1999, chapter 21; also still useful are A T H Smith, 1987 and Card, 1987. For more detailed (albeit not wholly up to date) analyses of the policing of industrial disputes, see Kahn *et al*, 1983; Geary, 1985; For a broader perspective, see McCabe and Wallington, 1988.
2. TULRCA 1992, s 15. At common law it was not unlawful for a union to authorise payment of fines for picketing offences by members after the offences were committed: *Drake v Morgan* [1978] ICR 56, QBD. See further para **6.116**.
3. *Ibid.*
4. Note also that public nuisance, as well as being a tort, is a common law crime, but in practice it has rarely been charged in the public order context. The Criminal Law Act 1977 provides that a person is guilty of criminal conspiracy if he or she agrees with any other person or persons that a course of conduct shall be pursued which will necessarily amount to or involve the commission of any offence or offences by one or more of the parties to the agreement if the agreement is carried out in accordance with their

intentions: s 1(1). However, an agreement to commit a summary offence not punishable with imprisonment 'in contemplation or furtherance of a trade dispute' (see further para **6.19** *et seq.*) is excluded from the ambit of this offence: TULRCA 1992, s 242. The maximum sentence of imprisonment for conspiracy cannot now exceed the maximum sentence for the substantive offence: Criminal Law Act 1977, s 3.

5. At most it may support the argument that picketing within its terms is not an 'unreasonable user' of the highway under the Highways Act 1980, nor without 'legal authority' for the purposes of TULRCA 1992, s 241.

The Trade Union and Labour Relations (Consolidation) Act 1992, s 241

6.76 The Trade Union and Labour Relations (Consolidation) Act 1992, s 241 is an updated version of offences originally contained in the Conspiracy and Protection of Property Act 1875 which were enacted specifically to deal with picketing.[1] Under the section, it is an offence to do one of five acts 'wrongfully and without legal authority' 'with a view to compelling'[2] another person to abstain from doing or to do any act which that person has a legal right to do or abstain from doing'. These acts are:

(a) using violence to or intimidating that person or his wife (sic) or children or injuring his property;

(b) persistently following that person about from place to place;

(c) hiding any tools, clothes or other property owned or used by that person, or depriving him of or hindering him in the use thereof;

(d) watching or besetting the house or other place where that person resides, works, carries on business or happens to be, or the approach to any such house or place; or

(e) following that person with two or more other persons in a disorderly manner in or through any street or road.

It now seems to be accepted that the term 'wrongfully and without legal authority' requires an activity to constitute at least a tort before it can give rise to liability under s 241;[3] without this requirement many forms of picketing would immediately be illegal as involving ' watching and besetting'. It is also arguable that picketing within the terms of s 220 is not 'without legal authority'. However, the protection afforded by the requirement that the activity should be tortious would be undermined almost entirely if the view of a Scottish court were accepted, to the effect that economic torts protected by the statutory immunities can nevertheless constitute the requisite 'wrongful' act because s 219 expressly applies only to proceedings in tort.[4] On the basis of this reasoning, any picketing which involves an inducement to breach a contract of employment or commercial contract could lead to a criminal charge, however few persons were involved. Given a maximum penalty of six months' imprisonment and a fine which currently stands at a maximum of £5,000, this would seem a wholly inappropriate result.[5] It has been suggested that an interpretation of s 241 which means that peaceful picketing can become a criminal offence merely because it involves the torts of inducing breach of contract or nuisance would be incompatible with Articles 10 and 11 of the ECHR as it would not be proportionate to the aim of protecting the 'rights of others'.[6]

1. The Public Order Act 1986 added a power of arrest and increased the maximum penalty to six months' imprisonment and a fine of level 5 on the standard scale (at the time of writing £5,000); see now s 241(2), (3).

2. Persuasion is not compulsion for this purpose: *DPP v Fidler* [1992] 1 WLR 91, DC.

3. *Ward, Lock and Co Ltd v OPAS* (1906) 22 TLR 327, CA; *Thomas v NUM (South Wales Area)* [1985] IRLR 136, ChD; cf. *J Lyons and Sons v Wilkins* [1896] 1 Ch 81 1, CA.

4. *Galt (Procurator Fiscal) v Philp* [1984] IRLR 156, High Ct of Justiciary. See para **6.17** *et seq.*

5. See note 1, above.

6. Hepple, forthcoming.

Highways Act 1980, s 137

6.77 The Highways Act 1980, s 137 makes it an offence 'in any way' to 'wilfully obstruct the free passage along a highway' without 'lawful authority or excuse'.[1] The latter requirement has been held by the courts to allow consideration of whether the user was 'reasonable'. This is a question of fact, depending on circumstances such as the length of time the obstruction continues, its location and purpose, and whether there was an actual as opposed to a potential obstruction.[2] It is arguable that picketing within the statutory immunity would be considered 'reasonable', but anything beyond that may not. A constable may arrest a person without warrant for this offence.

1. There is a maximum fine of level 3 on the standard scale established by the Criminal Justice Act 1982, s 37(2), as substituted by the Criminal Justice Act 1991, s 17(1) (at the time of writing, £1,000).

2. *Nagy v Weston* [1965] 1 All ER 78, QBD; see also *Hirst and Agu v Chief Constable of the West Yorkshire Police* (1986), 85 Cr App Rep 143, QBD (discussed Bailey 1987).

In *Jones v DPP* [1999] 2 All ER 257, HL, Lord Irvine LC (at 266) and Lord Hutton (at 293) drew on these authorities in determining the boundaries of the tort of trespass to the highway: see para **6.68**.

Obstructing a constable in the execution of his duty: the concept of a breach of the peace

6.78 The offence of obstructing a constable in the execution of his duty under the Police Act 1996, s 89(2) most frequently arises in the picketing context if pickets refuse to obey police instructions designed to prevent a breach of the peace.[1] The police and, indeed, all citizens have a common law power to take any steps necessary to prevent a breach of the peace on either public or private property;[2] such steps may include restricting the number of pickets present, ordering them to move away or, where appropriate, arresting them.[3] The police may also be empowered to prevent pickets approaching picket lines from some distance away provided that the police honestly and reasonably believe that the risk to the peace is real in the sense that it is 'in close proximity both in place and time'.[4] Although the concept of a breach of the peace is centuries old, its precise definition has been the subject of judicial controversy.[5] In *R v Howell* Watkins LJ stated that there was 'likely to be a breach of the peace whenever harm is actually done or is likely to be done to a person or in his presence to his property or a person is in fear of being so harmed through an assault, an affray, a riot, unlawful assembly or other disturbance'.[6] In 1981, in a differently constituted Court of Appeal, Lord Denning MR proposed a broader definition, affirming that there was a breach of the peace 'whenever a person who is lawfully carrying out his work is unlawfully and physically prevented by another from doing it'.[7] In a subsequent case before the Divisional Court, however, Collins J followed *Howell* in holding that there must be a risk of violence before there could be a breach of the peace, although such violence did not have to be perpetrated by the defendant: it was sufficient if its natural consequence was to provoke violence in others.[8] Finally, in *Nicol v DPP* Simon Brown LJ qualified that approach in stating that

> the court would surely not find a [breach of the peace] proved if any violence likely to have been provoked on the part of others would be not merely unlawful but wholly unreasonable—as, of course, it would be if the defendant's conduct was not merely lawful but such as in no material way interfered with the other's rights. *A fortiori* if the defendant was properly exercising his own basic rights, whether of assembly, demonstration or free speech.[9]

The approach represented by the last sentence of that dictum will be strengthened under the Human Rights Act 1998, although as this and other cases show, even before that time the courts have been prepared to give weight to the exercise by defendants of their Convention rights in deciding whether a police officer was justified in perceiving a breach of the peace.[10] However, the prospects for challenging the compatibility of police powers to act when they reasonably apprehend a breach of the peace with the rights protected by the Convention do not appear good, on the basis of current jurisprudence of the ECHR.[11] Indeed, as Fenwick remarks, the stance of the Court in the recent case of *Steel v UK*[12] 'in fact implies less tolerance of peaceful direct action than the stance taken in *Nicol* since the Court required only an interference with the rights of the others and the possibility of disorder in order to be satisfied regarding proportionality; no added requirement to show that the defendant rather than the other party was acting unreasonably was proposed'.[13] Nevertheless, even though the basic principle may remain in place, the courts may be expected to accord greater weight to the rights being exercised by defendants in deciding in any given situation whether the police had reasonable grounds for apprehending a breach of the peace in the face of an ostensibly peaceful picket. In particular, as we indicated in para **6.75**, the courts may be more sceptical of the adoption by the police of the six-picket guideline suggested by paragraph 51 of the Code of Practice in cases where there their apprehension of a breach of the peace is derived solely from the numbers present. A constable who interfered with the exercise of freedom of expression or assembly which could not be justified would have acted unlawfully and would not therefore be acting in the execution of his duty.[14]

---

1. This carries a maximum penalty of one month's imprisonment and/or a maximum fine of level 3 on the standard scale (at the time of writing, £1,000). The Police Act 1964, s 51(3) contained the predecessor to this provision.

2. *Thomas v Sawkins* [1935] 2 KB 249, KBD, a power preserved by the Police and Criminal Evidence Act 1984, s 17(6).

3. See, for example, *Piddington v Bates* [1960] 3 All ER 660, QBD; see also *Albert v Lavin* [1982] AC 546 at 565 and the Police and Criminal Evidence Act 1984, ss 17(6) and 25(6).

4. *Moss v McLachlan* [1985] IRLR 76, QBD (legality of a roadblock during the 1984–1985 miners' strike), discussed Morris, 1985a; see also Police and Criminal Evidence Act 1984, s 4.

5. See Fenwick, 1999, 506–511.

6. [1982] 1 QB 416, CA.

7. *R v Chief Constable of Devon and Cornwall, ex parte Central Electricity Generating Board* [1982] QB 458, CA, at 471.

8. *Percy v DPP* [1995] 1 WLR 1382, DC.

9. *Nicol and Selvanayagam v DPP* [1996] JP 155, at 163.

10. *Redmond-Bate v DPP* [1999] 163 JP 789.

11. *Steel v UK* judgment of 23 September 1998, (1999) 28 EHRR 603; *McLeod v UK* judgment of 23 September 1998, (1999) 27 EHRR 493. Cf. *Hashman and Harrup v UK* judgment of 25 November 1999 (order binding applicants over to keep the peace and not to behave *contra bonos mores* not 'prescribed by law' for the purposes of Article 10(2)).

12. Above.

13. Fenwick, 1999, 510. This decision also sits uneasily with the earlier decision of the Court in *Plattform 'Ärzte für das Leben' v Austria* judgment of 21 June 1988, (1991) 13 EHRR 204 that the state has a duty 'to take reasonable and appropriate measures to enable lawful demonstrations to proceed peacefully' (para 34) in the face of threatened disruption by counter-demonstrators (albeit this is 'an obligation as to measures to be taken and not as to results to be achieved' and the state has a wide choice of the means to be used: *ibid.*).

14. See further para **1.16**.

The Public Order Act 1986 and the Protection from Harassment Act 1997

6.79 The Public Order Act 1986 gives the police extensive powers to control 'public assemblies'[1] and 'public processions',[2] and it is an offence to organise, take part in, or incite others to take part in such an assembly or procession and knowingly fail to comply with conditions imposed by the police.[3] These conditions may be imposed either in advance or on the spot where the 'senior police officer'[4] reasonably believes that: (a) an assembly (or procession) may result in serious public disorder, serious damage to property or serious disruption to the life of the community; or (b) the purpose of the persons organising the assembly (or procession) is the intimidation of others with a view to compelling them not to do an act which they have a right to do,[5] or to do an act they have a right not to do. Such conditions as to the place, size and maximum duration of the assembly or procession may then be imposed as appear to the officer to be necessary to prevent these consequences occurring. In the case of pickets this may involve moving them away from a workplace entrance to avoid contact with those going into it or restricting them to times when other workers are not using the entrance, as well as restricting their number.[6] As we indicated in para **6.78** above, relying automatically on the six-picket limitation suggested in the Code of Practice to restrict numbers may be susceptible to challenge under the Human Rights Act 1998. The Act also lays down a requirement to give the police advance notice of 'public processions'.[7] The Act introduced five new statutory offences which may be relevant to the conduct of picketing.[8] These are (in declining order of seriousness) riot, violent disorder, affray, causing fear of violence or provoking it, and causing harassment, alarm or distress. All may be committed in both public and private places. In addition, the Criminal Justice and Public Order Act 1994 inserted into the Public Order Act 1986 a new offence of intentional harassment which, unlike the pre-existing offence, does not require a prior warning to cease the offending conduct. It is publishable by up to six months' imprisonment and a fine of £5,000. Finally, the Protection from Harassment Act 1997 created the offences of harassment and putting another in fear of violence, which we discussed in para **6.71** in the context of civil liability to which such conduct also may give rise. Harassment is publishable by a minimum of six months' imprisonment and/or a fine of up to level 5 on the standard scale; putting a person in fear of violence a maximum of five years' imprisonment, an unlimited fine, or both.[9]

---

1. Defined as 'an assembly of 20 or more persons in a public place which is wholly or partly open to the air': s 16. 'Public place' means any highway and place to which at the material time the public or any section of the public has access, on payment or otherwise, as of right or by virtue of express or implied permission.
2. Defined as a 'procession in a public place': *ibid.*
3. Ss 12 and 14.
4. Defined in ss 12(2) and 14(2).
5. For what the courts might view as 'intimidation' see *Thomas v NUM (South Wales Area)* [1985] IRLR 136, ChD.
6. See also s 14A of the Public Order Act 1986, inserted by the Criminal Justice and Public Order Act 1994, which permits a chief officer of police to apply to the council of a district where he reasonably believes that an assembly is intended to be held on land to which the public has no, or only a limited, right of access and *inter alia* may result in serious disruption to the life of the community. The council may make an order with the consent of the Secretary of State. See *Jones v DPP* [1999] 2 All ER 257, HL.
7. Public Order Act 1986, s 11.
8. *Ibid.*, ss 1–5.
9. Protection from Harassment Act 1997, ss 2, 4. See *R v Liddle* [1999] 3 All ER 816, CA, for guidelines on sentencing.

Picketing and the Human Rights Act 1998

6.80 We have indicated in our discussion of particular aspects of the liability of pickets those respects in which the Human Rights Act 1998 may modify their application.[1] In this paragraph we indicate briefly some general issues which are likely to be raised.[2] The articles of the ECHR most relevant to picketing are Article 10, which guarantees the right to freedom of expression, and Article 11, which guarantees the right to freedom of peaceful assembly. The jurisprudence on this aspect of Article 11 is relatively meagre, but the Court has affirmed that Article 11 must be considered in the light of Article 10, given that '[t]he protection of personal opinions, secured by Article 10, is one of the objectives of freedom of peaceful assembly as enshrined in Article 11'.[3] In practice, therefore, it would be foolhardy to overlook the principles governing Article 10, even if the case in question appeared more directly concerned with freedom of assembly. The ECtHR has accorded a wide meaning to the concept of 'expression', and it has been applied to protests which take the form of impeding activities of which demonstrators disapprove.[4] The case law therefore generally turns on whether an interference with the exercise of the right can be justified under Article 10(2). As we indicated in Chapter 1, in this respect the nature and context of the expression have been important: in deciding whether there is a 'pressing social need' for a restriction, whether the interference is 'proportionate to the legitimate aim pursued' and the reasons for it are 'relevant and sufficient', the margin of appreciation accorded to the state has varied, with, at one end of the scale, a wide margin of appreciation being given to 'commercial' expression, and at the other end a narrow margin where the expression is regarded as 'political'.[5] This 'categorisation' approach is not without its difficulties,[6] but if followed by domestic courts it will be crucial to determine the category into which picketing falls. In the United States, picketing has been regarded as protected speech on the ground that discussion of conditions in industry and the causes of labour disputes is indispensible to popular government.[7] However a Canadian writer has argued that it should best be regarded as commercial expression, 'since its main purpose is to encourage employees not to work and consumers not to buy'.[8] Where picketing is concerned with the provision of information, it is strongly arguable that regardless of its nature the courts should be wary of injuncting publication (more wary than the terms of the Human Rights Act 1998, s 12(3) would suggest[9]), and there is some support for the view that the 'categorisation' approach is less prevalent in the reasoning of the ECtHR where the interference with freedom of expression has taken the form of an injunction.[10] Where picketing consists essentially of attempting to persuade, it may be more difficult to challenge restrictions on conduct which fall outside the scope of the statutory immunities as failing to meet a 'pressing social need' or 'disproportionate'. A particular issue may be raised by secondary picketing, which, as we indicated in para **6.72** is entirely unprotected (a technical exception apart). As Hepple states, in the USA and Canada restrictions on this type of industrial action have usually been regarded as legitimate in order to prevent the spread of action to so-called neutrals.[11] It seems unlikely that domestic courts will be inclined to take a different view, although ILO jurisprudence on this issue should be noted.[12] Finally, as we have emphasised previously in this section, where pickets are subject to limitations on their numbers, it would seem appropriate for the courts to play closer regard to the exigencies of the particular situation rather than merely adopting the six-picket guideline recommended in the Code of Practice. Indeed, in the light of the Human Rights Act 1998, it would seem desirable for the Code of Practice to be amended.

1. See, in particular, paras **6.67**, **6.74**, **6.76** and **6.78**.

2. For more detailed discussion of Convention jurisprudence and of the HRA 1998, see Chapter 1. For a discussion of the issues raised by Articles 10 and 11 in relation to the broader freedom to demonstrate, see Fenwick, 1999.

3. *Ezelin v France* judgment of 26 April 1991, (1992) 14 EHRR 362, para 37.

4. See *Steel v UK* judgment of 23 September 1998, (1999) 28 EHRR 603 para 92; *Hashman and Harrup v UK* judgment of 25 November 1999, para 28.

5. See para **1.8**.

6. See Tierney, 1998; Lester, 1998a.

7. *Thornhill v Alabama* 310 US 88 (1940), S Ct; cf. *International Brotherhood of Teamsters v Vogt* 354 US 284 (1957), S Ct, where picketing was restrained when it prevented government from enforcing public policy (quoted Hepple, forthcoming).

8. Hogg, 1997, sec 40.8 (quoted Hepple, above).

9. S 12(3) provides that no relief which, if granted, might affect the exercise of the Convention right to freedom of expression is to be granted so as to restrain publication before trial 'unless the court is satisfied that the applicant is likely to establish that publication should not be allowed'. Note also s12(1),(2) on injunctions without notice, formerly known as *ex parte* injunctions.

10. *Observer and Guardian v UK* judgment of 26 November 1991, (1992) 14 EHRR 153; *Open Door Counselling and Well Women v Ireland* judgment of 29 October 1992, (1993) 15 EHRR 244 (information about abortion facilities); *Hertel v Switzerland* judgment of 25 August 1998, (1999) 28 EHRR 534 (views about the hazardous effect of microwave ovens); cf. *Markt Intern and Beerman v Germany*, judgment of 20 November 1989 (1990) 12 EHRR 161.

11. Hepple, forthcoming, quoting *Giboney v Empire Storage and Ice Co* 336 US 490 (1949), S Ct; *NLRB v Retail Store Employees Union* 447 US 607 (1980), S Ct; and *Retail, Wholesale and Department Store Union, Local 580 v Dolphin Delivery* (1986) 3 DLR (4th) 174, S Ct Can.

12. See para **6.29**.

INDUSTRIAL ACTION AND CONTRACTUAL RIGHTS

Sources and General Principles

6.81 The contractual position when workers take industrial action depends on whether the action constitutes a breach of their individual contracts.[1] Participation in a strike has generally been regarded by the courts as a breach of contract; whether this remains the case even after strike notice has been given depends upon the terms of that notice. Whether participation in other forms of industrial action constitutes a breach of contract depends upon the nature of the industrial action and the terms of the specific contract; if it does constitute a breach, notice of the action merely serves as notice of intended breach. Where industrial action constitutes a breach of contract, the employer has three remedies at its disposal: to sue individual workers in damages for the loss the industrial action causes; to withhold their pay; and, where the breach is sufficiently serious, to dismiss them without notice (although, depending upon the circumstances, employees may then be entitled to claim unfair dismissal).[2] However, the employer cannot obtain a remedy to force *employees* to work according to their contracts; the Trade Union and Labour Relations (Consolidation) Act 1992, s 236 prevents a court from ordering an employee[3] to work by way of an order for specific performance of the contract of employment or an injunction restraining a breach or threatened breach. The law also regulates formal 'no strike' agreements; under s 180 of that Act, the terms of a collective agreement which prohibit or restrict the right of workers to engage in a strike or other industrial action cannot be incorporated into an individual contract unless specified conditions are met.[4] A lock-out of workers by an employer may constitute a breach of the individual contract if workers are not given the notice of termination to which they are entitled; if it is a breach, workers may be entitled to loss of wages and other contractual benefits, at least where they can show that they were ready and willing to work during the lock-out period. As we discussed in Chapter 1, the Human Rights 1998 requires the courts to interpret the employer's managerial prerogative and the corresponding duty on employees to obey lawful and reasonable orders in a way which is compatible with the 'Convention rights'.[5] This may be material in assessing whether employers are entitled to issue a particular instruction to their workers (to submit to intimate body searches, for example), and whether workers have a correlative obligation to obey: a collective refusal to comply may not be regarded as a breach of contract if the employer had no contractual authority to issue the instruction in the first place.[6] However, for the reasons we explain in para **1.6** the current jurisprudence relating to the ECHR does not support the view that an entitlement to strike or take other forms of industrial action can, as such, be derived from the Convention, in contrast to the position under ILO Conventions 87 and 98, and the explicit protection accorded to the right to strike by the ICESPR and the ESC. If domestic courts follow this jurisprudence, rather than being persuaded to take a broader view of the right to freedom of association under Article 11, the contractual powers of employers in the context of industrial action will not be regarded as modified by the terms of Article 11, nor will the exercise by employers of their contractual powers constitute an interference with the exercise of the right.

---

1. It may also be crucial to the liability of dispute organisers in tort: see para **6.2** *et seq.* Surprisingly, whether the industrial action constitutes a breach of contract is irrelevant to many statutory rights: see para **6.91** *et seq.*

2. See para **6.92** *et seq.*

3. See App 1 for the definition of 'employee'. It would probably be difficult to persuade a court to grant specific performance of a contract by an individual worker, even if not an employee, on the extended application of the principle that this would 'turn contracts of service into contracts of slavery': *De Francesco v Barnum* (1890) 45 ChD 430, Fry LJ at 438.

4. For the definition of 'collective agreement', see para **4.70**. In practice, 'no-strike' agreements are likely to add little to existing constraints on workers: see para **6.84**.

5. This is derived from s 6(1), (3)(a); see further para **1.18**.

6. In the case of 'public authorities' (or 'pure' public authorities at least: see paras **1.16** and **1.17**), issuing an order to violate the Convention rights of others could be regarded as an unlawful act for the purposes of HRA 1998, s 6, and the order therefore one which an employee is entitled not to obey: see *Gregory v Ford* [1951] 1 All ER 121; *Lister v Romford Ice and Cold Storage Co Ltd* [1957] AC 555 (Viscount Simonds); *Morrish v Henlys (Folkstone) Ltd* [1973] ICR 482; in the case of other employers the argument rests on the points made in para **1.18** above. For discussion of the effect of failure to obey an order on unfair dismissal rights, see para **6.93**.

The Effect on the Individual Contract

Strikes

6.82 The courts have generally assumed that a strike, as a total cessation of work, will always constitute a breach of the contract of employment, regardless of the circumstances which provoked it.[1] Whether or not giving notice of a strike changes the position depends upon the terms of the notice given. The notice may explicitly evince an intention to break the contract, so enabling the employer to treat it as an anticipatory breach. Conversely, it may express an intention to terminate the contract. In that event, provided that a period of notice of sufficient length in relation to the individual participant has been given,[2] and that notice has expired before strike action begins, there will be no breach because the contract will have ended (provided that there are no additional constraints on termination).[3] However, it is rare for this to happen, and for good reason: collective resignation would be a very unwise course for workers to take, given that they would thereby forfeit their statutory employment protection rights, such as the maintenance of continuity of employment and any protection which they may be accorded against unfair dismissal.[4] In many cases, strike notices merely express an intention 'to strike', thereby leaving their legal effect for determination by the courts. There are powerful dicta which suggest that such notices should be regarded as notice of intended breach rather than of contractual termination, on the ground that strikers do not intend to leave their employment but, rather, to remain on terms other than those on offer by the employer.[5] The loss of individual statutory employment protection rights which would result from resignation reinforces the argument that ambiguous notices should be interpreted in this way.[6] In *Boxfoldia Ltd v NGA*,[7] Saville J broke with the conventional understanding in asserting that the meaning and effect of the words used in a strike notice should be examined in their context, with no preference for a particular construction. However, the details of his judgment indicate that even on this view the court is unlikely to find that notice of collective termination has been given without clear evidence of this. The union had given the employers by letter '14 days' notice of withdrawal of all NGA members' labour from the company'. The company claimed that the union had induced the employees to breach their contracts of employment and that, as this had not been preceded by a ballot, the union was liable in tort for damages. The union argued that the letter gave contractual notice of termination on behalf of all the NGA's members. Saville J considered that 'withdrawal of labour' was capable of referring to notice of termination, but on the facts found that this was not the case: the letter did not purport to be written by the union on behalf of or as agent for the employees, it did not communicate any decision by them to terminate their contracts, nor to give on their behalf the appropriate termination notice stipulated in their contracts. This finding suggests that, despite Saville J's earlier remarks, he, too, in practice required clear evidence in order to find that notice to terminate had been given. He also observed that there was nothing in the union's rules which gave it the requisite authority to terminate contracts on its members' behalf, and he refused to imply such authority from the union's power to instruct members to take industrial action and to publicise that instruction. On this reasoning, in the absence of express authority for a union to terminate its members' contracts, each striker would need to give notice of termination of employment on an individual basis or expressly authorise the union to give such notice on his or her behalf.[8] Where employees are required to give notice of differing lengths either of these procedures would be a complex organisational exercise. In view of the serious consequences for individuals of collective resignation, it is desirable that such obstacles exist to unions purporting to terminate their members' contracts of employment. It has been argued extra-judicially by Patrick Elias QC (now Elias J) that a defensive strike in response to a continuing repudiatory breach of contract by an employer should not be treated as a breach of contract by employees.[9] Two separate grounds are given for this. The first is that employees can lawfully initiate the strike by 'concerted constructive dismissals' which, provided that it is made clear that these are in response to the employer's repudiatory breach, would need no period of notice.[10] He argues that this would then allow employees to claim wrongful dismissal if not subsequently reinstated and (more tentatively) that they would not at this point be 'taking part' in industrial action and so would not thereby jeopardise their unfair dismissal rights. As it stands, this argument is open to the objection which we discuss above as to the inadvisability of employees terminating their contracts of employment. However, it could be invoked for the purposes of unfair dismissal to support the argument that the employees have been constructively dismissed because their existing contracts of employment have terminated prior to the industrial action starting, even though they remain in the employment.[11] However, if participants in industrial action wished to exercise their unfair dismissal rights they would need to be mindful of the time limit for claiming.[12] Elias's second argument is based upon the proposition that, by analogy with the position of employees, if the employer is not prepared to provide the whole of the consideration which is due to the employee under the contract of employment (for example, by cutting wages) the employee has the right to refuse to work.[13] A further possibility in relation to strike notices is that they may have the effect of suspending the contract of employment. This occurs in many legal systems, but, in the absence of statutory provisions, would require the presence of a contractual term giving employees the right to suspend.[14] It has been argued that if the terms of a collective agreement which forbids industrial action until a disputes procedure has been exhausted are incorporated into individual contracts then, on exhaustion of this procedure, a right to strike could be implied,[15] but there is no authority to support this proposition and we doubt that it could successfully be argued.

---

1. See, for example, Ewing, 1991. For a contrary argument, see Elias, 1994, summarised below.

2. The contractual period, subject to the minimum period set out in ERA 1996, s 86(2), where applicable.

3. It is possible that a 'no-strike' agreement may restrict the right of workers collectively to terminate their contracts during a dispute, but this restriction would need to have been incorporated in the contract of employment; see TULRCA 1992, s 180, discussed at para **6.84**.

4. See para **6.91** *et seq.*

5. *Rookes v Barnard* [1964] AC 1129, HL, Lord Devlin at 1204; *J T Stratford and Son Ltd v Lindley* [1965] AC 269 HL, Lord Denning at 285.. To date, the courts have not treated showing an intention to participate on a threatened or rolling strike if and when called upon to do so as a breach of contract: see *Ticehurst and Thompson v British Telecommunications plc* [1992] IRLR 219, CA.

6. See para **6.91** *et seq.*; see also *Simmons v Hoover Ltd* [1977] ICR 61 at 69, EAT, and *Barretts and Baird (Wholesale) Ltd v IPCS* [1987] IRLR 3 at 8, QBD.

7. [1988] IRLR 383, QBD.

8. See also *Ideal Casements Ltd v Shamsi* [1972] ICR 408, NIRC, where the need for authorisation by the rules for the giving of any form of strike notice by union officials was made clear. Custom and practice may also provide sufficient authority: *Heaton's Transport (St Helens) Ltd v TGWU* [1972] ICR 308, HL.

9. Elias, 1994. In *Simmons v Hoover* [1977] ICR 61 it was suggested that strikes in opposition to changes imposed by the employer in breach of contract should not be

treated as *repudiatory* breaches of the contract, but other judges have refused to accept even this view: *Wilkins v Cantrell and Cochrane (GB) Ltd*, [1978] IRLR 483, EAT; *Marsden v Fairey Stainless Ltd* [1979] IRLR 103, EAT.

10. *Ibid.*, 259. In *Wilkins v Cantrell and Cochrane (GB) Ltd*, above, the EAT held that going on strike in response to a repudiatory breach of contract by the employer should not be regarded as a termination of the contract. To the extent that the judgment may be taken to imply that employees are not in law entitled as part of a concerted campaign to terminate their contracts in response to a repudiatory breach, Elias argues that it is erroneous.

11. See *Hogg v Dover College* [1990] ICR 39, EAT; *Alcan Extrusions v Yates* [1996] IRLR 327, EAT.

12. A complaint must be presented to the employment tribunal before the end of the period of three months beginning with the effective date of termination (defined ERA 1996, s 97), or within such further period as the tribunal considers reasonable in a case where it is satisfied that it was not reasonably practicable for the complaint to be presented before the end of that period of three months: ERA 1996, s 111(2). See App 2 for the meaning of not 'reasonably practicable' in this context.

13. Authority for this is drawn from Lord Templeman's dictum in *Miles v Wakefield Metropolitan Borough District Council* [1987] IRLR 193 at 198 that '[i]f the employer declines to pay, the worker need not work' which Elias extends to the whole of the consideration.

14. Lord Denning's attempt in *Morgan v Fry* [1968] 2 QB 710 at 728 to introduce a general doctrine of suspension did not succeed: see *Simmons v Hoover Ltd* [1977] ICR 61, EAT. As Ewing, 1991 points out at 5–6, Lord Denning's approach would not, itself, protect employees without employers being additionally constrained from terminating their contracts with due notice.

15. Hepple, 1981b, para 495; see further para **6.84** for 'no-strike agreements'.

Industrial action short of a strike

6.83 Industrial action frequently falls short of a complete withdrawal of labour. Its effect upon the contract of employment depends upon its nature. Sometimes a refusal to perform a particular duty, or to handle particular goods, as instructed by the employer will clearly constitute a breach. Where it is not apparent that it does constitute a breach, the implied duty of co-operation may lead the courts to conclude that the employee should nevertheless obey the instruction to perform the task, even if the task in question constitutes the very subject-matter of the dispute.[1] Where the dispute concerns the imposition by the employer of new methods of performing work which the workforce refuses to accept, the court will have to decide whether the employer is contractually entitled to impose the change; if the methods can be viewed as different methods of performing the same task, rather than as a wholly different job, refusal to comply with the instruction will constitute a breach of contract.[2] An overtime ban will be a breach of contract if the employer is contractually entitled to demand overtime work; it will probably not be if overtime is voluntary on the worker's part, but, as we discuss below, the matter cannot be regarded as free from doubt.[3] A 'work-to-rule' is likely to be viewed as a breach of the implied duty of fidelity or co-operation, at least where the rulebook is construed as containing the lawful instructions of the employer to its workers on how they are to work. Authority for this view is given by *Secretary of State for Employment v ASLEF (No 2)*.[4] Although the decision does not mean that every work-to-rule will automatically be viewed as a breach of contract, the range of dicta in the case provide generous ammunition for the view that it will. A go-slow is likely also to be viewed as a breach.[5] The position where industrial action takes the form of a withdrawal of 'goodwill' or 'co-operation' depends upon the circumstances. In *Ticehurst and Thompson v British Telecommunications plc* the Court of Appeal affirmed that the implied term of faithful service was breached:

> when the employee does an act, or omits to do an act, which would be within her contract and the discretion allowed to her not to do, or to do, as the case may be, and the employee so acts or omits to do the act, not in honest exercise of choice or discretion for the faithful performance of her work but in order to disrupt the employer's business or to cause the most inconvenience that can be caused.[6]

This case concerned a managerial employee, but the dictum seems likely to be applied, *mutatis mutandis*, to all categories of worker.[7] Like Lord Denning MR in the *ASLEF* case, the judgment emphasises the intent with which an act is done; the court left open the position 'if the ill-intentioned course of conduct is shown to have had no significant consequences adverse to the employer and to be incapable of causing any such adverse consequences in future',[8] but the emphasis upon intent suggests that even this is likely to be deemed a breach. On this basis, even a ban on voluntary overtime could constitute a breach of the contract of employment if employees' refusal to provide it was deliberately designed to cause disruption, a view which seems to be extending the duty of co-operation beyond its legitimate limits. Finally, it should be noted that for industrial action short of a strike, giving notice cannot change its legal consequences; if the action itself breaches the contract, notice merely constitutes notice of intended breach.

---

1. See, in particular, *Sim v Rotherham Metropolitan Borough Council* [1986] IRLR 391, ChD; *Metropolitan Borough of Solihull v NUT* [1985] IRLR 211, ChD. See generally Fredman and Morris, 1987.

2. See, for example, *Cresswell v Board of Inland Revenue* [1984] IRLR 190, ChD. Where workers dispute the employers' right to force a change upon them, their only safe recourse is to the courts: see *MacPherson v London Borough of Lambeth* [1988] IRLR 470, ChD. However, their chances of obtaining an interim injunction to restrain the alleged variation of their contracts may not be great, and if the case went to full trial

it is difficult to predict what damages, if any, could be obtained. See also Deakin and Morris, 1998, 331–332.

3. The possibility that it could be a breach arises from the 'disruptive intent' approach in *Ticehurst and Thompson v British Telecommunications plc* [1992] IRLR 219, CA, discussed below.

4. [1972] QB 455. A number of grounds were offered for this view, including an implied term that the employee will not seek to obey lawful instructions in a wholly unreasonable way which has the effect of disrupting the system, the efficient running of which he is employed to ensure (Roskill LJ at 509), and an implied term that the employee must serve the employer faithfully with a view to promoting those commercial interests for which he is employed (Buckley LJ at 498). For Lord Denning it was the motive with which the act was done which rendered it unlawful (492), although this runs counter to the general principle that a bad motive does not render an otherwise lawful act unlawful. See Napier, 1972 for a discussion of the principles underlying the judgment in this case.

5. In *General Engineering Services Ltd v Kingston and St Andrew Corpn* [1988] 3 All ER 867, PC, at 869, a go-slow by firemen was classed as a 'wrongful repudiation of an essential obligation of their contract of employment' and their employer was not vicariously liable for their default.

6. [1992] IRLR 219, CA, Ralph Gibson LJ (with whom the other judges agreed) at 225.

7. The court stated (at 225) that it was necessary to imply into the contract of a manager who is given charge of the work of other employees an obligation to serve the employer faithfully within the requirements of the contract, a formulation put forward by Buckley LJ in *Secretary of State for Employment v ASLEF (No 2)*, above, note 4, at 498. The latter case was not concerned with managers and the implied term applies more widely than such groups.

8. Ralph Gibson LJ at 225.

The effect of 'no strike' agreements

6.84 In some areas of the private sector, collective agreements have been concluded which prohibit or restrict resort to industrial action.[1] These agreements attracted considerable controversy within the union movement at one time because of the symbolic significance of limiting recourse to industrial action. In practice, the legal effect of such agreements has been minimal at both the individual and the collective levels. At the collective level, if these agreements were to be legally enforceable, a party in breach would be liable to an injunction and to damages, and a union defendant would not be subject to the statutory limits on damages in tort.[2] In practice, however, most agreements have been no exception to the general practice not to insert the express statement of intent to render collective agreements legally enforceable.[3] In relation to the individual worker, because industrial action almost always constitutes a breach of the individual employment contract (see para **6.82** *et seq.*) a 'no-strike' agreement is unlikely to alter the legal position; the only additional constraint which it might impose is if it restricts the right of workers collectively to terminate their contracts during a strike.[4] In order to bind individual workers a 'no-strike' agreement must first be incorporated into the individual contract. The requirement for incorporation means that the restriction must be in a form which can be translated into an individual obligation rather than being one which is essentially collective in its nature.[5] A clause which merely states that 'there shall be no strikes or lockouts until the procedure for the settlement of disputes has been exhausted' seems unlikely to be capable of such translation. It is unclear what the nature of the obligation on the individual would be, and there is the additional difficulty that disputes procedures can usually be invoked only by the collective parties. More likely to be effective is a clause which attempts directly to translate the obligation into individual terms, such as a clause which states that there is incorporated in the contract of each employee a provision that during the course of any negotiations, conciliation or arbitration, he or she will not participate in any strike or other forms of industrial action.[6] However, even if the clause is appropriate for incorporation, additional statutory requirements must be met. The Trade Union and Labour Relations (Consolidation) Act 1992 provides that any terms of a collective agreement which prohibit or restrict the right of workers to engage in a strike or other industrial action, or have the effect of prohibiting or restricting that right, shall not form part of the individual contract unless the collective agreement is in writing; contains a provision expressly stating that those terms shall or may be incorporated into the individual contract; is reasonably accessible at his or her place of work to the worker to whom it applies and available for him or her to consult during working hours; and each trade union party to the agreement is independent.[7] The employer cannot contract out of these provisions either with the union or the individual worker.[8] Clauses in no-strike agreements which attempt to incorporate their provisions into individual contracts have been rare.[9] On occasion, employers have attempted to require employees to sign undertakings that they will not participate, or take any further part, in disputes as a condition of being allowed to return to work. The courts have held that a refusal to give such an undertaking does not, of itself, constitute a breach of the contract of employment.[10]

---

1. See Bassett, 1987; Lewis, 1990. In addition, in 1997 a collective agreement between management and unions at Government Communications Headquarters (GCHQ) committed the unions not to induce or authorise any form of industrial action by GCHQ staff if this would disrupt GCHQ operations, such a question to be determined by the Secretary of State. Entry into this agreement was the price which the unions paid for the restoration of staff rights to join national civil service unions after a ban was imposed on such membership in 1984: see Morris, 1985b.

2. See para **6.52** *et seq.*

3. Lewis, 1990, 38. The agreement at GCHQ referred to in note 1 above, unusually, is contractually binding. See para **4.70** for the provisions governing the legal status of collective agreements.

4. See para **6.82** for the argument (unsupported by authority) that where a disputes procedure whose terms had been incorporated into the individual contract had been exhausted a right to strike could be implied.

5. Cf. *National Coal Board v NUM* [1986] IRLR 439, ChD.

6. Lewis, 1990, 51.

7. TULRCA 1992, s 180. 'Strike' and 'industrial action' are not defined in this context. See para **4.70** for the definition of a 'collective agreement', App 1 for the definition of 'worker', and paras **2.6** and **2.7** for the definition of an 'independent trade union'.

8. TULRCA 1992, s 180(3).

9. Lewis, 1990, 37–38.

10. See *Ticehurst and Thompson v British Telecommunications plc* [1992] IRLR 219 at 228. *Chappell v Times Newspapers Ltd* [1975] ICR 145 also lends support to this view.

Employer Responses to Industrial Action in Breach of Contract

Dismissal

6.85 An employer may summarily dismiss a worker who is taking industrial action if the breach of contract is sufficiently serious to constitute a repudiation of the contract. This depends upon the facts. In general, strikes have been regarded as repudiatory.[1] It has been suggested, however, that strikes in opposition to changes made by the employer which breach the contract would not be repudiatory,[2] but other judges have refused to accept this view.[3] It is arguable that a protest strike of very short duration (for example, for a day or less) should not, without more, be considered a repudiation of the contract, but such authority as there is on the point suggests the contrary.[4] For industrial action short of a strike, a refusal to perform only a minor part of the employee's total duties should not, in principle, be seen as sufficiently serious to constitute repudiation, but it is difficult to predict how a court will view such action.[5] Where a breach is not repudiatory, an employer must give the requisite notice, and comply with any other contractual conditions, to terminate the contract lawfully. Where the employer fails to do this, however, the remedy would almost certainly be confined to damages; the discretionary power to grant injunctive relief against dismissal is exercised only in exceptional circumstances,[6] and the courts are unlikely to exercise it when employees cannot show that they are ready and willing to perform their side of the contract.[7] Any decision by an employer to dismiss employees should be taken in full cognisance of the unfair dismissal implications, which we discuss at para **6.92** *et seq.*

---

1. See *Simmons v Hoover Ltd* [1977] ICR 61 at 76, EAT.
2. *Ibid.* See also *Thompson v Eaton Ltd* [1976] ICR 336 at 342, EAT.
3. *Wilkins v Cantrell and Cochrane (GB) Ltd* [1978] IRLR 483, EAT; *Marsden v Fairey Stainless Ltd* [1979] IRLR 103, EAT. Cf the argument of Elias, 1994, summarised in para **6.82** above. Note ERA 1996, s 100(1)(d) in relation to employees who leave work for safety reasons, discussed at para **6.93.**
4. *Rasool v Hepworth Pipe Co Ltd* [1980] IRLR 88 (one-hour mass meeting during working hours without employer's consent a repudiatory breach of contract).
5. See *Wiluszynski v London Borough of Tower Hamlets* [1989] IRLR 259, CA, discussed at para **6.88**, where Nicholls LJ (at 264) with whom Mann LJ agreed, considered, *obiter*, that the claimants' refusal to answer councillors' queries was a repudiatory breach.
6. See, for example, *Irani v Southampton and South West Hampshire Area Health Authority* [1985] IRLR 203, ChD; *Robb v London Borough of Hammersmith and Fulham* [1991] IRLR 72, QBD, and see generally Deakin and Morris, 1998, 429–438.
7. In *Chappell v Times Newspapers Ltd* [1975] ICR 145, the Court of Appeal refused to grant an injunction to restrain employers from treating workers as having terminated their contracts of employment where the workers had been instructed by their union to take industrial action, although they had not yet breached their contracts as individuals, on the basis, *inter alia*, that in the light of union instructions they would not undertake to perform their part of the contract.

Damages

6.86 It is open to employers who suffer loss as a result of industrial action in breach of contract to sue each individual worker for the damages flowing from that breach, regardless of whether the breach is repudiatory.[1] However, each worker may be sued in contract only for the loss for which he or she was personally responsible.[2] In the case of assembly-line workers, for example, this would be the value of the lost production minus the costs which the employer would have had to incur as part of the process of production. Where the worker is a supervisor or a managerial worker, on the other hand, it may be harder to establish direct loss; the most likely measure is the extra cost to the employer of providing a replacement if this was necessary.[3] In practice, it has been extremely rare for employers to sue individual workers; in general they prefer to pursue a remedy in tort against the trade union or its officers. However, employers have been more willing in recent years to invoke the 'self-help' remedy of making some deduction from workers' pay (see para **6.87** *et seq.*), and in this context the existence of a right to sue for damages, even if it is not exercised as such, is significant.

---

1. For the principles which govern the measure of damages in contract see McGregor, 1997.
2. *National Coal Board v Galley* [1958] 1 WLR 16, CA. However, proof of inducing, fellow workers to break their contracts, or of conspiracy among workers to induce a breach, may give rise to liability in tort: see para **6.2** *et seq.* See also *Barretts and Baird (Wholesale) Ltd v IPCS* [1987] IRLR 3, QBD (discussed at para **6.8**), which suggests that a breach of contract *per se* could constitute unlawful means for the tort of interference with trade by unlawful means.
3. *National Coal Board v Galley*, above.

Withholding pay

6.87 The principles governing the circumstances in which employers may withhold pay from participants in industrial action are complex and not wholly consistent. It is clear that workers who go on strike have no right to be paid for the period of the strike. In addition, workers who refuse to comply with their full range of contractual obligations may be sent home without pay in the absence of any contractual term restricting the employer's right to do this.[1] It also seems that if partial working is imposed for only a proportion of the working week, employers may state that they are not prepared to accept less than the full range of duties and 'send the worker home' without pay for that proportion of the week. In *Miles v Wakefield Metropolitan District Council*[2] Mr Miles, a superintendent registrar of births, marriages and deaths, had refused to perform marriages on Saturday mornings for 14 months as part of a campaign for higher pay. He normally worked a 37-hour week, of which three hours were on Saturdays. The council told him that unless he was prepared to perform his full range of duties, he would not be required to attend work on Saturdays and would not be paid for doing so. Mr Miles nevertheless continued to do other work on Saturday mornings and when the council withheld three thirty-sevenths of his pay, he sued for the unpaid salary. The House of Lords held that the council was entitled to refuse his offer of reduced working on Saturdays, and his position was then the same as if he had withdrawn his labour completely for that period; he had no right to be paid for the work he had carried out on Saturdays. This decision is open to the objection that it conflicts with the common law approach that pay periods are non-divisible,[3] a point not addressed by any of their Lordships.

1. *Cresswell v Board of Inland Revenue* [1984] IRLR 190, ChD; see also *MacPherson v London Borough of Lambeth* [1988] IRLR 470, ChD; *Ticehurst and Thompson v British Telecommunications plc* [1992] IRLR 219, CA. However, in *Ticehurst* it was stated that evincing an intention to respond to a strike call by the union, if and when made, would not of itself have entitled the employers to refuse to permit the employee to work in a situation where the value of services received would not be reduced by the risk that at some future date the employee might refuse to perform her contract.

2. [1987] IRLR 193, HL; see also *Jakeman v South West Thames Regional Health Authority and London Ambulance Service* [1990] IRLR 62, QBD, where pay was withheld for periods for which the employer had refused to accept partial performance of duties. Mandatory interlocutory relief was sought by the claimant employees and refused.

3. *Cutter v Powell* (1795) 6 Term Rep 320. Cf also *Sim v Rotherham Metropolitan Borough Council* [1986] IRLR 391, ChD. See further Deakin and Morris, 1998, 291–296.

6.88 Where an employer allows workers to continue working on a restricted basis, the legal position as regards the employee's right to payment is confused. In *Royle v Trafford Borough Council*,[1] Park J refused to allow the council to deprive a teacher working restrictively of his entire wage on the basis that, having accepted imperfect performance, it could not then refuse to pay him anything for this. Another line of authority, however, holds that workers are not entitled under their contracts to any payment whatsoever. This view received support from Lords Templeman and Brightman, *obiter*, in *Miles*, although they considered that employees could claim payment on a *quantum meruit* basis for the amount and value of the work they had performed,[2] a view which was contested by Lord Bridge who questioned whether entitlement to a *quantum meruit* could replace entitlement to remuneration at the contractual rate.[3] It also accords with the principle upheld by the Court of Appeal in *Henthorn and Taylor v Central Electricity Generating Board*.[4] Here, the employers had refused to pay manual workers any wages for days when they were working to rule. The court rejected claims by two employees for unpaid wages on the basis that in order to claim money due under the contract, the claimants had first to prove that they themselves were willing to perform their contracts. Because they could not do this, they had no remedy. This view has been criticised on the ground, *inter alia*, that willingness to perform the contract is not relevant to a claim for money due in debt,[5] although it would not preclude a counterclaim. Argument may sometimes arise whether the employer has accepted imperfect performance. In *Wiluszynski v London Borough of Tower Hamlets*[6] Mr Wiluszynski, an estates officer in the council's housing directorate, as part of a campaign of limited industrial action, refused to answer queries from council members as he was contractually obliged to do. The council had informed him and other relevant employees that their presence on the premises was not required until they were prepared to resume normal working, and that were they to attend for work and undertake limited working this would be regarded as unauthorised and undertaken in a purely voluntary capacity. Mr Wiluszynski continued to attend work during the five weeks the action lasted, performing all his other duties. On resuming his normal duties, it took him about three hours to deal with the backlog of inquiries. When Mr Wiluszynski sued for unpaid salary, the Court of Appeal rejected the argument that the council had acquiesced in his work and taken the benefit of it; it had not given him any directions to work so as to contradict the statement that it would regard any work as voluntary, and he could not have been misled as to the genuineness of the employer's pronouncement. The council could not be expected physically to prevent the relevant staff from entering the premises. Mr Wiluszynski had failed to discharge a material part of his contractual duties[7] and the council was entitled to withhold his entire salary for the period. The reasoning in this case is open to question; the court relied upon the principle that employees who sue for remuneration must show that they are ready and willing to discharge their own obligations, which it took to be the principle upheld in *Miles.* Yet, if this were the case, there would be nothing to prevent an employer accepting imperfect performance and still refusing to pay, making discussion of whether there had been acceptance of such performance irrelevant. The combined effect of *Miles* (see para **6.87**) and *Wiluszynski* may suggest that those organising industrial action short of a strike would be best advised to restrict sanctions to limited quantifiable periods of time, with full performance in between. If employers wish to maintain services, whilst also making some deduction, this may satisfy honour on both sides.[8] Even then, however, the reasoning in *Wiluszynski* implies that employers may still be within their rights to withhold the entire salary on the basis that employees were not ready and willing to perform the contract in its entirety. There is a fundamental and unresolved conflict here. *Wiluszynski*, in particular, presents considerable problems for unions with members in essential services who may wish to maintain an emergency service yet would be unwilling to do this for no remuneration whatsoever. We would suggest that the most appropriate approach to the situation where employers accept partial performance is to argue that the employers have thereby waived their right to claim non-performance of the contract, without prejudice to a claim in damages for the loss caused by the employee's breach.

---

1. [1984] IRLR 184, QBD.
2. *Miles v Wakefield Metropolitan Council* [1987] IRLR 193, HL, Lord Templeman at 199; Lord Brightman at 195.
3. *Ibid.*, 195. See also Burrows, 1993, 280, who considers that the strength of the dicta by Lords Templeman and Brightman is weakened because it was not made clear that a

restitutionary analysis could only come into play once the employer had elected to terminate the contract.

4. [1980] IRLR 361, CA. See also *MacPherson v London Borough of Lambeth* [1988] IRLR 470, ChD. See para **6.89** below for the implications of industrial action on entitlement to the national minimum wage.

5. See Napier, 1986.

6. [1989] IRLR 259, CA. See also *Jakeman v South West Thames Regional Health Authority and London Ambulance Service* [1990] IRLR 62, QBD (mandatory interim relief refused to claimant employees who argued that partial performance of their contracts had been accepted by the employers).

7. The court rejected the view that the breach was insubstantial; although the amount of work involved was comparatively small, it was of considerable constitutional importance (Fox LJ at 262).

8. See McLean, 1990.

6.89 In *Royle v Trafford Borough Council*[1] the employee successfully challenged the employer's right to withhold the entire wage where it had accepted restricted working. There have been other cases where employees have challenged the employer's right to make even a partial deduction from wages. These arguments have not met with success. However the only attempt to provide a principled justification for deductions in this context has come from Scott J in *Sim v Rotherham Metropolitan Borough Council*.[2] Here, the defendant education authority had deducted a sum from the claimant teacher's salary to represent her failure to provide cover for an absent colleague for a 35-minute period during a campaign of industrial action. She sued to recover this amount claiming, first, that she had no contractual obligation to provide cover and, secondly, that if she had, the employer's remedy lay only in damages. Scott J held that her failure to provide cover constituted a breach of contract.[3] He also affirmed, however, that, given that she had been allowed to continue working, the contractual obligations on both sides remained on foot and she was entitled to her salary.[4] However, her claim to payment in full was subject to the employer's cross-claim for damages for the loss flowing from her breach. Applying the doctrine of 'equitable set-off', Scott J held that it would be unjust to allow the claimant to proceed without taking account of the loss to the employer, which in this case it was agreed was no less than the sum the employers had deducted. This decision allows employers to decide what sums reflect the damages to which they are entitled and puts the onus on the worker to challenge the deduction. In the case of assembly-line workers, for example, this could in theory be considerably more than the employee's contractual wages. The reluctance of the courts to grant interim relief during disputes to order the employer to make withheld payments compounds the difficulties for employees who may suffer hardship as a result.[5]

Moreover, the restrictions on deductions from wages imposed by the Employment Rights Act 1996 do not apply to deductions made on account of industrial action.[6] This means that employees who are dismissed for instituting legal proceedings on the matter who lack the requisite period of continuous employment will not qualify for protection against unfair dismissal.[7] The difficulties of quantifying loss in the case of clerical, managerial or professional workers[8] have not prevented this being a significant weapon for employers in the education sector, and in white collar areas of the civil service and local government where industrial action has traditionally taken the form of industrial action short of a strike.[9] It should be noted that all time during which a worker is 'engaged in taking industrial action' is excluded in respect of the time for which the national minimum wage is payable.[10] Thus, workers such as Wiluszynski would have had no minimum wage entitlement to the work which they actually did.[11] There is no definition of 'industrial action' in this context, and on the basis of the interpretation of this concept in relation to unfair dismissal even a ban on non-contractual duties could fall within it (see para **6.93**). By analogy with the unfair dismissal provisions, disputes may arise as to when a worker is 'engaged in taking' industrial action; it would seem to be confined to times when the worker individually is working restrictively (going-slow, for example), but it could conceivably be argued to extend to any period during which the worker has evinced an intention to participate in industrial action (such as a programme of rolling strikes) if called upon to do so.[12]

---

1. [1984] IRLR 184, QBD.

2. [1986] IRLR 391, ChD.

3. See Fredman and Morris, 1987, for a critique of this reasoning.

4. The difficulties presented by *Henthorn and Taylor v Central Electricity Generating Board* [1980] IRLR 361, CA (see para **6.88**) were not discussed.

5. See *Jakeman v South West Thames Regional Health Authority and London Ambulance Service* [1990] IRLR 62, QBD

6. ERA 1996, s14(5). In *Sunderland Polytechnic v Evans* [1993] IRLR 196 the EAT held, after examining Hansard, that an employment tribunal had no jurisdiction to examine whether a deduction from wages due to industrial action was authorised by the contract.

7. It is automatically unfair to dismiss an employee for the assertion of a 'relevant statutory right' (ERA 1996, s 104), and there is no minimum qualifying period of employment: ERA 1996, s 108. The protection does not apply, however, to infringements of contractual rights: see *Mennell v Newell and Wright (Transport Contractors) Ltd.* [1997] IRLR 519, CA.

8. In *Royle* above, note 1, a teacher had refused to admit an additional five pupils into his class of 31. A deduction of five-thirty-sixths was said to represent the 'notional value' of the services he had failed to perform. See also Morris and Rydzkowski, 1984, 160–161 on deductions in the NHS during the 1982 dispute. In *Jakeman v South West*

Thames Regional Health Authority and London Ambulance Service [1990] IRLR 62 QBD, the employer was seeking to rely on the losses it would otherwise incur in calling upon other agencies, such as the police and army, to help it out.

9. Elgar and Simpson, 1992, 50.

10. National Minimum Wage Regulations 1999, SI 1999/584, regs 15(6), 17(2), 18(2) and 21(4).

11. Simpson 1999a, 17–18; see also Simpson 1999b.

12. See para **6.94**.

Lock-outs

6.90 A lock-out is likely to constitute a breach of contract on the part of an employer unless (exceptionally) there is provision for suspension of the contract during a lock-out or notice of appropriate length to terminate the contract is given; merely giving notice to 'lock-out' may not be sufficient as this, like strike notice, can be interpreted as notice of intended breach.[1] Provided that employees can show that they were ready and willing to work during this period, they would be able to sue for any losses to them resulting from the breach.[2] Whether or not the breach is sufficiently serious to constitute a repudiation of the contract will depend on the facts;[3] the duration of the lock-out is likely to be a material factor here. Even if a lock-out is repudiatory, however, an employee would be ill-advised to resign in response; although they would have a wrongful dismissal claim based on breach of contract, there is no protection against unfair dismissal for employees dismissed during a lock-out unless the employer discriminates between 'relevant employees' or dismisses for a limited range of automatically unfair reasons,[4] and for the purposes of statutory redundancy payments an employee who leaves during a lock-out cannot claim to have been constructively dismissed.[5] This leaves the extraordinary situation that an employer can seek to impose new terms and conditions upon its workforce and then lock out with relative impunity those who do not accept them.[6] As we discuss in para **6.93** and **6.95**, the line between a strike and a lock-out, which is particularly crucial in the light of the new protection against dismissal for taking 'protected industrial action',[7] may not always be an easy one to draw. Where a proportion of an employer's workforce is taking industrial action and it wishes to lock out the remainder, the limited authority which exists on this point suggests that in the absence of a contractual right to suspend employees in these circumstances, the lock-out will constitute a breach of contract unless the employees have evinced a definite intention of participating in the action. In *Ticehurst and Thompson v British Telecommunications Plc*[8] the Court of Appeal rejected the employers' argument that the employee's evinced intention of future participation in a campaign of rolling strikes would alone be sufficient ground for them to refuse to allow her to work during the dispute unless it could be argued that the present value of her services would be reduced by such a risk. Similarly, a refusal to give an undertaking not to participate in any further action will not, of itself, justify a lock-out.[9] However, if the employee's contract permits the employer to lay off employees whose workload is reduced due to industrial action by other workers, they may forfeit their right to a statutory guarantee payment.[10]

---

1. In *Sanders v Ernest A Neale Ltd* [1974] ICR 565, NIRC, the court assumed for the purposes of argument that a lock-out was a breach of contract by the employer; similarly in *Chappell v Times Newspapers Ltd* [1975] ICR 145, CA. However, the Court of Appeal decision in *Express and Star Ltd v Bunday* [1987] IRLR 422 assumes that a lock-out will not necessarily constitute a breach.

2. *Henthorn and Taylor v Central Electricity Generating Board* [1980] IRLR 361, CA.

3. *Cummings v Charles Connell and Co (Shipbuilders) Ltd* [1969] SLT 25, Ct of Session.

4. See paras **6.102** and **6.103**.

5. ERA 1996, s 136(1),(2); see further paras **6.92** *et seq.*

6. See K. Miller and C. Woolfson, 1994, for a description of the use of this tactic by Timex in 1993.

7. See para **6.98**.

8. [1992] IRLR 219, CA; see Ralph Gibon LJ at 227.

9. *Ibid.*, 228. Note, however, that the remedies available to a worker in this situation may be limited. In *Chappell v Times Newspapers Ltd* [1975] ICR 145, the Court of Appeal refused to grant an injunction to restrain an employer from treating workers as having terminated their contracts of employment on the basis that they could be called upon to take industrial action, the grounds being that, even if the employers' action was not lawful, these workers could not affirm that they were ready and willing to perform their side of the contract. In such a case the sole remedy would be a claim for unpaid wages or damages for breach of contract.

10. ERA 1996, s 29(3); see further para **6.107**.

INDUSTRIAL ACTION AND STATUTORY RIGHTS

Sources and General Principles

6.91 We described in paras **6.81** *et seq.*, the treatment of industrial action by the common law, which does not accord it any protected status in considering its effect on the contract of employment and on remedies for breach.[1] Perhaps more surprisingly, legislation, too, has not until recently accorded employees any

additional protection; indeed, those taking industrial action have risked prejudicing a number of their statutory rights. In relation to unfair dismissal, the prevailing philosophy of all governments has been to exclude dismissals taking
place during industrial disputes from the purview of employment tribunals. This
is currently reflected in the Trade Union and Labour Relations (Consolidation)
Act 1992 s 238, which states that tribunals have no jurisdiction to determine fairness where at the date of dismissal the applicant was taking part in a strike or
other industrial action or the employer was conducting or instituting a lock-out.
However there is a limited measure of protection against victimisation of particular employees in the case of 'non-unofficial' industrial action only:[2] jurisdiction
is restored to the tribunal if it is shown that the employer did not dismiss all the
participants at the establishment taking part in the action on a particular day or
re-engaged one or more such employees within a three-month period. In that
event, the tribunal will then determine fairness in the normal way (provided that
the employee otherwise qualifies to claim). More recently, tribunals have been
afforded jurisdiction where the employee was dismissed (or in a redundancy
case, selected for dismissal) for specified reasons. This jurisdiction applies
regardless of whether the employee would otherwise qualify to claim, and dismissal for any of these reasons is automatically unfair. The most wide-ranging
of these reasons, introduced by the Employment Relations Act 1999 and applicable only to 'non-unofficial' action, is where the individual has been induced to
commit an act which by virtue of s 219 of the Trade Union and Labour Relations
(Consolidation) Act 1992 is not actionable in tort (styled 'protected industrial
action').[3] It is automatically unfair to dismiss an employee for taking protected
industrial action within eight weeks of that employee commencing it, or at a later
date if either the employee had stopped taking industrial action within the eight
week period or the employer had failed to take such procedural steps as would
have been reasonable to resolve the dispute. Other grounds upon which dismissal or selection for redundancy will be automatically unfair in this context
include specified activities relating to health and safety; acting, or standing for
election as, an employee representative or representative of the workforce; on
the grounds of pregnancy or childbirth; or for reasons relating to family leave.
It is notable that dismissal for trade union membership or activities is not
included in this list, although it is automatically unfair outside the context of
industrial action (see para **3.3** *et seq.*). Other dismissal rights are also affected by
industrial action: the Employment Rights Act 1996 provides that participants
risk losing all or part of the statutory redundancy payment to which they may
otherwise be entitled.[4] Statutory rights to payment during statutory minimum
notice periods are also put in jeopardy; if the employer gives notice but then terminates the contract in response to a repudiatory breach of contract by the
employee (which can include industrial action) during the notice period, no payment will be due for the balance of the original notice period.[5] Furthermore,
those who suffer financial loss against a background of industrial action may be

denied access to payments to which they may be entitled in other contexts. The Employment Rights Act 1996 removes entitlement to a guarantee payment in respect of a workless day if the failure to provide work occurs in consequence of industrial action involving any employee of the employer or an associated employer.[6] Under the Social Security Contributions and Benefits Act 1992, employees are disqualified from receiving statutory sick pay if there is a stoppage of work due to a trade dispute at their place of employment unless they can prove no 'direct interest' in the dispute.[7] Finally the social security benefits to which strikers are entitled are limited; the Jobseekers Act 1995 provides that a person is not entitled to a jobseeker's allowance for any week which includes a day where there is a stoppage of work due to a trade dispute at his or her place of work which causes him or her not to be employed on that day unless he or she can show that he or she was 'not directly interested in the dispute',[8] and entitlement to income support for strikers and their families is also restricted.[9] In relation to many of these provisions, similar restrictions apply to employees who have been locked out by their employer. Dismissal rights apart, only the continuity provisions provide a measure of protection to strikers. A week during any part of which an employee takes part in a strike does not count for the purposes of calculating continuous employment, but, in contrast to the usual position when a week cannot be credited to an employee, continuity remains unbroken.[10] It is notable that for the majority of provisions, there is no statutory definition of 'strike' or 'lock-out', despite the crucial importance of these concepts, nor is there any meaningful definition of the term 'industrial action'.[11] Those definitions which are afforded are not always compatible. For the purpose of the unfair dismissal provisions, 'strike' has recently been defined as a 'concerted stoppage of work'.[12] For the purpose of the continuity provisions, however, 'strike' is defined much more narrowly, and means:

(a) the cessation of work by a body of employed persons acting in combination, or
(b) a concerted refusal, or a refusal under a common understanding, of any number of employed persons to continue to work for an employer in consequence of a dispute,

done as a means of compelling their employer or any employed person or body of employed persons, or to aid other employees in compelling their employer or any employed person or body of employed persons, to accept or not to accept terms or conditions of or affecting employment.[13]

Although this would extend to strikes in support of other employees, it would not apply to political or other stoppages whose purpose is not related to compelling acceptance of terms of or affecting employment.

'Lock-out' is defined in analogous terms and means:

(a) the closing of a place of employment,
(b) the suspension of work, or
(c) the refusal by an employer to continue to employ any number of persons employed by him in consequence of a dispute,

done with a view to compelling persons employed by the employer, or to aid another employer in compelling persons employed by him, to accept terms or conditions of or affecting employment.[14]

These definitions apply also to the provisions governing notice rights and redundancy payments outlined above. They are not applied by statute to other contexts, however, although in the absence of any other definition, they may be seen as having some persuasive authority by courts and tribunals.

---

1. For the reasons we indicated in para **6.81**, it is unlikely that the Human Rights Act 1998 will alter this position.

2. We use the inelegant term 'non-unofficial' for two reasons: first, because there is no statutory definition (or use in this context) of the term 'official' industrial action; and secondly, because 'unofficial' as defined in the Act does not correspond to the commonly understood meaning of that term.

3. TULRCA 1992, ss 238(2B), 238A. For the scope of s 219, see paras **6.21** *et seq.*

4. ERA 1996, ss 140, 143, 144.

5. *Ibid.*, s 91(4). The right to payment is also excluded if the employee gives notice but participates in a strike as defined in s 35(5) before the notice expires: s 91(2).

6. *Ibid.*, s 29(3). See para **6.89** for the implications of industrial action for entitlement to the national minimum wage.

7. Social Security Contributions and Benefits Act 1992, s 153(3), Sched 11.

8. Jobseekers Act 1995, s 14. The Jobseekers Act replaced earlier measures with broadly equivalent provisions.

9. Social Security Contributions and Benefits Act 1992, ss 126 and 127. The law of social security lies outside the scope of this work: see further Ogus, Barendt and Wikely, 1995, 132–142 and 494–498; Bonner *et al*, 1999. For discussions of the policy considerations which have influenced the development of the law in this area, see Ewing, 1991, chapters 5–8; Mesher and Sutcliffe, 1986; Durcan and McCarthy, 1974; Gennard and Lasko, 1974.

10. ERA 1996, s 216.

11. The only definition is in TULRCA 1992, s 62(6) (rights of union members in relation to industrial action ballots), and is tautologous in stating that it means 'a strike or other industrial action by persons employed under contracts of employment'.

12. TULRCA 1992, s 246.

13. ERA 1996, s 235(5).

14. *Ibid.*, s 235(4).

Unfair Dismissal

Where industrial action is not 'unofficial'

6.92 As we indicated in para **6.91** above, an employment tribunal has no juris-diction to determine the fairness of a claim for unfair dismissal where at the date of dismissal the complainant was taking part in a strike or other industrial action or the employer was conducting or instituting a lock-out other than in two broad sets of circumstances.[1] The first is where it is shown that the employer discrimi-nated between those defined as 'relevant employees' within the meaning of the statute. We discuss this exception in para **6.95**. It is important to emphasise that this applies only where the employee would otherwise qualify to claim, and merely requires the employer to defend the claim in the normal way. The second applies where the employee was dismissed (or, in a redundancy case, selected for dismissal) on one of a number of specified grounds; here, the normal qualifica-tions need not be met and the dismissal is automatically unfair. The most notable automatically unfair reason, since the Employment Relations Act 1999, is that the employee was dismissed for taking 'protected industrial action' during the first eight weeks of his or her participation in the action, or at a later date in spec-ified circumstances.[2] We discuss this important exception to the general principle in para **6.98** *et seq.*, and the other grounds upon which selection is automatically unfair in para **6.102**. Although the first exception is likely to become more signif-icant in practice than the general principle, we discuss the general principle first because much of the case law which has been developed in that context will be rel-evant to discussion of 'protected industrial action'. At the time of writing, the protection against unfair dismissal for taking industrial action applies only to 'employees', despite the fact that a 'trade dispute' is defined in terms of a dispute between 'workers' and their employer.[3] This falls short of what is required by the freedom of association principles of the ILO. Article 11 of the ECHR accords the right to join a trade union for the protection of his interests to 'everyone'. As we explained in para **1.6**, the current jurisprudence relating to this article suggests that interference with the exercise of the freedom to take industrial action would not constitute a violation of it. However, it is conceivable that a domestic court would be persuaded to take a broader view of what the right to join a trade union embraces. If it were to take the view that it extended to participation in industrial action, a worker who was dismissed or otherwise penalised by a 'public author-ity' for taking industrial action may be able to bring an action against it for act-ing incompatibly with a Convention right (see further paras **1.16** and **1.17**). Where a private employer acted in this way, a court or tribunal may be persuaded in borderline cases to take an expansive view of the concept of an 'employee' in fulfilment of its obligation to give effect to legislation in a way which is compati-ble with Convention rights where it is possible to do so,[4] but clearly there would be limits to what that approach could offer.

1. TULRCA 1992, s 238.
2. *Ibid.*, ss 238(2B), 238A.
3. *Ibid.*, s 244(1); see further para **6.20**. The Secretary of State is empowered to extend this protection more widely (ERA 1999, s 23), but at the time of writing this power has yet to be exercised in this (or any other) context
4. Human Rights Act 1998, s 3; see para **1.14**.

6.93 The exceptions specified in para **6.92** apart, the employment tribunal's jurisdiction to determine the fairness of a claim for unfair dismissal is excluded where at the date of dismissal the complainant was taking part in a strike or other industrial action or the employer was conducting or instituting a lock-out.[1] 'Date of dismissal' in this context means, where the employee's contract of employment was terminated by notice, the date on which the employer's notice was given, and in any other case the effective date of termination.[2] 'Date' has been interpreted to mean 'time' of dismissal in this context.[3] This means that once an employer knows that industrial action has ended, it cannot dismiss employees later that same day. The wording and context of the statute strongly suggest that participation in industrial action need not be the reason for dismissal for the general exclusion to apply; the crucial issue is whether, judged objectively, employees were taking part in it (or locked out) at the time they were dismissed, and this is now supported by authority.[4] Under current case law, there is no scope to argue that the industrial action was engineered or provoked by the unreasonable or even the unlawful conduct of the employer.[5] Whether or not there is a 'strike', 'lock-out' or 'industrial action' taking place has been said by the courts to be a question of fact for the employment tribunal, acting as an industrial jury, to decide. The Trade Union and Labour Relations (Consolidation) Act 1992 defines a strike (unhelpfully) as a 'concerted stoppage of work',[6] but leaves the other terms undefined. The Court of Appeal has instructed tribunals to give the words 'industrial action' 'their natural and ordinary meaning', an approach which means that one tribunal may decide that there is 'industrial action', another the opposite, on the same set of facts, with the scope for appeal being confined to the argument that the tribunal has given the term a meaning which it could not reasonably bear (or if there is no evidence to support the findings of fact).[7] In relation to a 'lock-out', and before the 1992 Act 'strike', the courts have looked to the definitions offered for continuity purposes (see para **6.91**) whilst emphasising that these definitions should not be applied exclusively,[8] and it may be difficult to decide into which category a particular situation falls. The difficulty in distinguishing between a strike and a lock-out is a particularly serious matter given that the definition of 'relevant employee' differs in each case (see further para **6.95**) and there is no protection afforded to employees who are dismissed while locked out equivalent to that accorded to employees dismissed for taking 'protected industrial action'. The Court of Appeal has rejected the argument that a lock-out requires a breach of contract on the part of the employer, taking the view that although in some cases this might be critical, its materiality also depends upon the facts.[9] Thus, if an employer unilaterally introduces new technology which employees refuse to use and they are then told not to return to work until they are so willing, this may equally be perceived as a strike or a lock-out. The *laissez-faire* attitude of the higher courts in this area has caused particularly grave difficulty in the context of 'industrial action', leading to some conflicting, and arguably perverse, decisions. Thus, for several years it was generally accepted that industrial action was a collective activity which could not be taken by one employee alone, a view which accords both with the emphasis upon combination and concert in the statutory definitions of a strike and with industrial reality.[10] In 1993, however, the EAT held that it was open to a tribunal to find that a single employee could be taking part in 'industrial action',[11] so potentially exposing an employee who refuses on one occasion to carry out an instruction by the employer to dismissal without statutory redress.[12] In the same case the EAT also refused to characterise as perverse the tribunal's finding that the threat of industrial action itself was 'industrial action' on the basis that there was no prospect of negotiation before the following day, despite earlier (and, in our view, correct) authority to the contrary.[13] Finally, the Court of Appeal has affirmed that industrial action need not constitute a breach of the contract of employment (although if it does not involve a repudiatory breach, due notice of termination must be given by the employer before dismissing the employee).[14] Thus, a refusal to work overtime because of a wage dispute could constitute industrial action, notwithstanding that employees were under no contractual obligation to do this work. The court considered that this could be distinguished from a refusal to work overtime for other reasons (for example, attendance at a football match or personal reasons) by reference to its purpose—to put pressure on the employer. However, this approach, again, does not offer a solution in that it is probably unduly narrow in excluding disruptive action in protest at government policies or a demonstration of solidarity.[15] From another perspective, the interpretation of 'industrial action' may now required to be modified in the light of the Human Rights Act 1998. As we indicated in para **1.18** and **6.81**, the employer's managerial prerogative and the employee's correlative duty to obey lawful and reasonable orders must be interpreted by the courts and tribunals in the light of Convention rights. It is submitted that the duty to give effect to legislation 'so far as it is possible to do so' in a way which is compatible with Convention rights imposed by s 3 requires courts and tribunals not to regard as 'industrial action' a refusal by workers to obey an order which interferes with the exercise of a Convention right where such refusal does not constitute a breach of the contract of employment. Finally, there is now a statutory distinction between industrial action and stopping work for safety reasons. It is automatically unfair to dismiss an employee where the principal reason was that the employee 'in circumstances of danger which the employee reasonably believed to be serious and imminent and which he [or she] could not reasonably have been expected to avert' left, or proposed to leave, or (while the danger persisted) refused to return to his or her place of work or any dangerous part of it.[16] However, employees who stop work in order to exert pressure on an employer to improve safety conditions outside this specific situation, or to support other workers whose safety is at risk, will not be protected and are likely to be viewed as taking part in industrial action. Moreover, the statute does not deal directly with the contractual position of the employee who stops work or the position in tort of any individual who induces employees to stop work, although these may now be regarded as subject to the employer's statutory duty to give effect to appropriate procedures to be followed in the event of serious and imminent danger to persons at work, including enabling them to stop work and to require them to be prevented from resuming work.[17]

---

1. TULRCA 1992, s 238.

2. TULRCA 1992, s 238(5).The 'effective date of termination' where the contract is terminated without notice means the date the termination takes effect, or for an employee employed under a fixed term contract which expires without being renewed under the same contract, the date on which the term expires: TULRCA 1992, s 239(1); ERA 1996, s 97.An ultimatum that unless employees present themselves for work on a specific day they will summarily be dismissed does not constitute 'notice' for this purpose: *Bolton Roadways Ltd v Edwards* [1987] IRLR 392, EAT.

3. *Heath and Hammersey v JF Longman (Meat Salesman)* Ltd [1973] IRLR 214, NIRC. It is in the interests of both parties to record the time when this information was received by the employer; indeed, if the parties are not face to face a union may be well advised to confirm any oral communication by fax for evidential purposes.

4. *Faust v Power Packing Casemakers Ltd* [1983] IRLR 117, CA, *per* Stephenson LJ at 121; *Bolton Roadways Ltd v Edwards*, above, note 2; *Manifold Industries Ltd v Sims* [1991] IRLR 242 EAT (state of the employer's knowledge as to whether the employee was taking part in industrial action therefore irrelevant); *Jenkins v P and O European Ferries (Dover) Ltd* [1991] ICR 652, EAT. Cf. *McKenzie v Crosville Motor Services Ltd* [1989] IRLR 516, where the EAT held that it was for the employer to show that the reason for dismissal was participation in industrial action. In *Jenkins* the EAT accepted that *McKenzie* had put an unwarranted 'gloss' on the wording of the statute.

5. *Wilkins v Cantrell and Cochrane (GB)* Ltd [1978] IRLR 483; *Marsden v Fairey Stainless Ltd* [1979] IRLR 103, EAT. The arguments articulated by Elias, 1994 (see para **6.82**) would produce a different result but these have yet to be tested in the courts.

6. TULRCA 1992, s 246. In *Connex South Eastern Ltd v RMT* [1999] IRLR 249, CA a ban on overtime and rest-day working was said to constitute a strike for the purposes of deciding whether the action was authorised in a ballot. This definition of 'strike' has

been excluded for the purposes (only) of the question on the voting paper: see para **6.39**.

7. *Express and Star Ltd v Bunday* [1987] IRLR 422, CA; *Faust v Power Packing Casemakers Ltd* [1983] IRLR 117, CA.

8. *Express and Star*, above. In relation to a strike, some cases also referred to the definition offered by Lord Denning in *Tramp Shipping Corpn v Greenwick Marine Inc* [1975] ICR 261 at 266, CA.

9. *Express and Star*, above.

10. *Bowater Containers Ltd v Blake* (27 May 1982, unreported), EAT; see also *Coates and Venables v Modern Methods and Materials Ltd* [1982] IRLR 318 at 323, CA per Eveleigh LJ; cf. *McCormick v Horsepower Ltd* [1981] IRLR 217, CA (individual employee could be said to be on strike but not the same strike as other workers because community of purpose lacking).

11. *Lewis and Britton v E Mason and Sons* [1994] IRLR 4.

12. This is highly unlikely to constitute 'protected industrial action: see para **6.98**.

13. *Midland Plastics v Till* [1983] IRLR 9, EAT.

14. *Faust v Power Packing Casemakers Ltd*, above, note 4.

15. See also *Rasool v Hepworth Pipe Co Ltd (No 2)* [1980] IRLR 137, EAT. Note that TULRCA 1992, ss 146 and 152, on the one hand, and s 238 on the other are mutually exclusive: *Drew v St Edmundsbury Borough Council* [1980] IRLR 459, EAT: see further para **3.6.**

16. ERA 1996, s 100(1)(d). No minimum period of employment is required and there is no maximum age limit: ss 108, 109. By analogy with the protection against dismissal on trade union grounds (see para **3.3** *et seq.*), where the employee is claiming in circumstances where he or she would not otherwise be able to do so the employee must show that the reason falls within the statutory protection. The EAT has held that 'danger' covers any danger, however it originates, so covering, for example, dangers caused by the action of a fellow employee: *Harvest Press Ltd v McCaffrey* [1999] IRLR 778. Note also s 100(1)(e) ('other persons' in this context has been held to extend to members of the public: *Masiak v City Restaurants (UK) Ltd* [1999] IRLR 780, EAT). There is no limit on the compensatory award for unfair dismissal where an employee is dismissed, or selected for redundancy in a 'redundancy case', for reasons relating to health and safety: ERA 1996, s 124(1A).

17. The Management of Health and Safety at Work Regulations 1999, SI 1999 No 3242, reg 8. Note also the implied term that employers will take reasonable care for the health and safety of their employees: see Deakin and Morris, 1998, 319–323. *Quaere* whether in relation to inducing breach of contract the defence of justification would be accepted: see para **6.3**.

6.94 The issue of whether an employee was 'taking part' in a strike or other industrial action is also primarily a question for the employment tribunal, with scope to appeal only if the words are given a meaning of which they are not 'reasonably capable'.[1] With that reservation in mind, the cases offer guidance on some of the issues which this term raises. First, when does an employee begin to 'take part' in industrial action? What of the employee who is not due to work on the day when industrial action commences? There is authority to suggest that employees may begin to take part before their contractual obligation to work arises if they have made clear that they will withdraw their labour at that point.[2] Secondly, when does participation cease? What if the employee falls sick, for example? In this connection, it has been held that 'once men [*sic*] have stated that they will apply sanctions and do so they may be regarded as applying the sanctions either until they are discontinued or until they indicate an intention of stopping them'.[3] However, there is no authority on the position in relation to 'rolling strikes', whereby one group of employees comes out on strike one day, another the next. Should all employees who may be called upon to strike at some point be treated as 'taking part' from the outset? Conversely, should employees who have already been on strike be treated as 'taking part' throughout because they intend to strike again should they be called upon to do so? The third problem is that of the employee who fails to cross a picket line, perhaps for fear of abuse by strikers: should he or she be regarded as 'taking part' in the action? In *Coates and Venables v Modern Methods and Materials Ltd*[4] the Court of Appeal supported an objective approach to this question: an employer is entitled to assume that any employee who does not come to work during a strike is taking part in it. Stephenson LJ appeared to consider that expressing disagreement with the strike may alter the position;[5] for Kerr LJ, it was actions only which were material, although he suggested that if an employee was absent at the beginning of a strike for reasons unconnected with it, such as sickness or holidays, he or she would not be 'taking part'.[6] However, in a later case the EAT held that employees who were lawfully absent when the action started would be capable of 'taking part' if they associated themselves with the strike, attended at the picket line, or took part in the other activities of the strikers with a view to furthering their aims; taking part in a strike did not require a breach of the contractual obligation to work.[7]

---

1. *Coates and Venables v Modern Methods and Materials Ltd* [1982] IRLR 318, CA.
2. *Winnett v Seamark Bros Ltd* [1978] IRLR 387, EAT. Cf. *Naylor v Orton and Smith Ltd and D Twedell Engineering Ltd* [1983] IRLR 233, where the EAT upheld the employment tribunal's decision that a decision to impose an immediate overtime ban did not constitute industrial action; this decision presents the problem of defining when the action does begin (when the first employee refuses to work overtime?) and whether

other employees are taking part in the action as from that moment or only when they in turn refuse such a request.

3. *Williams v Western Mail and Echo Ltd* [1980] IRLR 222 at 224, EAT.

4. Above, note 1. See also *McKenzie v Crosville Motor Services Ltd* [1989] IRLR 516, EAT (incumbent upon employee who is absent from work to provide employer with the reason and during a strike, to maintain contact and ensure that the employer has the true picture so as to establish he is not withholding his labour). See para **6.93** note 4 for a criticism of another aspect of this decision, which confuses the issue of whether the employee was taking part in the strike with the fairness of the dismissal.

5. At 323.

6. At 325.

7. *Bolton Roadways Ltd v Edwards* [1987] IRLR 392, EAT. This approach is consistent with *Winnett v Seamark Bros Ltd*, above, note 2. See also *Rogers v Chloride Systems Ltd* [1992] ICR 198, EAT, where the EAT considered that had the applicant, who was on sick leave throughout the dispute, answered 'no' on being asked whether she would have returned to work on a specific date had she not been sick or whether she would have undertaken to work normally as soon as she was able, that would have been sufficient to constitute 'taking part'. Cf. *Hindle Gears Ltd v McGinty* [1984] IRLR 477 at 480, EAT ('circumstances would have to be very exceptional indeed before it could accurately be said of a servant [*sic*] lawfully absolved under his contract of employment on the grounds of ill-health from supplying any labour at all to his master that he had been engaged in the process of withdrawing labour').

6.95 The employer's protection against unfair dismissal claims by employees dismissed while taking part in industrial action or locked out is lost in two situations. The first is where it is shown that one or more 'relevant employees' of the same employer have not been dismissed.[1] It is, therefore, particularly important for employers to keep up-to-date and accurate lists of the names and addresses of their employees together with accurate sickness records. The second is where it is shown that any 'relevant employee' has, 'before the expiry of the period of three months beginning with the date of his dismissal been offered re-engagement and . . . the complainant has not been offered re-engagement'.[2] In relation to a strike or other industrial action, 'relevant employees' are 'those employees at the establishment of the employer at or from which the complainant works who at the date of his dismissal were taking part in the action'.[3] 'Date of dismissal' is likely to be interpreted as 'time' of dismissal, by analogy with the interpretation of this phrase in relation to the exclusion of jurisdiction.[4] Thus, if a number of employees returned to normal working on the morning of a particular day the employer could probably safely dismiss all those who had not done so later that same day. However, employers would be well advised to ensure that they have some clear documentary evidence of the time when the employees who had already returned to work had done so, for example a signing-on book or an employee attendance record card. There is no requirement that employees should receive any warning that they will be dismissed unless they return. There is no definition of 'establishment' either in s 238 or elsewhere in the Act, nor has its meaning arisen to date as an issue in the case law in this area. It is likely that the same guidelines applied in the context of redundancy consultation (see para **5.6**) would be applicable in this context. In relation to a lock-out, 'relevant employees' are more widely drawn to cover those who were 'directly interested in the dispute in contemplation or furtherance of which the lock-out occurred',[5] with no requirement that they should work at or from the complainant's establishment. 'Direct interest' is a concept borrowed from social security law and covers anyone whose terms of employment are likely to be immediately and automatically affected by the outcome of the dispute.[6] Whether or not employees were 'directly interested' is to be assessed on the date on which the lock-out occurred.[7] The scope of 'relevant employees' in the context of a lock-out was considered by the EAT in *Fisher v York Trailer Co Ltd*.[8] The employers were concerned that the employees who worked on the main container line at one of their factories were 'going slow'. They sent a letter to each of the 34 employees concerned which required them to give an undertaking that they would work at a normal incentive pace under the existing bonus scheme, failing which they would be suspended from the start of the next shift. On the next day no production occurred and the men held meetings. Subsequent to those meetings all but seven of the employees signed the document, and those seven were eventually dismissed. The EAT upheld the tribunal's finding that they had been dismissed while the employer was conducting a lock-out, and also held that employees who are 'directly interested' are not limited to those who remained locked out until the end of the dispute and, indeed, could extend to those who were not locked out at all.[8] In this case all 34 employees were 'relevant employees'. This decision shows that an employer who wishes to retain the immunity may need to dismiss a much wider range of employees than in the case of a strike. In practice, an employer may be well advised to argue that employees were taking part in industrial action rather than being locked out, so enabling a smaller pool to be at issue, unless this would mean that the dismissals would then be automatically unfair because they were due to the employees taking part in 'protected industrial action' or for some other specified automatically unfair reason (see paras **6.98** *et seq.*).

---

1. TULRCA 1992, s 238(2)(a).

2. *Ibid.*, s 238(2)(b).

3. *Ibid.*, s 238(3)(b). Where industrial action is 'unofficial' for some employees taking part in it but not others, the 'unofficial' participants remain 'relevant employees': *ibid*, s 238(3); see further para **6.103** *et seq.*

4. See *Heath and Hammersley v J F Longman (Meat Salesman) Ltd* [1973] IRLR 214, NIRC.
5. TULRCA 1992, s 238(3)(a).
6. *Presho v Department of Health and Social Security (Insurance Officer)* [1984] IRLR 74, HL.
7. *H Campey and Sons Ltd v Bellwood* [1987] ICR 311, EAT.
8. [1979] IRLR 385, EAT.

6.96 Where the employer's discriminatory treatment takes the form of re-engagement, this means:

> an offer (made either by the original employer or by a successor of that employer or an associated employer[1]) to re-engage an employee, either in the job which he held immediately before the date of dismissal or in a different job which would be reasonably suitable in his case.[2]

The offer must be made specifically to the individual; a general press advertisement inviting applications from the public at large constitutes merely an offer to treat for re-engagement,[3] in contrast to a communication which indicates that, should individuals apply for re-engagement, they will be re-engaged.[4] There is no requirement that the offer be made in writing,[5] and, indeed, mere tacit acceptance that employment is continuing will suffice.[6] To offer re-engagement an employer must have knowledge of the first job from which the employee had been dismissed, although this knowledge may be constructive (in the sense that the employer has the means of obtaining it) as well as actual, thus in practice placing the onus on the employer to make adequate inquiries about the worker's position before re-engaging him or her.[7] There is no definition of 'job' in the Trade Union and Labour Relations (Consolidation) Act 1992, but under the Employment Protection (Consolidation) Act 1978, s 153 (applicable before the entry into force of the 1992 Act) it was defined as 'the nature of the work which [the employee] . . . is employed to do in accordance with his contract and the capacity and place in which he is so employed', and this definition, which now appears in the Employment Rights Act 1996, s 235(1), also applies in this context.[8] The Court of Appeal has held that if an employee was offered re-engagement in the same capacity as before, there is no requirement that the terms and conditions of employment should be identical, although if the terms are considerably more disadvantageous, this may lead to an inference that that it is no longer the same job.[9] This decision means that employers may discriminate between employees to whom 're-engagement' is offered, in terms both of their respective positions under the disciplinary procedures and, at least in minor ways, of substantive terms and conditions. Moreover, the terms offered to employees, on either a uniform or selective basis, may be the very ones which were the subject-matter of the original dispute.[10] Where an employee is offered a different job, whether or not it is 'reasonably suitable' will probably depend, by analogy with cases relating to statutory redundancy payments, on whether it is substantially equivalent in terms of factors such as status, use of skill, and pay and benefits.[11] An applicant for unfair dismissal who presents a claim based upon selective dismissal or selective re-engagement must present it to an employment tribunal within six months of his or her own dismissal (or such further period as the tribunal considers reasonable where it is satisfied that it was not reasonably practicable for the complainant to comply with the time limit).[12]

---

1. See App 1.
2. TULRCA 1992, s 238(4).
3. *Crosville Wales Ltd v Tracey* [1993] IRLR 60, EAT.
4. This was the situation in *Williams v National Theatre Board Ltd* [1982] IRLR 377, CA, distinguished in *Crosville*, above.
5. *Marsden v Fairey Stainless Ltd* [1979] IRLR 103, EAT.
6. *Bolton Roadways Ltd v Edwards* [1987] IRLR 392 at 397, EAT: offer of re-engagement means 'that it is held open for the employee'.
7. *Bigham and Keogh v GKN Kwikform Ltd* [1992] IRLR 4, EAT. The need to make inquiries will be particularly important where, as in this case, the employer is decentralised and the employee is re-employed at a different site. If re-engagement resulted from a fraudulent application then it would be void: *ibid.*, 6.
8. TULRCA 1992, s 239(1) originally stated that s 238 shall be construed as one with Part V of EPCA 1978, and now states that it shall be construed as one with ERA 1996, Part X, to which the definition in ERA 1996, s 235(1) applies. For the application of the provision pre-TULRCA 1992, see *Williams v National Theatre Board* above, note 4.
9. *Williams v National Theatre Board* above, note 4. (30 strikers offered reengagement on the basis they were on second warning as regards their general conduct; one worker had an offer with no such conditions; all had been offered re-engagement). See Lord Denning MR's qualification to the general proposition at 379 (if the terms were unreasonable—half-pay or half-time, for example to a full-time worker, that may not constitute the same job)
10. Ewing, 1991, 59.
11. See, for example, *Hindes v Supersine Ltd* [1979] IRLR 343, EAT.
12. TULRCA 1992, s 239(2); see further App 2. Cf the usual position on unfair dismissal: see ERA 1996, s 111(2).

6.97 The claim that the employer has selectively dismissed or offered re-engagement within the meaning of the legislation must be established before the employment tribunal has jurisdiction to hear the claim. The date upon which discrimination between 'relevant employees' must be shown is the time when the tribunal either determines the substantive issue (involving determination of the jurisdiction point as well) or determines the jurisdiction point on a preliminary hearing.[1] This means that an employer who dismisses selectively, then finds during the course of a hearing for unfair dismissal that there was one relevant employee who was not dismissed, can defeat the claim by dismissing that employee before the hearing ends. (Any employee dismissed in those circumstances may, of course, be able subsequently to present an unfair dismissal claim and we suggest that the employer would have difficulty in defending successfully any such claim even if it were to argue that the dismissal was for 'some other substantial reason', but, depending on the numbers involved, this may be the cheaper option for the employer.[2]) Moreover, where the identity of an alleged 'relevant employee' is unknown to the employers, the tribunal may order the name of that person to be disclosed by the applicant(s) either before or at the hearing in order to enable the employer to know the case it has to meet, even though this may enable the employer to take action which would defeat the claim.[3] Less objectionably, an employer may defeat a claim for unfair dismissal based upon selective re-engagement by offering the applicant 're-engagement' before the end of the tribunal hearing.[4] Once jurisdiction is established, the tribunal will then consider whether the dismissal was fair or unfair according to general principles.[5] Thus, where an employee has been dismissed, or selected for dismissal, for reasons which constitute an automatically unfair dismissal, such as participation in union activities, the dismissal will be automatically unfair.[6] In cases of selective re-engagement, references to the reason or principal reason for which the complainant was dismissed are to be read as references to 'the reason or principal reason he has not been offered re-engagement'.[7] The relevant question is then 'not whether the initial dismissal was justified but whether the refusal to re-engage the applicants was justified when some employees have been taken back'.[8] Acts of gross misconduct during the dispute (for example, stealing or damaging company property) may justify selection for dismissal or failure to re-engage; an employee's conduct prior to the dispute may also be material. Thus, in one case the employer implemented the appropriate next stage of the disciplinary procedure against employees who had participated in a strike, and it was held that it was not unfair to dismiss those who were already on final warning.[9] In certain circumstances it may be fair to select particular employees for redundancy on the ground that they took part in industrial action when other potentially redundant employees did not.[10] For some years it was unclear whether participation in industrial action could constitute contributory fault, which can lead to a reduction in the basic and/or compensatory award for unfair dismissal.[11] In *Crosville Wales Ltd v Tracey (No 2)*[12] the House of Lords affirmed that any compensation due to the applicants in respect of their unfair dismissals, whose claims arose from the employers' selective re-engagement of those dismissed while taking part in industrial action, did not fall to be reduced because of their conduct in participating in industrial action because of the difficulty of allocating blame for the industrial action to any individual complainant.[13] However their Lordships stated obiter that individual blameworthy conduct additional to or separate from the mere act of participation in industrial action was in principle capable of amounting to contributory fault.[14] This means that individuals whose behaviour is perceived by a tribunal as 'over-hasty and inflammatory' may still be subject to a reduction in their compensation even if their dismissals are found to be unfair.[15]

---

1. *P & O European Ferries (Dover) Ltd v Byrne* [1989] IRLR 254, CA, modifying *McCormick v Horsepower Ltd* [1981] IRLR 217, CA.

2. ERA 1996, s 98(1)(b).

3. *P & O European Ferries*, above, note 1.

4. See, for example, *Highlands Fabricators Ltd v McLaughlin* [1984] IRLR 482, EAT.

5. Where the question of jurisdiction under TULRCA 1992, s 238 is determined as a preliminary issue, the result is binding upon the parties but the findings of fact which led the tribunal to reach its conclusion are not binding upon a differently constituted tribunal which determines the fairness or otherwise of the dismissal: *Munir v Jang Publications Ltd* [1989] IRLR 224, CA. However, the court considered that, given that the issue of jurisdiction would necessarily involve hearing evidence which would trespass on the issue of reasonableness, it was preferable not to hear the jurisdiction point as a preliminary issue.

6. See further para **3.3**.

7. TULRCA 1992, s 239(3).

8. *Edwards v Cardiff City Council* [1979] IRLR 303 at 305, EAT. In *Laffin and Callaghan v Fashion Industries (Hartlepool) Ltd* [1978] IRLR 448, EAT it was held that if a reason would not justify dismissal, it would not justify a refusal to re-engage.

9. *Bernard Matthews plc v Rowland* (24 May 1982, unreported) EAT.

10. See *Cruickshank v Hobbs* [1977] ICR 725, EAT, where three such circumstances were suggested: if the strike has 'caused or aggravated the redundancy'; after a long strike, difficulties of reintroducing the strikers due to technical or administrative changes during their absence; and if the friction which would arise from dismissing non-strikers and replacing them with strikers would impair morale and efficiency. Cf. *Laffin and Callaghan*, above, note 8 (unfair to select on basis solely of a 'loyalty test').

11. ERA 1996, ss 122(2) and 123(6).

12. [1997] IRLR 691, HL

13. It was agreed between the parties that, even though the claim only came into existence because of the selective re-engagement, the wording of the legislation meant that the relevant question in the context of the compensation provisions was whether an employee had contributed to his or her dismissal, not to the failure to be re-engaged.

14. [1997] IRLR 691 at 698.

15. Lord Nolan expressly endorsed, at 698, the judgment of Waite LJ in this case relating to contributory fault: see [1996] IRLR 91 at 98.

'Protected' Industrial Action

6.98 The Employment Relations Act 1999 has introduced a limited protection for those whose are dismissed for taking 'protected' industrial action in specified conditions; if one of these is met, the dismissal is automatically unfair. An employee takes 'protected industrial action' if he or she commits an act which (or a series of acts each of which) he or she is induced to commit by an act which by virtue of the Trade Union and Labour Relations (Consolidation) Act 1992, s 219 is not actionable in tort.[1] The provision does not cover 'unofficial' action, and so, in effect, is confined to situations where the industrial action is authorised or endorsed by the union of which the employee is a member, unless he or she is not a member of any union.[2] The restriction to protection of acts which are not actionable in tort *by virtue of s 219* constitutes a considerable limitation. First, it means that where industrial action is not actionable in tort at common law (for example, if it is confined to a ban on voluntary overtime, which may not constitute a breach of contract by those participating in it) employees will not be covered by the protection. Secondly, and more importantly in practice, s 219 does not afford protection against all the torts which those who induce employees to take part in industrial action may commit (see para **6.18**); thus, for example, it does not cover torts based upon breach of a statutory duty. Thirdly, protection under s 219 is conditional upon the union having met all the statutory requirements relating to ballots and notices to employers. The terms of the legislation (an act 'which is not actionable in tort') suggest that it will be sufficient that immunity is lost in relation only to one of a number of employers involved in the dispute. This will mean, therefore, that if a union fails to give only one employer the requisite notice of the action to be taken, all employees who have been induced by a call made by the union to take industrial action will lose any protection against dismissal. The definition of 'protected industrial action' in terms of immunity in tort means that employment tribunals may be required to decide complex issues relating to the scope of the economic torts, an activity for which they have not hitherto had experience as all such issues have previously been determined by the courts. The difficulties will be compounded by the fact that many of the decisions relating to the existence and ambit of these torts were decided in interim proceedings, in which it is sufficient to show that there is a serious question to be tried (see para **6.52** *et seq.*). Tribunals may also be required to decide whether the intricate provisions governing ballots and notices to employers have been complied with.[3] The legislation enables provision to be made for the adjournment and renewal of applications.[4] When an employer (or a third party) is bringing proceedings in the High Court against the union which has organised the industrial action in tort, it would seem sensible for tribunals to be required to adjourn the unfair dismissal hearing pending judgment on that claim, although only a full trial on the merits would provide the tribunals with an appropriate ruling on whether the industrial action was 'protected'. This could take a very long time, however, particularly if the question is appealed, an undesirable situation particularly given that the primary remedies for a claim for unfair dismissal are orders for reinstatement or re-engagement (even though in practice they are infrequently awarded). If no claim has been brought by an employer in tort, however, there would seem to be no basis on which an employment tribunal could refer the matter to the courts for decision.

---

1. TULRCA 1992, s 238A(1). See para **6.17** *et seq.* for the scope of s 219.
2. 'Unofficial' industrial action is defined in TULRCA 1992, s 237(2); see further para **6.104**. If the union repudiates an act during the course of a dispute and employees continue to take industrial action beyond the end of the 'working day' following the day on which the repudiation takes place, they will lose their entitlement to bring a claim: see s 238A(8). See s 237(5) (discussed in para **6.104**) for the definition of 'working day'.
3. For discussion of whether a union member may have a right of action against a union which prejudiced his or her unfair dismissal protection, see para **2.22**.
4. TULRCA 1992, s 239(4)(b).

6.99 It is not sufficient to attract protection that the employee was dismissed while protected industrial action is bring taken; the fact that the employee took protected industrial action must be the *reason* or principal reason for the dismissal (or, in a 'redundancy case' for selection for dismissal).[1] No minimum period of employment is required to claim, and there is no upper age limit barring claims.[2] However, by analogy with cases relating to dismissal for trade union reasons, where the employee would not otherwise qualify to claim unfair dismissal it will be for him or her to show that having taken protected industrial action was the reason for dismissal.[3] Although in cases where an employee would otherwise qualify to claim it is usually for the employer to show the reason for dismissal and that it acted reasonably in dismissing,[4] in this context the tribunal would not otherwise have jurisdiction if it is not shown that the employee was dismissed for taking protected industrial action. Effectively, therefore, the burden to show the reason will lie in all cases on the employee. As cases in the context of 'trade union' dismissals show, this may not be an easy test to satisfy, particularly where the decision is taken by a group of persons.[5] Moreover, employers may well be tempted to use the occasion of the industrial action to dismiss those whom it has been wishing to dismiss for other reasons, such as their poor performance or absence records, without going through the requisite disciplinary or performance procedures. Provided that they do not displace their immunity by discriminating between 'relevant employees' (see para

6.95 above),[6] or dismissing for a limited range of automatically unfair reasons (see para **6.102**), they will be able to do so with impunity. It is to be hoped that tribunals will scrutinise carefully the reasons given by, and conduct of, employers when dismissals take place against a background of industrial action. The confinement to situations where industrial action is the reason for dismissal stands in marked contrast to the general exclusion of jurisdiction, which applies where the employee is *taking part* in such action (see para **6.92** *et seq.*). It is also notable that the protection in this context applies only if the employee 'took' protected industrial action; it does not appear to extend to threatening to take it. Although participation in activities prior to a strike can constitute protected trade union activities,[7] it is unclear whether threatening to take industrial action would be covered by such protection.[8]

---

1. TULRCA 1992, s 238A(2); ERA 1996, s 105(7C). There is a 'redundancy case' where the reason or principal reason for dismissal is that the employee was redundant, and it is shown that the circumstances constituting the redundancy applied equally to one or more other employees in the same undertaking who held positions similar to that held by the employee and who have not been dismissed by the employer: ERA 1996, s 105(1), (9).
2. TULRCA 1992, s 239(1).
3. *Smith v Hayle Town Council* [1978] ICR 996; see further para **3.3**.
4. *Maund v Penwith District Council* [1984] IRLR 24, CA.
5. *Smith v Hayle Town Council*, above, note 3.
6. If they do so discriminate and those dismissed meet the qualification to claim unfair dismissal, the employer will have to defend the application in the normal way.
7. *Britool Ltd v Roberts* [1993] IRLR 481, EAT. Industrial action itself has been held not to be within this protection: *Drew v St Edmundsbury Borough Council* [1980] IRLR 459, EAT.
8. Note that in *Lewis and Britton v E Mason and Sons* [1994] IRLR 4, EAT, a finding that threatening to take industrial action could, of itself, constitute industrial action was not regarded as perverse, but cf. *Midland Plastics v Till* [1983] IRLR 9, EAT: see further para **6.93**.

6.100 The protection against dismissal for having taken protected industrial action applies in three sets of circumstances. The first is where the dismissal takes place 'within the period of eight weeks beginning with the day on which the employee started to take protected industrial action'.[1] It is notable that the protection is framed in terms of the employee's own participation. This will make it crucial to determine when the employee individually started to take such action, a matter which, as we discussed in para **6.94**, may not be easy to determine, particularly in relation to rolling strikes and overtime bans. The second is if the dismissal takes place after the end of the eight-week period and the employee had stopped taking protected industrial action before the end of that period,[2] so preventing subsequent victimisation. Once again, this is linked to the employee's own participation and the discussion in para **6.94** remains equally pertinent in this context. An employee who wishes to cease to take protected industrial action and who is absent from work for other reasons, such as illness or holiday, would be well advised to ensure that he or she records in writing to the employer that his or her participation in the action has ceased. The third is where the dismissal takes place after the end of the period, the employee had not stopped taking protected industrial action before the end of the period, and 'the employer had not taken such procedural steps as would have been reasonable for the purposes of resolving the dispute to which the protected industrial action relates'.[3] In determining whether an employer has taken such steps, tribunals are directed to have regard in particular to whether the employer or union complied with the procedures established by any applicable collective or other agreement; whether either party offered or agreed to commence or resume negotiations after the start of the protected industrial action; and whether either party unreasonably refused, after the start of the protected industrial action, a request that conciliation services be used, or mediation services in relation to procedures to be adopted for the purposes of resolving the dispute.[4] However no regard may be had to the merits of the dispute.[5] If the fairness of an employee's dismissal rests upon it establishing that it falls within this category, it is likely to be expected to be particularly contentious. It will therefore be important for both unions and employers to ensure that they maintain full records of all meetings and other forms of communication with the other party throughout the dispute. A claim for unfair dismissal must be brought within six months of the complainant's dismissal (or within such further period as the tribunal considers reasonable where it is satisfied that it was not reasonably practicable for the complainant to comply with the time limit).[6] However in the event that the complaint is upheld, no order for reinstatement or re-engagement may be made until *all* employees have ceased to take protected industrial action in relation to the relevant dispute.[7] This was justified by the Government on the dual grounds that it would 'make no sense' for tribunals to issue re-employment orders when 'the employees are unwilling to work', and that the terms of settlement of the dispute may include reinstatement of those dismissed.[8]

---

1. TULRCA 1992, s 238A(3). The selection of the eight-week period was justified by the Government as 'putting some pressure on both parties' while also providing them 'with sufficient opportunity to hold constructive negotiations and to explore thoroughly all avenues that might lead to a resolution': Mr. Ian McCartney, Minister of

State, Department of Trade and Industry, Official Report of Standing Committee E, 9 March 1999, 6.15pm. Novitz, 2000 remarks (at 387) that this imposes a threshold not contemplated by international labour standards.

2. *Ibid.*, s 238A(4).
3. *Ibid.*, s 238A(5).
4. *Ibid.*, s 238A(6). If the CAC has imposed a 'method' of collective bargaining upon the parties pursuant to the statutory recognition procedure, it will be important to determine whether this has been complied with.
5. *Ibid.*, s 238A(7).
6. *Ibid.*, s 239(2). See App 2.
7. *Ibid.*, s 239(4)(a).
8. Mr. Ian McCartney, above, note 1, 6.45 pm.

6.101 The protection accorded to employees by this provision has some notable limitations, in addition to those which have been identified already. First, it offers no protection to those who are dismissed when locked-out by the employer (possibly in breach of contract), although the justification for according an eight-week breathing space[1] applies equally in this context. This is unfortunate both on policy and on technical grounds; as we saw in para **6.93** the line between a strike and a lock-out may be a difficult one to draw, and the designation of this issue as largely one of fact limits the scope for appeal where a decision is short of perverse. Secondly, in contrast to other automatically unfair reasons for dismissal, there is no accompanying protection against subjection to a detriment short of dismissal. However there may be a way round this lacuna if a detriment is imposed which is a fundamental breach of contract, such as demotion or a unilateral cut in wages or which breaches the implied term of trust and confidence,[2] and so constitutes constructive dismissal, which falls within the definition of dismissal in this context.[3] 'Constructive dismissal' occurs when 'the employee terminates the contract under which he is employed (with or without notice) in circumstances in which he is entitled to terminate it without notice by reason of the employer's conduct'.[4] The fact that the concept is framed in terms of termination of the *contract* rather than the relationship means that employees may claim to have been constructively dismissed, and so mount a claim for unfair dismissal, while remaining in the employer's employment.[5] The employer would no doubt wish to argue that the action had been taken in response to the employee's own fundamental breach of contract in engaging in industrial action. Such action by the employer would then, however, constitute an acceptance of the employee's breach, and could thus be analysed as a (direct) dismissal by the employer, which is also framed in terms of termination of *the contract* under which the employee is employed.[6] This analysis does not deal with the situation where the detriment imposed by the employer falls short of a fundamental breach of contract, but it may go some way towards correcting this legislative omission. Finally in this context we would wish to draw attention again once again to the current confinement of protection to employees (so breaching international standards) rather than the wider category of workers who constitute the legitimate party to a trade dispute.[7]

---

1. See para **6.100**, note 1.
2. On developments in this duty, see Brodie, 1998.
3. TULRCA 19992, s 239(1).
4. ERA 1996, s 95(1)(c).
5. *Hogg v Dover College* [1990] ICR 39, EAT; *Alcan Extrusions v Yates* [1996] IRLR 327, EAT.
6. ERA 1996, s 95(1)(a); see *Hogg* and *Alcan*, above.
7. See para **6.92**.

Other Automatically Unfair Reasons for Dismissal

6.102 The exclusion of the jurisdiction of an employment tribunal to determine the fairness of an employee's dismissal in the circumstances described in para **6.92** does not apply where it is shown that the reason or principal reason for dismissal, or, in a redundancy case, for selecting the employee for dismissal,[1] was for one of a limited number of specified reasons, which render the dismissal automatically unfair. Unlike dismissals for taking 'protected industrial action', this applies to those dismissed while locked out as well as those dismissed for taking industrial action. The specified reasons are, in brief, specified activities relating to health and safety; acting, or standing for election, as an employee representative or representative of the workforce; on the grounds of pregnancy or childbirth; and for reasons relating to maternity or parental leave, or time off for dependants.[2] There is no minimum period of employment required to qualify to claim, nor is there an upper age limit barring claims.[3] The comments which we made in para **6.99** about the burden of proof on the complainant, and the difficulties which this presents, apply equally in this context. An employee will need to rely on these provisions only when the employer has dismissed non-selectively within the meaning of the legislation and the provisions relating to 'protected industrial action' which we described in para **6.98** *et seq.* do not apply. It is difficult to envisage circumstances where an individual would be able to show that he or she had been dismissed for any one of those reasons where all those participating in the action have been dismissed. It is notable that there is no protection against dismissal on grounds of trade union membership or participation in union activities in this context.

1. There is a 'redundancy case' where the reason or principal reason for dismissal is that the employee was redundant, and it is shown that the circumstances constituting the redundancy applied equally to one or more other employees in the same undertaking who held positions similar to that held by the employee and who have not been dismissed by the employer: ERA 1996, s 105(1),(9).
2. TULRCA 1992, s 238(2A).
3. ERA 1996, ss 108, 109.

Where Industrial Action is 'Unofficial'

6.103 An employee has no right to complain of unfair dismissal, even if selective, if at the time of dismissal he or she was taking part in an 'unofficial' strike or other 'unofficial' industrial action[1] unless it is shown that he or she was dismissed (or in a 'redundancy case' selected for dismissal) for one of the reasons specified in para **6.102** above, or, additionally, for making a 'protected disclosure' within the terms of the Employment Rights Act 1996, ss 43A–43L.[2] As we indicated in that paragraph, these automatically unfair reasons do not include selection for dismissal on grounds of union activities, thus enabling employers to dismiss with impunity the 'ringleaders' behind industrial action as long as they do so while they are taking part in the industrial action. The provision described in para **6.93** for stoppages in circumstances of serious and imminent danger applies in this context[3] and, indeed, may be particularly significant if the circumstances are such that no union official is involved in instigating the stoppage and it may otherwise be deemed to be 'unofficial' industrial action. However, once again employees who stop work in order to exert pressure on an employer to improve safety standards outside the specific situation covered by the statute, or to support other workers whose safety is at risk, will not be protected and are likely to be viewed as taking part in 'industrial action'. As in the context of dismissal for 'non-official' action, the wording of the statute indicates that participation in industrial action need not be the reason for dismissal; the crucial question is whether employees were 'taking part' at the 'time' they were dismissed.[4] 'Time of dismissal' for this purpose means, where the employee's contract of employment is terminated by notice, when the notice is given; where it is terminated without notice, when the termination takes effect; and where the employee is employed under a contract for a fixed term which expires without renewal under the same contract, when that term expires.[5] Thus, it is made explicit in the statute that once an employer knows that industrial action has ended, it cannot dismiss employees later that day. The meaning of 'strike', 'other industrial action' and 'taking part' is discussed in paras **6.93** and **6.94**. There is no immunity against liability in tort for any person who organises industrial action in protest at the dismissal of an employee who participated in unofficial action and who is thereby deprived of protection against unfair dismissal.[6]

---

1. TULRCA 1992, s 237.
2. *Ibid.*, s 237(1A). It is curious that the same protection in relation to protected disclosures is not accorded to participants in 'non-unofficial' action.
3. ERA 1996, s 100(1)(d).
4. The case law on TULRCA 1992, s 238 also supports that view: see para **6.93**. As in that context, the current case law does not afford scope to argue that the industrial action was provoked by the employer, although cf. Elias, 1994.
5. TULRCA 1992, s 237(5). In the context of non-unofficial action, the term 'date of dismissal' is used, but in *Heath and Hammersey v JF Longman (Meat Salesman) Ltd* [1973] IRLR 214, the NIRC interpreted this to mean 'time' of dismissal.
6. TULRCA 1992, s 223. In *British Railways Board v RMT* (17 September 1992, unreported), QBD, industrial action had no immunity on this basis.

6.104 The policy underlying the introduction of this aspect of the legislation governing industrial action was to ensure that industrial action fell into one of two categories: either it is 'unofficial' or it is action for which a trade union is legally liable, in which case a ballot and prior notices to employers are required in order for immunity in tort to be retained.[1] There is a presumption that industrial action is 'unofficial' in relation to a particular employee unless one of three conditions applies.[2] First, if he or she is a member of a trade union and the action is authorised or endorsed by that union.[3] Secondly, if he or she is not a member of a trade union but there are among those taking part in the industrial action members of a union by which the action has been authorised or endorsed.[4] Thirdly, if none of those taking part in the industrial action is a union member.[5] The crucial issue is whether any participant was a union member at the time when he or she began to take part in the industrial action;[6] thus, employees cannot resign from the union once the industrial action has started in order to protect their union against legal liability on the one hand, whilst retaining protection for themselves against selective dismissal on the other. The question whether industrial action has been 'authorised or endorsed' by a trade union is determined according to the principles laid down in the Trade Union and Labour Relations (Consolidation) Act 1992, s 20(2). We discuss these principles fully in para **6.13** *et seq.* In summary, an act is attributed to a union if it was done, authorised or endorsed by one of three categories of person: first, by a person empowered by the union rules so to act; secondly, by the principal executive committee, president or general secretary; and, thirdly, by any other committee of the union or any other official, whether employed by it or not. Where liability arises from an act by a person who falls within the third category, the union can avoid liability if the act is repudiated by the executive, president or general secretary as soon as reasonably practicable after coming to the knowledge of any of them.[7] Once an act has been repudiated, the participants in industrial action have a short period within which to end their action before being exposed to selective dismissal; the legislation provides that 'industrial action shall not . . . be treated as unofficial before the end of the next working day after the day on which the repudiation takes place'.[8] A 'working day' means 'any day which is not a Saturday or Sunday, Christmas Day, Good Friday or a bank holiday under the Banking and Financial Dealings Act 1971'.[9] The definition does not, therefore, allow for any variation according to the working patterns of the individual enterprise or individual employees. Thus, if a participant in unofficial industrial action is not due to work the day following a repudiation by the union, or is unable to attend work due to illness, he or she will have to ensure that the employer is aware that his or her participation in the industrial action has come to an end; failure to do this will entitle the employer to assume continued participation and will therefore expose the employee to dismissal.[10] It may be sufficient to protect an employee's interests that the organiser of the industrial action informs the employer of the cessation of sanctions,[11] but given the uncertainty which may surround unofficial action an employee would be best advised to make clear his or her individual position (preferably in writing) to the employer. There is no safety net for employees who are unaware of the repudiation, regardless of the reason for this. Although, for a repudiation to be effective in removing liability from the union, written notice must be sent to each member of the union who the union has reason to believe is taking part in the action (and to the employer of every such member), there is no requirement for members to receive such notice before the protection against selective dismissal is removed; it is assumed that union members will be in sufficient communication with their representatives and with each other to receive this information through other channels. However, it is unclear whether a repudiation which is treated as ineffective for the purposes of union liability may also be treated as ineffective in the context of protection against unfair dismissal. The legislation states that the question whether industrial action is to be taken as authorised or endorsed by the union shall be determined by reference to the facts as at the time of dismissal.[12] However, this does not mean that the matter is free from doubt. It is conceivable that an employer may find that the tribunal has jurisdiction to examine the fairness of the dismissal of a dismissed employee because the union failed to follow the procedures to ensure that the repudiation was effective, although it is highly unlikely that this is what the legislation intended. The same comment applies with respect to subsequent behaviour by the executive, president or general secretary which is inconsistent with the purported repudiation; this can be constituted, *inter alia*, by a failure to confirm the repudiation in accordance with the statute up to three months afterwards.[13] It is a notable feature of the legislation that whether the organisation of industrial action is attributable to a union for the purpose of determining liability in tort is determined by the ordinary courts, but in relation to the position of an individual employee it is determined by employment tribunals. If an employer found that industrial action which had appeared to be 'unofficial' at the time of dismissal turned out not to be so, it would be open to it to avoid the tribunal having jurisdiction over the claim in accordance with the principles described in para **6.97** (avoiding discrimination between 'relevant employees') unless the dismissal fell within the circumstances in which dismissal for 'protected industrial action' is automatically unfair, or the dismissal was automatically unfair for other reasons, in which case it would not be possible to avoid the jurisdiction of the tribunal.

---

1. *See Unofficial Action and the Law*, Cm 821, 1989.

2. TULRCA 1992, s 237(2).

3. *Ibid.*, s 237(2)(a). See para **2.4** for the definition of a 'trade union'.

4. *Ibid.*, s 237(2)(b). There is no requirement that these other participants should be 'employees' rather than 'workers': see App 1 for definitions of these terms. Note that action may be 'unofficial' in relation to some employees and not others; an individual may be a member of a union which has not authorised or endorsed the action even though another union has and thus not fall within either of the first two categories.

5. *Ibid.*, s 237(2).

6. TULRCA 1992, s 237(6). However, membership of a trade union 'for purposes unconnected with the employment in question' shall be disregarded: *ibid.* This would cover, for example, a 'resting actor' who is a member of Equity but temporarily engaged in different employment.

7. Repudiation involves an 'open disavowal and disowning of the acts of the officials concerned' *Express and Star Ltd v NGA (1982)* [1985] IRLR 455 at 459, QBD.

8. TULRCA 1992, s 237(4). In the course of debate on the Employment Relations Act 1999, Mr. Ian McCartney, Minister of State, Department of Trade and Industry, claimed that '[t]here is no evidence that the existing time limit has caused problems in the past. For example, no one has suggested that the time period is too short for the workers concerned to learn of the repudiation, or that there is insufficient time for them or the employer to adapt their behaviour': Official Report of Standing Committee E, 9 March 1999, 6.45 pm.

9. *Ibid.*, s 237(5).

10. *See Williams v Western Mail and Echo Ltd* [1980] IRLR 222, EAT, and the discussion in para **6.94**.

11. *In Williams v Western Mail and Echo Ltd*, above, the court stated (at 224) that 'once men [*sic*] have stated that they will apply sanctions and do so they may be regarded as applying the sanctions *either until they are discontinued* [our italics] or until they indicate an intention of stopping them'. However, in that case the action was supported by the union. In the case of unofficial action, it may be much less clear when the sanctions have been discontinued.

12. TULRCA 1992, s 237(4).

13. *Ibid.*, s 21(6); see para **6.14**.

Redundancy Payments

6.105 The effect of taking industrial action upon the right to receive a statutory redundancy payment is complex. The basic principle, contained in the Employment Rights Act 1996, s 140(1), is that an employee is not entitled to a redundancy payment where the employer, being entitled to terminate the contract of employment without notice by reason of the employee's conduct, terminates it in one of three ways. The first is to terminate it without notice. The second is to give shorter notice than would otherwise be required. The third is to give full notice, but to accompany this by a written statement that the employer would be entitled to terminate the contract without notice by reason of the employee's conduct. This principle applies to employees who take part in industrial action other than a strike which constitutes a repudiatory breach of contract. In *Simmons v Hoover Ltd* [1] the EAT affirmed that this was the case both where there is a single dismissal (ie a dismissal for redundancy, not explicitly for misconduct) as well as a double dismissal (dismissal for redundancy followed by dismissal for misconduct); thus, an employer who gives insufficient notice of redundancy but then discovers misconduct on the part of the employee is relieved of liability. [2] Where the employer follows the procedure set out in s 140(1) and the dismissal takes place within the 'obligatory period', [3] the employment tribunal has discretion to award all or part of the redundancy payment if it considers this 'just and equitable'. [4] However, in *Simmons v Hoover Ltd* the court considered that this applied only where there were two dismissals, [5] a view which benefits employers who act wrongfully by giving insufficient notice on a single dismissal.

---

1. [1976] IRLR 266, EAT.

2. *X v Y Ltd* (1969) 4 ITR 204, Employment Tribunal.

3. Defined in ERA 1996, s 136(4): for an employer who gives the minimum period of notice required to terminate the contract lawfully, the actual period of notice; in any other case, the period equal to that minimum period which expires when the employer's notice expires (so if the minimum period is three weeks but the employer gives six, the last three weeks of the six-week period).

4. ERA 1996, s 140(3), (5).

5. Above, note 1, at 271–272.

6.106 The Employment Rights Act 1996, s 140(1) is modified in the case of strikes (for which the same definition applicable in relation to continuity of employment applies).[1] An employee who has been dismissed who then takes part in a strike retains the right to payment provided that the strike occurs during the obligatory period of the employer's notice.[2] In *Simmons v Hoover Ltd* the Employment Appeal Tribunal considered that this exception applied only where there was a 'double' dismissal and the strike followed the redundancy notice; where the redundancy followed the strike, s 140(1) would apply (taking part in a strike constituting 'employee's conduct' within that section).[3] Where an employee goes on strike after receiving notice of redundancy, the employer may serve a written notice requesting the employee to agree to extend the contract by the number of days the strike lasts.[4] If the employee does not comply, the right to a redundancy payment is lost unless the employee can show that he or she was unable to comply or that it was reasonable not to comply, in which case the tribunal has a discretion to award some or all of the payment.[5] There is no protection for employees who terminate their contracts without notice in response to a lock-out which constitutes a repudiatory breach of contract by the employer; such termination is expressly excluded from the definition of 'constructive dismissal' in this context, so denying employees any right to a statutory redundancy payment.[6] There is a clear danger that employees who lack appropriate advice may be manipulated into resigning by employers who may initiate a lock-out by proposing terms which they can predict will be unacceptable to the workforce, knowing that redundancies would in any case be imminent. It is difficult to appreciate the policy justification for this state of affairs.

---

1. ERA 1996, s 235(5); see para **6.91**.

2. *Ibid.*, s 140(2),(5). 'Obligatory period' is defined in s 136(4): see para **6.105**, note 3. Thus, if an employee who should receive two months' notice receives three and goes on strike immediately and is then dismissed, s 140(1) will apply and the right to a redundancy payment will be lost; he or she must wait a month before being protected by s 140(2).

3. [1976] IRLR 266 at 270, EAT. If the employee has been dismissed for redundancy, goes on strike and the employer does nothing, the right to a payment will be retained: *Sanders v Ernest A Neale Ltd* [1974] ICR 565 at 575, NIRC. Note that s 140(3), according tribunals discretion to award some or all of a statutory redundancy payment (see para **6.105** above) is excluded when the contract is terminated by reason of the employee taking part in a strike.

4. ERA 1996, ss 143,144. The notice must contain specified information.

5. *Ibid.*, s 143(5).

6. *Ibid.*, s 136(2). The same definition applies in this context as for continuity purposes: s235(5); see further para **6.91**.

Guarantee Payments

6.107 An employee who has been continuously employed for not less than one month[1] is entitled to payment by the employer for days when he or she is not provided with work for a maximum of five days in any three-month period subject to certain conditions being met.[2] This entitlement is lost if the failure to provide work occurs in consequence of a strike, lock-out or other industrial action[3] involving any employee of his or her employer or of an associated employer.[4] It follows therefore that an applicant employee's claim for a guarantee payment will in these circumstances fail even though he or she was not involved in the industrial action. Collective agreements (or other agreements) which provide for payments in a wider range of circumstances than the statute (for example which exclude payment only where the dispute involves the employer's own employees) remain effective provided that their terms have been incorporated into employees' individual contracts of employment. However, any agreement which purports to limit the right further than the legislative exception (for example, by excluding payment where the lay-off is caused by a strike involving a third party employer other than an associated employer) will be ineffective in this respect unless the employees are covered by an exemption order.[5]

---

1. Ending with the day before that in respect of which payment is claimed: ERA 1996, s 29(1). See App 1 for the meaning of 'employee'.
2. ERA 1996, ss 28–35. A number of other conditions must be satisfied. The maximum amount is varied periodically: on 1 February 2000 (and at the time of writing) it stood at £16.10 per day. Note that certain classes of employees are excluded from claiming: see ERA 1996, s 199(2), 200(1).
3. These terms are not defined in this context; see para **6.93** for their interpretation in the context of unfair dismissal.
4. ERA 1996, s 29(3); see App 1 for the definition of 'associated employer'.
5. *Ibid.*, s 35.

Continuity of Employment

6.108 Many individual employment protection rights are dependent upon an employee having a specified period of continuous employment with an employer.' In general, if a week occurs which cannot be credited to an employee, continuity is destroyed, so that any weeks previously credited to that employee are wiped out.[2] The position where an employee goes on strike constitutes an exception to that rule. Any week during which an employee takes part in a strike,[3] however short, does not count for the purpose of calculating an employee's period of continuous employment, but continuity remains unbroken so that the periods of employment before and after the strike can be aggregated.[4] This principle applies even if the employee is dismissed during the strike and then re-employed once the strike is over.[5] As far as lockouts are concerned, if the employee's contract continues in existence, the week during which the lock-out occurs counts for continuity purposes.[6] However, if there is no contract in existence during that week, the position is the same as for a strike; the week does not count but continuity remains unbroken.[7]

---

1. See ERA 1996, ss 210–219 and App 1.
2. ERA 1996, s 210(4).
3. Defined in ERA 1996, s 235(5); see para **6.91**.
4. *Ibid.*, s 216(1),(2). See also s 211(3).
5. *Hanson v Fashion Industries (Hartlepool) Ltd* [1980] IRLR 393, EAT.
6. ERA 1996, s 212.
7. *Ibid.*, s 216(3); see also s 211(3). 'Lock-out' is defined in s 235(5); see para **6.91**.

THE RIGHTS OF TRADE UNION MEMBERS

Sources and General Principles

6.109 There are a variety of avenues, both common law and statutory, by which trade union members may challenge their union's support for industrial action and measures ancillary thereto. At common law, individual members may apply to the High Court for declaratory and/or (more commonly) injunctive relief if their union calls or supports industrial action which is not authorised by the union's rules. They may also seek to challenge disciplinary measures taken against them by the union for failing to obey instructions to participate in such action (and, arguably, also in certain circumstances for failing to participate in action which is authorised under the rules). As far as statute is concerned, there are four provisions of the Trade Union and Labour Relations (Consolidation) Act 1992, as amended, which are relevant to industrial action. First, s 62 empowers union members who have been, or are likely to be, induced by the union to take part in industrial action which does not have the support of a ballot conducted in accordance with the statutory requirements to apply to the High Court for an order preventing any further inducement. Secondly, under ss 64–67 members who have been disciplined for opposing, or failing to participate in or support, any strike or other industrial action may complain to an employment tribunal, regardless of whether the action has the support of a ballot or is lawful under the union's rules. Thirdly, s 15 prohibits unions from paying any penalty for an offence or contempt of court on behalf of any individual, or indemnifying an individual in respect of any such penalty and gives individual members the right to bring proceedings in the High Court on the union's behalf to recover any payment where the union unreasonably fails to do this. Lastly, s 16 enables members who claim that the union trustees have allowed, or will allow, unlawful application of the union's property or have complied, or are proposing to comply, with an unlawful direction to them under the union rules, to apply to the High Court for an order to prevent this. The order may include removal of any or all of the trustees.

Common Law Rights

6.110 As discussed in para **2.12** *et seq.*, every trade union member has a contractual right to ensure that the affairs of the union are conducted in accordance with the constitution laid down in the union rules and may sue for breach of contract if the union does not act in accordance with its rules. Union support for industrial action may be challenged on the ground that the rules do not permit industrial action in the circumstances in question or, more likely, that the correct procedure has not been followed. Thus, for example, if industrial action is called without the support of a ballot, where a ballot is required by the union rules,[1] or if the requisite majority has not been obtained, a union member may apply to the High Court for relief. This form of relief will continue to be material despite the comprehensive statutory balloting procedures described in para **6.30** *et seq.* and the specific remedy available to union members in the event of non-compliance, if union rules require a higher majority that the legislation stipulates, for example. Even if the rules do ostensibly permit the action, there is some authority that it is beyond the powers of a union deliberately to embark upon activities, including industrial action, which would be bound to involve offences against the criminal law (although not activities which carry only the risk of such acts).[2] This doctrine, if accepted, could be relevant to certain kinds of picketing and also industrial action by specific groups of workers.[3] It has also been argued on occasion, with less success, that union rules cannot authorise industrial action which would lead to the commission of a tort; in *Thomas v NUM* the court refused to hold that picketing was outside the union's powers merely because it was 'almost certain' that the union had exposed itself to liability for interference with contract, although the question whether action which was bound to constitute any other tort would be similarly treated was left open.[4] Clearly if this argument were to be accepted it would expose a high proportion of campaigns to challenge. Like employers, union claimants commonly seek an interim injunction to restrain the union from carrying out or continuing allegedly unlawful activities, and the same principles which we described in paras **6.53** *et seq.* apply. In this context, the power to order sequestration of a union's assets in the event that it acts in contempt of court, or to appoint a receiver to manage and control its assets, may be particularly important.[5]

---

1. *Porter v NUJ* [1980] IRLR 404, HL; *Taylor v NUM (Derbyshire Area)* [1984] IRLR 440, ChD.

2. See *Thomas v NUM (South Wales Area)* [1985] IRLR 136 at 153, ChD. See Ewing, 1985, 164–165; 174–175; Elias and Ewing, 1987, 237–240.

3. Such offences could include mass picketing, which is likely to contravene TULRCA 1992, s 241 (see para **6.76**); breach of s 240 of that Act (which makes it an offence wilfully and maliciously to break a contract of service or of hiring, knowing or having reasonable cause to believe that the probable consequences of so doing will be to endanger human life, cause serious bodily injury, or expose valuable property to destruction or serious injury), for which there are no reported prosecutions but which could nevertheless be relevant in this context; and industrial action which breaches health and safety legislation. For specific groups which are subject to constraints on industrial action, see Morris, 1991, and for an overview, Deakin and Morris, 1998, 933–937.

4. Above, note 2, at 154, 153; see also the references cited in note 2, above. In *Sherard v AUEW* [1973] ICR 421, CA, the judgment of Lord Denning MR suggests that the possibility that industrial action may be tortious is not a ground for restraining the union from calling the strike (but see also para **6.112** below). Cf. *NSFU of Great Britain and Northern Ireland v Reed* [1926] Ch 536 at 539–540, ChD (unlawful for a union to call a strike where there was no trade dispute).

5. See para **6.61**. Both these measures were taken during the 1984–1985 miners' strike and the 1988 P & O dispute. See *Clarke v Heathfield* [1985] ICR 203, CA. See now also TULRCA 1992, s 16, discussed in para **6.117**.

6.111 Trade union members may challenge the decision to take industrial action in three principal ways: first, they may wish to restrain the union from taking the action at all; secondly, they may seek to restrain the unauthorised expenditure of money, such as strike pay, in support of the action; and, thirdly, they may refuse to participate in the action and wish to forestall or challenge disciplinary action being taken against them for this refusal.[1] The case law arising out of the 1984–1985 miners' strike illustrates all three of these processes in operation.[2] The strike was held to contravene the rules both of the National Union of

Mineworkers and of some of the constituent area unions because of non-compliance with the rules relating to ballots and, as such, it was declared unlawful.[3] This meant that instructions or directions issued by the unions to the membership to strike, not to work, or not to cross picket lines were similarly unlawful, and the claimants could disregard them with impunity.[4] Injunctions were granted which, variously, restrained the defendant unions from taking disciplinary action against the respective claimants for refusing to comply with such directions or instructions, and from instructing or seeking to persuade members not to work or cross picket lines by describing the strike as official or by threatening disciplinary action.[5] In subsequent proceedings, the claimants successfully sought an injunction to restrain one area union from further using its funds for the purposes of the strike, such as payments to pickets and striking miners.[6] However, the court refused to grant summary judgment on the claim for damages against the secretary and/or treasurer of the union for breach of contract and/or breach of trust in relation to payments already made; although the defendants were liable to reimburse the union, it was open to the majority of members to resolve that no action should be taken to remedy this wrong and this eventuality could not be ruled out in the 'wholly unprecedented' circumstances surrounding the case.[7] The fact that the NUM could not use its own funds to support the strike did not prevent another union making payments to the NUM to assist the conduct of the strike or to alleviate hardship among the families of striking miners, given that these purposes came within the general objects of that union.[8]

---

1. Elias and Ewing, 1987, 236.

2. See *ibid.*, 119–132; Ewing, 1985.

3. *Taylor v NUM (Derbyshire Area)* [1984] IRLR 440, ChD; *Taylor and Foulstone v NUM (Yorkshire Area) and NUM* [1984] IRLR 445, ChD.

4. See the *Derbyshire* case, above.

5. *Ibid.* In the *Derbyshire* case the union was also restrained from implementing the suspension from membership of the claimants. An additional reason the national union was disabled from imposing any disciplinary penalty was that it had no power under the rules to do this. In *Clarke v Chadburn (No 2)* [1984] IRLR 350, ChD the court held void for illegality a rule giving the national union such a power because it was passed in defiance of a court order restraining such a resolution being passed owing to one area being unable to mandate its delegates on the matter.

6. *Taylor v NUM (Derbyshire Area) (No 3)* [1985] IRLR 99, ChD. An injunction to this effect was initially granted without notice (formerly known as *ex parte*). The rules expressly allowed payments to be made for strikes called within the rules and the court held that it was impossible to imply consistently with that a power to make a similar allowance to members on strike in breach of the rules. (See also *YMA v Howden* [1903] 1 KB 309, CA and [1905] AC 256, HL, on which the Court relied.)

7. *Taylor v NUM (Derbyshire Area) (No 3)*, above, 107–108.
8. *Hopkins v NUS* [1985] IRLR 157, ChD. However, it seems to have been accepted that once the sequestration order was made against the NUM, a payment which was liable to be seized by the sequestrators was not within the objects of the NUS. A payment for alleviating distress would not be liable to seizure.

6.112 Where a union seeks to discipline a member for non-participation in industrial action, by expulsion or otherwise, the power to do this must be clearly present in the union rules. This may be achieved either by a rule which specifically relates to industrial action or by a broader rule which permits disciplinary action for conduct prejudicial or detrimental to the interests of the union (howsoever phrased). As we have indicated in para **6.111**, the exercise of disciplinary power may be challenged on the ground that the industrial action in question was not authorised by the union rules. Even where industrial action was within the rules, however, it may still be possible in certain circumstances to argue that disciplinary action is invalid at common law.[1] First, a direct instruction to union members to commit a tort would be unlawful.[2] Thus, a rule which empowered a union to compel its members to take industrial action, whether or not they thereby committed a tort, would be void. However,

> [i]n practice . . . rules do not take this form. Rather they will permit various bodies within the union to call industrial action in certain circumstances, and the rule will make no reference at all to any unlawful acts which might thereby be committed. In these circumstances the court will construe the rule so as to permit the union to do what is lawful, and the rule itself will be valid.[3]

Nevertheless, there remain some situations where an instruction will inevitably involve the commission of a tort: an order to 'sit-in' would constitute an order for a member to commit a trespass, and picketing, particularly mass picketing, may, in certain circumstances (for example, if clearly designed to obstruct access to premises), fall within this category.[4] Where members are required to take action which will involve the union but not them as individuals in the commission of a tort, it has been suggested that a member could not be disciplined for non-compliance, even though he or she could not prevent the action taking place on this ground,[5] but this view remains unsupported by any other authority.[6] Secondly, there is some slender authority to suggest that it may be unlawful for a union to discipline a member who fails to strike in breach of a procedure agreement,[7] although this argument rests largely upon one possible interpretation of a single decision. An alternative explanation of that decision is that the union's instructions caused the claimant to break his contract of employment, but this is not compatible with a Court of Appeal ruling that an instruction to break an employment contract is not *per se* unlawful.[8] Thirdly, where taking industrial action conflicts with the fiduciary duties which directors and possibly other managers owe to their company, there is authority to suggest that the courts will give priority to the fiduciary obligation.[9] Lastly, in *Esterman v NALGO*, Templeman J appeared to allow a species of 'conscientious objection' clause, considering that there may be circumstances where, even if a union had the power under its rules to order the action, the member would be justified in concluding that the order was one to which it had no right to demand obedience and which, as a loyal member of the union, he or she felt bound to disobey.[10] The facts of this case were highly unusual,[11] and, although this dictum has never been expressly disavowed, it has not been followed in subsequent cases.

---

1. We focus here upon substantive grounds of challenge; the procedural grounds which apply generally (see para **2.12** *et seq.*) will also apply in this context. The categorisation here is derived from Elias and Ewing, 1987, chapter 7.

2. See Treitel, 1999, Chapter 11 for the effect of a contract to commit a tort.

3. Elias and Ewing 1987, 242.

4. See further paras **6.68** *et seq.*

5. Lord Denning MR in *Sherard v AUEW* [1973] ICR 421 at 433: no steps should be taken against a member who thought it right not to participate in industrial action not in furtherance of a trade dispute.

6. Lord Denning's view may have been influenced by the fact that the Industrial Relations Act 1971 (now repealed) made disciplinary measures in those circumstances unlawful.

7. *Partington v NALGO* [1981] IRLR 537, Ct of Sess, Lord Allanbridge at 542; see also *Porter v NUJ* [1979] IRLR 404, CA, Lord Denning MR at 407 (decision upheld HL ([1980] IRLR 404) without reference to this point).

8. *Porter v NUJ*, above. Moreover, if this was the basis of the decision in *Partington*, above, the court failed to address the relevance of TULRCA 1992, s 180 (see para **6.84**) to the question of incorporation of the collective agreement into the individual contract. (As it was agreed that the collective agreement was a term of the individual contract, no consideration was given to its appropriateness for incorporation.)

9. *Boulting v ACTT* [1963] 2 QB 606,CA.

10. [1974] ICR 625 at 633–634, ChD.

11. This point was emphasised by Templeman J at 632. Moreover, the decision must be seen in the light of the fact that there was doubt under the rules whether the union had the authority to give the instruction it did; to argue that the doctrine applies even where conformity with the rules is clear would be a much wider proposition.

6.113 In practice, challenges to disciplinary measures connected with industrial action, particularly where that action is lawful under the union rules, are most likely now to be brought under the statutory right not to be 'unjustifiably disciplined' contained in the Trade Union and Labour Relations (Consolidation) Act 1992, ss 64–67. However, the common law remains of relevance for two reasons: first, because it offers the possibility of injunctive relief, whereas the statute provides only for financial compensation; and, secondly, because the statute requires a disciplinary 'determination' to have been made whereas on occasion the courts have been prepared to grant a remedy at an earlier stage, sometimes restraining the union from holding even an initial inquiry into whether there has been a breach of the union rules. Thus in *Esterman v NALGO* Templeman J considered that no reasonable tribunal could *bona fide* conclude that disobedience to the strike call in question demonstrated unfitness to be a member of the union as charged and he granted an interim injunction to restrain any disciplinary action (although emphasising that this should be done only in 'exceptional circumstances').[1] In *Porter v NUJ*[2] the House of Lords also took a highly interventionist approach, holding that since there were serious issues of disputed fact as to the lawfulness of the strike call and whether the union was entitled to take disciplinary proceedings against the claimants, the balance of convenience lay clearly in favour of maintaining the *status quo*, by which the claimants remained members of the union, until the trial. This meant that the union would have been forced to undertake potentially lengthy litigation had it wished to proceed with the disciplinary measures.[3] In the later case of *Longley v NUJ*,[4] the Court of Appeal took a very different approach, emphasising that the courts should be slow to prevent domestic tribunals adjudicating upon a matter in the first instance. The court approved the statement of the trial judge that '[a] domestic tribunal which has not embarked upon a hearing should not be restrained unless it has acted improperly or it is inevitable that it will do so';[5] even where it was shown that no reasonable tribunal could uphold the complaint, unless there was persuasive evidence to suggest that the issues had been prejudged or that the prescribed procedures would not be followed, it was preferable to leave the complaint to be heard by the domestic tribunal.[6] This approach accords with that of the legislation and, if followed, would make it much more difficult for claimants to forestall the disciplinary process.

---

1. [1974] ICR 625, ChD, at 632. As Davies and Freedland, 1984, 606, point out: 'In practice the test applied seemed to be more like whether a reasonable member might consider the call for industrial action a breach of the union's rules or even simply unwise'.

2. [1980] IRLR 404, HL.

3. Cf. Lord Diplock, above, at 406, who stated that for the claimants loss of a union card would constitute a serious handicap whereas for the union it was merely

'vengeance . . . postponed'. *Quaere* whether the current non-enforceability of the closed shop (see para **3.17** *et seq.*) would influence judicial attitudes today?

4. [1987] IRLR 109, CA.

5. Nourse LJ at 112, with whom the other judges agreed.

6. Nourse LJ emphasised (at 112) that the standard of 'reasonableness', although objective, was to some extent conditioned by the practices and traditions of the union which was, in the first instance 'in a far better position to define and apply [it] than the court'. Ralph Gibson LJ, in a judgment whose tenor strongly emphasised non-interventionist arguments, suggested (at 114) that there might be a case for prior restraint if the tribunal had in the past 'misconstrued and misapplied' the rules and was likely to do so again, an approach which, if followed, would have potentially wide implications.

Statutory Rights

The right to a ballot

6.114 A trade union member who claims that members of the union, of which he or she is one, are likely to be, or have been, induced by the union to take (or to continue to take) part in industrial action which lacks the support of a ballot may apply to the High Court for an order restraining such inducement.[1] The 'inducement' need not be effective.[2] Industrial action is deemed to lack the support of a ballot unless the statutory requirements for conducting a ballot (including, where applicable, the provisions relating to the independent scrutineer) have been met, the union has not called on its members to take part in the action to which the ballot relates before the date of the ballot, and the call is made by a specified person.[3] The requirements for conducting a valid ballot are described in paras **6.30** *et seq.*[4] Where the court upholds a member's application, it must make an order requiring the union to take steps to ensure that there is no (or no further) inducement of members to take (or to continue to take) part in the industrial action and that no member takes industrial action as a result of any prior inducement.[5] Interim relief may be granted for this purpose.[6] Failure on the part of the union to comply with the order would constitute contempt of court.[7]

---

1. TULRCA 1992, s 62. An act is done by a union if it was authorised or endorsed by the union according to the principles in TULRCA 1992, s 20(2)–(4); see further para **6.13** *et seq.* 'The court' in relation to England and Wales means the High Court: s 121.

2. *Ibid.*, s 62(6). The inducement may be ineffective because the member is unwilling to be influenced by it or for any other reason.

3. *Ibid.*, s 62(2).

4. Note also the effect on liability in tort of failing to conduct a ballot in accordance with the statutory requirements. The union need not hold separate ballots for the purpose of this provision and in order to retain immunity in tort: *ibid.*, s 62(9). There also circumstances in which an individual employer or third parties (under the statutory right of action: see para **6.11)** may be able to seek a remedy in circumstances where this course would not be open to union members, for example if a relevant employer who is not informed of the ballot result: ss 226(1)(b), 231A.

5. TULRCA 1992, s 62(3).

6. *Ibid.*, s 62(4).

7. See para **6.61** *et seq.*

The right not to be unjustifiably disciplined

6.115 An individual who is, or at any time has been, a member of a trade union has the right not to be 'unjustifiably disciplined' by that union and may be awarded substantial financial compensation if this right is infringed.[1] Much of the conduct which may found a claim for 'unjustifiable discipline' relates to non-participation in, or opposition to, industrial action.[2] The right is enforced by way of complaint to an employment tribunal in the first instance.[3] It forms an addition to, not a substitute for, other rights which may be available to the individual; thus, the member may still sue for breach of contract if the disciplinary action infringes the union rules.[4] However, the statutory right exists irrespective of whether the action is lawful under the rules or, indeed, whether it has the support of a ballot. The introduction of this provision attracted considerable criticism in Parliament from the right, as well as the left, of the political spectrum, one argument from the former being that it would undermine the representativity of the ballot by discouraging those opposed to the action from voting against it if they knew that they would be protected against retaliatory action for non-participation. From an early stage the ILO Committee of Experts on the Application of Conventions and Recommendations has condemned the provision as being in conflict with Article 3 of Convention 87 on Freedom of Association and Protection of the Right to Organise on the ground that this requires that union members should be permitted when drawing up their constitutions and rules to determine whether or not it should be possible to discipline members who refuse to participate in lawful strikes or other industrial action.[5] It has also been regarded by the Committee of Independent Experts (now the ECSR) as incompatible with the right to organise guaranteed by Article 5 of the ESC.[6] It is notable that, given the clear view that these restrictions breach international standards, the Labour Government has taken no steps to date to remove these restrictions, and shows no intention of doing so. There are four kinds of conduct particularly relevant to industrial action which could found a complaint were a member to be disciplined for engaging in it.[7] The first is failing to participate in or support any strike or other industrial action (whether by members of the trade union in question or by others) or indicating opposition to, or a lack of support for, such action. Industrial action is not defined in this context.[8] The second form of conduct is failing to contravene, for a purpose connected with such a strike or other industrial action, a requirement imposed on that person by or under a contract of employment, which in this context includes any agreement between that individual and a person for whom he works or normally works.[9] As discussed in para **6.81** *et seq.*, most forms of industrial action constitute a breach of the contract of employment. The term 'any agreement' covers the self-employed and is also sufficiently wide to include an agreement entered into between the employer and member after the industrial action has begun, for example, that the member will take on additional duties during the industrial action or will be paid a bonus for continued working. In addition, it protects workers recruited after the industrial action has started. The third is asserting (whether by bringing proceedings or otherwise) that the union, or any of its officials, representatives, or trustees of its property, has contravened, or is proposing to contravene, any requirement which is, or is thought to be, imposed by or under the union rules or any other agreement or by or under any enactment or rule of law.[10] However this does not apply where the assertion was false and the individual believed this or acted otherwise in bad faith.[11] Encouraging another person to make, or attempt to vindicate, such an assertion is also protected. The fourth form of protected conduct is encouraging or assisting a person to perform an obligation imposed on him or her by a contract of employment (in the extended sense of the term as defined above). This last provision protects a member who attempts to persuade others to continue working, at least where the industrial action constitutes a breach of contract, regardless of whether the action is supported by a majority of the workforce. However, its application is not confined to industrial disputes. The inclusion of this protection undermined the justification afforded by the Conservative Government for the introduction of these restrictions, which was that 'every union member should be free to decide for himself whether or not he wishes to break his contract of employment and run the risk of dismissal without compensation'.[12] Their retention now that there is at least limited protection against dismissal for participating in 'protected industrial action' (see para **6.98**) is even more difficult to justify.

---

1. TULRCA 1992, s 64. See paras **2.27** and **2.28** for further details of this right, and para **2.27** for the definition of 'disciplined'. In *NALGO v Killorn and Simm* [1990] IRLR

464, EAT it was held that naming a member as a strikebreaker in a branch circular with the intention of causing her embarrassment constituted 'unjustifiable discipline'

2. TULRCA 1992, s 65(2)–(4).

3. TULRCA 1992, s 66. There is a right of appeal to the EAT on questions of law and the EAT also hears applications for compensation where the union fails to reverse the effect of a decision which constitutes unjustifiable discipline.

4. *Ibid.*, s 64(5). However the only remedies for infringement of the statutory right are those conferred by the statute (although see also s 64(3)). Unlike the common law position (see paras **6.111**–**6.113**), the statutory right arises only when a disciplinary 'determination' has been made; it does not allow the individual to forestall the disciplinary process: see *TGWU v Webber* [1990] IRLR 462, EAT (discussed in para **2.27**). However, it is conceivable that a union's breach of s 64 could constitute unlawful means in an action in tort by a third party, particularly in the light of *Associated British Ports v TGWU* [1989] IRLR 305, CA (see para **6.8**). The government did not accept an amendment proposed to exclude this possibility: Lord Wedderburn, HL Debs, Vol 485, col 511, 7 March 1988.

5. See Report III, Pt 4A, 1989, 237; see further paras **1.19** and **1.20**.

6. See para **1.21**. See also Leader, 1991 where it argued that the measure also impinges on trade unionists' right to freedom of association under Art 11 of the ECHR in forcing them to keep within their ranks individuals who refuse to take part in industrial action. See further Chapter 1 for discussion of the scope of freedom of association.

7. TULRCA 1992, s 65. See para **2.27** for discussion of the remaining reasons. The section also covers 'proposing to engage in, or doing anything preparatory or incidental to' such conduct: s 65(4). It is sufficient if the specified conduct constitutes one of the reasons for disciplining the member or that something is believed by the union to amount to such conduct: s 65(1). Note the rider to s 65(5) discussed in para **2.27**, which was inserted to protect bodies which maintain professional standards. Persons holding office or employment under the Crown on terms which do not constitute a contract of employment are deemed to have a contract for the purposes of these provisions: s 65(8).

8. See para **6.91** for the definition of a 'strike' in other contexts. In *Knowles v FBU* [1996] IRLR 617, the Court of Appeal held that 'the question of what is industrial action for the purposes of s 65 . . . is a mixed question of fact and law. In large measure it is a question of fact, but the facts have to be judged in the context of the Act which plainly contemplates that industrial action is a serious step'. It was 'necessary to look at all the circumstances. These circumstances will include the contracts of employment of the employees and whether any breach of or departure from the terms of the contract are involved, the effect on the employer of what is done or omitted, and the object which the union or the employees seek to achieve': Neill LJ at 621.

9. TULRCA 1992, s 65(7). See App 1 for the general definition.

10. 'Official' is defined in *ibid.*, s 119 and covers both union officers and a person elected or appointed in accordance with the union rules to be a representative of union members or some of them, including employees of the same employer as members whom he or she represents. It thus includes shop stewards. 'Representative' means a person acting or purporting to act in his or her capacity as a member of the union or on the instructions or advice of a person acting or purporting to act in that capacity or in the capacity of an official of the union: s 65(7).

11. *Ibid.*, s 65(6).
12. *Trade Unions and their Members* Cm 95, 1987, 7–8.

Prohibition on indemnities for unlawful conduct

6.116 At one time several trade unions made provision in their rules for indemnifying members, in particular officials, for specified unlawful acts. At common law, provided that their rules so permitted, unions were free to resolve to make payments in respect of offences already permitted but not future ones.[1] This practice is now prohibited: it is unlawful for union property to be applied in or towards:

(a) the payment for an individual of any penalty which has been or may be imposed on him for an offence[2] or for contempt of court;
(b) the securing of any such payment, or
(c) the provision of anything for indemnifying an individual in respect of such a penalty.[3]

Although these provisions may apply in a wide range of contexts, in practice they are likely to be most relevant in relation to industrial action. 'Penalty' includes an order to pay compensation and an order for the forfeiture of any property.[4] The statute does not include the legal expenses of defending a prosecution or contempt case; whether a payment or indemnity for the former is lawful depends, first, upon whether it is authorised by the union rules and, secondly, whether or not it is open to challenge on public policy grounds.[5] Civil damages are also excluded from the statutory restriction; whether or not individuals may be indemnified in this regard depends upon the union rules. Since the removal of union immunity from liability in tort in 1982 (see para **6.1**) indemnities for individuals in this context have become less significant. Union 'property' is not defined, but it clearly extends beyond money, and 'the provision of anything' in (c) covers non-monetary property which could be converted into money.[6] There may be difficulty in deciding when something becomes the 'property' of the union, however; what if a union organises a voluntary collection specifically to indemnify a member who has been required to pay a fine, for example? Where unions merely administer the property of others, for example an anonymous (or named) non-union donor, for a prohibited purpose, they should be careful to ensure that they can account for this if challenged.[7] Conversely, they may not apply union property for a prohibited purpose through a third-party holding agency. The statutory restriction is without prejudice to any other provision, such as the union rules, which may restrict the application of union property.[8] If union property is applied for a prohibited purpose for the benefit of a particular individual, the payment is recoverable from that individual or, in the case of an application of property, that person is liable to account to the union for the value of the property.[9] A union member who claims that a failure by the union to bring or continue proceedings to this end is 'unreasonable' may apply to the High Court for an order authorising the applicant to bring or continue the proceedings on the union's behalf and at the union's expense.[10] These provisions are without prejudice to any other remedy available to the union, its trustees, or individual members.[11] Initially these constraints on the use of union property were condemned by the ILO's Committee of Experts on the Application of Conventions and Recommendations as incompatible with Article 3 of Convention 87 in that they 'den[ied] trade unions the right to utilise their funds as they wish for normal and lawful trade union purposes'.[12] In more recent reports, however, the Committee took a less confident tone, appearing to acknowledge the Conservative Government's case which included the argument that where penalties were imposed on an individual, rather than a union, this would 'imply a clear finding of wilful and unlawful action by that individual'.[13] However it has maintained the view that indemnification in respect of legal liabilities incurred on behalf of the union should be possible. The ECSR (formerly the CIE) which supervises the ESC also takes the view that in principle unions should be free to use their property as they consider appropriate.

---

1. *Drake v Morgan* [1978] ICR 56, QBD; cf. *Thomas v NUM (South Wales Area)* [1985] IRLR 136, ChD.

2. The Secretary of State may by order designate offences in relation to which the section does not apply: TULRCA 1992, s 15(5). At the time of writing no such order has been made.

3. TULRCA 1992, s 15.

4. *Ibid.*, s 15(4).

5. See *Drake v Morgan*, above, note 1, at 61.

6. It seems that the statute does not apply to the use of branch property where the union rules clearly specify that this is not the property of the union: *News Group Newspapers Ltd v SOGAT 82 (No 2)* [1986] IRLR 227, CA.

7. TULRCA 1992, s 30 (see para **2.32**) may be of assistance to a member wishing to challenge such a transaction.

8. *Ibid.*, s 15(6)(a).

9. TULRCA 1992, s 15(2). There may be problems if the value of the property has diminished in the hands of the individual, possibly merely by virtue of transfer of ownership (as with a car). The purpose of the section would appear to be that the original value should be restored to the union (Honeyball, 1988, para 7.12). Such proceedings will normally be able to be brought in the county court.

10. *Ibid.*, s 15(3).

11. *Ibid.*, s 15(6)(b).

12. Report III (Part 4A), ILO, Geneva, 1989, 237.

13. *Ibid.*, 1992, 245.

Remedy against trustees for unlawful use of property

6.117 All property belonging to a trade union must be vested in trustees on trust for the union.[1] A union member may apply to the High Court regarding the trustees' use of union property on two separate grounds.[2] The first is if or she claims that the trustees have so carried out, or are proposing so to carry out, their functions as to 'cause or permit' any unlawful application of the union's property. This would seem to cover releasing funds to further an unlawful purpose; it would certainly cover using union funds to support unlawful industrial action by the union itself or, indeed, by any other union. The power to complain if trustees are 'proposing' a course of action gives members a wide preventative power which may be particularly significant in the context of industrial disputes. The second is if the member claims that the trustees have complied, or are proposing to comply, with an unlawful direction which has or may be given, or purportedly given, under the union rules. Thus, even if the trustees are specifically empowered by the rules or the trust instrument to act in a particular way, or are obliged to obey the directions of the union's executive, the member may have a remedy.[3] Where the court is satisfied that a member's claim is well-founded, it shall make such order as it considers appropriate.[4] This may include power to require the trustees (if necessary on behalf of the union) to take specified steps for protecting or recovering union property (including, presumably, obliging them to take legal proceedings against any relevant person); power to appoint a receiver of the union's property;[5] or power to remove one or more trustees. However, the court has less discretion where union property has been applied in contravention of a court order, or in compliance with a direction which contravenes a court order, or the trustees were proposing to apply property in such a way; it must then remove all the trustees except any individual trustee who satisfies it that there is good reason for allowing him or her to remain.[6] The removal of all the trustees will not necessarily lead to the appointment of a receiver; the court has the power to appoint new trustees itself under the Trustee Act 1925.[7] An interim injunction may be awarded under this provision,[8] which is without prejudice to any other remedy which may lie in respect of a breach of trust by the trustees of a union's property.[9] The union members are protected against being disciplined for the exercise of this right.[10]

---

1. TULRCA, 1992, s 12.

2. *Ibid.*, s 16(1). A person is not entitled to make an application in respect of property which has already been unlawfully applied or a direction which has already been complied with unless he was a member at the time of that application or compliance: s 16(2). Given that union property is held on trust for the union, members would appear not to be direct beneficiaries of the trust so their *locus standi* to bring an action for

breach of trust, other than where there has been a breach of the union rulebook, is uncertain: cf. *Hughes v TGWU* [1985] IRLR 382, ChD.

3. Under the general law, trustees are bound to obey only the lawful instructions of the union's executive committee: *Clarke v Heathfield (No 2)* [1985] ICR 606, ChD, at 614.

4. TULRCA 1992, s 16(3). The statutory language suggests that the court is obliged to make an order but Mr Patrick Nicholls stated in Committee that the court retained discretion to decide not to make an order: House of Commons, Official Report of Standing Committee F, col 305, 10 December 1989.

5. A restriction on the appointment of a receiver over union funds in the Trade Union Act 1871 was repealed by the Industrial Relations Act 1971 (now itself repealed).

6. TULRCA 1992, s 16(4).

7. S 41.

8. TULRCA 1992, s 16(5).

9. *Ibid.*, s 16(6).

10 *Ibid.*, s 65(2)(c).

APPENDIX 1

DEFINITIONS

In this Appendix we set out the definitions of terms that occur frequently throughout the text, and which are not defined elsewhere. We confine ourselves, in the main, to legislation which is relevant to collective labour law.

1. Employer

In broad terms, an employer is a person or group of persons, including a partnership, who or which employs an employee or worker. In a partnership employees are normally regarded as being employed by all the partners and a change of identity of the partners does not break continuity of employment: ERA 1996, s 218(5). For statutory purposes the definition of employer varies according to the context in question. We set out below the main statutory definitions:

TULRCA 1992, s 295—'employer', in relation to an employee, means the person by whom the employee is (or, where the employment has ceased, was) employed.

TULRCA 1992, s 296(2)—'employer', in relation to a worker, means a person for whom one or more workers work, or have worked or normally work or seek to work.

TULRCA 1992, s 235, in relation to the requirement for a ballot before industrial action for whose organisation a union is deemed responsible, states that references to a contract of employment include any contract under which one person personally does work or performs services for another and *employer* and other related expressions *shall be construed accordingly* (our italics).

ERA 1996, s 230(4)—'employer', in relation to an employee or a worker, means the person by whom the employee or worker is (or, where the employment has ceased, was) employed.

NMWA 1998, s 54(4)—'employer', in relation to an employee or a worker means the person by whom the employee or worker is (or, where the employment has ceased, was) employed.

TUPE 1981, reg 2(1)—'employee' means any individual who works for another person whether under a contract of service, or apprenticeship or otherwise but does not include anyone who provides services under a contract for services and *references to a person's employer shall be construed accordingly* (our italics).

National Minimum Wage Regulations 1999, reg 2(1)—'employer' has the meaning given to it by s 54(4) of NMWA 1998 but, in relation to a worker (as defined in s 54(3) of the Act), includes in addition, (except in paragraph (6) of reg 12)—
(a) an agent or principal in relation to whom, by virtue of s 34(2) of the Act, the provisions of the Act have effect as if there were a worker's contract between him and an agency worker for the doing of work by the agency worker, and
(b) an employer of a home worker who is a worker by virtue of s 35 of the Act.

Under *ERA 1999, s 23(4) (b)* the Secretary of State may by order make provision as to who are to be regarded as the employers of individuals.

2. Employers' Association

TULRCA 1992, s 122 defines an employers' association as an organisation (whether temporary or permanent) which either:
(a) consists wholly or mainly of employers or individual owners of undertakings of one or more descriptions and whose principal purposes include the regulation of relations between employers of that description or those descriptions and workers or trade unions; or
(b) which consists wholly or mainly of
   (i) constituent or affiliated organisations which fulfil the conditions specified in paragraph (a) (or themselves consist wholly or mainly of constituent or affiliated organisations which fulfil those conditions), or
   (ii) representatives of such constituent or affiliated organisations
and whose principal purposes include the regulation of relations between employers and workers or between employers and trade unions, or the regulation of relations between its constituent and affiliated organisations.
References in the Act to employers' associations include combinations of employers and employers' associations.

ERA 1996, s 235(1) adopts the same definition.

3. Associated Employers

TULRCA 1992, s 297 and *ERA 1996, s 231* both state that any two employers shall be treated as associated if—
(a) one is a company of which the other (directly or indirectly) has control, or
(b) both are companies of which a third person (directly or indirectly) has control;
and 'associated employer' shall be construed accordingly.

The fact that two employers are 'associated' does not mean that an employee of one of those employers is an employee of the other. However, certain rights may be conferred on an employee in relation to an employer who is an associated employer of his or her employer: see, for example, ERA 1996, s 115(1) (order for re-engagement). In addition, the concept is important in relation to continuity of employment. If an employee of one employer is taken into the employment of another who, at the time when the employee enters his or her employment, is an associated employer of the first employer, the employee's period of employment at that time counts as a period of employment with the second employer and the change of employers does not break the continuity of the period of employment: ERA 1996, s 218(6). Whether employers are associated may also be important in the context of certain trade union rights including the definition of recognition, determining the minimum number of workers employed for the purposes of the mandatory recognition procedure, and the disclosure of information provisions. The definitions in TULRCA 1992, s 297; ERA 1996, s 231 means that at least one of the employers must be a limited company[1] and therefore partnerships and many employers in the public sector are excluded.[2] The importance of one of the employers being a limited company is exemplified by decisions relating to the meaning of 'control'. The test is not who runs the business on a day-to-day basis but, rather, who has the right to control the company by a majority of the votes in a general meeting.[3] The position is uncertain where nobody has overall voting control, although there is authority to suggest that where there are 50:50 shareholdings in two companies they cannot be associated employers because nobody is in control.[4]

---

1. But see *Pinkney v Sandpiper Drilling Ltd* [1989] IRLR 425, EAT, (companies formed into a partnership of companies can be 'associated employers') and *Hancill v Marcon Engineering Ltd* [1990] IRLR 51, EAT: the company need not be incorporated in the UK if it can be likened in its essentials to a company limited under the Companies Act.
2. See, for example, *Gardiner v London Borough of Merton* [1980] IRLR 472, CA; *Hasley v Fair Employment Agency* [1989] IRLR 106, NI CA. In some contexts special provision is made for public sector workers.

3. *Secretary of State for Employment v Newbold* [1981] IRLR 305, EAT, but see also *Payne v Secretary of State for Employment* [1989] IRLR 352, CA, where a finding that a shareholder held her share as a nominee of her husband was decisive in determining his voting control.
4. *South West Launderettes Ltd v Laidler* [1986] IRLR 305, CA; cf. *Tice v Cartwright* [1999] ICR 769, EAT.

4. Employment Categories

There are a variety of contractual arrangements under which one individual may work for another. The work may be on a full-time or part-time basis, permanent or temporary, on the employer's premises or elsewhere, paid for by a regular wage or by the job. The law currently makes a basic distinction between individuals who are, on the one hand, 'employees', and who work for another under a contract of employment (or service) and those who work under some other form of arrangement. Many statutory rights, including the right to claim unfair dismissal and a statutory redundancy payment, are available only to 'employees'. In addition, certain rights and obligations will be implied by the courts into contracts of employment, which may not be applicable to other forms of working relationships. For statutory purposes, the position is further complicated by the creation of two other employment categories: a 'worker', and a person who 'personally does work or performs services for another'. The parties may choose to stipulate the legal nature of their relationship in the contract by, for example, stating that the worker is an 'employee'. This does not bind the courts and employment tribunals, which will always look behind a label to ascertain the true nature of the employment relationship,[1] although the label may determine the issue in cases of genuine ambiguity.[2] The scope for appeal against the decision of a tribunal depends on whether the terms of the contract have been reduced to writing. The House of Lords has held that if the parties intend all the terms of their contract (apart from any implied by law) to be contained in a document or documents, the construction of those documents is a question of law. However, if the intention of the parties, objectively ascertained, has to be gathered partly from documents but also from oral exchanges and conduct, the terms of the contract are a question of fact (as is the question whether the parties intended a document or documents to be an exclusive record of their terms of agreement).[3] Designation of this issue as a question of fact means that the decision of the tribunal cannot be challenged on appeal unless it is perverse or based on a misdirection of law.[4] This means that differently constituted tribunals may come to differing conclusions on similar facts but these decisions will nevertheless be unappealable.

1. See, for example, *Ferguson v John Dawson & Partners (Contractors) Ltd* [1976] 3 All ER 817, CA; *Young and Woods Ltd v West* [1980] IRLR 201, CA.
2. *Massey v Crown Life Insurance Co Ltd* [1978] ICR 590, CA.
3. *Carmichael v National Power Plc* [2000] IRLR 43, HL.
4. *Lee v Chung and Shun Shing Construction and Engineering Co Ltd* [1990] IRLR 236, PC.

(a) Employee

TULRCA 1992, s 295(1), ERA 1996, s 230(1) and NMWA 1998, s 54(1) state that 'employee' means an individual who has entered into or works under (or, where the employment has ceased, worked under) a contract of employment.

TUPE 1981, reg 2(1) states that 'employee' means any individual who works for another person whether under a contract of service or apprenticeship or otherwise but does not include anyone who provides services under a contract for services.

'Contract of employment' is defined in ERA 1996, s 230(1) as a 'contract of service or apprenticeship, whether express or implied and (if it is express) whether oral or in writing'. TULRCA 1992, s 295 defines it merely as 'a contract of service or of apprenticeship'. In some contexts, however, it is wider: see, for example, TULRCA 1992, s 235 where it extends to 'any contract under which one person personally does work or performs services for another'. See also TULRCA 1992, s 65(7) and TUPE 1981, reg 2(1). Since there is no statutory definition of 'contract of service' it is necessary to rely solely upon the case law. (The question whether a worker is 'an employee' is relevant also in other contexts, including tax and social security status, vicarious liability and health and safety legislation). In relying on the case law, there is a further difficulty because, although the courts and employment tribunals endeavour to weigh up all the relevant factors to decide the issue, this balancing exercise is unscientific in nature and sometimes unpredictable in result. At one time the courts placed great emphasis upon the extent of an employer's control over a worker; if the employer could tell the worker not only what work to do but also how to do it the worker was an employee.[1] This test may be useful in relation to unskilled workers but it is less suited to situations where the worker has specialised skill and training. Another test, the 'organisational' or 'integration' test, asks whether the worker is an integral part of the employer's business or only accessory to it.[2] Nowadays the courts and tribunals tend to look at all the features of the relationship, of which the element of control is but one.[3] Previous practice in relation to tax and social security contributions and the parties' intentions will be relevant, although they are not conclusive. One question of particular importance is whether the individual can be seen as an entrepreneur performing services 'as a person in business on his own account'.[4] This, in turn, requires consideration of several factors, including:

> whether the man [*sic*] performing the services provides his own equipment, whether he hires his own helpers, what degree of financial risk he takes, what degree of responsibility for investment and management he has, and whether and how far he has an opportunity for profiting from sound management in the performance of his task.[5]

Exclusive service for one employer will point towards employee status but the ability to work for others will not point conclusively against it.[6] However, the courts place particular emphasis on the fact that employee status requires both sides to be subject to some degree of obligation; if a worker has no obligation to accept work when it is offered on any given occasion, and the employer has no obligation to provide it, the individual is not an employee,[7] although mutual obligations may be inferred from a course of dealing over time.[8] The consequent exclusion of purely casual workers may, on occasion, conflict with the entrepreneurial test. It has been argued by many commentators that the tests used by the courts to determine employment status are ill-equipped to deal with the variety of relationships in the contemporary labour market and, indeed, that the basis of entitlement to employment protection rights should be changed.[9] The Secretary of State is empowered by the Employment Relations Act 1999, s 23 to extend rights conferred on individuals under that Act, the Trade Union and Labour Relations (Consolidation) Act 1992, the Employment Rights Act 1996 and any instrument made under the European Communities Act 1972 to 'individuals who are of a specified description'.

---

1. See, for example, *Performing Rights Society Ltd v Mitchell and Booker (Palais de Danse) Ltd* [1924] 1 KB 762, KBD; *Mersey Docks and Harbour Board v Coggins and Griffiths Ltd* [1947] AC 1, HL.
2. *Stevenson Jordan and Harrison Ltd v MacDonald and Evans* [1952] 1 TLR 101, CA.
3. *Ready-Mixed Concrete (South-East) Ltd v Minister of Pensions and National Insurance* [1968] 2 QB 497, QBD. Freedom to delegate performance on a regular basis will be inconsistent with a contract of employment—*Ready-Mixed Concrete*, above; *Hitchcock v Post Office* [1980] ICR 100, EAT. *Express & Echo Publications Ltd v Tanton* [1999] IRLR 367, CA. See also *Secretary of State for Trade and Industry v Bottrill* [1999] IRLR 326, CA where it was held that the fact that an individual was a controlling shareholder, whilst significant, was not determinative of the issue as to whether he or she was an employee and that on the facts it was open to the tribunal to find that a genuine contractual relationship existed.

4. *Market Investigations Ltd v Minister of Social Security and National Insurance* [1969] 2 QB 173, QBD; *Lee v Chung and Shun Shing Construction and Engineering Co Ltd* [1990] IRLR 236, PC.

5. *Market Investigations Ltd*, above, at 184. See also *Hall v Lorimer* [1994] ICR 218, CA.

6. *Market Investigations Ltd*, above, note 4.

7. See *Clark v Oxfordshire Health Authority* [1998] IRLR 125, CA, stressing the importance of mutual obligations subsisting over the entire duration of the relevant period and *O'Kelly v Trusthouse Forte plc* [1983] IRLR 369, CA; *Nethermere (St Neots) Ltd v Taverna and Gardiner* [1984] IRLR 240, CA; *McLeod v Hellyer Brothers Ltd* [1987] IRLR 232, CA; *McMeechan v Secretary of State for Employment* [1995] IRLR 353, CA. See also *Carmichael v National Power plc* [2000] IRLR 43, HL, where the applicants were held not to be employees in the absence of the irreducible minimum of mutual obligation necessary to create a contract of service.

8. *Nethermere (St Neots) Ltd v Taverna and Gardiner*, above.

9. See Leighton, 1986; Wedderburn, 1986, chapter 2; Hepple, 1986; Collins, 1990, Deakin and Morris, 1998, 149–171, 232–234.

(b) Worker

TULRCA 1992, 296(1) states that 'worker' means an individual who works, or normally works or seeks to work

(a) under a contract of employment, or

(b) under any other contract whereby he undertakes to do or perform personally any work or services for another party to the contract who is not a professional client of his, or

(c) in employment under or for the purposes of a government department (otherwise than as a member of the naval, military or air forces of the Crown) in so far as such employment does not fall within paragraph (a) or (b) above.

This definition covers self-employed workers as long as they contract to provide work or services personally.[1]

ERA 1996, s 230(3) and *NMWA 1998, s 54(3)* state that 'worker' means an individual who has entered into or works under (or, where the employment has ceased, worked under)

(a) a contract of employment; or

(b) any other contract, whether express or implied and (if it is express) whether oral or in writing, whereby the individual undertakes to do or perform personally any work or services for another party to the contract whose status is not by virtue of the contract that of a client or customer of any profession or business undertaking carried on by the individual;

and any references to a worker's contract shall be construed accordingly.

Note also the special definitions of agency workers and home workers in NMWA 1998, ss 34 and 35.

ERA 1999, s 13 states that 'worker' for the purposes of the right to be accompanied in disciplinary and grievance hearings means an individual who is—

(a) a worker within the meaning of ERA 1996, s 230(3),

(b) an agency worker (defined in ERA 1999, s 13(2)),

(c) a home worker (defined in ERA 1999, s 13(3)),

(d) a person in Crown employment within the meaning of ERA 1996 s 191, other than a member of the naval, military, air or reserve forces of the Crown, or

(e) employed as a relevant member of the House of Lords staff or the House of Commons staff within the meaning of ERA 1996, s 194(6) or 195(5).

Somewhat confusingly, 'worker' has other statutory definitions in other contexts. For example, in relation to a 'trade dispute' with an employer, 'worker' under TULRCA 1992, s 244(5) means a 'worker' employed by that employer, or a person who has ceased to be so employed if his or her employment was terminated in connection with the dispute or if the termination of his or her employment was one of the circumstances giving rise to the dispute. By contrast, the general definition of 'worker' under the Act includes an individual who works or normally works or seeks to work even if not employed by a specific employer: TULCRA 1992, s 296. In the light of these differences, it is particularly important to examine carefully the definition which applies to the statutory provision at issue.

---

1. See *Broadbent v Crisp* [1974] ICR 248, NIRC. There must be some contractual obligation to complete the work in question: *Writer's Guild of Great Britain v BBC* [1974] ICR 234, NIRC and *Edmonds v Lawson QC*, [2000] IRLR 391, CA (unreported). On the exclusion of those with contracts with professional clients, see *Carter v Law Society* [1973] ICR 113, NIRC.

(c) Persons Personally Doing Work or Performing Services for Another

Distinct from the concepts of 'employee' and 'worker', there is the category of persons 'personally doing work or performing services for another'.[1] In relation to secondary industrial action and industrial action ballots, TULRCA 1992 defines a 'contract of employment' as including 'any contract under which one person personally does work or performs services for another': ss 224(6) and 235. The emphasis is therefore placed on personal work and services, much as in the legislation relating to unlawful discrimination where 'employment' is defined as including employment under a contract personally to execute any work or labour: SDA 1975, s 82(1); RRA 1976, s 78(1); DDA 1995, s 68(1). It also reflects aspects of the definition of a 'worker' (see (b) above).

---

1. For judicial interpretation of this concept, see *Hugh-Jones v St John's College* [1979] ICR 848, EAT; *Quinnen v Hovells* [1984] IRLR 227, EAT; *Mirror Group Newspapers Ltd v Gunning* [1986] IRLR 27, CA; *Loughran v Northern Ireland Housing Executive* [1998] IRLR 593, HL.

APPENDIX 2

Time Limits for Employment Tribunal Claims

Employment tribunals have jurisdiction to hear complaints under numerous statutes.[1] It is of crucial importance for there to be strict adherence to the time limit specified in relation to the right in question but a tribunal generally has jurisdiction to grant an extension of time when it considers that the complaint was presented within such further period as it considers reasonable where it is satisfied that it was not reasonably practicable for the complaint to be presented before the end of the relevant period. There is considerable case law on what is meant by the words 'reasonably practicable'. Most of these cases are in the context of claims for unfair dismissal. The onus is on the applicant to satisfy the tribunal that it was not reasonably practicable to present the claim in time.[2] 'Reasonably practicable' has been interpreted as 'reasonably feasible'.[3] 'Reasonably practicable' is largely a question of fact for the tribunal, and unless it misdirects itself, it will be difficult to sustain a successful appeal. In the light of this, previous cases are of limited value but afford some general guidance. The time limits are often strictly construed against the applicant, particularly if he or she has engaged 'skilled advisers' which has been held to include in this context solicitors,[4] trade union officers[5] and a Citizens Advice Bureau[6] but not an employee of an employment tribunal.[7] In *London International College Ltd v Sen*[8] Bingham MR questioned whether these cases were really purporting to lay down a rule of law that an applicant who consults a solicitor can no longer say that it was not reasonably practicable for him or her to comply with the time limit even if the advice is wrong, as this is essentially a question of fact. It has been held that a late presentation by just one day had the effect of debarring a tribunal from entertaining the application[9], although the originating application can be presented up to midnight on the last day[10]. The date from which time starts to run depends on the wording of the relevant statutory provision. A number of the time limits within which complaints before tribunals must be presented begin with the date of the act complained of. This means that the date itself counts for the purposes of computation of the period. If a tribunal holds that it was not reasonably practicable to present a claim in time, the extension of time allowed will be for such period as it considers reasonable. There is no fixed limit and each case is considered on its own facts and in the light of the applicant's reasons for the delay.[11] These time limits for the presentation of claims are jurisdictional rather than procedural and therefore cannot be waived by the employer. This is contrasted with common law claims to the High Court where the general rule is that if a claim is brought out of time the court will not normally, of its own volition, bar the claim if the defendant is prepared to allow it to proceed.

---

1. They also have a limited jurisdiction to hear certain contractual claims, see Employment Tribunals Extension of Jurisdiction (England and Wales) Order 1994, SI 1994/1623.

2. *Porter v Bandridge Ltd* [1978] IRLR 271, CA.

3. *Palmer and Saunders v Southend-on-Sea Borough Council* [1984] IRLR 119, CA. See also *Schultz v Esso Petroleum Co Ltd* [1999] 3 ALL ER 338 where the Court of Appeal held that in assessing whether or not something could or should have been done within the limitation period, while looking at the period as a whole, attention will in the ordinary way focus on the closing rather than the early stages.

4. *Dedman v British Building and Engineering Appliances Ltd* [1973] IRLR 379, CA.

5. *Union Cartage Co Ltd v Blunden* [1977] IRLR 139, EAT.

6. *Riley v Tesco Stores Ltd* [1980] IRLR 103, CA.

7. *Jean Sorelle Ltd v Rybak* [1991] IRLR 153, EAT.

8. [1993] IRLR 333 at 336.

9. *Haigh v Lewis & Co (Westminster) Ltd* [1973] ITR 360, NIRC; *Pruden v Cunard Ellerman Ltd* [1993] IRLR 317, EAT; *University of Cambridge v Murray* [1993] ICR 460, EAT.

10. *Post Office v Moore* [1981] ICR 623, EAT.

11. *Marley (UK) Ltd v Anderson* [1996] IRLR 163, CA.

APPENDIX 3

List of Employment Tribunals

ASHFORD	Tufton House Tufton Street Ashford Kent TN23 1RJ Tel: 01233 621 346 Fax: 01233 624 423
BEDFORD	8–10 Howard Street Bedford MK40 3HS Tel: 01234 351 306 Fax: 01234 352 315
BIRMINGHAM	Phoenix House 1–3 Newhall Street Birmingham B3 3NH Tel: 0121 236 6051 Fax: 0121 236 6029
BRISTOL	1st Floor The Crescent Centre Temple Back Bristol BS1 6EZ Tel: 0117 929 8261 Fax: 0117 925 3452

BURY ST. EDMUNDS	100 Southgate Street Bury St Edmunds Suffolk IP33 2AQ Tel: 01284 762 171 Fax: 01284 706 064
CARDIFF	2nd Floor Caradog House 1–6 St Andrew's Place Cardiff CF10 3BE Tel: 029 2037 2693 Fax: 029 2022 5906
EXETER	10th floor Renslade House Bonhay Road Exeter EX4 3BX Tel: 01392 279 665 Fax: 01392 430 063
LEEDS	Fourth floor Albion Tower 11 Albion Street Leeds LS1 5ES Tel: 0113 245 9741 Fax: 0113 242 8843
LEICESTER	King's Court 5a New Walk Leicester LE1 5TE Tel: 0116 255 0099 Fax: 0116 255 6099

LIVERPOOL	1st Floor
	Cunard Building
	Pier Head
	Liverpool
	L3 1TS
	Tel: 0151 236 9397
	Fax: 0151 231 1484
LONDON NORTH	19–29 Woburn Place
	London
	WC1H 0LU
	Tel: 020 7 273 8640
	Fax: 020 7 273 8686
LONDON SOUTH	Montague Court
	London Road
	West Croydon
	CR0 2RF
	Tel: 020 8 667 9131
	Fax: 020 8 649 9470
MANCHESTER	Barlow House
	Minshull Street
	Manchester
	M1 3DZ
	(temporary address)
	Tel: 0161 833 0581
	Fax: 0161 832 0249
NEWCASTLE UPON TYNE	Quayside House
	110 Quayside
	Newcastle Upon Tyne
	NE1 3DX
	Tel: 0191 260 6900
	Fax: 0191 222 1680

NOTTINGHAM	3rd floor Byron House 2a Maid Marian Way Nottingham NG1 6HS
	Tel: 0115 947 5701 Fax: 0115 950 7612
READING	5th floor 30–31 Friar Street Reading RG1 1DY
	Tel: 0118 959 4917 Fax: 0118 956 8066
SHEFFIELD	14 East Parade Sheffield S1 2ET
	Tel: 0114 276 0348 Fax: 0114 276 2551
SHREWSBURY	Prospect House Belle Vue Road Shrewsbury SY3 7AR
	Tel: 01743 358 341 Fax: 01743 244 186
SOUTHAMPTON	3rd Floor Duke's Keep Marsh Lane Southampton SO1 1EX
	Tel: 023 8 063 9555 Fax: 023 8 063 5506
STRATFORD (London)	44 The Broadway Stratford E15 1XH
	Tel: 020 8 221 0921 Fax: 020 8 221 0398

APPENDIX 4

List of Offices of Advisory, Conciliation and Arbitration Service in England and Wales

---

HEAD OFFICE

Brandon House
180 Borough High Street
London
SE1 1LW

Tel: 020 7 210 3613
Fax: 020 7 210 3645

MIDLANDS REGION

Warwick House
6 Highfield Road
Edgbaston
Birmingham
B15 3ED

Tel: 0121 456 5856
Fax: 0121 456 5466

Anderson House
Clinton Avenue
Nottingham
NG5 1AW

Tel: 0115 969 3355
Fax: 0115 969 3085

NORTHERN REGION

Commerce House
St. Alban's Place
Leeds
LS2 8HH

Tel: 0113 243 1371
Fax: 0113 247 0429

NORTHERN REGION	Westgate House Westgate Road Newcastle Upon Tyne NE1 ITL
	Tel: 0191 261 2191 Fax: 0191 232 5452
NORTH WEST REGION	Commercial Union House 2–10 Albert Street Manchester M60 8AD
	Tel: 0161 833 8585 Fax: 0161 833 8515
	Cressington House 249 St Mary's Road Garston Liverpool L19 0NF
	Tel: 0151 427 8881 Fax: 0151 427 2715
SOUTH AND WEST REGION	Regent House 27a Regent Street Clifton Bristol BS8 4HR
	Tel: 0117 946 9500 Fax: 0117 946 9501
	Westminster House Fleet Road Fleet Hants GU13 8PD
	Tel: 01252 811 868 Fax: 01252 811 030
LONDON, EASTERN AND SOUTHERN AREAS	Clifton House 83–117 Euston Road London NW1 2RB

Tel: 020 7 396 5100
Fax: 020 7 396 5159

39 King Street
Thetford
Norfolk
IP24 2AU

Tel: 01842 750 432
Fax: 01842 750 433

Suites 3–5
Business Centre
1–7 Commercial Road
Paddock Wood
Kent
TN12 6EN

Tel: 01892 837 273
Fax: 01892 837122

WALES

3 Purbeck House
Lambourne Crescent
Llanishen
Cardiff
CF4 5GL

Tel: 029 2076 1126
Fax: 02920 751 334

Website Address: www.acas.co.uk

To order publications:
ACAS Reader Limited
P.O. Box 16
Earl Shilton
Leicester
LE19 8ZZ

Tel: 01455 852225

APPENDIX 5

List of Other Relevant Offices

EMPLOYMENT APPEAL
TRIBUNAL

Audit House
58 Victoria Embankment
London
EC4Y 0DS

Tel: 020 7 273 1041
Fax: 020 7 273 1045
Web site:
www.employmentappeals.gov.uk

CERTIFICATION OFFICER

Certification Office for Trade Unions and
Employers' Associations
Brandon House
180 Borough High Street
London
SE1 1LW

Tel: 020 7 210 3734/5
Fax: 020 7 210 3612

CENTRAL ARBITRATION
COMMITTEE

Third Floor, Discovery House
28–42 Banner Street
London
EC1Y 8QE

Tel: 020 7 251 9747
Fax: 020 7 251 3114
Web site: www.cac.gov.uk

INTERNATIONAL LABOUR
ORGANISATION

UK Office, London
International Labour Office
Millbank Tower
21–24 Millbank
London
SW1 PQP

Tel: 020 7 828 6401
Fax: 020 7 233 5925
E-mail: london@ilo.org.

Regional Office for Europe, Geneva:
International Labour Office
4, route des Morillons
CH-1211 GENEVA 22

Tel: + 44.22.799.6666
Fax: + 41.22.799.6061
E-mail: europe@ilo.org
ILO Headquaters, Geneva:
International Labour Office
4, route des Morillons
CH-1211 GENEVA 22

Central tel: + 41.22.798.8685
Central fax: + 41.22.799.6111
Web site: www.ilo.org

EUROPEAN COURT OF
HUMAN RIGHTS

Council of Europe
F-67075 Strasbourg-Cedex
France

Tel: 33 (0) 3 88 41 2018
Fax: 33 (0) 3 88 41 2730
Web site: www.echr.coe.int

COUNCIL OF EUROPE

67075 Strasbourg-Cedex
France

Tel: 33 (0) 3 88 41 20 00
Fax: 33 (0) 3 88 41 27 80
Web site: www.coe.fr

APPENDIX 6

We set out below a model recognition agreement between an employer and a trade union. The clauses in the agreement are examples only and will need to be amended, depending on the nature of the business and the extent to which the union is recognised for collective bargaining by the employer. In some cases, agreements of this nature are of considerably greater length, particularly if they append the terms and conditions of employment which are incorporated into employees' contracts of employment. We do not, however, recommend this as it is preferable for a recognition agreement and terms and conditions of employment negotiated pursuant to it to be recorded separately.

RECOGNITION AGREEMENT
BETWEEN
[EMPLOYER] AND [TRADE UNION]

1 This Agreement is made between [Name of Employer] of [address] ['X'] and [Name of Trade Union] of [address] ['Y'], hereinafter referred to collectively as 'the parties'.

2 [X] and [Y] agree on the importance of the role of collective bargaining and the importance of good industrial relations between [X] and its employees and [Y].

3 [X] and [Y] are committed to a working environment free from discrimination, giving equality of opportunity for all those who are employed by [X].

4 [X] and [Y] will at all times act under this Agreement in a spirit of mutual trust and co-operation. The parties agree to use all reasonable endeavours to reach agreement on all issues, and to explore solutions that recognise the needs of the other party. Whilst it is recognised that some conflicts of interest are bound to arise, the parties accept that with good industrial relations they can be resolved in a responsible and constructive way.

5 [X] agrees to give recognition to [Y] for negotiation purposes in those units of the business of [X] [in England and Wales] as defined in Appendix A of this Agreement.

6 In order to assist the involvement of both parties in this Agreement, [X] agrees, where possible and appropriate, to provide information necessary for [Y] properly to represent its members. [Y] agrees to provide, where available and appropriate, information to assist [X] in understanding the concerns of [Y's] members. The parties to this Agreement undertake to respect the confidentiality of all information provided, other than that required to be provided under the Trade Union and Labour Relations (Consolidation) Act 1992 s.181, and undertake to respect any restrictions regarding access to the information, or all embargoes (whether or not in writing) regarding the timing of announcements and notices.

7 The spirit and intention of this Agreement is to bring about a prompt and satisfactory settlement of any problem or grievance. No industrial action, threats, embargoes or departures from normal working will take place until the procedures established under this Agreement have been exhausted.

8 Items agreed to be negotiable are listed in Appendix B of this Agreement.

9 A Negotiating Committee will be established:

- in each of the units set out in Appendix A
- for identified areas/groups of employees within any particular units
- to discuss matters that are common to two or more of these units

10 Each Negotiating Committee will deal exclusively with those matters specific to the specified unit.

11 Meetings of each Negotiating Committee shall be as mutually agreed between the parties. Meetings will be held within [ ] days of a formal request being submitted by either party. A quorum for the meetings of the Negotiating Committee shall be not less than [ ]. Minutes of the meetings of each Negotiating Committee shall be taken, circulated to the parties in draft form and subsequently agreed.

12 The parties agree that informal working parties will, from time to time, be established outside the meetings of the Negotiating Committee to discuss matters of mutual concern and interest, with a view to resolving any problems or difficulties and increasing understanding and co-operation between the parties.

13 All agreements reached between them shall be in writing and be signed by duly authorised representatives of the parties.

14 The parties can agree to refer any differences between them that are not resolved through the discussions in the appropriate Negotiating Committee to ACAS for conciliation. The parties agree that a matter can be referred to conciliation at any stage if it is clear that no further progress is likely to be achieved in the Negotiating Committee.

15 If there is no agreement to refer a matter to ACAS for conciliation, the parties agree that either party can record a formal disagreement, at a Negotiating Committee or in writing. In these circumstances, a Negotiating Committee meeting will normally be convened within [ ] days of a formal disagreement being recorded to allow further discussions with a view to reaching agreement. If agreement is not reached between the parties at this stage, either party has a right unilaterally to refer to ACAS for conciliation.

16 If, under the auspices of the Negotiating Committee or ACAS conciliation, agreement is reached, both parties will agree a timetable for implementation of any such agreement. In the event that no agreement can be reached between the parties or through the auspices of ACAS, procedures will be regarded as complete.

17 The parties agree that the contents of Appendix A will be reviewed from time to time and amended on the basis of changes to the structure of [X].

18 If, as part of the review, [Y] is shown to the reasonable satisfaction of [X] to have a membership level of above [ ]% in a particular unit, [X] will recognise [Y] in that unit and Appendix A will be amended accordingly. If [Y] is shown by [X] to have a membership level below [ ]% in a particular unit then [Y] will cease to be recognised in that unit and Appendix A will be amended accordingly. In these circumstances, [X] and [Y] undertake, if so requested by the other party, to supply relevant information to an independent third party appointed jointly by the parties, for the purpose of examining and verifying information relating to the membership records of employees in the relevant unit of [X].

19 Changes to this Agreement can only be made with the written consent of both parties, duly signed and authorised by the parties.

20 This Agreement can be terminated by either party, giving not less than three months' written notice to each other. Written notice shall be given at the appropriate address set out in paragraph 1 of this Agreement.

21 This Agreement will terminate forthwith upon a merger by [Y] with any other body, whether a trade union or otherwise.

ABC
for and on behalf of [X]
Dated [   ] [2000]

DEF
For and on behalf of [Y]

APPENDIX A
Units of [X] in England and Wales which recognise [Y]
for the purposes of Negotiation

In each of the following units one or more Negotiating Committees will be established under the terms of paragraph 9 of this Agreement:
[Examples]
Plastics Division
Transport Division
Quality Control Division
Head Office

APPENDIX B
Matters agreed as Negotiable

[Y] is entitled to represent the interests of its members in the units set out in Appendix A in respect of matters set out below. In particular the following are agreed to be matters for negotiation at the appropriate Negotiating Committee:
[Examples]
Salary
Annual reviews of salary
Hours of work
Holidays
Disciplinary Procedures
Performance Procedures
Grievance Procedures
Maternity Leave
Paternity Leave
Sickness Absence Procedures

Matters that are not recognised as negotiable under this Appendix do not come within the procedures under this Agreement unless both parties agree in writing.

Bibliography

ADAMS, ROY J (1999), 'Why statutory recognition is bad labour policy: the North American experience' 30 *Industrial Relations Journal* 96–100.

ALCOCK, A (1971), *History of the International Labour Organisation* (Macmillan, London).

ARLIDGE, ANTHONY, DAVID EADY and A.T.H. SMITH (1999), *Arlidge, Eady and Smith on Contempt* (Sweet and Maxwell, London).

AUERBACH, SIMON (1988) 'Injunction Procedure in the Seafarers' Dispute' 17 *Industrial Law Journal* 227–238.

—— (1989), 'Injunctions Against Picketing' 18 *Industrial Law Journal* 166–170.

—— (1990), *Legislating for Conflict* (Clarendon Press, Oxford).

BAILEY, SUZANNE (1987), 'Wilfully Obstructing the Freedom to Protest?' *Public Law* 495–502.

BAIN, GEORGE SAYERS (1970), *The Growth of White-Collar Unionism* (Clarendon Press, Oxford).

BAMFORTH, N (1999), 'The Application of the Human Rights Act 1998 to Public Authorities and Private Bodies' 58 *Cambridge Law Journal* 159–170.

BARNARD, CATHERINE (1996) *EC Employment Law* (Wiley, Chichester).

—— (1999), 'The Working Time Regulations' 28 *Industrial Law Journal* 61–75.

—— and IVAN HARE (2000), 'Police Discretion and the Rule of Law: Economic Community Rights versus Civil Rights' 63 *Modern Law Review*, forthcoming.

BASSETT, PHILIP (1986), *Strike Free: New Industrial Relations in Britain* (Macmillan London).

BEATSON, JACK (1991), *The Use and Abuse of Unjust Enrichment: Essays on the Law of Restitution* (Clarendon Press, Oxford).

—— (1995), 'Public Law Influences in Contract Law' in *Good Faith and Fault in Contract Law* ed Jack Beatson and Daniel Friedmann (Clarendon Press, Oxford).

BECK, MATTHIAS and CHARLES WOOLFSON (2000), 'The regulation of health and safety in Britain: from old labour to new labour' 31 *Industrial Relations Journal* 35–49.

BELLACE, JANICE R (1997), 'The European Works Council Directive: Transnational Information and Consultation in the European Union' 18 *Comparative Labor Law Journal* 325–361.

BEN-ISRAEL, R (1988), *International Labour Standards: The Case of Freedom to Strike* (Kluwer, Deventer).

—— (ed) (1994), *Strikes and Lock-outs in Industrialised Market Economies* (Kluwer, Deventer-Boston).

BENEDICTUS, ROGER (1979), 'Closed Shop Exemptions and Their Wording' 8 *Industrial Law Journal* 160–171.

BERCUSSON, BRIAN (1977), 'One Hundred Years of Conspiracy and Protection of Property: Time for a Change' 40 *Modern Law Review* 268–292.

—— (1978), *Fair Wages Resolutions* (Mansell, London).

BIRKS, PETER and CHIN NYUK YIN (1995), 'On the Nature of Undue Influence in Good Faith and Fault in Contract Law' in *Good Faith and Fault in Contract Law* ed Jack Beatson and Daniel Friedmann (Clarendon Press, Oxford).

BONNER, DAVID, IAN HOOKER and ROBIN WHITE (1999), *Non-Means Tested Benefits: The Legislation* 14th edn (Sweet and Maxwell, London).

BOWERS, JOHN, SIMON JEFFREYS, BRIAN NAPIER and FRASER YOUNSON (1998, as updated), *Transfer of Undertakings* (Sweet and Maxwell, London).

—— JACK MITCHELL and JEREMY LEWIS (1999), *Whistleblowing: The New Law* (Sweet and Maxwell, London).

BRILLAT, REGIS (1996), 'A New Protocol to the European Social Charter Providing for Collective Complaints' *European Human Rights Law Review* 52–62.

BRODIE, DOUGLAS (1998), 'Beyond Exchange: The New Contract of Employment' 27 *Industrial Law Journal* 79–102.

BROWN, D and AILEEN MCCOLGAN (1992) 'UK Employment Law and the International Labour Organisation: The Spirit of Co-operation?' 21 *Industrial Law Journal* 265–279.

BROWN, WILLIAM (2000), 'Putting Partnership into Practice in Britain' 38 *British Journal of Industrial Relations* 299–316.

—— SIMON DEAKIN and PAUL RYAN (1997), 'The Effects of British Industrial Relations Legislation 1979–1997' 161 *National Institute Economic Review* 69–83.

—— SIMON DEAKIN, MARIA HUDSON, CLIFF PRATTEN and PAUL RYAN (1998), *The Individualisation of Emnployment Contracts in Britain*, Department of Trade and Industry Employment Relations Research Series 4 (Department of Trade and Industry, London).

BROWNE-WILKINSON, LORD (1992) 'The Infiltration of a Bill of Rights' *Public Law* 397–410.

BURROWS, ANDREW (1993), *The Law of Restitution* (Butterworths, London).

CARD, RICHARD (1986), *Public order–the new law* (Butterworths, London).

CARLEY, MARK and MARK HALL (2000), 'The Implementation of the European Works Councils Directive' 29 *Industrial Law Journal* 103–124.

CARTY, HAZEL (1988), 'Intentional Violation of Economic Interests: The Limits of Common Law Liability' 104 *Law Quarterly Review* 250–285.

Chitty on Contracts (1999), 28th edn (Sweet and Maxwell, London).

CLAYDON, TIM (1996), 'Union De-Recognition: A Re-Examination' in *Contemporary Industrial Relations* ed Ian J Beardwell (Oxford University Press, Oxford).

CLEMENTS, LUKE, NUALA MOLE and ALAN SIMMONS (1999), *European Human Rights: Taking a Case under the Convention*, 2nd edn (Sweet and Maxwell, London).

CLERK and LINDSELL (1995), *Clerk and Lindsell on Torts*, 17th edn and supplements (Sweet and Maxwell, London).

COLLINS, HUGH (1990), 'Independent Contractors and the Challenge of Vertical Disintegration to Employment Protection Laws' 10 *Oxford Journal of Legal Studies*, 353–380.

CRAVEN, MATTHEW (1998), *The International Covenant on Economic, Social and Cultural Rights*, (Clarendon Press, Oxford).

CREIGHTON, BREEN (1993) 'Freedom of Association' in *Comparative Labour Law and Industrial Relations in Industrialised Market Economies*, 5th edn, ed R Blanpain and C Engels (Kluwer, Deventer-Boston).

CULLY, MARK, STEPHEN WOODLAND, ANDREW O'REILLY and GILL DIX (1999), *Britain at Work* (Routledge, London).

DAVIES, PAUL (1996), 'The European Court of Justice, National Courts and the Member States' in *European Community Labour Law: Principles and Perspectives* ed Paul Davies, Antoine Lyon-Caen, Silvanna Sciarra, and Spiros Simitis (Clarendon Press, Oxford).

—— and MARK FREEDLAND (1983), *Kahn-Freund's Labour and the Law* (Stevens and Sons, London).

—— and MARK FREEDLAND (1984), *Labour Law: Text and Materials* 2nd edn (Weidenfeld and Nicolson, London).

—— and MARK FREEDLAND (1993), *Labour Legislation and Public Policy* (Clarendon Press, Oxford).

DE SMITH, STANLEY, LORD WOOLF, and JEFFREY JOWELL, (1995, supplement 1998) *Judicial Review of Administrative Action* (Sweet and Maxwell, London).

DEAKIN, SIMON and GILLIAN S MORRIS (1998), *Labour Law*, 2nd edn (Butterworths, London).

DICKENS, LINDA and GEORGE SAYERS BAIN (1986), 'A Duty to Bargain? Union Recognition and Information' in *Labour Law in Britain*, ed Roy Lewis (Basil Blackwell, Oxford).

DOYLE, BRIAN (1980), 'A Substitute for Collective Bargaining? – The Central Arbitration Committee's Approach to Section 16 of the Employment Protection Act 1975' 9 *Industrial Law Journal* 154–166.

DOYLE, BRIAN J (1996), *Disability Discrimination: Law and Practice* (Jordans, Bristol).

DUNN, STEPHEN and JOHN GENNARD (1984), *The Closed Shop in British Industry* (Macmillan, London).

Dunn, Stephen and Martyn Wright (1993), *Managing Without the Closed Shop* (Centre for Economic Performance Discussion Paper No 118, London School of Economics).

Durcan, JW and WEJ McCarthy (1974), 'The State Subsidy Theory of Strikes: An Examination of Statistical Data for the Period 1956–1970' 12 *British Journal of Industrial Relations* 26–47.

Elgar, Jane and Bob Simpson (1992), *The Impact of the Law on Industrial Disputes in the 1980s* (Centre for Economic Performance, London School of Economics).

—— —— (1994), 'A Final Appraisal of "Bridlington"? An Evaluation of TUC Disputes Committee Decisions 1974–1991' 32 *British Journal of Industrial Relations* 47–66.

—— —— (1996), *Industrial action ballots and the law* (Institute of Employment Rights, London).

Elias, Patrick (1979), 'Admission to Trade Unions', 8 *Industrial Law Journal* 111–113.

—— (1994), 'The Strike and Breach of Contract: A Reassessment' in *Human Rights and Labour Law: Essays for Paul O'Higgins* eds KD Ewing, CA Gearty and BA Hepple (Mansell, London).

—— and John Bowers (no date given), *Transfer of Undertakings: The Legal Pitfalls* (FT Law and Tax, London).

—— and Keith Ewing (1982), 'Economic Torts and Labour Law: Old Principles and New Liabilities' 41 *Cambridge Law Journal* 321–358.

—— and Keith Ewing (1987), *Trade Union Democracy, Members' Rights and the Law* (Mansell, London).

Evans, Stephen (1987), 'The Use of Injunctions in Industrial Disputes' 25 *British Journal of Industrial Relations* 419–435.

—— and Roy Lewis (1987), 'Anti-Union Discrimination: Practice, Law and Policy' 16 *Industrial Law Journal* 88–106.

—— and Roy Lewis (1988), 'Labour Clauses: From Voluntarism to Regulation' 17 *Industrial Law Journal*, 209–226.

Ewing, Keith (1985), 'The Strike, the Courts and the Rule-Books' 14 *Industrial Law Journal* 160–175.

—— (1991), *The Right to Strike* (Clarendon Press, Oxford).

—— (1994), *Britain and the ILO* 2nd edn (Institute of Employment Rights, London).

—— (1999), 'Freedom of Association and the Employment Relations Act 1999' 28 *Industrial Law Journal*, 283–298.

—— (2000), 'Dancing with the Daffodils?' 50 *Federation News* 1–22.

Fenwick, Helen (1999), 'The Right to Protest, the Human Rights Act and the Margin of Appreciation' 62 *Modern Law Review* 491–514.

Fitzpatrick, Barry (1983), 'Time Off: Recent Developments in the Court of Appeal', 12 *Industrial Law Journal* 258–261.

FREDMAN, SANDRA (1987), 'The Right to Strike: Policy and Principle' 103 *Law Quarterly Review* 176–182.

—— (1992), 'The New Rights: Labour Law and Ideology in the Thatcher Years' 12 *Oxford Journal of Legal Studies*, 24–44.

—— and GILLIAN S. MORRIS (1987), 'The Teachers' Lesson: Collective Bargaining and the Courts' 16 *Industrial Law Journal* 215–226.

—— and GILLIAN S. MORRIS (1989), *The State as Employer: Labour Law in the Public Services* (Mansell, London).

—— and GILLIAN S. MORRIS (1991), 'Public or Private? State Employees and Judicial Review' 107 *Law Quarterly Review* 298–316.

GALL, GREGOR and SONIA MCKAY (1994), 'Trade Union Derecognition in Britain 32 *British Journal of Industrial Relations* 433–448.

—— and SONIA MCKAY (1999), 'Developments in Union Recognition and Derecognition in Britain 1994–1998' 37 *British Journal of Industrial Relations* 601–614.

GEARY, ROGER (1985), *Policing Industrial Disputes 1893–1985* (Cambridge University Press, Cambridge).

GENNARD, J and R LASKO (1974), 'Supplementary Benefits and Strikers' 12 *British Journal of Industrial Relations* 1–25.

GERNIGON, BERNARD, ALBERTO ODERO and HORACIO GUIDO (1998), 'ILO principles concerning the right to strike' 137 *International Labour Review* 441–481.

GOFF, LORD of Chievely and GARETH JONES (1998), *The Law of Restitution* 5th edn (Sweet and Maxwell, London).

GOLD, MICHAEL and MARK HALL (1994), 'Statutory European Works Councils: the Final Countdown?' 25 *Industrial Law Journal* 177–186.

GOSPEL, HOWARD and GRAEME LOCKWOOD (1999), 'Disclosure of Information for Collective Bargaining: the CAC Approach Revisited' 28 *Industrial Law Journal* 233–248.

—— and PAUL WILLMAN (1981), 'Disclosure of Information: the CAC Approach' 10 *Industrial Law Journal* 10–22.

GRAY, KEVIN and SUSAN FRANCIS GRAY (1999), 'Civil Rights, Civil Wrongs and Quasi-Public Space' *European Human Rights Law Review* 46–102.

GROSZ, STEPHEN, JACK BEATSON and PETER DUFFY (2000), *Human Rights: The 1998 Act and the European Convention* (Sweet and Maxwell, London).

GUNNINGHAM, NEIL and RICHARD JOHNSTONE (1999), *Regulating Workplace Safety: Systems and Sanctions* (Oxford University Press, Oxford).

HALL, MARK (1996), 'Beyond Recognition? Employee Representation and EU Law' 25 *Industrial Law Journal* 15–27.

—— and PAUL EDWARDS (1999), 'Reforming the Statutory Redundancy Consultation Procedure' 28 *Industrial Law Journal* 299–318.

HARRIS, DJ (1984), *The European Social Charter* (University Press of Virginia, Charlottesville).

—— M O'BOYLE and C WARBRICK (1995), *Law of the European Convention on Human Rights* (Butterworths, London).

HARVEY (1972 as updated), *Harvey on Industrial Relations and Employment Law* (Butterworths, London).

HENDY, JOHN (1998), 'The Human Rights Act, Article 11 and the Right to Strike' [1998] *European Human Rights Law Review* 583–616.

—— (2000), 'Caught in a Fork' 29 *Industrial Law Journal* 53–60.

HEPPLE, BA (1970), 'Intention to Create Legal Relations' 28 *Cambridge Law Journal* 122–137.

—— (1981a), 'A Right to Work?' 10 *Industrial Law Journal* 65–83.

—— (1981b), *Hepple and O'Higgins: Employment Law* 4th edn (Sweet and Maxwell, London).

—— (1982), 'The Transfer of Undertakings (Protection of Employment) Regulations' 10 *Industrial Law Journal* 29–40.

—— (1986) 'Restructuring Employment Rights' 15 *Industrial Law Journal* 69–89.

—— (2000), 'Supporting collective bargaining: some comparative reflections' in *Employment Relations in Britain: 25 years of the Advisory, Conciliation and Arbitration Service*, eds Brian Towers and William Brown (ACAS and Blackwell, Oxford).

—— (forthcoming), 'Freedom of Expression and the Problem of Harassment' in *Freedom of Speech and Freedom of Information*, eds J Beatson and Y Cripps (Oxford University Press, Oxford).

—— and ANGELA BYRE (1989), 'EEC Labour Law in the United Kingdom – A New Approach' 18 *Industrial Law Journal* 129–143.

—— and MARTIN MATTHEWS (1991), *Tort: Cases and Materials* 4th edn (Butterworths, London).

HOGG, PETER W (1997), *Constitutional Law of Canada* 4th edn (Carswell, Scarborough, Ontario).

HOLLINGSWORTH, MARK and CHARLES TREMAYNE (1989), *The Economic League: The Silent McCarthyism* (National Council for Civil Liberties, London).

HONEYBALL, SIMON (1988), *A Guide to the Employment Act 1988* (Butterworths, London).

HUNT, MURRAY (1997) *Using Human Rights Law in English Courts* (Hart Publishing, Oxford).

—— (1998), 'The "Horizontal" Effect of the Human Rights Act' *Public Law* 423–443.

INSTITUTE OF PERSONNEL MANAGEMENT (1987), *Contract Compliance: The UK Experience* (IPM, London).

JACOBS, ANTOINE (1986), 'Collective Self-Regulation' in *The Making of Labour Law in Europe*, ed Bob Hepple (Mansell, London).

—— (1998), 'The Law of Strikes and Lock-outs' in *Comparative Labour Law and Industrial Relations in Industrialised Market Economies* ed R Blanpain and C Engels (Kluwer, Deventer-Boston).

JAMES, PHIL (1992), 'Reforming British Health and Safety Law: A Framework for Discussion' 21 *Industrial Law Journal* 83–105.

JAMES, PHILIP and DAVID WALTERS (1997), 'Non-Union Rights of Involvement: The Case of Health and Safety at Work', 26 *Industrial Law Journal* 35–50.

JAY, ROSEMARY and ANGUS HAMILTON (1999), *Data Protection law and practice* (Sweet and Maxwell, London).

JONES, GARETH and WILLIAM GOODHART (1996), *Specific Performance* 2nd edn (Butterworths, London).

JONES, MICHAEL A and ANNE MORRIS (1985), 'Picketing, the Closed Shop and Enforcement of the Employment Acts' 14 *Industrial Law Journal* 46–50.

JONES, TIMOTHY H (1995), 'The Devaluation of Human Rights under the European Convention' *Public Law* 430–449.

KAHN, PEGGY, NORMAN LEWIS, ROWLAND LIVOCK and PAUL WILES (1983), *Picketing: Industrial Disputes, Tactics and the Law* (Routledge and Kegan Paul, London).

KIDNER, RICHARD (1983), *Trade Union Law* 2nd edn (Stevens, London).

—— (1984), 'Trade Union Democracy: Election of Trade Union Officers' 13 *Industrial Law Journal* 193–211.

—— (1991), 'Unjustified Discipline by a Trade Union' 20 *Industrial Law Journal* 284–291.

LAVENDER, NICHOLAS (1997), 'The Problem of the Margin of Appreciation' *European Human Rights Law Review* 380–390.

LAWS, THE HON SIR JOHN (1993), 'Is the High Court the Guardian of Fundamental Constitutional Rights?' *Public Law* 455–466.

LAWSON, R.A. and H.G. SCHERMERS (1999), *Leading Cases of the European Court of Human Rights*, 2nd edn (Ars Aequi Libri, Nijmegen).

LEADER, SHELDON (1991), 'The European Convention on Human Rights, The Employment Act 1988 and the Right to Refuse to Strike' 20 *Industrial Law Journal* 39–59.

LECHER, WOLFGANG and STEFAN RÜB (1999), 'The Constitution of European Works Councils: From Information Forum to Social Actor? 5 *European Journal of Industrial Relations* 7–25.

LEIGH, IAN (1999), 'Horizontal Rights: The Human Rights Act and Privacy: Lessons from the Commonwealth' 48 *International and Comparative Law Quarterly* 57–87.

—— and LAURENCE LUSTGARTEN (1999), 'Making Rights Real: The Courts, Remedies, and the Human Rights Act' 58 *Cambridge Law Journal* 509–543.

LEIGHTON, PATRICIA (1986), 'Marginal Workers' in *Labour Law in Britain* ed Roy Lewis (Basil Blackwell, Oxford).

LEOPOLD, JOHN W (1997), 'Trade Unions, Political Fund Ballots and the Labour Party' 35 *British Journal of Industrial Relations* 23–38.

LESTER, LORD (1998a), 'Universality versus Subsidiarity: A Reply' *European Human Rights Law Review* 73–81.

LESTER, LORD (1998b), 'Opinion: The Art of the Possible – Interpreting Statutes under the Human Rights Act' *European Human Rights Law Review*, 665–675.

Lewis, Roy (1979), 'Collective Agreements: The Kahn-Freund Legacy' 42 *Modern Law Review* 613–622.

—— (1990), 'Strike-free Deals and Pendulum Arbitration' 28 *British Journal of Industrial Relations* 32–56.

Lightman, Gavin (1987), 'A Trade Union in Chains: Scargill Unbound – The Legal Constraints of Receivership and Sequestration' *Current Legal Problems* 25–54.

McBride, Jeremy (1999), 'Protecting life: a positive obligation to help' 24 *European Law Review* Human Rights Survey, HR43–HR/54.

McCabe, Sarah and Peter Wallington (1988), *The Police, Public Order and Civil Liberties* (Routledge, London).

McCarthy, WEJ (1964), *The Closed Shop in Britain* (University of California Press, Berkeley and Los Angeles).

McCarthy, Lord (1999), *Fairness at Work and Trade Union Recognition: Past Comparisons and Future Problems* (Institute of Employment Rights, London).

McGhee, John (2000), *Snell's Equity* 30th edn (Sweet and Maxwell, London).

McGoldrick, Dominic (1994), *The Human Rights Committee* (Clarendon Press, Oxford).

McGregor, Harvey (1997), *McGregor on Damages*, 16th edn (Sweet and Maxwell, London).

MacInnes, John (1985), 'Conjuring Up Consultation: The Role and Extent of Joint Consultation in Post-War Private Manufacturing Industry' 23 *British Journal of Industrial Relations* 93–113.

McLean, Hazel (1990), 'Contract of Employment – Negative Covenants and No Work, No Pay' 49 *Cambridge Law Journal* 28–31.

McMullen, John (1998, as updated), *Business Transfers and Employee Rights*, (Butterworths, London).

Mahoney, Paul (1997), 'Universality versus Subsidiarity in the Strasbourg Case Law on Free Speech: Explaining Some Recent Judgments' *European Human Rights Law Review,* 364–379.

Marginson, Paul (2000), 'The Eurocompany and Euro Industrial Relations' 6 *European Journal of Industrial Relations* 9–34.

—— Mark Gilman, Otto Jacobi and Hubert Kreiger (1998), *Negotiating European Works Councils: an Analysis of Agreements under Article 13* (European Foundation for the Improvement of Living and Working Conditions).

Markesinis, Basil (1999), 'Privacy, Freedom of Expression and the Human Rights Bill: Lessons from Germany' 115 *Law Quarterly Review* 47–88.

Markesinis, B.S. and S.F. Deakin, *Tort Law*, 4th edn (Clarendon Press, Oxford).

Marriot, Jane and Daniel Nicol (1998), 'The Human Rights Act, Representative Standing and the Victim Culture' *European Human Rights Law Review,* 730–741.

MARTIN, RODERICK, PATRICIA FOSH, HUW MORRIS, PAUL SMITH and ROGER UNDY (1991), 'The Decollectivisation of Trade Unions? Ballots and Collective Bargaining in the 1980s' 22 *Industrial Relations Journal* 197–208.

MESHER, JOHN and FRANK SUTCLIFFE (1986) 'Industrial Action and the Individual' in *Labour Law in Britain* ed Roy Lewis (Blackwell, Oxford).

MILLER, DOUG and JOHN STIRLING, 'European Works Council Training: An Opportunity Missed?' (1998) 4 *European Journal of Industrial Relations* 35–49.

MILLER, KENNETH and CHARLES WOOLFSON (1994), 'Timex: Industrial Relations and the Use of the Law in the 1990s' 23 *Industrial Law Journal* 209–225.

MILLS, SHAUN (1997) 'The International Labour Organisation, the United Kingdom and Freedom of Association: An Annual Cycle of Condemnation' *European Human Rights Law Review* 35–53.

MILLWARD, NEIL, ALEX BRYSON and JOHN FORTH (2000), *All Change at Work?* (Routledge, London).

MORRIS, GILLIAN S (1985a), 'Road Blocks and Bail Conditions' 14 *Industrial Law Journal* 109–111.

—— (1985b), 'The Ban on Trade Unions at Government Communications Headquarters' *Public Law* 177–186.

—— (1986), *Strikes in Essential Services* (Mansell, London).

—— (1991), 'Industrial Action in Essential Services: The New Law' 20 *Industrial Law Journal* 89–101.

—— (1993), 'Industrial Action: Public and Private Interests' 22 *Industrial Law Journal* 194–210.

—— (1994a), 'Freedom of Association and the Interests of the State' in *Human Rights and Labour Law: Essays for Paul O'Higgins*, eds K.D. Ewing, C.A. Gearty and B.A. Hepple (Mansell, London).

—— (1994b), 'The New Legal Regime for Prison Officers' 23 *Industrial Law Journal* 326–331.

—— (1998), 'The Human Rights Act and the Public/Private Divide in Employment Law' 27 *Industrial Law Journal* 293–308.

—— (1999), 'The European Convention on Human Rights and Employment: To Which Acts Does it Apply?' *European Human Rights Law Review* 496–511.

—— with STEPHEN RYDZKOWSKI (1984), 'Approaches to Industrial Action in the National Health Service' 13 *Industrial Law Journal* 153–164.

MOWBRAY, ALASTAIR (1997), 'The European Court of Human Rights' Approach to Just Satisfaction' *Public Law* 647–659.

NAPIER, BRIAN (1972), 'Working to Rule – A Breach of the Contract of Employment?' 1 *Industrial Law Journal* 125–134.

—— (1986), 'The Contract of Employment' in *Labour Law in Britain* ed Roy Lewis (Basil Blackwell, Oxford).

—— (1987), 'Breach of Statutory Duty and Unlawful Means in Strike Law' 46 *Cambridge Law Journal* 222–224.

NEAL, ALAN C (1990), 'The European Framework Directive on the Health and Safety of Workers: Challenges for the United Kingdom?', 6 *International Journal of Comparative Labour Law and Industrial Relations*, 80–117.

NIELSEN, RUTH and ERICA SZYSZCZAK (1997), *The Social Dimension of the European Community*, 3rd edn, Handelshojskolens Forlag, Copenhagan.

NOVITZ, TONIA (1998), 'Freedom of Association and "Fairness at Work" – An Assessment of the Impact and Relevance of ILO Convention No 87 on its Fiftieth Anniversary' 27 *Industrial Law Journal* 169–191.

—— (2000), 'International Promises and Domestic Pragmatism: To What Extent will the Employment Relations Act 1999 Implement International Labour Standards Relating to Freedom of Association' 63 *Modern Law Review* 379–393.

O'DAIR, RICHARD (1991), 'Justifying an Interference with Contractual Rights' 11 *Oxford Journal of Legal Studies* 227–246.

OGUS, AI, EM BARENDT and NJ WIKELEY (1995) *The Law of Social Security* 4th edn (Butterworths, London).

O'HIGGINS, PAUL (1991), 'The European Social Charter' in *Human Rights for the 1990s* ed Robert Blackburn and John Taylor (Mansell, London).

OLIVER, DAWN (1999), *Common Values and the Public-Private Divide* (Butterworths, London).

ORTH, JOHN V (1991), *Combination and Conspiracy: A Legal History of Trade Unionism 1721–1906* (Clarendon Press, Oxford).

PANNICK, DAVID (1998), 'Principles of interpretation of Convention rights under the Human Rights Act and the discretionary area of judgment' *Public Law* 545–551.

POOLE, THOMAS (2000), 'Judicial Review and Public Employment: Decision-Making on the Public-Private Divide' 29 *Industrial Law Journal* 61–67.

REDGRAVE, ALEXANDER, JOHN HENDY and MICHAEL FORD (1998), *Health and Safety*, 3rd edn (Butterworths, London).

REID, KAREN (1998), *A Practitioner's Guide to the European Convention on Human Rights* (Sweet and Maxwell, London).

ROWE, NICOLA and VOLKER SCHLETTE (1998), 'The Protection of Human Rights in Europe after the Eleventh Protocol to the ECHR' 23 *European Law Review* HR 3–16.

ROYLE, TONY (1999), 'Where's the Beef? McDonald's and its European Works Council' 5 *European Journal of Industrial Relations* 327–347.

SALES, PHILIP and DANIEL STILITZ (1999), 'Intentional Infliction of Harm by Unlawful Means' 115 *Law Quarterly Review* 411–437.

SAMUEL, LENIA (1997), *Fundamental Social Rights: Case law of the European Social Charter* (Council of Europe Publishing, Strasbourg).

SELWYN, NORMAN (1969), 'Collective Agreements and the Law' 32 *Modern Law Review*, 377–396.

SIMPSON, BOB (1979), 'Judicial Control of ACAS' 8 *Industrial Law Journal* 69–84.

—— (1987), 'The Labour Injunction, Unlawful Means and the Right to Strike' 50 *Modern Law Review* 506–516.

—— (1989), 'The Summer of Discontent and the Law' 18 *Industrial Law Journal* 234–241.

—— (1993) 'Individualism versus Collectivism: an Evaluation of Section 14 of the Trade Union Reform and Employment Rights Act 1993' 22 *Industrial Law Journal* 181–193.

—— (1994), 'Bridlington "2"' 23 *Industrial Law Journal* 170–174.

—— (1999a), 'A Milestone in the Legal Regulation of Pay: The National Minimum Wage Act 1998' 28 *Industrial Law Journal* 1–32.

—— (1999b), 'Implementing the National Minimum Wage – the 1999 Regulations' 171–182.

SINGH, RABINDER, MURRAY HUNT and MARIE DEMETRIOU (1999), 'Is there a Role for the "Margin of Appreciation" in National Law after the Human Rights Act?' *European Human Rights Law Review* 15–22.

SMITH, ATH (1987), *The Offences against Public Order* (Sweet and Maxwell, London).

SMITH, J, P. EDWARDS and M. HALL (1999), *Redundancy Consultation: A Study of Current Practice and the Effects of the 1995 Regulations* (DTI, Employment Relations Research Series, No 5, London).

SMITH, IT and GH THOMAS (1996), *Smith and Wood's Industrial Law* 6th edn (Butterworths, London).

SMITH, JC (1999), *Smith and Hogan Criminal Law* 9th edn (Butterworths, London).

SMITH, PAUL, PATRICIA FOSH, RODERICK MARTIN, HUW MORRIS and ROGER UNDY (1993), 'Ballots and Union Government in the 1980s' 31 *British Journal of Industrial Relations* 365–382.

SPENCEr, JR (1989), 'Public Nuisance – A Critical Examination' 48 *Cambridge Law Journal* 55–84.

SPRY, ICF (1997), *The Principles of Equitable Remedies: Specific Performance, Injunctions, Rectification and Equitable Damages* (LBC Information Services, Sydney).

SWEPSTON, LEE (1997), 'Supervision of ILO Standards', 13 *The International Journal of Comparative Labour Law and Industrial Relations*, 327–344.

SUPPERSTONE, MICHAEL (1997), 'The ambit of judicial review' in *Judicial Review*, ed Michael Supperstone and James Goudie, 2nd edn (Butterworths, London).

TIERNEY, STEPHEN (1998), 'Press Freedom and Public Interest' *European Human Rights Law Review* 419–429.

TOULSON, R.G. and C.M. PHIPPS (1996), *Confidentiality* (Sweet and Maxwell, London).

TOWERS, BRIAN (1999), *Developing recognition and representation in the UK: how useful is the US model?* (Institute of Employment Rights, London).

TOWNSEND-SMITH, RICHARD (1991), 'Refusal of Employment on Grounds of

Trade Union Membership or Non-Membership: The Employment Act 1990' 20 *Industrial Law Journal*, 102–112.

TREITEL, GH (1999), *The Law of Contract* 10th edn (Stevens and Sons, London).

TURPIN, COLIN (1989) *Government Procurement and Contracts* (Longman, London).

UNDY, ROGER, PATRICIA FOSH, HUW MORRIS, PAUL SMITH and RODERICK MARTIN (1996), *Managing the Unions: The Impact of Legislation on Trade Unions' Behaviour* (Clarendon Press, Oxford).

—— and RODERICK MARTIN (1984), *Ballots and Trade Union Democracy* (Basil Blackwell, Oxford).

VALTICOS, N and K SAMSON (1998) 'International Labour Law' in *Comparative Labour Law and Industrial Relations in Industrialised Market Economies* 6th edn, ed R Blanpain and C Engels (Kluwer, Deventer-Boston).

VALTICOS, NICOLAS and GERALDO VON POTOBSKY (1995), *International Labour Law* (Kluwer, Deventer-Boston).

VAN ALSTYNE, WILLIAM W. (1967–1968), 'The Demise of the Right-Privilege Distinction in Constitutional Law' 81 *Harvard Law Review* 1439–1464.

VAN DIJK and VAN HOOF (1998), *Theory and Practice of the European Convention on Human Rights*, 3rd edn (Kluwer, The Hague)

WADE, HWR (1998), 'The United Kingdom's Bill of Rights' in *Constitutional Reform in the UK: Practice and Principles* (Hart Publishing, Oxford).

WEBB, SIDNEY and BEATRICE WEBB (1920), *The History of Trade Unionism*, new edn, (Longmans, Green and Co, London).

WEDDERBURN, LORD (1986), *The Worker and the Law* 3rd edn (Penguin, Harmondsworth).

—— (1989), 'Freedom of Association and Philosophies of Labour Law' 18 *Industrial Law Journal* 244–254.

—— (1991), *Employment Rights in Britain and Europe: Selected Papers in Labour Law* (Lawrence and Wishart, London).

—— (1992a), 'Inderogability, Collective Agreements, and Community Law' 21 *Industrial Law Journal* 245–264.

—— (1992b), 'Contempt of Court: Vicarious Liability of Companies and Unions' 21 *Industrial Law Journal* 51–58.

—— (1997), 'Consultation and Collective Bargaining in Europe: Success or Ideology?' 26 *Industrial Law Journal* 1–34.

—— (2000), 'Collective Bargaining or Legal Enactment: The 1999 Act and Union Recognition' 29 *Industrial Law Journal* 1–42.

WEEKES, BRIAN, MICHAEL MELLISH, LINDA DICKENS and JOHN LLOYD (1975), *Industrial Relations and the Limits of Law: The Industrial Effects of the Industrial Relations Act 1971* (Blackwell, Oxford).

WEIR, TONY (1997), *Economic Torts* (Clarendon Press, Oxford).

WEISS, MANFRED (1996), 'Workers Participation in the EU' in *European*

Community Labour Law: Principles and Perspectives ed Paul Davies, Antoine Lyon-Caen, Silvana Sciarra and Spiros Simitis (Clarendon Press, Oxford).

WOOD, STEPHEN and JOHN GODARD (1999), 'The Statutory Union Recognition Procedure in the Employment Relations Bill: A Comparative Analysis' 37 *British Journal of Industrial Relations* 203–244.

YOUNSON, FRASER R (1989), *Employment Law and Business Transfers: A Practical Guide* (Sweet and Maxwell, London).

ZUCKERMAN, AAS (1993), 'Interlocutory Remedies in Quest of Procedural Fairness' 56 *Modern Law Review* 325–341.

Index